International Financial Policy

Essays in Honor of Jacques J. Polak

INTERNATIONAL FINANCIAL POLICY

Essays in Honor of

Jacques J. Polak

Edited by Jacob A. Frenkel and Morris Goldstein

International Monetary Fund • De Nederlandsche Bank

1991

The article by Richard N. Cooper, "What Future for the International Monetary System?" appeared in *The Evolution of the International Monetary System: How Can Efficiency and Stability Be Attained?* edited by Yoshio Suzuki, Junichi Miyake, and Mitsuaki Okabe (Tokyo: University of Tokyo Press, 1990) and is reprinted with permission.

This book was designed and produced by the IMF Graphics Section; photograph by Denio Zara.

Library of Congress Cataloging-in-Publication Data

International financial policy : essays in honor of Jacques J. Polak / edited by Jacob A. Frenkel and Morris Goldstein.
    p. cm.
Published in association with De Nederlandsche Bank.
Includes bibliographical references.
ISBN 1-55775-196-X
    1. International finance—Congresses. 2. International Monetary Fund—Congresses. I. Frenkel, Jacob A. II. Goldstein, Morris, 1944– . III. Polak, J. J. (Jacques Jacobus), 1914– .
HG203.I573 1991
332'.042—dc20   91-46087
                                         CIP

Price: US$30.00

Please send orders to:
International Monetary Fund, Publication Services
700 19th Street, N.W., Washington, D.C. 20431, U.S.A.
Tel.: (202) 623-7430   Telefax: (202) 623-7201

Preface

In recognition of Jacques J. Polak's outstanding contributions to international economics and his distinguished service at the International Monetary Fund, the IMF and De Nederlandsche Bank jointly sponsored a conference to honor him. The conference was held in Washington, D.C., on January 13–15, 1991. In the course of his association with the IMF, which spans over forty years, Jacques J. Polak has served the IMF in various capacities, including Economic Counsellor and Director of Research, and member of the Executive Board representing Cyprus, Malta, the Netherlands, Romania, and Yugoslavia. In these positions—as well as through his writings—Jacques Polak has had a major influence on the shape of the postwar international monetary system and on the IMF's role in that system.

The papers included in this volume were prepared for the conference by a group of eminent scholars—friends and former colleagues of Jacques J. Polak. The papers deal with a variety of subjects, ranging from the future of the international monetary system to the sequencing of reforms in Eastern Europe. Through publication, it is hoped to disseminate to a wider audience some of the foremost thinking on a number of the major policy issues of the day.

Special thanks are due to W.F. Duisenberg and his colleagues at De Nederlandsche Bank for their ideas in planning the conference and for their generous support. The editors are extremely grateful to the authors for their contributions and for their cooperation in preparing the papers for publication. They also wish to thank Jonathan Ostry for assisting with the scheduling, Roberto Brauning and Patricia Kane of the External Relations Department for supervising the logistics of the conference, and Adriana Vohden for secretarial assistance. Finally, Esha Ray of the External Relations Department did her usual masterful job in editing the volume for publication.

The views expressed in the papers are those of the authors and do not in any way represent those of the IMF, De Nederlandsche Bank, or the organizations with which the contributors are associated.

JACOB A. FRENKEL

MORRIS GOLDSTEIN

Contents

PART FIVE. EXTERNAL ADJUSTMENT AND POLICY ASSIGNMENT

Contributors

VICTOR ARGY, Professor of Economics, School of Economic and Financial Studies, Macquarie University, Sydney

EDWARD M. BERNSTEIN, Guest Scholar, The Brookings Institution, Washington, and former Director of Research, International Monetary Fund, Washington

RICHARD N. COOPER, Maurits C. Boas Professor of International Economics, Harvard University, Cambridge, Massachusetts

W. MAX CORDEN, Professor of International Economics, School of Advanced International Studies, The Johns Hopkins University, Washington

ANDREW CROCKETT, Executive Director, Bank of England, London

J. DE BEAUFORT WIJNHOLDS, Deputy Director, De Nederlandsche Bank, Amsterdam

W.F. DUISENBERG, President, De Nederlandsche Bank, Amsterdam

JACOB A. FRENKEL, Governor, Bank of Israel, Jerusalem, and former Counsellor and Director of Research, International Monetary Fund, Washington

HANS GENBERG, Professor of Economics, Graduate Institute of International Studies, Geneva

JOSEPH GOLD, former General Counsel and Director, Legal Department, and now Senior Consultant, International Monetary Fund, Washington

MORRIS GOLDSTEIN, Deputy Director, Research Department, International Monetary Fund, Washington

H. ROBERT HELLER, President, VISA International, San Mateo, California

ALEXANDRE KAFKA, Executive Director, International Monetary Fund, Washington

PETER B. KENEN, Walker Professor of Economics and Finance, and Director, International Finance Section, Princeton University, Princeton, New Jersey

MOHSIN S. KHAN, Senior Advisor, Research Department, International Monetary Fund, Washington

ROBERT MUNDELL, Professor of Economics, Columbia University, New York

RUDOLF R. RHOMBERG, former Deputy Director, Research Department, International Monetary Fund, Washington

ROBERT SOLOMON, Senior Fellow, The Brookings Institution, Washington

ALEXANDER K. SWOBODA, Director and Professor of Economics, Graduate Institute of International Studies, Geneva

A. SZÁSZ, Executive Director, De Nederlandsche Bank, Amsterdam

JAN TINBERGEN, Professor Emeritus, Erasmus University, The Hague, and Nobel Laureate in Economics

JOHN WILLIAMSON, Senior Fellow, Institute for International Economics, Washington

PART ONE
Overview and Reflections

1

Major Themes in the Writings of Jacques J. Polak

Jacob A. Frenkel, Morris Goldstein,
and Mohsin S. Khan

Jacques Polak was born in the Netherlands in 1914. He received his doctorate in economics in 1937 from the University of Amsterdam. His first professional work was with Professor Jan Tinbergen. In 1937 he began his international service as an economist with the League of Nations. He was a member of the Netherlands delegations to the 1944 Bretton Woods Conference establishing the International Monetary Fund and to the Atlantic City conference that established the United Nations Relief and Rehabilitation Administration (UNRRA). During this period, he served at the Netherlands Embassy in Washington. From 1944 to 1946, he was Assistant Financial Adviser, and then Economic Adviser, to the Director General of UNRRA.

Jacques Polak joined the staff of the International Monetary Fund in January 1947, serving first as Chief of the Statistics Division, and then as Assistant Director, Deputy Director, and from 1958, as Director, of Research. In 1966, he also became the Economic Counsellor of the Fund, a position which he held until his so-called retirement from the Fund staff in 1979. That retirement was of course one of the shortest on record. After serving briefly as Adviser to the Managing Director, Jacques Polak was elected in January 1981 as Executive Director of the Fund for the constituency of Cyprus, Israel, the Netherlands, Romania, and Yugoslavia. He served with distinction as an Executive Director until 1986, when he, for want of a better term, retired for a second time. Since then, he has, in addition to engaging in a full agenda of research and writing, served

3

as a Consultant with the World Bank, as a Senior Adviser to the Development Center of the Organization for Economic Cooperation and Development (OECD), and, since 1987, as President of the Per Jacobsson Foundation. It makes you wonder what tasks Jacques could be lining up for his third retirement.

While all this was going on, Jacques Polak was writing. His first publication appeared in 1937. His most recent one appeared a few weeks ago, and we have it on good information that several more papers are in the pipeline. During the intervening 53 years, the international economics literature had the benefit of more than ninety papers and six books from the pen of Jacques Polak.[1] Anyone who thinks he can become well acquainted with Jacques Polak's work in a long weekend ought to think again, perhaps in terms of a sabbatical.

In this paper, we have eschewed any attempt to survey and to evaluate all of Jacques Polak's writings, in large part because we were not confident we could do justice to the breadth and depth of that work in a single paper of moderate length. Instead, we have set for ourselves the more limited task of identifying and commenting on three major themes that have underlain much of Jacques Polak's writings and that have particular significance for the ongoing work of the International Monetary Fund. These three themes are (1) the international spillover effects of national economic policies; (2) the monetary approach to the balance of payments; and (3) the functioning of the international monetary system.

Before proceeding to those themes, we wish to highlight four characteristics of the broader body of Jacques Polak's writing.

To begin with, Polak's writings are overwhelmingly *policy oriented*. The practical motivation for each paper or study is always readily apparent. This is not an economist with a set of solutions in search of problems. Quite the contrary. Even a cursory perusal of Jacques Polak's writings provides a good outline of the issues confronting international economic policy over the past five decades. Thus in the early 1940s, Polak is concerned with how to design an optimal rationing system for a wartime economy.[2] In the mid-1940s, he goes on to analyze how countries attempting to reconstruct their war-ravaged economies should manage their foreign borrowing and

---

[1] See Annex I for a bibliography of works by Jacques J. Polak. All references in this paper to Polak's writings are to this bibliography.
[2] Polak (1941).

investment programs.[3] In the latter part of that decade, as countries are just learning their way with the new par value system, Polak attempts to draw the lessons of earlier exchange rate adjustments, to assess the merits of alternative methodologies for identifying the equilibrium exchange rate, and to provide quantitative estimates of the effect of exchange rate depreciation on Europe's exports to the dollar area.[4] When in early 1950 the issue of a European payments union was under discussion, Polak is involved with a set of (internal) papers that lays out the strengths and weaknesses of existing proposals, along with his own proposal for clearing European payments imbalances through the Fund.[5] In response to the concern in the early 1950s that when the United States sneezes the rest of the world catches pneumonia, Polak refines his earlier pioneering empirical work on the nature of the international business cycle, so that a better appreciation of the empirical values of the relevant parameters can be obtained.[6] What has come to be known as "the Polak model" provides in the late 1950s a theoretically elegant, but also eminently practical, answer to the pressing issue of how to calculate the rate of domestic credit creation consistent with a targeted improvement in the balance of payments.[7] In a similar vein, Polak's work on international liquidity and the SDR in the late 1960s responds directly to concerns about a possible shortage of international liquidity.[8] This same preoccupation with using economic theory and econometrics to shed light on "live" policy issues carries on in Polak's writings in the 1970s and 1980s—be it in the context of writing codes of conduct for a heterogenous exchange rate system under the Second Amendment to the Fund's Articles of Agreement, or in designing a mechanism for an orderly diversification of reserve holdings in the face of a weak U.S. dollar,[9] or in thinking about how developing countries will be able to finance their development objectives in the aftermath of the debt crisis.[10] A paper he published earlier this year is right on the regression line: it analyzes the issue

---

[3] Polak (1943a).
[4] Polak (1947a, 1948c, 1949b, and 1949c).
[5] Polak (1950b, 1950d, and 1950g).
[6] Polak (1952b and 1956).
[7] Polak (1957a).
[8] Polak (1965, 1967a, 1967b, and 1970a).
[9] Polak (1980).
[10] Polak (1989a).

of whether currency convertibility is an indispensable element in the transition process in Eastern Europe.[11]

A second characteristic of Polak's work is the continuing search for *empirical regularities* that can aid the policymaking process. To Polak, theory and measurement are merely two sides of the same coin. Indeed, many of his papers follow a similar organizing framework: state the problem to be analyzed and its relevance, lay out the necessary economic theory, review the existing empirical evidence and then add your own to it, and finally, draw the implications for economic policy. In many cases, the policy implications hinge directly—as they should—on the empirical findings. In a similar vein, some of the theoretical models themselves are constructed with a keen eye toward the availability of data so that they can be applied by practitioners. And when the existing data are inadequate or even misleading, Jacques Polak is ready with suggestions about how those data can be improved.

Already in his earliest published papers, Polak undertakes to provide estimates of some fundamental parameters. Thus, for example, in his classic 1939 paper on "The International Propagation of Business Cycles," he concludes from his regression analysis that for the average industrial country a 1 percent change in the "world" business cycle induces a change of $3/4$ of 1 percent in the "national" business cycle, other things being equal.[12] Likewise in 1939, he estimates the marginal propensity to consume out of labor income in the United States to be about 0.95, and then uses that estimate to derive the Keynesian income "multiplier."[13] By 1951, he is able on the basis of several of his earlier empirical papers to put forth the judgment that a rough working figure for the price elasticity of demand for exports of industrial countries is on the order of one to two.[14] By this time, he has also developed estimates that confirm that the "pass-through" of exchange rate changes into export prices differs across periods of boom, slump, inflation, and hyperinflation;[15] that the export demand effects of currency depreciation differ markedly as between unilateral and simultaneous devaluations; and that income-demand and export-supply effects can often dominate

---

[11] Polak (1991a).

[12] Polak (1939a).

[13] Polak (1939b).

[14] Polak (1951d). This is very close to the consensus estimate offered by Goldstein and Khan (1985), nearly thirty-five years later.

[15] Polak (1950c).

the relative-price effects of a devaluation.[16] In an important 1955 paper with William H. White on "The Effect of Income Expansion on the Quantity of Money," Polak goes on to develop estimates of the (public's) income and interest rate elasticities of demand for money, of the (commercial banks') interest rate elasticity of supply of money, and of the income elasticity of demand for imports.[17] This acute interest in the key structural parameters of the world economy also remains evident in Polak's more recent work. His 1989 study, *Financial Policies and Development*, looks carefully at the (real) interest rate elasticity of saving and investment in developing countries.[18] This careful attention to the numbers permits Polak in his policy recommendations to not only offer views on which policy instruments should be changed but also on how much they should be changed.

This practical quantitative bent also surfaces in the theoretical models that Polak himself constructs. Nowhere is this more apparent than in his famous 1957 paper ("Monetary Analysis of Income Formation and Payments Problems") that introduced the Polak model to the profession.[19] The great appeal of this model, particularly for economists in the field, probably owed as much to its economical data requirements as to its theoretical elegance. Polak recognized that if calculation of the effects of monetary changes on income or the balance of payments had to depend on national income accounts, then the model's application would of necessity be severely constrained—since, at that time, these data were either unavailable or of notoriously poor quality for most developing countries. In contrast, a model that leaned on basic monetary and balance of payments data would have a distinct advantage. The Polak model is such a model. In fact, even what now seems like a curious emphasis on demonstrating that *average* propensities (to import and to hold money) would be good approximations to marginal propensities, carries justification when seen in this light. For as Polak shows, if average propensities are equal to marginal ones, then the model is further simplified so that one simple ratio, namely, that of money to imports, can be used to calculate the ratio of domestic assets to foreign assets that an economy can afford in the long run.

---

[16] Polak (1949c).
[17] Polak (1955a).
[18] Polak (1989a).
[19] Polak (1957a).

This was not quite making bricks without straw, but it certainly moved us a lot closer to it at a time when very little straw was available.

Taking account of data limitations in theoretical work is one thing. Being complacent about those limitations is quite another. Jacques Polak was never comfortable with the view that the quality of international data was a technical issue that should be left to statisticians alone. Thus, for example, his 1954 paper on "Conceptual Problems Involved in Projections of the International Sector of Gross National Product" explores in some detail the reasons why the smallness of the international sector in national income accounts is, to a large extent, arbitrary.[20] He also advances specific proposals for how that arbitrariness could be reduced. Similarly, his 1959 article on "Financial Statistics and Financial Policy" provides a concise appraisal of the potential rate of return from developing flow-of-funds accounts, including an insightful discussion of the key differences between banks and other financial intermediaries.[21]

Yet a third characteristic of Jacques Polak's work is its *innovative* nature. We testify to some of that in the themes outlined later in this paper. So too do other papers presented at this conference. Still, we would be remiss in this review if we didn't note that at least two of Jacques' contributions, while less known than his work on economic fluctuations, on the monetary approach and on the international monetary system, are also highly significant.

By now, everyone who works on balance of payments and exchange rate issues employs the "absorption approach" as an integral part of their analytic tool kit. Whether the subject is the "twin deficits" in the United States or the reconstruction of Eastern European economies, the tack of looking to the private and public sector income-absorption balances as the counterpart to the current account has become almost second nature. Sidney Alexander's classic 1952 paper, "Effects of a Devaluation on a Trade Balance," is widely regarded as the first, definitive exposition of the absorption approach. Without wishing to take anything away from Alexander's path-breaking analysis, we would submit that Jacques Polak too was in the delivery room. The best indication of Polak's contribution can be found in a hitherto unpublished, 1948 paper, entitled "Depreciation to Meet a Situation of Overinvestment," prepared in response

---

[20] Polak (1954c).
[21] Polak (1959).

to Mexico's proposal for a depreciation of its currency.[22] In that paper, Jacques distinguishes among three causes of a loss of reserves: a price level that is too high due to domestic monetary inflation; structural difficulties in the balance of payments (e.g., natural resources that produce exports have become exhausted); and an extremely high demand for output in home use in the form either of domestic investment or a government deficit. He notes that whereas in the first and second cases, the loss of reserves is often accompanied by unemployment, the third case usually implies full employment. It is this third case on which he focuses. He then goes on to argue that a depreciation can restore equilibrium in the balance of payments "only if it eliminates the excess demand for resources which gave rise to it." He notes further that there may be "many instances where no reasonable amount of depreciation can achieve stability, since the rate of investment (private and governmental) is incompatible with the demand for consumption at levels of full employment. In such a situation, it will be necessary to cut investment (if consumption cannot be reduced by direct measures), rather than to rely on the haphazard allocation of resources by a rapidly falling rate of exchange."[23] Also included in the paper is a statement of the basic absorption identity (current account = government deficit + domestic investment − domestic saving). The way in which a depreciation is seen by Polak as reducing absorption is by the forced saving associated with the rise in prices. Specifically, he envisages a shift in income from groups (workers) with relatively low marginal propensities to save and subject to low taxation to groups (entrepreneurs) with higher saving and taxation propensities.

The analysis of the channels by which absorption is reduced is less comprehensive than in Alexander's later paper, but the basic idea is clearly there. Further corroboration of Polak's early appreciation for the central message of the absorption approach is contained in his discussant's comments at the 1951 meetings of the American Economic Association. Here, he argues

> I submit that the analysis of exchange rate changes would become much more useful if it did not start out from two, four, or eight elasticities, but from a simple social accounting identity, viz., that the existence of a balance-of-payments deficit implies that the country

---

[22] Polak (1948d).
[23] See this volume, p. 49.

absorbs more resources in consumption and investment than it produces. Therefore, if devaluation is to cure this deficit, it must either
increase production with consumption and investment constant, or
decrease consumption and investment with output constant, or achieve
some combination of the two. This I think is the more useful starting
point for a discussion of the effects of a change in an exchange rate.[24]

A second major innovation relates to the modeling of import
behavior in developing countries. A prominent feature of modern
global trade models is that import behavior is specified differently
for industrial countries than for developing ones. For the former, the
volume of imports is typically specified as a function of the level of
real income (in the importing country) and of the level of relative
import prices. In contrast, import volumes in developing countries
are treated as a function of their foreign exchange receipts or of the
level of their international reserves. This distinction was, for example, a key feature of the foreign sector in the Brookings Quarterly
Econometric Model of the United States in the mid-1960s; it remains
virtually intact in the latest (1990) version, MULTIMOD Mark II, of
the Fund's global macroeconomic model.

Again, Jacques Polak set the pattern. As far as we can tell, he first
introduced the imports/reserves nexus in his 1952 paper on ''The
Postwar International Cycle.''[25] Like many of Polak's ideas, this one
seems to have been motivated by a puzzle. Polak noticed that
during the 1946–52 period, there were severe cyclical movements in
international trade and reserves, even though the domestic
economies of almost all (industrial) countries exhibited remarkable
stability around a rising trend. After rounding up and then dismiss-
ing the usual suspects, Polak hit upon the observation that a key
difference between the prewar and postwar periods was the general-
ity of inadequate reserves in the latter period. He argued that there
were in fact only a handful of countries (the United States, Switzerland, Belgium, Canada, and Cuba) that could regard losses of
reserves with equanimity. In all other cases, he saw reserve fluctuations as playing a dominant role in import policy. From this, he
concluded that

the fact that the great majority of countries now tends to bring about or
make short run adjustments of imports to the exchange position rather

---

[24] Polak (1951d), p. 181.
[25] Polak (1952b).

than have them fluctuate through internal adjustment . . . has led to an international cyclical mechanism that is fundamentally different from that of the inter-war period.[26]

The conclusion that a function relating imports to foreign exchange availability is particularly relevant to the situation of the developing countries comes later. Specifically, it emerges in his joint 1962 paper with Rudolf Rhomberg on "Economic Stability in an International Setting." It is here that they hypothesize that the developing countries have typically had to adjust their imports to "their foreign exchange receipts on account of exports, inflow of private capital, and aid . . . . Broadly speaking, therefore, it is not an inaccurate description of the behavior of these countries as a group to say that they have had to adjust their imports to their exports . . . ."[27]

It would not be difficult to identify other areas in international economics where Polak has been an innovator. To quickly just mention a few more, there is the derivation (with Ta-Chung Liu) of the stability conditions for a devaluation in the multicountry case,[28] the specification of a money supply function,[29] the introduction of a control-group methodology for estimating the effects of devaluation,[30] and the properties of alternative currency baskets.[31]

A fourth characteristic of Jacques Polak's work is the *attention paid to country circumstances*. This may, at first blush, seem an odd thing to highlight. Yet we think it accounts, along with the insistence on a rigorous theoretical framework, for a good part of the quality control that one sees in all of Polak's writings. To Jacques Polak, just because one could see the forest was no reason to ignore the trees. Aggregation across countries comes at the end of Polak's empirical papers, after he has already satisfied himself that the individual country results make sense. Polak's 1943 study on "The National Income of the Netherlands Indies, 1921–1939," provided early experience in analyzing the structure of an individual economy.[32] So too we suspect did Jacques' tenure as a research assistant and collaborator of Professor Tinbergen. In any case, this fascination with how

---

[26] Polak (1952b), p. 253.
[27] Polak and Rhomberg (1962a), p. 113.
[28] Polak and Liu (1954b).
[29] Polak and White (1955a).
[30] Polak (1951a).
[31] Polak (1974).
[32] Polak (1943c).

individual economies operate, and with the differences among them, is always there. Thus, in his *An International Economic System*, the empirical application of his model is first given in 25 chapters, *one per subject country*.[33] Similarly, in a joint 1960 paper with Lorette Boissonneault that provides extensive empirical tests of the Polak model, one finds separate tables and charts for each of 39 subject countries![34] And when an estimate arises that doesn't seem right, Polak is prepared to pursue the factors involved, whether it is inventory fluctuations in the United States that are distorting the income-elasticity results, or supply developments in Western European countries that are distorting the estimates of the demand effects of a devaluation. Moreover, if superior data are available for a single country—even a small one—that will permit him to test a hypothesis of general interest, he will show no hesitation to proceed. It is a research strategy that one encounters infrequently—perhaps too infrequently—today.

We turn next to the three themes outlined earlier.

I. International Spillovers of National Economic Policies

In reviewing Jacques Polak's work, one cannot but be struck by his consistent interest in the following three questions: (1) what determines fluctuations in income and in balance of payments positions; (2) how can the spillover effects of national economic policies best be modeled and estimated; and (3) what can be done by policymakers to deal with the external and internal sources of economic instability?

To lend some perspective to Polak's involvement with this theme, it is relevant to recall the status quo in the late 1930s when Jacques began toiling in this vineyard. The economics profession was just starting to debate and to absorb the policy implications of Keynes's *General Theory*. Chief among these perhaps was the proposition that fluctuations in income would be driven primarily by fluctuations in domestic investment via the "multiplier." It was also a time when the modern system of national income accounts was just in its infancy. There was of course no possibility of studying economic

---

[33] Polak (1953).
[34] Polak and Boissonneault (1960).

interactions across countries by linking national econometric models, since such national models simply did not exist for the vast majority of countries. The ravages of the Great Depression were still very much in evidence; there was a vivid memory of the unhappy experience with competitive devaluations; capital controls and import restrictions were pervasive; and spillover effects of national economic policies took place primarily through the trade account of the balance of payments.

Put simply, what Jacques Polak did was to help extend the quantitative study of economic fluctuations to the open economy. To fluctuations in domestic investment, he added fluctuations in *exports* as an important factor in the business cycle. He also put forward a method of specifying economic interactions across countries that did not depend on the existence of national economic models, namely, the world trade model. By applying the techniques of correlation and multiple regression analysis—themselves only newly developed by Tinbergen at the Cowles Commission—Polak was also able to provide quantitative estimates of international spillovers. In addition, by including competitiveness as a determinant of exports and of income, his world trade model would be capable of handling exchange rate questions, as well as more straightforward income interactions.

Mark I of the Polak world trade model appeared in a remarkable 1939 paper entitled "The International Propagation of Business Cycles."[35] Here, Polak specifies a reduced-form relationship between an individual country's economic cycle (i.e., its index of industrial production) and three explanatory variables: the "world" cycle (an index of world industrial production); the individual country's exchange rate against the world (essentially an effective exchange rate designed to measure competitiveness); and a trend (to capture the country's secular development). The two main hypotheses were that there would be a positive correlation between the cycle of a country and that of the rest of the world, and a negative correlation between the national cycle and the price of the country's currency relative to other currencies. In brief, Polak finds that this small set of explanatory variables does indeed explain much of the fluctuation of economic activity in each of his eight subject countries over the 1920–36 period. Also, the signs of the correlations are as hypothesized. The sizes of the estimated coefficients seem reason-

---

[35] Polak (1939a).

able to Polak, with one notable exception, namely, the very high coefficient on the world cycle in the equation for the United States. Characteristically, Polak refuses to accept this at face value and goes on to argue that what this equation is indicating is a reverse causation from the U.S. cycle to the world cycle. Following up that line of inquiry, he is able to isolate the independent influence of the world on the U.S. economy, arriving at a (much lower) figure more in keeping with the relatively low degree of openness of that economy. In the latter part of this article, Polak uses Tinbergen's structural model of the Dutch economy to gauge not only the impact of world events on the Dutch economy but also the value of the domestic multiplier.

Mark II was first presented to the Econometric Society in 1949 (Polak (1950a)) and appeared in full in 1953 in the volume *An International Economic System*. By this time, the model has become a set of structural equations that would be quite familiar to today's global trade modelers. Exports are a function of world exports and an index of competitiveness. Income is a function of exports. Imports are a function of domestic income and of relative import prices. Finally, the model is closed with an identity that establishes the equality of exports and imports. Empirical tests are then conducted on each of the structural equations, so that the estimated income and relative-price elasticities of demand can be obtained. The regressions are first run on an individual-country basis and aggregated only at the end. Income elasticities tend to be better determined than the estimated price elasticities.

This global trade model, simple as it was, made it possible to obtain quantitative answers to questions about international spillovers that hitherto could be addressed only qualitatively. In the final chapter of *An International Economic System*, Polak takes the model through a few of its paces. He asks to what extent the decline in economic activity in the United States between 1929 and 1932, and the resulting reduction in the supply of dollars, was responsible for the reduction in world trade in the Depression. Using his estimate of the world trade multiplier, along with some supplementary analysis of the evolution of the U.S. balance of payments position, Polak is able to arrive at the estimate that roughly three fifths of the decline in world trade from 1929 to 1932 was attributable to events in the United States. By implication, Polak also concludes that import restrictions played only a minor role in the world trade decline.

By now, it has of course become possible to "link" together

national econometric models in order to simulate the spillover effects of national economic policies. Still, much of the structure of Polak's early trade model is embedded in the present generation of global trade models—including the notion that spillover effects are heavily influenced by the change in imports induced by a change in exports, that is, by what Jacques labeled the international "reflection ratio." A second pillar on which today's modeling of interdependence stands was erected by two prominent Research Department colleagues of Jacques Polak, namely, Marcus Fleming and Robert Mundell.[36] With the aid of the Mundell-Fleming model, it became feasible to gauge the spillover effects of monetary and fiscal policies, to bring the influence of interest-sensitive international capital flows into the picture, and to isolate the effect of the exchange rate regime (i.e., fixed versus floating exchange rates) on the transmission process. Add to this Polak-Mundell-Fleming framework a forward-looking expectations scheme, the requisite balance sheet constraints, and reasonable steady-state properties, and one has the nucleus of the modern open-economy macroeconomic model.

Jacques Polak's interest in the spillover effects of national economic policies did not stop at the border between econometric modeling and policy recommendations. In the early 1960s, Polak in fact began to concentrate on the types of policies and institutional changes that might bring greater stability to the world economy. It is possible to discern three interrelated strands within Jacques' overall line of thought on this topic.

One deals with measures that might help to stabilize the imports of developing countries by reducing the instability of their export receipts. In this connection, Polak was impressed by the magnitude of the fluctuations that routinely took place in the export prices and volumes of primary producing countries. He also noted that when the developing countries reduced their imports, there was a nontrivial feedback on the exports and incomes of the industrial countries. This suggested to Polak that there could be merit in establishing a mechanism that would compensate (developing) countries for temporary fluctuations in their export receipts that were predominantly beyond their control. In a 1962 paper with Rudolf Rhomberg on "Economic Instability in an International Setting," the authors are already musing about the order of magnitude of the resources

---

[36] Fleming (1962) and Mundell (1968).

necessary to carry out a program of full compensatory financing.[37] We suspect that it was more than coincidence that in 1963, a compensatory financing facility was established in the Fund. While that facility has since undergone a number of extensions and modifications, its basic purpose of preventing temporary, exogenous shocks from throwing good policies in developing countries offtrack, has remained close to Polak's original conception.

A second strand is concerned with the management of international liquidity. This is a topic that we shall be discussing in greater depth in Section III of this paper. For now, it is enough to note that Polak has consistently argued that proper management of international liquidity can help individual countries to maintain a stable level of aggregate demand.

The third strand goes directly to policy formation in the industrial countries. In Polak's view, the primary responsibility for keeping the world economy on an even keel inevitably rests with the main industrial countries.[38] It should come as no surprise, therefore, that he has also been an active participant in the long-running debate on the merits and limits of *economic policy coordination*. Polak's first paper on the subject, "International Coordination of Economic Policy," appeared in 1962.[39] Since then, he has returned to the subject on at least four occasions, most recently, in 1989.[40]

Polak has no quibble with the basic rationale for policy coordination. Given the existence of international externalities and international public goods, it is useful to have some mechanism that induces countries to take better account of the international effects of their national policy decisions. Polak likewise seems comfortable with the proposition that joint policymaking can in principle be more effective in achieving certain objectives than decentralized policymaking, if only because the former always retains the latter as a default option. Nor does Polak have any difficulty with the claim that policy coordination can produce significant benefits by making national policymakers better informed about the policies and policy intentions of their colleagues in other countries (although he would probably call this policy "collaboration" rather than policy "coordination").

---

[37] Polak and Rhomberg (1962a).
[38] Polak (1962b).
[39] Polak (1962b).
[40] Polak (1981a, 1984c, 1989b, and 1989c).

Jacques Polak has pushed the debate on policy coordination forward by reminding us of the formidable constraints that limit the scope for policy coordination in practice, by highlighting the advantages of a decentralized approach to adjustment, and by offering explicit suggestions for the focus of multilateral surveillance. We consider each of these aspects in turn.

Much has been made of the obstacles to policy coordination thrown up by different views among countries on how policy instruments affect policy targets, by the proclivity to treat certain policy instruments as objectives in themselves, and by the differing incentives to coordinate implied by differences in openness across countries. Yet it was left to Polak to draw attention to an additional obstacle that may well be the most constraining in practice. We refer here to the marked tendency for international bargaining to come *after* domestic bargaining. As emphasized in Polak's 1981 publication, *Coordination of National Economic Policies* (prepared for the Group of Thirty), the compromise of objectives at the national level is nowadays often so delicately balanced as to leave relatively little room for further compromise at the international level.[41] The experiences of trying to fashion a budget agreement in the United States, of agreeing on the financing of German unification, and of implementing structural reform in Japan attest amply to the point at hand. In view of the multiple constraints facing policy coordination, Polak has argued that it is likely to be most successful when spillover effects are obvious, when obligations are specific in nature and compliance can thus be readily observed, and when participants have committed themselves to observe certain policy rules or codes of conduct.

Jacques Polak's endorsement of the "decentralized" or "atomistic" approach to adjustment reflects his strong view that a more centralized approach carries a greater risk of delaying needed policy changes. This is because the centralized approach offers no technical solution to the question of how to share the collective adjustment burden and is thus a prime target for protracted political posturing and scapegoating. In contrast, so Polak argues, the decentralized approach to adjustment, long followed in the IMF's individual country consultations as well as in the OECD's Working Party No. 3, is not prone to this malady, since it places on each country experiencing a large imbalance the responsibility to bring that imbal-

---

[41] Polak (1981a).

ance down. By "adjustment," Polak means maintaining a surplus or deficit on current account that is not in excess of what the country can finance over the medium term. We can do no better in explaining the rationale for the decentralized approach than to quote from Polak's 1989 paper on "Strengthening the Role of the IMF in the International Monetary System":

> There are a number of good reasons for this decentralized approach. First, almost all countries' policies are overwhelmingly more important for their own economic health than in terms of their impact on the world economy . . . .
>
> Second, the decentralized approach provides a practical . . . answer to the question of which countries should take action and how much: Each country with a substantial unsustainable external disequilibrium should take enough action to reduce its disequilibrium to manageable proportions.
>
> Third, the approach is likely to place the adjustment burden largely on the country where the disequilibrium originates. That country will have a large surplus or deficit, while the resulting deficits or surpluses in all other countries will tend to be much smaller in proportion to their trade flows.[42]

We are less convinced than Jacques about the sufficiency of the decentralized approach to adjustment. As he himself concedes, the decentralized approach hardly distinguished itself in say, the ten-year period leading up to the Plaza Agreement of 1985; indeed, it was the very dissatisfaction with the decentralized approach—including the protectionist pressures associated with the large overvaluation of the U.S. dollar and the large existing payments imbalances among the three largest industrial countries—that provided the impetus for the revival of policy coordination. Nor is it obvious that the risk of delaying needed policy adjustments will consistently be higher with a coordinated approach. After all, it could be argued that free-riding will be diminished when the major players are asked to make policy adjustments simultaneously as part of a coordinated policy package; in contrast, with an uncoordinated approach, each country can legitimately claim that its own imbalance reflects in part policy inadequacies elsewhere, and that it will only tackle its own problems when there is assurance that others are simultaneously dealing with theirs. Finally, we would note that the identification of

---

[42]Polak (1989c), pp. 59–60. For an alternative view, see Frenkel, Goldstein, and Masson (1990).

a "sustainable" current account imbalance has proved to be a tougher nut to crack analytically than Polak perhaps implies in his definition of adjustment. For example, who would be willing to go to the stake to defend a net capital inflow for the United States of $50 billion rather than $100 billion—yet the difference between such numbers surely carries nontrivial implications for adjustment. In fact, this same difficulty of identifying sustainable capital flows plagues estimates of "equilibrium" exchange rates as well.[43]

As part of his recent appraisal of the policy coordination process, Polak has also put his finger on a key unresolved question: how can a satisfactory, *global* level of economic activity be assured? His other concerns notwithstanding, this is an area where Polak sees the need to temper the disaggregated approach to adjustment with some central guidance. He does not regard any single indicator, such as an index of primary commodity prices, as providing a reliable diagnosis. Instead, he looks to a more judgmental assessment of the prevailing state of the world economy to provide the appropriate "slant" to individual-country adjustment actions. Polak's comments at the conference on "Macroeconomic Policies in an Interdependent World," sponsored by the Brookings Institution, the Centre for Economic Policy Research, and the IMF, outline his preferred solution to this thorny issue:

> There is one thing that a process of adjustment to imbalances does *not* ensure, namely, a satisfactory level of world activity.... The prevailing state of the world economy should set the direction, positive or negative, in which the balance of the adjustment impacts of individual countries is slanted. There is no reason to expect the separate adjustment actions of individual countries to conform to this rule. In some contexts, policy coordination may rather easily provide the answer. Where differential monetary policies are used by a group of major countries, their actions should be based on a judgment of the direction in which interest rates in the world in general should move. In an inflationary context, deficit countries should raise their rates.... By contrast, in a deflationary context, surplus countries should lower their rates....
>
> This raises a major challenge for international organizations: to guide the decentralized adjustment process, on which they have to rely even with an active Group of Seven, to the desired result in terms of aggregate demand.[44]

---

[43] Frenkel and Goldstein (1988).
[44] Polak (1989b), p. 377.

II. The Monetary Approach to the Balance of Payments

The view that the balance of payments is essentially a monetary phenomenon gained widespread popularity during the 1960s and 1970s. The monetary approach contains at least two basic insights into balance of payments analysis. First, the balance of payments position of a country reflects decisions on the part of its residents to accumulate or run down their stock of money balances. It is this process of monetary adjustment that gives rise to balance of payments surpluses and deficits. Second, in an open economy operating under fixed exchange rates, the money supply is not controlled by the monetary authorities; it is the domestic component of the monetary base (domestic credit) that is the relevant monetary policy variable, rather than the overall monetary base, since the latter is an endogenous variable responding to changes in international reserves.

The monetary approach to the balance of payments has had a long history in the Fund as well as outside.[45] The distinction between money of external origin (international reserves) and money of domestic origin (domestic credit) probably goes back in the Fund at least as far as a 1946 paper by Triffin.[46] Certainly, the relationship between monetary factors and the balance of payments was recognized by Fund staff involved in designing stabilization and adjustment programs with member countries in the late 1940s and early 1950s. At that time, the work in the Fund was described as "the quantity theory of money in an open economy," or as "monetary and balance of payments analysis," or most commonly, as "financial programming."[47]

Jacques Polak was a pioneer in the development of the monetary approach in the Fund. What Polak set out to do in a series of papers written over two decades was to integrate monetary and credit factors into balance of payments analysis and to derive a formal relationship between policy measures and balance of payments outcomes. The framework he developed, which is incorporated in a set of balance sheet and behavioral relationship linking assets and liabilities of the banking system to the balance of payments, yielded

---

[45] Frenkel and Johnson (1976) and Mundell (1968).
[46] Triffin (1946).
[47] Rhomberg and Heller (1977).

a unique relationship between changes in domestic credit and changes in international reserves. Just as important, this framework could be used fruitfully for setting policy. In many respects, it was a fundamental breakthrough. Almost thirty-five years after his seminal 1957 paper was published, virtually all Fund-supported adjustment programs still exploit this key linkage between domestic credit and the balance of payments and still employ domestic credit ceilings as a performance criterion.[48] Impressive too is the extent to which the monetary approach has subsequently been successfully applied to help explain the behavior of endogenous open-economy variables that were taken as exogenous in the original formulation. Thus, the 1970s and the 1980s witnessed the development of a monetary approach to international capital flows[49] and to the determination of floating exchange rates.[50]

A 1955 paper by Polak and William H. White on "The Effect of Income Expansion on the Quantity of Money" took as its point of departure the stylized empirical fact that in some countries money and income expansion were positively related, while in others the relationship was negative. Negative co-movements were difficult to justify using the standard closed-economy business cycle models of the time.[51] Polak and White illustrated how a monetary approach could provide analytical support for the proposition that an expansion of income would be accompanied by a fall in the money supply. The basic reasoning went as follows: higher incomes will lead to higher imports (and exports will also tend to decline as more resources are absorbed internally). The balance of payments will go into deficit, and the fall in the stock of international reserves—provided that the central bank did not expand credit to offset the effect of the loss of reserves—will lead to a decline in the money supply. Formally, the sign of the relationship between money and income depends on the respective sizes of velocity, the marginal propensity to import, the reserve ratio of the banking system, and the interest elasticities of the demand and supply of money. In general, if the interest elasticity of the demand for money was larger (smaller) than the interest elasticity of money supply, the money stock would fall (rise).

---

[48] International Monetary Fund (1987) and Robichek (1985).
[49] Kouri and Porter (1974).
[50] Frenkel and Mussa (1985).
[51] Polak and White (1955a).

This hypothesis was tested and the data tended to support the authors' conclusions. The empirical tests performed by Polak and White are interesting in that not only are estimates for the interest elasticities derived—via the use of charts—but also a dynamic period-by-period analysis is conducted. The latter enabled the authors to estimate that the lag in the response of the money supply to changes in nominal income was typically less than one year.

There are two aspects of the Polak-White paper that are particularly relevant to the development of the monetary approach. First, one of the main elements of this approach, namely the endogenous nature of the money supply, is outlined and tested. Second, the transmission mechanism between the money supply and income, working primarily via interest rates, is spelled out.

It is also worth noting that the Polak-White model yields quite a different answer for the effects of an *exogenous* increase in income than does, say, a later "Chicago" version of the monetary approach.[52] The latter would suggest that an expansion in income would increase the demand for money. If the supply of domestic credit was fixed, this rise in the demand for money could only be satisfied from abroad, that is, through an increase in international reserves. Thus, there would be a positive relationship between changes in income and changes in the money supply in an open economy, irrespective of the relative sizes of the interest elasticities of money demand and money supply.[53] The Polak-White paper was followed by three papers that placed Jacques Polak's indelible stamp on the monetary approach to the balance of payments. In 1957 he published his classic piece, "Monetary Analysis of Income Formation and Payments Problems," which contained the simple framework now known as the "Polak Model."[54] In a subsequent 1960 joint paper with Lorette Boissonneault, some of the main properties of the Polak model were tested.[55] A later (1971) paper with Victor Argy developed a more general model of the balance of payments, and compared its analytical properties with those of the original Polak model.[56]

The 1957 paper brought together the various strands of thinking

---

[52] Frenkel and Johnson (1976).

[53] See also Mundell (1968) for the relationship between the rate of growth of output and the balance of payments.

[54] Polak (1957a).

[55] Polak and Boissonneault (1960).

[56] Polak and Argy (1971b).

on monetary developments, absorption, and the balance of payments into a very simple, albeit rich, structural model. This model contains two behavioral relationships: an import demand function and a quantity theory of money equation designed to explain nominal income. Two identities, for the balance of payments (equal to exports minus imports plus net capital flows) and for the money supply (equal to domestic credit of the banking system and the domestic currency value of net international reserves), are used to close the system.

Polak stressed that to integrate monetary analysis into income analysis, domestic credit had to be the policy, or control, variable. To illustrate how the Polak model works, consider the case of a temporary expansion in domestic credit. The increase in domestic credit initially raises the money supply, and from the quantity theory of money relationship, nominal income rises. However, the increase in nominal income causes imports to increase, and given exports and net capital flows, the balance of payments worsens. The resulting fall in international reserves pushes the money supply down, and the process is reversed. In the long run, the expansion in domestic credit is matched by a loss of international reserves.

This one-for-one relationship between changes in domestic credit and international reserves is, of course, the fundamental equation of the monetary approach to the balance of payments. But Polak went further and offered both short-run solutions and an explicit formulation of the channels through which domestic credit expansion affected the balance of payments.

To use the Polak model to formulate policy, one simply need choose a target value for the endogenous variable, say the level of international reserves; calculate values for the exogenous variables in the system (exports and capital flows); and then solve for the expansion in domestic credit that would be consistent with the target. The Polak model thus provides analytical justification (under a fixed exchange rate regime) for the use of credit ceilings as a performance criterion in adjustment programs supported by the Fund. By monitoring the expansion in domestic credit, one can determine if the program is "on track" in achieving the targeted increase in international reserves.

In the same 1957 paper, Polak also demonstrated how one could go about applying the model, by obtaining values for the key ratios needed—namely, velocity, the average propensity to import, and the ratio of the money supply to imports. His sample included some 48 industrial and developing countries over the period 1950–54. In

Polak and Boissonneault, more extensive tests of the model were undertaken for a group of 39 countries using the period 1948–58. It was concluded that the model predicted imports (the only endogenous component of the balance of payments) reasonably well from monetary data. In Polak and Argy, a more general model is developed. On the face of it, this model has a very Keynesian-looking structure, except that it retains the central identity expressing the money supply as the sum of domestic credit and international reserves. This model, considered to be more relevant for economies with developed financial structures, places considerable emphasis on the role of interest rates in money demand and in international capital flows. The Polak model is nested within this expanded model and can be obtained by setting both the interest elasticity of money demand and the interest-responsiveness of capital flows equal to zero. While some differences between the two models are found with respect to the short-run effects of changes in domestic credit on the balance of payments, these differences do not alter any of the principal propositions of the monetary approach. In the long run, the two models yield identical results. The conclusions drawn by Polak on the basis of his earlier papers therefore do not appear to be narrowly model-specific.

While the Polak model has a simple—even rudimentary—structure, the simplicity is somewhat deceptive. It turns out in fact to be an extremely versatile model that can be applied easily across countries. Furthermore, it is a flexible model that can be extended in many ways without disturbing the key results. Indeed, the popularity of this model, both as an analytical device and as a policymaking tool, stems in many respects from its general adaptability. This adaptability can perhaps best be illustrated by considering two extensions of the Polak model: first, to include an explicit treatment of output; and second, to introduce exchange rates and interest rates as additional policy instruments.

In Polak's papers on the monetary approach, no attempt is made to split nominal income into its price and real output components. Since there may well be situations in which one is interested in ascertaining the effects of policies on the balance of payments, prices, and output, the use of only nominal income can be considered restrictive. One might even say that there is a "missing equation," much along the same lines as in the quantity-theory-of-money determination of nominal income.[57] Our own view is that

---

[57] Friedman (1970).

since the nominal income equation in the model is basically a variant of the quantity theory of money, it is output that is left unspecified.

There are many ways of introducing output determination into the Polak model without affecting its essential properties. One option—albeit one that Polak finds less than satisfactory[58]—is to combine the Polak model with a version of an open economy, neoclassical growth model.[59] Introducing an additional equation for capacity output, and making appropriate modifications to the model, allows one to analyze the behavior of prices and output separately. The resulting model has properties very similar to those of the original Polak model: an expansion in domestic credit will raise prices, increase output, and worsen the balance of payments. Other alternatives could also be considered. For example, it is possible to have both capacity output and actual output determined endogenously in the model, using a growth equation for the former and an aggregate supply equation for the latter. Again, the main Polak conclusions are unaffected, reinforcing the robust nature of the original model.

One cannot choose targets for nominal income and the balance of payments independently in the Polak model since there is only one policy instrument available, namely, domestic credit. Another policy tool is called for, and again there are a number of possibilities. Here, we consider the exchange rate and interest rates.

The Polak model—consistent with the spirit of the monetary approach to the balance of payments—assumes fixed exchange rates. In actual practice, however, exchange rate adjustments often play a key role in adjustment programs. As such, it seems natural to introduce the exchange rate into the specification.[60] One way of doing so is to add an identity that links changes in the overall price level to the weighted sum of changes in the domestic price level (or price of nontradables) and the foreign price level (adjusted by exchange rate changes). With the inclusion of this identity, the model takes on an additional equation, an additional endogenous variable (domestic prices), and an additional policy instrument.[61] The import equation can also be modified to incorporate relative prices and the exchange rate. The policymaker can then attain

---

[58] Polak (1990a).

[59] Khan and Montiel (1989) and Khan, Montiel, and Haque (1990).

[60] Note that as soon as one introduces changes in the exchange rate, the complex but important element of *expectations* enters the picture.

[61] Khan, Montiel, and Haque (1990).

independently the targeted values for the balance of payments and for nominal income.

Another policy instrument would be interest rates. While Polak's work reflects his awareness of the role of interest rates in the domestic money market and in international capital flows,[62] he chose to treat the rate of interest as an endogenous variable. But in a developing country context, interest rates are often an administered policy instrument. If a rise in interest rates (including rates on bank deposits) results in an increased demand for domestic financial assets (and for money in particular), then for a given change in domestic credit, the balance of payments would improve.[63]

Jacques Polak has in fact just recently returned to the topic of interest rate policy in developing countries in his (1989) book, *Financial Policies and Development*.[64] While this book deals with the wider issues of development and external debt, much of what it says about the effects of interest rate policies on saving, investment, and growth has a bearing on the balance of payments as well. Here, we focus exclusively on the analytical and empirical aspects of interest rate policy.

The analytical framework begins with the standard proposition that, given the growth rate of the labor force, an increase in real output is the result of an increase in investment (total saving) and of its productivity or efficiency. Where capital markets are perfect, average (and marginal) productivities of investment projects are equalized and, therefore, one can postulate a uniform, aggregate average (and marginal) productivity of capital. When capital markets are imperfect, the marginal products of investment projects are not equalized, and the question then arises of how resources should be allocated.

Polak considers two possible allocative mechanisms: (1) a command economy where the government taxes away all private saving and directs it into different investment projects; and (2) a decentralized market mechanism, where there are banks and other financial institutions, and where competition for savings occurs via interest rates, dividends, and the like. The command system is suboptimal because it is unlikely that the government will allocate resources on a cost-benefit basis and without political interference; for example, the authorities often have a strong preference for public enterprises

---

[62] Polak and White (1955a), Polak and Argy (1971b), and Polak (1976a).

[63] The interest rate here is the own rate of return.

[64] Polak (1989a).

over private ones. The second allocative mechanism approximates the banking and capital markets found in advanced countries. Not surprisingly, it is the latter mechanism that Polak prefers.

Polak notes that while the market mechanism functions with a reasonable degree of efficiency in the industrial countries, efficiency is much lower in developing countries where domestic capital markets are fragmented both geographically (partly due to poor communications and transport) and vertically (official markets coexisting with unofficial ones). He argues that an important consequence of such fragmentation is that the system fails both to secure the maximum saving out of a given level of income, and to allocate it to the most productive investment projects. In Polak's world, savings, investment, and growth can be raised by reducing fragmentation and by increasing interest rates.

One of Polak's key points is that by maintaining real interest rates that are positive and close to market rates, developing countries can promote economic growth. While acknowledging the statistically weak effect of interest rates on private saving found in other studies, Polak argues that increasing interest rates can have powerful beneficial *allocative* effects. To bolster his case, Jacques presents (pooled cross-section, time-series) regression equations where the rate of economic growth is the dependent variable and where the real interest rate is a robust explanatory variable (with a positive coefficient). The equations utilize a sample of 40 developing countries and cover the 20-year period through the mid-1980s.

Polak's policy prescription is orthodox: raise interest rates to their market equilibrium level (to the extent that this is known), so as to spur saving, investment, and growth. Another part of Polak's policy recommendations is the call for decontrol of interest rates *conditional* on a sufficient degree of competition among banks and on effective bank supervision. If these conditions are not satisfied, Polak suggests the continuation of regulated interest rates (assuming that implementation will display some flexibility).[65]

III. The Functioning of the International Monetary System

Jacques Polak served on the Fund staff for 33 years. Since Jacques himself has noted that "the broadest job description for the Fund is

---

[65] See also Villanueva and Mirakhor (1990).

its responsibility for the functioning of the international monetary system,"[66] it was almost inevitable that a good portion of his professional writing would deal with the system. It is perhaps easiest if we divide our remarks on this theme into two parts: the exchange rate system and international liquidity.

Curiously enough—especially so in a field where there are very few nonaligned participants—one would search in vain for a clear signal in Polak's writings as to whether he is a fixed-rate man or a floater. This is of course not because he attaches little importance to the evolution of the exchange rate system. Quite aside from his academic writings on the subject, Jacques was also one of the principal contributors to Article IV—which lays out obligations regarding exchange arrangements under the Second Amendment to the Fund's Articles of Agreement—as well as to the existing principles underlying the Fund's surveillance over exchange rate policies.[67] It would seem instead that Polak has simply not found the fixed/floating regime issue to be an illuminating one without recourse to particular systemic and individual country circumstances. Thus, for example, Polak has frequently in his writings paid tribute to the extraordinary success enjoyed by the world economy in the quarter century following World War II and has regarded the par value system as an important element making for stability.[68] At the same time, he has noted that the success of Bretton Woods, at least up until the mid-1960s, reflected an implicit contract that would not necessarily be transferable to other situations. This contract specified that the dominant economic power (the United States) would maintain domestic economic stability and that other countries, as compensation for giving up monetary policy independence, would import stability from the center. But if the dominant country lapsed seriously in its financial discipline, the others would likely seek other mechanisms of stability. Nor is it likely that the dominant economic power would be willing to subordinate its monetary policy to that of other countries for the sake of a fixed exchange rate, even if some other country exhibited superior inflation performance.

Polak has also emphasized that the greatly expanded role of private capital markets now puts any system of stable exchange

---

[66] Polak (1989c), p. 52.
[67] See International Monetary Fund, *Selected Decisions and Selected Documents of the International Monetary Fund*, Sixteenth Issue (Washington, 1991).
[68] Polak (1988c).

rates under strong pressures. These pressures can be overcome if the participating countries place high value on the maintenance of the fixed exchange rate and if they are prepared to go quite far in adjusting national policies to the exchange rate constraint. As far as the world's major trading countries are concerned, Jacques expresses some skepticism about their willingness to meet this test. In his 1988 paper on "The Choice of an Exchange Rate Regime," he observes that " 'the best will in the world' to subordinate national monetary and fiscal policies to an exchange rate system of that nature is not in evidence."[69] In short, conditions need to be propitious for the establishment and durability of a fixed rate system; otherwise, some variant of "managed" floating will probably be the outcome.

In much the same way, Polak has declined to offer blanket recommendations on exchange rate policy for either individual countries or for groups of them, preferring instead to adopt a case-by-case approach. Polak's summing-up of a recent (1990) conference on "Choosing an Exchange Rate Regime in Smaller Industrial Countries" provides insight into the types of factors that he considers important in the regime decision. These include the country's track record on inflation; the "credibility" advantages of foreclosing certain courses of action on monetary policy (and in this context, the merits of a hard exchange rate commitment vis-à-vis granting greater independence to the central bank); the value of changes in the nominal exchange rate, relative to other adjustment mechanisms, in responding to country-specific real economic shocks (particularly in primary producing countries subject to unusually large terms-of-trade fluctuations); the effects of real exchange rate variability on the efficiency of resource allocation; the nature of the government's loss function; and the geographical pattern of the country's foreign trade.[70] Since these factors obviously differ across countries, Polak does not regard the observed heterogeneity of exchange arrangements as disturbing in itself, although he also cautions that the actual regime choices made by countries may sometimes simply be incorrect.

If Jacques Polak has been agnostic about the optimal exchange arrangement, he has been zealous about the key attributes that a well-functioning exchange rate *system* ought to possess. He has in

---

[69] Polak (1988c), p. 133.
[70] Polak (1990b).

particular stressed the need for the system to encourage disciplined and stable macroeconomic policies at the national level, to identify as early as possible—and to discourage—disequilibrium real exchange rates, and to adopt rules, guidelines, or understandings about countries' adjustment responsibilities. A few words on each of these desiderata are in order.

Polak would not, we think, be willing to go so far as to suggest that disciplined monetary and fiscal policies would be sufficient to generate a stable system of exchange rates. But he is certainly right to emphasize that it is a necessary condition.[71] Consistent with this message, right up front in Article IV, is the exhortation to members to "endeavor to direct [their] economic and financial policies toward the objective of fostering orderly economic growth with reasonable price stability" and "to seek to promote stability by fostering orderly . . . economic and financial conditions." In Polak's discussions of exchange rate policies, it is always the dog wagging the tail—not the other way around.

We also strongly support Polak's second tenet that disequilibrium real exchange rates, generated under whatever form of exchange arrangements, can impose sufficiently large welfare costs as to justify oversight by the international community. If the entreaty to members in Article IV and in the surveillance guidelines to "avoid manipulating exchange rates or the international monetary system" was written on stone tablets, it might be shortened to "thou shalt not have the wrong exchange rate." The tricky part of course is how to recognize a "wrong" exchange rate before it gets too far out of line. In this connection, it is worth paraphrasing the so-called pointers included in the surveillance guidelines as indicating the need for discussion between the Fund and a member country. There are five of them: (1) protracted large-scale intervention in one direction in the exchange market; (2) an unsustainable level of official or quasi-official borrowing or lending for balance of payments purposes; (3) the introduction, substantial intensification, or prolonged maintenance, for balance of payments purposes, of restrictions on, or incentives for, either current transactions or payments, or for the inflow or outflow of capital; (4) the pursuit, for balance of payments purposes, of monetary and other domestic financial policies that provide abnormal encouragement or discouragement to capital flows; and (5) behavior of the exchange rate that appears to be unrelated to

---

[71] Polak (1976b).

underlying economic and financial conditions. Note that whereas the first four pointers might legitimately be viewed as symptoms of a misalignment, the fifth pointer almost seems like a definition of the disease itself. This fifth pointer was included to cover the misalignment of a floating rate and thereby, to place "floaters" under standards of surveillance equivalent to those of "fixers." But the exercise also illustrates another message that surfaces in Polak's work on the system: neither markets nor governments can be counted on always to set exchange rates at an appropriate level. If multilateral surveillance over exchange rates is to be effective, it will have to deal with *both* sources of misalignment. The appearance of disequilibrium exchange rates for key currencies in both the latter days of Bretton Woods as well as in the latter days of unmanaged floating (1984–85) supports that verdict.

In Section I of this paper, we discussed Jacques Polak's endorsement for a "disaggregated" approach to adjustment. This is really part and parcel of Polak's broader view that the adjustment process will work well only if members of the system understand clearly what their obligations are. Here, Jacques sees some significant advantages in a rule-based framework. For one thing, it decreases the need for discretionary policy coordination since the rule itself, assuming it is a good one, will take care of the needs of the system. In this connection, it is well to recall that Polak was deeply involved in the work of the Committee of Twenty on the reform of the international monetary system, including the recommendation in its 1974 report for a universal system of asset settlement.[72] As Polak notes in a 1989 comment on policy coordination and surveillance, the aim of that effort was to make it more difficult for deficit countries to finance deficits by incurring liabilities, thus avoiding adjustment.[73] This was to be buttressed by reserve indicators that would signal the need for adjustment on the part of deficit and surplus countries alike, and by means of sanctions that would be set off when the reserve indicators pointed to large and persistent disequilibria. In the event, the Committee of Twenty's recommendations were stillborn. More fundamentally, the growth of private capital markets turned the Committee's adjustment rule on its head: instead of universal asset settlement, the world moved closer to universal

---

[72] Committee on Reform of the International Monetary System and Related Issues (Committee of Twenty) (1974).
[73] Polak (1989b).

liability settlement, as more and more countries found they could finance payments deficits by tapping the private markets. Since the demise of the Committee of Twenty and the coming into force of the Second Amendment, there has been a revival of policy coordination and more "management" of key-currency exchange rates, but little in the way of a more rule-based orientation for the adjustment process.

Part of the story is that it has proved extremely difficult to design policy rules that would be robust to significant changes in the operating environment; witness, for example, the downgrading of monetary targeting in major industrial countries. Part of it is that there is perhaps less agreement than in the 1960s or 1970s about what constitutes a "sustainable" current account position in a world of continuing capital market integration and innovation. And part of it is also that it may well be intrinsically more difficult to write tight guidelines for a managed floating regime in the absence of publicly announced target zones. The existing surveillance principles clearly have their limitations. While broad enough to cover a wide array of exchange arrangements, they are not specific enough to guide the adjustment process in an automatic fashion. Nor do the practices that they prohibit account for the bulk of policy inadequacies. For example, the absence of either "manipulation" of exchange rates or of policies undertaken for "balance of payments purposes" alone, such as exchange controls or excessive borrowing, is unlikely to be sufficient to produce satisfactory exchange rate or balance of payments outcomes.[74]

To Jacques Polak, while agreement on rules that put certain policy options "out of bounds" would be the preferred path to strengthening the exchange rate system, it is not necessary to insist that rules be enshrined in the statutes of international organizations. What counts, after all, is results. In this sense, firm understandings could be a useful second best. In a 1989 commentary, Jacques offers a clue as to what he has in mind: "In what has been called the present non-system, it might not be beyond the realm of the possible for central bankers to have a firm understanding about avoiding competitive interest rate escalation even in situations in which their finance ministers could not reach agreement on the coordination of fiscal or other policies."[75] More food for thought.

---

[74] Crockett and Goldstein (1987).
[75] Polak (1989b), p. 376.

We move next to the other half of the international monetary system, namely provisions for the supply and management of international liquidity, including the creation and evolution of the SDR. The separation is of course artificial. The very reason why Jacques Polak has been so interested in international liquidity is that its inadequacy could threaten the expansion of the world economy, as well as progress toward a liberal system of trade and capital movements. The exchange rate system and the arrangements for international liquidity were thus *both* seen by Polak as facilitating mechanisms for more fundamental economic objectives.

As usual when there was a potential threat to the system, Polak was part of the first division to hit the beach. Although the First Amendment to the Articles of Agreement went into effect in July 1969 and the Governors of the Fund voted for the first allocation of SDRs a few months later, Polak's involvement began much earlier. As noted in Section I of this paper, Polak was already writing in the early 1960s about an inadequacy of international reserves in the developing countries as a source of economic instability.[76] At the same time, and of more immediate danger, there was the prospect—most persuasively laid out by Robert Triffin—that the gold exchange standard based on a fixed dollar price of gold would inevitably produce either a reserve shortage or a breakdown of the system itself. All of this was taken up in official discussions, beginning in the fall of 1963, and involving the Deputies of the Group of Ten, the Executive Board of the Fund, the two groups combined, and the Ministers of the Group of Ten. The agreed solution to the dilemma was to give more elasticity to the supply of reserves by creating an international reserve asset (the SDR) that was not the liability of any national government, and by allocating SDRs "to meet the long-term global need...to supplement existing reserve assets."[77]

Enough to say that Jacques Polak was instrumental in developing most of the original economic features of the SDR. Since then, he has worked tirelessly to improve the attractiveness and usefulness of the SDR in the face of changing circumstances. In the process, he has also been the most eloquent spokesman and writer for why the SDR still has a future.

As Jacques has chronicled in a number of his recent writings,

---

[76] Polak and Rhomberg (1962a).
[77] Article XVIII, Section 1 of the IMF's Articles of Agreement.

things have worked very differently than anticipated at the time of the SDR's birth.[78] Under the twin assumptions that other sources of reserves would grow modestly and that SDRs would be allocated, as and when needed, to meet the long-term global demand for reserves, it was then envisaged that the SDR could by the end of the century account for over half of total world reserves and would eventually become "the principal reserve asset in the international monetary system."[79] But before the first basic period of allocation (1970–72) was completed, the ruptures in the system that the SDR was intended to prevent—an increase in the dollar price of gold and the cessation of official convertibility of the dollar into gold—occurred anyway. More importantly, the supply of other reserves in fact grew immodestly, as liability settlement in reserve currencies become more and more widespread. This in turn made any threat of a global reserve shortage seem distant. Proposals for increasing the share of SDRs in official reserve portfolios via "substitution accounts" did not garner the requisite support. This was true both of the Committee of Twenty's proposal for a mandatory substitution of SDRs for reserve currencies and perhaps also official gold,[80] and of the proposal in the late 1970s for a voluntary substitution account to permit an orderly off-market diversification out of the dollar.[81] Nor have more recent proposals for postallocation redistribution of SDRs (toward the developing countries) elicited the necessary backing. Moreover, changes in the characteristics of the SDR—moving to a five-currency basket and to a market interest rate and cutting the amount of red tape associated with its use—never proved sufficient to induce a significant increase in demand for the asset. To make a long story short, after the initial allocation of SDR 9.3 billion, there has been only one other allocation (in 1979–81); the total amount allocated has thus stood at SDR 21.4 billion since 1981, and the SDR's share of total nongold reserves has been on a slowly but steadily declining trend, to a level that now stands at roughly $3\frac{1}{2}$ percent.

These developments, however, in no way diminish the contributions that Polak's writings have made to the still ongoing debate on

---

[78] Polak (1988a and 1989c).

[79] Article VIII, Section 7, and Article XXII of the IMF's Articles of Agreement.

[80] Committee on Reform of the International Monetary System and Related Issues (Committee of Twenty) (1974).

[81] Polak (1980).

the management of international liquidity and to our understanding of the nature of internationally created reserve assets.

In his 1988 article on "The Impasse Concerning the Role of the SDR," Polak offers four main reasons why it would be unwise for the international community to allow the SDR to fade away, in favor of an almost exclusive reliance on private capital markets.[82] In the first place, Jacques argues that reserves obtained by borrowing from commercial banks always carry the risk of melting away just when they are most needed, namely when banks are unwilling to roll over loans that fall due. What is good for the commercial banks is not always good for the world economy. The very need for a Baker initiative to induce banks to resume their credit activities to a broad group of countries is a case in point. Reserves obtained through SDR allocation will not melt away. In this sense, one has to think beyond just the quantity of reserves to their quality. "Owned" reserves are better than "borrowed" reserves.

Second, despite the growth of private cross-border lending, there remain a group of (developing) countries that cannot borrow from the private credit markets, in large part because of their impaired credit history. This can be so even when these countries begin to implement serious adjustment and reform packages. In the absence of SDR allocation, many of these countries will have to reduce imports, with adverse consequences for their future economic growth, in order to "earn" the reserves they need to hold. SDR allocation can ease this painful conflict between growth and reserve adequacy, particularly for low-income countries.

Third, while countries with the highest credit rating can borrow reserves at close to the London interbank offered rate (LIBOR), other countries with lower ratings have to pay a spread or risk premium—again, even if they are now following reasonable economic policies. Polak argues that SDR allocation saves countries this margin since the IMF, operating as a kind of credit collective, can within certain limits provide credit more cheaply than the market. Moreover, this implicit subsidy to less creditworthy countries need not be matched by an implicit tax on the creditors of the SDR system so long as the borrowers follow responsible policies.

Fourth and finally, there is a case for keeping the SDR alive and in good working order as a "safety net for future contingencies." Implicit here are the notions that there could in the future be some

---

[82]Polak (1988a).

"systemic" shock that would make it desirable to back up both the private markets and the official swap network among major central banks, that such a safety net cannot be created anew quickly but rather has to be already in place, and that modest, regular SDR allocations would keep that safety net from becoming an insignificant share of total reserves.

In that same article, Polak also meets head on what is perhaps the single most potent objection to SDR allocation, namely, that it can act as a disincentive to adjustment at a time when adjustment is in fact very much needed. Put in other words, SDR allocation involves unconditional credit when conditional credit is what is called for. It is interesting to note that Polak's disagreement with opponents of SDR allocation is *not* one based either on a different diagnosis of the economic situation in the developing world or on a different conception of the role of the Fund. Polak fully accepts that there is a pressing need in many developing countries for comprehensive and strong programs of macroeconomic adjustment and of structural reform and that the Fund's conditional extension of credit is a natural counterpart to this. Similarly, Polak has always taken the "monetary character" of the Fund seriously, in the sense of emphasizing that the financing of the Fund from the reserves of member countries does and should place constraints on the quality of its lending. Polak's position is instead based on numbers. More specifically, Jacques sees no reason why modest allocations of SDRs should interfere in a significant way with the adjustment process. When annual access limits under stand-by and extended arrangements are on the order of 90 percent to 110 percent of Fund quotas and when actual access in many cases is close to half of that, he finds it hard to accept that annual SDR allocations amounting to, say, 5 percent to 10 percent of Fund quotas would "make an appreciable difference to the ability of countries in difficulties staving off the need for adjustment."[83] The overriding priority of adjustment may preclude large SDR allocations, but it need not militate against smaller ones.

The task of launching and gaining acceptance for a new reserve asset or common currency is never easy. Difficult analytical issues have to be faced right from the outset. For example, if the asset is to be defined as a "basket" of existing currencies, there is the question of how the weights in the basket should be adjusted in the case of a

---

[83] Polak (1988a), p. 182.

devaluation of one of the component currencies so as not to weaken the value of the new asset itself. Likewise, how should one set the interest rate on the new asset? Does perhaps the new asset's "diversification" qualities justify a "security discount," or do any restrictions on the use of the new asset, or its lack of "reputation," argue for a compensating interest rate differential? What official support, if any, is needed to overcome the inertia and costs of switching out of existing assets, if the new asset is to make it in the private sector? If the new asset is to be usable for exchange market intervention, what institutional arrangements would facilitate its use by commercial banks? What guidelines are most appropriate for the institution that issues the new asset so that the quantity supplied is neither inflationary nor deflationary? Jacques Polak has addressed each of these issues and more in his series of articles on the characteristics and valuation of the SDR (most of them published in the IMF's Pamphlet Series).[84] Those who are seeking to introduce other new common currencies or reserve assets (e.g., the "Hard ECU") will no doubt profit from his insights.

IV. Closing Remarks

We have attempted in this paper to illustrate how Jacques Polak's writings of the past fifty years have enriched the theory and practice of international economics. Other papers prepared for this conference in his honor will supplement the areas that we have chosen to highlight. And we are confident that Jacques will make all of our efforts obsolete by continuing to introduce new ideas and policy proposals. We in the Research Department of the Fund are inspired by having such a tough act to follow.

REFERENCES

Alexander, Sidney S., "Effects of a Devaluation on a Trade Balance," *Staff Papers*, International Monetary Fund (Washington), Vol. 2 (April 1952), pp. 263–78.

Committee on Reform of the International Monetary System and Related Issues (Committee of Twenty), *International Monetary Reform* (Washington: International Monetary Fund, 1974).

---

[84]Polak (1971a, 1974, 1979a, and 1979c).

Crockett, Andrew, and Morris Goldstein, *Strengthening the International Monetary System: Exchange Rates, Surveillance, and Objective Indicators,* IMF Occasional Paper No. 50 (Washington: International Monetary Fund, February 1987).

Fleming, J. Marcus, "Domestic Financial Policies Under Fixed and Floating Exchange Rates," *Staff Papers,* International Monetary Fund (Washington), Vol. 9 (November 1962), pp. 369–80.

Frenkel, Jacob A., and Michael Mussa, "Asset Markets, Exchange Rates, and the Balance of Payments," Chap. 14 in *Handbook of International Economics,* Vol. 2, ed. by Ronald W. Jones and Peter B. Kenen (Amsterdam: North-Holland, 1985).

Frenkel, Jacob A., and Morris Goldstein, "Exchange Rate Volatility and Misalignment: Evaluating Some Proposals for Reform," in *Financial Market Volatility* (Kansas City: Federal Reserve Bank of Kansas City, 1988).

———, and Paul R. Masson, "The Rationale for, and Effects of, International Economic Policy Coordination," in *International Policy Coordination and Exchange Rate Fluctuations,* ed. by William H. Branson, Jacob A. Frenkel, and Morris Goldstein (Chicago: University of Chicago Press, 1990).

Frenkel, Jacob A., and Harry G. Johnson, eds., *The Monetary Approach to the Balance of Payments* (London: Allen & Unwin, 1976).

Friedman, Milton, "A Theoretical Framework for Monetary Analysis," *Journal of Political Economy* (Chicago), Vol. 78 (March/April 1970), pp. 193–238.

Goldstein, Morris, and Mohsin S. Khan, "Income and Price Effects in Foreign Trade," Chap. 20 in *Handbook of International Economics,* Vol. 2, ed. by Ronald W. Jones and Peter B. Kenen (Amsterdam: North-Holland, 1985).

International Monetary Fund, *Theoretical Aspects of the Design of Fund-Supported Adjustment Programs,* IMF Occasional Paper No. 55 (Washington: International Monetary Fund, September 1987).

Johnson, Harry G., "Towards a General Theory of the Balance of Payments," in *International Trade and Economic Growth: Studies in Pure Theory* (London: Allen & Unwin, 1958).

Khan, Mohsin S., and Peter J. Montiel, "Growth-Oriented Adjustment Programs: A Conceptual Framework," *Staff Papers,* International Monetary Fund (Washington), Vol. 36 (June 1989), pp. 279–306.

———, "A Marriage Between Fund and Bank Models? Reply to Polak, *Staff Papers,* International Monetary Fund (Washington), Vol. 37 (March 1990), pp. 187–91.

———, and Nadeem U. Haque, "Adjustment with Growth: Relating the Analytical Approaches of the IMF and the World Bank," *Journal of Development Economics* (Amsterdam), Vol. 32 (January 1990), pp. 155–79.

Kouri, Pentti J.K., and Michael G. Porter, "International Capital Flows and Portfolio Equilibrium, *Journal of Political Economy* (Chicago), Vol. 82 (May/June 1974), pp. 443–67.

McKinnon, Ronald I., *Money and Capital in Economic Development* (Washington: Brookings Institution, 1973).

Mundell, Robert A., *International Economics* (New York: Macmillan, 1968).

Rhomberg, Rudolf R., and H. Robert Heller, "Introductory Survey," in *The Monetary Approach to the Balance of Payments* (Washington: International Monetary Fund, 1977).

Robichek, E. Walter, "Financial Programming as Practiced by the IMF," (unpublished; Washington: World Bank, January 1985).

Triffin, Robert, "Esbozo General de un Análisis de las Series Estadísticas Monetarias y Bancarias de América Latina sobre Bases Uniformes y Comparables," in *Memoria: Primera Reunión de Técnicos sobre Problemas de Banca Central del Continente Americano* (Mexico City: Bank of Mexico, 1946), pp. 410–30.

Villanueva, Delano, and Abbas Mirakhor, "Strategies for Financial Reforms: Interest Rate Policies, Stabilization, and Bank Supervision in Developing Countries," *Staff Papers*, International Monetary Fund (Washington), Vol. 37 (September 1990), pp. 509–36.

ANNEX I

Jacques J. Polak—A Bibliography, 1937–91[1]

Publieke Werken als vorm van Conjunctuurpolitiek (Public works as a form of business cycle policy), doctoral dissertation ('s-Gravenhage: Nijhoff, 1937).

"Conjunctuur: Theorie en Beinvloeding" (Business cycles: theory and policy), *Fundament* (Amsterdam), Vol. 5 (1938), pp. 1–16.

(1939a), "The International Propagation of Business Cycles," *Review of Economic Studies* (Cambridge, England), Vol. 6 (February 1939), pp. 79–99.

(1939b), "Fluctuations in United States Consumption, 1919–1932," *Review of Economic Statistics* (Cambridge, Massachusetts), Vol. 21 (February 1939), pp. 1–12. "A Correction" (May 1939), p. 88.

---

[1] This bibliography includes a selection of unpublished papers in the RD, RES, and DM series of the International Monetary Fund. Most of these papers may be found in Jacques J. Polak, *Collected Papers*, Vols. 1 and 2, available in the IMF-World Bank Joint Library.

(1939c), "Études Statistiques de la Structure Économique," in Société des Nations, Institut International de Coopération Intellectuelle, Réunion d'Études sur l'Application du Calcul des Probabilités (Geneva, 1939).

"Rantsoenering van Consumptiegoederen" (Rationing of consumption goods), *De Economist* (Haarlem), Vol. 88 (February 1940), pp. 102–21.

"Rationing of Purchasing Power to Restrict Consumption," *Economica* (London), Vol. 8 (New Series) (August 1941), pp. 223–38.

(1943a), "Balance of Payments Problems of Countries Reconstructing with the Help of Foreign Loans," *Quarterly Journal of Economics* (Cambridge, Massachusetts), Vol. 57 (February 1943), pp. 208–40.

(1943b), "European Exchange Depreciation in the Early Twenties," *Econometrica* (Chicago), Vol. 11 (April 1943), pp. 151–62.

(1943c), *The National Income of the Netherlands Indies, 1921–1939* (New York: Netherlands and Netherlands Indies Council of the Institute of Pacific Relations, 1943); reprinted in *Changing Economy in Indonesia*, Vol. 5: National Income, ed. by P. Creutzberg (The Hague: Nijhoff, 1979).

"On the Theory of Price Control," *Review of Economic Statistics* (Cambridge, Massachusetts), Vol. 27 (February 1945), pp. 10–16.

(1946a), "International Investment—Discussion," *American Economic Review, Papers and Proceedings* (Menasha, Wisconsin), Vol. 36 (May 1946), pp. 713–15.

(1946b), *Economic Recovery in the Countries Assisted by UNRRA* (Washington: United Nations Relief and Rehabilitation Administration, 1946).

(1947a), "Exchange Depreciation and International Monetary Stability," *Review of Economic Statistics* (Cambridge, Massachusetts), Vol. 29 (August 1947), pp. 173–82.

(1947b), "The Foreign Trade Multiplier," *American Economic Reivew* (Menasha, Wisconsin), Vol. 37 (December 1947), pp. 889–97; "A Restatement" (with G. Haberler), pp. 906–907.

(1947c), "Begrotingsevenwicht in de Na-Oorlogse Overgangsperiode" (A balanced budget in the postwar transition period) in *Economie en Maatschappij* (Groningen: P. Noordhof, 1947).

(1947d), "Statistical Activities of the International Monetary Fund," in *International Statistical Conferences Proceedings* (Washington), Vol. 2 (1947), pp. 65–75.

(1948a), "Balancing International Trade: A Comment on Professor Frisch's Paper," *American Economic Review* (Menasha, Wisconsin), Vol. 38 (March 1948), pp. 139–42.

(1948b), "Europe's Terms of Trade," RD-594 (unpublished; Washington: International Monetary Fund, May 1948).

(1948c), "A Note on Purchasing Power Parity Computations," RD-620 (unpublished; Washington: International Monetary Fund, May 1948).

(1948d), "Depreciation to Meet a Situation of Overinvestment," RD-707 (Washington: International Monetary Fund, September 1948); see Annex II below.

(1949a), "The 'Real Income Effect' of Exchange Depreciation," RD-1005 (unpublished; Washington: International Monetary Fund, March 1949).

(1949b), "Exchange Rate Adjustment as a Quantitative Problem," RD-854 (unpublished; Washington: International Monetary Fund, June 1949).

(1949c), "Effect of Exchange Depreciation on the Value of Europe's Exports to the Dollar Area," RD-873 (unpublished; Washington: International Monetary Fund, August 1949).

(1949d), "National Income in the Quota Formula," RD-954 (unpublished; Washington: International Monetary Fund, December 1949).

(1950a), "An International Economic System," Compte-Rendu du Congrès de Colmar, 12–14 Septembre 1949, *Econometrica* (Chicago), Vol. 18 (January 1950), pp. 70–73.

(1950b), "An Economic Analysis of the European Trade and Payments Proposals," RD-966 (unpublished; Washington: International Monetary Fund, January 1950).

(1950c), with T.C. Chang, "Effect of Exchange Depreciation on a Country's Export Price Level," *Staff Papers*, International Monetary Fund (Washington), Vol. 1 (February 1950), pp. 49–70.

(1950d), "European Clearing Through the Fund," RD-991 (unpublished; Washington: International Monetary Fund, February 1950).

(1950e), "Note on the Measurement of Elasticity of Substitution in International Trade," *Review of Economics and Statistics* (Cambridge, Massachusetts), Vol. 32 (February 1950), pp. 16–21.

(1950f), "The Statistical Activities of the International Monetary Fund," *Bulletin*, Institut International de Statistique (The Hague), Vol. 32, Part 2 (1950), pp. 191–97.

(1950g), "The European Payments Union," RD-993 (unpublished; Washington: International Monetary Fund, March 1950).

(1950h), with Jan Tinbergen, *The Dynamics of Business Cycles: A Study in Economic Fluctuations* (Chicago: University of Chicago Press, 1950).

(1950i), "The 'Optimum Tariff' and the Cost of Exports," *Review of Economic Studies* (Cambridge, England), Vol. 19, No. 1 (1950–51), pp. 36–41.

(1951a), "Contribution of the September 1949 Devaluations to the Solution of Europe's Dollar Problem," *Staff Papers*, International Monetary Fund (Washington), Vol. 2 (September 1951), pp. 1–32.

(1951b), "Dollar Export Retention Quotas in Europe," RES-72 (unpublished; Washington: International Monetary Fund, September 1951).

(1951c), "Reconsideration of the Cross Rate Problem," RES-41 Revised (unpublished; Washington: International Monetary Fund, October 1951).

(1951d), "International Trade Theory—Discussion" (American Economic Association Annual Meetings, December 1951), published in *American Economic Review, Papers and Proccedings* (Evanston, Illinois), Vol. 42 (May 1952), pp. 179–81.

(1952a), "De Stabiliteit van het Wisselkoersmechanisme" (The exchange stability problem), review of G. Stuvel's book, *De Economist* (Haarlem), Vol. 100 (July/August 1952), pp. 481–94.

(1952b), "The Postwar International Cycle," RES/52/17 (Washington: International Monetary Fund, September 1952); published in *The Business Cycle in the Post-War World*, Proceedings of a Conference Held by the International Economic Association, Oxford, September 1952, ed. by Erik Lundberg (London: Macmillan, 1955).

An International Economic System (Chicago: University of Chicago Press, 1953; London: Allen & Unwin, 1954).

(1954a), "Commodity Currency Proposals," DM/54/1 (unpublished; Washington: International Monetary Fund, January 1954).

(1954b), with Ta-Chung Liu, "Stability of the Exchange Rate Mechanism in a Multi-Country System," *Econometrica* (Chicago), Vol. 22 (July 1954), pp. 360–89.

(1954c), "Conceptual Problems Involved in Projections of the International Sector of Gross National Product," in *Long-Range Economic Projection*, Studies in Income and Wealth, Vol. 16 (Princeton: Princeton University Press, 1954).

(1955a), with William H. White, "The Effect of Income Expansion on the Quantity of Money," *Staff Papers*, International Monetary Fund (Washington), Vol. 4 (August 1955), pp. 398–433.

(1955b), "The Economics of *Scrabble*," *American Economic Review* (Menasha, Wisconsin), Vol. 45 (September 1955), pp. 648–52.

"The Repercussions of Economic Fluctuations in the United States on Other Parts of the World," *Staff Papers*, International Monetary Fund (Washington), Vol. 5 (August 1956), pp. 279–83.

(1957a), "Monetary Analysis of Income Formation and Payments Problems," *Staff Papers*, International Monetary Fund (Washington), Vol. 6 (November 1957), pp. 1–50.

(1957b), "The Capacity of the Banking System to Finance Development," *Memoria*, Reunión de Técnicos de los Bancos Centrales del Continente Americano, Fifth (Bogota), Vol. 2 (1957), pp. 169–81.

"Financial Statistics and Financial Policy," *Staff Papers*, International Monetary Fund (Washington), Vol. 7 (April 1959), pp. 1–8.

With Lorette Boissonneault, "Monetary Analysis of Income and Imports and Its Statistical Application," *Staff Papers*, International Monetary Fund (Washington), Vol. 7 (April 1960), pp. 349–415.

"De Onderscheiding Tussen Interne en Externe Inflatoire Factoren" (Distinction between internal and external inflationary factors), *De Economist* (Haarlem), Vol. 109 (June 1961), pp. 385–95.

(1962a), with Rudolf R. Rhomberg, "Economic Instability in an International Setting," *American Economic Review, Papers and Proceedings* (Evanston, Illinois), Vol. 52 (May 1962), pp. 110–18.

(1962b), "Internationale Coördinatie der Economische Politiek," paper presented to the Vereniging voor de Staathuishoudkunde (Netherlands Economic Society), December 9, 1961; translation published as "International Coordination of Economic Policy," *Staff Papers*, International Monetary Fund (Washington), Vol. 9 (July 1962), pp. 149–81.

"Basic Requirements of the International Monetary Structure," DM/63/26 (unpublished; Washington: International Monetary Fund, May 1963).

"The Report of the International Monetary Fund," *American Economic Review, Papers and Proceedings* (Evanston, Illinois), Vol. 55 (May 1965), pp. 158–65.

(1967a), "Some Facts About Those SDRs," *Banking* (New York), Vol. 60 (November 1967), pp. 42–43.

(1967b), "The Outline of a New Facility in the Fund," *Finance & Development* (Washington), Vol. 4 (December 1967), pp. 275–80.

(1968a), "IMF en Wereldbank als Internationale Organisaties" (The IMF and the World Bank as international organizations), *Economisch Statistische Berichten* (Rotterdam), Vol. 53 (April 1968), pp. 349–51.

(1968b), "El Problema de la Inflación Severa," *Boletín Mensual* (Mexico City), Vol. 14 (September 1968), pp. 489–93.

(1968c), "Have Economists Said Their Final Word in the Fight Against Inflation?" *Finance & Development* (Washington), Vol. 5 (September 1968), pp. 10–12.

"Stabilization and Growth," in *International Development: Proceedings of the Tenth World Conference, March 6–9, 1969*, Society for International Development (Dobbs Ferry, New York: Oceana Publications, 1969).

(1970a), "Money—National and International," in *Essays in Honour of Thorkil Kristensen* (Paris: Organization for Economic Cooperation and Development, 1970); reprinted in *International Reserves: Needs and Availability* (Washington: International Monetary Fund, 1970).

(1970b), "The Present Working of the International Monetary System" (unpublished; Washington: International Monetary Fund, 1970).

(1970c), "Special Drawing Rights—The First Six Months," *Børsen* (Copenhagen), Supplement to No. 15 (1970), p. 10.

(1971a), *Some Reflections on the Nature of Special Drawing Rights*, IMF Pamphlet Series No. 16 (Washington: International Monetary Fund, 1971).

(1971b), with Victor Argy, "Credit Policy and the Balance of Payments," *Staff Papers*, International Monetary Fund (Washington), Vol. 18 (March 1971), pp. 1–24.

"Reform of the International Monetary System: A Sketch of Its Scope and Content," paper submitted to the Executive Board of the International Monetary Fund, March 7, 1972; printed in *The International Monetary Fund, 1972–1978*, Vol. III: Documents, ed. by Margaret Garritsen de Vries (Washington: International Monetary Fund, 1985), pp. 3–17.

"Valuation and Rate of Interest of the SDR," IMF Pamphlet Series No. 18 (Washington: International Monetary Fund, 1974).

(1976a), "Exchange Rates and Interest Rates," SM/76/106 (Washington: International Monetary Fund, May 1976).

(1976b), "The Fund After Jamaica," *Finance & Development* (Washington), Vol. 13 (June 1976), pp. 7–11.

With Robert A. Mundell, eds., *The New International Monetary System* (New York: Columbia University Press, 1977).

(1979a), *Thoughts on an International Monetary Fund Based Fully on the SDR*, IMF Pamphlet Series No. 28 (Washington: International Monetary Fund, 1979).

(1979b) "The Evolution of the International Monetary System," comments on the 1979 Per Jacobsson Lecture at Belgrade, September 1979 (Washington: Per Jacobsson Foundation, 1979).

(1979c), "The SDR as a Basket of Currencies," *Staff Papers*, International Monetary Fund (Washington), Vol. 26 (December 1979), pp. 627–53.

(1979d), "The EMF: External Relations," in *The European Monetary Fund: Internal Planning and External Relations*, Proceedings of the Second International Seminar on European Economic and Monetary Union held at the International Center for Monetary and Banking Studies (Geneva, December 1979).

(1979e), "International Coordination of National Economic Policies," in *U.S.-European Monetary Relations*, ed. by Samuel I. Katz (Washington: American Enterprise Institute for Public Policy Research, 1979).

"The International Monetary System and the Dollar: Some Thoughts on a Substitution Account in the Fund," presented to the Georgetown University Bankers Forum, Washington, September 29, 1980; printed in *IMF Survey* (Washington), October 27, 1980, pp. 337–39.

(1981a), *Coordination of National Economic Policies*, Occasional Paper No. 7 (New York: Group of Thirty, 1981).

(1981b), "The SDR and Other IMF Matters," in *Global Monetary Anarchy*, ed. by Randall Hinshaw (Beverly Hills: Sage Publications, 1981).

(1982a), review of *The Collected Writings of John Maynard Keynes*, Vol. 26, in

Journal of Economic Literature (Nashville, Tennessee), Vol. 20 (March 1982), pp. 83-85.

(1982b), "IMF en Derde Wereld" (The IMF and the third world), *Aspecten*, Ministry of Foreign Affairs (The Hague, April 1982).

(1982c), "Financial Problems of Nonoil Developing Countries," in *International Reserves, Exchange Rates, and Developing-Country Finance*, ed. by Norman C. Miller (Lexington, Massachusetts: Lexington Books, 1982).

(1983a), "Exchange Rate Regimes and Policy Interdependence—Concluding Remarks," *Staff Papers*, International Monetary Fund (Washington), Vol. 30 (March 1983), pp. 208-11.

(1983b), "Neutraal Geld" (Neutral money), a review article in *Economisch Statistische Berichten* (Rotterdam), Vol. 68, No. 3414 (July 20, 1983), pp. 651-52.

(1983c), "Monetarist Policies on a World Scale," in *Monetarism, Economic Crisis and the Third World*, ed. by Karel Jansen (London: F. Cass, 1983).

(1984a), "Internationaal Beleid met Betrekking tot Betalingsbalansproblemen—1973 tot 1983" (International policies concerning balance of payments problems—1973 to 1983) in Vereniging voor de Staathuishoudkunde (Netherlands Economic Society), *De Financieel-Economische Crisis in de Wereld* (The world financial and economic crisis) (Leiden: Stenfert Kroese, 1984).

(1984b), "The Role of the International Monetary Fund," in *The International Monetary System: Forty Years After Bretton Woods* (Boston: Federal Reserve Bank of Boston, 1984).

(1984c), "Is er een Nieuw Bretton Woods Nodig?" (Is there a need for a new Bretton Woods?), *Economisch Statistische Berichten* (Rotterdam), Vol. 69, No. 3464 (July 18, 1984), pp. 656-60.

"Mobilizing International Finance for Global Trade and Development—Concluding Address," Global Interdependence Center, Philadelphia, December 1985.

(1988a), "The Impasse Concerning the Role of the SDR," in *The Quest for National and Global Stability*, ed. by Wietze Eizenga, E. Frans Limburg, and Jacques J. Polak (Dordrecht: Kluwer, 1988).

(1988b), "The History of Dutch Macroeconomic Modelling (1936-86)—Comments," in *Challenges for Macroeconomic Modelling*, ed. by W. Driehuis and others (Amsterdam: North-Holland, 1988).

(1988c), "The Choice of an Exchange Rate Regime," in *Development Issues in the Current International Monetary System: Essays in Honour of Byanti Kharmawan*, ed. by Dahlan M. Sutalaksana (Singapore: Addison Wesley, 1988).

(1988d), "Economic Policy Objectives and Policymaking in the Major Industrial Countries," in *Economic Policy Coordination: Proceedings of an International Seminar Held in Hamburg*, Wilfried Guth, Moderator (Washington: International Monetary Fund and HWWA-Institut für Wirtschafts-forschung-Hamburg, 1988).

(1989a), *Financial Policies and Development* (Paris: Development Center of the Organization for Economic Cooperation and Development, 1989).

(1989b), "The Role of International Institutions in Surveillance and Policy Coordination—Comments," in *Macroeconomic Policies in an Interdependent World*, ed. by Ralph C. Bryant and others (Washington: Brookings Institution, Centre for Economic Policy Research, and International Monetary Fund, 1989).

(1989c), "Strengthening the Role of the IMF in the International Monetary System," in *The International Monetary Fund in a Multipolar World: Pulling Together*, ed. by Catherine Gwin and Richard E. Feinberg (New Brunswick, New Jersey: Transaction Books, 1989).

(1990a), "A Marriage Between Fund and Bank Models? Comment on Khan and Montiel," *Staff Papers*, International Monetary Fund (Washington), Vol. 37 (March 1990), pp. 183–86.

(1990b), "Summary" in *Choosing an Exchange Rate Regime: The Challenge for Smaller Industrial Countries*, ed. by Victor Argy and Paul De Grauwe (Washington: International Monetary Fund, 1990).

(1990c), *Financial Policies and Development*, Occasional Papers, No. 11, International Center for Economic Growth (San Francisco: ICS Press, 1990).

(1991a), "Convertibility: An Indispensable Element in the Transition Process in Eastern Europe," in *Currency Convertibility in Eastern Europe*, ed. by John Williamson (Washington: Institute for International Economics, 1991).

(1991b), *The Changing Nature of IMF Conditionality*, Essays in International Finance No. 184 (Princeton, New Jersey: Princeton University Press, 1991).

(1991c), "International Policy Coordination and the Functioning of the International Monetary System—A Search for Realism," in *The Reality of International Economic Policy Coordination*, ed. by H. J. Blommestein (Amsterdam: North-Holland, 1991).

ANNEX II

Depreciation to Meet a Situation of Overinvestment

Jacques J. Polak

September 10, 1948

This paper has been written in connection with Mexico's proposal for exchange depreciation. Although the relative order of magnitude of some of the figures reflects approximately Mexican conditions, the objective of the paper is not to derive conclusions which are directly applicable to the situation of Mexico, but rather to provide a framework of the general considerations which would have a far wider applicability.

Summary

The question whether exchange depreciation will bring equilibrium in the balance of payments, and the mechanism by which it will achieve this equilibrium, depends to a considerable degree on the cause of the disequilibrium. If the cause is a high level of investment, accompanied by a state of practically full employment, little effect can be expected from the improved competitive conditions on the import and export side, both because the spread between foreign and domestic prices is not likely to remain large and because any increase in exports or substitution of domestic goods for goods previously imported will create additional domestic inflationary pressure, most of which will ultimately make itself felt in additional demand for imports. Probably more considerable effects result from the shift of real income from the population as a whole to exporters, where it is more likely to be taxed or saved. This effect of depreciation, similar to that of inflation in a closed economy, cannot be increased at will by increasing the rate of depreciation; it is limited by the extent to which, and the time during which, it is possible to reduce the real income and hence the consumption of the rest of the population. If the initial import surplus, which has to be eliminated, is in excess of the total demand for resources which can be set free by depreciation, the residual excess demand for resources will have to be cut by a reduction in government expenditure, an increase in taxation, or a reduction in investment.

I. Cause of Loss of Reserves

In general, one may distinguish between three categories of causes which may lead to an unfavorable balance of payments and a loss of reserves.

(1) The country may have a price level which is too high, due usually to domestic monetary inflation. This is the situation most usually indicated as "overvaluation."
(2) The country may have structural difficulties in its balance of payments; its export products may find difficulties in foreign markets where other countries' products are preferred, or the natural resources which produce exports may become exhausted; or again, demand in the country may show a shift from domestic to foreign products.
(3) The country may have an extremely high demand for output for

home use in the form of either domestic investment (e.g., industri-
alization or a building boom), or, if there is a government deficit,
for government use. In this situation prices need not be out of line,
and exports may continue to flow, in particular during a period of a
general sellers' market.

This memorandum is concerned with the third case—where the loss
of reserves is due to overinvestment and depreciation is resorted to in
order to stop this drain. It will analyze in particular the mechanism by
which the change in the rate will tend to stop the loss of reserves.

In the first and second cases mentioned (overvaluation and structural
difficulties in the balance of payments), the loss of reserves is often
accompanied by unemployment, in particular in the export industries.
In the third case, on the other hand, the loss of reserves is usually
accompanied by full employment, as the demand for output for purposes other than consumption, that is to say government deficit and
domestic investment, is in excess of the amount which is currently
made available from domestic saving. Initially, the deficiency in saving
is likely to be met by a loss of reserves as resources are drawn from
abroad by means of an import surplus to fill the gap. The import
surplus produces an equilibrium in the following way:

Government deficit + domestic investment = domestic saving +
(imports − exports).

The possibility of an import surplus as an outlet for excessive inflationary pressure is available only in an "open economy" with a certain
international margin. In a closed economy (or, what comes to the same
for purposes of inflation, an open economy without available reserves)
no such safety valve is available, and prices will tend to rise immediately in response to an inflationary pressure. Usually such a rise of
prices will tend toward a new equilibrium by the occurrence of "forced
saving." "Forced saving" is essentially a shift of income as a result of
high, or rising, prices, from lower-income groups to higher-income
groups. The shift is likely to be from persons (such as workers), subject
to low taxation and with a low marginal propensity to save, to persons
(entrepreneurs) subject to high marginal taxation and with a high
marginal propensity to save. This shift of income tends, at least temporarily, to increase tax receipts and saving and thus to restore the
balance between government expenditure and domestic investment, on
the one hand, and government receipts and saving, on the other hand.
In an open economy, however, this process does not start immediately.
The loss of reserves gives the country a breathing space during which it
can have both "excessive" domestic investment and relative price
stability. There will always be a certain tendency of prices to rise as
foreign supplies are not substitutable for all domestic commodities. In
various bottleneck spots in the economy, prices will rise considerably
before foreign supplies would be attracted. Even the relative price

stability is, however, essentially a temporary phenomenon, a postponement of the full inflationary price rise. The loss of reserves cannot go on forever. As reserves become exhausted and the inflationary tendencies are not stopped, depreciation becomes inevitable.

Depreciation in a free economy introduces at one moment a rise in prices somewhat similar to that which the loss of reserves had postponed. The price rises due to depreciation are distributed over the economy in a different way than those due to inflation in a closed economy. After depreciation, only two sets of prices rise, at least initially: the cost of imported commodities in local currency and the price in local currency obtained for exports (assuming a somewhat elastic foreign demand). Subsequently, price increases are likely to spread. But the initial rise in prices at the periphery of the economy will have by itself certain stabilizing effects on the economy very similar to those of inflation in a closed economy. They have other effects, following from the fact that relative prices are changed on both the import and the export side, which may affect the volume of imports and exports. Conventional economic theory has been concentrated on these latter effects of exchange depreciation. They are, however, of relatively minor influence as a stabilizing factor in a country which enjoys practically full employment as a result of overinvestment. We shall discuss the effects of the change of relative prices first.

Exchange depreciation can produce stability, that is, an equilibrium in the balance of payments only if it eliminates the excess demand for resources which gave rise to it. The initial position of loss of reserves was a *real*, not a *monetary*, phenomenon, arising from an excess of demand. To stop the loss it will be necessary to change some or all of the real factors so that no excess demand for resources remains. It is not obvious in itself that depreciation can achieve this result. There may be many instances where no reasonable amount of depreciation can achieve stability, since the rate of investment (private and governmental) is incompatible with the demand for consumption at levels of full employment. In such a situation, it will be necessary to cut investment (if consumption cannot be reduced by direct measures), rather than to rely on the haphazard allocation of resources by a rapidly falling rate of exchange.

In some instances exchange depreciation may make possible an import surplus if it leads to capital inflow. Depreciation may reverse previous capital flight; it may also make the economy more attractive to foreign capital for investment purposes. In this way the amount of internal adjustment necessary may be reduced to the extent that the inflow of capital permits the continued use of foreign resources as an addition to domestic resources. In the following analysis, this possible effect of depreciation has not been taken into account. The assumption of practically full employment implies also that the effect of depreciation on exports is small, if any. Primarily, therefore, the problem studied is the manner and the extent of the compression of imports as a result of depreciation.

II. Effect of Depreciation via a Change in Relative Prices

According to conventional theory, exchange depreciation will improve the balance of payments by changing relative prices. On the export side, this would make the commodities of the depreciating country more competitive. Hence it would increase the volume and, on reasonable assumptions, also the dollar value of exports. On the import side, the rise in prices of imported commodities compared with those of domestic commodities would tend to reduce the demand for imports by substituting domestic commodities for imported commodities. Hence the volume of imports, and, assuming their price in dollars to be constant, the dollar value of imports would be reduced. Thus the balance of payments would improve on both sides. Additional foreign resources would become available from exports and less foreign resources would be required for imports. The amount of depreciation necessary to bring payments into balance would depend on the elasticities involved on the import and the export side. Given the balance to be worked off, it would be possible to select such a rate that the improvement on the two sides would just equal this amount. At the new rate so determined, the balance of payments would be in equilibrium.

It would appear, however, that in the situation under consideration—that of overinvestment—the improvement of the balance of payments along these lines will be small. This is due to three sets of limitations:

(1) the effect of practically full employment in the export industries;
(2) low elasticity of substitution on the import side; and
(3) offsets due to increase in domestic activity.

Full Employment in Export Industries

If there is practically full employment, and hence very inelastic supply, in the export industries, it is likely that the export price will rise almost immediately to the extent of the depreciation. This effect is the more likely to occur if the country exports a relatively standard product for a large market in which it has only a small share.[1] In that situation, the export price in terms of dollars is practically given. It will be possible to expand exports only as the domestic consumption of exportable supplies is reduced by the higher price. To what extent this will occur will depend on the proportion of total production of exportable com-

---

[1]Cf., J.J. Polak and T.C. Chang, "The Effect of Exchange Depreciation on a Country's Export Price Level," RD-628 (Washington: International Monetary Fund, June 30, 1948). [Later published as Polak (1950c); see Annex I above.]

modities which is exported. If this proportion is small, the relative effect on exports of a reduction in domestic consumption may be considerable. In the rather general case where most exportable commodities are produced primarily for the foreign market, little if any increase of the volume of exports by a restriction of domestic consumption will be possible.

In terms of real resources, it is clear from the assumption of full employment in the export industries that no additional volume of exports can be made available, except by reducing domestic consumption, and that hence given the dollar price of the exportable commodities the value of exports in dollars cannot increase appreciably. Thus in a situation of full employment the possible improvement of the balance of payments on the export side due to depreciation would in most cases appear to be small.

Low Elasticity of Substitution on the Import Side

It has generally been found that the price elasticity of demand for imports is low, in particular for agricultural and mining countries. Of 13 countries of this type for which calculations were made by T.C. Chang, only one, Canada, was found to have an elasticity in excess of unity; for six the elasticity was less than 0.5 and for six between 0.5 and 1.[2] Although there are probably some reservations with respect to the precise statistical accuracy of these measurements, it would still appear probable that countries which are relatively little industrialized would have only a limited elasticity of substitution on the import side.

Depreciation will, no doubt, produce a certain effect on imports by the "income effect" of imports becoming more expensive. Even though there would be no possibility whatsoever to substitute domestic commodities for imported commodities, there would be a general tendency on the part of all those persons whose incomes in terms of local currency had remained the same to consume less as the cost of living had gone up due to the rise in prices of imported commodities. The reduction of consumption which they would be forced to make by the rise of import prices would be made in part by a reduction in the consumption of imported commodities. Thus, there would be a reduction in the demand for imports by all those whose incomes in terms of local currency had remained the same. But the reduction in real income (money income corrected for price changes) of these persons will be largely offset by an increase in the real income of exporters. If the export income remains the same in terms of dollars, its local currency value will increase in proportion to the depreciation. Hence the money income in terms of local currency of the exporting community will in-

[2]T.C. Chang, "International Comparison of Demand for Imports," *Review of Economic Studies* (London), Vol. 13(2), No. 34 (1945–46), pp. 53–67, at p. 64.

crease in proportion to the depreciation. As long as domestic prices remain constant, the cost of living index will rise by a much smaller proportion and the real income of exporters will increase nearly in proportion to the depreciation. The net effect of depreciation in reducing real income will be equal to the amount of depreciation times the import surplus; and only a relatively small fraction of this would be reflected in a reduction in imports.

Offsets Due to Increase in Domestic Activity

Thirdly, an expansion of domestic activity and income as a result of substitution of domestic commodities for goods previously imported will tend to increase imports. This comes about in the following way. Let us assume that as a result of the rise in prices of imported commodities compared with the prices of domestic commodities, substitution of imports by domestic commodities takes place to an amount equivalent to $50 million. Fifty million dollars of purchasing power which was previously drained off in the form of imports will then be spent on additional domestic commodities. For this to be possible at all we must of course assume that there is not completely "full" employment, but that some leeway is available for additional production of commodities and services for local consumption. This additional production however will increase income by approximately the same amount. A part of the additional income will be saved, a part spent on domestic commodities and services, and the remaining used for additional imports. The receivers of the additional income in the second round will distribute their income in the same way between saving, domestic consumption, and imports.

This process will continue in a number of successive rounds of declining magnitude. In each round income will be smaller than in the preceding one because the part of the income of the preceding round which has been spent on imports and saved does not contribute to the formation of·new income in the next round. The final total increase in income can be estimated if we assume certain numerical values for the "marginal propensity to save" and the "marginal propensity to import." If the marginal propensity to save is 0.1 and the marginal propensity to import, 0.2,[3] the total increase of income will be $125 million as a result of the initial increase of income of $50 million. Of the $125 million increase in income, 30 percent, or $37.5 million, would be spent on imports; thus the net decrease of imports would be $12.5 million, that is, 25 percent of the initial decrease. For other values of the two propensities, the amount found would of course be different; but,

---

[3]It should be noted that for many countries the marginal propensity to import is much higher than the average propensity to import (the ratio of imports to national income). Cf. data for many countries given by Chang, ibid.

in any case, given a relatively high marginal propensity to import and a relatively low marginal propensity to save, which no doubt characterize the economies of most developing countries, the percentage of the amount of additional income "leaked away" would tend to be relatively large.[4] The initial effects of additional exports will be reduced in the same way.

We may combine these observations with those made earlier concerning the changes in exports and imports as a result of depreciation. We assume that there is no increase in the value of exports in terms of dollars and that the elasticity of substitution on the side of imports equals one third. We assume further, for the sake of argument, a depreciation of 20 percent, that is, a rise in import prices in local currency by 25 percent. The volume of imports and hence the dollar value of imports would then decrease by one third of 25 percent, or say 8 percent. We assume an initial value of imports of $500 million and of exports of $400 million. The initial reduction in imports would then amount to roughly $40 million. The net saving in imports as a result of an initial shift of $40 million from imports to domestic production would be a small proportion of this, say $10 billion.

To this should be added the "income effect" mentioned above. Real income would be reduced on this account by an initial amount of 25 percent of $100 million, or $25 million. Similar to the effect of increases in income, this initial reduction would lead to further reductions in income as various consumers reduced their purchases of domestic commodities. The ultimate reduction in income on this account would be $62.5 million, and the corresponding reduction in imports 30 percent of this amount, or nearly $19 million.

The total net effect might therefore be in the order of $30 million. If exports were to increase by 10 percent, the total net effect would not be improved much; it would increase to, say, $40 million.

It would follow from this that, on the assumptions made, the effects of depreciation via changes in relative prices would be insufficient to eliminate the deficit. After a relatively short period, moreover, the effects would all tend to be reduced if prices in the depreciating country started to rise, either by direct competition or by a "sympathetic" upward movement. This would reduce both the price spread and the impact of higher import prices on real income. A greater degree of depreciation, which in itself would have larger effects, would tend to be

---

[4]The percentage leaked away may also be found by the ratio of the marginal propensity to import over the sum of the marginal propensity to import and the marginal propensity to save. Assuming throughout a marginal propensity to import of 0.3, this ratio would be 85 percent for a marginal propensity to save of 0.05, 75 percent for a marginal propensity to save of 0.1, and 60 percent for a marginal propensity to save of 0.2.

relatively more subject to neutralization by an upward movement of prices in the depreciating country.

For these reasons, in the case of a relatively large deficit, depreciation would require to be supplemented to a very considerable extent by policies calculated to increase saving, to reduce private investment, to reduce government deficit expenditure, or to increase government revenue. In part, however, depreciation itself may produce some of these results or may make policies in this direction more readily feasible.

In considering these latter effects of depreciation, it is useful to turn the attention to a discussion of inflation in a closed economy. It will appear from this that there may be quite considerable stabilizing effects from depreciation very much in the same way as a rise in prices operates in the direction of equilibrium under inflationary conditions in a closed economy.

III. Inflation in a Closed Economy

The operation of inflation as an equilibrating force in a closed economy may be briefly described as follows. The movement of prices in a closed economy tends to restore equilibrium, or a position of a moving equilibrium, by shifting real income from those with fixed or slowly adjusting incomes to entrepreneurs (including farmers). This shift in real income is effected by (1) high prices and (2) rising prices. High prices reduce the real income of persons with fixed money incomes, such as *rentiers* and pensioners. Rising prices reduce the real income of all those groups in the population whose money incomes are not adjusted instantaneously, but only with a certain lag and often incompletely, to increases in prices. Industrial workers are the most important group of the population in this category. Even when money wages are raised from time to time to compensate fully the preceding increase in the cost of living, the lag involved in this adjustment makes real wages at any moment lower than they would be at a stable price level. The amount of real income which is thus shifted towards the employer and entrepreneurial group of the population depends on a number of factors such as the amount of real income received by that part of the population which depends on fixed incomes, the level of prices, the rate of increases of prices, and the speed and completeness of the adjustment of wages to increase in the cost of living. In a situation such as the one described, prices will tend to rise continuously although possibly with interruptions and with leaps and bounds, as long as the basic inflationary conditions persist. There will in fact be a tendency for prices to rise faster and faster as the share in the total real income of those receiving fixed incomes is further reduced and as the adjustment period of money wages becomes shorter.

Why is the transfer of real income a stabilizing force? It has two stabilizing effects, both of which are due to the fact that the shift in real income produced by inflation tends, on the whole, to move income from low-income groups to high-income groups. In the first place, the high-income groups will be subject to a higher rate of taxation. As Keynes put it, "The profiteers become, so to speak, tax-collecters for the Treasury."[5] Secondly, the higher-income groups will normally have a higher marginal propensity to save than the low-income groups. Thus the rise in prices will both reduce the government deficit and increase saving. In a situation of completely free inflation, prices will tend to rise at a rate which will produce the necessary changes in these two magnitudes to offset the initial excess inflationary pressure.

Other factors may, however, offset in part or in whole the tendency towards equilibrium. High profits may lead to an increased rate of investment. The rise in prices itself may lead to the speculative accumulation of commodity stocks in anticipation of further price increases. These tendencies towards increased investment may outweigh the stabilizing tendencies. If that situation occurs, prices will rise faster and faster and the rate of price increase may approach infinity, as shown by the experience of Germany in the early 1920s and of Greece, Hungary, and China in the 1940s. The economic system is then "explosive." No equilibrium situation can be achieved except by a change in the basic inflationary factors, for example, by a sharp reduction in government expenditure, an increase in taxation, measures to restrict investment, and/or assistance from abroad permitting a temporary import surplus.

IV. Shift in Real Incomes Through Depreciation

We have dealt at some length with the case of inflation in a closed economy because it has an important bearing on the situation of countries which depreciate in a position of full employment.

In such a situation, depreciation may produce an equilibrium in the balance of payments even though the classical effects may be almost negligible. Depreciation will then operate in a way similar to inflation in a closed economy. The real income of exporters will be increased, while the reduction in real income will bear primarily on the population at large. If exporters constitute a small fraction of the population, mainly entrepreneurs and corporations, a large part of the increase may go into taxes (either existing income or profit taxes, or ad hoc export taxes), or savings. If the initial depreciation is large enough to thus produce equilibrium in the economy via increased saving and increased government revenue, stability will be reached at the new rate. If not, and in particular if an upward movement of wages and other low incomes gradually nullifies the shift in real income, a continuous depreciation

---

[5]John Maynard Keynes, *How to Pay for the War: A Radical Plan for the Chancellor of the Exchequer* (London: Macmillan, 1940), p. 65.

will be necessary. Under certain conditions this depreciation may be rapid and may be reinforced by that special form of speculative investment provided in an open economy by "capital flight." If that situation occurs, the development in an open economy may be "explosive" (as in a closed economy), and the rate of exchange will fall further and further and with increasing speed until measures are taken to correct the basic inflationary situation.

The amount of the shift in real income and hence the amount of the anti-inflationary effect which can be achieved by depreciation is not unlimited. The effect does not increase proportionately with the degree of depreciation. If depreciation were to become too large and import prices would rise too much, the pressure for wage increases would become greater. Beyond a certain point the net effect would become zero as real wages could be no further compressed. It might indeed well become negative: a small reduction in real income which can be achieved by a moderate rise in prices would be likely to be wiped out as wages would have to be adjusted in any case if prices rose to a considerable extent. The optimum amount which could be achieved would probably be the amount corresponding to the maximum increase in the cost of living which would not yet lead to a wage adjustment. This would be an optimum from the limited point of view of the restriction of inflationary pressure by depreciation only; it would of course not be an optimum from a social point of view.

Let us assume again a 20 percent depreciation. On the basis of a value of exports of $400 million, this would lead to an increase in the income of exporters of the local currency equivalent of $100 million. Also assume that imports constitute, say, 15 percent of national income and that there would be some immediate rise in domestic prices, in particular in commodities actively competing with imports and in export commodities which are also consumed domestically. If measures are taken to keep down price increases and if a general reduction of the inflationary pressure is achieved, it might be that prices (possibly after a little initial speculative boom) would settle down at a level increased by, say, one fourth of 25 percent, or roughly by 6 percent. This might well be near the maximum amount of the rise in the cost of living which would be tolerable without wage increases. It would shift to exporters a net increase in their real income of 25 percent minus 6 percent, or roughly $80 million. If this entire amount were taxed or saved, a very considerable dent in the inflationary pressure could be made; but such an extremely favorable result is not likely to be achieved. Part of the additional real income of exporters will no doubt be devoted to additional consumption of both domestic and imported commodities; and the increased profitability of the export industry may also lead to some increase in investment for which capital equipment and some raw materials will have to be imported. On balance, an improvement of the balance of payments of, say, $40 million on account of the shift in real income would appear quite a considerable success; and the achievement of this rate of improvement would probably mean the imposition of new taxes to channel towards the government part of the windfall income of the export industries.

V. Summary of Effects

Taking the figures computed in the previous sections at their face value, the net effect on the balance of payments of a 20 percent depreciation (i.e., a 25 percent increase in the dollar price) would, under the assumptions made, amount to $80 million a year. No precise numerical significance should, of course, be attributed to this result. The purpose of the exposition was primarily to make clear the various factors which are at work and to give some impression of their relative importance. The effects of the shift in real income in particular depend to a large extent on government policy. They can be supplemented by further disinflationary measures on private investment or government expenditure; or they may be neutralized by large expenditures on subsidies or relaxation of anti-inflationary vigilance.

One thing is clear: a depreciation which would raise foreign prices in terms of local currency by double the amount (i.e., a depreciation by 33 1/3 percent, increasing foreign prices by 50 percent) would not yield the double result. Many effects, particularly the effects via the shift of real income, are not proportional to the degree of depreciation. Too heavy a depreciation might produce numerous increases in the domestic price level and might possibly set off speculative tendencies which might prove hard to control.

If a situation of a large balance of payments deficit due to overinvestment is met by depreciation, the latter policy, in order to be successful and not merely to provide temporary relief, will require to be supplemented by direct policies aiming at a reduction of the excess demand for investment and governmental purposes.

2

The Early Years of the International Monetary Fund

Edward M. Bernstein

It is not usual for a predecessor to bear witness to the high qualities of his successor. Actually, I have expressed appreciation of Jack Polak many times in many ways, and I am honored to be asked to do it again.

Jack was among the first economists to join the Research Department of the International Monetary Fund. In a staff that included Allan Fisher, Robert Triffin, Maurice Allen, Sidney Alexander, and Marcus Fleming, among others, Jack was pre-eminent. That is why I chose him to be the Assistant Director and then the Deputy Director of Research. When I left the Fund in January 1958, I did it without regret because I knew that Jack was there to succeed me.

The Fund was an exciting place for economists, particularly in its formative years. That was because new approaches were needed to deal with international payments problems. The classical gold standard, as it existed before World War I, was thought to be free of exchange rate problems because the gold value of currencies was regarded as immutable; and balance of payments deficits and surpluses were said to be automatically adjusted by the specie flow they generated. Under the Bretton Woods system, members were required to establish par values for their currencies denominated in gold or the U.S. dollar of July 1944, but the par value could be changed if necessary to correct a large and persistent payments problem. A member could draw on the Fund to supplement the use of its own reserves in meeting a temporary payments deficit, but it was expected to take measures to adjust its payments position. Such an international monetary system required oversight by the Fund and constant study and analysis by its staff.

The Bretton Woods Agreement entered into force in December 1945, the Fund was organized by June 1946, and it was ready to begin operations by October 1946. Before the Fund could undertake exchange transactions, however, it had to establish initial par values for the currencies of its members. The Fund recognized the difficulty of determining an appropriate pattern of exchange rates at a time when many of its members had only just begun to recover from the disruption and devastation of war, when controls of all kinds were still in effect, and when inflation in varying degree was in progress throughout the world. Nevertheless, the Fund decided to begin operations, and the Research Department was instructed to prepare papers on the initial par value of the currencies of its 39 members.

It would have been futile to attempt a purchasing power parity analysis of currencies for which there had not been a free exchange market for seven years or more during which the relative international economic position of the members of the Fund had changed enormously. Instead, the Research Department decided that the test of the initial par value should be how it would affect a country's trade. Because of extreme shortages, most countries in Europe and Asia would continue to limit their imports through exchange controls. The one function that the exchange rate could perform, and the most important at that time, was to enable countries to restore their exports and to re-establish their position in world markets. As the first *Annual Report* of the Fund said: "We recognize that in some cases the initial par values that are established may be found incompatible with the maintenance of a balanced international payments position at a high level of domestic economic activity."[1] When that occurred the par value could be changed.

As expected, the need to devalue the European currencies came coincidentally with the 1949 recession. I had recently visited a number of European members to discuss their payments situation. When I raised the question of devaluation in the Netherlands, I was told that it would devalue the guilder at the same time and to the same extent as sterling. That was also the attitude of most countries I visited. In the spring of 1949, the U.S. Executive Director pressed the staff to hold discussions with the Executive Board on the devaluation of the European currencies. I did not want the Fund to hold such discussions before there was a proposal from a member to

[1]International Monetary Fund, *Annual Report of the Executive Directors* (Washington, 1946), p. 12.

change the par value of its currency. Anything said or written by the staff on devaluation would be instantly sent by the Executive Directors to the countries they represented. That could precipitate speculation and prevent the orderly change of existing par values.

Instead of holding such discussions, the Managing Director proposed that he and I go to London to discuss the payments situation and the exchange rate. The Bank of England informed the Fund that it did not want the Managing Director to come to London at that time as it would be regarded as a signal of an imminent devaluation. However, it was willing to receive me and, at my suggestion, Maurice Allen. We had a full discussion of Britain's payments problem in the course of which I said to Governor Cobbold that I hoped he had not ruled out devaluation of sterling as a way to deal with the payments deficit. The Governor assured me he had not.

In September 1949, the United Kingdom proposed a 31 percent devaluation of sterling. Other European members, except France and Belgium, proposed the same devaluation of their currencies. It is interesting to note that after World War I, these same countries had followed the sterling rate from 1919 to 1924, depreciating against the dollar when Britain removed the wartime peg and returning to the historical parity when Britain restored the gold standard. Now, as then, these countries assumed that Britain would be their principal European competitor in world trade. The Research Department prepared papers recommending approval of the devaluations, although it still did not know what exchange rates in Europe would be necessary for a balanced pattern of international payments after the reconstruction was completed.

Although the Fund had approved devaluations in these and other instances, was that all that was to be done to eliminate the payments deficit? Fortunately, the Research Department had developed a theory of adjustment in 1948. Mexico had prospered during the war and had accumulated large reserves. In 1948, the expansion turned into inflation, the current account went into deficit, capital fled from the peso to the dollar, and the reserves fell rapidly. Mexico proposed a 44 percent devaluation of the peso which the Fund approved. In connection with the devaluation, Jack Polak wrote a paper, ''Depreciation to Meet a Situation of Overinvestment,'' which became the Fund's guide on adjustment policies.[2] He pointed out that the current account deficit represented the excess of domestic

---

[2] See Chapter 1, Annex II in this volume.

investment over saving and the devaluation would not restore the balance of payments unless the excess investment was eliminated. When Sidney Alexander joined the Research Department we asked him to go over our earlier reports to see which should be published. He selected Jack's paper, elaborated the analysis, and published it as "Effects of a Devaluation on a Trade Balance."[3]

I was introduced to Jack's monetary approach to the balance of payments in 1950. The price of coffee rose by about two thirds in 1949–50. Coffee was a major export of seven Latin American countries. The Fund was afraid that the increased foreign exchange receipts would be dissipated in a surge of imports that could not be sustained if the price of coffee fell from its peak. I wrote a paper on how the increase in exchange receipts would work its way through the economy and into the monetary system, with suggestions how to add more of the receipts to reserves. I was revising a draft of this paper, "The Price of Coffee and Monetary Policy," when Jack showed me a series of equations which he had developed as a general theory of how the money supply and the balance of payments interacted with each other.

It was never easy to separate the views expressed by a member of the Research Department in a Fund memorandum from ideas that came out of discussions with other members of the staff. In the papers on balance of payments adjustment, however, the basic ideas all came from Jack Polak. I acknowledged this at a conference in 1956, sponsored by the National Bureau of Economic Research, where I gave a paper on "Strategic Factors in Balance of Payments Adjustment," published under my name.

While the Research Department was learning more about how the international monetary system worked, we also had to fight off those who wanted us to tilt with the windmills of the 1930s. In the discussions before the Bretton Woods Conference, many countries said that the main cause of the postwar balance of payments problems would be a recurrence of a great depression in the United States. Keynes had written that this was the basic reason for establishing the International Clearing Union. The U.S. Treasury rejected this view. We said that the Great Depression was the result of the interaction of wartime inflation and the subsequent restoration of the gold standard at unrealistic exchange rates. This will not happen

---

[3] See *Staff Papers*, International Monetary Fund (Washington), Vol. 2 (April 1952), pp. 263–78.

again, we said, if there is an International Stabilization Fund that maintains orderly exchange arrangements. Nevertheless, we agreed that if a deep and prolonged depression caused a general scarcity of dollars—that is, large and persistent deficits—members of the Fund would be allowed to place restrictions on their exchange transactions with the United States.

Fear of a great depression gradually faded, but fear of a dollar shortage, however, persisted for about ten years. In its last stage, it was attributed to a greater increase of productivity in the United States than in other countries. The Fund insisted that there was no dollar shortage. The current account deficits of Europe, financed by aid from the United States, reflected a shortage of real resources for reconstruction that would soon come to an end. And if productivity actually did increase at a higher rate in the United States than in other countries, that would not cause payments difficulties if wages were increased as much as the increase in productivity, a point made in *Questions and Answers on the International Monetary Fund*, a document issued at Bretton Woods. I spent two years trying to persuade Donald MacDougal not to publish his book on a permanent dollar shortage.

By late 1957, I began to feel that my usefulness at the Fund had come to an end. I was having differences with the U.S. Executive Director and the Managing Director. I could see that changes would have to be made to adapt the Fund to new conditions in the world economy. The Bretton Woods system was based on the assumption that the United States would avoid inflation through its fiscal and monetary policies, and that other countries would be impelled to follow similar policies because of the importance they attached to stability of the dollar exchange rate for their currencies. It had become evident that the United States was no longer as dominant in world trade and finance as it had been and that some changes in the operations of the Fund would have to be made to take account of this. I thought that the Fund would be more receptive to new ideas if they came from other members of the staff.

There have been great changes in the Fund since I left. Some have helped to meet the Bretton Woods objectives. They include measures and facilities that gave members greater access to the resources of the Fund, especially in times of emergency, and the First Amendment to the Fund's Articles of Agreement, authorizing it to issue SDRs. I am sure that Jack Polak and Joseph Gold, the economic and legal advisers of the Fund, felt that the changes that they sponsored would strengthen the Bretton Woods system.

On the other hand, the Second Amendment to the Fund Agreement abandoned the par value system and legitimized floating exchange rates. It assumed that most countries would have floating rates, although a member could establish a par value for its currency, but not in gold. Groups of members could also make arrangements to link the exchange rates for their currencies, which some members of the European Community have done. However, the Fund could not restore a widespread system of stable but adjustable par values unless approved by 85 percent of the voting power.

The system of floating rates has not worked as expected. When the United States abandoned the par value of the dollar, it believed that the balance of payments would be automatically adjusted without too much change in exchange rates and without as much dependence on restrictive policies. In fact, fluctuations in the dollar exchange rates for the major currencies have been huge and the U.S. deficits on current account have reached record heights in the past ten years. Nor did floating exchange rates give the Federal Reserve greater freedom on monetary policy in this period.

It is a serious mistake to think that a country can be indifferent to the foreign exchange value of its currency—whether under a par value or floating rate system. The exchange rate is an integral part of monetary policy, along with the monetary aggregates and interest rates. When the dollar rises and falls as much as it did in 1980–90, it cannot be simply due to underlying economic conditions which do not change so much so quickly. Rather, the dollar must have been undervalued in one part of this period and overvalued in another. An overvalued currency is like a too-tight monetary policy—it holds down the rise of prices, but it also slows the growth of output. And an undervalued currency is like a too-easy monetary policy—it stimulates the growth of output, but it also facilitates a rise of prices.

It is time for the members of the Fund to consider whether it is now possible to establish a more orderly, less volatile, exchange rate system, embracing the dollar, the yen, and the European currencies. The Fund as the overseer of the international monetary system has the primary responsibility for proposing changes in the present exchange rate system. The Research Department, which has always been the source of innovation at the Fund, has the technical competence to make such a study. If it needs assistance, I shall be glad to give them help. I'll do what I always did in the Research Department—I'll assign the job to Jack Polak.

PART TWO

The International Monetary System

Changing Perspectives on the International Monetary System

Robert Solomon

In his long and distinguished career at the International Monetary Fund, Jacques Polak was intimately involved with most of its activities. Among those were the functioning and reform of the international monetary system. He was "present at the creation" of Bretton Woods in 1944 and has witnessed, and contributed to, the many alterations in the system since then. As one reviews the evolution of the international monetary system, one finds it almost impossible to detect an aspect of that subject about which Jacques Polak has not written.

What I propose to do in this paper is to examine the way preoccupations about the international monetary system have changed over the years since Bretton Woods. Whose preoccupations? Mainly those of officials, who are the ones with the power to reform the system, but I shall not ignore the views of academics. I shall follow a "then" and "now" procedure: depicting the concerns that were prevalent in the 1950s and the 1960s and comparing them with current concerns.

The functioning of the international monetary system is usually discussed in terms of adjustment, liquidity, and confidence. I shall concentrate on the first two of these. Confidence refers to the potential switching by monetary authorities from one reserve asset to another, especially conversions of reserve currencies into gold. While other stability problems may afflict the system, that particular danger no longer exists. What is possible is the switching from one reserve currency to another and that has been happening but apparently has not created significant instability in recent years.

I. Balance of Payments Adjustment—Then

In the 1950s and 1960s, exchange rates were pegged and were expected to be altered, if at all, only in the event of "fundamental disequilibrium." Such alterations occurred only *in extremis*; a crisis was often required to bring about or make acceptable a change in par values under the Bretton Woods system. In the early 1960s, the prevailing attitude among officials of the major industrial countries was that their exchange rates should remain fixed. In 1964 the Group of Ten characterized the international monetary system as a structure based on "fixed exchange rates and the established price of gold."[1]

In the early postwar years, it was widely believed that the "dollar shortage" would persist for a long time on the basis of the technological prowess of the United States and its supposed rapid rate of productivity growth. The dollar shortage implied a potentially larger U.S. current account surplus than actually existed, since most countries were restricting imports from the "dollar area." It was thought that other countries would be unable to finance the corresponding current account deficits. Thus the United States accepted other countries' restrictions on dollar imports. U.S. policy also sought to encourage capital flows to the rest of the world so as to make it possible for other countries to increase both their dollar imports and their gold and dollar reserves. The focus of adjustment was on Europe and Japan; the aim was to help those countries achieve sustainable balance of payments positions and to do so without resort to import restrictions. It was assumed that the United States could ignore its own balance of payments. The decline in the U.S. trade surplus from its 1947 peak of $10.1 billion (4.3 percent of gross national product (GNP)) was welcomed, but it was believed that a repressed demand for U.S. exports existed throughout the world.

As it turned out, Western Europe staged a remarkable recovery during and after the Marshall Plan (1948–52). Output and productivity rose rapidly (more rapidly than in the United States), exports

---

[1] Ministerial Statement of the Group of Ten and Annex Prepared by Deputies, August 1964.

grew markedly, international reserves were reconstituted, and, in 1958, convertibility on current account was established.

In these conditions, the flow of private U.S. capital to Europe increased. The United States developed an overall balance of payments deficit as reflected in a decline in its reserve assets (mainly gold) and an increase in its foreign liabilities. Actually this deficit appeared as early as 1950, during the Marshall Plan, but it was not labeled as a "deficit" at that time. It was called, in IMF *Annual Reports* and elsewhere, "a net transfer of gold and dollars" to the rest of the world and was welcomed as a sign that war-torn countries were recovering, since they were able to accumulate reserves instead of spending all their receipts on imports. Only in the late 1950s and early 1960s did U.S. deficits come to be frowned upon in Europe and to be worried about by U.S. officials. I believe that the first time an IMF *Annual Report* used the word deficit to characterize the U.S. balance of payments was in 1960, covering the year 1959.

Attention was focused much more on reserve changes than on current account positions. In fact, the U.S. current account was almost steadily in surplus; between 1950 and 1970 it was in deficit only in three years: 1950, 1953, and 1959. In the 1950s, the current account surplus averaged $0.6 billion a year; in the 1960s, it was $3.3 billion a year, dwindling late in the decade under the impact of the Viet Nam war. The overall deficit was the product of an excess of capital outflow over the current account surplus. The U.S. balance of payments statistics showed what was then called a "liquidity deficit" (the decrease in reserves plus the increase in liabilities to both official and private holders abroad). The liquidity deficit amounted to $1.7 billion a year, on average in 1950–59, but ranged above $3 billion a year in 1958–60. In the 1960s, the liquidity deficit averaged $2.6 billion a year. The official settlements deficit (adopted in the mid-1960s and initially called the balance settled by official transactions, which counted only liabilities to foreign monetary authorities) was smaller: $1.2 billion a year in the 1950s and $1.1 billion a year in the 1960s.

Finance ministers and central bank governors became quite exercised about the U.S. deficits in the late 1950s and early 1960s. In fact, President Kennedy is said to have coupled the U.S. balance of payments deficit with nuclear war as the two dangers that he feared most. The concern expressed in Europe was partly that the United States was exporting inflation via its balance of payments deficits. And both European and U.S. officials worried about the deteriorating net reserve position of the United States.

By today's standards those deficits appear trivial. Were they trivial when we scale them back to the magnitudes of those earlier decades? The official settlements deficit amounted to 0.3 percent of U.S. GNP in the 1950s and less in the 1960s. Relative to the GNP of the six member countries of the European Community plus the United Kingdom, the entire U.S. official settlements deficit came to about 0.6 percent a year in the 1950s and half that much in the 1960s. It seems evident that in most of the 1950s and 1960s, the U.S. deficits were rather small, but they appeared large in 1958–60. In those three years, the official settlements deficit averaged $3 billion a year, and the gold and dollar reserves of the industrial countries of Western Europe rose by about 50 percent.

While the United States was in "overall deficit" and Europe as a whole was in overall surplus in most of the 1960s, some European countries had occasional deficits that created problems for them: Italy in 1963–64, the United Kingdom in 1964–67 (culminating in the sterling devaluation of November 1967), and France in 1968–69 (leading to the franc devaluation of August 1969). Each of these countries was forced to adopt stringent domestic policy measures to cope with its deficit.

But in the United States and the surplus nations of Europe (Japan was not yet regarded as a country in surplus) balance of payments adjustment measures were few and far between. The U.S. Treasury and Federal Reserve devised a number of techniques to protect the U.S. reserve position but these can hardly be called adjustment measures. The income tax cut proposed by the Kennedy Administration in 1963 was regarded as an opportunity to alter the mix of fiscal and monetary policy so that higher interest rates might discourage capital outflows. And beginning in 1963, a number of direct restrictions on capital outflows were adopted.

Among European countries in surplus, Germany and the Netherlands appreciated their currencies by 5 percent in 1961. Germany and Switzerland later attempted to restrict capital inflows with penalty reserve requirements on foreign-owned deposits. In late 1968, Germany raised border taxes on exports and reduced them on imports and, in September 1969, this was replaced by a revaluation of the deutsche mark.

It is evident that an asymmetry existed in the reasons for exchange rate adjustment as between countries in surplus and countries in deficit. Those in deficit devalued when their reserves were running low and doubt arose as to their ability to finance continued external deficits. Those in surplus revalued because they wished to avoid the monetary effects of the inflow of foreign exchange that their central banks were forced to purchase in order to maintain their exchange parities.

In the late 1960s, the current account surplus of the United States declined sharply, while that of Europe and Japan increased. And in 1967–69, the exchange rates of three major countries had been changed. This led to greater attention even in official circles to the adjustment process in general and to the possible need for greater exchange rate flexibility in particular. The earlier notion that exchange rates should remain fixed among industrial countries was giving way. The IMF undertook a study of *The Role of Exchange Rates in the Adjustment of International Payments*, published in the autumn of 1970, which guardedly suggested more prompt adjustment of par values.

Members of the academic community organized the Bellagio group in 1963–64 (under the leadership of Fritz Machlup, William Fellner, and Robert Triffin) and issued a report that, among other proposals, recommended more frequent changes in exchange rates "than currently contemplated by major governments.[2] Later the so-called Bürgenstock group held conferences and published a volume of papers on exchange rate flexibility.[3]

While some officials in Germany, Italy, and the Netherlands were sympathetic to increased flexibility, those in the United States who had such sympathy faced a dilemma: under the existing international monetary arrangements, with the dollar convertible into gold for monetary authorities at the fixed price of $35 an ounce, the dollar could not be devalued without setting off a run on the U.S. gold stock. All the United States could do was to urge countries in surplus to revalue their currencies upward. And Europeans looked upon this asymmetrical approach with little enthusiasm.

Thus nothing came of the impulse to reform the system so as to provide for greater flexibility of exchange rates.

And apart from Germany's small revaluation in 1969, no exchange rate adjustments were made to reverse the sharp decline of the U.S. current account surplus. As for other adjustment measures, the

---

[2] *International Monetary Arrangements: The Problem of Choice—Report on the Deliberations of an International Study Group of 32 Economists* (Princeton, New Jersey: Princeton University Press, 1964), p. 102.

[3] *Approaches to Greater Flexibility of Exchange Rates: The Bürgenstock Papers*, edited by George N. Halm (Princeton, New Jersey: Princeton University Press, 1970).

United States imposed stringent controls on the outflow of capital in early 1968 and, rather too late, tightened its fiscal policy while the Federal Reserve pursued a restrictive monetary policy. This led to a large flow of short-term capital to the United States, via U.S. bank borrowings from their branches in the Eurodollar market, which created an official settlements surplus that masked the deterioration in the current account. But the United States moved into mild recession in late 1969. As Federal Reserve policy eased and interest rates declined, short-term capital flowed out and the dollar holdings of European countries rose rapidly, setting the stage for the crisis of 1971.

In August 1971, the United States abandoned convertibility into gold and the way was prepared for the floating regime that started in March 1973.

II. Balance of Payments Adjustment—Now

The past decade has featured substantial current account imbalances—principally the U.S. deficit and the surpluses of Germany and Japan. In the first half of the decade these imbalances were associated with the fiscal policies being pursued; the United States developed a large budget deficit, while budgetary policy in Germany and Japan shifted toward surplus. Exchange rates moved to accommodate the fiscal-monetary mixes, and the 80 percent appreciation of the U.S. dollar in 1980–85—the largest movement of a real exchange rate of an industrial country in modern history—helped to produce the U.S. current account deficit, which at its peak in 1987 amounted to 3.6 percent of GNP. Japan's surplus also peaked in 1987 at 3.6 percent of GNP (in 1986, it was only slightly smaller in dollar terms but amounted to 4.4 percent of GNP). Germany's surplus was at its maximum in 1989 at 4.6 percent of GNP. In the 1960s, the United States had been in steady current account surplus; its largest surplus, in 1964, came to 1.0 percent of GNP. Japan was mostly in deficit in the 1960s, but in 1969 it had a current account surplus equal to 1.2 percent of GNP. Germany's largest surplus of the 1960s, in 1968, was equal to 2.2 percent of GNP. Thus, current account imbalances were larger, relatively as well as absolutely, in the 1980s than earlier.

What can be said about balance of payments adjustment in recent years? First, it has to be noted that the notion of an overall balance or even an official settlements balance is hardly mentioned these days. With a few exceptions—notably 1987, when official intervention in foreign exchange markets was heavy—current account imbalances have been financed mainly by flows of private capital.

If we ask what policies have been directed to reducing the current account imbalances, we can point to the Plaza Agreement of September 1985, which was aimed at encouraging a depreciation of the dollar that had already begun in February of that year. But the Louvre Accord of February 1987 was aimed at stabilizing exchange rates among the Group of Six even though most forecasts pointed to a continuing U.S. current account deficit at those exchange rates. We can also take note of the "6 trillion yen" domestic expansion program adopted by Japan in 1987 based on the Mayekawa report and the recent budgetary measures in the United States.

It is evident that payments imbalances do not evoke the same degree of concern as in the past. The rest of the world seems quite prepared to live with what might be called a persistent U.S. current account deficit. Some Americans express concern because of the buildup of gross foreign debt that will burden the future. But many observers, official as well as academic, have come to the view that current account imbalances reflect decisions regarding saving and investment and do not require policy reactions. Moreover, such imbalances can be financed easily in today's world of high capital mobility.

One of the most dramatic changes between "then" and "now" is the increase in the mobility of capital. As the result of the abandonment of capital controls and the development of telecommunications and computer technology, new financial instruments have appeared, information now spreads instantaneously throughout the world, and transactions can be carried out without delay. The consequence has been an enormous increase in gross international capital flows. For example, between 1973 and 1989, the foreign liabilities of banks in industrial countries increased elevenfold while their aggregate liabilities rose fivefold; annual foreign purchases and sales of U.S. Treasury bonds and notes rose from $4 billion to $4 trillion.

What can be said about attitudes toward exchange rates? In the 1970s, there was discussion about "clean" versus "dirty" floating but that has disappeared. Official intervention in foreign exchange markets is now regarded as normal but its limitations as a basic influence on exchange rates are recognized.

Exchange rate overshooting is a live concern and this has led to well-known proposals for target zones but no action in this direction has been taken. The attempt at exchange rate management begun at the Plaza by the Group of Seven and continued at the Louvre does not qualify, in my view, as a major reform.

The European Monetary System (EMS)—the most important reform of the exchange rate regime since 1973—seems to have evolved toward a fully fixed rate system. By this I do not mean to say that no further EMS realignments will occur but that most EMS members will try very hard to avoid such changes, given the credibility they have achieved and their aspirations to form a European monetary union. Whether the world will swing back toward something like the exchange rate regime of the 1950s and the 1960s is not an irrelevant question.

One other element in the present system is the procedure of macroeconomic policy coordination among the nations of the Group of Seven. This process is still in its infancy, but it strikes me as a valuable recognition of the increased interdependence that has occurred in the past quarter century. I regard it as a preoccupation that aims at more fundamental goals than the preoccupations of the 1960s.

III. International Liquidity—Then

By international liquidity was meant world reserves. For an individual country, international liquidity "means, most commonly, the command of its monetary authority over foreign exchange for use in intervening in the foreign-exchange market to support the exchange value of its currency. By intervening, the monetary authority can delay or avoid (1) the adoption of the domestic economic policies that would be required to adjust the economy so as to restore immediate payments balance at the current exchange rate, or (2) the adjustments that would be brought about by a change in the exchange rate."[4] Generally, liquidity consisted of gold and foreign exchange holdings. Among industrial countries, foreign exchange was mostly in the form of dollars.

In the system of almost fixed exchange rates of the 1950s and the 1960s, monetary authorities were sensitive about the level of their reserves and regarded it as desirable that reserves should grow as their economies grew and their international transactions increased over time. The Bretton Woods agreement made no provision, systematic or otherwise, for the growth of world reserves (except for

---

[4] *International Monetary Arrangements: The Problem of Choice*, op. cit., p. 29.

the provision in the IMF Articles for a uniform change in par values —that is, a general increase in the price of gold—which was impractical if the dollar was to remain a reserve currency). As it turned out, the main sources of reserve growth were that portion of gold production that found its way to official reserves ($300 million a year in 1952–69) and increases in the official liabilities of the United States ($750 million a year in 1950–69). A U.S. official settlements deficit, like a deficit of any other country, increased the reserves of the rest of the world. But a U.S. deficit financed by increased dollar holdings of monetary authorities abroad increased other countries' reserves without reducing those of the United States.

Thus the world relied on U.S. official settlements deficits for growth of reserves. This led to two types of dissatisfaction with the existing system. In Europe, Jacques Rueff, who became an economic adviser to General de Gaulle when the latter returned to head the French Government in 1958, expressed unhappiness with an asymmetrical system in which U.S. deficits did not, as in the case of other countries, lead to a loss of reserves and consequent pressure to adopt policies to reduce the deficits; President de Gaulle in turn spoke of the "exorbitant privilege" the United States had under existing international monetary arrangements. And French officials came forward with a proposed reform: a new "collective reserve unit" (CRU) linked to gold and designed to replace the dollar as a reserve asset as well as to meet the need for reserve growth.

In the United States, at Yale, Robert Triffin formulated his famous dilemma: if the U.S. deficits were eliminated, the world supply of reserves would not grow enough to satisfy the demand; but if this source of reserve growth continued, instability might ensue as U.S. liabilities increased relative to U.S. reserve assets.

In these circumstances, it was decided in the autumn of 1963 that the Group of Ten would undertake an "examination of the outlook for the functioning of the international monetary system and its probable future need for liquidity." While U.S.-French differences were papered over in this study, it in turn led to the formation of a study group to examine proposals for the creation of reserve assets.

Over the next five years, treasury and central bank officials and IMF staff members busied themselves with this subject—in the Group of Ten, in combined meetings of the Group of Ten with the Executive Directors of the IMF, and, finally, in crisis meetings of the finance ministers and central bank governors of the Group of Ten in 1967 and again in March 1968. All this activity led, in 1969, to agreement on the creation of SDRs in the IMF.

This agreement was facilitated by the gold crisis that erupted after the devaluation of sterling in November 1967. The central banks of the major industrial countries had formed a gold pool in 1960 to try to stabilize the market price of gold. While this arrangement permitted the central banks to buy gold for a while, the devaluation of sterling led to market expectations of a possible dollar devaluation, which would mean an increase in the dollar price of gold. Thus, private purchases of gold increased sharply. In early 1968 the speculation shifted from an expected dollar devaluation to the prospect that the gold pool would be abandoned and the market price would rise. At a weekend meeting at the Federal Reserve Board in March 1968 the remaining gold pool members (France had dropped out) agreed to adopt a two-tier system: to stop selling gold in the market in an effort to stabilize the market price but to continue to transact gold with each other at the official price of $35 an ounce. This meant that there probably would be no additional flows of gold into official reserves. In a sense, gold was demonetized at the margin.

Also, from 1964 through 1968, world reserves in the form of gold and dollars had *decreased* by more than $4 billion as the result of official sales of gold into the market up to March 1968 and U.S. official settlements surpluses in 1966 and 1968 (and continuing in 1969).

Another rationale for the creation of SDRs was that additions to world reserves would serve to reconcile countries' balance of payments aims. It was argued that if one added up the goals of countries concerning growth of their reserves, including the desire of the United Kingdom and France to reconstitute reserves that had been depleted during their balance of payments crises, the positive number that resulted was greater than any potential supply of new reserves. The implication was that unless the demand for reserves was satisfied, nations might pursue policies that were too restrictive. Thus a decision was taken in 1969 to create SDRs.

By the time the first SDR activation occurred at the beginning of 1970, short-term capital was flowing out of the United States back to the Eurodollar market and other countries' dollar reserves were rising again. The system was headed for the dollar crisis of 1971.

IV. International Liquidity—Now

Very little attention is paid now, at least among industrial countries, to international liquidity. Developing countries, which have been oppressed by heavy debts and much-reduced capital inflows, have had more reason to be concerned with their reserve levels.

Gold reserves have barely altered over the past twenty years, except for the transfer by members of the EMS of some of their gold holdings to a central institution. While gold remains in reserves and is so reported, it has lost most of its monetary function. It has become a commodity and is part of the national patrimony like the Louvre or the Prado.

Foreign exchange reserves grew, on balance, in the 1980s after declining from 1980 through 1983. The increase from 1980 to 1989 was $339 billion, or about 90 percent. Of this amount, only about one third consisted of reported official claims on the United States. Another 31 percent represented claims on other countries. The share of dollars in total foreign exchange holdings fell from 78 percent in 1978 to 60 percent in 1989. But these changes in the amount and composition of foreign exchange reserves have aroused little interest in recent years. Discussion of a substitution account in the IMF, which would permit monetary authorities to turn in foreign exchange for SDRs, has virtually ceased. And one hears little about additional SDR allocations—the latest of which was in 1981.

Within the EMS, of course, reserves are of greater importance since intervention in foreign exchange markets is obligatory.

If one were to identify the world's principal economic and financial problems, international liquidity would be far down on the list. That is why this section of my paper is so short. There is little to say on the subject in regard to the present system. One can imagine reforms that would enhance the function of and need for reserves, including the SDR, but that is beyond the scope of this paper.

V. Concluding Comment

The key factor explaining the contrasts between "then" and "now" with respect to both adjustment and liquidity is the enormous increase in the international mobility of capital. It helps to account for the larger current account imbalances now and the relative indifference to them, since they are mostly financed privately. It helps to explain the volatility of exchange rates. It helps to explain the lack of concern about the level and composition of reserves. And, finally, it accounts for the increased interest in international policy coordination.

4

Monetary Integration in Europe

Andrew Crockett

Economic and monetary union is now in the forefront of the European agenda. An intergovernmental conference, aimed at proposing the necessary amendments to the Treaty of Rome, was formally opened in mid-December 1990. It is expected to complete its work during the course of 1991, so that the proposed Treaty amendments can be ratified by national parliaments during 1992.

There remains, however, much to discuss. While most countries are agreed that a single currency managed by an independent central bank should be the objective from the outset, the United Kingdom has proposed an evolutionary approach. This would involve the creation of a common (not single) currency, which could eventually develop into a single currency "if peoples and governments so choose."[1]

Beyond the disagreement about whether it is wise to specify the exact nature of an eventual monetary union at the present time, there is also a range of views concerning the speed of progress toward union and the nature of transitional arrangements. Some favor the continuation of broadly the current arrangements (i.e., the exchange rate mechanism (ERM), anchored by the deutsche mark) for an extended period, until the European Community is ready to move to a single currency. Others support the creation of a new institution at a relatively early stage. Some favor the creation of deadlines as a means of stimulating progress, while others believe

---

The views expressed in this paper are those of the author and not necessarily of the Bank of England.

[1]Speech by John Major, then the Chancellor of the Exchequer, to the German Industry Forum on June 20, 1990, "Economic and Monetary Union: Beyond Stage One."

there should be strict conditions before any move is made from one stage to the next.

The current discussions are not, of course, the first time that the European Community has addressed the issue of monetary union. In 1970, the Werner Report proposed a plan for moving to irrevocably fixed currencies within ten years.[2] This plan effectively foundered with the breakdown of the Bretton Woods system and the onset of the exchange rate volatility that characterized the 1970s. Thereafter, monetary authorities revised their aims to the less ambitious goal of creating "a zone of monetary stability" based on the stable but adjustable parities of the ERM.[3]

How have circumstances changed in the twenty or so years since the Werner Report? And are the chances of success greater now than they were then? The purpose of this paper is to re-examine these issues in the light of the debate initiated by the publication of the Delors Report.[4] The substantive analysis begins (Section I) with an assessment of the underlying case for monetary union, from an economic standpoint. Many of the arguments involved are familiar from the optimum currency area literature, but recent contributions[5] have extended this analysis in several directions.

Section II addresses itself to transitional issues. The Delors Report was rather skimpy on transitional issues. The assumption was that in the process of monetary union there could be a gradual transfer of functions and responsibilities from national central banks to a central institution. Subsequent analysis, however, has suggested that the *gradual* transfer of monetary functions is not really very practical.

Section III of the paper analyzes in some more detail the "Hard ECU" proposal of the U.K. authorities. This proposal has received a

[2] Commission of the European Communities, *Report to the Council and the Commission on the Realization by Stages of Economic and Monetary Union in the Community* (Werner Report), Supplement to Bulletin 11 of the European Community (Luxembourg, 1970).

[3] Resolution of the European Council of December 5, 1978 on the establishment of the European Monetary System (introduction, paragraph 1); see Commission of the European Communities, *European Economy* (Luxembourg), No. 3 (July 1979), pp. 95–97.

[4] Committee for the Study of Economic and Monetary Union (Delors Committee), *Report on Economic and Monetary Union in the European Community* (Luxembourg, 1989).

[5] Richard E. Baldwin, "On the Microeconomics of the European Monetary Union," in *The Economics of EMU*, Special Edition No. 1 to *European Economy*, Commission of the European Communities (Luxembourg, 1991).

rather bruising reception in certain quarters, in part because the U.K. Government has been isolated in not wishing to commit itself to the ultimate achievement of single currency. Section IV therefore examines some of the criticisms that have been made of the Hard ECU. The conclusion is that the Hard ECU proposal is indeed technically feasible and can be used to address some of the transitional problems that have so far been inadequately dealt with in other proposals.

I. The Costs and Benefits of Monetary Union

The traditional optimum currency area literature[6] identified the elimination of transactions costs and the trade-creating effects of lower exchange rate variability as being the principal benefits of extending the domain of a single currency. The cost, of course, is the loss of the exchange rate instrument as a means of responding to disturbances that affect different regions differently.

In an exceptionally thorough and professional study of the consequences of monetary union,[7] the Commission of the European Communities has attempted to quantify these costs and benefits and has also identified other ways in which monetary union can have an impact on national economies. The Commission study identifies 16 different mechanisms by which economic and monetary union can affect economic performance. These mechanisms are grouped under five main headings, shown in Table 1.[8] The Commission wisely does not attempt to arrive at a "bottom line" that provides a quantified balance of benefits versus costs. The tone of the report, however, is that the benefits are greater than the earlier literature has suggested, and the costs much smaller and transitory. Moreover, since many benefits accrue at the conclusion of the transition process, the advantages of rapid progress are overwhelming.

Without necessarily denying that the advantages of a single currency could eventually come to outweigh the costs, it is possible to be skeptical about some of the hyperbole in the Commission paper. The following analysis considers in turn the various mechanisms

---

[6]Yoshide Ishiyama, "The Theory of Optimum Currency Areas: A Survey," *Staff Papers*, International Monetary Fund (Washington), Vol. 22 (July 1975), pp. 344–83.

[7]"One Market, One Money: An Evaluation of the Potential Benefits and Costs of Forming an Economic and Monetary Union," *European Economy*, Commission of the European Communities (Luxembourg), No. 44 (October 1990).

[8]Ibid., p. 26.

Table 1. Economic Mechanisms Generating Benefits and Costs, by Stages of EMU, as in the Delors Committee Report

	Stage I	Stage IIIa (Fixed Exchange Rates)	Stage IIIb (Single Currency)
Efficiency and growth			
Exchange rate variability and uncertainty	+	+ +	+ +
Exchange transaction costs	•	+	+ +
Extending 1992 to economic union	•	+	+
Dynamic gains	•	+	+ +
Price stability			
Price discipline	+	+ +	+ +
Institutions conducive to stability-oriented monetary policy	•	+	+ +
Transitional costs of disinflation	– –	–	–
Public finance			
Autonomy, discipline, and coordination	– / +	– / +	– / +
Lower interest-rate costs (less seigniorage losses)	– / +	+	+ +
Public sector efficiency	+	+	+
Adjustment without exchange rate changes			
Loss of nominal exchange rate instrument	–	– –	– –
Adjustment of real wage levels	– / +	– / +	– / +
Lesser country-specific shocks	+	+ +	+ +
Removal of external constraints	•	+	+ +
International system			
ECU as international currency	•	+	+ +
Improved international coordination	•	+	+ +

Note: + = benefit; – = costs; and • = insignificant or uncertain. The comparisons are between the stages and a baseline case that assumes completion of the single market and membership of the European Monetary System's exchange rate mechanism.

Source: Commission of the European Communities, "One Market, One Money: An Evaluation of the Potential Benefits and Costs of Forming an Economic and Monetary Union," *European Economy* (Luxembourg), No. 44 (October 1990), p. 26.

that the paper identifies. (The sections that follow correspond to the groupings of mechanisms shown in Table 1.)

Efficiency and Growth

Four mechanisms contributing to higher efficiency and growth are distinguished. The first is the reduction in exchange rate variability and uncertainty, which is considered to generate strong benefits. The basis of this claim is the observation that, during the period 1987–89, nominal exchange rate variability among ERM participants averaged 0.7 percent monthly, while among non-ERM participants it averaged 1.9 percent. Fully fixed exchange rates would eliminate this variability and hence, it is implied, remove a costly source of uncertainty in economic activity.

Econometric evidence on the damage exchange rate variability does to trade is pretty inconclusive.[9] But even if it is accepted that wide swings in exchange rates (such as those that occurred in the 1980s between the U.S. dollar, the yen, and the deutsche mark) have adverse effects on resource allocation, it is much more debatable whether the relatively minor movements within the narrow bands of the ERM have the same consequences. It is these fluctuations that the move from present arrangements to full monetary union will eliminate. Such small and short-term fluctuations can be hedged against at relatively minor cost.

There are, in addition, a number of further considerations that should make one cautious about concluding that eliminating nominal exchange rate flexibility within the Community is an unambiguous source of benefit. First, as the Commission paper itself concedes, nominal exchange rate variability is not the same as real exchange rate variability. It is the latter that is the more relevant for purposes of competitiveness and resource allocation. Second, reduction of exchange rate variability vis-à-vis partner countries within the Community is not the same thing as reduction in overall exchange rate variability (i.e., including third currencies such as the U.S. dollar and the Japanese yen). Third, and most importantly, a reduction in exchange rate uncertainty is only welfare-enhancing if it is associated with a reduction in the *overall* level of uncertainty facing economic agents. If the elimination of exchange rate movements means that exogenous or policy-induced disturbances give rise to additional fluctuations in other variables (inflation or employment, say) then welfare will not necessarily be improved. It is not impossible, indeed, that welfare will decline, if exchange rate movements are a lower-cost method of adjustment to the sorts of disturbances to which the economies concerned are prone.

The second source of efficiency gains from monetary union is to be found in the elimination of transactions costs. How great these costs are has proved difficult to measure. The Commission's study is

---

[9] *Exchange Rate Volatility and World Trade: A Study by the Research Department of the International Monetary Fund*, IMF Occasional Paper No. 28 (Washington: International Monetary Fund, 1984).

easily the most careful so far, and produces an estimate of cost savings of approximately $\frac{1}{2}$ of 1 percent of Community gross domestic product (GDP). (This appears to be an upward rounding, as the estimate presented at the conclusion of the Commission's quantitative analysis is in the range of 0.3–0.4 percent of GDP.)[10] Although the Commission considers its estimates "conservative," and they are certainly lower than in other published studies,[11] they nevertheless contain some sources of potential overestimation. Some of the costs related to currency exchange (e.g., the holding of zero-yielding balances in foreign exchange) are private costs but not social costs. The expenses borne by the private sector are offset by seigniorage income to issuing central banks. And the estimate of in-house costs of currency exchange is derived from a questionnaire returned by only six companies. The small size of the sample, combined with the unexplained divergence in individual responses, make the use of this data very suspect.

It is also worth noting that the Commission's estimates suggest that, for large member states, the reduction of transactions costs from moving from ERM membership to a single currency is likely to fall in the range of 0.1–0.2 percent of GDP. Such savings are worth having, but they are small in comparison with the potential costs and benefits from other mechanisms.

The next two efficiency-enhancing mechanisms in the Commission's paper are the effects of extending the 1992 program and the dynamic gains from higher economic efficiency. The first of these is of course a highly important aspect of economic integration in Europe. It is likely to have substantial beneficial effects in the long term (although it is possible to quibble with the Commission's unquestioning acceptance of the proposition that "greater Community involvement" in fields such as education, environment, and commercial policy can be expected to "yield considerable net benefits"). The consequences of measures toward greater economic integration are, however, outside the scope of the current analysis, which is concerned only with the direct implications of *monetary* union.

The assessment of dynamic gains from greater economic efficiency, the last of the four mechanisms under the general heading of

---

[10] "One Market, One Money" (see footnote 7), p. 68.

[11] Alex Cukierman, "Fixed Parities versus a Commonly Managed Currency and the Case Against 'Stage I'," Ministry of Finance (Paris, June 21, 1990).

efficiency, should probably be characterized as a pure guess. For example, "estimates show that if EMU reduced the risk premium in the required rate of return by a moderate amount (0,5 percentage points) there could be a substantial growth offered [sic] over the long run, accumulating to perhaps 5% of GDP."[12] This argument is in fact an extension to the dynamic level of the proposition that a reduction in exchange rate variability can be considered to offer a reduction in the overall risk premium in the required rate of return. To the extent that it does so, it is reasonable to suppose that benefits will be felt in dynamic efficiency and a higher rate of capital accumulation, as well as in improved static efficiency.

The central question, however, is whether alternative adjustment mechanisms can work sufficiently smoothly to ensure that eliminating exchange rate movements will indeed lead to a reduction in uncertainty. As was suggested earlier, there is no *necessary* reason why a reduction in uncertainty should result. It can be argued that where risks and uncertainties are inherent in the economy, the suppression of exchange rate variability will simply cause these uncertainties to be reflected in other markets.

Monetary Union and Price Stability

The next set of mechanisms that the Commission considers is related to price stability. Put briefly, the argument is that (1) price stability is a benefit; (2) monetary union produces a more conducive environment for the pursuit of price stability; and (3) the transitional costs of disinflation will be less under monetary union.

Most economists would probably no longer challenge the view that price stability provides a conducive environment for sustainable growth. (This is not in itself a *mechanism* to affect economic performance, but a statement of the premise on the basis of which monetary arrangements could affect performance.) The mechanism itself is of a political economy nature. It is argued that a new European central bank would be designed in such a way (i.e., with greater political independence) as to make it less susceptible to political pressures for monetary accommodation. This may or may not be true. To the extent that it is true, it is not an argument for monetary union; it is an argument for independent central banks. Only if the desired degree of central bank independence is itself

---

[12] "One Market, One Money" (see footnote 7), p. 21.

constrained by the absence of monetary union would it be necessary to abandon national currencies to get the benefits of price stability.

As to the proposition that monetary union lessens the transitional costs of reducing inflation, this seems to rest on the argument that a new Community central bank would have greater credibility, and would thus contribute to better price stability than a continuation of current arrangements based on the ERM. This proposition is certainly not incontrovertible. The current ERM is based on the anti-inflationary credibility of the Deutsche Bundesbank, and the demonstrated willingness of other countries to peg to a deutsche mark anchor. It is to be hoped that a new central monetary institution would in time acquire the credibility of the Bundesbank; but it seems fanciful to assume that it would begin life with such credibility.

Monetary Union and Public Finance

The next set of arguments falls in the area of public finance. It is argued, first, that the absence of independent monetary policies will require a greater weight to be placed on national budgetary policies for stabilization and adjustment purposes. This in turn will require greater policy coordination and surveillance. The Commission considers that this could be accounted either a benefit or a cost. A more neutral assessment would surely put it in the "costs" column; to the extent that policy coordination produces benefits, it can be achieved with or without monetary union; to the extent that it is *required* to make monetary union effective, it implies what fiscal adjustments have to be introduced that were not considered necessary on their own merits.

Further budgetary consequences will ensue if monetary union leads to a lower general level of inflation. Governments will *lose* access to some of the seigniorage revenues generated by inflation, but will *gain* through the lower inflation premiums they have to borrow. The Commission paper concludes (rightly, in my view) that the gains of lower interest rates will outweigh the losses of seigniorage. Note, however, that these gains are the result of lower inflation, rather than of monetary union per se. The argument for a positive effect of monetary union therefore depends upon the assertion that price stability will have a higher priority in a monetary union than under alternative monetary arrangements.

Lastly, in the area of public finance, it is argued that public authorities will come under increased pressure to harmonize those taxes and expenditures that fall on potentially mobile factors of production. This effect is due to the removal of barriers to factor mobility following the completion of the single market. It does not depend at all on monetary union. Moreover, it is difficult to see why it should be considered an unambiguous benefit, as the Commission does, given the well-known risk that public goods may be underprovided in such competitive circumstances.[13]

The Effects of Monetary Union on Adjustment Costs

The next broad way in which monetary union can affect economic performance is through the elimination of the exchange rate as a mechanism of adjustment. This has previously been assumed to be the main source of costs in widening a currency area. Much of the literature on optimal currency areas concentrates on identifying the factors that determine the extent of these costs.[14]

Generally speaking, adjustment costs will be greater in the absence of the exchange rate instrument (1) if economies are subject to country-specific real economic disturbances, and (2) if other adjustment mechanisms, such as factor mobility and factor price flexibility, are deficient. Countries can find themselves subject to country-specific shocks requiring different adjustment responses either if the composition of their output and trade differs, or if the response of domestic costs and prices to common stimuli is different (e.g., if there are differences in inflation proneness). If the exchange rate is not available to play a role in adjusting to such disturbances, other mechanisms have to be called into play, chiefly greater factor price flexibility and increased factor mobility. If these mechanisms are insufficiently effective, the response will have to be felt through variations in the level of output and employment.

The Commission argues that the loss of the exchange rate instrument, though a significant cost, should not be exaggerated. They note that nominal exchange rate adjustments have already been limited under the ERM. Moreover, competitiveness adjustments will

---

[13] Frederick van der Ploeg, "Macroeconomic Policy Coordination Issues During the Various Phases of Economic and Monetary Integration in Europe," in *The Economics of EMU*, Special Edition No. 1 to *European Economy*, Commission of the European Communities (Luxembourg, 1991).

[14] See, for example, Peter B. Kenen, "The Theory of Optimum Currency Areas: An Eclectic View," in *Monetary Problems of the International Economy*, ed. by Robert A. Mundell and Alexander K. Swoboda (Chicago: University of Chicago Press, 1969).

remain possible through differential rates of cost inflation, and the completion of the single market will both reduce the incidence of country-specific shocks and make them easier to adjust to.

The Commission is undoubtedly right to say that *active* use of the exchange rate instrument is unlikely to be effective in securing improved economic performance. What is at issue, however, is whether the residual likelihood of competitiveness divergence is great enough to warrant the retention, at least for the time being, of the safety valve of exchange rate adjustment.

Over time, the completion of the single market should play an important role in integrating economic structures, harmonizing wage bargaining, and increasing factor mobility. But these changes will not be complete on January 1, 1993. Cultural and linguistic consider-ations suggest that it will take many years for the legislative pro-gram of 1992 to have its full effect on economic behavior. And the economic impact of German unification—although no doubt itself a unique event—is a useful reminder that unexpected country-specific disturbances remain a distinct possibility.

It cannot be excluded, therefore, that exogenous developments will have differential impacts, of significant size, on individual countries. Nor can it be excluded that costs and prices may diverge in a way that would be very costly to correct through the mechanism of variations in levels of real economic activity. If economic activity has to be maintained at suboptimal levels for extended periods to enable the fixed exchange rate to be maintained, the costs could easily exceed the efficiency gains resulting from a single currency.

What all this suggests is that it would be prudent to allow the process of integration to proceed further before finally abandoning the instrument of the exchange rate. At the very least, it would seem essential to wait until the full effects of the 1992 program have been felt, and a complete cycle of successful experience with ERM (i.e., a cycle without forced realignments) has occurred before moving to a single currency.

International Effects

The final mechanism identified in the Commission paper is the advantage to the Community of having a single currency in the international arena. To the extent that the single currency is used more widely outside the Community than individual national cur-rencies are used currently, seigniorage gains will be reaped. And the greater weight of the Community in international affairs will enable discussions in the Group of Seven to be conducted among a smaller number of players. These effects are hard to quantify, but would seem unlikely to give rise to a major change in Community welfare.

All in all, therefore, a more skeptical assessment of the potential costs and benefits of monetary union leads to a less eupeptic judgment than that reached by the Commission. Despite the multiplicity of mechanisms by which European monetary union (EMU) is said to affect economic performance, the key costs and benefits of moving to a single currency boil down to, on the one hand, the reduction of exchange rate uncertainty and, on the other, the potential costs of the nonavailability of the exchange rate as an instrument of adjustment. It has been argued above that these costs are inversely related to the degree of economic integration and convergence. This suggests that the issues of transition—how to move from 12 currencies to 1, and how fast to do so, are of particular importance. To these issues we now turn.

II. Transitional Issues

There are two main transitional issues. First, at what speed is it appropriate to make progress toward monetary union? Second, what intermediate steps are possible to ease the transition to the eventual goal of a single monetary policy conducted by a single monetary authority? (Left aside for the moment is the question of whether one should define the ultimate goal at the outset, as desired by 11 countries, or whether one should focus only on the next step in an evolutionary process without commitment to a predetermined end-point, as in the British preference.)

Concerning speed, some participants in the debate have favored rapid progress to full monetary union. For example, the European Commission, in its paper of August 21, 1990,[15] suggested that Stage II of monetary union should begin on January 1, 1993, and that after a brief "training period" for the new European central bank, Stage III with the single monetary policy, should begin "shortly thereafter." More recently, the summit at Rome in October 1990 recorded that 11 countries favored beginning Stage II on January 1, 1994, and

---

[15] Commission of the European Communities, "Economic and Monetary Union" (Brussels, August 21, 1990).

taking a decision to move to Stage III within three years after that date.

The argument in favor of this means of progress is that by imposing institutional constraints and deadlines, countries will be obliged to achieve the necessary degree of convergence in order to be able to meet the discipline of a single currency and a single monetary policy.

There are, however, potential risks in such a rapid progression. Monetary union implies an irrevocable fixing of exchange rates (and eventually a single currency) with a single rate of interest throughout the Community. If monetary union were to take place before competitiveness had been broadly harmonized, or before underlying inflation rates had converged, then the necessary convergence would have to be obtained through shifts in the level of economic activity. Consider a country that enters a monetary union with a weak competitiveness position and an underlying inflation rate above that of its partners. After union, it will be unable to have a nominal interest rate different from that of the rest of the union, so that the *real* interest rate will initially be lower than elsewhere. Lower real interest rates will stimulate economic activity and help keep inflation above the Community average until the cumulative loss of competitiveness causes unemployment to rise. Thereafter, of course, activity will have to be kept sufficiently depressed to bring inflation *below* the Community average for as long as it takes to restore full-employment competitiveness. Most historical experience suggests this would be a long process, particularly if the Community average inflation rate is as low as is to be hoped.

The costs of conjunctural adjustment would be significantly reduced if, by the time exchange rates were locked, substantial convergence had already been achieved in key economic variables such as inflation rates, interest rates, external competitiveness, relative cyclical positions, and budget balances. It can be argued, therefore, that a better priority than fixing a date for transition from stage to stage of monetary union would be to design an agenda for achieving and maintaining convergence. Convergence would then lead to additional steps to union, rather than union enforcing a possibly costly path to convergence.

A further reason for moving cautiously in abandoning the possibility of exchange rate adjustment lies in the fact that the European Community does not have income transfer mechanisms to cushion the effects of divergent economic developments. In most cases where a single currency is used, there is also a single government, or at least a large federal budget. This enables redistributive mechanisms, operating through social security provisions and the progressive income tax, to be called into play. It is not likely that such mechanisms will be created at the European level, and more overt means of income transfer from one national authority to another, beyond those already in place, would certainly encounter political resistance. (Such resistance is perhaps not surprising, since experience suggests that such direct income transfers can impede, as well as assist, necessary adjustments.)

Quite apart from cyclical or conjunctural differences among European economies, there is still a significant lack of convergence in underlying economic structure. Europe is, in this respect, some distance from becoming an optimum currency area. For one thing, the countries comprising the Community are at very different stages of economic development: the disparity in income levels between Community members is much greater than that between, say, individual states of the United States.[16] Moreover, the mobility of factors of production between member states still falls short of that prevailing in other single currency areas. While it is true that the single European act will remove all formal barriers to the movement of goods, services, labor, and capital, barriers of custom and tradition, to say nothing of language, will for some time continue to inhibit labor mobility. And capital movements may continue to be limited by portfolio preferences and institutional rigidities.[17] This means that factor mobility cannot be relied upon as a means of cushioning differential economic shocks in quite the same way as would be possible for other single currency areas.

In addition, there is still apparently a significant difference in the inflation proneness of different European countries. Even among members of the narrow band of the ERM, retail price inflation in 1990 ranged from around 2 1/2 percent (Netherlands, Germany) to over 6 percent (Italy). In countries that are not members of the narrow band, inflation rates were generally even higher. Until these

---

[16] In the United States, the highest per capita income state (Connecticut) had a per capita income in 1987 2.1 times greater than that of the state with the lowest income level (Mississippi). In Europe, the comparable multiple is 5.0 (Denmark: Portugal). See U.S. Bureau of the Census, *Statistical Abstract of the United States: 1990* (110th edition, Washington, 1990); and Organization for Economic Cooperation and Development (1988).

[17] Martin Feldstein and Charles Horioka, "Domestic Saving and International Capital Flows," *Economic Journal* (London), Vol. 90 (June 1980), pp. 314–29.

underlying divergences are eliminated (and it is not unreasonable to suppose that, with time, they will be) there may be significant costs in arrangements that in effect suppress the manifestation of such divergences.

What all this adds up to is the fact that the Community is still in a situation where the costs of giving up the possibility of using monetary and exchange rate policies to adjust to differences in economic situations are potentially significant. Over time such costs should diminish as the effects of the single market work themselves through, increasing the level of basic economic integration, and as divergences in the economic cycle and in underlying fiscal positions are reduced.

How far these trends would have to go before the benefits of a single currency would outweigh the costs of forgoing independent monetary policies is, of course, a matter of judgment. But a good case can be made for proceeding cautiously, and not making an irrevocable jump until the integrating impulse of current trends, in particular the 1992 program, has more chance to make itself felt.

A second danger in a rapid progression to a single currency, without an intermediate transitional stage, is that a known and trusted system—that of the exchange rate mechanism based on the anchor of the deutsche mark—would be abandoned in favor of an untried system—that of a new European System of Central Banks. This is not a change that should be undertaken lightly. Monetary stability is sufficiently important that confidence in the strength of any new institutional arrangement should be established before the existing one is abandoned.

It may be asked why a new institution cannot simply be designed in the Bundesbank mold, with effective political and operational autonomy. This would allow it to produce the same degree of price stability that the Bundesbank has achieved. This view falls into the trap of assuming that legislative arrangements can produce operational credibility. This is surely a simplistic interpretation of how a central bank achieves a reputation for anti-inflationary monetary policy. No central bank, however independent it is in a formal sense, can be impervious to the pressures of public opinion. The Bundesbank has acquired its credibility not simply through the independence conferred on it by statute but following a long period of exercising that independence in skillful monetary management. During this period, the aversion of the German people to inflation (born of historical experience) has been augmented by a realization that price stability provides the best basis for sustained and stable economic growth.

A new institution would start with no such inherited legitimacy. If, in addition, it began its life in circumstances where there were significant divergences among member countries in inflation performance and budget deficits, as well as in underlying living standards, it might face substantial political pressures. As noted above, persistent divergences in inflation could lead to corresponding divergences in competitiveness, and eventually to growing unemployment in the less competitive regions. If unemployment were high in large parts of the Community, and if, in addition, these were regions where average income levels were already below those elsewhere, political pressures could become very great indeed.

There is a point beyond which a central bank, however independent in formal terms, cannot ignore such pressures if it is to retain its political legitimacy (and, indeed, its formal independence). It would be unfortunate (at best) and disastrous (at worst) if a new European central bank began its life in circumstances where there was a major economic and political tug-of-war going on between parts of the Community seeking monetary easing to avoid politically damaging unemployment and regions seeking tight money to assure price stability.

The conclusions of the foregoing are twofold. First, it is desirable to allow steps toward monetary union to take place in an evolutionary and pragmatic way. The locking of currencies on the basis of a predetermined schedule, without regard to the extent of underlying economic integration, would carry significant risks. Second, it would be desirable to provide for a period in which any new institution that was expected to be responsible for monetary policy in a monetary union could acquire operational experience and market credibility *before* being given sole powers.

III. The Hard ECU Proposals

The U.K. Hard ECU proposals are intended to address these difficulties. They are designed to achieve a number of objectives. First, they acknowledge the desire of many Community countries to maintain the momentum of institutional development by establishing, at a relatively early date, a Community monetary institution with meaningful powers. Second, they seek to avoid the risk that premature locking of parities would occur before adequate convergence in economic performance had been achieved. Third, they are designed to promote further convergence in economic performance beyond the end of Stage I. Fourth, they allow the establishment of a new Community currency, while avoiding a confusion of responsibilities between national and Community monetary authorities. Fifth, they give the Community the opportunity to gain experience in joint management of a common money, without abandoning or undermining the tested system of the ERM, and its anchor, the deutsche mark.

These objectives are to be achieved by the creation of a new common currency, the Hard ECU (henceforward HECU) that would be issued and managed by a new Community institution in such a way as to provide both a firm anti-inflationary anchor and a Community currency. This new currency could gradually acquire market standing and eventually displace national currencies.

The following paragraphs describe some of the key features of the proposal. In Section IV some of the objections that have been raised are examined.

The Nature of the New Currency

The U.K. proposal involves redefining the ECU as a new currency, rather than a currency basket as in the present definition. There are, in principle, several ways in which a new currency might be given the anti-inflationary credentials it would need to be a satisfactory focal point for Community monetary policy. One would be simply to give the managers of the HECU the mandate to pursue price stability, and the necessary instruments and autonomy to pursue that objective. This approach has a number of attractions, but its drawback is that it does not provide any security (beyond the basic mandate) that operations would in fact be conducted in the desired way. Hence, the HECU managed in this way might take additional time to establish its role.

Another possibility would be to define the HECU in terms of a commodity basket or, more ambitiously, in terms of a purchasing power index.[18] This would be a direct means of achieving the fundamental objective of any monetary standard, that of preserving price stability. However, it also has a number of well-known practical disadvantages.

---

[18] A.A. Walters, *Sterling in Danger: The Economic Consequences of Pegged Exchange Rates*, Chapter 7 (London: Fontana/Collins, 1990).

The U.K. proposal therefore suggests that the HECU be defined so that it could never be devalued against any other ERM currency. In other words, its central rate, which could be changed only as part of a more general realignment, would always move up in step with whichever happened to be the strongest currency. The HECU would be subject to the same (narrow) margins of variation as the other ERM currencies, whose central rates would over time become increasingly fixed, though not irrevocably so.

The Issuing Institution

The HECU would require an institution to issue and manage it. Under the U.K. proposals this institution is illustratively named the European monetary fund (EMF) and is owned and controlled by participating national central banks as shareholders. Participating central banks would subscribe capital in agreed proportions reflecting their relative economic weight. (Capital or guarantees would be needed because the EMF would incur financial risks as a result of its market activities. It is to be expected, however, that the EMF would make profits over time. In this case, capital subscriptions would provide the "key" for determining the distribution of net income.)

If absolute credibility were to attach to the commitment to maintain the value of the HECU, such a commitment would need to be unlimited. It would be the task of the management of the EMF to limit the extent of possible loss, balancing that risk against the requirements of creating a competitive and durable new currency. The EMF would essentially be a deposit-taking and currency-switching institution.[19] Its business would consist of receiving deposits in national currencies (probably, but not necessarily, channeled through commercial banks) out of which it would acquire a portfolio of claims denominated in national currencies; in return it would issue liabilities denominated in HECU. The EMF would be free to accept and convert national currencies on demand at an exchange rate determined in the market. It would however have an *obligation* to buy HECU for national currencies at an intervention point set at the HECU's lower margin of variation against national currencies. It would also have an obligation to *acquire* national currencies against HECU at the upper end of the range.

[19]Joe Grice, "The U.K. Proposals for a European Monetary Fund and a 'Hard ECU': Making Progress Towards Economic and Monetary Union in Europe," *Treasury Bulletin* (London), Autumn 1990, pp. 1–9.

The EMF would need to offer interest on its HECU liabilities, in order that the demand for them would be sufficient to keep the HECU within its prescribed margins of fluctuation against other ERM currencies. Initially, it seems likely that HECU interest rates would need to be administratively set. There could be different rates for a range of maturities, adjusted as necessary to keep the HECU at the desired point in the ERM band. At a more mature stage in the HECU's development, and probably only when it had been comple-mented by the provision of a central clearing and settlement system for commercial banks participating in HECU-denominated business, a more significant demand might emerge for non-interest-bearing, operational deposits. In time, numbers of commercial banks might hold operational balances in HECU at the EMF. If and when this occurred, these balances would be a means whereby the new insti-tution could exert increasing influence on monetary conditions throughout the system.

Managing the EMF's Portfolio

The management of the EMF's portfolio of liabilities would be relatively straightforward and would be constrained by the need to keep the exchange value of the HECU within its ERM margins. The management of the EMF's asset portfolio poses more difficult ques-tions. One objective would be to contain the risk of loss arising from a mismatch—by currency, maturity, or interest rate—with the liabili-ties described above. A second objective would be to exert appropri-ate pressure for policy action on the issuing central bank(s) of the currency(ies) that were offered for conversion to the EMF. The objective would be to ensure that the *combined* effect of the EMF's own money creation—through the generation of HECU monetary liabilities—and the influence it exerted on the money creation by national central banks was consistent with the anti-inflationary ob-jectives of the Community as a whole.

To give the EMF the necessary power to influence the money creation of national central banks, it is envisaged that it would be empowered to require issuing central banks to repurchase, against hard currency, balances in their currency which the EMF acquired, and possibly also to provide a maintenance of value guarantee in terms of HECU. In effect, central banks would be required to support their respective currencies within their ERM bands by spending hard-currency reserves. This would both safeguard the EMF against loss and provide leverage on the policies of national central banks. The mechanism by which pressure would be exerted on national central banks to correct any tendency to laxity in monetary policy is broadly similar to the one that operates under present ERM arrangements. Policy weakness leads to a decline in the exchange rate and a loss of net reserves when the currency concerned reaches the bottom of its margin of fluctuation.

There remains, however, a range of options over how the EMF's power to require national currencies to be repurchased might be exercised. At one extreme, full discretion might be left to the EMF's management regarding the amounts of national currency that the institution might hold (and therefore the amounts that would need to be presented to national banks for repurchase); as well as regarding the currencies that would be acceptable to it in the event of repurchase. Alternatively, or in addition, maintenance of value guarantees might in some cases be deemed sufficient protection for its national currency holdings up to a certain point, perhaps in association with monetary policy undertakings by the relevant national bank. In another variant, the obligation to redeem national currency balances might be automatic.

The obligation on national central banks to repurchase their currencies would, as just noted, exert monetary discipline through the familiar mechanism of reserve loss. National authorities would be obliged to spend their own reserves or to purchase reserves with their own currency (in both cases extinguishing an equivalent amount of domestic base money), or borrow reserves in the market. To limit or reverse such reserve loss, a national central bank would have to raise its interest rates. This would tend to depress national currency creation, and thereby restore the appropriate Community-wide stance of monetary policy. The harder the monetary discipline to be exerted on individual countries of issue, the greater the need to insist on immediate and full redemption in external assets.

If the EMF were to manage the HECU in a passive way (e.g., by simply matching interest rates on the hardest ERM currency), this would, as noted above, replicate the mechanisms of current arrangements. A more proactive monetary role for the EMF would envisage the possibility of outbidding equivalent interest rates on national currencies. This would enable the EMF to exert upward pressure on Community-wide interest rates. At the same time, it would involve greater exposure to risk of loss. The trade-off between monetary leverage and exposure to loss would depend on the degree of maturity of development and acceptability of the HECU.

Interest Rate Policy

The immediate purpose of managing HECU interest rates would be to influence the exchange rate of the HECU against other currencies. A range of possibilities would be available. At one extreme, the EMF could pursue an entirely passive or nonmanaged approach, in which it would set HECU interest rates close to those on corresponding maturities of the strongest of other ERM currencies. In that case, the rate of growth of the HECU would depend purely on the market's view of (1) the EMF's commitment to maintaining its exchange value, as reflected in the credibility of the guarantees provided by its shareholders; (2) the usefulness of the new currency as a payments medium, which would depend in part on the rate at which an associated clearing and settlement system developed; and (3) the value of the option that the new currency would in effect provide for its holders in the event of a realignment. If its reputation were at least on a par with that of the central bank with the strongest currency, the EMF might, by virtue of the option afforded by the HECU, find that it could set the HECU deposit rate below that on the strongest national currency and still see some substitution of HECU for other deposits. The greater any expectation of a forthcoming devaluation of the hitherto strongest currency, the larger would be the margin by which HECU interest rates could diverge below those on that currency.

In a more managed approach, it would be open to the EMF to raise the interest rate on HECU relative to rates on national currencies. It would do this either by raising the rate offered on HECU deposits or by raising the rate at which it lent HECU to relieve market shortages created by its sales of HECU. In the early stages, a higher interest rate on HECU would be the only available means of provoking additional demand for HECU assets, other things being equal. The EMF, which would be called upon to satisfy the additional demand, might well face the choice between, on the one hand, selling increasing amounts of its own HECU liabilities, to maintain its desired level of rates, and, on the other hand, allowing market interest rates on HECU assets to fall away from the desired level.

The stronger the EMF's resolve to keep HECU interest rates up, the greater would be its ability to sell HECU assets or issue HECU liabilities, and the greater would be the pressure on national central banks to move their interest rates up in parallel. The strength of this pressure would also depend on how widely the HECU was used in commercial transactions.

Admittedly an operation of this sort would expose the EMF to some financial risk. This might in practice imply some limitation on its willingness to act for long in this kind of way. In the longer run, the key means of enhancing the new currency's role would be to secure its reputation as a currency subject to low inflation expectations, backed up by an efficient clearing and settlement system. This should enable a negative risk premium to be established against even the strongest currency. That, in turn, would permit low HECU lending rates, which would enhance its appeal for borrowers.

IV. Criticisms of the HECU Proposal

As noted earlier, the HECU proposals have attracted a number of criticisms, on political as well as economic grounds. This section surveys a number of the main reservations that have been expressed.

A first criticism is that the proposals provide no clear link with, or commitment to, the ultimate objective of Stage III of EMU. It is, of course, true that in putting forward its proposal, the U.K. Government has not accepted the goal of a single currency. But, while the plan does not itself involve an eventual move to a single currency, it certainly does not preclude such a move. Indeed, insofar as it promotes disciplined monetary policies throughout the Community and the progressive attainment of price stability, it helps provide an essential precondition for any move to a single currency.

A second criticism is that the operations of the EMF and the constraints and obligations it would impose on national monetary authorities would represent an undesirable loss of national sovereignty. It is certainly true that participation in the EMF would constrain national central banks to accept the disciplines set by the EMF in managing the HECU. But this would not be fundamentally different from the current situation, since national authorities have to take account of external market pressures in formulating policy. Each national authority would continue to have the option to manage its own currency, subject to the constraints imposed by membership of the ERM. In extreme circumstances, it would retain the right to request a change in its central rate or even to withdraw from the mechanism altogether.

Third, at a more technical level, it is argued that the HECU would not develop without artificial incentives. Its relative strength and stability would not be sufficient to compensate for its unfamiliarity as a transactions medium. This argument is based on a strand of literature that points out that an established national currency has a considerable power to resist replacement by an outside currency, even when the intrinsic properties of the latter are clearly superior. Thus, even in countries with very high inflation (Brazil, Argentina) the national currency remains the principal circulating medium.

This argument clearly has a strong basis in observed experience, but cannot necessarily be extrapolated to the European case. If a common currency were given equality to compete with national currency (through the removal of legal impediments and the provision of effective cross-Community payment and settlement systems) it might well perform better. Conferring legal tender status on the HECU could provide a useful additional incentive to its use, though the importance of this step should not be exaggerated. A growing recognition that the new currency was a potential future single currency might further enhance its acceptability.

Nevertheless, it is perhaps unlikely that a new currency such as the HECU would quickly find its way into everyday retail use. This does not, however, undermine the case for the HECU. Its primary importance in the early stages of development would lie in its role as a noninflationary standard for the ERM and as a wholesale instrument in financial markets.

Fourth, it is argued that to encourage holding of HECU, rates would have to be set above those on other strong currencies, thus imparting upward pressure to interest rate costs across the Community. This seems to misunderstand the character of the HECU. From the outset the new currency would have an appeal as a store of value that was devaluation proof relative to national currencies within the Community. The required interest return could therefore be correspondingly low. At the same time, the low rate of interest payable would compensate borrowers of HECU whose income or assets were still largely denominated in national currencies for the currency risk that they would be undertaking.

It is not possible to predict exactly where rates would need to be set to ensure the EMF met its primary obligation that the HECU should never be devalued and progressively to attract savers and borrowers to use the new medium. But over time short-term HECU rates should settle below even the interest rates for comparable assets denominated in the strongest of national currencies.

A fifth objection is that the HECU would not have the hedging characteristics of the basket ECU, since it would not be composed of the national currencies of member states. But the HECU would be a different product, satisfying a different market need, namely stability as a store of value and low interest rates; in this sense what it would be offering is a hedge against inflation. It would have additional appeal of being a common currency for the Community as a whole, whose management and development would be the responsibility of a Community body, the EMF. At the same time, the private markets would not be deprived of the means of hedging against movements in Community currencies and interest rates. Positions could still be taken in baskets of Community currencies, either synthesized to a standard formula or tailored to a particular need.

A sixth objection that has been advanced to the U.K. proposal is that competition between the HECU and the basket ECU would be harmful to the development of a common currency. This is because of the confusion that might be created by the coexistence of two different types of ECU. It has to be recognized, of course, that there would be an initial period in which instruments in both HECU and basket ECU would exist alongside one another. But this presents no particular difficulties. Unless the contracting parties in the private ECU markets agreed otherwise, existing contracts in basket ECUs could be worked out on the basis of their original contractual terms. But from its inception the HECU would be expected to become the main vehicle for new contracts.

A seventh question concerns the inflationary potential of the HECU. It is argued that the primary objective of the EMF would be exchange rate stability rather than price stability, and that the introduction of the HECU as a parallel currency would provide an additional source of credit creation that would complicate the management of monetary policy within the Community. Although this criticism has gained some currency, it is neither the intention nor the likely outcome of the proposal that exchange rate stability should be given primacy over price stability. The premise of the proposal is that any arrangements for moving beyond Stage I should ensure, to the maximum degree possible, anti-inflationary pressure and convergence toward stable prices.

The HECU proposal is designed to provide strong safeguards against the concerns expressed in the Delors Report about the inflationary potential of parallel currencies. In the first place, the creation of HECU can only come about when national currencies are surrendered to the EMF in exchange for HECU claims. Therefore, at the point of creation of HECUs there would be an equivalent extinction of national currency. In addition, further safeguards are provided. The responsibility of the EMF to ensure that the HECU could not be devalued against other national currencies provides an assurance that the EMF would operate the policy instruments at its disposal to maintain sufficiently tight monetary conditions in the Community as a whole. This would be reinforced by the repurchase obligation (possibly backed up by a maintenance of value guarantee by member states). To the extent that the EMF received national currencies, it would always have the right to put these currencies back to national central banks in exchange for "hard" assets. Thus, if a national monetary authority was running an excessively loose monetary policy, and this was resulting in the national currency concerned being exchanged for HECU-denominated deposits, the national central bank would find itself either losing reserves, or having to underwrite the HECU value of the national currency holdings of the EMF.

Lastly, there is the objection that the existence of a common currency would result in confusion over the ultimate responsibility for monetary policy. In fact, the HECU proposal is designed to eliminate ambiguity in this regard. Each national monetary authority would remain responsible for its own monetary policy, while the EMF would have responsibility for the maintenance of value of the HECU. There would similarly be no ambiguity about the objective of the EMF as the managing authority for the HECU. It would be to maintain the value of the HECU in terms of the strongest currency and to ensure that continuous downward pressure on inflation was maintained.

5

Some IMF Problems After the Committee of Twenty

Alexandre Kafka

This paper sketches the development of the Fund's regulatory and financial functions since the abandonment of the reform efforts of the Committee of Twenty.[1] It comments on possibilities today of strengthening the Fund's influence over the policies of its members and, thereby, over the working of the international monetary system —being listened to, not necessarily obeyed. The paper eschews discussion of the choice of the global exchange rate system.[2]

One main conclusion is that the *scope* of the Fund's regulatory powers (except over the global exchange rate system), as well as of its financial functions, has been extended. Nevertheless, the Fund has lost *influence* over the major countries. This is due to the end of the par value system and to the fact that these countries no longer borrow from it. The Fund's influence over its borrowing members is

I am indebted for their help to many colleagues at the Fund, including Jacques J. Polak himself.

[1]The Committee of Twenty—the Committee of the Board of Governors of the International Monetary Fund on Reform of the International Monetary System and Related Issues—was established in 1972. Its members were governors of the Fund, ministers, or others of comparable rank. The Committee presented its final report, together with an *Outline of Reform*, in 1974.

[2]Attempts to revive the par value system ended—so far—at the September 1973 meeting in Paris of the Deputies of the Committee of Twenty, that is, before the Committee's last session in July 1974. There is increased sympathy for "stable but adjustable" rates as an instrument to achieve monetary stability.

On the remaining functions of the Fund, see especially Peter B. Kenen, *Financing, Adjustment and the International Monetary Fund* (Washington: Brookings Institution, 1986).

substantial, if at times controversial. The Fund's approach to financing has changed in many respects. The number of financing arrangements with the Fund has grown, including, importantly, countries qualifying for concessional finance. Moreover, the Fund has become an increasingly important catalyzer of other institutions' lending. Nothing suggests that the Fund's role could be usefully merged at this time into that of any other existing international financial institution. The Fund's macroeconomic expertise justifies a separate institution. That the Fund to some extent competes in that area with other international financial institutions is neither an argument for a merger nor necessarily a disadvantage. In discussing the Fund one must remember that the term is shorthand for the governments that constitute the international financial community and, more precisely, for the governments holding—on any given decision—the necessary majority of the institution's voting power.

The second main conclusion of the paper is that without any change in its regulatory powers it might be possible to increase the Fund's influence through changes in its financing policies. The risks to the Fund should be tolerable. The changes could affect the Fund's relations with major members as well as other members. They might comprise the practice of conditionality, the cost of Fund credit, and the settlement system. Also, intensified attempts to demonstrate to countries the advantages of cooperation through and with the Fund will be particularly relevant. Success in respect of major countries would undoubtedly be limited at best. Efforts would be needed to overcome at the same time the borrowers' "adjustment fatigue" and the creditor countries' "assistance fatigue."

Section I of this paper discusses the remaining regulatory functions of the IMF. The financial functions of the IMF are discussed in Section II. Section III suggests some means of strengthening the Fund's influence.

I. The Regulatory Functions of the IMF After the Collapse of the Par Value System

The IMF's regulatory jurisdiction[3] remains ample (despite loss of its legal powers over choice of the global exchange rate system). The

---

[3] Designed to promote the purposes of the Fund, as set out especially in Article I of the IMF's Articles of Agreement. Article IV mentions "sound economic growth" as an "essential purpose."

Fund maintains its jurisdiction and surveillance over exchange rate policies for the purpose of (1) the prevention of their abuse for achieving "unfair" competitive advantage and (2) for promoting stability and the undefined concept of "a stable system of exchange rates."[4] Exchange restrictions (and aspects of trade restrictions for balance of payments purposes) continue under the jurisdiction and surveillance of the IMF. The rule that restrictions are not to be used, except temporarily, is meeting with increased support among countries of all kinds of economic structures, and irrespective of whether or not they borrow from the Fund—a very important development.

Properly to carry out its functions, under present circumstances, the Fund has extended its surveillance from exchange rates to those "fundamental" policies that are widely believed to determine exchange rates in the longer run. This extension is a natural development. Except in the case of "fundamental disequilibrium," the par value system had required the subordination of other policies to exchange rate stability. Hence, once that system had been abandoned, a wider scope of surveillance became necessary to assure any kind of stability in the exchange area. There is, however, a distinction between those policies that proximately affect exchange rates—including intervention, where the Fund has adopted guidelines[5] designed to avoid short-term abuse of exchange rates—and those policies that influence exchange rates through their effect on underlying conditions. The latter are subject to less close surveillance.[6] The replacement of the par value system by mere surveillance through the Fund has had a major impact on the Fund's influence. This is because the inherent international policy coordination of a par value system that functions has by no means been replaced by deliberate multilateral policy coordination, whether through Fund or other entities' surveillance.

The Interim Committee (formally an advisory body to the Board of Governors of the Fund, its top authority) is de facto a new decision-making entity at ministerial level.[7] Its recommendations can address

---

[4] Article IV.

[5] See International Monetary Fund, *Selected Decisions of the International Monetary Fund and Selected Documents*, Sixteenth Issue (Washington, 1991), p. 9, et seq.

[6] François Gianviti, "The International Monetary Fund and External Debt," *Recueil des Cours*, Vol. 215, 1989-III (Dordrecht: Nijhoff), pp. 205–86, at p. 266, et seq.

[7] Its creation was recommended by the Committee of Twenty, whose structure the former copies. The Articles also contemplate its replacement by a Council formally empowered to make decisions.

all matters subject to the Articles of Agreement.[8] But the Fund's jurisdiction is too narrow for some purposes, where "cross-issue" bargaining (comprising issues beyond those under the Fund's jurisdiction) could be helpful. To the extent this is true, the purposes of the Fund involving multilateral coordination can find support through attempts at coordination of policies in other fora. Such a forum is (or was) Working Party 3 of the Organization for Economic Cooperation and Development. The Group of Seven (as well as fora such as the Group of Three or the Group of Five) appears to have had some successes (e.g., the Plaza and Louvre Agreements); but more recently (i.e., the aftermath of the Stanhope retreat), its objectives and achievements seem to have been modest at best. In any case, the Group of Seven does not necessarily take into account the interests of the entire international financial community. And while the Managing Director of the IMF attends the multilateral surveillance meetings of the Group of Seven, he does not attend all their meetings and may, therefore, not even be able on all occasions to convey the views on the matters under discussion of the member groups not represented. It should also be noted that, since there are almost always divergences between "the majors,"[9] wider representation could, on occasion, help in building an effective consensus among them, in addition to protecting the interests of the "non-majors."

When the Committee of Twenty concluded its work, most academics—and many others—probably thought that its greatest success was its failure to reinvigorate the par value system. Today the

---

[8] Including those pertaining to the Executive Board, the usual decision-making body of the Fund. The Council foreseen in Schedule D, but never established, would exercise de jure the Interim Committee's de facto powers. It is preferable (not only speaking as an Executive Director from a developing country) that the Council should not have come into existence. Jurisdictional disagreements between the Executive Board and the Council could occur; strictly speaking, such disagreements between the former and the Interim Committee are impossible. Open disagreements could be very disruptive and could, moreover, be reflected in a disruption of the relationship between management and the Executive Board. Nor would it be practical to attribute to the Council a different jurisdiction than to the Executive Board. Since the Council would make decisions by voting, rather than by consensus, as the Interim Committee, the influence on the forum of the developing country members would be smaller.

[9] Joseph Gold, "The Group of Five in International Monetary Arrangements," *Contemporary Problems of International Law: Essays in Honour of Georg Schwarzenberger on his Eightieth Birthday*, ed. by Bin Cheng and E.D. Brown (London: Stevens and Sons, 1988), pp. 86–115.

matter is, perhaps, seen differently. In any case, however, despite its loss of jurisdiction over the choice of the global exchange rate system, the Fund retains regulatory powers over a wide area of the international monetary system. But the Fund's influence is more than ever dependent on the material incentives it can offer members by its policies, including its ability to lend its own (and catalyze the lending of other) resources.[10]

II. The Financial Functions of the Fund

The purpose of the financial functions of the Fund remains[11] to lend to members[12] so as to give confidence to them to correct balance of payments disequilibrium without resorting to measures "destructive of . . . prosperity." Due to the growth of the international capital market, the dichotomy of the membership has acquired major significance: on one hand, industrial countries plus a small if slowly growing number of others that can (again) borrow freely from that market; on the other hand, most developing countries—that depend for their finance mostly on the IMF and other official or private lenders catalyzed by the Fund. (There are, however, official lenders whose relationship with the borrower is primarily political; the Fund's role could be subdued in such cases.[13]) An important development is the growing skepticism of Fund creditors on how much the Fund should lend to other members; this skepticism is also reflected in overly cautious quota increases. Among the underlying causes of this attitude, new standards of policy courage expected by Fund creditors from other countries (if not from themselves) could be noted,[14] as well as the lack of decisiveness of debtor countries in tackling their problems. One may also mention the

---

[10]This latter statement must be carefully defined, however. As noted earlier, the major countries today voluntarily follow certain of the policies advocated by the Fund —for example, with respect to restrictions—that they did not do to the same extent before 1973.

[11]As defined in Article I(v).

[12]Temporarily, under adequate safeguards.

[13]For example, the recent loan of the European Community to Greece, which did not wish to submit to a Fund arrangement.

[14]However, as already suggested above, in earlier years of the Fund's existence, differences of view between the Fund and countries with potential creditor positions in it on one hand and potential borrowers from the Fund on the other hand frequently arose from differences in perception of the effect of economic policies; this is now less common.

length of the debt crisis, due to its initial misdiagnosis as a mere liquidity problem; this in turn delayed debt relief as the unavoidable strategy instead of additional borrowing.

The dichotomy noted has reduced the availability to the Fund of the material incentives that previously strengthened its influence even over its most important members. The skepticism noted has had some effect on the Fund's willingness to finance and thereby influence other members. But in this respect one must be careful to describe correctly what has occurred. There has been a considerable increase in maximum potential access to Fund credit over recent years. Yet, in the 1980s, there was no clearly rising overall trend in the volume of Fund loans (drawings) even in nominal terms though such a trend need not have been incompatible with the revolving nature of Fund drawings. We note, however, that such a trend seems to have started in 1990 (Table 1).

The Mechanics

During the period considered here, major changes occurred in the mechanics of the Fund's financial activities.[15]

---

[15] Access to the Fund's resources under the tranche policy requires a waiver if it implies that the Fund's holdings of any currency would exceed 200 percent of quota —that is, access to Fund resources without waiver and including the reserve tranche is limited to 125 percent of quota and Fund net lending to 100 percent of quota. But it has become much easier to obtain waivers. Anticipating developments commented on below, access to Fund credit *in addition* to purchases that "float" above the credit tranches can reach 440 percent of quota in case of need and has no specified limit in exceptional circumstances.

In the early days of the Fund, stand-by arrangements were sometimes as short as six months. The maturity of Fund loans was initially limited to three–five years, but has since been extended; ordinary resources can be lent for four–ten years, resources borrowed by the IMF for four–ten years, with repayments on a linear schedule. The purpose of these extensions was to accommodate particularly the least developed countries where more complicated and time-consuming measures—including structural ones—may have to be adopted to bring about the most effective and least painful adjustment. Although equal disbursements (drawings) per period are the rule, front- and back-loading are not unknown.

Conditionality was present from a very early period onward. The initial distinction was between the gold (we would now say, reserve) tranche, the first credit tranche, and the upper credit tranches. Access to the gold tranche was *practically* (though not formally) automatic (the member's request was given the "overwhelming benefit of the doubt") but subject to repurchase. Access to the reserve tranche has now become formally automatic and exempt from repurchase. Among the upper credit tranches, there is no formal distinction but the size of access is, in practice, certainly taken into account in determining the strength of conditionality (see below). Initially,

Table 1. Financing Under IMF Facilities, 1981–91

(In billions of U.S. dollars)

(Financial Years Ending April 30)	1981	1982	1983	1984	1985	1986	1987	1988	1989	1990	1991
IMF purchases											
Under credit tranche policies[1]	4.18	5.86	6.42	8.70	5.29	4.07	3.66	3.46	2.48	5.15	5.49
CFF and CCFF[2]	0.90	1.79	3.89	1.16	1.38	0.73	0.84	2.06	0.31	1.15	2.81
Buffer stock financing facility	—	—	0.36	0.10	—	—	—	—	—	—	—
Loan disbursements											
Under SAF	—	—	—	—	—	—	0.20	0.59	0.38	0.60	0.27
Under ESAF	—	—	—	—	—	—	—	—	0.34	0.58	0.54
Total purchases and loan disbursements	5.08	7.66	10.67	9.96	6.67	4.81	4.70	6.11	3.51	7.48	9.11
Changes in gross international financial flows (IMF-based data)											
To industrial countries	—	—	100	132	208	413	548	471	564	386[3]	—
To developing countries	—	—	34	11	4	2	22	–6	11	–13	—
To others[4]	—	—	25	140	64	123	233	95	244	58	—
Total change in claims	—	—	159	183	276	538	803	560	819	431	—

Sources: International Monetary Fund, Treasurer's Department; International Monetary Fund, *Annual Report, 1991*; and International Monetary Fund, *International Capital Markets: Developments and Prospects*, various issues.
[1] First credit tranche, upper credit tranches, and extended Fund facility.
[2] CCFF replaced CFF in August 1988.
[3] First three quarters of 1990.
[4] Includes offshore centers and some identified cross-border changes in accounts of centrally planned economies.

Initially the financial function of the IMF was exercised exclusively through the "tranche policy"—that is, loans ("drawings") and "stand-by arrangements" for medium-term *general* balance of payments purposes. Various (other) lending "facilities" began to be introduced in the 1960s. With one significant exception, they were addressed essentially to problems of developing countries. They can, with some imprecision, be divided into two types.

The Type I facilities comprise the compensatory financing facility (CFF), now succeeded by the compensatory and contingency financing facility (CCFF); the buffer stock financing facility, and the former oil facilities, as well as the present oil window of the CCFF (and, in a sense, emergency assistance by the Fund). They were initially designed to enable the IMF to grant assistance quickly and without negotiation of a program of adjustment where a self-reversible balance of payments problem beyond the country's control was involved. Under these circumstances, access was practically auto-

---

phasing—disbursement ("drawing") in installments—was not required to be present in *all* stand-by arrangements. The change came after the 1967 stand-by arrangement with the United Kingdom, where the rule was established that all stand-by arrangements beyond the first credit tranche had to be phased. But even the so-far sacrosanct rule that the first credit tranche is to be exempt from phasing and, therefore, from the usual sanction against violation of understandings has recently been questioned. It should be understood that phasing is neither an absolute nor the only guarantee of implementation of accepted conditions by borrowers. In its absence, countries must consider that deviations will affect access under future arrangements; it does not, in any case, protect against deviations from agreed conditions after drawing and conditionality. Hence, one of the developments over time in the tranche policy has been "prior conditions"—that is, policy action required of countries before approval of the stand-by (or other) arrangement.

A second development has been the requirement, as a performance clause, of consultations during the stand-by (or other) arrangement; this entitles the Fund to require a change in the other performance clauses if it is not satisfied that the existing ones remain adequate. Moreover, the financial assistance of the Fund was on occasion given through genuine "stand-by arrangements"—that is, arrangements under which disbursements were not made upon conclusion of the arrangement but only if—and when—a balance of payments need developed subsequently. More recently, there has been increased interest in monitoring agreements, where no financial arrangement is involved. This type of relationship reflects the Fund's "catalytic" role in promoting financing from other lenders for countries without independent access to the international capital market. It may also avoid conflict that could arise when commercial banks' new money agreements with debtor countries would otherwise require pari passu disbursements of Fund resources and bank "new money."

matic.[16] The Type I facilities could thus also be used in the cases contemplated instead of a bridging credit facility, which the Fund does not possess. The Fund can deploy its tranche policy quickly, but an automatic facility can be even quicker. Only the 1974 and 1975 oil facilities were used extensively by industrial countries; they were the most automatic of all facilities.

The Type II facilities address general balance of payments problems in a more generous and slightly longer-term fashion than the tranche policy. They comprise the extended Fund facility (EFF) and—while available—the supplementary financing facility (equipped later with an interest rate subsidy), as well as the enlarged access policy; and three concessional facilities not financed from the General Resources Account, viz., the Trust Fund, and, later, the structural adjustment facility (SAF) and the enhanced structural adjustment facility (ESAF). Here, access was invariably not automatic but subject to negotiation of a program with conditionality and phasing (beyond the first credit tranche which is rarely used alone).

The different (initial) approach to Type I and Type II facilities regarding conditionality is explained by the need of the Fund to protect the revolving character of its resources and by the fact that it lends for policy purposes. Conditionality protects the Fund's pur-

---

[16] Subject only to an undertaking to collaborate with the Fund on solving any contemporaneous balance of payments problems not of a nature to disappear automatically. When access to the CFF was first increased, it was made subject, beyond a first tranche, to a requirement that the borrower *had* in the past collaborated with the Fund.

The CFF, established after abandonment of UN attempts to create a *grant* facility with similar purpose, was the first of three facilities available to supply finance to members suffering from reversible export revenue reductions independent of the member's control. This facility, like the other Type I facilities, was outside the traditional tranche policy; it "floated" against the reserve as well as the credit tranches, permitting the drawing on the compensatory facility while leaving the reserve and first credit tranches intact and available, if the member country so desired. In several other respects also, it represented a fundamental change in Fund practices. The facility was destined for primary producing (rather than all member) countries although this was not a formal limitation.

The buffer stock financing facility, a Type I facility similar to the CFF, was established for the financing of member countries' contributions to international buffer stocks. The oil facility was a temporary special facility for countries facing the effects of the first oil shock, which was used by industrial and developing countries in equal proportions. It is significant that it was the least conditional of all facilities. The recent "oil element" of the CCFF is a modest copy of the oil facility.

poses and resources to the extent that this can be done by tying disbursements to observance of policies designed to re-establish a sound balance of payments (Type II); it can be dispensed with where reversal of the balance of payments problems can be expected to be automatic (Type I). Since the protection offered the Fund by conditionality makes it possible to grant access without further complications as long as the conditions are fulfilled, it is desirable that conditions of access to the Fund's resources should be precisely defined. One consequence of this attitude is, however, that even a trivial violation of the conditions leads to interruption of disbursements. Such interruption, even if brief (see below), can prove damaging to a country's market access.

Trends

From the early until the middle 1980s, access to both Type I and Type II facilities expanded. However, in the mid-1980s average access[17] in quota terms[18] under arrangements in the General Resources Account has remained essentially unchanged after a temporary increase up to 1983 (Table 2) and again in 1990 and 1991. Concessional loans (financed outside the General Resources Account), however, have been increasing in the second half of the 1980s (Table 3). It is also noteworthy that regular Fund charges have greatly increased by comparison with market rates (Table 4).

The (apparent) retrenchment in Fund General Resources Account lending after the mid-1980s followed its great expansion after the conclusion of the work of the Committee of Twenty: viz., the oil shocks of 1973 and 1979, the recession of the early 1980s, and the debt crisis; while the impact of the Middle East crisis and Eastern European restructuring appears to be leading to renewed expansion of Fund lending. Retrenchment after the earlier oil shocks was logical, but retrenchment while the debt crisis continues may appear to have been precipitate. The moment when Fund credit is to be

---

[17] As regards the CFF, a distinction was explicitly established between those cases where the export shortfall was clearly the result of events outside the control of the shortfall country and those where there might also be other causes. In the latter case, access either because of export shortfalls or because of increases in cereal import costs was—beyond certain limits—made subject to additional conditions (e.g., adoption of a program supported by a financial arrangement with the Fund) with all their complications and delays of negotiation, implying an interruption—in principle—of drawings in cases even of trivial noncompliance.

[18] A similar statement applies in nominal terms.

**Table 2. Average Annual Access Limit Under Arrangements in the
General Resources Account, 1981 – September 1991**

(In percent of quota)

Year	Annual Access Limit(s) (Including Enlarged Access from 1981)	Average Annual Access	Lowest Annual Access	Highest Annual Access
1981	200	100	25	225
1982	150	100	44	150
1983	150	107	61	150
1984	102–125	60	35	102
1985	95–115	49	32	70
1986	90–100	42	25	90
1987	90–110	42	18	80
1988	90–100	41	21	51
1989	90–110	51	15	90
1990	90–110	51	30	101
1991[1]	90–110	54	22	100

Source: International Monetary Fund, Treasurer's Department.
[1] January–September 1991.

restricted after a period of expansion cannot be determined solely on the basis of mechanical rules. From that point of view, the rise in net repurchases by countries with recent debt-servicing problems[19] in the late 1980s was hardly felicitous.

Retrenchment for Type I facilities[20] relied on limiting automatic access by requiring overwhelming likelihood that balance of payments "need"—a concept as important and as vague as "fundamental disequilibrium"—was determined by self-reversible circumstances. With this exception, access beyond a minimum was made conditional as under Type II facilities.[21] For the latter (as for the tranche policy) prior actions, or a period of formal or informal monitoring, are also required increasingly to establish a favorable

---

[19]International Monetary Fund, *World Economic Outlook, May 1991* (Washington), Table A44.

[20]Though access limits were maintained at their previous maximums in *nominal* terms; since those limits were based on average quota increases, they reduced nominal maximum access in terms of quota for countries whose quotas had increased less than the average. Also, average quota increases did not match increases in any of the usual comparators, for example, inflation.

[21]A major change in the CFF occurred when it was joined with a new contingency financing facility into a combined compensatory and contingency financing facility (CCFF). As distinct from the compensatory facility, the contingency facility was designed to be attached to stand-by and extended arrangements to compensate unexpected future exchange revenue needs. The facility, however, is extraordinarily complicated (despite a recent attempt at simplification).

track record before access to Fund financing. Thus, effective access to Type I and Type II facilities (like access under the tranche policy) is in practice determined by use of the "case-by-case" approach. This approach is designed to preserve *uniformity* of treatment in the face of different circumstances—rather than *equality* in terms of quantifiable or otherwise precise criteria. This poses a problem: mechanical uniformity may be inappropriate, yet discretion—rightly or wrongly—can appear to be arbitrary and, therefore, prejudice potential borrowers' confidence.

Factors Affecting the Trends

Some of the ideas and other developments that have contributed to the trend in financial assistance by the Fund have already been noted. Other suggestions have included the idea that the Fund should stress policy advice, while financing would be replaced by more rapid adjustment; at most, the Fund should catalyze outside resources rather than lend its own resources. It is not clear how any of these policies could work. Where would the resources come from, since private lenders are mostly retrenching rather than expanding while official lenders are also reticent? How persuasive vis-à-vis cofinanciers (and even borrowers) could the Fund be if it were not to risk its own resources? Are there no practical limits to speed of adjustment?

To the propensity of some member countries to retrench on the Fund's financing, the arrears problem has contributed powerfully. Arrears to the Fund became a major problem for it only after the eruption of the debt crisis in 1982. The Fund's attitude was, from the outset, to refuse formally to reschedule debt owed to it, although it does refinance in fact and the Articles of Agreement permit it formally to reschedule repurchases[22] and to postpone payment of charges by accepting local currency.

Yet rescheduling need not discourage resumption of service to the Fund by the defaulting country. On the contrary, unless a country is

---

[22] Instead of rescheduling, the Fund applies a succession of exhortations to a country in arrears, but during this period is not paid. Even if it could apply the ultimate sanction of compulsory withdrawal (which requires an 85 percent majority of the voting power), it has no means of exacting payment of amortizations (repurchases), though it may impose extra charges on other members to offset arrears of interest payments (charges).

Repurchases can be explicitly rescheduled. Charges can be paid in local currency and, therefore, rescheduled until the local currency debt of the member country has to be repurchased.

Table 3. IMF Arrangements in Effect as of Financial Years Ended April 30, 1953–90

Financial Year	Number of Arrangements as of April 30					Amount Committed as of April 30 (In millions of SDRs)				
	Stand-by	EFF	SAF	ESAF	Total	Stand-by	EFF	SAF	ESAF[1]	Total
1953	2				2	55.0				55.00
1954	3				3	112.50				112.50
1955	3				3	112.50				112.50
1956	3				3	97.50				97.50
1957	9				9	1,194.78				1,194.78
1958	9				9	967.53				967.53
1959	11				11	1,013.13				1,013.13
1960	12				12	351.38				351.38
1961	12				12	416.13				416.13
1962	21				21	2,128.63				2,128.63
1963	17				17	1,520.00				1,520.00
1964	19				19	2,159.85				2,159.85
1965	23				23	2,154.35				2,154.35
1966	24				24	575.35				575.35
1967	25				25	591.15				591.15
1968	31				31	2,227.36				2,227.36
1969	25				25	538.15				538.15
1970	23				23	2,381.28				2,381.28
1971	18				18	501.70				501.70
1972	13				13	313.75				313.75
1973	12				12	281.85				281.85
1974	15				15	1,394.00				1,394.00
1975	12				12	337.25				337.25
1976	17	2			19	1,158.96	284.20			1,443.16
1977	17	3			20	4,672.92	802.20			5,475.12
1978	19	3			22	5,075.09	802.20			5,877.29

1979	15	5			20	1,032.85	1,610.50			2,643.35
1980	22	7			29	2,340.34	1,462.85			3,803.19
1981	22	15			37	5,331.03	5,464.10			10,795.13
1982	23	12			35	6,296.21	9,910.10			16,206.31
1983	30	9			39	9,464.48	15,561.00			25,025.48
1984	30	5			35	5,448.16	13,121.25			18,569.41
1985	27	3			30	3,925.33	7,750.00			11,675.33
1986	24	2			26	4,075.73	831.00			4,906.73
1987	23	1	10		34	4,313.10	750.00	327.45		5,390.55
1988	18	2	25		45	2,187.23	995.40	1,357.38		4,540.01
1989	14	2	23	7	46	3,054.05	1,032.30	1,566.25	954.97	6,607.57
1990	19	4	17	11	51					
1990/December	17	4	10	14	45	3,597.02	7,834.40	1,109.64	1,370.20	13,911.26

Source: International Monetary Fund, *Annual Report*, various issues.
[1] Includes undisbursed amounts under SAF arrangements that were replaced by ESAF arrangements.

Table 4. IMF Charges, 1951 – October 1991
(In percent per annum)

Financial Years	Average Rates of Charge					U.S. Government Ten-Year Bond	Six-Month Eurodollar
	On ordinary resources		On borrowed resources	On combined ordinary and borrowed resources (weighted)			
	Basic rate	Adjusted for burden sharing		Basic rate	Adjusted for burden sharing		
1951/55	1.85	—	—	—	—	2.68	—
1956/60	1.96	—	—	—	—	3.58	—
1961/65	2.62	—	—	—	—	4.01	—
1966/70	2.92	—	—	—	—	5.53	6.94
1971/75	3.31	—	—	—	—	6.85	8.34
1976/80	4.64	—	7.43	6.11	—	8.45	8.89
1981/85	6.35	—	11.37	8.33	—	12.38	12.64
1986/90	6.57	7.23[1]	8.09	7.22	7.49[1]	8.60	7.98
1987/90	6.46	7.23	7.80	7.03	7.49	8.37	7.96
1990/October 1991	8.30	9.58	9.34	8.66	9.50	8.67	8.33

Source: International Monetary Fund.
[1] 1987–90 (burden sharing began in 1987).

defaulting "capriciously," payment on the original terms may be felt to involve an intolerable sacrifice; then rescheduling—like "Chapter 11" under U.S. bankruptcy laws—is likely to strengthen the ability of the Fund to press a country in default to adjust its policies so as to enable it to repay although on a rescheduled basis. Rescheduling, therefore, can protect the interests of the Fund and of the rest of the international financial community, as well as those of the debtor country. This has now been recognized in practice through the adoption of the "intensified collaborative strategy" including the "rights approach." While this approach might by some be seen as the ultimate in disguised rescheduling, it is certainly an intelligent, if belated innovation. Under it, a member country that accepts to follow a program monitored by the Fund will receive its help in obtaining bridging credits from governments or others to clear its arrears. It will then be able to conclude a financial arrangement with the Fund which will enable it to repay its bridging credits. If necessary, it may be allowed, under its monitored program, to earn "rights" to drawings larger than those otherwise available under a financial arrangement. The technique is experimental and has so far been applied only in the case of one country (but may soon be applied to a second one). The total resources made available to the first country in the first year, nevertheless, exceeded those necessary to clear the arrears by rather little. The technique is to be limited to the countries that had protracted arrears at the end of 1989. In the case of other countries cooperating with the Fund, the latter would, however, be prepared to show them sympathetic consideration in solving their arrears problem.

The increasing comparative cost of the Fund's credit has already been noted. It is generally justified as necessary to encourage Fund creditors to maintain or increase their net creditor positions. But the Fund is a cooperative institution, and it may be asked whether such an institution need require its loans to be remunerated (as was not always the case) close to a Group of Five borrowing rate.[23]

III. How to Strengthen the Fund's Influence

The Fund's policy influence has been affected by the developments sketched in the two preceding sections. The main challenge is

---

[23] The Fund has not recently used its power to graduate charges according to the time loans remained outstanding.

to attempt to enhance, through the Fund, the international community's influence over the major Fund members but also over others.[24]

Attempts to reinvigorate the Fund's influence, if at all feasible, must be limited, for the time being, to what can be achieved particularly through the persuasiveness with which the Fund's technical competence endows it and through its financial functions. I am not suggesting that encouraging countries to borrow from the Fund or otherwise is a panacea.

Encouraging Access

It would be particularly important, though difficult, to encourage major countries to borrow from the Fund. As long as almost no country could feel "safe" from having to become a borrower from the Fund, one can surmise that all countries were inclined to be careful about conditions of access, rather than some being overwhelmingly interested in making access easier and others—the major countries—in making it more limited. Thus, it is for consideration whether it could be helpful if even those countries that presently are not in need of borrowing from the Fund could be induced in one way or another from time to time to do so (this would go beyond inducing members to use their reserve tranche—as the United States did once or twice in earlier times).

But how could this be accomplished? Nobody in his senses would wish to restrict international capital flows, whose availability makes many countries certain for all practical purposes to be able to escape the need to borrow from the Fund. That they may indeed wish to

---

[24] See John H. Williams, "The Adequacy of Existing Currency Mechanisms Under Varying Circumstances," *American Economic Review, Papers and Proceedings* (Evanston, Illinois), Vol. 27 (March 1937), pp. 151–68, and "Currency Stabilization: The Keynes and White Plans," *Foreign Affairs* (New York), Vol. 21 (July 1943), pp. 645–58.

Re-establishment of the par value system might contribute to meeting the main challenge mentioned, if it comprised the major countries. There can presently be no realistic expectation of such a development. It is also difficult to see how a "tripolar" system could significantly and realistically differ from the "system" we have today—nor what it could contribute to meeting the main challenge; apparently, it would be less binding or organized than the late Professor Williams' "key currency" proposal and perhaps no more so than the Tripartite Agreement of the late 1930s. (United States, *Annual Report of the Secretary of the Treasury on the State of the Finances, for the Fiscal Year Ended June 30, 1937* (Washington: U.S. Government Printing Office, 1938), pp. 258–62.)

avoid doing so, need be no sign of a desire to follow irrational policies, but of a difference of opinion on what is the "right" policy and particularly of what is politically possible. But it may be possible to induce more members to borrow in two other ways.

The first method to induce borrowing would be a change, originally suggested by former Managing Director H. Johannes Witteveen, in the official settlement system for countries not accepting genuine free floating. Such countries would be required to settle part of their payments balances in resources borrowed from the Fund or SDRs,[25] that is, in assets, the creation or use of which is subject to international control through the Fund.

Another approach would be a degree of liberalization of access to the Fund's resources. It could mean a reduction in the rate of charge; on occasion, even an increase in the benefit of the doubt given to aspiring drawers from the Fund about the feasibility of their program or increased flexibility of maturities of drawings, as long as neither change led to excessive or excessively long net use of the Fund's resources by members.

In these ways, use of Fund resources could become somewhat attractive even to members with ample access to the capital market. The motive why major countries might agree to create conditions that would induce or oblige them to borrow from the Fund would be their desire to strengthen the Fund for the benefit of all its members.

One industrial country member[26] not requiring Fund financial assistance has employed monitoring agreements with the Fund to encourage implementation of policies against domestic pressures. It is conceivable that such agreements could, in time, become more acceptable than they are now to countries not requiring to borrow from the Fund and also strengthen the Fund's influence[27] over the major countries, if they perceived that their acceptance of such program encourages other major countries to do the same, with

---

[25] It may not be essential for this purpose to change the Articles of Agreement.

A system that—with modification—might meet this problem has been described in the report of the Technical Group on Intervention and Settlement, *Documents of the Committee of Twenty* (Washington: International Monetary Fund, 1974), p. 112, et seq.

[26] Belgium.

[27] Particular problems in recent years have been three oil problems (1973-74, 1979 and, again, recently) and the debt problem. We have already made some comments on both. They have thrown up a number of complications.

At the beginning of the debt crisis, there was a genuine threat to the banking system in some countries. The Fund by offering its own resources was able to prevail

mutual benefit. But such a development must no doubt take considerable time, if it is at all likely.

The Practice of Conditionality

The idea of liberalizing access to the Fund's resources brings us to possible changes in the practice of conditionality. Criticism, much of it misplaced, of the practice of conditionality is sometimes presented as the need for respect for sovereignty; it could be more convincingly based on the need to give a country as wide a latitude for decision making as possible, where this can be done while protecting the Fund's purposes and resources. It would be conceivable to replace conditionality in part by collateral, but this is hardly likely to be of wide applicability. That conditionality could usefully be replaced by higher and varied levels of interest rates (''charges'') must be doubted; similarly for reversing the abandonment, since shortly after the Second Amendment, of interest rates rising as a function of time of net use of Fund resources. To rely purely on trust instead of

---

upon banks to reschedule debts on a large scale although for short periods, but this was the wrong solution in the light of the nature of the crisis as it subsequently revealed itself. At present there are again threats to banks in one or two countries, but the debt problem of developing countries is not any more the major problem they are facing.

Involvement with countries in respect to their commercial bank debt has created a considerable number of complications both for the Fund and for countries and banks themselves. It is natural for the Fund to wish to avoid becoming directly involved in negotiations between banks and member countries, but the Fund nevertheless has to take a view in all those cases where financing assurances do not cover all of a country's credit needs. In those cases, the Fund has gradually accepted to disburse despite the fact that a country may continue to accumulate arrears when an agreement with the banks that would seem sensible to the international financial community represented by the Fund cannot be arrived at. In such a situation, however, the question arises whether closer involvement by the Fund would not impress upon the negotiations an outcome that could often be more helpful than it is at present. In some cases, the Fund has been placed into an embarrassing situation by the insistence of banks on certain conditions precedent to drawings from them which would force the Fund to go beyond what it conceives to be a correct measure of balance of payments needs in making available its own financial assistance. On the other hand, the Fund has sometimes had an excessively narrow conception of a country's balance of payments needs that should include the need to finance enhancements to be offered to banks. Moreover, the Fund has sometimes found it necessary to agree to larger drawings because earlier decisions had limited loans for a type of enhancement (set asides) to a proportion of drawings, though augmentation, reserved for collateralization of debt-service reduction, is related not to drawings but to quotas. These problems are illustrations of what we have earlier called unnecessary complications in the Fund's policies.

performance clauses would not recommend itself to the Fund's creditors. Nevertheless, some liberalization of conditionality, as already mentioned, would be conceivable without danger to the Fund or its creditors. Another possibility could be less frequent testing dates of Fund performance clauses. The trend has been in the opposite direction. There is no reason not to try to reverse it.

Among Fund conditions, periodic reviews as performance clauses under an arrangement with the Fund require special mention. In these reviews, countries must often come to an agreement with the Fund on whether the existing arrangement is still appropriate in the face of changing circumstances even though all its specific performance clauses may have been met. This means that one advantage of conditionality for the member country is lost, namely, assured access as long as those clauses are met. The question, therefore, arises whether members should not be given the choice to link access *only* to *reviews* or *only* to *specific performance clauses* rather than having to link them to both types. In the latter hypothesis, thought might have to be given to the formulation of these clauses—to avoid excessive imprecision as well as excessive detail.

It has also been suggested that the availability of waivers for program modifications tends to relieve many of the problems that conditionality would otherwise cause. In reality, waivers may not be particularly helpful. The mere interruption of disbursements even for a short time may undermine creditworthiness. Delays in Fund disbursements that are conditions for access to other credits can play havoc with the use of the latter. On repeated occasions it has been suggested that quantified conditions should foresee an upper and lower limit so that an infraction not exceeding the extreme limit would not lead to an interruption of disbursements. But dual limits would in practice be meaningless because the extreme limit would become the only effective one. Nor would a slight modification of this approach, which has been suggested, be helpful. Under such a modification there would be a single limit but successive, increasingly insistent and possibly more public warnings would be issued by the Fund to a country that was approaching its limit. But contact between a member country with an arrangement and the Fund is close enough so that such warnings are issued in any case privately. Public warnings could be destructive of the country's credit.

Design of Programs

Changes in the design of programs could also be helpful in encouraging potential borrowers to come to the Fund, at an early stage of their payments problem. Thus, the Fund's experience with Eastern Europe has drawn attention to the importance of social safety nets in the design of programs, or, in more general terms, to the need for contemplating broad political and social problems as well as economic ones. Greater emphasis on these two problems in future programs could make it more attractive for members to enter into arrangements with the Fund and thereby strengthen its influence. The members attracted by such changes might still not be the major countries, but a larger set of the nonmajors.

Another proposal is to replace performance criteria in nominal terms (e.g., the public sector borrowing requirement) by criteria in real terms (e.g., the "operational" public sector balance). Since reduction in inflation is seen as one necessary purpose of a Fund arrangement, discarding nominal criteria altogether would not make sense. Yet, the use of real criteria along with nominal ones can indicate whether policies went seriously wrong in all or only some respects. Other suggestions have been to limit conditionality to matters directly affecting the international financial community—especially the external balance—rather than extend it to instrument variables, such as the budgetary balance (real or nominal); only if external balance conditionality fails would implementation of performance criteria relating to other variables be required. This could appear attractive; but it may lead, at least, to delays in corrective action.

Other aspects of program design have come in for comment as well. The Fund is often accused of limiting its arsenal of acceptable instruments to fiscal and monetary policy—the consequence of relying more on demand than on supply policy. To switch the emphasis would require a larger Fund—on which some comments are made below—or a greater propensity of the international financial community to allow its assistance to be catalyzed by the Fund. One instrument would be greater use of contingency clauses. The Fund has, so far, not had attractive experiences with such clauses. The Fund is also accused of orthodoxy. There certainly continues to be an emphasis on sustainable budgetary and monetary policies and on "realistic" exchange rates, but the Fund has been prepared to accept various forms of "incomes policies" especially in relation to cases of so-called inertial inflation. In fact, what seems to some excessive confidence in exchange rate "anchors"—a particularly dangerous type of orthodoxy—is increasingly displayed by some—but only some—in the Fund, as a means of reversing expectations, in the direction of stability—even where the preconditions of the functioning of anchors are not in place.

Maturities and the Monetary Character of the Fund

The question of maturities also deserves additional comment. For drawings occasioned by self-reversible balance of payments needs, appropriate maturities could be established coupled with a return to the previous practice of automaticity of access or, at any rate, less conditionality than at present.

On the other hand, it may be doubted whether the length of maturities of drawings, in the Type II facilities, has been adequate for dealing with some of the balance of payments problems that these facilities are supposed to address. One could say that longer maturities transform the Fund into a development finance institution. The economist will always find it hard to distinguish between balance of payments and development financing.

Another way of looking at this matter is the question of the preservation of the "monetary character" of the Fund. This refers to the need that the counterpart of Fund lending, that is, the net creditor positions in the Fund, should be unquestionably liquid. But this danger does not exist as long as the Fund's liquid liabilities do not exceed its liquid resources. In calculating the latter, one must consider that the Fund's gold can be mobilized to supplement the Fund's other assets. One must also note that the General Arrangements to Borrow (GAB) can be activated in case the Fund's liquidity became a question as this would constitute a systemic crisis, precisely one of the situations contemplated by the GAB. If all these matters are taken into account, some further extension of Fund maturities could be contemplated without fear. It is also relevant in this context that the liquidity of credits on the Fund is less correlated with the specific purposes of loans to borrowing members than with the overall stance of their policy.

Other Problems

More recently, the Fund has taken on a possibly vast and risky new task: technical assistance to the Soviet Union and/or its successor republics. The needed resources could be found from members, from the market, or—not desirably—at the expense of borrowers or other recipients of technical assistance.

When (and if) the Fund has to give financial assistance to the U.S.S.R. or its successor republics, a major financial problem may be created. It could require, one would think, rather long-term funds. While the Articles of Agreement could be interpreted to authorize longer-term lending by the Fund even of its own resources, the Fund has so far stuck essentially to medium-term lending. It is by no means clear that avoidance of longer-term lending by the Fund, as suggested earlier, was always appropriate.

In this connection, a few more words could be said on ways of making the resources at the Fund's disposal more flexible. Timely and more generous increases in quota could be used; the SDR mechanism could be resurrected and modified in various forms; and one might recall a proposal of the Canadian authorities at Bretton Woods, which, however, would require a change in the Articles of Agreement to give the Fund authority to compel members to lend to it up to 50 percent of quota.

6

What Future for the International Monetary System?

Richard N. Cooper

This paper discusses some problems with present international arrangements and suggests that the time has come to begin contemplating a common currency among the industrialized democracies. This idea is much too radical to garner much political support in the near future. But it does offer a way to overcome a number of difficulties that these economies now face, and which are likely to become more, not less, serious in the coming years. So despite its novelty, a common currency provides a focal point for analysis, which may in turn suggest intermediate steps that accomplish some of the same results with less political commitment.

Before we turn to the present and the future, it is worth considering past international monetary arrangements and how they performed. The first section of the paper, therefore, reviews briefly six types of international monetary arrangements that have existed during the past century. It then turns to an evaluation of the strengths and weaknesses of the current arrangement of floating exchange rates subject to ad hoc management. Throughout, the focus will be on the arrangements among the major economies of the day, basically Europe, North America, and in the last 30 years, Japan. During the earlier period, these arrangements encompassed many "peripheral" areas as well, by virtue of their colonial status. How peripheral countries relate to the international monetary core is an interesting and important topic, but it is necessary first to be clear on relationships at the core.

I. Past International Monetary Systems

History is complex, and it would take us too far afield to enter into a detailed exposition of the workings of different international monetary systems. But every system must address two fundamental questions, and it is worthwhile to sketch how different systems addressed these questions, both in theory and in the way the theory was modified in practice. The two fundamental questions concern how the international monetary system envisions that countries will adjust to "disturbances" to economic relations among countries (the adjustment problem) and how it envisions that adequate, internationally acceptable means of payment will be provided (the liquidity problem).

The history of the past century can be divided roughly into six periods, excluding the two world wars and their immediate aftermath, each of which involved a somewhat different international monetary system covering the major countries. Of course, this division inevitably involves some stylization, since history evolves continuously; in some cases the shift from one system to another is gradual and involves antecedents, and not all countries move together.

The six systems are the gold-specie standard (1879–1913); the gold exchange standard (1925–31); freely floating exchange rates (1919–25, 1933–36); the Bretton Woods system, early phase (1947–59); the Bretton Woods system, late phase (1959–73); and managed flexible exchange rates (1973–present).

Gold-Specie Standard

Under the gold-specie standard, national money and acceptable means of payment were the same, namely, gold coins of standard weight and fineness. These might be re-minted into different national coins, although foreign coins sometimes also circulated domestically. Thus both domestic and international liquidity were satisfied in principle from new gold production. If this proved inadequate, as it did for prolonged periods, most notably from the 1870s to the mid-1890s, the increased liquidity was supplemented domestically by a rapid expansion of new forms of payment, notably banknotes and demand deposits in banks (Triffin (1964)) and by a prolonged decline in the price level, which raised the real value (in commodities) of a given volume of gold money. Wholesale prices fell by 40 percent to 55 percent in all the major countries between 1873 and 1896 (Cooper (1982)).

The theory of the adjustment mechanism under the gold standard was simple, and it was clearly and concisely stated by David Hume in 1752 (Cooper (1969)). A transfer (for example, reparations, or a capital investment) from country A to country B raised the money stock in B and lowered it in A. As a result, prices would fall in A and rise in B, and A would in consequence enlarge its trade surplus (or reduce its deficit), make the real transfer in goods, and earn the gold back until monetary and payments equilibrium was restored.

How the adjustment mechanism worked in practice is still controversial. First, much less gold actually moved internationally than the theory would suggest (Bloomfield (1959)). Second, Viner's (1924) classic study of large capital inflows into Canada before World War I suggested that although price movements could be discerned, especially of nontradable goods against tradable goods, the price movements were far smaller and worked to accomplish changes in trade flows more rapidly, than he and his teacher Taussig expected. Later analysis suggested that a substantial part of the adjustment was accomplished by changes in spending—up in the receiving country, down in the sending country—associated with the transfer itself. Recently, McKinnon (1988a) has argued that there is no presumption one way or the other about which way the sending country's terms of trade will change, and with a fully integrated capital market, there need not even be any change in domestic (that is, nontradable) prices. The key point is that adjustment is accomplished partly through changes in spending, or absorption, and partly through changes in prices, especially the prices of nontradables.

Gold Exchange Standard

The adjustment mechanism under the gold exchange is similar to that under the gold standard. In this case, the downward pressure on prices in the sending country is mediated by the banking system, which operates on fractional gold reserves. In fact, the period of the gold exchange standard was dominated by economic stagnation in the leading country, the United Kingdom, but that was related to the exchange rate at which the United Kingdom returned to gold convertibility rather than to the nature of the standard itself. Its period was too short to discover if adjustment eventually would have taken place.

The novelty of the gold exchange standard was to conserve gold by removing it from circulation and concentrating it in the hands of the leading banks, even going beyond that by encouraging banks, including smaller central banks, to hold short-term claims on other countries, mostly in sterling, secondarily in dollars. Thus national currencies began to play a role as international means of payment. Moreover, this period also saw extensive use of loans from one central bank to another as a temporary source of liquidity. Again, the period was too short to reveal the potential problem of relying on growth of the ratio of the gold-convertible currency holdings relative to a more slowly growing stock of monetary gold, a problem underlined later by Triffin (1960).

Floating Exchange Rates

Floating exchange rates during the interwar period were not thought of as a "system" at all, but rather as an unavoidable but temporary expedient during a turbulent time until a more stable system could be re-established. The "adjustment process" worked by a market price—the exchange rate—clearing the market for foreign exchange, much as the price of strawberries clears the market for strawberries. If for any reason home demand for a foreign currency rose, the exchange rate of that currency would appreciate to ration the demand to what was available at the new price. The most comprehensive examination of floating exchange rates during this period (Nurkse (1944)) found them to be a major source of disturbance rather than a source of smooth adjustment, and that view strongly influenced the re-establishment of fixed exchange rates under the Bretton Woods system.

International liquidity in the sense of an internationally accepted means of payment was not necessary under these arrangements, since residents would buy the foreign currencies they needed in the foreign exchange markets, and the banks need not hold international reserves. Because this arrangement was considered temporary, however, central banks had their eye on the longer term and continued to hold gold. In 1919–20 and again in 1929–33 there was a sharp drop in wholesale prices, so the real value of monetary gold rose. In addition, both the United Kingdom and the United States devalued their currencies against gold (that is, they redefined the gold content of a pound and a dollar) in the 1930s, and that also increased the monetary value of gold reserves.

Bretton Woods—Early Phase

The Bretton Woods system was the first international monetary system to be designed from scratch. It stipulated fixed exchange rates, but recognized that with national full employment commitments, "fundamental disequilibria" might arise from time to time and it called for a discrete change in exchange rates, with international approval. It was taken for granted that monetary and fiscal policy would be used to achieve domestic equilibrium, as defined by each country. International disequilibria were to be financed in the short run, drawing if necessary from the new International Monetary Fund.

There was a major adjustment in exchange rates in 1949, but thereafter exchange rate changes of leading currencies were rare. Instead, adjustment was achieved by differential liberalization of trade and payments. Many countries were in a suppressed disequilibrium following World War II and maintained tight restrictions over trade and payments. These restrictions were gradually relaxed, country by country, as conditions permitted. Not until the end of 1958 did Western European countries abandon controls on current account transactions, and many maintained restrictions on outward capital movements long after that.

Curiously, the Bretton Woods system made no provision for a secular rise in international liquidity. Since the United States held a disproportionate share of the world's monetary gold reserves (more than 70 percent) in the late 1940s, the gold reserves of other countries could be built up in part by drawing on those of the United States, as well as from new production. In addition, however, countries accrued substantial balances of U.S. dollars, as under the gold exchange standard. It should be noted that the world economy grew much more rapidly in the 1950s than anyone dared to expect in the 1940s. The rapid growth in production and trade seemed to call forth a corresponding growth in demand for international reserves, which was satisfied in large part by U.S. Treasury bills, thought to be better than gold since they bore interest and for monetary authorities were convertible into gold at the U.S. Treasury on demand. These circumstances gave rise to the celebrated Triffin (1960) dilemma: how could the world economy grow without additional dollars, yet how could the gold convertibility of the dollar remain credible as U.S. liabilities to foreign monetary authorities grew continually relative to the U.S. gold stock?

Bretton Woods—Late Phase

The conceptual underpinnings of the Bretton Woods system remained the same, but the scope for differential payments liberalization as the mechanism of adjustment diminished. Some modest exchange rate adjustments among major currencies occurred during the 1960s (the deutsche mark in 1961, the pound sterling in 1967, the French franc in 1969), but for the most part, countries were spared the need to adjust by a large and growing U.S. payments deficit, financed by a buildup in dollars held by central banks. When this buildup became unacceptably great, the Bretton Woods system broke down. It broke down basically because discrete changes in exchange rates, the key feature of its adjustment mechanism, are incompatible with the high mobility of private capital, which had resumed by the late 1960s. Any anticipated change in official exchange rates evoked a huge movement of speculative capital, which played havoc with domestic monetary policy. The emergence of any "fundamental disequilibrium," especially if it was in the world's largest economy, was bound to be financially destabilizing under these circumstances.

In the late phase of Bretton Woods, the question of international liquidity, omitted earlier, was addressed systematically, and the result was creation of a new kind of international fiat money, the SDR, to be held and used by central banks. The SDR was designated to become the centerpiece of the international monetary system, to be created as needed to serve the world's need for international liquidity. In fact, total SDR creation has amounted so far to only about $25 billion, less than 10 percent of official foreign exchange reserves.

Managed Floating, 1973–Present

Since 1973 the major currencies have been floating with respect to one another, but the floating has been subject to market intervention by the monetary authorities—sometimes heavy intervention—to influence the movement of exchange rates. And most European currencies since March 1979 have been linked through the European Monetary System (EMS) in a Bretton Woods type system combined with permissible variation in market exchange rates around the central rates, and occasional changes (11 in all from 1979 through 1989) in central rates.

Under floating exchange rate arrangements, it is supposed that the main mechanism of adjustment will be changes in real exchange rates brought about by market-induced changes in nominal rates, supported as appropriate by changes in fiscal policy designed to maintain overall balance in the economy. (Within the EMS, of course, adjustment is similar to what it was supposed to be under the Bretton Woods system.) In fact, it is difficult to interpret the period of floating as behaving in this way, since manifestly exchange rates did not always move in such a way as to reduce current account imbalances. But interpretation of the historical record is complicated by two factors. First, macroeconomic policy, and especially fiscal actions, were not always conducive to international balance. On the contrary, in the early 1980s the United States pursued a markedly expansionist fiscal policy, combined with a tight monetary policy, while Japan, Germany, and the United Kingdom introduced strong fiscal contraction. The combination produced heavy upward pressure on the U.S. dollar, which in turn led to a sharp deterioration of the U.S. current account and corresponding increases in the surpluses of Japan, Germany, and, for a period, the United Kingdom (which was also influenced by increasing production of North Sea oil). In this instance, exchange rate movements "disequilibrated" the current account.

But in doing so, perhaps they were serving the broader role of equilibrating economies. That brings us to the second problem of interpretation: in an integrated world economy, there is no special merit in assuring balance in each country's current account position. On the contrary, for a variety of reasons at particular times some countries will be net savers and others net investors, and one of the useful functions of an integrated economy is to channel savings to investment. If the integrated economy crosses national boundaries, the savings may also be expected to cross national boundaries, and sometimes for substantial periods of time. As a consequence, we do not have a clear, operational definition of international equilibrium. At a minimum, "sustainable" capital movements should be set against the current account, but unfortunately the actual purchases of foreign assets do not carry labels that tell us whether they are sustainable or not. Drawing the line at "long-term" investments will not do, since the definition of short-term (with original maturities under one year) is itself arbitrary, and in an integrated market many financial instruments, whatever their original maturity, may be purchased for short-term or speculative motives, while some short-term credits (for example, trade credits) may be expected to grow predictably in total over time.

Another dividing line often suggested is between official monetary transactions and all others. This suggestion introduces the other characteristic of a monetary system, international liquidity. Under a system of freely floating exchange rates, there should be no need for international liquidity, that is, officially held international means of payment. But in fact we have not had free floating, and the growth of official foreign exchange reserves during the period of floating has been phenomenal (Table 1), despite the widespread view that liquidity was excessive at the end of 1972 before floating began.

The growth in international liquidity has been satisfied overwhelmingly by the acquisition of foreign exchange reserves. There has been only one allocation of SDRs (in three tranches) since 1973, amounting to less than $15 billion. The dollar has continued to be the preferred currency, but the official holdings of deutsche mark and Japanese yen have grown even more rapidly, starting from a much lower base. In addition, the members of the European Monetary Compensation Fund have opened unlimited lines of short-term credit for one another. Gold, the traditional reserve asset, continues to be held by many monetary authorities, but it is virtually never used. Indeed, there is no generally accepted method of valuation, since the official price remains $42 an ounce, while the market price has ranged from $200 to $800, and has remained in the vicinity of $400 an ounce for several years.

Much of the explosive growth in reserve holdings has been voluntary and desired, lending support to Harrod's long contention that demand for reserves would be higher under floating exchange rates, not lower as economic theorists generally contended. The voluntary acquisition of reserves makes it inappropriate to consider a balance on current account plus net private capital movements a suitable measure of payments equilibrium. Some of the reserve acquisition,

Table 1. End-of-Year International Reserves
(In billions of U.S. dollar equivalents)

Holdings	1945	1960	1970	1980	1985
Gold[1]	33.3	38.0	37.2	41.8	40.1
U.S. gold holdings	20.1	17.8	11.1	11.2	11.1
Foreign exchange[2]	14.3	18.6	44.6	370.8	378.7
U.S. liabilities	4.2	11.1	23.8	157.1	172.8
Other[3]	—	3.6	10.8	36.5	62.5
Total reserves	47.6	60.2	92.5	449.1	477.7
Addendum: World exports	34.2	113.4	280.3	1,844.6	1,783.0

Sources: Board of Governors of the Federal Reserve System, *Federal Reserve Bulletin*; and International Monetary Fund, *International Financial Statistics*.
[1] At official prices of $35 an ounce before 1980 and $42 an ounce in 1980 and 1985.
[2] Reported assets differ from U.S. reported liabilities by minor differences in concept, by measurement error, by official holdings of foreign exchange other than dollars, and by official deposits in the Eurocurrency market.
[3] SDRs and reserve positions in the IMF.

particularly the large official acquisition of U.S. dollars in 1987, took place not to satisfy a growing demand for reserves, but to brake the depreciation of the dollar against other leading currencies, particularly the yen and the deutsche mark. So increases in official foreign exchange holdings reflect a mixture of motives, being partly a consequence of defensive exchange rate actions under managed floating.

II. A Brief Evaluation

What do we want of an international monetary system? I suggest (1) that it should contribute to our basic economic objective of growth with low inflation; (2) that to that end and for its own sake it should help reduce the uncertainties economic agents face as close as possible to the minimum intrinsic in nature and the economic system; (3) that it should permit diversity in the national pursuit of economic and social objectives with a view to maintaining harmonious relations among nations; and (4) that it should do all this as unobtrusively as possible.

In terms of such aggregate indicators as real economic growth, variability of inflation, and predictability of growth and inflation, the Bretton Woods system, while it lasted, was a superior performer compared with previous periods and compared with the current managed float (Table 2). In terms of long-term price stability, the gold standard performed best, although the reasons remain poorly understood, since both short- and medium-term price variability was sizable.

III. The Case for Flexible Exchange Rates

Two quite different traditions argue in favor of flexible exchange rates. The monetarist tradition (Friedman (1953)) emphasizes the feature of flexible exchange rates that insulates a national economy from external monetary disturbances, from inflationary impulses that may be coming from abroad. This tradition emphasizes that under fixed exchange rates or market intervention, monetary expansion abroad will lead to reserve outflows for the expanding country, but it will also lead to reserve inflows, hence monetary expansion, for the country that is not expanding. If the economy is operating at full capacity, this expansion will lead to domestic inflation. By

**Table 2. Variance of Quarterly Forecast Errors (Times 1,000)
for the United States**

	Nominal GNP	Price Level	Real GNP
Gold standard			
1890(1)−1914(4)	2.98	0.25	2.83
1915(1)−1931(3)	1.80	0.60	1.41
No clear standard			
1931(4)−1941(4)	5.64	0.24	4.02
1942(1)−1951(1)	0.67	0.60	0.78
Bretton Woods			
1951(2)−1971(3)	0.13	0.02	0.11
Fluctuating rates			
1971(4)−1980(4)	0.13	0.02	0.14

Note: Quarterly forecasts are made by using a Kalman filter with respect to expected level and expected rate of change on past data for each series.
Source: Meltzer (1986), p. 141.

eschewing exchange market intervention and allowing the currency to appreciate, this imported inflation can be avoided. In the smooth and frictionless world of economic models, flexible exchange rates provide perfect insulation against monetary impulses, positive or negative, coming from the rest of the world.

There is also a Keynesian tradition that supports flexible exchange rates, or, more accurately, changes in exchange rates. It operates on the assumption that the economic system will be hit by "exogenous" disturbances from time to time; that for any single country, these disturbances may include the policies of other countries; and that the country will need to "adjust" to these disturbances. Under a competitive market system with continuous market clearing, any needed adjustment is spread throughout the system via price signals, and the loss of output will be minimal and short-lived. But with various rigidities in the formation of prices and wages, such as exist in all modern economies, some of the need for adjustment will be thrown on output and employment, thus producing economic waste. The possibility of changing exchange rates introduces an element of price flexibility into this system replete with price rigidities. Under some circumstances, movements in exchange rates may substitute for product or labor market price flexibility, achieve adjustments in real wages and prices, and thereby avoid some of the loss in output. In this view of the world, the possibility of exchange rate movements introduces an additional element of flexibility into the economy. It is noteworthy that while the monetarist and the Keynesian schools emphasize different aspects of exchange rate flexibility, and the monetarist school in particular underlines the need for full flexibility rather than merely for changes in the exchange rate, the two schools at this level of generalization are quite compatible.

IV. Problems with Flexible Rates

In spite of these arguments for exchange rate flexibility, there are a number of worrisome features about the present arrangements of floating exchange rates subject to occasional official management. First, as Tobin (1988) has pointed out, major adjustments to external disturbances may require changes in the overall price level between one country and another. To the extent that governments treat their price levels as policy targets, adjustment via this mechanism is thwarted. If price level targeting is wholly successful, and if relative prices are sticky—which was the starting point of the Keynesian rationale for floating rates—national action will offset the effect of exchange rate movements. Thus, for example, if the U.S. dollar depreciates in response to some external disturbance, leading to price increases in the United States, the Federal Reserve may tighten monetary policy in order to avoid "inflation." The Deutsche Bundesbank, in contrast, eases monetary action in order to avoid "deflation." In this way adjustment is shifted to output after all.

Second, the imperfect competition that leads to sticky prices may have a further implication, as Krugman (1989), elaborating an analysis by Dixit, has recently pointed out. Fixed market entry costs not only will slow the process of adjustment to changes in the exchange rate, but will actually create a band of variation in which, for the relevant industries, no adjustment will take place. The profit incentive must exceed a certain threshhold before entry is worthwhile. Once entry has taken place, and the costs of entry have been sunk, the profit disincentive must move correspondingly far to make exit the proper strategy. This difference between marginal cost on entry and on exit will be reinforced by uncertainty about future exchange rates. It may make sense for a firm to hold onto its market at prices even below its current marginal costs, if the costs of re-entry after exiting the market are high, and if there is a sufficient probability that the conditions for re-entry—for example, a sufficiently large movement in the exchange rate—will recur.

The implication of this market feature is that exchange rates may have to swing very far in order to achieve real adjustment, since industries subject to significant entry and exit costs will be unresponsive to movements in exchange rates of a relatively minor character. In this respect, flexible exchange rates are not an especially efficient mechanism of adjustment since, when measured against long-run comparative advantage, misallocations of resources may be induced, and then persist for a long period of time, in response to exchange rate fluctuations. One might have in mind the United States in the mid-1980s, for instance, when many foreign firms, attracted by the profit possibilities created by an exceptionally strong dollar, entered the U.S. market profitably and then hung on tenaciously even after the dollar depreciated substantially, in some cases beyond the point at which profitability continued.

Third, a high variability of real exchange rates may reduce total investment in the sectors of the economy open to international competition. When a currency has depreciated strongly, profits in tradables will be high and cash flow will be good, but firms will be reluctant to invest in productive capacity because the cheap currency is not expected to last. They will simply enjoy their windfall profits and perhaps invest more in market opening, as discussed above. When a currency is strongly appreciated, on the other hand, even though the situation is expected by management to be temporary, profits and cash flow will be low, leading to low investment because of credit rationing and because of skeptical, risk-averse boards of directors. Although many other factors have undoubtedly also played a role, it is perhaps not a mere coincidence that investment in plant and equipment in the member countries of the Organization for Economic Cooperation and Development has been depressed since the inauguration of floating exchange rates in 1973, compared with the 1950s and 1960s. In particular, Europe failed to invest much when profits were high and rising as a result of a strong dollar in the period from 1983 to 1985.

Fourth, since firms cannot hedge their investments in future production—as distinguished from a particular sale—through financial markets, they will do so by investing abroad, across currency zones, even if that means giving up some of the advantages of cost and scale associated with exporting from their home bases or some other lower-cost location. Because some of this diversification takes place through takeovers and buyouts, one possible further consequence is greater world concentration in certain industries, leading to a reduction of worldwide competition.

Fifth, at the national level businesses will seek to blunt what they consider unequal competition by urging an increase in trade barriers. Business firms generally feel they can cope with the market uncertainty that attends any growing, dynamic economy, as long as their competitors are subject to the same ups and downs. What they find intolerable is being placed at a competitive disadvantage with respect to their leading competitors for reasons unrelated to decision making in the firms, or indeed in the industry. Present exchange rate arrangements violate this strong desire, insofar as a firm can suddenly find itself facing much stiffer competition (or much less, but that is rarely a cause for concern) as a result of an exchange rate movement, which has its origins in the arcane world of finance. Certainly U.S. firms, and organized labor, greatly increased their pressure on the U.S. Government in the period 1983–85 for some form of relief against overcompetitive imports during the period of an exceptionally strong dollar. It is noteworthy that under the gold standard, while national price levels moved substantially, they tended to move in parallel instead of moving relative to one another.

These various factors involve a misallocation of resources arising from the uncertainties associated with exchange rate flexibility. Whether monetary arrangements can be improved is a complex question, which depends in part on whether exchange rate uncertainty is simply the surface manifestation of uncertainties intrinsic to the economic system as a whole, or whether exchange rate dynamics actually add to the uncertainties faced by those who must make decisions on production and investment, that is, on present and future output of the economy. It also depends on whether a superior set of arrangements can be found, one that reduces whatever incremental uncertainties market-determined exchange rates contribute to the economic system while preserving or finding an adequate substitute for the contribution that changes in exchange rates may make to reducing the costs of adjustment to those changes which dynamic economies will inevitably have to make from time to time.

Whether high volatility in floating exchange rates reflects the uncertainties in the economic system and instabilities in economic policies or adds to them is a source of unresolved controversy. It is difficult to sustain the view, however, that foreign exchange markets reflect accurately and faithfully only the disturbances exogenous to the economic system, plus the net impact of governmental actions,

Chart 1.   United States – Germany: Real Exchange Rate Changes
(In percent per month)

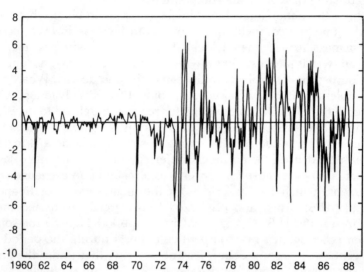

Source: Dornbusch (1988).

which may themselves either dampen volatility or augment it. Chart 1 shows the monthly changes in the U.S. dollar-deutsche mark exchange rate, corrected for differential movements in wholesale prices, during 1960–88. The increase in volatility following the inauguration of floating in 1973 is dramatic.

There is a growing body of evidence to support the view that practitioners have long held, namely, that financial markets have a dynamic of their own and are occasionally subject to bandwagon effects, or speculative bubbles, whether these be rational or irrational. Shiller (1984) has shown that U.S. stock prices have frequently followed paths that are very difficult to explain except in terms of fashion or social psychological dynamics. Indeed, one of the principal bases for stock selection by some specialists, chartism, presupposes that stock prices follow distinctive patterns that are basically unrelated to what is happening in the economy. To the extent that substantial numbers of investors adopt this basis of stock selection, chartism can become self-fulfilling provided the chartist prices stay within the wide bounds set by liquidation value of the firms and the competition for funds provided by yields on long-term bonds.

More recently, Krugman (1985 and 1989) has shown that the appreciation of the dollar in 1983–85 cannot have been based on fundamentals alone, even though some appreciation could have been expected on the basis of the configuration of monetary and fiscal policies in the United States, on the one hand, and in Japan, Germany, and the United Kingdom on the other. Krugman's analysis starts with the observation that the "market" must have expected a subsequent depreciation of the dollar at a rate no greater than the interest differential between comparable assets denominated in dollars, yen, and deutsche mark. On generous assumptions about the effect of such expected depreciation on trade flows, Krugman shows that U.S. external debt would have grown explosively, that is, unsustainably. This simple calculation suggests that market participants were not paying adequate attention to the underlying fundamentals, but rather were following their own lead in a bubble, until it burst in early 1985, with encouragement from heavy purchases of deutsche mark by the Bundesbank.

Moreover, Frankel and Froot (1987) have shown on the basis of survey data that short-run exchange rate expectations are extrapolative, that is, they project recent rate movements forward into the near future, even when the movement is away from the "long-run"—6 to 12 months—view of what the exchange rate will be. Thus, exchange rate movements are subject to bandwagon effects in the short run. Over a longer period, exchange rate expectations seem to be regressive to recent past levels, according to the survey data. But of course market movements are a series of short runs.

These observations provide circumstantial evidence that the foreign exchange market, with its own dynamic, can introduce disturbances into the real side of the economy. At least on some occasions, it adds to the uncertainties that decision makers on production and investment must face. But is there anything that can be done about it? Are there exchange rate arrangements that are superior to the unstructured managed floating we have had, in the sense of reducing the uncertainty without incurring high costs in some other dimension, and especially in the costs of adjustment to the disturbances that will inevitably occur from time to time?

V. Proposals for Reform

A number of suggestions have been put forward. Tobin (1982) has suggested a modest tax on foreign exchange transactions to discourage short-term transactions of low social utility, with the presumption that that will reduce exchange rate volatility. Williamson and Miller (1987), Kenen (1988), McKinnon (1984 and 1988b), and Cooper (1984) have made proposals for introducing greater stability into exchange rate movements directly, but with different techniques and emphases.

A Transactions Tax

A small tax, say 25 basis points (0.25 percent), could be imposed on all transactions that involve converting one currency into another, including forward transactions. (Some go further and suggest a small tax on all financial transactions, but that is not discussed here.) Such a tax would raise the cost of all cross-currency transactions, but it would be so small that it could be expected to have virtually no effect on trade in goods and services and on long-term capital flows. But the tax would impose a relatively large cost on short-term in-and-out transactions. For instance, 50 basis points for a two-way transaction would require an interest differential of more than 25 percent per annum to cover it for a weekly turnaround and over 100 percent per annum for a daily turnaround. Such a tax would reduce greatly the huge volume of foreign exchange transactions that now occurs ($700 billion a day in New York alone), most of which are interbank transactions. The aim of the tax would be to reduce short-term exchange rate volatility and encourage greater emphasis on longer-term transactions, which presumably are socially more valuable.

In fact, however, the impact of such a tax on short-term volatility is entirely unclear. To the extent that banks, corporate treasurers, and other short-term traders are "market makers," like securities specialists, their activities should be stabilizing and reduce short-run volatility. Taxing them out of short-term transactions would in that event lead to an increase in volatility. But to the extent that these traders seek quick short-term gains, must guess very short-run market developments, and therefore are subject to bandwagon effects, their activities may increase short-run volatility, and a transactions tax would reduce it.

In either case, a transactions tax would not prevent the emergence of major misalignments, such as those that occurred in the mid-1980s, except insofar as those arise from the cumulative effect of a series of short-run extrapolative expectations, which might not get started in the presence of a tax. Presumably one characteristic of a cumulative exchange rate movement in the "wrong" direction is that each participant feels he can reverse his position at the right moment, before the crowd turns, or at least ahead of it. The crowd could turn at any time, even in the near future. To that extent, a transactions tax could inhibit major speculative currency movements, but it is unclear that it would be enough to prevent them.

To be effective, the transactions tax would have to be introduced in all leading financial centers; otherwise, transactions would move to the tax-free centers, something that is increasingly possible with modern communications. But it would not be necessary to get universal agreement on the tax. It would suffice to stipulate that disputes arising over foreign exchange transactions could not be adjudicated in countries of the leading financial centers unless the tax had been paid. Since it takes years to establish a reputation for fair and impartial dispute settlements, a small tax would be unlikely to drive transactions to tax-free countries without such reputations.

A tax represents one proposal for reducing exchange rate volatility. That is not a certain outcome, however, nor is the avoidance of significant misalignment. Other proposals focus on commitments to affect exchange rate movements directly.

Target Zones

Williamson and Miller (1987) have proposed that the major countries establish "target zones" for their exchange rates. The basis for establishing the target zones would be a calculation for each country of a "fundamental equilibrium exchange rate," which in turn would be based on mutually agreed upon current account targets for each country. These equilibrium rates would be recalculated at regular intervals so they could move in response to new information, but presumably they would move slowly. They in turn would be translated into a set of mutually consistent nominal exchange rates, which would represent the center of the target zone. At first, the zone around these central rates would be wide, say ±10 percent, to encompass substantial initial deviation from the target current account positions, but the zones could gradually be narrowed over time, once the current account targets were achieved.

Monetary authorities would intervene in exchange markets—and, more important, adjust their monetary policies—as exchange rates reached the edges of the target zone. These edges could be either hard—well-defined rates, which are not to be surpassed—or soft—presumptive points of intervention and "leaning" by authorities, but without a firm commitment that the boundaries will never be crossed.

With n countries and only $n-1$ exchange rates among them, there would be a degree of freedom in monetary policy. This would be directed toward aggregate demand in the community as a whole. Put another way, if a given exchange rate approached the edge of the zone, whether one country tightened its monetary policy to affect the rate or the other country loosened would depend on the overall state of aggregate demand. Each country, in addition to having a current account target, would also have a target for growth in nominal demand, chosen in a way to be mutually consistent with those of other countries, and national fiscal policies would be directed toward achieving these aggregate demand targets.

The effect of this system in operation would be to limit the movement of exchange rates and thus prevent the emergence of major misalignments of the kind that occurred in the 1980s. It would not, however, eliminate short-run volatility of exchange rates, and the uncertainties they create, unless the target zones were quite narrow, which is not envisaged. While it is possible for businessmen to hedge against unexpected exchange rate movements for particular transactions, it is not possible to hedge for an investment or a commitment to a marketing strategy that will take a number of years to mature. So this source of uncertainty would remain.

The Williamson-Miller proposal is ambitious in its demands on policy coordination among major countries and on the skillful manipulation of monetary and fiscal instruments by national authorities. It is especially ambitious with respect to the coordination of policy targets—real effective equilibrium exchange rates and growth in national nominal aggregate demand. Agreement on the key underpinnings for calculation of real effective equilibrium exchange rates—current account targets, plus the bearing of exchange rates on their achievement—is particularly demanding, not least because the setting of current account targets would be an intrinsically arbitrary exercise in a world of high capital mobility and open markets for goods and services. For concreteness, consider the case of Canada. As a high-income country, it should perhaps run a current account surplus, contributing to the transfer of real resources to the lower-income developing countries. But in every respect except income, Canada itself is a "developing country," and indeed Canada has run current account deficits throughout most of its existence as an independent state. How should we determine what Canada's current account position should be in the future? Or, for that matter, the current account position of the United States, which by compari-son with Europe and Japan is also a developing country, with its population growing relatively rapidly, increasingly through immi-gration, as in the nineteenth century.

Kenen (1988) advocates something like an extension of the EMS to include the United States, Japan, and possibly other countries. He supports hard exchange rate margins with a band width of at least 10 percent, much larger than the EMS band, so that changes in central rates, which must occasionally be made, need not affect market rates and hence would not provide a one-way speculative option when accurately anticipated. Kenen would also increase the visible reserves available for intervention, by analogy with the EMS, especially for the United States, by creating a modified substitution account into which the United States would deposit gold and others would deposit dollars.

On the choice of central rates, Kenen takes the view that that is less relevant than the procedures for changing them. If they are not right, that is, are needed for adjustment, they should be altered. He would give weight (but not mechanically) to a host of indicators, especially changes in relative price competitiveness, as in the EMS, but in the end, changes in central rates would be discretionary, to be negotiated among all the relevant parties.

Key Currency Monetary Coordination

McKinnon (1984 and 1988b) concentrates attention on just three countries and their currencies: the United States, Japan, and Ger-many, although he assumes several other currencies will be linked to the deutsche mark through the EMS. He would at first confine movement of exchange rates among the three key currencies within a 10 percent band, like Kenen, but over time he would gradually reduce the width of the band so that the exchange rates among the three key currencies eventually showed little or no movement. In addition, McKinnon departs from the other two proposals by select-ing the central rates to which the exchange rates are to converge on the basis of purchasing power parity. Concretely, McKinnon would construct broad-based indices of tradable goods, and would choose exchange rates that equate the value of a comparable basket of these goods (McKinnon and Ohno (1988)). Nominal exchange rates would then remain fixed except insofar as changes were required to offset relative changes in purchasing power parity as defined by the baskets. Monetary policy in each of the countries would be dedicated to maintaining the fixed exchange rates; monetary policy in the three countries taken together—close coordination would be required—would be dedicated to maintaining stability in the prices of the baskets of tradable goods, as was advocated over half a century ago by Keynes (1930). Such a target implies moderate inflation as measured by the consumer price index, because of its component of services.

A Common Currency

Cooper (1984) would go a step further than McKinnon by institutionalizing the close monetary cooperation in coherent management of a single currency for the industrialized democracies. So long as national currencies are distinct, under distinct management, the possibility of major changes in nominal and real exchange rates exists, and that possibility is itself a source of uncertainty to investors so long as memories of the 1970s and the 1980s persist. The most effective way to eradicate exchange rate uncertainty is to eradicate exchange rates, that is, to introduce a single currency. A single currency would require a single monetary authority, which would represent a bold, even radical step—one that governments and their publics are not yet ready to contemplate seriously, much less undertake. So unlike the proposals discussed above, which are put forward with the near future in mind, this proposal has to be envisioned in a longer time frame, into the next century. Still, it carries the logic of a return to fixed exchange rates to its full conclusion, and for that reason is worth exploring more fully.

The institutional aspects of a common currency are not so difficult to imagine: they could be constructed by analogy with the U.S. Federal Reserve System, which is an amalgam of 12 separate Reserve Banks, each issuing its own currency. One could imagine an open market committee for all or any subset of the industrial democracies that would decide the basic thrust of monetary policy for the group as a whole. On it could sit representatives of all member countries, with votes proportional to gross national product. At one extreme the representatives could be ministers of finance; at the other they could be outstanding citizens chosen by their governments for long terms solely for the purpose of managing the monetary system. An obvious interim (and possibly permanent) step would be to appoint the senior governors of existing central banks.

National central banks could continue as the national components and agents of the new international Board of Bank Governors, and indeed could remain the issuers of currency, just as the 12 District Federal Reserve Banks do in the United States. If national sentiment called for it, currency designations—pounds, deutsche mark, yen, francs, dollars—could even be retained on nationally issued currency. The central point is that monetary policy would be out of the hands of any single government. Governments could not finance their budget deficits through monetary expansion, and the national currencies would exchange at fixed exchange rates. Most commercial transactions do not involve currency at all, so all commercial and bank transactions could take place in a common unit of account. A common currency would of course eliminate exchange rate uncertainty not only for commercial transactions, but also for financial transactions, so a unified capital market would develop throughout the area covered by the currency. By the same token, however, changes in nominal exchange rates could not be used any longer as part of the adjustment process. More will be said about this below.

A common currency could create serious adjustment problems if the exchange rates among the precedent currencies were not right at the time of conversion into the common currency. For this reason also, such a move cannot be consummated until major disequilibria have been eliminated. Purchasing power parity conditions, such as those suggested by McKinnon, must be met at least approximately; in addition, uncovered interest parity over all maturities should obtain at least approximately, implying no expectation of future changes in exchange rates.

For the participating countries, international and national currency would become identical, and liquidity needs would be satisfied by decisions by the Board of Bank Governors to increase the money supply.

VI. Evaluation of the Single-Currency Proposal

One objection that will be raised immediately against a single money for the industrialized democracies is that it involves ceding too much sovereignty to an international entity (in this case, the Board of Bank Governors). This is a misguided objection. Ultimate sovereignty continues to reside with the national governments. It is an exercise of sovereignty, not an abrogation of sovereignty, to agree on a common endeavor with other sovereign nations. The key question that should be asked is whether, on balance, the particular exercise of sovereignty leaves the participants better or worse off. It would limit the freedom of action of individual governments in the monetary arena. But the economies of these nations are becoming increasingly interdependent, and that economic interdependency increasingly limits the efficacy of individual actions in the areas of macroeconomic policy, taxation, and financial regulation. So retaining full freedom of action may turn out to be largely empty short of withdrawal into autarky, which would be extremely costly. A cooperative endeavor, while reducing national freedom of action, will restore effectiveness to joint action.

What of the adjustment process? The principal argument for exchange rate flexibility is that it may reduce the costs of adjustment to various economic disturbances. It should be kept in mind, however, that the requirements for efficient adjustment depend on the nature of the disturbances; and the nature of the disturbances in turn depend in part on the nature of the monetary system.

In particular, disturbances to national economies that are wholly or largely monetary in nature will be greatly diminished or eliminated altogether when the nations share a common currency, with no chance (short of major political disturbance) of changes in exchange rates among national monies. This would apply, for instance, to shifts in asset preferences among national financial claims motivated by expected changes in exchange rates, or to differential inflation among nations in tradable goods. Differences in national wage settlements not based on changes in productivity cannot be ruled out under a common currency, but they are much less likely in the presence of a common currency and extensive trade between nations. So at least some disturbances for which changes in exchange rates might be helpful hardly exist under a common currency.

What about disturbances to the real side of the economy, such as the discovery or exhaustion of natural resources, the technological changes that have differential effects among sectors, or the divergent rates of growth between demand and supply among nations?

With respect to technological change and discovery or exhaustion of resources, three observations can be made concerning economic adjustment in the industrialized democracies. First, most of the adjustment will have to take place within the three regions of the United States, Japan, and the European Community. Sectors, especially resource-based sectors, are often concentrated geographically, and changes in technology or the pattern of demand will require consequential adjustment among them. Such adjustments now take place within these economic areas. But exchange rate changes facilitate adjustment between countries, not within them. Yet these three economies taken as a whole are large and diversified; so little adjustment is likely to be required between them. Second, major disturbances at the global level, such as the oil price increases of the 1970s, are likely to affect all three regions in roughly the same way, although not of course identically. Third, the differential effects that remain once the first two points are taken into account are likely to be manageable within the parameters established by the natural growth and retirement of the labor force and the .capital stock. Changes in real income and in domestic relative prices (for example, between tradables and nontradables) will help to bring about the adjustment, without substantial changes in output.[1]

With respect to differential growth in national (or regional) demand and output, such discrepancies, whether merely cyclical or reflecting more durable changes in saving behavior, can easily be accommodated by capital movements motivated by relatively small differences in yield within an integrated capital market, such as would obtain over a common currency area under modern conditions.

Possibly the greatest source of disturbance between large and diversified economies would arise from significant and opposite changes in fiscal policy. If one country pursued fiscal expansion while another was contracting substantially, that could create significant adjustment problems, and changes in exchange rates might assist the adjustment. But two things should be said about this possibility. First, it is desirable to be able to use fiscal action, within limits, to affect aggregate demand at the national or regional level. The adoption of a common currency, far from preventing this, would enhance the desirability of fiscal flexibility. Thus, it may be undesirable to allow or encourage exchange rates to adjust in response to discrepant fiscal actions, since such adjustment both affects the structure of output (for example, between tradables and nontradables) and weakens the demand effects of the fiscal actions (for example, by leading to a fall in net exports attendant upon a fiscal expansion).

---

[1]In this regard, Krugman (1989) exaggerates the changes in output—or under flexible rates, in the real exchange rate—required to achieve a given adjustment between two large and diversified economies. McKinnon (1988a), based on Jones (1975), argues persuasively that change in the terms of trade need not be large to accommodate a disturbance between two multisectored economies that are reasonably flexible, and it may not be necessary at all.

Second, however, fiscal deficits would have to be financed exclusively in the (integrated) capital market. So long as a government's credit was good, it would have no trouble borrowing. As the ratio of public debt to tax revenues grew, however, the market would require higher yields to be willing to take that government's securities. There would be market signals indicating when one government was markedly out of line with the others in terms of growing indebtedness. Thus, while fiscal freedom of action would be unimpaired, it would be limited by the ability to service public debt. It would undoubtedly be useful to have informal discussions concerning the framing of fiscal action among all the participants; but formal coordination of fiscal action would not be necessary, and full harmonization would not be desirable.

The above points can be summed up briefly by saying that in the not very distant future nominal exchange rate flexibility among major currencies may create more disturbances for the real productive side of national economies than it corrects.

REFERENCES

Bloomfield, Arthur I., *Monetary Policy Under the International Gold Standard, 1880–1914* (New York: Federal Reserve Bank of New York, 1959).

Cooper, Richard N., "The Gold Standard: Historical Facts and Future Prospects," *Brookings Papers on Economic Activity: 1* (1982), Brookings Institution (Washington), pp. 1–43, reprinted in Richard N. Cooper, *The International Monetary System: Essays in World Economics* (Cambridge: MIT Press, 1987).

———, "A Monetary System for the Future," *Foreign Affairs* (New York), Vol. 63 (Fall 1984), pp. 166–84, reprinted in Richard N. Cooper, *The International Monetary System: Essays in World Economics* (Cambridge: MIT Press, 1987).

———, ed., *International Finance* (Baltimore: Penguin Books, 1969).

Dornbusch, Rudiger., "The McKinnon Standard: How Persuasive?" *Cato Journal* (Washington), Vol. 8, No. 2 (Fall 1988), pp. 375–83.

Frankel, Jeffrey A., and Kenneth A. Froot, "Using Survey Data to Test Standard Propositions Regarding Exchange Rate Expectations," *American Economic Review* (Nashville, Tennessee), Vol. 77 (March 1987), pp. 133–53.

Friedman, Milton, "The Case for Flexible Exchange Rates," in *Essays in Positive Economics* (Chicago: University of Chicago Press, 1953).

Jones, R.W., "Presumption and the Transfer Problem," *Journal of International Economics* (Amsterdam), Vol. 5 (August 1975), pp. 263–74.

Kenen, Peter B., *Managing Exchange Rates* (London: Routledge, 1988).

Keynes, J.M., *A Treatise on Money*, Vol. 2 (London: Macmillan, 1930).

Krugman, Paul, "Is the Strong Dollar Sustainable?" in *The U.S. Dollar: Prospects and Policy Options* (Kansas City: Federal Reserve Bank of Kansas City, 1985).

——, *Exchange-Rate Instability* (Cambridge: MIT Press, 1989).

McKinnon, Ronald I., *An International Standard for Monetary Stabilization* (Washington: Institute for International Economics, 1984).

—— (1988a), "An International Gold Standard Without Gold," *Cato Journal* (Washington), Vol. 8, No. 2 (Fall 1988), pp. 351–73.

—— (1988b), "Monetary and Exchange Rate Policies for International Financial Stability: A Proposal," *Journal of Economic Perspectives* (Nashville, Tennessee), Vol. 2, No. 1 (Winter 1988), pp. 83–103.

——, and Kenichi Ohno, "Purchasing Power Parity as a Monetary Standard" (unpublished; San Francisco: Federal Reserve Bank of San Francisco, October 1988).

Meltzer, Allan H., "Some Evidence on Comparative Uncertainty Experienced Under Different Monetary Regimes," in *Alternative Monetary Regimes*, ed. by Colin Dearborn Campbell and William R. Dougan (Baltimore: Johns Hopkins University Press, 1986).

Nurkse, Ragnar, *International Currency Experience: Lessons of the Interwar Period* (Geneva: League of Nations, 1944).

Shiller, Robert J., "Stock Prices and Social Dynamics," *Brookings Papers on Economic Activity: 2* (1984), Brookings Institution (Washington), pp. 457–98.

Tobin, J., "A Proposal for International Monetary Reform," in *Essays in Economics* (Cambridge: MIT Press, 1982).

——, "Are There Reliable Adjustment Mechanisms?" in *Toward a World of Economic Stability: Optimal Monetary Framework and Policy*, ed. by Yoshio Suzuki and Mitsuaki Okabe (Tokyo: University of Tokyo Press, 1988).

Triffin, Robert, *Gold and the Dollar Crisis* (New Haven: Yale University Press, 1960).

——, *The Evolution of the International Monetary System: Historical Reappraisal and Future Perspectives*, Princeton Studies in International Finance No. 12 (Princeton, New Jersey: Princeton University Press, 1964).

Viner, Jacob, *Canada's Balance of International Indebtedness* (Cambridge: Harvard University Press, 1924).

Williamson, John, and Marcus Miller, *Targets and Indicators: A Blueprint for the International Coordination of Economic Policy* (Washington: Institute for International Economics, 1987).

7

Failings of the SDR
Lessons from Three Decades

Rudolf R. Rhomberg

A few days ago, on January 1, 1991, the SDR came of age. The first SDRs were allocated on that date in 1970. These SDRs, and with them the SDR system as a whole, just became 21 years old, thus reaching the traditional age of majority. Quite apart from the special occasion provided by this conference, it would be appropriate to celebrate this birthday by reflecting on the history of the SDR, its promises as a baby, its failings as a teenager, and its future. As a staff member of the Research Department until 1987, I had participated in a number of earlier reviews of this kind. Indeed, I remember a period of years during which a presentation to the Executive Board on the reassessment of the need for further SDR allocations became a routine biennial task of the staff. Nevertheless, I welcome this further opportunity to go over some of this ground once again, especially since some distance in time and my present private position may allow a new perspective.

This conference honoring Jacques J. Polak provides an excellent opportunity—perhaps it would be better to say a mandate—to talk about the SDR. It would certainly be a grave omission in any appreciation of Jacques Polak's work to leave out his contributions to the conception, planning, negotiation, implementation, and operation of the SDR. That this is so follows immediately from the converse observation that it is not possible to give an account of the genesis and the development of the SDR without dealing at every turn with Polak's contributions. I would like to let this general tribute stand for the many additional references to Polak's thought and writings that it would have been appropriate to make throughout the body of this paper.

For purposes of the questions to be taken up below, events during the years of gestation before the actual birth of the SDR may well be more important than those that have occurred during its life span. It is, therefore, necessary to consider developments over a period of about three decades. It is not intended, nor would it be possible in this short paper, to review this history at all comprehensively. The plan is rather to recall selected developments that help focus attention on a number of questions that will then be asked in an attempt to identify possible reasons for the failure of the SDR to live up to the high expectations with which it was brought into the world.

It may be best to state at the outset that I do not presume to know the ultimate answer to the question of why the SDR has to date not played a more central role in the evolution of the international monetary system. I hope, however, to advance a number of ordered hypotheses with the objective of aiding a discussion of the reasons for this—dare I say it?—magnificent failure.

I. Salient Historical Observations

To begin with, it is relevant to recall the great difficulties encountered in the conception, elaboration, and establishment of the SDR system. A decade elapsed between the first explicit statement (by Triffin in 1959 and 1960) of the problem for which the deliberate creation of international reserves was suggested as a remedy and the time when the remedy was ready to be applied. The last half of that period was spent in intensive and difficult negotiations about the objective of deliberate reserve creation, about the character of the reserve claims to be created, and about various fundamental and operational features.

At times, it did not seem that the negotiating parties could reach common ground. To give just one example: the two chief protagonists, France and the United States, both switched sides in the dispute over the purpose and character of a new reserve medium; but they did so in such a perfectly choreographed way that, for some time, they were always on opposite sides. When France and other European countries in 1964 expressed interest in a new reserve unit to replace U.S. dollars in their reserves, the United States showed little enthusiasm and stressed the importance of credit facilities in supplying international liquidity.[1] A year later, the United States, under a new Treasury Secretary, Henry Fowler, had come to prefer reserve units to a credit facility as a more acceptable replacement for gold, whose international monetary role was intended to be diminished after the gold pool arrangements were abandoned in March 1968. The French authorities were appalled by the thought of replacing gold—rather than U.S. dollars—and nearly withdrew from the whole endeavor. In the end, they were brought back only when the United States and other negotiators bowed to their insistence on giving the new medium a credit character—hence the name special drawing rights—to make clear that it was not "international money."

Similar disputes took place in the years 1965–68 about many other aspects of deliberate reserve creation, including country participation (universal or selective), decision making, the possible transfer of resources entailed in the process of reserve creation, valuation of the new medium, rules for its use and transfer, and others. It is true that there came a point in 1968 when final agreement on an SDR scheme was reached, with the implication that all of the earlier disagreements had been resolved and that the system could go into regular operation. Before long, it became clear, however, that a kind of periodic renegotiation of the SDR agreement was inherent in the need to decide from time to time on the allocation of SDRs, particularly in light of the requirement of a large voting majority (85 percent) for these decisions.

Agreement on allocations was reached only twice in the 21-year history of the SDR, at its inception and again in 1978. In both cases, consensus was attained only after considerable reluctance on the part of some members (whose votes were necessary for passage) was overcome by linking SDR allocation to other measures, including increases in Fund quotas, in a political package and by keeping the proposed allocations relatively small and reducing the normal allocation period from five years to three. At other times, no consensus on generating additional SDRs could be reached even though a majority of members (but less than the required 85 percent) regularly supported such a policy. SDR allocations, which had been anticipated to become annual events except in unusual circumstances, occurred thus in only 6 of the past 21 years.

In the light of this history, proponents of the SDR have at times raised the question of whether it would have been preferable to let

---

[1] See Robert Solomon, *The International Monetary System, 1945–1976: An Insider's View* (New York: Harper & Row, 1977), pp. 66–67.

the periodic decisions on allocation deal, not with the amount to be allocated in a subsequent time span, but rather with any change in the previously established rate of allocation. Lack of the required majority for a new decision would then leave the rate of allocation unchanged. To be sure, such a rule might just substitute one inflexibility for another. More important, it is not likely that such automatic allocation could have been agreed on in 1968 or, if such agreement could have been achieved, it might have held up—possibly indefinitely—the activation of the SDR scheme through the first allocation, which had to meet special criteria in addition to those prescribed for any decision to allocate.

These reflections show that there can be no substitute for continuous consensus in any international agreement that depends for its operation on periodic reaffirmation, for example, on quota increases in the Fund or allocations through the SDR account. A momentary consensus achieved by the assemblage of a political package containing attractions for different negotiating parties can be successful when eventual agreement is the final act required for implementation, for instance, in a trade agreement or the settlement of border disputes. In the SDR system, by contrast, participating countries are, in effect, asked every few years—at times they were asked more than once a year—whether they still agreed that the scheme as originally envisaged was of benefit to themselves as well as to the international community. Unwillingness to support such reaffirmation may indicate that at least some members have second thoughts about important aspects of the agreement.

The second historical observation attempts to probe into possible reasons for this apparent change of attitude of the international community or, at any rate, of some major countries. Was there a fundamental change in underlying conditions between the 1960s and the 1970s that made an SDR system properly designed for the earlier period unsuitable later on? Or was the SDR already inadequate at the time it was being readied for implementation? It is, of course, true that, shortly after SDR allocations commenced, the international monetary system changed radically through the abandonment of the gold exchange standard and the system of fixed par values. Under floating exchange rates the role of international reserves, and thus also the position of the SDR, was fundamentally altered. But this reflection may be considered to beg the question of whether the international monetary system may have changed in part because of an inadequacy of reserves and whether it could have developed quite differently if SDRs had been introduced earlier and on a larger scale. Somewhat deeper probing is, therefore, necessary.

In 1959 and 1960, Robert Triffin posed a broad qualitative question about the viability of the gold exchange standard. With growing world demand for reserves outstripping the growth of gold supplies at a given price of gold, two developments were possible: if the demand for reserves were accommodated, an increasing excess of liquid liabilities of the reserve center (the United States) over its gold holdings would destroy confidence in the gold convertibility of the principal reserve currency (the U.S. dollar); if, on the other hand, the reserve center resisted this tendency through prudent policies fostering external balance, the world would be plagued by progressively worsening reserve shortages and deflation until it was driven to resort to other monetary arrangements. Since the gold exchange standard could not survive in either case, it would be better, Triffin argued, to adopt a new system right away and replace currency reserves by some international money, which could consist of deposits in the IMF whose volume would be regulated by the Fund's credit policies.[2]

When these results came to be seriously discussed in the middle of the 1960s, a curious truncation of Triffin's argument had occurred. The part dealing with the growing deficits of the reserve center and the loss of confidence in convertibility had been lopped off. It was assumed that the United States would follow prudent policies and achieve (or come close to) balance in its external accounts. The resulting reserve shortage would then need to be alleviated by deliberate reserve creation. According to this thinking, the main problem was a quantitative one, namely, to determine the gap between the demand for reserves, on one hand, and the accretion in reserve accounts of newly produced gold and perhaps some marginal amount of reserve currencies, mainly U.S. dollars, on the other hand. In the Managing Director's proposal on SDR allocation for the first basic period, put forward in September 1969, the annual supply of new reserves other than SDRs was projected at $0.5 billion in gold and $0.5–1.0 billion in U.S. dollars. The largest part of the annual reserve increase in the early 1970s would, according to the proposal, be the SDR allocation of $3.0–3.5 billion.

The other part of Triffin's analysis—probably meant to be the major branch of his overall argument—received less and less atten-

---

[2] A number of other plans put forward in the early 1960s responded to the same dilemma but were less radical. For instance, the plan set forth by Edward Bernstein in those years relied on widening the list of reserve currencies rather than on the replacement of the principal reserve currency by an international asset.

tion in the liquidity discussions of the second half of the 1960s. This part had to do with what would happen if policies in the reserve center were not such as to restrict the supply of the reserve currency and preserve confidence in it. Instead of global reserve shortages, one should then, according to Triffin, expect a plentiful supply of reserves accompanied by disturbances emanating from the loss of confidence in the reserve currency. Raising world reserves through supplementary allocations of a new reserve asset unaccompanied by other measures would not be the right remedy in these circumstances, and it might, indeed, be counterproductive.

In the event, this was the branch of the Triffin scenario that actually materialized. In 1970 foreign exchange reserves rose, not by $0.5–1.0 billion, but by $12 billion; in 1971, they increased by $30 billion, and the gold exchange standard broke down when the United States officially terminated the gold convertibility of the U.S. dollar in August of that year. The system had successfully evaded the Scylla of reserve shortages only to fall prey to the Charybdis of erosion of confidence in the principal reserve currency.

This story has a sequel, which has to do with later attempts to use the SDR as a means of improving the quality of reserves and thereby to strengthen the international monetary system. When the first allocation period ended in 1972, it was clear that there was no need for further SDR allocations to alleviate a threatening shortage of reserves. During the next several years, some large industrial Fund members opposed SDR allocation as being unwarranted under the relevant criterion in the Fund Articles, which had been given the purely quantitative cast that characterized the discussions of the late 1960s (with new SDRs supplementing existing reserve assets when needed). Even though other members favored renewed allocation, partly because of expected favorable distributional effects, they could not muster the required voting majority, and no SDR allocations took place in the years 1973–78.[3]

In these circumstances, qualitative aspects of the SDR system were being rediscovered. This discussion had two dimensions: first,

---

[3] In commenting on this paper at the conference, Alexandre Kafka recalled that the discussions in 1972 on SDR allocations in the second basic period (1973–77) might well have resulted in agreement on some allocation, perhaps at a lower rate than in the first basic period, except for the attempt by representatives of developing countries to force a higher rate of allocation through blocking agreement on a proposal at a lower rate. The resulting impasse illustrates a danger inherent in the requirement of a high qualified majority in decision making.

the quality of the SDR as an asset (e.g., with respect to its valuation, interest rate, and usability) and, second, the contribution that the SDR could make to the stability of the monetary system by replacing —rather than being added to—other reserve assets. The first of these concerns prompted a series of much-needed improvements in the asset quality of the SDR, which brought it closer—but probably not close enough—to qualifying for a role as substitute for currency reserves. Meanwhile, the second consideration—replacing reserve currencies by SDRs—made explicit what had always been a latent rivalry between these two asset classes.

The new emphasis on quality, both of the SDR and of international reserves as a whole, bought a new lease on life for the SDR at the end of the 1970s. The third installment of the Fund's official history has a major part entitled "Resurgence of the SDR in 1978," which ends with the sentence "The SDR seemed to be on the verge of coming into its own."[4] A new allocation of SDRs for a three-year period (1979–81) had been agreed as part of a package and, more important, consideration was given once again to the establishment of a substitution account through which Fund members could exchange part of their U.S. dollar holdings for SDRs.

The idea of a substitution arrangement was not new. In a way, it marked a return to the Triffin proposal of almost two decades earlier. What is often less well remembered is that the notion of replacing reserve currencies by SDRs had also been considered in the wake of the breakdown of the gold exchange standard in the early 1970s as a means to deal with what was seen as a "dollar overhang." A report prepared in March 1972 by the Fund staff (under the direction of Jacques Polak) at the request of the Board of Governors proposed, as part of the reform of the international monetary system, the "consolidation" of reserve currency holdings by replacing them with SDRs, adding that "measures should be taken to discourage the growth of official balances in such currencies."[5] These ideas were left behind, however, when the Committee of Twenty failed to agree on a reform plan.[6]

---

[4]Margaret Garritsen de Vries, *The International Monetary Fund 1972–1978*, Vol. II (Washington: International Monetary Fund), p. 900.

[5]*Reform of the International Monetary System: A Sketch of Its Scope and Content* (March 7, 1972), reprinted in de Vries, op. cit., Vol. III, pp. 3–15, at pp. 6–7. In the subsequent report by the Executive Directors to the Board of Governors on this subject, the presentation was more tentative, but it retained the idea of a substitution account.

[6]In 1974, there was discussion in the Fund of a possible gold substitution account, but it did not attract support from most industrial countries.

The renewed discussions in 1978–80 of a substitution arrangement to reduce dependence of the system on U.S. dollar reserves and permitting, in effect, currency diversification of reserves without putting pressure on exchange markets appeared to be quite promising to the very end. They ultimately failed, however, when no other source than a pledge of the Fund's gold holdings could be found for the needed exchange guarantee securing the financial integrity of the substitution account, which would hold U.S. dollars but have its liabilities denominated in SDRs. A sudden reversal in the early months of 1980, just before the crucial Interim Committee meeting in Hamburg, in the protracted decline of the exchange value of the U.S. dollar may also have reduced the urgency with which substitution for U.S. dollars was sought. The anticipated consensus quickly evaporated and the substitution proposal was shelved.

I have dwelt on this episode at some length because it may have been a crucial turning point in the history of the SDR, if not of the international monetary system. What was lost at that juncture was the prospect of strengthening international monetary control by substituting a single monetary asset whose supply can be regulated by the international community for existing stocks of unmanaged and unmanageable national currency reserves. It put out of reach, for the time being, the objective stated in the IMF's Articles of Agreement of "promoting better international surveillance of international liquidity" (Article VIII, Section 7).

Speaking at the beginning of the 1990s, one may well ask how important it is in today's world to be able to exercise international control over world liquidity. Over time, views on this subject have been affected by developments in the international monetary system, and this will be the subject of the next historical observation.

When the SDR system was put in place, its architects and the world at large had high expectations with respect to the degree of control over international liquidity that these new arrangements would make possible. This faith was not noticeably diminished by the awareness that the SDR system would permit deliberate reserve expansion but could not as easily be used if a reduction of world reserves was indicated. Any "cancellation" of SDRs, although permitted by the new Articles of Agreement, would for political reasons be difficult to achieve in practice and would in any event require the existence of a stock of previously allocated SDRs commensurate with the intended reduction in reserves. Nevertheless, a firm belief in the determination of the United States to pursue effective adjustment policies and a somewhat cloudy view of the future role of international capital markets in providing foreign exchange reserves made it seem improbable that there would ever be an excess, rather than a shortage, of reserves. The Fund's *Annual Report* for 1968 (p. 16) states boldly that the new facility "will permit the Fund to *assure* an appropriate level of international reserves" (emphasis added). These high hopes were quickly disappointed, and three years later the *Annual Report* (for 1971, p. 35) allowed that, as experience had shown, the ability to create an international reserve asset "of itself is not sufficient to regulate the volume of aggregate international reserves, and that further problems remain to be tackled if the reserve system as a whole is to be made responsive to deliberate management."

The failing of the SDR system, as constituted, frustrated any hope to employ international reserve management so as to help keep the world economy on a desirable path, in other words, to conduct international monetary policy, quite apart from other difficulties that would be encountered in such an attempt.[7] Since SDR management could not assure direct control over global reserves, an alternative control mechanism was suggested in 1975 by the fifth Managing Director of the Fund, H. Johannes Witteveen. Guidance of the evolution of world reserves through SDR management might still be possible, even in the presence of substantial foreign exchange reserves, if member countries agreed to hold a prescribed minimum proportion of their total reserves in the form of SDRs. This suggestion was, as far as I know, never explored to any depth, but I had always felt that it faced fundamental difficulties.

In corresponding domestic monetary arrangements, the demand for credit—and thus spending—by the public can be influenced through variation in the amount of central bank money and its effects on the permissible credit extension by commercial banks as intermediaries. In the international monetary system, by contrast, the member governments are not intermediaries passing signals sent by the Fund's decisions on SDR allocation to a set of ultimate spenders, but they are themselves members of the "public" whose spending decisions are to be influenced. There is danger, therefore, that the signals would come at them upside down, as it were, and trigger a response opposite from that which is intended. Consider,

---

[7] See J. J. Polak, "Money—National and International," in *Essays in Honour of Thorkil Kristensen* (Paris: Organization for Economic Cooperation and Development, 1970); reprinted in *International Reserves: Needs and Availability* (Washington: International Monetary Fund, 1970).

for instance, a situation in which inflationary developments and a tendency toward excessive growth of foreign exchange holdings were intended to be reined in by abstention from SDR allocation, or even by cancellation of SDRs. Members would in this case either have to buy SDRs from others with excess holdings, or they would have to accelerate spending in an attempt to bring foreign exchange reserves down to the prescribed multiple of their SDR stocks. All countries together could not easily succeed in cutting foreign exchange reserves,[8] and inflationary pressures would tend to be increased, rather than reduced.

Ideally, members with excess foreign exchange holdings in this example would allow their currencies to appreciate instead of inflating expenditures. For such a reaction to serve the intended purpose, however, it would have to be planned some time ahead because of the slow and initially perverse effect of exchange rate changes on foreign exchange reserves. It is too optimistic to expect this kind of well-planned exchange rate adjustment to be typical of member countries in these circumstances. In any case, all countries together could not appreciate their currencies simultaneously. A system of SDR-reserve ratios is thus not likely to enable the international community to conduct effective surveillance over international liquidity through its policy of SDR allocation.

We may, I think, conclude that international control of world liquidity through the SDR system is not feasible in the presence of large holdings of foreign exchange reserves and the potential for generating additional supplies of them. The world economy has, of course, now found a self-regulating way of providing needed liquidity through market mechanisms, much like the private domestic money advocated by Professor Hayek. There has been little complaint about the level of world liquidity, but there is at times dissatisfaction with the resulting exchange rates and with the domestic and trade policies that give rise to the trade flows, capital movements, and exchange rates regarded as objectionable. Since the choice of an international monetary system is being taken up in other papers at this conference, these thoughts will not be further pursued here.

Two additional matters arising in past SDR discussions should be briefly mentioned. The first of these concerns the absence of a full

---

[8]Unless the reserve currency countries cooperated by running large external surpluses.

and vigorous private market in SDR-denominated instruments and of associated clearing facilities. This topic was discussed by the Committee of Twenty, as well as on subsequent occasions in the context of the possibility of using SDRs directly in intervention in foreign exchange markets. Deliberations in the Executive Board in 1980–81 about the possibility of Fund borrowing in private markets (presumably in terms of SDRs) also generated interest in the development of private SDR markets and clearing facilities.

Private SDR-denominated instruments were made possible by the currency-basket method of valuation, which provided a convenient unit of account for commercial multicurrency assets. The use of such instruments expanded rapidly in the second half of the 1970s and the early 1980s. Since then, however, these instruments have ceased to grow and, indeed, contracted. This reversal contrasts with the continued vigorous expansion in private instruments and markets denominated in the ECU, which had received active support from institutions and members of the European Community.

The hesitant and at times retrograde development of private SDR markets may have a number of causes, but one that is no doubt prominent among them is the lack of integration between official and private SDRs. In the absence of a clearing mechanism for SDR-denominated assets, commercial banks and other private transactors are not encouraged to develop instruments and modalities for private cross-border transactions in this denomination. Moreover, official holders are unable to conduct market intervention in SDRs, which marks a decided disadvantage for that international asset in comparison with reserve currencies.

In national monetary systems, profit-motivated commercial banks take it upon themselves to develop a private payments system on the basis of relatively small balances of official money (chiefly their deposits at the central bank and circulating currency). In an international monetary system based on a central reserve asset, it would fall to a large extent to the member governments, if they chose to do so, to promote within and across their jurisdictions the development of a private financial system based on that asset and to agree on the elaboration of appropriate clearing facilities. But member governments are less motivated to engage in this task than are commercial banks acting in the national monetary system. Indeed, insofar as the SDR may be perceived in some reserve centers as a rival money in international finance, whose development could eventually entail constraints on national policymaking, the attitude of national monetary authorities toward the development of a more prominent role of the SDR in the private international payments system would under-standably be a cautious one. Interest in such developments has, therefore, been barely kept alive by academic economists, as well as by a small number of Executive Directors and staff work done at their request.

The second aspect to be briefly mentioned concerns the valuation of the SDR. At its inception, the SDR was issued under a gold-value guarantee, although developments in the early 1970s quickly showed that this did not mean an SDR whose purchasing power followed the market price of gold but rather one defined in terms of the U.S. par value expressed in gold. When that par value was suspended in 1973, a new method of valuation of the SDR had to be sought. The present method, under which the value of the SDR is equal to the value of a basket of currencies, defines that value as a nominal magnitude whose purchasing power fluctuates with the weighted-average purchasing power of the currencies composing the basket. As an alternative, the notion of an asset that would tend to maintain its purchasing power, either in some degree or as fully as possible, was raised at least twice: first, in the deliberations of the Committee of Twenty—under the heading of "a stronger capital value" for the SDR—and again when the Executive Board discussed possible valu-ation schemes. On this latter occasion, the thought of a "real SDR" was quickly squelched on the grounds that indexing the SDR, as any indexing of a financial asset, would tend to undermine efforts directed against inflation.

A central reserve asset of constant purchasing power over goods and services that are produced or available, say, in the five major industrial countries would provide an important alternative to na-tional currencies in official reserve holdings and could represent a monetary "anchor" in a system of otherwise nominal assets and magnitudes.[9] Private instruments denominated in this unit, presum-ably with a low interest rate, should also be expected to be quite attractive in international financial markets, and even in domestic markets to the extent monetary authorities permit such a rival money to evolve. All the same, this idea never came under active consideration.

---

[9] See Warren L. Coats, "In Search of a Monetary Anchor: A 'New' Monetary Standard," IMF Working Paper No. 89/82 (Washington: International Monetary Fund, 1989).

II. Why Has the SDR Failed?

By the "failure of the SDR" I simply mean its gradual disappearance when measured in relation to other important magnitudes in the world economy, such as reserves, trade, and income.

One of the difficulties met in addressing the question of why the SDR may have failed is to keep that question apart from other issues with which it is closely linked, such as the relative desirability of alternative monetary systems. One system might benefit from, or even require the presence of, a central monetary asset like the SDR. This would be true of a system of essentially fixed but at times adjustable exchange rates in which gold or a similar commodity asset is not to be used as a central pivot and in which the asymmetries of a standard based on one of the national currencies are to be avoided. Another system, say, one characterized by floating of exchange rates among most or all member countries or among major economic blocs, may not need such a central asset and may be able to formulate its rules with respect to policy interaction and adjustment in terms of other ratios and relations. It is my aim to comment on the failure of the SDR without having to make an assumption about the relative merit of such monetary systems. This should, I believe, be possible, just as one can ask what brought down a certain monarchy at a certain time without being forced to accept the superiority of the republican form of government as the only valid answer.

All the same, it is true that the SDR was introduced as an instrument needed if the par value system was to be preserved. Since that system vanished so soon after the arrival of the SDR, the first question presenting itself is whether this was a case of "too little and too late." The SDR did come late, ten years after Triffin's alarms, four–five years after the Fund staff had started to warn about incipient inadequacies of international reserves. The first SDR allocation antedated the beginning of the end of the par value system only by one year and a half, not enough time for it to exercise a sufficient effect preventing the collapse of that system. "Little" is also a word well applied to the effort made on behalf of the existing monetary system through SDR allocation.

Nevertheless, the phrase "too little and too late" would be misleading if it were intended to convey the thought that the ultimate outcome might have been different if only SDRs could have been allocated somewhat earlier and in somewhat larger volume. The par value system did not go down because of reserve shortages, not even because of a shortage of gold, but because of inadequate adjustment policies in major countries. The SDR system was not designed to affect adjustment policies so compellingly as to remedy this flaw in the par value system. Only a much more radical reform that would have permitted a phasing-out of currency reserves could —perhaps— have eliminated the asymmetrical operation of adjustment pressures characterizing the dollar-centered par value system. Efforts in the late 1970s to get on a track leading in this direction through the establishment of a substantial substitution account (an amount of SDR 50 billion was mentioned at the time) did indeed come too late.

A second possible reason for the failure of the SDR could be a wrong design of the asset in some of its various detailed features regarding its valuation, the determination of its interest rate, the rules about holding, using, and transferring SDRs, and others. This hypothesis is not plausible. In the first place, many of these features, perhaps most of them, have been changed since they were first set down so as to adapt them to changing conditions or make them consistent with altered concepts agreed among participants. Changes in the valuation of the asset have already been mentioned. The interest rate paid to SDR holders has been fundamentally altered from a very low fixed rate appropriate for an asset that was nicknamed ''paper gold'' to a rate calculated weekly on the basis of interest rates in money markets of financial centers. The requirement of mandatory reconstitution of previously used SDR holdings was abolished. And numerous improvements were made in the rules determining the usability of the SDR.

Generally speaking, few difficulties were encountered in this process of improving the SDR. If other broadly agreed changes had become desirable, there is little doubt that they could also have been achieved. If there were any initial technical shortcomings in the design of the SDR, they should not be held responsible for the subsequent decline in the role of this asset.

There may be one technical feature, which was up for consideration when a new method of valuation for the SDR had to be found in 1973–74, that could have been more fully explored than it was: an SDR of constant purchasing power. This might have been an interesting alternative to an SDR defined as a basket of currencies, which cannot easily distinguish itself from a similar collection of the same currencies without the basket. With given prices of apples, oranges, and bananas there is a limit to how much can be charged for a basket (or perhaps just a bag?) of fruit. By contrast, a basket of fruit guaranteed not to spoil would have quite a different attraction. However that may be, the suggestion of an SDR of constant real value was summarily dismissed. It is doubtful, of course, that this one feature would by itself have reversed the decline of the SDR, but if a reform package had been agreed following the deliberations of the Committee of Twenty, this modification might have deserved a place in the list of desiderata.

A third hypothesis could be that the SDR system was not viable because it was set up to achieve the wrong objective. There can perhaps be different versions of this hypothesis depending on the objectives considered appropriate by various proponents. It could be argued, for instance, that the SDR should have been specifically designed to replace U.S. dollars, as France and some other European members had initially intended, rather than to replace gold. In a par value system, this would have guarded not only against a possible reserve shortage (Triffin's secondary concern), which could have been met by making larger supplies of the new asset available, but also against inadequate U.S. balance of payments adjustment (Triffin's primary concern), which would be precluded by the requirement of "asset settlement," that is, by the need to settle any foreign deficit of the United States by drawing down its reserve assets rather than by increasing its U.S. dollar liabilities. Moreover, such a redirection of the objective of the SDR system would also have solved the problem of international control over world liquidity, because foreign exchange reserves would have gradually been phased out except for working balances.

Such a fundamental reorientation of the SDR facility would probably have had to be planned from the start of serious negotiations about deliberate reserve creation. It could not easily have been accomplished by later amendment of the facility actually put in place at the end of the 1960s. At least two major changes of the SDR system installed by the First Amendment of the Articles would have been required.

First, since substantial foreign exchange holdings in excess of working balances already existed at the time, SDRs would have had to be issued in the first place by substitution for existing currency balances and only secondarily by allocation. This would also have required a solution to the problem on which the substitution account proposal failed in 1980, namely, coverage of the exchange risk to which the substitution facility would be exposed. This could have been attempted through exchange guarantees extended by the issuers of currencies—an idea generally resisted by them—or, if the basket method of valuation could have been anticipated in the 1960s, by issuing SDRs against bundles of currencies in such a way that the distribution of currencies deposited in the substitution account matched that in the valuation basket.

A second major change required would have been the provision of rules implementing an asset settlement system that would prevent reserve currency countries from settling balance of payments deficits by allowing their currency liabilities to increase. This change requires primarily the adherence by other countries to rules against the accumulation of foreign exchange holdings beyond working balances. The most effective way—perhaps the only effective way—to ensure compliance with such a rule is to make the international reserve asset somewhat more attractive in its yield, security, and usability characteristics than the most attractive national currency.

These concepts, which are controversial even now, were simply not contained in the vocabulary available to the negotiators in the 1960s. It is rather unlikely, therefore, that a fully operational system of this type could have been designed at the negotiating table. Nevertheless, it could have been given a good start and completed over time as the full requirements of such a system became revealed through experience. Perhaps one should say that this *could* have been attempted, provided there had been broad agreement on this specific objective of deliberate reserve creation and, more generally, on the high degree of international cooperation and policy coordination necessary to implement it. To the extent that it was not a lack of foresight and imagination, but a lack of collective political will, that accounts for the failure to create a viable international reserve system to replace the gold exchange standard, another possible cause of the demise of the SDR has to be considered.

This fourth and last hypothesis of why the SDR may have failed is that it was never really wanted by some important member countries. According to this view, the negotiations leading to the introduction of the SDR facility may have generated a certain momentum, which at an accidental confluence of maximum enthusiasm by supporters and minimum resistance by opponents carried the proposed system on to full elaboration, acceptance, ratification, and even first activation, with some of the latter steps completed in part because of the political pressure of a process that had already come a long way. When stock had finally been taken after this effort was spent, a sufficiently large voting minority almost invariably opposed further allocation of SDRs and any aggressive development of the

SDR system.[10] This account would also explain the hesitation—perhaps hostility is not too strong a word—with which major financial centers approached the development of private SDR markets and associated arrangements. Encouragement of such private initiatives could have been an effective way of fostering the evolution of the SDR into a viable and central part of the international monetary system and thus into a more serious rival of national currencies in international finance.

What still would have to be explained by an adherent to this hypothesis is how it was possible for the SDR to come into existence if members with enough voting power to block what for brevity's sake might be called "pro-SDR decisions" were in fact opposed to the SDR facility. The answer may be that governments shift their stance on a particular issue in accordance with the way it interacts with other, perhaps broader, developments. The United States, as the largest member country whose voting power suffices by itself to block major decisions on SDRs, may be taken as example.

It will be recalled that the United States was not in favor of deliberate reserve creation in the form of reserve units as long as these were perceived to be intended as replacement of U.S. dollars in world reserves. Such a replacement would clearly have put pressure on the U.S. balance of payments and on the U.S. dollar exchange rate. It was thus likely to be seen as detrimental to U.S. interests. A little later, as gold convertibility problems increased, the United States embraced the idea of using deliberately created reserve units as a supplement to its dwindling gold reserves and perhaps even as a worldwide substitute for gold. This was the phase at which the SDR scheme was negotiated and its detailed features were set. The United States provided leadership in this process and helped to bring along the most reluctant major industrial country, France. Eventually, the SDR amendment was passed and ratified by most members, and after an interval also by France.

This phase at the end of the 1960s may have been the window of opportunity for the SDR. A short time later the United States found a more direct way of reducing the role of gold in the international monetary system. After the gold window was closed, it was not clear that SDRs entailed benefits for the United States: a gold

---

[10] A modified version of this hypothesis would point to changing circumstances, such as unexpectedly high reserve growth and increasing inflation, as justifying a changed attitude toward the new reserve creation scheme.

supplement was no longer needed, a supplement to, or substitute for, U.S. dollar holdings in global reserves was not favored, and the transfer of resources implied by the relatively low SDR interest rate was not intended. If the SDR had not come into existence before, it is not likely that it would have seen the light of day, say, in 1972 or later.

The fate of the SDR is, of course, not determined by the United States alone. Some other industrial countries have in recent years joined with the United States in opposition to SDR allocations, generally on the grounds that they could not be justified by a shortage of other reserves, as required by the Articles of the Agreement, and that they could be inflationary.[11] Nevertheless, in the light of U.S. veto power over decisions requiring an 85 percent majority, the example of changing influences that may have affected the U.S. attitude toward the SDR is important and revealing. It may throw light on past developments as well as on the future of the SDR.

A caveat should be added. I cannot claim to have studied in depth the historical record of actions and attitudes of the United States with respect to the SDR. In any case, governments do not reveal the motives for their actions. Indeed, as collective bodies composed of executive, legislative, and judicial entities, together with commissions, chambers, associations, and committees, they may not even be conscious of their motivation. The motivation of governments, or "countries," is a category of the historian. And historical perception changes over time, partly because the record may be studied more deeply as time goes on, but mainly because history is not so much a collection of facts as a collection of interpretations, which in turn depend on changing perspectives and filters through which the record is examined.

The foregoing observation should make clear the limited intention of this review. It holds up for examination the proposition that the SDR came into existence at an extremely propitious moment, which was both preceded and followed by circumstances either unsuitable or, at any rate, much less favorable to its birth and development. If there be validity in this view, it would also explain the anemic existence of the SDR in comparison with its prophesied glorious

---

[11] See Jacques J. Polak, "The Impasse Concerning the Role of the SDR," in *The Quest for National and Global Economic Stability*, ed. by Wietze Eizenga, E. Frans Limburg, and Jacques J. Polak (Dordrecht: Kluwer, 1988), pp. 175–89.

development. It now barely maintains life, like a plant set into unsuitable soil.

Is there, nevertheless, a future for the SDR? The answer to this question depends in large measure on the evolution of the international monetary system, a topic treated in other papers before this conference and beyond the scope of this contribution. I would like to make just three remarks in this context.

First, to the extent that the system moves away from direct participation of individual countries, large or small, and drifts in the direction of agglomeration into a few big blocs, the usefulness of a central monetary asset is probably lessened. The blocs make their own monetary arrangements on the basis of a dominant national currency or a regional reserve unit, like the ECU. For relations among the blocs, exchange rate adjustments are likely to be more important than concerns over international liquidity. All the same, one should not completely write off an international reserve asset even in these circumstances. As exchange rates within blocs are stabilized or become fixed, exchange rates between blocs may tend to become more volatile. At some time in the future, efforts may be directed at the reordering of interbloc monetary relations. An SDR, which would in this case probably have to be given a new valuation, could play a role in such an endeavor.[12]

Second, the events of the late 1960s and again those of the late 1970s suggest that interest in an international reserve asset increases when a dominant reserve asset weakens and no other asset is in a position to take its place. The SDR was established when gold was phased out and before a pure dollar system was fully accepted. The substitution account proposal almost succeeded in 1979–80 when the exchange value of the U.S. dollar had suffered a long decline and when many countries were not yet prepared to switch their reserve holdings from U.S. dollars to other national currencies. Such a monetary power vacuum could occur again and, if it did, the international community might well be inclined to fall back on the SDR.

Third, there is in any event every reason for preserving the SDR, even if its present usefulness is limited and its future is uncertain.

---

[12] The ideas put forward by Richard N. Cooper's paper "What Future for the International Monetary System?" at this conference are relevant in this context; see Chapter 6 in this volume. (Also published in *The Evolution of the International Monetary System: How Can Efficiency and Stability Be Attained?* ed. by Yoshio Suzuki, Junichi Miyake, and Mitsuaki Okabe (Tokyo: University of Tokyo Press, 1990).)

There is, for one thing, the need of a unit of account and perhaps also for a medium of exchange to make possible the operation of the Fund. This by itself would be a sufficient justification for the SDR. But apart from this reason, there is also the consideration that the existence of an international reserve asset permits a wider choice of international monetary arrangements than would otherwise be available. Some such arrangements require the existence of such an asset, especially if there is reluctance to return to gold or a single national currency for the central monetary functions on which some systems depend. Experience shows that events precipitating changes in the international monetary system usually arrive rapidly and with unpredictable timing. The creation of an international reserve asset, by contrast, takes a substantial amount of time. When a monetary system becomes so burdensome that it has to be changed, there would not be time to elaborate and install a facility like the SDR.[13] Unless such a facility already existed, the choice among monetary systems facing the international community would be limited to those systems that do not require a man-made central asset. The principle that "more choice is better than less choice" may be seen as an important reason for keeping the SDR alive.

---

[13] This argument for keeping the SDR alive is made by Polak in "The Impasse Concerning the Role of the SDR," op. cit., p. 180.

Role of the International Monetary Fund

PART THREE

Role of the
International Monetary Fund

8

Borrowing by the IMF
Ultra Vires and Other Problems

Joseph Gold

Jacques J. Polak has been a delegate to the Bretton Woods Conference, a senior official on the staff of the International Monetary Fund (IMF), and an Executive Director of the organization. I can think of only one other person who has had such a career, but the services of Jacques Polak were performed over a considerably longer period. His impact on the policies and practices of the IMF has been pervasive and will be enduring. As a close colleague of his in the longest stretch of his tripartite career, I have found it difficult to choose a single aspect of the IMF on which to contribute an essay in his honor. My choice has been determined finally by the fact that he was one of the small group that took the initiative to recommend and negotiate the first borrowing agreement and by the further fact that little has been written in a systematic way about the powers of the IMF to borrow, its practice in the exercise of the powers, and the effects of that practice.

I. Borrowing by IMF Under Article VII

Origin of Power to Borrow

The IMF has had a power to borrow under the first version and the amendments of the IMF's Articles of Agreement (Articles).[1] The

---

The views expressed in this paper should not be taken to be those of the IMF or anyone other than the author, unless they are clearly attributed to someone else or to the IMF itself.

[1] All references to the IMF's Articles of Agreement are to the present Articles, that

origin of the power was the contest between John Maynard Keynes
and Harry Dexter White on the fundamental character of the organization they foresaw, particularly in providing monetary resources to
its member states. Keynes advocated an International Currency (or
Clearing) Union that would be able to create a new international
reserve asset, bancor, to meet the needs for liquidity of members in
balance of payments difficulty. Members in surplus would willingly
accept this asset.[2] Keynes contemplated quotas for debit balances in
the Union, but ''[t]here need be no limit to the amount of a credit
balance.''[3] White, however, preferred an organization in which the
burden on each member would not be open-ended or as extensive
as whatever its surplus might be. He preferred a subscription equal
to a defined quota, which would be negotiated and known. His
view prevailed. A member would negotiate its original quota, and
although the IMF might be willing to adjust quotas at any time, an
adjustment could not be made without the member's consent.[4] The
provision requiring the member's consent was safeguarded by another provision, under which acceptance by all members was neces-

---

is, the treaty as modified by amendment, unless the original Articles or a particular
Amendment is cited.

The following abbreviations have been used in this paper:

BIS	Bank for International Settlements	SAMA	Saudi Arabian Monetary
ESAF	Enhanced structural adjustment		Agency
	facility	SDR	Special drawing right
GAB	General Arrangements to Borrow	SFD	Saudi Fund for Development
IMF	International Monetary Fund	SFF	Supplementary financing facility

[2] The creation of official liquidity by the IMF was accepted by the membership
when it adopted the First Amendment, under which the IMF was authorized to
allocate SDRs to members. The IMF retains this authority under the present Articles.
A member's obligation to accept transfers of SDRs from other members is subject to
quantitative limits and other qualifications (Article XXV, Sections 4 and 5 (First
Amendment); Article XIX, Sections 4 and 5).

[3] *The Collected Writings of John Maynard Keynes*, Vol. 25, ed. by Donald Moggridge
(Macmillan and Cambridge University Press for the Royal Economic Society, 1980),
p. 118. (See also p. 457: ''The absence of a rigid maximum to credit balances does not
impose on any member state, as might be supposed at first sight, an unlimited
liability outside its own control. The liability of an individual member is determined,
not by the quotas of the other members, but by its own policy in controlling its
favourable balance of payments.'') Keynes's ideas on the rate of interest payable by
debtor and creditor members under his proposals, and on the pressures that were to
be applied to them if they remained persistent debtors and creditors, went through
many transformations.

[4] Article III, Section 2 (original); Article III, Section 2(*d*).

sary for amendment of the safeguard.[5] The political and financial importance of both the absolute and the relative sizes of quotas justified other safeguards. Decisions on the adjustment of quotas, whether the decisions related to a single member or to members in general, could be taken only by the Board of Governors and only by a high majority of the voting power of all members.[6] As the Board of Governors was likely to be composed mostly of persons holding ministerial rank, they would probably give weight to political considerations that affected the distribution of power, benefits, and burdens. Furthermore, each Governor would be able to speak for his own country and would cast separately the number of votes allotted to the country for which he spoke, in contrast to the practice in the Executive Board in which most Executive Directors would perform their functions for a constituency of members and would reflect the views of the group in taking positions. All the safeguards mentioned here were in the original Articles and have been retained in the present version.

The explanation of the difference between the approaches of Keynes and White is obvious. Keynes expected the United Kingdom to be in deficit in its balance of payments, and his concern was to ensure that the new organization would have adequate resources for taking care of his country's needs as well as the needs of other countries in a similar predicament during a postwar period of uncertain duration. White was confident that his country would be one of the few countries in surplus following the war, and would certainly have the largest surplus.

---

[5] Article XVII(*b*) (original); Article XXVIII(*b*). Unanimous acceptance has been a condition for the amendment of only three provisions.

[6] Article III, Section 2 (original); Article III, Section 2(*c*). The Second Amendment increased the majority from 80 percent to 85 percent of the total voting power in accordance with a policy of reducing the number of different majorities required for decisions of the IMF. On the admission of a new member, the question is sometimes asked why, in contrast to the majority for increasing a quota, an original quota can be determined by the lowest of all majorities, the majority of votes cast. The explanation is that the IMF was regarded as potentially a universal organization. A high majority for membership could impede the admission of an applicant. An unfair original quota was unlikely to be offered, because, as was made explicit by the Second Amendment (Article II), the terms for membership are to "be based on principles consistent with those applied to other countries that are already members." The Articles do not specify criteria for the adjustment of quotas. An adjustment in an individual quota might upset a balance among quotas that some members might prefer to maintain until a general adjustment of quotas.

The compromise made to accommodate Keynes, at least to some extent, was the IMF's power to borrow to augment the resources derived from subscriptions. Keynes cited this power in a letter to Joan Robinson, who, it seems, had criticized the project for an IMF in the form in which it was emerging. The power to borrow, he wrote, could be exercised in order to enable the IMF to waive the twelve-month and cumulative limits[7] on a member's outstanding use of the IMF's resources and permit it to make a larger use.[8] "The quotas," he wrote, "are a minimum, not a maximum. The U.S. representatives were always eager to explain to us that this is strictly how they regarded them." He made the further point that the decision to grant a waiver could be taken by a majority vote, by which he meant that a special high majority would be unnecessary. Nevertheless, he expected the IMF to be "very chary" of borrowing the currency of a member that was in short supply in the IMF, except to give that member an opportunity "to find another way out."[9] In expressing these views, Keynes seems to have been saying that a country in surplus that caused undue difficulties for other members could lend its currency to the IMF, while taking other measures to reduce or eliminate its surplus, and in this way avoid a declaration of scarcity by the IMF that would authorize other members to discriminate against the member in surplus.[10]

There is ample evidence to support Keynes's version of the U.S view. The U.S. Treasury issued its *Questions and Answers on the International Monetary Fund* on June 10, 1944, a few days before the preliminary drafting conference at Atlantic City and the subsequent Bretton Woods Conference. The answer to Question 5 stated that:

> The Fund may sell foreign exchange for additional local currency, even when its holdings exceed the prescribed limits, if the Board of Directors approves the sale and the member country is taking satisfactory measures to correct the disequilibrium or to reduce the excess local currency holdings of the Fund.[11]

The answer to Question 15 explained in detail why the United States preferred the approach based on quotas and subscriptions

---

[7] Article V, Section 3(a)(iii) (original).

[8] The reference was to Article V, Section 4 (original).

[9] *The Collected Writings of John Maynard Keynes*, Vol. 26 (see footnote 3 above), pp. 130–31.

[10] Article VII, Section 3(b) (original).

[11] *The International Monetary Fund 1945–1965: Twenty Years of International Monetary Cooperation*, Vol. III: Documents, ed. by J. Keith Horsefield (Washington: International Monetary Fund, 1969), p. 143.

and rejected the approach of the Currency Union. The answer concluded with these words:

> Fourth, if the operations of the Fund reveal a need for additional resources for its successful functioning, such resources can be secured through the borrowing power of the Fund, without the indirect compulsion inherent in the creation of credit.[12]

In the answer to Question 5, this view was expanded somewhat:

> The Fund's resources will probably be adequate for all ordinary needs of member countries. When the Fund has been strengthened and a larger proportion of its assets are in the form of gold, it will undoubtedly be able to meet even extraordinary needs for any particular currency or currencies. In the meantime, if the Fund should find its holdings of any member currency inadequate, it may borrow the needed amounts of that currency with the approval of the member country concerned and on terms and conditions agreed between them.[13]

The U.S. Treasury, therefore, did not expect that there would be much need to exercise the IMF's power to borrow, and to this extent the Treasury shared Keynes's opinion. The reasons, however, were different. Keynes was expressing a principle to guide the IMF's exercise of the power: the IMF should invoke the power to give the member in troublesome balance of payments surplus sufficient time to deal with this disequilibrium. The Treasury's explanation of the reason why exercise of the power would be infrequent was related to the IMF's stock of gold. Members would pay part of their subscriptions in gold. Subscribed gold would be supplemented over time by the repurchase obligations of members using the IMF's resources that accrued in gold, in accordance with the formulas prescribed by the Articles, and also by possible purchases of gold by the IMF from members.[14] The importance of the IMF's gold stock was that the IMF could compel a member to sell its currency to the organization in return for gold, thus reducing the need for borrowing by the organization.[15] Keynes and White would have been surprised if they could have foreseen the abundant use the IMF has

---

[12] Ibid., p. 154. See also p. 142.

[13] Ibid., p. 144.

[14] Under Article V, Section 6 of the original Articles, a member desiring to obtain, directly or indirectly, the currency of another member for gold, was bound to sell the gold to the IMF for the currency, provided the sale could be made with "equal advantage." This obligation did not prevent a member from selling in any market gold newly produced within the member's territories.

[15] Article VII, Section 2(ii) (original and First Amendment).

made of its original and its expanded powers to borrow. Notwithstanding the U.S. Treasury's view on the use of gold, the Articles did not require the IMF to sell gold before trying to borrow. Nor was any priority given to borrowing, even though the power to borrow was set forth in the provision on replenishment before the power to sell gold. Any inclination to infer that one measure took priority over the other would have been incompatible with the language that preceded both powers: "The Fund may...take either or both of the following steps." This formulation has been retained by the present Articles. The original and the current provisions of Article VII on replenishment are appended to this paper.

Problems of Interpreting Article VII

Article VII has given rise to many problems of interpretation, some of which are noted here:

"Scarce Currencies"

Article VII has always included three powers of the IMF. In the original treaty, Article VII was headed "Scarce Currencies," and the title of the three provisions in which the powers were set forth referred either to "scarcity" or to "scarce currencies." First, the IMF could find that a general scarcity of a particular currency was developing. The IMF could then inform members of this fact, issue a report on the causes of the scarcity, and make recommendations for bringing it to an end. Second, the IMF could take either or both of two actions to replenish its holdings of a member's currency described in the title of the provision as "scarce." Third, if it was evident that the demand for a currency threatened the IMF's ability to supply it, the IMF could formally declare the currency scarce. The effect was to authorize discrimination by other members against the issuer of the scarce currency. This last provision was the "scarce currency clause" of legendary importance in the negotiation of the original Articles.[16]

The provisions seemed to follow a logical order. A widespread or worldwide shortage of a currency might develop, and to counteract it the IMF could apply the sanction of private and public oppro-

---

[16] Roy Harrod records how, on reading the proposed clause for the first time, "I could not believe my eyes or my brain.... I felt an exhilaration such as only comes once or twice in a lifetime," and he rises to even higher peaks of enthusiasm.—*The Life of John Maynard Keynes* (New York: Harcourt, Brace, 1951), pp. 544–45.

brium. A scarcity in the world could lead to a scarcity in the IMF because of the drain on its resources. A member could prevent a scarcity in the IMF and could avoid the sanction of mobilized shame by lending to the organization. In borrowing, the IMF was not imposing a sanction, but if the member did not lend adequate amounts, the IMF could resort to the severe sanction of the scarce currency clause.

One problem raised by Article VII was whether a condition of resort to the second provision (borrowing) was action by the IMF under the first provision (the report) or possibly the third provision (the declaration of scarcity). Did scarcity have one, two, or three meanings under the three provisions? The IMF concluded that there were indeed three meanings and that they were independent of each other. The independence of the third from the first meaning was made explicit in the third provision ("whether or not it [the IMF] has issued a report . . . "). The IMF held that the independence of the second provision from the other two was implied, so that there was no reason to reduce the apparently unlimited scope of the discretionary authority suggested by the clause "if it [the IMF] deems such action [borrowing] appropriate."[17] This understanding gave the IMF a more effective discretion to borrow than any other conclusion, because it freed the IMF from the unpleasant necessity of imposing a sanction under the first or the third provision as a prelude to borrowing. For many years in the life of the IMF, sanctions were a rebarbative idea for conduct contrary to the purposes of the IMF, but in those years the breach of financial obligations was unthinkable.

The Second Amendment put the issue of the relationship among the provisions on the matter of scarcity beyond controversy. The heading of Article VII became "Replenishment and Scarce Currencies" instead of "Scarce Currencies." The original order of the

---

[17] This conclusion was reinforced to some extent by the drafting history of the provision. The earlier version of the provision as proposed jointly by the U.S. and British delegations at Bretton Woods was entitled "Operations for the Purpose of Preventing Currencies from Becoming Scarce," and the IMF was authorized to borrow if "it deems such action appropriate to prevent the currency of any member from becoming scarce."—*Proceedings and Documents of the United Nations Monetary and Financial Conference*, U.S. Department of State Publication 2866 (Washington: U.S. Government Printing Office, 1948), hereinafter referred to as *Procs. and Docs.*), pp. 31, 449. A later proposal was that the IMF could borrow if it deemed such action appropriate "to maintain necessary balances of any currency" (*Procs. and Docs.*, pp. 526, 669).

provisions was abandoned, and the provision giving the IMF power to replenish its holdings of a currency was placed first. In addition, the word "scarce" was suppressed in the amended title of that provision.

"Replenish"

The IMF's power to borrow has always been to "replenish" its holdings of a member's currency.[18] The ordinary modern meaning of the word is to fill up again, although there is an archaic meaning of simply filling a need completely, somewhat in the Biblical sense of fruitfulness. Was the IMF's power limited, in accordance with the modern sense, to borrowing a member's currency in an amount that raised the IMF's holdings of the currency to the level, but not beyond, of the actual currency subscription made by the member originally or to the ideal currency subscription of 75 percent of quota if that amount had been exceeded originally?

An argument could have been made for a third limit: replenishment could increase the IMF's holdings of a member's currency to the level of the member's quota. The argument would have run along these lines. The concept of replenishment applied to both borrowing and the obligation of a member to transfer its currency to the IMF in return for gold. At Bretton Woods, an inconsistency was pointed out between suggested provisions on borrowing and on the authority of members to buy their currency from the IMF with gold.[19] The language of the latter proposal was that "a member country may repurchase from the Fund for gold any part of the latter's holdings of its currency."[20] The purpose of this proposal was to harden the IMF's resources by allowing a member to substitute gold for any part of its currency held by the IMF if the member was reluctant to have these holdings put into circulation by sales to other members.[21]

The inconsistency was that the IMF could require a member to provide its currency for gold, but the member could counteract this transaction at once or at any time later by reacquiring the currency with gold. The dilemma was resolved by allowing a member to

---

[18] But the word "replenish" did not appear in earlier drafts of the provision (see footnote 17 above).

[19] *Procs. and Docs.*, pp. 825–26.

[20] Ibid., pp. 33, 158, 653, 665, 775.

[21] For the same reason, the ideal gold subscription of 25 percent of quota was called "a minimum" (Article III, Section 3(*b*) (original)).

purchase its currency with gold only to the extent that the IMF's holdings exceeded the level of the member's quota.[22] The rationale of this limited authorization was that a member should be able at any time to avoid incurring the charges levied on the IMF's holdings of the member's currency in excess of quota.

An argument might have been made, therefore, that as the member would be able to buy with gold the IMF's holdings of its currency in excess of quota, even if the excess was borrowed, replenishment should not enable the IMF to borrow currency that increased holdings beyond the level equivalent to quota. The argument would not have been persuasive, however, because a member intending to reacquire its currency, at least at the time of proposed borrowing by the IMF, could refuse to lend or to concur in loans of the currency to the IMF by others.

The decisive argument against the original or the ideal currency subscription or the quota as the limit up to which the IMF's holdings could be increased by borrowing was that the IMF could arrange to borrow a larger amount but to call for it in installments that were disposed of in the IMF's transactions in such a way that the limit, whatever it might be, was never transcended. Immediate disposition, however, made it an inconvenient and empty ceremony to negotiate loans for advances in installments. The problem would have been complicated further if there was little or no room for borrowing below the limit. Whatever the size of a borrowing, however, the effect of the immediate disposition of the contractual amount was that at the end of the day on which the IMF received the amount, its holdings of the currency would be the same as they were at the beginning of the day. It could be said, therefore, that replenishment was given the archaic meaning of filling the IMF's need whatever it might be.

This meaning, however, has not been the only one the IMF has observed. Sometimes, the ordinary or modern meaning has guided practice and has had the effect of limiting replenishment to amounts that did not increase the IMF's holdings of a currency beyond the level of the ideal currency subscription of 75 percent of quota. This practice was followed when the currency obtained by replenishment was to be retained by the IMF and not used in immediate transactions. The practice, though, was the consequence of pragmatic considerations rather than semantics. For example, before the

---

[22] Article V, Section 7(*a*) (original).

Second Amendment of the Articles, if the IMF's holdings of a member's currency were increased above 75 percent of the member's quota, repurchase obligations might accrue for the member that would require it to reduce the IMF's holdings to the level of 75 percent. (It is for this reason that 75 percent has been referred to as the ideal currency subscription, because the obligation to repurchase could accrue simply because a member had made a larger original currency subscription.) Furthermore, if replenishment were allowed to increase the IMF's holdings of a member's currency beyond the level of quota, the member would be required to pay charges to the IMF on the holdings in excess of quota. The absurd situation would then have been that the member paid charges to the IMF while the IMF paid interest to the member on the borrowing.

If the accrual of repurchase obligations were the only pragmatic consideration, the level to be observed if the IMF retained currency received in replenishment would now be the quota. The Second Amendment substituted that level for 75 percent of quota as the level above which the IMF's holdings of a currency are subject to an obligation of repurchase. The pragmatic considerations, however, are more complex: any addition of a member's currency to the IMF's holdings in the General Resources Account can affect the member's position in the IMF by making the position less beneficial or more detrimental. For example, in some circumstances, the IMF's acquisition of a member's currency can reduce the amount of remuneration the IMF pays to the member. The reduction of this benefit can be suffered even though the IMF's holdings are not raised to or beyond the "remuneration norm." The norm is the percentage of a member's quota that enters into the IMF's calculation of the extent to which the norm exceeds the IMF's average daily balances of the member's currency. The IMF pays remuneration on the amount by which the average of daily holdings is below the norm.[23]

The practical importance of not retaining borrowed currency in the General Resources Account can create a dilemma. The IMF seeks to comply promptly with a member's proper request for resources. To comply, the IMF may have an immediate need for the resources promised to it under existing borrowing agreements. Prompt compliance with unprogrammed calls for advances under borrowing agreements, however, can complicate a lender's management of its reserves. The IMF had to adapt its practice as a condition of borrow-

---

[23] Article V, Section 9.

ing from the Saudi Arabian Monetary Agency (SAMA) to assist in the financing of transactions under the IMF's policy on enlarged access. Under agreements of 1981 and 1984 with SAMA, the IMF undertook to give substantial advance notice of its intention to make calls,[24] and it agreed also to make repayments on fixed dates.[25] For similar reasons, the IMF established special value dates for transactions with members under the enlarged access policy financed with borrowed resources and for repurchases in respect of such transactions.[26] Currency received from SAMA before the IMF could use it in transactions or received from members before the IMF could use it in the repayment of borrowing from SAMA made it necessary to hold the currency in a suspense account pending use so as to avoid bringing the currency into the General Resources Account immediately on receipt and affecting the rights and obligations in the IMF of the issuer of the currency.[27] The establishment of suspense accounts raises the question whether the IMF should borrow resources for unforeseeable future needs in contrast to borrowing resources to meet predictable requests by members.

The technique of the suspense account did not solve all problems, because eventually the currency would have to be brought into the General Resources Account for immediate use in transactions of the IMF with members or in operations to repay SAMA. These transactions and operations would be conducted on the basis of the SDR as the IMF's unit of account. The SDR value of the currency at the time of disbursement by the IMF might differ from the SDR value at the date of receipt. The IMF decided, therefore, that it had an implied power to invest the currency in specified deposits or marketable obligations denominated in the SDR.[28] Under another implied power, the currency could be exchanged at the time of deposit in the suspense account for the currency of another member in which an investment was to be made.

The power to borrow, therefore, has been a source of authority from which the IMF has been able to derive various implied powers

---

[24] International Monetary Fund, *Selected Decisions of the International Monetary Fund and Selected Documents*, Annex to Fourteenth Issue (Washington, 1989), pp. 79, 111–12; hereinafter referred to as *Selected Decisions, Annex*. (The Sixteenth Issue has no Annex.)

[25] Ibid., pp. 80, 111–12.

[26] Rule G-4(b) and (c).

[27] International Monetary Fund, *Selected Decisions*, Sixteenth Issue (1991), pp. 339–40.

[28] *Selected Decisions*, Sixteenth Issue (1991), pp. 340–41.

that are deemed to be both necessary and appropriate to make the borrowing power effective. A condition for the recognition of an implied power under a treaty is subject to a third test: the power must not be inconsistent with the express provisions of the treaty. The insistence by a potential lender on certain terms as the conditions on which it is willing to lend does not automatically justify the conclusion that the terms are consistent with the express or implied provisions of the Articles. This principle was a source of controversy in the negotiation of the General Arrangements to Borrow (GAB), but finally it was agreed that the principle had to be observed.[29]

Lenders

The IMF can borrow a member's currency from the member itself or from any other source, whether located inside or outside the member's territories. No limitation is placed on potential lenders: they can be the member whose currency is to be borrowed, other members, official institutions of the member or of any other member, nonmembers or their official institutions, international organizations, or private entities. No member or other entity, official or nonofficial, approached for a loan is compelled to lend. The terms and conditions of a loan are subject to agreement between the IMF and the lender, but as seen already the terms and conditions must be consistent with the Articles and must not be a pretext for what would be, in effect, an ad hoc modification of the Articles without observing the requirements for amendment.

If the IMF proposes to borrow a member's currency from a lender other than the member, the IMF must obtain the member's concurrence. The reason for this requirement is that the IMF should not interfere with the member's domestic monetary policies or impede the member's own ability to borrow, particularly in the market. The IMF is not empowered to manage the markets.

A subtlety lurks in the word "concurrence." The corresponding word in the original Articles was "approval." The Second Amendment made the substitution because the words have different connotations in the Articles and in the IMF's practice. In seeking "approval," the IMF is not entitled to exert pressure on the member to approve on the ground that there is a presumption the member will

---

[29] Erin E. Jacobsson, *A Life for Sound Money: Per Jacobsson, His Biography* (Oxford: Clarendon Press, 1979), pp. 375–85.

approve: the two parties are on an even plane. "Concurrence," however, connotes a presumption in favor of the member's acquiescence in the IMF's request. Good faith requires that the member should have a bona fide reason for withholding concurrence and should explain its position to the IMF if concurrence is withheld.

The IMF has not borrowed from private lenders, although the Interim Committee of the IMF's Board of Governors and other official bodies have shown tentative interest in the practice, usually by favoring study of it by the Executive Board and staff. The Bretton Woods legislation of the United States had provided that neither the President nor any person or agency acting on behalf of the United States should make a loan to the IMF unless Congress by law authorized such action. In November 1983, Congress amended the legislation by providing that neither the President nor any person or agency acting on behalf of the United States should consent to borrowing by the IMF, other than borrowing from a foreign government or other official public source, of funds denominated in U.S. dollars, unless the Secretary of the Treasury transmits notice of such borrowing to both Houses of Congress at least 60 days before the date on which the borrowing is scheduled to take place.

On March 15, 1985, the Treasury, acting in response to a statutory direction, transmitted a report to Congress expressing its opposition to proposals for borrowing dollars in the private market. Such borrowing, the Treasury concluded, "although feasible, could have an adverse impact on the cooperative international monetary character of the IMF and the ability of the United States to influence IMF policies."[30] It seems, therefore, that the United States is not likely to concur in a proposal of the IMF to borrow dollars in the market, unless the Treasury changes its attitude because the dangers foreseen in 1985 are thought to have disappeared.

Borrowed Resources

In all versions of the Articles, the resources the IMF has been empowered to borrow under Article VII have been limited to "any member's currency." This limitation excludes authority to borrow the currency of a nonmember, even from the nonmember itself, and

---

[30] For a detailed discussion of the subject matter of the paragraph to which this footnote is attached, including a critique of the reasons advanced by the Treasury, see Joseph Gold, "Borrowing by the International Monetary Fund from Nonofficial Lenders," *International Lawyer* (Chicago), Vol. 20 (1986), pp. 455–83, at p. 464.

even though the IMF has borrowed from Switzerland as a nonmember. The fundamental reason for the limitation is that, although the Articles require each member and the IMF to maintain the value of the IMF's holdings of the member's currency, there would be no such obligation on the IMF, members, or a nonmember to maintain the value of the IMF's holdings of the nonmember's currency if the IMF could borrow that currency.[31] Even though a nonmember's contractual obligation to lend to the IMF may be and has been expressed in the SDR as the IMF's normal unit of account,[32] the nonmember would not be bound by that form of denomination to maintain the SDR value of the IMF's holdings of the nonmember's currency if the IMF could receive it. When the IMF borrowed from Switzerland in the past, the agreement specified that advances under it were to be made in a member's currency.[33]

Another consequence of the limited power of the IMF to borrow under Article VII is that the IMF has not been able to borrow gold or SDRs. Even before the role of gold was reduced by the Second Amendment, the IMF could not borrow gold. The fundamental reason was that the IMF was not authorized to sell gold to members requesting use of the IMF's resources under Article V. The most important use the IMF could make of gold was to compel a member to provide its currency for gold in replenishment of the IMF's holdings of that currency. Therefore, if the IMF needed to replenish its holdings of a currency, the IMF could borrow the currency or sell gold already held to obtain the currency but could not borrow gold in order to sell it for the currency.

Another, perhaps less important, reason for denying the IMF the power to borrow gold may have been the paradox that the power might reduce the IMF's stock of gold. The lender might insist on repayment in gold, but the repurchase obligation of a member receiving balance of payments assistance from the IMF, either with

---

[31] Article V, Section 11(*a*). Thus, even though under Article XIX(*a*) of the original Articles the IMF could decide that a member's holdings of a nonmember's currency specified by the IMF were to be included in the calculation of a member's monetary reserves on the basis of which repurchase obligations were determined, the IMF could not receive in a nonmember's currency the portion of a repurchase obligation that accrued in that currency. The Articles have contained no provision permitting departure from the prohibitions relating to a nonmember's currency even if the nonmember were to agree by contract to maintain the value of any holdings of its currency by the IMF.

[32] Article V, Section 10(*b*).

[33] *Selected Decisions*, Sixteenth Issue (1991), pp. 312, 317.

the borrowed gold (if that transaction had been permitted by the Articles) or with the proceeds of the sale of borrowed gold, might not accrue in gold. The provisions of the Articles on repurchase were tightly drawn and mandatory. If, then, the IMF had been authorized to borrow gold and exercised that power with a contractual obligation to repay in gold, the IMF would have had to draw down its gold holdings to discharge its undertaking.

One of the modifications of Article VII by the Second Amendment was the substitution of SDRs for gold as the resource with which the IMF can require the replenishment of its holdings of a currency.[34] This change was one of the many such substitutions made throughout the Articles in order to diminish the role of gold. Although an objective of the Second Amendment was to make the SDR ''the principal reserve asset in the international monetary system,''[35] the IMF was not empowered to borrow SDRs. An effort was made to include this power in the revised Articles, but the effort did not succeed. The refusal may seem all the more surprising because although the IMF could not provide gold to members for balance of payments assistance, the IMF can now provide SDRs for this purpose.[36]

It follows that the reason for denying a power to borrow SDRs cannot be that the IMF is unable to make them available to a member as balance of payments assistance. If the IMF were empowered to borrow SDRs, it would be able to provide them to members. These members might have to dispose of the SDRs at once for currencies, if, for example, the member was intervening in the

---

[34] The IMF was empowered by the First Amendment (Article XXV, Section 7(d)) to require a member to replenish the IMF's holdings of currency with SDRs, but the power to replenish with gold under Article VII was not amended. No limit was placed on the power to replenish with gold, but the First Amendment adopted three limits or conditions on the use of SDRs for replenishment: (1) a member could not be required to accept further SDRs if the member's holdings of SDRs were equivalent to its so-called acceptance limit; (2) in exercising its power of replenishment the IMF had to pay ''due regard'' to the principles for designating members to receive SDRs; and (3) before requiring a member to accept SDRs in replenishment the IMF had to consult the member. The present Articles have retained the first two and abandoned the third of these qualifications of the power to borrow, in order to enhance the status of the SDR.

[35] Article VIII, Section 7; Article XXII.

[36] Under Article XXV, Section 7(f) of the First Amendment, the IMF could take that action only by agreement with the member requesting balance of payments assistance.

market or discharging obligations. It was deemed advisable, therefore, to empower the IMF to borrow currency only and not SDRs.

A more powerful motive for objection by some negotiators may
have been the fear that if the IMF were able to borrow SDRs, it
might be tempted to make allocations in the hope of being able to
borrow a substantial proportion of them, instead of seeking an
increase in quotas. Adjustment of a member's quota and loans to
the IMF require legislative approval in some countries, including the
United States, but support for an allocation of SDRs might not. The
uneasiness of the U.S. Congress about allocations is evident in a
statutory enactment of 1983, which provides that neither the President nor anyone else acting on behalf of the United States shall vote
to allocate SDRs without consultations, at least 90 days prior to any
such vote, by the Secretary of the Treasury with the Chairman and
ranking minority members of specified committees and appropriate
subcommittees of the Senate and the House of Representatives. The
consultations must include an explanation of the consistency of the
proposed allocation with the Articles, and in particular with the
criterion of a long-term global need to supplement reserves as it
appears in the Articles.[37]

Against the background of this legislative provision, consider a
procedure that has been suggested for funneling SDRs into the
General Resources Account of the IMF notwithstanding the inability
of the IMF to borrow SDRs for use in transactions conducted
through that Account. The IMF would conclude that the conditions
of the Articles for an allocation of SDRs were met, but a decision
would be taken only if there was the assurance that a sufficient
number of newly allocated SDRs would be brought into the General
Resources Account under the following scheme. A participant
(Patria) would agree to lend to the IMF an amount of the currencies
of other participants equivalent to the SDRs Patria had agreed to
make available to the IMF under the scheme, and the IMF would
undertake in the borrowing agreement to use the borrowed currencies only in accordance with the scheme. Simultaneously with this
operation, the IMF would purchase SDRs from Patria with the
currencies borrowed from it.[38] When the arrangement had run its

---

[37] Pub. L. No. 91-599(1970); Pub. L. No. 94-564(1976); Pub. L. No. 98-181(1983).

[38] The purchase by the IMF would be carried out under Article V, Section 6(a):
"The Fund may accept special drawing rights offered by a participant [in the Special
Drawing Rights Department] in exchange for an equivalent amount of the currencies
of other members."

course, the IMF would resell to Patria, for the currencies of other participants, the amount of SDRs the IMF had received from Patria,[39] or would pay the equivalent of them in currency if the IMF could not provide SDRs. Other steps would be necessary to restore the situation of all parties, including the members that benefited from the IMF's acquisition of the SDRs. Each step in this series, taken alone, would be authorized by the language of a provision of the Articles.

The weakness of the scheme is that in some and perhaps many legal systems such a scheme would be considered a "step transaction." All the steps would be treated as a single transaction designed to achieve an objective contrary to law. Thus, in England, the House of Lords, the highest judicial tribunal, has held, in *United City Merchants (Investments) v. Royal Bank of Canada* [1983] 1 A.C. 168, that an even longer staircase constituted a "step transaction" and was really "a monetary transaction in disguise" designed to evade exchange control provisions. According to this analysis, the scheme described above would be considered a borrowing of SDRs in disguise and *ultra vires*.[40] The principle of good faith in the interpretation of treaties is fundamental in international law and should require the conclusion that the step transaction described here would be a *détournement de pouvoir*. If there is an ambiguity or an inadvertent gap in legal provisions, courts may be less likely to invalidate a step transaction, but they are unlikely to tolerate an attempt to evade a prohibition or a denial of authority. The absence of an express power of the IMF to borrow SDRs is neither ambiguous nor inadvertent.

"Transactions"

The IMF can borrow currencies under Article VII only for use in "transactions" conducted through the General Resources Account. The IMF has no power to borrow for the purposes of the other two Accounts of the General Department (namely, the Special Disbursement Account and the Investment Account). Furthermore, the IMF is unable to borrow for the purpose of "operations," even if they

---

[39] Article V, Section 6(*b*): "The Fund may provide a participant, at its request, with special drawing rights for an equivalent amount of the currencies of other members."

[40] Ebere Osieke, "The Legal Validity of Ultra Vires Decisions of International Organizations," *American Journal of International Law* (Washington), Vol. 77 (1983), pp. 239–56.

are conducted through the General Resources Account. The Articles define "transactions" as exchanges of monetary assets by the IMF for other monetary assets, and "operations" as other uses or receipts of monetary assets by the IMF.[41] The most obvious "transaction" is the IMF's sale of currencies or SDRs in return for the purchasing member's currency. The repayment of borrowing by the IMF is a leading example of an "operation." When the IMF repays, it discharges an obligation and does not receive an asset: the IMF gets nothing that it can hold or use.[42]

The Second Amendment brought about a reduction in the IMF's power to borrow by making two changes in the Articles. First, authority to borrow if the IMF deems such action appropriate to replenish its holdings of any member's currency was qualified by adding "needed in connection with its [the IMF's] transactions." Second, definitions of "transactions" and "operations" were included in the Articles for the first time.

It follows from the definitions that the IMF is unable to borrow currencies to repay its indebtedness. A reason for this limitation is that members are required to terminate their use of the IMF's resources on time, and the IMF is expected to manage its financial activities in such a way that it should have no difficulty in repaying its indebtedness without incurring new indebtedness. Some of the negotiators of the Second Amendment were not enthusiastic about borrowing and even more were uncomfortable with the prospect of prolongation of the IMF's indebtedness. In addition, the negotiators of the Second Amendment thought it desirable to avoid any implication that because the IMF had a power to borrow to repay its indebtedness, the IMF might be willing to permit use of the IMF's resources by members beyond the assigned period. Yet another reason for the change in the power to borrow was the nervous reaction of some negotiators to the newly minted definitions of transactions and operations. Transactions were reasonably clear and limited, but the concept of operations was a residual category of unlimited and undefined scope. The breadth of the word "operations" was troubling and provoked the fear that it might include questionable activities, although no examples were cited. Inability to

---

[41] Article XXX(h).

[42] The IMF has decided that the repayment by a member of a loan received from another member is an operation. See Article XIX, Section 2(c) and *Selected Decisions,* Sixteenth Issue (1991), pp. 389–92.

foresee examples gave rise to an anxiety that was relieved by limiting the power to borrow.

Lenders could be confident that when a member repurchased in respect of a transaction with the IMF financed with borrowed resources, the IMF would necessarily have the resources with which to repay the lender if the borrowing agreement correlated repurchases by members and repayments by the IMF. To encourage potential lenders further, the IMF has sought to endow claims by lenders with attractive characteristics. One characteristic has been that a lender is able to obtain repayment by the IMF before the due date if unfavorable changes develop in the balance of payments position of the lender.[43]

The assumption that the IMF will have no difficulty in repaying a lender with ordinary resources when a member repurchases in respect of a transaction financed with the borrowing cannot be made when a lender requests early repayment. To give the lender confidence of early repayment, the IMF has negotiated contractual rights to borrow from other lenders to repay a lender requesting early repayment. The IMF negotiated such a term before the Second Amendment when the IMF borrowed from a group of lenders under a single agreement with them or from a number of lenders under individual but standardized agreements in support of the same specified policy of the IMF. The GAB falls within the first of these two categories; the agreements for loans in support of the oil facilities of 1974 and 1975 and the supplementary financing facility (SFF, 1977) fell into the second category.

A term of this kind had become so entrenched in the IMF's practice that the term continued to be included in the GAB when it was revised in 1983, five years after the Second Amendment. As the repayment of a loan is an "operation" of the IMF and not a "transaction," borrowing to make the settlement is not authorized

---

[43] Improvements in the quality of loan claims have gone beyond the assurance to lenders that the IMF will not challenge a lender's representation of a need for early repayment in accordance with the criterion of need as defined in the loan agreement. (The technical jargon for this assurance is that the IMF will give the lender "the overwhelming benefit of any doubt".) In addition, claims can be transferred, sometimes freely at the lender's will to designated transferees and to other transferees if the IMF has given its consent, and sometimes with the necessity for the IMF's consent in all cases. A transferee may be assured that it will stand in the shoes of the transferor for all purposes under the transferor's loan agreement. Claims carry interest and were guaranteed formerly in terms of gold and are guaranteed now in terms of the SDR as the IMF's current unit of account.

by the Second Amendment. The IMF has suffered a regrettable loss of authority. The term in question is now *ultra vires* and should be deleted from the GAB. Even if the term is not deleted, a participant in the GAB could validly refuse to lend for what was interpreted to be an *ultra vires* purpose.

Efforts to Authorize Borrowing for "Operations"

In the drafting of the Second Amendment a proposal was made to include operations among the activities for which the IMF could borrow. The supporters of the suggestion were content not to insist on it against the opposition, because they assumed that the IMF would manage its currency resources in such a way that the amount to be borrowed for transactions could be estimated after making allowance for the resources needed to finance operations. As a precaution against too lavish or too loose an estimate of the amounts to be borrowed for transactions, however, the word "needed" was introduced into the provision to give the impression that estimates should be conservative. The fact that members could be compelled to accept SDRs for replenishment of the IMF's currency resources made some drafters more willing to draft a narrower provision on borrowing than had been included in the original Articles.

Toward the end of the negotiations on the Second Amendment, there was a return to the issue of borrowing for operations. A strong attempt was made to include in the Articles authority for the IMF to engage at least in all operations and transactions in SDRs that were permitted between members, between members and other holders of SDRs prescribed by the IMF, or between prescribed other holders.[44] The argument for the proposal was the illogicality of a narrower authority for the IMF itself than for members and other holders of SDRs. The main argument in opposition was again uncertainty about the categories of future operations in SDRs that members and other holders might be permitted to engage in. This argument prevailed, though unresponsive in logic, because at the late stage at which the proposal was made there was widespread

---

[44] International Monetary Fund, *Documents Relating to the Second Amendment of the Articles of Agreement of the International Monetary Fund*, Vol. II: Minutes, Part 3 (Washington, 1980), pp. 2552–58, 2579–81. Members and prescribed other holders have been authorized to make loans of SDRs to members or other holders (*Selected Decisions*, Sixteenth Issue (1991), pp. 381–83, 390–92).

reluctance to endure further delay in completing the already lengthy negotiation of the Second Amendment.

The advocates of the idea that the IMF should be authorized to engage in all the categories of operations and transactions in SDRs that were permitted for others then retreated to an even more humble proposal. The IMF should be authorized at least to engage in the one operation of borrowing SDRs. Impatience to wind up the negotiations was responsible for rejecting this proposal also, but there was another reason for opposing it. Some of the negotiators were discomfited by the thought that the IMF might pay interest on the borrowing of SDRs at a rate higher than the rate of interest paid on holdings of SDRs and the rate of remuneration paid to members whose currencies were used in the IMF's activities.[45]

Majorities

The Executive Board is the organ that exercises the IMF's power to borrow. As a special majority for the exercise of the power is not required, the Executive Board can decide to borrow by the basic, which is also the lowest, majority for taking decisions: the majority of the votes actually cast.[46] The basic majority continues to suffice for decisions to borrow, notwithstanding the explosive increase in the number of categories of decisions for which special majorities were made necessary by the Second Amendment. A reason for the modest majority is that a decision to borrow does not bind any member or other entity to lend or any member to concur in a borrowing when concurrence is necessary.

The majority for decisions to borrow implies that they were not considered matters of high policy involving political interests or the development of the international monetary system. They were re- garded as operating decisions, much like decisions to adopt policies on the use of the IMF's resources and to approve transactions under the policies, for which the same majority suffices. Sales of gold by the IMF provide the IMF with additional resources in the form of currency, and therefore are still a form of replenishing currency resources, even though the sales are now authorized by Article V instead of Article VII. That sales of gold presuppose willing pur- chasers heightens the similarity to borrowing currency, and so too

---

[45] Article V, Section 9.
[46] Article XII, Section 5(c).

does the fact that if the IMF sells gold, it must consult the member for whose currency the gold is to be sold. The Second Amendment, however, is designed to prevent restoration of the role of gold by the IMF. Therefore, obligations with respect to gold, including the obligation of members to purchase gold from the IMF for the replenishment of its currency resources, have been abrogated. Decisions by the IMF to sell gold under its present residual powers on gold require a majority as high as 85 percent of the total voting power of the membership.[47]

Established Encouragements to Lend

The Articles offer two special benefits to members that can be considered encouragements to lend or rewards for having done so. One benefit is that for two categories of decisions related to the use of the IMF's general resources, a member's voting power is increased on the basis of net sales by the IMF of the member's currency. The amount of the increase is limited to ensure that voting power will not be modified too radically, particularly for the benefit of the strong at the cost of the reduced voting power of the weak. The formula for the calculation permits an increase that takes account of the IMF's sales of subscribed and borrowed currency up to a maximum amount equal to the member's quota.[48] The maximum effect of the formula is that the adjustment of voting power cannot exceed 25 percent of the voting power based on quota. Adjustment, however, has not had much influence in the affairs of the IMF. The categories of decisions for which adjustment is required are few, the size of adjustments is not substantial, and the occasions on which adjustments could affect the outcome are perhaps rare. It is unlikely that the adjustment of voting power has been a real incentive for members to lend to the IMF.

The second benefit, and probably a more effective one if members are in a strong enough position to make loans, is offered by a different provision. The two members that have made available to the IMF the largest average amounts of resources in use in the two years before a biennial election of Executive Directors may each appoint an Executive Director for the next biennial period if these

---

[47] Article V, Section 12(c), (e).

[48] Article XII, Section 5(b). Joseph Gold, *Voting and Decisions in the International Monetary Fund* (Washington: International Monetary Fund, 1972), pp. 30–43.

members do not appoint an Executive Director because they have one of the five largest quotas.[49] The calculation for this purpose takes into account average resources subscribed or lent by a member and in outstanding use without limit. This provision does not adjust voting power and so can produce no distortion in it among members.[50]

Aspects of Practice Under Article VII

Reasons for Borrowing

The IMF has never attempted to formulate a general policy on when to initiate negotiations to borrow (or on when to compel replenishment by sales of gold before the Second Amendment or by sales of SDRs now). The Articles are admirably vague in providing only that the IMF may borrow if it "deems such action appropriate." It has been said sometimes that subscribed resources take care of normal needs of the IMF and that borrowing can take care of abnormal or exceptional needs. It is, of course, difficult to distinguish between normal and abnormal or exceptional needs, particularly in view of the frequency with which the IMF has entered into agreements to borrow. Four of the last five Managing Directors of the IMF, including the present Managing Director, have taken the initiative to propose borrowing, and the fifth was in office when the First Amendment, to create the SDR, was negotiated.

Abnormal or exceptional need, if indeed there is such a criterion, embraces a variety of ideas, which may be recognized either separately or in some sort of combination as the justification for borrowing in the circumstances that have developed. One idea is that a current or prospective demand for use of the IMF's resources places, or is likely to place, an uncomfortable strain on the resources that are, or will be, suitable for use. A second idea is that the international monetary system faces a present or looming threat. The inadequacy of the IMF's sources, even if there is no other alleged threat to the system, is sometimes considered a threat in itself. A

---

[49] Article XII, Section 3(c).

[50] A sixth or seventh appointment of an Executive Director might upset a desirable composition of the Executive Board, but the Board of Governors can exercise a flexible power to modify the number of seats on the Executive Board (Article XII, Section 3(b)).

third idea is that an improvement in the international monetary system is within reach with the help of additional resources.

Inadequate resources by hypothesis make the case for replenishment according to the first idea. To defend the system against threat or to achieve improvement of the system may make replenishment necessary or advisable to enable the IMF to do what is appropriate in the circumstances. It is difficult to be categorical in selecting a single motive for each resort to borrowing. One example of borrowing[51] in which the predominant impulse can be considered relief from strain on the IMF's resources is the borrowing to help finance the enlarged access policy (1981). The purpose of the policy has been to "provide balance of payments assistance to members facing serious balance of payments imbalances that are large in relation to their quotas"[52] and needing a relatively long period for adjustment and a maximum period for repurchase longer than the traditional three to five years.

Present or prospective strain on the IMF's resources may be the result of outstanding use or reasonably foreseeable requests of considerable magnitude because of the number of existing policies of the IMF, the unusually large amounts that can be provided under one or more of them, commitments to provide resources under stand-by arrangements already approved by the IMF, delay in the effectiveness of a general review of quotas, or a combination of some of these circumstances. Delay in the effectiveness of the Eighth General Review of Quotas showed that borrowing for a brief period might be advisable as well as borrowing for longer periods to relieve both short-run and more prolonged strain.

Borrowing by the IMF to finance transactions under its oil facilities of 1974 and 1975 can be regarded as an example of borrowing to resist a threat to the international monetary system. The policy was designed to assist members to deal with the impact on their balances of payments of the increased costs of importing petroleum and petroleum products without the introduction or intensification of restrictions on trade and payments.

---

[51] For the texts of most agreements to borrow under Article VII, see *Selected Decisions* as follows: original GAB and associated agreements (Ninth Issue, 1981), pp. 105–33; current GAB and associated agreements (Sixteenth Issue, 1991), pp. 286–305; supplementary financing facility (Sixteenth Issue, 1991), pp. 330–39; enlarged access policy (Fourteenth Issue, Annex, 1989), pp. 76–164; oil facility, 1974 and 1975 (Ninth Issue, 1981) pp. 188–200.

[52] *Selected Decisions*, Sixteenth Issue (1991), p. 112.

The GAB is an example of borrowing to facilitate an improvement in the international monetary system. The GAB, which entered into force on October 24, 1962, is of historic interest for many reasons, including the fact that it was the first experiment by the IMF in arranging to borrow. The environment in which the GAB was negotiated was described as follows in the original preamble: "In order to enable the International Monetary Fund to fulfill more effectively its role in the international monetary system in the new conditions of widespread convertibility, including greater freedom for short-term capital movements, ..."[53]

The GAB was intended to help the IMF improve the system by encouraging the spread of convertibility and freedom for exchange markets that began at the end of the 1950s, but the GAB demonstrates the difficulty of choosing a single motive to explain a borrowing arrangement. One reason why it seemed advisable to consider borrowing was an announcement by President Kennedy that the United States might use the IMF's resources. The announcement was welcomed but created concern that the IMF's resources might then be inadequate to meet the requests of all members that might need assistance. Therefore, assurance of the adequacy of the IMF's resources in the special circumstances that were foreseen was an important objective of the GAB.

The preambular language of the GAB as quoted above was changed in 1983 so that it now reads: "In order to enable the International Monetary Fund to fulfill more effectively its role in the international monetary system, ..."[54] Thus, the emphasis on the original motive for the GAB has been softened, and the primary purpose is more the defense than the improvement of the international monetary system. Even the original text of the GAB was ambiguous in this respect, because it referred also to borrowing in support of an exchange transaction or stand-by arrangement of the IMF that the Managing Director considered necessary "to forestall or cope with an impairment of the international monetary system." This language, as well as other provisions, which reflected the sense that the GAB was for the benefit of the United States and its

---

[53] For a detailed account of the origin, terms, and history of the development of the GAB, see Michael Ainley, *The General Arrangements to Borrow*, IMF Pamphlet Series No. 41 (Washington: International Monetary Fund, 1984), and Joseph Gold, *Legal and Institutional Aspects of the International Monetary System: Selected Essays*, Volume II (Washington: International Monetary Fund, 1984), pp. 478–511.

[54] *Selected Decisions*, Sixteenth Issue (1991), pp. 286–329, at p. 286.

hegemonic currency, or mainly for the benefit of that member and the dollar, is still present in the current text. The GAB is now usually regarded by members and others as an arrangement reserved for dealing with emergencies that threaten the system.

Although a strain on the IMF's resources has not been considered in itself the justification for invoking the GAB, the need for supplementary resources has always been a condition. In other words, the GAB is not available even if there is a need to replenish the IMF's resources unless there is an actual or threatened impairment of the international monetary system, but equally the GAB is not available even though there is an actual or threatened impairment if the IMF can respond to it effectively with the resources already available to it.

Special Policies and Transactions

It will be apparent from the discussion so far that the IMF has borrowed in support of such special policies on the use of its resources as the oil facility, the SFF, and the enlarged access policy. The IMF concluded that it would not have been able to establish such policies without borrowing. In addition, however, the IMF has borrowed, not to finance a special policy, but to finance commitments under stand-by arrangements or transactions under its basic policy, the so-called credit tranche policy. The GAB is an arrangement that was designed for this latter purpose and was not associated with a new policy on the use of the IMF's resources that the IMF would have been unable, or at least reluctant, to establish without the assurance of borrowing specifically in support of the policy.

The existence of the GAB deterred participants from lending to the IMF outside those arrangements to finance assistance under the credit tranche policy. In the 1960s, there was some disposition within the IMF staff to negotiate a ring of bilateral borrowing agreements so as to avoid the complicated procedures of the GAB and to get firm assurances of loans by individual members. It was hoped by this strategy to circumvent the obstruction the participants in the GAB had erected by agreeing among themselves that their joint acquiescence would be necessary as a condition of lending by any of them under the GAB. In addition, the strategy might have enabled the IMF to avoid the demand for concomitant sales of some of its gold that the participants, when approached for loans, had insisted on as a condition of their acquiescence in activation of the

GAB. The efforts of the IMF to negotiate a competing ring of bilateral agreements failed.

In 1966, however, the IMF did enter into a bilateral borrowing arrangement of a unique character in its practice. Italy had accumulated large reserves of U.S. dollars and wished to obtain a guarantee in some form of the gold value of at least part of these holdings. Italy would probably have requested the conversion of some of its holdings with gold or lire by the United States. Lire could be purchased by the United States from the IMF for the conversion of dollars under Article VIII, Section 4, the provision on the obligation of a member to convert foreign official holdings of its currency. If the United States purchased lire under the provision, the effect would be to increase the entitlement of Italy to make purchases from the IMF, the value of which was guaranteed in relation to gold. A conversion by means of such a transaction by the United States, however, was not feasible at the time because the IMF's holdings of lire were at too low an ebb. The solution was an arrangement by which the IMF borrowed lire from Italy and sold them in a transaction with the United States, which used them to redeem Italy's holdings of an equivalent amount of dollars. As a result of this arrangement, Italy obtained a right, guaranteed in gold value, to repayment by the IMF in lire or another convertible currency or in gold itself.[55] The financial terms of the agreement to borrow from Italy were patterned on those of the GAB.

The arrangement as described above provided an impetus for further efforts on the part of the management and staff of the IMF to arrange a series of bilateral loan agreements of a stand-by character. They could be either in standard form or they could vary with the circumstances and according to the wishes of a potential lender. To promote the idea, it was suggested that the borrowings might be used exclusively for financing members' transactions in the gold tranche.[56] The object was to induce members to lend by offering

---

[55] It was not overlooked by some observers that the IMF's policies on the selection of currencies for use in its transactions would have justified the sale of other strong currencies when the IMF's holdings of lire were low. The issuers of all the currencies sold, and not simply Italy, would then have benefited from the arrangement by improving their gold tranche positions in the IMF.

[56] The gold tranche represented a net use the IMF had made of a member's subscription. The IMF gave members the assurance, de facto before the First Amendment and de jure under it, that a member would be able to make automatic and unconditional use of the IMF's resources in an amount equivalent to the member's gold tranche.

them a guarantee of the safety of their gold tranche—their reserve assets in the IMF. The offer was not a sufficient inducement, perhaps because gold tranches seemed safe enough, and no arrangements of the kind proposed were entered into.

For the present purpose, the borrowing from Italy demonstrates the flexible use that can be made of Article VII, Section 2. In particular, the episode shows that borrowing is feasible even if it is not in support of a new policy of the IMF on the use of its resources, or associated with an improvement in the international monetary system, or intended to forestall or deal with a threat to the system. It might be said, however, that in protecting the gold stock of the United States by making it unnecessary for Italy to demand gold from the United States in performance of its undertaking to buy and sell gold with other members for the settlement of international transactions, the borrowing helped in a modest way to avoid a threat to the system.

Joint and Single Lenders

A distinction has been drawn between borrowing by the IMF from a group of lenders jointly and borrowing from lenders separately. The latter kind of borrowing may be from a single member or from a number of members under individual agreements but for a common purpose. The archetype of joint lending is the GAB. The joint character of the arrangement is evident, for example, in the provision that the GAB was not to become effective unless a specified number of potential participants with a specified total of credit commitments adhered to the GAB as contracting parties. Other terms provide for joint procedures of the participants—which they have supplemented by understandings among themselves—and for proportionate loans of the currencies of participants in a borrowing, as well as proportionate repayments to lending participants. A feature of an agreement such as the GAB is that as there is only one agreement between the IMF and the participants as a group, the terms and conditions are necessarily the same for all participants unless special provisions are included for a nonmember participant, such as those made for the Swiss National Bank.

A joint arrangement such as the GAB can be distinguished from the practice followed in borrowing from 7 members or central banks to help finance the 1974 oil facility and from 12 such lenders for the purpose of the 1975 oil facility. The IMF established standard terms and offered them to potential lenders, but subject to the understanding expressed in the IMF's decision to borrow that the terms and conditions could be adapted for good reason in individual cases, such as domestic legal requirements or the character of the lending institution. Clearly, this qualification was not meant to encourage substantive departures from the standard form of agreement, and in particular from the financial terms. The IMF did not enter into a joint agreement with all lenders under these arrangements. The possible lenders to be approached for the GAB and the oil facility arrangements were chosen by the IMF, but the lenders for the oil facility did not constitute themselves into a group or follow common procedures. Nevertheless, the IMF's decision to authorize borrowing for the oil facility contained undertakings on proportionate calls for advances under the individual agreements and on proportionate repayments. These undertakings were not included in the agreements and so were not subject to individual negotiation.

A feature of the agreements, however, was that the IMF could call for loans from a lender under an existing agreement either to finance transactions under the oil facility or to repay a borrowing by the IMF from a lender under another agreement of the same kind. This term was evidence that the lenders regarded themselves as having common interests.

The provision enabling the IMF to borrow to repay indebtedness incurred to finance transactions under the oil facility followed the precedent of the original GAB. Under that arrangement, if the IMF's holdings of currencies in which early repayment of a participant's claim should be made were not wholly adequate, the IMF could approach individual participants to provide the necessary balance under the GAB. They were not bound to make loans for this purpose, and therefore the GAB prescribed the form in which the IMF would make repayment if they refused to lend. Borrowing to repay indebtedness under the original GAB (or the oil facility) created no legal problem, because until the Second Amendment became effective the IMF's power to borrow was not restricted to the financing of "transactions." It will be recalled that the provision of the GAB on borrowing to repay indebtedness[57] has not been amended in the revised GAB and that the provision cannot be reconciled with the present Articles.

The arrangements to borrow from 14 members and central banks to finance the SFF followed the model of the earlier arrangements to

[57] *Selected Decisions*, Sixteenth Issue (1991), p. 292.

finance the oil facility. The IMF entered into individual agreements but again based on a common form. The IMF reserved somewhat more flexibility to accept departures from that form: the terms and conditions would be "uniform to the maximum extent possible." The IMF undertook a commitment to observe proportionality in calling for advances, but again with the prospect of greater diversity under the SFF. For the purpose of the oil facility, the IMF would "take into account" the formula for proportionality, but in the case of the SFF the IMF would observe the formula "subject to such operational flexibility as the Fund may find necessary." The IMF gave no commitment on proportional repayments. The agreements included authority to borrow from a lender to repay another lender under the SFF, but these agreements also were entered into before the Second Amendment.

The discussion so far has noted three distinct techniques for borrowing: a joint agreement with lenders to finance transactions of the IMF but not for the purpose of a special policy; a set of separate agreements in more or less standardized form to finance transactions under a special policy of the IMF; and a single agreement to finance a single transaction of an unusual character. All these techniques have provided for the lender to make loans to the IMF. Two further techniques will now be noted. One of them has been an agreement with the IMF in such form as is appropriate when a lender links its lending in some way with the GAB, and therefore not for the purpose of financing transactions under a special policy of the IMF. The agreements in this form have been few but diverse in form and content.

In 1974, the Swiss Confederation entered into an agreement with the IMF under which the Confederation undertook to consider lending resources directly to a participant in the GAB when the IMF activated the GAB for the benefit of the participant. The terms and conditions of this agreement with the IMF were to some extent, but not broadly, assimilated to those of the GAB.

In contrast to this agreement, the Swiss National Bank, in 1976, entered into an agreement with the IMF to lend to the IMF for the purpose of helping to finance transactions under a stand-by arrangement approved by the IMF for the United Kingdom. The IMF had activated the GAB for the benefit of the United Kingdom under the stand-by arrangement. The terms and conditions of this agreement with the Swiss National Bank were closely assimilated to those of the GAB. Again, in 1977, the Swiss National Bank entered into a similar agreement with the IMF in similar circumstances, but on this occasion for the benefit of Italy.

The borrowings by the IMF under the 1976 and 1977 agreements were not made under the 1974 agreement with the Swiss Confederation, and they differed from that earlier agreement in expressing a commitment related to a specific stand-by arrangement of the IMF instead of a general understanding not designed for the benefit of a particular member. These two agreements can be grouped with the agreement to borrow from Italy for the purpose of facilitating the conversion of dollar holdings—even though the purpose of the two agreements was not unusual—rather than grouping them with agreements of general association with the GAB. The Swiss National Bank became a participant in the GAB in 1983, which raised the number of participants from 10 to 11, and eliminated the need for an association agreement on the part of Switzerland.

The other agreement of association with the GAB was entered into by Saudi Arabia on the occasion of the revision and substantial enlargement of the GAB in 1983. Most of the provisions of this association agreement parallel corresponding provisions of the GAB. The association agreement, like the GAB, is of a stand-by character, running for five years but subject to renewal, with the expectation that it will be renewed. In this respect, the GAB and the association agreement of Saudi Arabia differ from all other borrowing agreements of the IMF so far, because these other agreements have not been timeless in concept. They have been designed for financing particular policies that are subject to expiration or for financing a specified stand-by arrangement or transaction.

The fifth technique to be noted relates to borrowing by the IMF in accordance with agreements for financing transactions under the enlarged access policy. Of these 22 agreements with members, central banks, and the Bank for International Settlements (BIS), all have been for borrowing over the short term, 1 over the medium term, and 18 over the longer term. The technique of these agreements differs from other techniques for borrowing from a number of lenders in support of the same policy on the use of the IMF's resources. The difference is not that individual agreements have been entered into, but that the agreements have been entered into at different dates over a substantial number of years, are not standardized, and indeed vary much more among themselves than under any other technique for borrowing from more than one lender for a common purpose. The agreements contain little evidence of an interrelationship among them, even though the enlarged access policy was not to become effective until the borrowing agreements contemplated by the IMF were concluded. Even if there is little or no legal interrelationship among agreements, individual lenders may have resolved not to enter into an agreement to lend unless other prospective lenders undertook a similar obligation.

Agreements to help finance transactions under the enlarged access policy are examples of the fifth technique. A complex agreement for medium-term borrowing for this purpose was entered into by the IMF with SAMA in 1981, followed by a supplementary agreement in 1984 and amendments in 1986. A few terms of these agreements have been incorporated in other agreements, but on the whole the agreements with SAMA have not been a model for wider use. In 1981, the IMF entered into an agreement with the BIS in support of the enlarged access policy, but in a form that differed from the agreement with SAMA and from pre-1981 agreements. Also in 1981, the IMF decided ("the readiness decision") that it would stand ready to enter into an agreement with any member, the central bank or other agency of any member, or any official entity prescribed by the IMF as a holder of SDRs, on terms and conditions substantially the same as those of the 1981 agreement with the BIS, except as those terms and conditions might be adjusted and supplemented by the provisions of the readiness decision. The IMF entered into 17 agreements on the model of the 1981 agreement with the BIS.

Later in the 1980s, the IMF entered into agreements with the BIS, SAMA, the Government of Japan, and the National Bank of Belgium, but not in accordance with the terms of the readiness decision. Subsequent amendments were made in all these agreements. The terms and conditions differed from the model of the readiness decision and differed even among these four agreements, notwithstanding the fact that the IMF considered them at the same time and that they entered into force at the same date.

An unusual feature of the 1981 agreement with SAMA is that although there was no explicit relationship between that agreement and any other agreement that the IMF might enter into, SAMA obtained a guarantee that, given the contingencies mentioned below, it too would have the benefit of any more favorable terms enjoyed by other lenders under subsequent agreements entered into by the IMF. The subsequent agreements thus referred to were not confined to those that might be for the support of the enlarged access policy, but the period of two years mentioned in the next paragraph as part of the first (but not the second) contingency gave some assurance that the other agreements also would be for financing the enlarged access policy.

The contingencies for activation of the guarantee were that the IMF entered into an agreement with a member or its central bank (1) during the period of two years following entry into force of the agreement with SAMA, on financial terms in the later agreement that could reasonably be regarded by either SAMA or the IMF as more favorable to the lender than those of the agreement with SAMA, or (2) contained provisions under which the IMF waived immunity from judicial process with respect to the settlement of disputes. In either situation, SAMA and the IMF would consult at the request of SAMA and with a view to amending the SAMA agreement in order to give SAMA comparable financial terms or a comparable waiver of immunity with respect to loans by SAMA under the agreement and notes issued by the IMF as a result of borrowing under the agreement. A similar consultation for the purpose of reaching agreement on an amendment is to be held at the request of SAMA if, at any time while any loan by SAMA under the agreement is outstanding, the IMF issues notes containing a more extensive waiver of immunity than has been made available to the holders of notes, whoever they might be, issued by the IMF under the SAMA agreement.

SAMA insisted on another safeguard: if at any time while a loan by SAMA under its agreement was outstanding, the IMF gave security in respect of indebtedness under any other borrowing agreement, SAMA was to have equal and ratable security for outstanding loans under its agreement. In addition, if the IMF created other indebtedness that ranked ahead of its indebtedness under the SAMA agreement, repayment to SAMA was to rank pari passu with such other indebtedness in respect of the priority of repayment.

In view of the diversity of practice developed so far, it may be useful to express some broad distinctions between leading characteristics of many of the agreements mentioned so far.

1. A joint agreement of the IMF with lenders; individual agreements with lenders.
2. An agreement regarded as permanent (though subject to periodic renewal); agreements regarded as impermanent.
3. Agreements in support of the credit tranche policy; agreements in support of a special policy.
4. Individual agreements in support of the same policy and in more or less standard form; agreements in support of the same policy but not in such form.
5. Agreements to finance various stand-by arrangements or transactions under the same policy; agreements to finance a single stand-by arrangement or transaction.

Procedure

The normal procedure for borrowing is that the Managing Director initiates and negotiates a proposal to borrow from entities he regards as appropriate potential lenders in the circumstances giving rise to the proposal. The Managing Director proposes the amount and the financial and other terms and prepares draft agreements. Usually, he approaches potential lenders after the Executive Board has decided, or at least reacted favorably to his recommendation, that a special policy on the use of the IMF's resources should be adopted, if indeed he thinks that a special policy is advisable and that it should be financed wholly or partly with borrowed resources.

The Managing Director has sometimes negotiated with potential lenders individually, and sometimes with a group of them at the same time as on the occasions when he negotiated the GAB and financing for the SFF. The agreements that emerge from these negotiations become effective only after they are approved by both the willing lenders or group of willing lenders and the Executive Board. The degree of collegiality among lenders, the relative amounts they are willing to lend, the interrelationships among the agreements, the adherence of all parties to a single agreement or the use of individual agreements have depended to some extent on the procedure followed by the Managing Director in negotiating the agreements. Often in the history of the IMF, procedure has had a decisive influence on substance, with the consequence that procedure itself has sometimes been controversial.[58]

Contractual Obligation and Discretion to Lend

In the negotiation of the GAB, participants were fearful that the strength of the United States in the IMF might be powerful enough to enable that member to use the resources of the IMF, supplemented by resources advanced under the GAB, without meeting the criteria of the credit tranche policy that all members are supposed to satisfy. The GAB provided, therefore, and still provides, that a proposal by the Managing Director for loans under the GAB becomes effective only if accepted by the participants and then ap-

---

[58] See Joseph Gold, *Legal and Institutional Aspects of the International Monetary System: Selected Essays* (Washington: International Monetary Fund, 1979), pp. 217–37 ("International Monetary System and Change: Relations Between Mode of Negotiation and Legal Technique"); pp. 238–91 (" 'Political' Bodies in the Fund").

proved by the Executive Board. The participants have agreed in an independent instrument of their own ("the Baumgartner letter" of December 15, 1961) on the procedure they will follow for deciding whether to accept a proposal. If, in reacting to a proposal, the participants are not unanimous, they vote, with voting power proportioned to the amounts of their participation in the GAB, and with special majorities of the number of participants and the volume of voting power required for a decision to accept a proposal. The participant that is to be the beneficiary of borrowing by the IMF under the GAB is not entitled to vote in this procedure. In all these matters, the participants have departed, as they are free to depart, from the model of the Articles on voting power and decisions. If the participants decide to accept a proposal, further consultations are held with the Managing Director on the amount to be provided by each of the participants that are going to make loans.

It is obvious that the GAB does not impose an obligation on any participant to lend when the Managing Director proposes to borrow from participants. The GAB raises the question whether it is an international agreement, because in systems of national law a commitment to "lend" only if "the lender" sees fit is not regarded as a contract.[59] The management, staff, and many members of the IMF have always disliked the discretionary character of the GAB, but not for reasons of legal taxonomy: the objection is that the IMF has no assurance that resources will be forthcoming to finance transactions or support a particular policy. The IMF, however, could not reasonably object to the reservation of a similar discretion by the Swiss Confederation in its former agreement for association with the GAB and by Saudi Arabia in its present association agreement.

The IMF has not entered into any other borrowing agreement under Article VII in which the potential lender has reserved the discretion to decide whether to comply with a call for advances under the agreement. Nevertheless, although all other agreements bind the lender to lend on call by the IMF, participants have some other discretionary rights with respect to their commitments. The right to request early repayment has been discussed already. In addition, a participant in the GAB on which the Managing Director proposes to make calls may protest in the procedure under the Baumgartner letter that, because of the participant's present and

---

[59] Ibid., pp. 446–68 ("On the Difficulties of Defining International Agreements: Some Illustrations from the Experience of the Fund").

prospective balance of payments and reserve position, calls should not be made on it or should be made for an amount smaller than is proposed. The other participants then consult among themselves in order to provide substitute amounts. If a proposal for a call on a participant has become effective, the participant may give notice to the IMF that, for the reason mentioned above, calls should no longer be made or should be made for a smaller amount. The Managing Director may then propose to other participants that they should provide substitute amounts. The original proposal remains effective unless and until it is settled that other participants will provide substitute amounts.[60]

The association agreement with the Swiss Confederation while in force contained a provision enabling the lender to withhold or reduce requested advances under an effective proposal because, in the lender's opinion, its present and prospective balance of payments and reserve position justified this reaction. The present association agreement with Saudi Arabia contains a similar provision.

The association agreement with the Swiss Confederation gave it an unchallengeable right to react in this way, but in the case of Saudi Arabia, a member of the IMF, its representation receives "the overwhelming benefit of any doubt." The practical effect of this inspissated formulation, however, is that a challenge by the IMF of the alleged justification of the present and prospective balance of payments and reserve position, though not legally precluded, is highly unlikely. A similar formulation has been used in the standard borrowing agreements to help finance the SFF, except that in those agreements the reference to the balance of payments and reserve position included no mention of the prospective position. The formulation of the overwhelming benefit of any doubt goes back to the time when the original Articles prevented a de jure undertaking by the IMF that it would not challenge requests for transactions in the gold tranche.[61] The de facto assurance left open the possibility, though slim, of challenge by the IMF. Inclusion of the language in borrowing agreements has been considered useful because the possibility of challenge, though again remote, gives the IMF the oppor-

---

[60] Under the 1976 and 1977 agreements of the Swiss National Bank to lend for helping to finance transactions under stand-by arrangements for the United Kingdom and Italy, the Bank was entitled to reduce its commitment proportionately if the total amount of possible calls under the GAB for the benefit of these members was reduced below a specified amount.

[61] See footnote 56.

tunity to contest a lender's clearly unjustifiable effort to derogate from its commitment to comply with calls.

The agreement with Saudi Arabia in support of the enlarged access policy includes a different provision. Saudi Arabia may represent to the IMF that the country's balance of payments and reserve position does not justify further calls and may request the IMF to suspend such calls. The IMF is able to determine whether or not suspension is justified. No mention is made of the overwhelming benefit of any doubt in response to the representation, perhaps because of skepticism that a representation would be sustainable. The standard form of agreement for borrowing from central banks and other official institutions in support of the enlarged access policy on terms similar to those of the agreement with the BIS does refer, however, to the overwhelming benefit of any doubt that the IMF gives to a lender's representation with respect to the balance of payments and reserve position. A similar provision appears in the agreements with Japan and the National Bank of Belgium in support of the enlarged access policy.

Lenders

It is sometimes said that the concept of the IMF as an international monetary organization is that the monetary authorities of members pool a portion of the national reserves for use by the IMF in accordance with its Articles. This concept is clearer than ever in the present Articles, under which a member pays part of its subscription in SDRs or the currencies of other members selected by the IMF; and the member is bound, if requested when its currency is purchased from the IMF, to exchange it for a currency deemed by the IMF to be "freely usable" if the purchased currency is not itself of that character.[62] As replenishment under Article VII provides the IMF with resources that supplement subscriptions, it is logical to assume that members should be regarded as the primary potential lenders. It has been seen that the origin of the IMF's power to borrow was the desire to find a compromise with those who, like Keynes, favored an open-ended commitment as the responsibility for the proper functioning of the international monetary system that members in balance of payments surplus should bear.

The IMF's practice in borrowing under Article VII has recognized the desirability of lending by members, including their official

---

[62] Article III, Section 3; Article V, Section 3; Article XXX(f).

institutions that exercise national monetary functions, as a manifestation of the responsibility of members for the effective functioning
of the IMF. It is clear, however, that the proper functioning of the
international monetary system has been given greater weight insofar
as realization of that objective depends on adequacy of the IMF's
resources. Therefore, Article VII has always empowered the IMF to
borrow resources from any willing lenders. Lenders that are not
members are referred to simply as "some other source," without
limitation, and to make it clear that there is no limitation, it is added
that they may be "either within or outside the territories of the
member" whose currency the IMF deems it appropriate to borrow.
In view of the breadth of the IMF's power to borrow, it must be
understood that the concept of pooling some portion of members'
monetary reserves is not preclusive: the IMF may borrow resources
that are not part of a member's monetary reserves. Furthermore,
there is not even a condition that the lenders must be subject to the
jurisdiction of the member whose currency the IMF borrows, although the need for the member's concurrence enables it to control
the IMF's borrowing of the currency from both domestic and external entities willing to lend.

The IMF has relied most heavily on borrowing from the monetary
authorities of members, and even when the IMF has borrowed
under Article VII from other sources, it has borrowed from official
entities within the international monetary system: Switzerland, its
National Bank, and the BIS. The IMF has not borrowed hitherto
from nonofficial entities, although there has been some flirtation
with the idea because of difficulty or delay in increasing quotas.[63]

The IMF and its members have been unwilling to risk weakening
the status of the IMF as the central institution of the international
monetary system by diluting the sense of responsibility of the
membership for the IMF and the system that might result from
looking to the market for replenishing the General Resources Account. In addition, members have not wanted to risk the reduction
of their influence over the policies of the IMF.

Nevertheless, the borrowing agreement with one lender, SAMA,
has important features that would be of interest to nonofficial
lenders. Indeed, the agreement with SAMA could result in financial
obligations of the IMF to nonofficial obligees, which they would be
able to enforce by judicial process. These features of the agreement

---

[63] See Joseph Gold, "Borrowing by the International Monetary Fund from Nonofficial Lenders," *International Lawyer* (Chicago), Vol. 20 (1986), pp. 461–62, 465.

were unprecedented in the experience of the IMF. In the negotiation of the agreement, SAMA was represented by private American legal advisers who may have sought safeguards, not only because of their experience with commercial lending, but also because of the fears inspired by the action of the United States in freezing official assets of the Islamic Republic of Iran. The amount that could be borrowed under the agreement with SAMA was substantial. Repayment might be made in U.S. dollars and the dollars might be held within the reach of the prescriptive jurisdiction of the United States.

The unusual terms and conditions, some of which have been referred to already, include covenants with respect to equal and ratable security; pari passu treatment of indebtedness in the ranking of lenders for repayment; and comparable benefits if the IMF should agree to more favorable financial terms or waivers of immunity under subsequent borrowing agreements with other lenders. A default under any subsequent security arrangement between the IMF and another lender was to be deemed a default under the agreement with SAMA, and on default SAMA could terminate its agreement and demand accelerated repayment. Any question between SAMA and the IMF concerning their rights and obligations that did not relate to interpretation of the Articles and could not be settled by agreement was to be submitted to arbitrators.

The agreement with SAMA authorizes it to assign its claims against the IMF under the agreement to certain specified official entities, but there is nothing original in that provision. The contrast with earlier practice is to be found in another, and as at the date of entry into the agreement, completely novel set of provisions. At any time, SAMA could request the IMF to deliver promissory notes in bearer form in exchange for any part of any claim to repayment. No limitations were placed on possible transferees of the bearer notes, so that they could be official or private holders. If SAMA retained notes, it could demand payment of them by the IMF in any currency, other than U.S. dollars, included in the basket of currencies by reference to which the value of the SDR is defined.

The bearer of a note could demand payment of it by any one or more of the financial institutions acceptable to SAMA that the IMF was required to designate as paying agents in Frankfurt, London, New York, Paris, and Tokyo. The bearer of a note had the option to demand payment by a paying agent outside New York by a check drawn on a bank in New York. The notes were to be governed by and construed in accordance with the laws of the State of New York. If the IMF failed to pay any amount due under a note or an interest coupon attached to it, the bearer could sue in designated courts in New York, England, or the Canton of Geneva. For this purpose, the IMF irrevocably waived its immunity from suit in these courts, and also from execution of a final judgment in any member country or in Switzerland. The IMF undertook to appoint agents to receive process in any action instituted in the courts in which the IMF waived immunity from suit. If the IMF failed to comply with a request for notes, the rights and obligations of SAMA and the IMF were to be determined not by the provisions of the agreement but by the provisions of the model note appended to the agreement.

Whether the terms of the agreement with SAMA outlined above will become precedents for future borrowing agreements under Article VII cannot be predicted. The 1981 agreement with the BIS did not contain the novel provisions of the agreement with SAMA that have been outlined above. The standard agreements for borrowing from central banks and other official institutions on terms similar to the 1981 agreement with the BIS, however, did contain terms and conditions on the issuance of bearer notes that resemble the provisions of the agreement with SAMA on this matter. The probable reason was not so much the fear of another freeze of assets by the United States as the effort to fortify the case that the loans were squarely within the investment powers of the central banks and other lenders. Later, a freeze by the United States of Libya's official assets did occur, but it did not impel the BIS, the Government of Japan, or the National Bank of Belgium to insist on the inclusion of provisions with respect to bearer notes in their subsequent agreements with the IMF in 1984.

Beneficiaries

With only one exception, the borrowing agreements of the IMF under Article VII have not been entered into for the express purpose of financing use of the IMF's resources by a selected number of specified members. The special policies in support of which the IMF has borrowed have included criteria for use of the resources under the policies, but the members likely to meet the criteria were not named.

A different procedure was followed in the case of an agreement that was not for the support of a special policy: the agreement was the original GAB. Under it, the IMF could borrow only to finance use of the IMF's resources by the eight participating members and the two members whose central banks were participants. This limitation provoked sharp and sustained criticism on the part of numerous nonparticipants. The participants replied that the GAB made more of the IMF's ordinary resources available for use by other members than would have been available if the GAB had not reduced strain on the resources. Eventually, however, revision of the GAB opened up the possibility of borrowing by the IMF to finance the use of its resources by nonparticipants without any specified selection among them.

Borrowing to finance transactions by nonparticipants, however, is subject to restrictive conditions that do not apply to borrowing for the benefit of participants. First, the use of the IMF's resources by nonparticipants financed wholly or partly by borrowing under the GAB must meet the IMF's more demanding standards of conditionality. Second, the Managing Director may initiate the procedure leading to borrowing for the benefit of nonparticipants only if he considers that the IMF "faces an inadequacy of resources to meet actual and expected requests for financing that reflect the existence of an exceptional situation associated with balance of payments problems of members of a character or aggregate size that could threaten the stability of the international monetary system."[64] Third, in making proposals for calls for this purpose, the Managing Director must pay due regard to potential calls for the benefit of participants.

Switzerland as a nonmember could not have the benefit of the revised GAB even though the Swiss National Bank became a participant in the GAB with effect from April 10, 1984. The Articles do not allow a nonmember to use the IMF's resources. Switzerland's position was prima facie less advantageous than it had been under its agreement for association with the GAB. Switzerland could not use the IMF's resources as a result of that agreement also, but it provided that Switzerland would consider making resources available to a participant in the GAB only under an implementing agreement that required reciprocal financial assistance between Switzerland and the participant if Switzerland wished to have reciprocity.[65]

Some Institutional Effects of Borrowing

In an investigation of the institutional effects of borrowing by the IMF, the Group of Ten comes to mind immediately, because it

---

[64] *Selected Decisions*, Sixteenth Issue (1991), p. 296.

[65] For a description of some financial features of the IMF's borrowing arrangements, see Treasurer's Department, *Financial Organization and Operations of the IMF*, IMF Pamphlet Series No. 45 (Washington: International Monetary Fund, Second Edition, 1991).

emerged solely as a result of the GAB. The Managing Director and his assistants who negotiated the GAB foresaw the possibility that the ten potential lenders might assume a de facto collective personality and act through their Governors and Executive Directors as a steering group in the IMF, in which they would have a substantial preponderance of voting power. Evidence of the attempt to forestall this development can be detected in certain provisions of both the original and the current version of the GAB. The effort by the IMF's negotiators to have these provisions included in the GAB succeeded, but this success did not prevent the emergence of the Ten as a de facto collectivity. Almost at once, the participants assumed the role that had been feared and began to take initiatives in matters involving the IMF, to the vast annoyance of members that were not participants and the disappointment of the IMF's negotiators.

Only a few comments need be made here on the Group of Ten. The Group sometimes has justified its activities by claiming to have a de jure function as a kind of instrumentality of the IMF, with the provisions of the GAB as the Group's charter. In more recent years, the Group has viewed the will of the ten, and now eleven, countries as the source of its birthright, rather than the agreement of these countries with the IMF.

The view that the Group of Ten has been responsible in one way or another for the creation of other durable groups in the international monetary system is not too extreme. This view is safe enough to help explain the formation of the Group of Twenty-Four by developing countries, but it may be that in addition the Group of Ten has had some influence in bringing the Groups of Five and Seven into existence as clubs designed to be even more exclusive in composition than the Group of Ten. In any event, there is no doubt that adverse reactions to the Group of Ten by nonparticipants in the GAB has been a major political influence in establishing the model for the composition of important bodies within the IMF. These bodies are not organs of the IMF and they do not take decisions of the IMF or bind its members, but they deal with issues of policy on which the guidance of persons having ministerial rank is advisable or necessary for the resolution of contested issues within the organization. To be effective, these bodies must not be excessive in size, but their composition must be seen to be a microcosm of the total membership of the IMF. The only model, it is now clear, that meets this test of what has been called legitimacy is the structure of the Executive Board. This model determined the composition of the Committee of Twenty, and now controls the composition of the

Interim Committee. The composition of the Development Committee follows the model of the Executive Board of the IMF and of the World Bank for alternating periods of two years.

Another consequence of the GAB has been clarification of an important aspect of the authority of members to use the IMF's resources. As recalled earlier, a primary objective of the original GAB was to supplement the IMF's resources to help it assist members that suffered outflows of short-term capital in the new conditions of greater freedom for the markets. A problem that had to be solved before negotiation of the GAB could be undertaken was the effect of the prohibition in the original Articles of "net use" of the IMF's resources to meet "a large or sustained outflow of capital" from a member country. The IMF was empowered by the Articles to request a member to exercise controls to prevent such use, and a member that did not comply could be declared ineligible to use the IMF's resources. These provisions are still included in the Articles.[66] In 1946, the United States, attempting to meet the concern of Congressional and other critics, requested the IMF to adopt an authoritative interpretation of the Articles on the proper use of the IMF's resources. In response to the request, the IMF decided that use of the IMF's resources was "limited" to temporary assistance in financing balance of payments deficits on current account for monetary stabilization operations.[67]

The interpretation ignored much language in the Articles on capital transfers and was too restrictive. The words "large" and "sustained" were the main issues in a re-examination in 1961 of the interpretation and of all relevant provisions in the new conditions of the day and in the light of the practice already followed by the IMF. "Sustained" was not a lofty hurdle, because it could be surmounted by understanding the word to refer to timely repurchase by a member that was using the IMF's resources. Repurchase would be facilitated by reflows of short-term capital. As for "large," that word ceased to be an obstruction once it was realized that the measurement made to determine whether use was "large" could take account of the volume of resources available to the IMF.[68] If they were supplemented adequately by borrowing, the IMF could

---

[66] Article VI, Section 1(*a*) (original and present Articles).

[67] *Selected Decisions*, Sixteenth Issue (1991), p. 55.

[68] The meaning of "large" could not be rigidly determined by the size of quotas in view of the IMF's wide powers under Article V, Section 4 to waive limits on the use of the IMF's resources related to quotas.

conclude that, notwithstanding capital outflow from a member, there was sufficient leeway for its use of the IMF's resources in accordance with the provisions of the Articles without prejudice to the IMF's ability to supply resources for financing deficits on current account.

The way was open to negotiation of the GAB. The clarification meant also that the problem did not arise in connection with any of the subsequent borrowing agreements of the IMF. These agreements have enabled the IMF to expand existing policies and initiate new policies on the use of its resources.

A policy made possible in this way has sometimes helped to settle disputed issues of the IMF's practice. For example, at one time there was a division of opinion on the propriety of including in stand-by arrangements a term that interrupted a member's right to make further purchases if the member introduced new or intensified existing restrictions on trade transactions. Some critics objected to this practice on the ground that the IMF's jurisdiction to approve or disapprove restrictions was confined to restrictions on payments and transfers for current international transactions and did not extend to restrictions on the trade or other current account transactions themselves. The decision on the oil facility, however, provided that a member would not be able to make purchases under the policy unless the IMF was satisfied that the member was not introducing or intensifying restrictions on payments and transfers for current international transactions or on the transactions themselves.

The true issue was not the IMF's regulatory jurisdiction to approve or disapprove restrictive measures but the proper use of the IMF's resources. It has now become normal practice to include in stand-by or extended arrangements a term that suspends a member's right to make new uses of resources under an arrangement if the member "imposes [or intensifies] import restrictions for balance of payments reasons" or "imposes [or intensifies] restrictions on payments and transfers for current international transactions."[69] After suspension, consultations are held to determine in what circumstances the right to make new uses can be resumed.

---

[69] *Selected Decisions*, Sixteenth Issue (1991), pp. 129, 134. The use of the IMF's resources explains the contrast between the practice discussed in the text and the proposed voluntary declaration on trade and other current account measures, which has not and will not take effect even though it was carefully drafted to avoid any assertion of regulatory jurisdiction by the IMF over trade and other current account measures for balance of payments reasons (ibid., pp. 366–69).

For some of its practices, the IMF has had to make a distinction between borrowed resources and other ("ordinary") resources of the General Resources Account. (The correct distinction is between ordinary and borrowed resources and not the frequently made distinction between "owned" and "borrowed" resources, because the IMF owns both of them.) Under the enlarged access policy, the IMF's charges for the use of its resources financed by borrowing exceed the charges for use financed with ordinary resources. The net cost of borrowing and an additional margin enter into determination of the first of these two categories of charges.[70] To ensure fairness among members using resources under the enlarged access policy, the IMF has adopted a decision on the proportions of the two kinds of resources to be drawn on in financing use by members under the enlarged access policy.[71] A similar practice has been followed for the SFF.[72] Under both the enlarged access policy and the SFF, a distinction has been made between the two kinds of resources for the purpose of repurchase also. A longer period may be allowed before repurchases must be made in respect of use financed with borrowed resources.[73]

Another consequence of borrowing is the IMF's conclusion that it is advisable to adopt guidelines—a word the IMF understands to connote a degree of flexibility—on the combined total of outstanding borrowing by the IMF and unexecuted contractual undertakings to lend (or to consider lending) to it. A number of conflicting considerations entered into determination of the guidelines. For example, lenders might wish to set a limit lower than the one preferred by members likely to use the IMF's resources: the lenders might dwell on protection of their claims to repayment while other members might wish to be assured that the IMF would have sufficient resources to meet their needs. However, members in both classes might not favor a limit too high in relation to quotas, so as not to discourage consensus on increases in quotas. At the same time, too low a limit might provoke frequent negotiations on increases in

---

[70] Rules and Regulations, Rule I-6(5). Furthermore, if transactions under the enlarged access policy have been financed with amounts available under the decision on supplementary financing and resources borrowed under the enlarged access policy, the former amounts are deemed to have been used before the latter amounts (*Selected Decisions*, Sixteenth Issue (1991), p. 115).

[71] *Selected Decisions*, Sixteenth Issue (1991), pp. 118–19.

[72] Ibid., pp. 190–91.

[73] Ibid., pp. 115, 191. Rules and Regulations, Rule G-4(c).

quotas and might shake the confidence of lenders in the soundness of the IMF's capacity to repay indebtedness.

The guidelines as adopted declare that the IMF will not allow the total of outstanding borrowing and the unused portions of all types of credit lines under Article VII to exceed the range of 50 percent to 60 percent of total quotas. In calculating the total of outstanding borrowing and the unused portions of credit lines, the IMF applies a special formula to the GAB and associated borrowing agreements, because not all participants and associated lenders might be in a balance of payments and reserve position that would justify contemporaneous lending by them.

If the total reaches 50 percent, the Executive Board must assess the situation, but while the assessment is being made the total may be allowed to rise to 60 percent. Assessment of the situation would give the IMF the opportunity to consider whether quotas rather than borrowing should be increased. Article III, Section 2(a) requires the IMF to conduct a review of quotas at intervals of not more than five years, and therefore the IMF may conduct a review and propose the adjustment of quotas at any time before the five years have elapsed.

If "major" developments should occur, or if there should be a "significant" change in the GAB or associated agreements, the Executive Board must review the guidelines and may adjust them. Whatever the proportions for borrowing may be from time to time under the guidelines, the proportions are not to be considered targets for borrowing.

The guidelines include no explicit asset or liquidity ratio, that is, a relationship of total borrowing to the total of assets the IMF regards as usable according to its economic criteria, with due account taken of potential needs for all purposes. This omission from the guidelines avoids such complications as the changing calculation of "usable" assets, but it does not follow that the asset ratio is regarded as irrelevant.

II. Direct Loans by Lenders to Members

All but one of the arrangements discussed so far have been agreements (1) to lend to the IMF (2) for the purpose of augmenting the resources formerly held by the IMF in the General Resources Account and since the Second Amendment in the General Resources Account of the General Department. The one exception has been the agreement by which the Swiss Confederation associated itself with the GAB. The parties to that agreement were the Swiss Confederation and the IMF, but it was provided that to make the agreement effective the Confederation would consider entering into an individual "implementing agreement" with any participant in the GAB requesting such an agreement.[74] Under an implementing agreement, direct loans would be made by the lender to the participant. The agreement to which the IMF was a party was a kind of *stipulation pour autrui*, a concept which in national law would give rise to the question whether a third-party beneficiary could assert an entitlement to the benefit of the agreement.[75]

The procedure to be followed was that if the Managing Director made proposals for calls on participants under the GAB for the benefit of a participant that had entered into an implementing agreement, he would propose to the Swiss Confederation that it should make a specified amount of resources directly available to the participant. The terms and conditions for the timing of repayment were to correspond, to the maximum extent practicable, to the terms and conditions of the GAB. Furthermore, the IMF agreed that, at the request of a party to an implementing agreement, the IMF would make any determination, or use its good offices, to facilitate the operation of the implementing agreement, although without accepting any responsibility or liability as the result of these activities.

An issue that had to be resolved as a condition of entry into the association agreement was whether the IMF possessed authority to enter into such an agreement. Article VII was broad enough to authorize the IMF to borrow from a nonmember, but the agreement with the Swiss Confederation provided for possible loans to

---

[74] *Selected Decisions*, Sixteenth Issue (1991), p. 307.

[75] See, for example, John Kidd, "Privity of Contract Under Attack in Australia: Some Implications of the Trident Insurance Case," *Business Law Review* (London), Vol. 11 (April 1990), pp. 113–15.

The principle affirmed by the International Court of Justice is one of international law, but the national law of a country may not recognize the principle unless domestic measures have been taken to make it effective under that law. For English law, see *Maclaine Watson & Co. Ltd. v. Department of Trade and Industry* [1989] 3 All E.R. 523; *Arab Monetary Fund v. Hashim & Others (No. 3)* [1990] 3 W.L.R. 139, [1990] 2 All E.R. 769. Swiss law regards international organizations constituted by treaty as juridical persons without further action. (Christian Dominicé, "Le Tribunal fédéral face à la personnalité juridique d'un organisme international," *Zeitschrift für Schweizerisches Recht* (Basle), Vol. 108, No. 5, Part 1 (1989), pp. 517–38.

participants in the GAB and not to the IMF. Article IX, Section 2 declares that the IMF has full juridical personality, and, in particular, the capacity to contract. Article IX, Section 1, however, provides that to enable the IMF to fulfill its functions, the status, immunities, and privileges set forth in Article IX were to be accorded to the IMF "in the territories of each member." Switzerland was not a member. It was concluded that the IMF had "objective legal personality" and therefore the power to contract with nonmembers to fulfill the purposes of the IMF. The International Court of Justice had recognized that "fifty States, representing the vast majority of the members of the international community, had the power, in conformity with international law, to bring into being an entity [the United Nations] possessing objective international personality, and not merely personality recognized by them alone."[76] The IMF could be said to have a similar power.

An advantage of the technique embodied in the association agreement was that while the IMF has no power to borrow the currencies of nonmembers, the Swiss Confederation could agree to lend Swiss francs to a participant with which an implementing agreement had been made. The association agreement referred only to the "resources" that the Swiss Confederation might lend, and the total was expressed as equivalent to an amount denominated in Swiss francs.

The technique of an agreement in this form has not been followed as a precedent for associating a lender with borrowing arrangements negotiated under Article VII. It remains, however, a possibly useful technique for the direct provision of loans to a member, whether the lender is a member or a nonmember. The technique might be particularly useful when for some reason borrowing by the IMF would be beyond its powers because of the constraints on those powers as discussed in this paper, but the agreement would have to be for an object consistent with the purposes of the IMF. It will be seen below that the IMF has entered into an agreement for direct loans by a lender to members by way of association with borrowing agreements of the IMF negotiated under the authority of Article V, Section 2(b) and not Article VII.

---

[76] *I.C.J. Reports* 1949, p. 185. Finn Seyersted, "Is the International Personality of Intergovernmental Organizations Valid Vis-à-Vis Non-Members?" *Indian Journal of International Law* (New Delhi), Vol. 4 (1964), pp. 233–68; Joseph Gold, *Membership and Nonmembership in the International Monetary Fund* (Washington: International Monetary Fund, 1974), pp. 456–63 ("Objective International Personality and Nonmembers").

III. Borrowing Under Article V, Section 2(*b*)

The Power to Borrow Under Article V, Section 2(*b*)

A new era in the history of borrowing by the IMF has begun with the inclusion of Article V, Section 2(*b*) in the Second Amendment:

> If requested, the Fund may decide to perform financial and technical services, including the administration of resources contributed by members, that are consistent with the purposes of the Fund. Operations involved in the performance of such financial services shall not be on the account of the Fund. Services under this subsection shall not impose any obligation on a member without its consent.

No comparable provision was included in the original Articles. The provision is an unusual one in treaty law, and some trepidation was expressed about its breadth in the negotiation of the Second Amendment.

Although there was such concern, the provision is narrower than other proposals that were made. For example, it was proposed that the IMF should be empowered to create new Departments, in addition to the General Department and the Special Drawing Rights Department which would be established by express direction of the Articles, and to adopt the provisions that would govern a new Department. Another proposal was that the IMF should be authorized to establish new Accounts within the General Department, beyond the three to be created by the amended Articles, and to decide which provisions of the Articles or newly fashioned provisions should govern a further Account. A third proposal, of special interest for the present purpose, was that all resources borrowed by the IMF should be managed through the medium of one of these techniques. The objection to the techniques, which prevailed, was that they would constitute de facto amendments of the Articles without respecting the procedure for amendment. This objection could not be made to Article V, Section 2(*b*) because even before the Second Amendment the IMF had relied on an implied power of similar character to establish the Trust Fund that was an essential element in the compromise on the treatment of gold by the proposed Second Amendment. In fact, the Trust Fund was largely the inspiration for Article V, Section 2(*b*).

Borrowing from Nonmember

Borrowing is deemed to be authorized by the clause in the provision "including the administration of resources contributed by members." A power to borrow had been included in the instrument creating the Trust Fund.[77] Although the resources are said to be those contributed by members, the IMF has borrowed under the provision from a nonmember, the Swiss Confederation, as a means of financing the enhanced structural adjustment facility (ESAF).[78] Perhaps this borrowing was deemed to be authorized by an implied power analogous to the express power of Article V, Section 2(*b*). It is always difficult to decide whether or to what extent an express power displaces the possibility of implying analogous powers. Does an express power make it impossible to hold that an alleged implied power of an analogous kind meets the test for implied powers that they must be consistent with the express provisions of the treaty?

If the power to borrow from a nonmember is an implied power, would it be equally possible to imply a power to borrow from the market under Article V, Section 2(*b*) notwithstanding the language of the provision that refers to "resources contributed by members"? The contrast with the broad empowering language of Article VII, Section 1 is striking. An equally strong contrast is the absence of any express direction to seek the concurrence of a member under Article V, Section 2(*b*) if the IMF were to borrow a member's currency from some source other than the member itself.

One difficulty with the view that the IMF is authorized to borrow from the market under the provision involves the reference to "services." For whom would the services be performed? If they were regarded as performed for the benefit of the private parties making the loans, the IMF would be undertaking an unusual function. The beneficiaries of the borrowed resources undoubtedly would be members, because of the condition that the services must be consistent with the purposes of the IMF, but this condition does not mean that the "services" would be rendered to them. The problem considered here does not arise in connection with Article VII, Section 1, because the word "services" does not appear in that provision.

An alternative to the theory of an implied power to justify borrowing from nonmembers is possible and preferable. The clause that begins with the word "including" can be understood to mean that the financial and technical services mentioned in the clause are

---

[77] *Selected Decisions*, Sixteenth Issue (1991), p. 416.
[78] *Selected Decisions*, *Annex*, pp. 21–26.

exemplary and not exhaustive.[79] The IMF's administration of resources borrowed from lenders other than members would be a further example of authorized financial and technical services. The problem of the consistency of authorized services with the purposes of the IMF would still arise.

In agreeing to lend to the IMF for the purpose of the ESAF, the President of the Swiss Confederation made a number of unusual statements in his letter dated April 15, 1988 to the Managing Director.[80] He explained in some detail that the ESAF was monetary in character, by which he seemed to be clarifying that in his view it was authorized by the purposes of the IMF, and that at the same time it was consistent with Swiss legislation on international cooperation with respect to development. The object of this analysis may have been to prevent criticism that the agreement was *ultra vires* either under the Articles or, perhaps of greater interest, under Swiss law, because the beneficiaries of the ESAF are confined to low-income developing countries and the aim is to support programs of structural adjustment that will substantially strengthen the balance of payments and promote growth.

The President also stated that, as the Swiss Confederation was a nonmember of the IMF and was not "represented on the Executive Board," the Confederation should be informed and consulted before the IMF took any decision to amend the instrument or the lending policy of the ESAF. He proposed, and the Managing Director agreed on behalf of the IMF, that there should be periodic meetings between representatives of the IMF as Trustee of the ESAF and representatives of the Confederation to exchange views and information, as well as the transmission of documentation to the Confederation that would be necessary to keep it abreast of developments affecting the ESAF.

The letter suggests the broader question whether a lender, whatever its character, is entitled, under general principles of law and in the absence of a contrary term of the agreement, to be consulted before the IMF takes a decision to amend a policy for the financing

---

[79] The Commentary in the *Report on the Proposed Second Amendment* states that "[t]he financial services include the administration of resources contributed by members or by others" (Part II, D.2), but does not explain the principle on which the reference to "others" is based. *Proposed Second Amendment to the Articles of Agreement of the International Monetary Fund: A Report by the Executive Directors to the Board of Governors* (Washington: International Monetary Fund, 1976), p. 19.

[80] *Selected Decisions, Annex*, pp. 25–26.

of which the lender has agreed to lend. A further question that arises is whether a lender is entitled to terminate its agreement to make advances under an agreement if the lender considers an amendment of the policy unsatisfactory.

Constraints on Power to Borrow

Express Constraints

It has been seen that the letter from the President of the Swiss Confederation implies that a policy for which the IMF borrows as Trustee under Article V, Section 2(*b*) should be demonstrably consistent with the purposes of the IMF and therefore *intra vires*. Consistency with the IMF's purposes is one of the few express constraints on exercise of the power to borrow under the provision. A second express constraint is that no obligation can he imposed on a member under the provision without the member's consent. A prima facie third constraint is that the resources the IMF can administer under the provision are contributed by members, but, as discussed above, a case can be made for accepting contributions by a nonmember, and the IMF has not refrained from administering resources contributed by one of them.

The final express constraint is that activities conducted under the provision "shall not be on the account of the Fund." The rationale of Article V, Section 2(*b*) is thus made obvious: the IMF can perform voluntary financial services, provided that they do not involve a present or potential reduction in the assets of the IMF or an increase in its liabilities, subject to the possible qualification discussed in the next paragraph. A condition of the IMF's services is that the contributor of the resources or some other entity must bear any loss incurred in the course, or as the result, of the IMF's administration of the resources, even if the loss can be attributed to maladministration of any kind. The condition does not apply to technical services, but the IMF is able to charge for them. It was expected that financial obligations would not be undertaken or liabilities arise in the performance of technical services.

There is no difficulty in understanding contributed resources to include resources lent to the IMF. Nor is there any difficulty in understanding the provision to mean that the IMF can take the initiative to suggest that resources should be donated or lent. In the negotiation of the provision, however, it was thought that members would take the initiative to seek the services of the IMF, as is evident from the opening words ("If requested, the IMF may . . . ").

This assumption made it possible to reach a compromise with those who had doubts about the wisdom of the provision. Requests for services could be complied with by the IMF, but on the strict condition that the IMF would not accept liability and the reduction of its assets in the General Department.

If the IMF takes the initiative to seek loans, it is all the more likely that the lenders approached in this way, aware of the immunization of the three Accounts of the General Department and the emergence of members' arrears in the financial activities of the IMF, will press for safeguards that repayment will be made.

The question arises whether, notwithstanding the language of Article V, Section 2(*b*), the IMF would be able to sell gold, transfer the proceeds in excess of the former official price to the Special Disbursement Account,[81] and use those proceeds to repay borrowing contracted under Article V, Section 2(*b*). The provision authorizing the sale of gold permits the excess proceeds to be used for "operations and transactions that are not authorized by other provisions of this Agreement but are consistent with the purposes of the" IMF. The question is whether this language authorizes uses of the proceeds that are contrary to the express constraint in Article V, Section 2(*b*) that operations involving the performance of financial services "shall not be on the account of the Fund."

A principle of interpretation is that all provisions of a treaty must be respected. According to this principle, the language of Article V, Section 2(*b*) would be a limitation on the provision authorizing use of the proceeds of the sale of gold. The strongest argument for authorization is that any use of the proceeds of the sale of gold in operations and transactions not authorized by other provisions is contrary to the Articles. A logical distinction, it could be argued, cannot be drawn between uses that are contrary to an express provision (such as Article V, Section 2(*b*)) and uses that go beyond express authority. The latter uses are contrary to implied prohibition.

The Executive Board, when drafting the Second Amendment, did not intend this latter interpretation. The Executive Board's Commentary on the Second Amendment makes the following statement in explaining Article V, Section 2(*b*):

> Operations and transactions involved in the performance of these financial services would not be on the account of the Fund. That is to

---

[81] Article V, Section 12(*f*).

say, the assets in the Accounts of the General Department or any assets in the Special Drawing Rights Department would not be available to meet obligations or liabilities incurred in the course of these services.[82]

This statement clarifies that the protection of the IMF's assets against risk conferred by Article V, Section 2(*b*) extends to the assets held in all the Accounts of the General Department. The assets therefore include those held in the Special Disbursement Account. The only assets in that Account are proceeds of the sale of gold in excess of the former official price, the obligations in which the proceeds are invested, and the income of investment.

The prohibition of financial risk on the part of the IMF is absolute. The prohibition is not a privilege or an immunity that the IMF can waive. The IMF is unable, by means of a waiver, to accept contractual liability under Article V, Section 2(*b*) that would encumber holdings in the General Department. In addition, the IMF cannot be held responsible in tort, or under any other head of liability, for maladministration of contributed resources. Resources held in an account administered under Article V, Section 2(*b*), however, are also assets of the IMF, even though they are held by the IMF as Trustee, and as such they are within the ambit of the IMF's privileges and immunities.[83]

The inability of a lender to the IMF under Article V, Section 2(*b*) to obtain repayment from, or in some other way reach, the resources of the IMF held in the Accounts of the General Department may give a potential lender pause in deciding whether to lend. As noted earlier, the emergence of arrears on the part of some members as the result of transactions conducted through the General Resources Account may cause anxiety about the repayment of loans by the IMF to members contracted under Article V, Section 2(*b*) and the consequent inability of the IMF to repay loans made to it. Therefore, action has been taken, or ideas adumbrated, to give assurances to potential lenders to encourage them to lend for the purpose of the ESAF.

The most obvious assurance is the structure of the ESAF Trust itself as governed by its Trust Instrument. The operations and

---

[82] Commentary, *Report on Proposed Second Amendment* (cited in footnote 79), Part II, D.2, p. 19.
[83] Article IX. Whether assets administered by the IMF are assets of the IMF depends on the legal technique used. Assets held by the IMF as Trustee are assets of the IMF. See Commentary, *Report on Proposed Second Amendment* (cited in footnote 79), Part II, D.2, p. 19.

transactions of the Trust are conducted through the elaborate structure of a Loan Account, a Reserve Account, and a Subsidy Account. Loans may be made to the IMF as Trustee for the benefit of the Loan Account or the Subsidy Account. Disbursements by the Trustee to eligible members, repayments by them, and repayments by the Trustee to lenders are made through the Loan Account. The purpose of the Subsidy Account is to ensure that eligible members will pay no more than a highly concessional rate of interest on disbursements to them without prejudice to the Trustee's ability to pay interest to lenders. The difference between the two rates of interest is to be financed by annual donations, but in exceptional circumstances the IMF may borrow from official lenders to prefinance donations that have been firmly committed. Repayments of loans for the benefit of the Subsidy Account and interest are paid from the donations when made, income from investment, and proceeds of the liquidation of investment. The assets held in the Reserve Account, which come from various specified sources but without power for the Trustee to borrow for the benefit of that Account, are used to make payments of principal and interest to lenders to the extent that all other resources available for those purposes are inadequate. If, in such circumstances, the resources of even the Reserve Account are inadequate, the Trustee must review the situation in a timely manner.

It will be apparent from this greatly simplified sketch of the ESAF Trust how difficult, and indeed impossible, it may be to give lenders total assurance that they will receive payments of principal and interest in accordance with the contractual terms, given the absence of authority for the IMF to commit assets not subject to the ESAF Trust for these purposes. Part of the complexity of the ESAF Trust and the difficulty of giving assurance to lenders, however, must be attributed to the special circumstance of the IMF's desire to provide assistance at highly concessional rates of interest to developing countries with low income. The ESAF Trust need not be a precedent for the administration of other resources borrowed under Article V, Section 2(*b*) for the purpose of other trusts.

Another attempt of the IMF to give lenders an express assurance that the financial terms of their loan contracts with the IMF in support of the ESAF will be performed at the due dates or without prolonged delay after those dates is set forth in the decision of the IMF that adopts the annexed Trust Instrument:

> 2. The Fund is committed, if it appeared that any delay in payment by the Trust to lenders would be protracted, to consider fully and in

good faith all such initiatives as might be necessary to assure full and expeditious payment to lenders.[84]

This statement is carefully drafted to constitute no more than an obligation—if it can be regarded as an obligation at all—to "consider" initiatives, although the word "committed" might be interpreted to convey a promissory intent.

The idea has been advanced that the IMF might possibly sell some of its gold to raise proceeds in order to route the amount in excess of the former official price from the Special Disbursement Account to the Reserve Account of the ESAF to repay borrowing contracted under Article V, Section 2(b) for financing that facility.[85] The authority of the IMF to use proceeds in this way has been discussed earlier in this paper.[86]

Paragraph 2 of the decision adopting the Trust Instrument avoids the sharper language that the drafters of "comfort letters" sometimes adopt by referring, for example, to a "policy" of ensuring that another entity, such as a subsidiary, will meet certain liabilities that are not liabilities of the entity that is the author of the letter. Comfort letters have produced much litigation and scholarly debate.[87]

The authors of the letters intend to acknowledge a moral but not a legally enforceable liability. A comfort letter can create an unfortunate dilemma: if a court holds that the letter is legally enforceable, the party tendering it is frustrated; and if it is held not to be legally

---

[84] *Selected Decisions*, Sixteenth Issue (1991), p. 26.

[85] "Directors accepted that the proposals that had been put forward to safeguard the resources lent to the Trust were adequate to provide the necessary assurance to potential creditors. Although noting the views of some Directors, I have repeated that the phrase 'all such initiatives as might be necessary' had to be understood to include the possible use of gold." (Ibid., p. 44.)

[86] Suppose, however, that the IMF did sell gold for the purpose discussed in the text. "A trustee has an established right of indemnity in respect of debts and liabilities incurred in favour of third parties provided that these debts and liabilities are properly incurred." (R.A. Hughes, "The Right of a Trustee to a Personal Indemnity from Beneficiaries," *Australian Law Journal* (North Ryde, New South Wales), Vol. 64 (September 1990), pp. 567–79, at 567, footnote omitted). This remedy of trust law, if applicable, would seem to add nothing substantive to a defaulting member's obligation to repay the loan made to it by the Trustee, unless the IMF could claim that the member was bound to transfer to the IMF the equivalent in gold of the amount sold by the IMF.

[87] *Kleinwort Benson Ltd. v. Malaysia Mining Corporation Berhad* [1989] 1 W.L.R. 379; *Soc. anon. Viuda de José Tolra v. Société régionale de développement du Languedoc-Roussillon (Sodler), Recueil Dalloz Sirey* (Paris), No. 10 (March 9, 1989), *Jurisprudence*, pp. 112–15;

enforceable, the recipient is disappointed. The IMF would not be subject to suit by a lender, but there could be disputes about the binding quality of the assurance given by paragraph 2 of the decision quoted above and by any other representations.

As a third assurance, the Executive Board has taken a decision authorizing the Managing Director to confirm to lenders that he did not intend to propose to the Executive Board borrowing in excess of SDR 6 billion for the Loan Account of the ESAF except after consultation with all creditors regarding the justification for such additional borrowing and the adequacy of the resources of the Reserve Account in relation to further borrowing.[88] The purpose of the decision is to assure lenders of a contemplated total of SDR 6 billion that the Trust will have the resources necessary for repaying this amount.

Another idea in the nature of an assurance to lenders relates not to the repayment of borrowing but to the lender's use of the IMF's general resources.[89] According to this idea, if a member having a claim against the ESAF Trust were to represent that it had a need for liquidity not exceeding its claim because of developments in its reserves in the sense of Article V, Section 3(b)(ii), and the IMF, having taken into account the amount of the requested purchase, agreed that the purchase was justified, the member would be able to use the IMF's general resources.

Article V, Section 3(b)(ii) certainly authorizes a member to use the IMF's general resources because of "developments in its reserves," but there remain two questions. First, according to the idea, lending to the ESAF, which must mean the claim to repayment arising from such lending, "could" be considered by the IMF to be part of a

Ibrahim Najjar, "L'autonomie de la lettre de confort," *Recueil Dalloz Sirey* (Paris), No. 32 (October 5, 1989), *Chronique*, pp. 217–21; A.D.M. Forte, "Letters of Comfort or Letters of Cold Comfort," *Journal of Maritime Law and Commerce* (Cincinnati), Vol. 21 (January 1990), pp. 99–109; Georg A. Wittuhn, "Kleinwort Benson Limited v. Malaysian Mining Corporation Berhad—A Comparative Note on Comfort Letters," *McGill Law Journal* (Montreal), Vol. 35 (March 1990), pp. 490–504; Ian Brown, "The Letter of Comfort: Placebo or Promise?" *Journal of Business Law* (London), July 1990, pp. 281–91. The comfort letter must be distinguished from the letter of intent. (Ralph B. Lake and Ugo Draetta, *Letters of Intent and Other Precontractual Documents: Comparative Analysis and Forms* (Stoneham, Massachusetts: Butterworth Legal Publishers, 1989), pp. 13–14.)

[88] *Selected Decisions*, Sixteenth Issue (1991), p. 50.

[89] Ibid., p. 48.

member's "official reserves." Perhaps the verb "would" has been avoided because two of the published borrowing agreements show that the lenders under them are not members' monetary authorities (Caisse Centrale de Coopération Economique of France and the Export-Import Bank of Japan).[90] To treat the claims of such lenders as part of a member's "official reserves" would be unconventional, unless this expression is to be distinguished from "monetary reserves," in which event an interpretation of "reserves" in Article V, Section 2(b)(ii) would be implied. The Articles before the Second Amendment used the expression "monetary reserves," but the present Articles refer to "reserves," "reserve assets," or "reserve position." The Articles do not refer to "official reserves," but the expression "their [members'] official holdings of gold and foreign exchange" can be found in some contexts.

The second question is the meaning of the statement that if the liquidity problem can be addressed on its own, there would be no need for an adjustment program to solve the balance of payments problem. This statement should not be understood to mean that the use of the IMF's general resources to meet liquidity problems only would not be subject to conditionality. The statement should be taken to mean that the resources would be available because of the assumption that a member's policies already in place satisfied the criteria of conditionality applicable to the tranche in which the transaction would take place. In such circumstances, an adjustment program of different or modified policies would not be necessary. The member's only problem would be liquidity and not the correction of its policies. Since the First Amendment, the Articles have denied the IMF authority to permit new unconditional uses of its resources. The theory of this denial is that needs for such liquidity can be met by allocations of SDRs, provided that there exists a long-term global need to supplement reserves.[91] The negotiators of the First Amendment intended in this way to avoid the anomaly that although a majority of 85 percent of the total voting power of members is required for allocations of SDRs, a majority of the votes

---

[90] Not all agreements have been published.

[91] *Establishment of a Facility Based on Special Drawing Rights in the International Monetary Fund and Modifications in the Rules and Practices of the Fund: A Report by the Executive Directors to the Board of Governors Proposing Amendment of the Articles of Agreement*, April 1968, Section 34 (*The International Monetary Fund 1966–1971: The System Under Stress*, Volume II: Documents, ed. by Margaret Garritsen de Vries (Washington: International Monetary Fund, 1976), pp. 69–70).

cast is sufficient for decisions on policies related to the use of the IMF's general resources.

The necessity for conditionality is expressed by the requirement in Article V, Section 3(a) that the IMF must adopt policies on the use of its resources. An unconditional use would not be a policy: it would be a negation of the requirement of a policy. To understand the statement as accepting the possibility of an unconditional use would be contrary not only to Article V, Section 3(a) but also to Article V, Section 2(b), because the administration of contributed resources would then be "on the account of the Fund."

It is difficult to see why the liquidity problem for which use of the general resources might be justifiable would be tied so rigidly to the amount of the lender's claim. If the liquidity problem was larger, the member should qualify for broader use of the general resources in the circumstances that have been postulated. Limiting the use to the amount of the claim to repayment might give the impression that after all an unconditional use was contemplated for that amount.

Finally, it has been suggested that the assurance to lenders of prospective purchases by them from the IMF could be given some attractive characteristics. For example, the IMF could decide, by an 85 percent majority of total voting power, that special repurchase periods could be permitted in respect of the purchases and that a member's reserve tranche would not be reduced by the purchases. Nothing in these characteristics requires them to be attached to unconditional use.

The emphasis on assurances and the chafing against the restraint that financial services must not be on the account of the IMF can be understood as a consequence of the initiative taken under Article V, Section 2(b). It is useful to repeat that the assumption with which that provision was adopted was that normally, or at least frequently, a member or members would take the initiative to contribute resources, and that the IMF would respond by agreeing to administer them. If, as in the case of the ESAF, the IMF takes the initiative to raise contributed resources, and members respond with loans, lenders may feel the need for assurances that they would not expect if they had taken the initiative to provide resources.

Unexpressed Constraints

A possible implied constraint on borrowing has been mentioned already. If borrowing is contracted on the understanding that it is for financing a particular policy of the IMF, whether the borrowing

is under Article V, Section 2(*b*) or Article VII, the lender might insist
that a change in the policy gives it the right to terminate the
agreement to lend, even though the right is not made explicit by the
agreements. It would be wise, therefore, for the IMF to consult the
lender before a change was made.

The IMF can give an express undertaking not to change any
provisions, or certain specified provisions, of a Trust Instrument
that authorizes borrowing by the IMF. The provisions can relate not
only to the terms and conditions for borrowing but also to the
character of the policy in support of which the IMF borrows. The
Trust Instrument of the ESAF contains such an undertaking.[92]

Often when the IMF borrows resources under Article V, Section
2(*b*), it does indeed administer them under a Trust Instrument. A
second unexpressed constraint arises from this practice. A trustee is
bound by certain duties that are inherent in the concept of trusteeship. To take one example, a trustee cannot engage in "self-dealing"
in administering a trust, and so the IMF is not permitted to invest in
the claims of lenders to the trust no matter how attractive these
claims may be. For the same reason, the IMF cannot invest assets of
the trust in the IMF's obligations.[93]

A third constraint not expressed in Article V, Section 2(*b*) is that
even as trustee the IMF cannot borrow SDRs under the provision.
The reason is not the same as for the similar constraint on borrowing
under Article VII. That provision is formulated restrictively so as to
preclude the borrowing of SDRs. The IMF can hold SDRs only in the
General Resources Account,[94] and the organization has no authority
to prescribe itself as an other holder of SDRs in its capacity as
trustee.[95] Trusteeship gives the IMF new duties but does not change
its legal personality. The IMF cannot prescribe a trust itself as a
holder of SDRs, because a trust is not a legal entity in the sense of
being a bearer of rights or a subject of duties. The trustee is the legal
entity that owns the trust property, acquires claims, and incurs

---

[92] *Selected Decisions*, Sixteenth Issue (1991), p. 41.

[93] Joseph Gold, *Legal and Institutional Aspects of the International Monetary System: Selected Essays*, Volume II (Washington: International Monetary Fund, 1984), pp. 862–75 ("Trust Funds in International Law: The Contribution of the International Monetary Fund to a Code of Principles").

[94] Article XVII, Section 2.

[95] Article XVII, Section 3. Furthermore, a trustee may not invest trust assets in claims against itself, and SDRs are liabilities of the IMF in the liquidation of the Special Drawing Rights Department.

liabilities in administering the trust, although the trustee does so in the interests of the beneficiaries.[96]

The ESAF Trust Instrument refers to loans or donations of SDRs, but although the language is not free from ambiguity, it is not quite said that the IMF can hold SDRs in its capacity as Trustee:

> Loans or donations to the Trust may also be made in or exchanged for SDRs in accordance with such arrangements as may be made by the Trust for the holding and use of SDRs.[97]

The language beginning with the phrase "in accordance" should be understood to mean that the arrangements to make loans or donations in SDRs or to exchange the proceeds of loans or donations for SDRs would have to involve qualified holders of SDRs acting for the benefit of the Trust.[98] A loan of SDRs can be made directly to a member by another member or a prescribed holder of SDRs, whether or not on the initiative of the IMF, because loans of SDRs have been authorized by the IMF as permitted operations in SDRs.[99] An exchange of currency for SDRs between members is authorized by the Articles[100] and between members and prescribed holders has been authorized by decisions taken pursuant to the Articles.[101]

Freedom from Constraints

Borrowing under Article V, Section 2(b) is free from most of the constraints that apply to borrowing under Article VII. For example, the problems associated with the need for replenishment of the IMF's holdings of a currency in the General Resources Account do not arise, and, however advisable it may be to obtain the concurrence of the issuer of a currency to be borrowed under Article V, Section 2(b), concurrence is not a legal requirement. The power to borrow under Article V, Section 2(b) is not limited to use of the borrowed currency in "transactions": borrowing can be entered into

---

[96] See International Monetary Fund, *Documents Relating to the Second Amendment of the Articles of Agreement of the International Monetary Fund*, Volume II: Minutes, Part 3 (Washington, 1980), p. 2557.

[97] *Selected Decisions*, Sixteenth Issue (1991), p. 28. For "Trust" in this and other provisions of the Trust Instrument, read "Trustee."

[98] See ibid., pp. 386–87.

[99] Ibid., pp. 390–92.

[100] Article XIX, Section 2.

[101] Article XVII, Section 3; *Selected Decisions*, Sixteenth Issue (1991), pp. 381–83.

for the purpose of "operations" without transgressing the Articles. The doctrine of uniformity, which requires that all members that meet the criteria for use of the IMF's resources under a particular policy must be entitled to the benefit of the policy, does not apply to a policy financed with resources borrowed under Article V, Section 2(b). The beneficiaries can be one or more members selected by the lenders if the IMF is willing to administer resources contributed for such a purpose.[102]

The terms and conditions of the operations and transactions the IMF can enter into with the resources it borrows and administers under Article V, Section 2(b) are not subject to the provisions of the Articles or of the IMF's subordinate law that govern the conduct of operations and transactions through the General Resources Account, unless the IMF decides that some of those provisions are to apply by analogy.[103] The terms and conditions can be highly concessional and can be adopted by decisions of the IMF that do not require special majorities of voting power. Transactions under Article V, Section 2(b) can take the form of loans by the IMF instead of the exchange of currencies, and if loans are the chosen technique the complications of maintaining the value of the IMF's holdings of currency do not arise.

Lending to the IMF under Article V, Section 2(b) may be free from national constraints also, whether legal or financial, that apply to lending by members under Article VII. The character of the policy of the IMF for which a "contribution" is made for administration by the IMF may be such that the loan can be undertaken by an official institution of a member under the institution's own legal authority, from its own funds, and without an impact on the national budget, even though the member itself may lack authority to lend to the IMF without special measures or procedures under its law. The result may be that traditional monetary reserves are not pooled in support of policies financed under Article V, Section 2(b). The IMF has borrowed from development institutions because of the content of structural adjustment programs followed by developing countries

---

[102] It is true that the original GAB was entered into under Article VII for financing transactions of the ten participants with the IMF under the credit tranche policy. The GAB did not exclude any member from the benefit of that policy. On the contrary, the justification of the GAB advanced by the participants was that it benefited nonparticipants indirectly by reducing the strain on the IMF's ordinary resources and making them more readily available for use by nonparticipants.

[103] See, for example, *Selected Decisions*, Sixteenth Issue (1991), p. 39.

that qualify for assistance under the ESAF. Another consequence can be considerable diversity among the borrowing agreements entered into to finance a policy under Article V, Section 2(*b*), even if certain standard terms are prescribed by the Trust Instrument in accordance with which the agreements are made. The agreements to provide resources to the IMF for the Loan Account of the ESAF Trust have had the characteristics noted here.

Practice connected with the ESAF Trust demonstrates also that a lender can agree with the IMF under Article V, Section 2(*b*) to make associated loans to a member. The Saudi Fund for Development (SFD) agreed (1989) with the IMF that if a member entered into an arrangement with the IMF under the ESAF, the SFD would make associated loans to the member in accordance with the terms of an agreement between the member and the SFD. The associated loans are to be used to finance imports of the recipient country that are defined as eligible for this purpose. The loans are made through a special account financed by the SFD and administered by the IMF as agent for the SFD.[104]

It may seem surprising that the IMF has undertaken to administer an account for financing specified imports rather than the general balance of payments. The question the arrangement raises is whether it complies with the condition in Article V, Section 2(*b*) that the services the IMF undertakes must be consistent with its purposes. The condition must be observed even if the arrangement is considered technical and not financial. Perhaps the justification in this case is the breadth of the imports or the notional amalgamation of the resources with all the resources borrowed by the IMF for financing the ESAF. If the conditions of Article V, Section 2(*b*) are not met, the failure is not cured by the fact that the IMF is acting as an agent of the lender. In undertaking the service, the IMF would be no more justified by the concept of agency than it would be if it undertook as agent to handle the export of pencils for a member. The controversy over the GAB settled the issue long ago that the powers of the IMF are governed by the treaty and cannot be enlarged or diminished by agreement with a member.

The arrangement with the SFD creates a third approach in the IMF's practice to the recruitment of resources by means of loans. The first approach is, of course, an agreement between the IMF and a lender that provides for resources to be made available by the

---

[104] *Selected Decisions, Annex,* pp. 67–76.

lender to the IMF, which receives and disburses them in the capacity of a principal. The lender's commitment to advance resources to the IMF may be firm or it may be subject to the lender's ad hoc consent when approached by the IMF for an advance under the agreement.

The second approach is an agreement by which Patria associates itself with an agreement of the first kind between the IMF and Terra, but Patria provides no resources to the IMF. Instead, Patria agrees with the IMF to make resources available directly to a third member, Regio, under a separate agreement between Patria and Regio, subject to such terms as the IMF has prescribed by its agreement with Patria, the condition that the IMF has decided to provide resources to Regio, and the further condition that Patria is satisfied that the terms of its separate agreement with Regio are met.

The third approach is similar to the second, except that Patria transfers resources to the IMF for disbursement, but subject to the same conditions as have been mentioned in connection with the second approach. According to the third approach, the IMF receives and disburses the resources provided by Patria, but in both steps as agent for Patria and not as principal. The IMF holds the resources, but not as a borrower. In the case involving the SFD, in which the third approach has been followed, the only loans are those made by the SFD to recipient countries (such as Regio in the example cited above).

The second approach permits a loan of SDRs to be made directly between members (Patria and Regio), but the third approach would not enable a member to lend SDRs by transferring them to the IMF as disbursing agent for passing them on to members. An advantage for the IMF and for lenders to it of both the second and third approaches in such an arrangement as the ESAF Trust is that loans pursuant to these approaches place no burden on the resources of the Reserve Account of the Trust.

IV. The Case for Borrowing

Ever since the IMF embarked on borrowing with the negotiation of the GAB there have been frequent declarations by the IMF, its officials, or members that the IMF should not have to rely on borrowing to supplement its resources in order to enable it to perform its functions effectively. This opposition has almost completely abated in relation to the GAB, particularly after the expansion of total commitments under it from the original equivalent of

US$6 billion to the present SDR 17 billion, and more particularly after the concurrent amendments that permit the IMF to borrow in certain circumstances for financing the transactions of nonparticipants in the GAB. Discontent with the GAB has declined because the resources that can be advanced under it are now regarded as a fund for emergencies that could threaten the stability of the international monetary system. For that reason, however, the GAB is less likely to be relied on than in the past, especially now that it has become common practice and almost commonplace for the IMF to borrow without recourse to the GAB if difficult conditions develop in which augmentation of the IMF's resources is advisable.

The basic objection to reliance on borrowing is that the IMF cannot respond as promptly and as adequately as it should to the changes that can develop in international financial and economic conditions. The IMF lacks this flexibility because it must negotiate borrowing, and there is no certainty that it will succeed. It is also possible that the IMF can succeed only on terms that are considered not altogether favorable to it or to beneficiary members in some respects. A further objection that could be made is that the anxiety to borrow has led to certain exercises of the powers to borrow that raise questions about whether they are *intra vires*.

Disquiet about borrowing by the IMF has not prevented interest in developing new techniques for borrowing. For example, officials have expressed interest from time to time in borrowing under Article VII from nonofficial lenders. It is thought that this technique might avoid the difficulties encountered in negotiating with official entities. Some members have been cautious about the volume of claims on the IMF they hold, while private entities, it is assumed, might welcome the opportunity to hold such claims.

Some ambivalence about borrowing can be suspected, even on the part of those who profess the wish to eliminate the practice, because the new provision, Article V, Section 2(*b*), has become the launching pad for new forms of borrowing as well as other projects. A major reason for this development in the practice of the IMF on borrowing is the broad exemption of activities under the provision from legal constraints that apply to Article VII and the General Resources Account. Article V, Section 2(*b*) gives the IMF considerable maneuverability, so that the IMF might find it useful to exercise this freedom even if its subscribed resources were deemed satisfactory for traditional activities.

The major disadvantage of borrowing under Article V, Section 2(*b*) is that a wall, intended to be impregnable, protects the resources the IMF holds in the General Department against liabilities and obligations related to the performance of financial services under the provision. The IMF has tried to assure lenders that borrowing will be repaid on time and that ways may be found to repay them if difficulties about repayment should nevertheless arise.

Even if the IMF were not prevented by Article V, Section 2(*b*) from using proceeds of the sale of gold in excess of the former official price to repay borrowing contracted under the provision, there might still be problems. In the United States, for example, Section 5 of the Bretton Woods Agreements Act, as amended by Public Law 95-147(1977), provides that:

> Unless Congress by law authorizes such action, neither the President nor any person or agency shall on behalf of the Unites States...(g) approve either the disposition of more than 25 million ounces of Fund gold for the benefit of the Trust Fund established by the Fund on May 6, 1976, or the establishment of any additional trust fund whereby resources of the International Monetary Fund would be used for the special benefit of a single member, or of a particular segment of the membership, of the Fund.

If this provision applies to the sale of gold to raise proceeds for the repayment of borrowing in accordance with trust arrangements established under Article V, Section 2(*b*), and the provision is not amended, the authorization of Congress would be necessary to enable the Executive Director appointed by the United States to vote in favor of the sale. If Congress did not provide this authorization, a proposed sale would be vetoed, because a majority of 85 percent of the total voting power of members is necessary for a decision to sell gold.

Part of the case against borrowing is that lenders can demand special advantages, whether the borrowing takes place under Article VII or under Article V, Section 2(*b*). These advantages, if conceded, can be incorporated in the borrowing agreement or can be extrinsic to it. It must be said at once that advantages for a lender are not necessarily disadvantages for the IMF, but the possibility that they might be can help to explain the doubts about borrowing as an acceptable feature of the life of the IMF. Some official opposition to borrowing from nonofficial sources has certainly been based on the influence over the policies of the IMF that these lenders might try to exert and, if they were to succeed, the consequent reduction in the influence of members in the affairs of the IMF and the international monetary system.

Contractual terms favorable to a lender might be financial or nonfinancial. Contractual terms of a financial character have already led to modifications in the IMF's practice, such as the institution of suspense accounts for resources the IMF receives before it can use them and the extension of its powers of investment. The waiver of the IMF's immunity from suit and from the execution of adverse judgments are examples of terms that may or may not be financial. The IMF would probably have preferred not to concede such terms, as is suggested by the normal practice of providing in the IMF's borrowing agreements that disputes are to be settled to the mutual satisfaction of the contracting parties. Contractual terms that have been particularly unwelcome to the IMF are those that reserve to the lender the option not to lend when approached by the IMF for loans to it or to a member under the agreement. The ancestor of such a term was, and still is, a feature of the GAB. The Baumgartner letter shows that the participants have reserved the right to judge for themselves whether the program of the member for whose benefit the IMF wishes to invoke the GAB is satisfactory, even though the Managing Director will already have reached a favorable judgment.[105]

The willingness of a lender to lend may be dependent on advantages it seeks that are not included in the borrowing agreement. SAMA's massive loan agreement of 1981 was accompanied by a substantial ad hoc increase in Saudi Arabia's quota in the IMF. The use of Saudi Arabia's subscription and SAMA's loans to the IMF have given Saudi Arabia the power to appoint an additional Executive Director as the result of the biennial calculations made for this purpose.[106] Furthermore, an understanding was reached at the time of the 1981 agreement that, as a safeguard for lenders, the IMF would consider a limit on the volume of borrowing, and such a limit has now been established. An advantage that a lender seeks may be not only outside its agreement with the IMF but also outside the IMF. The agreements of the Swiss Confederation and SAMA for association with the GAB were responsible for the seats Switzerland and Saudi Arabia have occupied in meetings of the Group of Ten. The case of Switzerland produced the anomaly of a voice for a nonmember in the affairs of the IMF.

---

[105] *Selected Decisions*, Sixteenth Issue (1991), p. 300. See also the association agreement of the SFD with the ESAF, under which the SFD determines the eligible imports for which loans will be made.

[106] Article XII, Section 3(c); Section 18 of the IMF's By-Laws.

However persuasive the arguments against borrowing may be, it is unlikely that it will ever be regarded as a practice the IMF should renounce. Experience demonstrates that increases in quotas are difficult to negotiate, that negotiations do not result in agreement to provide the IMF with resources adequate to the tasks it should undertake, and that such agreements as are reached become effective only after unhelpful delay. Even if subscribed resources should ever become adequate, borrowing under Article V, Section 2(*b*) might still be considered attractive as a technique for giving financial assistance to poorer members without the constraints that are imposed by other provisions and policies.

If increases in quotas were to provide the IMF with resources deemed adequate at the time to meet the needs of the IMF under all its policies, circumstances might develop that subject the resources to unforeseen strain. For instance, one or more members with large quotas may wish to use the IMF's resources or may request early repayment of loan claims to meet unexpected difficulties in their balances of payments, with the consequence that the resources available, according to the IMF's economic criteria, for use by other members are reduced to an uncomfortable level. The distribution of surpluses and deficits among members may produce a similar stringency if the surpluses are enjoyed by members with quotas too small to provide the IMF with sufficient usable resources to meet all legitimate needs.

For any one of the reasons mentioned above, Managing Directors may demonstrate their activism as much in the future as in the past by initiating projects to borrow on the most favorable terms that they can negotiate.

ANNEX I

A. Original Articles

Article VII. Scarce Currencies

Section 1. *General scarcity of currency*

If the Fund finds that a general scarcity of a particular currency is developing, the Fund may so inform members and may issue a report setting forth the causes of the scarcity and containing recommendations designed to bring it to an end. A representative of the member whose currency is involved shall participate in the preparation of the report.

Section 2. *Measures to replenish the Fund's holdings of scarce currencies*

The Fund may, if it deems such action appropriate to replenish its holdings of any member's currency, take either or both of the following steps:

(i) Propose to the member that, on terms and conditions agreed between the Fund and the member, the latter lend its currency to the Fund or that, with the approval of the member, the Fund borrow such currency from some other source either within or outside the territories of the member, but no member shall be under any obligation to make such loans to the Fund or to approve the borrowing of its currency by the Fund from any other source.

(ii) Require the member to sell its currency to the Fund for gold.

Section 3. *Scarcity of the Fund's holdings*

(*a*) If it becomes evident to the Fund that the demand for a member's currency seriously threatens the Fund's ability to supply that currency, the Fund, whether or not it has issued a report under Section 1 of this Article, shall formally declare such currency scarce and shall thenceforth apportion its existing and accruing supply of the scarce currency with due regard to the relative needs of members, the general international economic situation, and any other pertinent considerations. The Fund shall also issue a report concerning its action.

(*b*) A formal declaration under (*a*) above shall operate as an authorization to any member, after consultation with the Fund, temporarily to impose limitations on the freedom of exchange operations in the scarce currency. Subject to the provisions of Article IV, Sections 3 and 4, the member shall have complete jurisdiction in determining the nature of such limitations, but they shall be no more restrictive than is necessary to limit the demand for the scarce currency to the supply held by, or accruing to, the member in question; and they shall be relaxed and removed as rapidly as conditions permit.

(*c*) The authorization under (*b*) above shall expire whenever the Fund formally declares the currency in question to be no longer scarce.

B. Present Articles

Article VII. Replenishment and Scarce Currencies

Section 1. *Measures to replenish the Fund's holdings of currencies*

The Fund may, if it deems such action appropriate to replenish its holdings of any member's currency in the General Resources Account needed in connection with its transactions, take either or both of the following steps:

(i) propose to the member that, on terms and conditions agreed between the Fund and the member, the latter lend its currency to the Fund or that, with the concurrence of the member, the Fund borrow such currency from some other source either within or outside the territories of the member, but no member shall be under any obligation to make such loans to the Fund or to concur in the borrowing of its currency by the Fund from any other source;

(ii) require the member, if it is a participant, to sell its currency to the Fund for special drawing rights held in the General Resources Account, subject to Article XIX, Section 4. In replenishment with special drawing rights, the Fund shall pay due regard to the principles of designation under Article XIX, Section 5.

Section 2. *General scarcity of currency*

If the Fund finds that a general scarcity of a particular currency is developing, the Fund may so inform members and may issue a report setting forth the causes of the scarcity and containing recommendations designed to bring it to an end. A representative of the member whose currency is involved shall participate in the preparation of the report.

Section 3. *Scarcity of the Fund's holdings*

(*a*) If it becomes evident to the Fund that the demand for a member's currency seriously threatens the Fund's ability to supply that currency, the Fund, whether or not it has issued a report under Section 2 of this Article, shall formally declare such currency scarce and shall thenceforth apportion its existing and accruing supply of the scarce currency with due regard to the relative needs of members, the general international economic situation, and any other pertinent considerations. The Fund shall also issue a report concerning its action.

(*b*) A formal declaration under (*a*) above shall operate as an authorization to any member, after consultation with the Fund, temporarily to impose limitations on the freedom of exchange operations in the scarce currency. Subject to the provisions of Article IV and Schedule C, the member shall have complete jurisdiction in determining the nature of such limitations, but they shall be no more restrictive than is necessary to limit the demand for the scarce currency to the supply held by, or accruing to, the member in question, and they shall be relaxed and removed as rapidly as conditions permit.

(c) The authorization under (b) above shall expire whenever the Fund formally declares the currency in question to be no longer scarce.

.

.

.

9

Recent Evolution of Fund Conditionality

Azizali F. Mohammed

Policy-based lending by the Fund goes under the rubric of "Fund conditionality." Three elements are involved: (1) the general policy approach; (2) the particular choice and mix of policy instruments; and (3) the specification of intermediate target variables as performance criteria for the purpose of monitoring program implementation. The contribution of Jacques J. Polak to laying the intellectual foundations of the Fund's policy approach is described in another paper submitted to this conference.[1] This paper focuses on the evolution of the substantive aspects of conditionality in the last decade. While some of the adaptations described here may appear to have moved quite far afield from the elegant simplicity of the "Polak model," the basic framework of analysis underlying Fund-supported adjustment programs derives directly from the key linkages between financial policy instruments and desired balance of payments outcomes that were forged in that model.

I. Basic Conditionality

The Fund's current policy approach emphasizes two elements: achieving macroeconomic balance and reducing distortions created by interference with the operation of markets, including price and wage rigidities, inappropriate taxes and subsidies, trade restrictions,

---

[1]Jacob A. Frenkel, Morris Goldstein, and Mohsin S. Khan, "Major Themes in the Writings of Jacques J. Polak," Chapter 1 in this volume.

and other direct controls. Since countries turn to the Fund for financial assistance when they have an imbalance in their external payments, the restoration of overall balance between domestic absorption and aggregate supply becomes the dominant objective. However, this has to be combined with incentive policies to move resources into the foreign trading sector, so that treating the balance of payments disequilibrium is not at the expense of growth.

The frequently heard characterization of the Fund's approach as "demand management" and its objective as "stabilization" has never been correct. Even in the earliest programs, the deployment of the exchange rate instrument and the inclusion of reforms affecting producer prices of major export commodities were strong evidence of the fact that Fund prescriptions went beyond demand management measures in order to switch resources into the balance of payments. The Fund also attached importance to appropriate interest rates, in order to promote savings and an efficient allocation of resources. An emphasis on trade liberalization also showed the Fund's concern with the efficient use of resources in the tradable goods sector.

The IMF also introduced its extended Fund facility in 1974 to enable it to help members "suffering serious payments imbalance relating to structural maladjustments in production and trade and where prices and cost distortions have been widespread" as well as in economies "characterized by slow growth and an inherently weak balance of payments position which prevents pursuit of an active development policy."[2]

It is useful to recall this history because most of the changes in Fund conditionality that emerged in the last decade represent less a break than an elaboration of earlier policies. A few changes, however, may have been of a different character. For example, the Fund has tried to influence the behavior of creditors, especially the commercial banks, in the aftermath of the debt crisis. Yet to the extent that the use of Fund resources by a borrowing member is conditioned upon the evoking of specific responses from other parties, these changes have significant implications for the Fund's role in the international financial arena.

This paper focuses, however, on adaptations of conditionality that apply to the borrowing member directly. These cover (1) an explicit

---

[2]International Monetary Fund, *Selected Decisions and Selected Documents of the International Monetary Fund*, Sixteenth Issue (Washington, 1991), p. 105.

concern with helping to restore growth in the economy by prescribing structural reforms; (2) an effort to protect programs from going offtrack because of unexpected contingencies; (3) a growing concern with the prolonged use of Fund resources; and (4) an effort to take account of the impact of adjustment measures on the poor.

II. Evolution in the 1980s

Growth-Oriented Adjustment

The Fund's purposes (Article I) provide that it contribute "to the development of the productive resources of all members" through facilitating "the expansion and balanced growth of international trade." In helping member countries deal with their balance of payments difficulties, a concern with how to encourage growth can thus be regarded as an extension of its systemic responsibilities. What happened in the 1980s was an explicit recognition that, for payments adjustment to be durable, there had to be a restoration of growth in the economy or at least an effort to incorporate a growth factor into the design of an adjustment program. This realization was driven home in the aftermath of the debt crisis. An earlier assumption that the middle-income, heavily indebted countries were facing only a liquidity problem was discarded by the mid-1980s[3] in favor of the notion that restoration of their creditworthiness necessitated their return to sustained growth.

A similar conviction applied in the case of the low-income countries. In formulating programs under the Fund's structural adjustment facility (SAF), introduced in 1986, the eligible countries were expected to develop macroeconomic and structural policy objectives, as well as the measures they intended to adopt during a three-year period. These measures would be incorporated in a policy framework paper (PFP) to be reviewed by the Executive Directors both of the IMF and the World Bank. While some observers expressed an apprehension that these procedures were tantamount to applying "cross-conditionality," most borrowers under the SAF saw the PFP-process as an efficient means of catalyzing and coordinating financial assistance in support of their adjustment programs. An

---

[3] This was the essence of the "Baker Plan," that is, countries had to "grow out of their debts" and only if GDP growth was faster than the growth of debt could debtor countries hope to resume normal market access.

enhanced structural adjustment facility (ESAF) was created at the end of 1987. Programs to be supported by ESAF were expected to incorporate structural measures that would be particularly ambitious in scope and timing. The basic idea of ESAF programs was to foster growth and achieve a substantial strengthening of the balance of payments position, sufficient to allow exceptional financing to be discontinued after the three-year program period. The fact that both SAF and ESAF programs were financed on concessional terms (of 0.5 percent annually), with repayments spread over ten years (starting five and a half years after each disbursement), meant that the international community was prepared to recognize that the normal terms applicable to Fund financial assistance (repayment in three to five years with charges close to market rates) were too onerous for low-income countries undertaking growth-oriented adjustment programs in the prevailing difficult circumstances.

Protecting Against Contingencies

While effective implementation has always been at the heart of program success or failure, there was until recently no provision to take account, in advance, of the main factors that could disrupt programs during the course of implementation. A compensatory financing facility (CFF), created as far back as 1963, did provide financing to offset temporary shortfalls in export earnings arising from circumstances largely outside the country's control.[4] This was extended in 1976 to cover an excess in cereal import costs and in 1990 to cover excess oil import costs (on a temporary basis). No conditionality applied if the country had a satisfactory balance of payments except for the effect of the export shortfall or the excess in cereal import costs. Over the years, however, the application of the CFF tended to become more conditional, as payments problems were found to go beyond these specific and reversible adversities. Countries were expected, in such circumstances, to cooperate with the Fund in finding appropriate solutions to their balance of payments difficulties.

An aspect that came into sharper focus in the 1980s was the importance of helping a member implementing a Fund-supported

---

[4] As noted in Frenkel, Goldstein, and Khan (Chapter 1 in this volume, p. 16), the basic purpose of the CFF of "preventing temporary, exogenous shocks from throwing good policies in developing countries offtrack, has remained close to Polak's original conception."

program to obtain financing (in addition to that provided in support of the program) to cover part of the net effect on its balance of payments of external shocks. It was seen as suitable to cover unfavorable deviations beyond the member's control in key current account variables that are easily identifiable as well as highly volatile (e.g., key export or import prices or international interest rates). Initially, contingency mechanisms were incorporated into arrangements with Mexico in respect of oil revenues in order to help facilitate that country's debt negotiations with its banks.[5] The experience gained in this transaction provided a precedent for complementing the CFF with an approach to help keep programs on track in the face of unpredictable exogenous developments. Often in the past, the response by creditors to countries surprised by external adversity would be to insist upon more adjustment. The new facility, the compensatory and contingency financing facility, enabled the Fund to provide "fallback financing," thereby encouraging governments to adopt measures sometimes touching the outer limits of political acceptability with some degree of assurance that the international community would be prepared to compensate them for plain bad luck. The contingency element is coming into greater use to handle unpredictable changes in world oil prices in tandem with the compensatory financing of excess oil import costs in the wake of the Middle East situation.

Assuring Medium-Term Viability

The past decade has witnessed a mounting concern with the incidence of prolonged use of Fund resources of which the problem of arrears owed to the Fund can be treated as a special case.[6] Overdue obligations have risen from almost none at the beginning of the decade to over SDR 3 billion owed by nine countries at the end of 1990. While it is not germane to this paper to discuss measures adopted by the Fund to protect its financial position directly or to deal with countries in arrears, the existence of arrears on the part of a few members has sensitized the Fund to the importance of preventing their emergence on the part of other members. This has meant an even stronger emphasis on the quality

---

[5] See Joseph Gold, "Mexico and the Development of the Practice of the International Monetary Fund," *World Development* (Oxford), Vol. 16 (October 1988), pp. 1127–42.

[6] There is, however, no direct link between prolonged use and arrears to the Fund.

of programs and increased concern with the capacity of countries to meet their obligations to the IMF. The staff now discusses explicitly with the authorities of a country its capacity to repay. The staff also undertakes a careful evaluation of associated financial arrangements with other creditors and donors; the sensitivity of any shortfalls in financing for the viability of the program and actual flows is closely monitored. The authorities are also expected to acknowledge their readiness to adapt their policies quickly to unexpected developments.

In cases of prolonged use, attention is given to levels and phasing of access, with a view to reducing outstanding Fund credit over time. Continued access requires stronger policy justification. In cases where a country's record of payments performance indicates difficulties in meeting obligations punctually, a closer examination of the cash flows is undertaken with a view to assuring the Fund that there would be sufficient resources available to meet obligations to the Fund as and when they fall due. Finally, in cases where projections indicate a doubt that viability would be attained in the medium term if certain assumptions were not fulfilled, the Fund seeks additional and clear expressions of support from the international community to the effect that the Fund would be treated as a preferred creditor.

These developments have led the Fund to be increasingly unwilling to see its resources being used as part of "gap-filling" exercises and to put greater weight on the buildup of the borrowing countries' reserves. The Fund has also tended to give much greater weight to the adoption of corrective measures of a durable character, especially in the fiscal area, while being unprepared to accept measures that are of a "band-aid" type, or measures that would lose effectiveness with the passage of time.

Protecting the Poor

The Fund has traditionally taken the view that it is a country's prerogative to make social and distributional choices in its adjustment, growth, and development processes. It has also felt that disorderly adjustment is often most damaging to poor groups who are least able to protect themselves from, say, the adverse consequences of open or repressed inflation and that policies that form part of an orderly adjustment process can result in a lasting improvement in the circumstances of the poor.

However, the acute difficulties that confronted many developing countries in the aftermath of the debt crisis have focused attention on the adversities than even an orderly adjustment process can create for some of the most vulnerable elements of society in the short run.

Two elements in program design have been identified to help ameliorate adverse effect on the poor: the implications of different sequencing of policy measures, and the specific nature of revenue and expenditure measures. It is recognized that the speed with which key prices and incomes change in response to policy measures can produce excessive and unintended consequences that are hurtful to certain groups of the poor because of inadequate infrastructure or imperfect markets and lack of access to information. Efforts can be made, to the extent feasible, to coordinate the timing of changes in certain administered prices so as to avoid unintended changes in relative product and factor prices. Also, the level and composition of public expenditures have important implications for poor groups, especially consumption subsidies, expenditures on social services, and transfers under social security and similar arrangements.

The Fund has sought to improve its understanding of the channels through which economic policies affect poor groups. It has given increasing emphasis to an appropriate policy mix for protecting the poor in the adjustment process. In many programs, the pass-through of exchange rate changes on domestic prices of imported essential products, and other adjustments in administered prices, have been made gradually so as to spread their impact on real incomes, and the attendant fiscal burden has been financed through an increase in taxation. Other programs have included wage supplements for low-level public employees affected by price increases. Some recent programs have incorporated social safety nets consisting of funds for unemployed workers, pensioners, or other poor people. The funds for unemployed workers have been aimed both at providing workers with training for alternative employment and at helping them maintain their income during an initial period of unemployment. To help public employees who would lose their jobs as a result of fiscal retrenchment, some programs have made specific budgetary provisions for severance pay, training, or financial assistance.

The basic issue that confronts the international community is the trade-off between such efforts to protect the poor and the implications for the speedy reduction of macroeconomic imbalances. How to incorporate distributional concerns effectively into program design without placing an undue strain on scarce administrative resources is another challenge, especially when recommending the replacement of generalized subsidies with programs targeted to ensure a more effective delivery of benefits to the poorest. To some extent, the trade-offs could be ameliorated if it were possible to mobilize additional domestic and foreign resources, specifically for the purpose of helping to put in place well-designed measures to mitigate short-run adverse effects on the poor. To this end, the Fund has been working in a complementary manner with the World Bank, as well as with United Nations agencies, bilateral aid agencies, church groups, and nongovernmental organizations to catalyze additional resources for poverty alleviation, and to protect the poor, in the context of adjustment programs supported by the Fund.

III. Adaptations to Eastern Europe

The Fund's dealings with Eastern European countries that are launched on a transition from centrally planned to market-oriented economies are much too recent to allow for more than a few issues to be raised on how the Fund's conditionality is, or ought to be, adapting to handle the unique problems of these countries. For what these countries are attempting is a transformation that goes far beyond any adjustment of macroeconomic imbalances. The massive changes in institutions—legal, political, and in the organization of the economy—are emerging from a strictly indigenous experience and could not possibly be engineered from the outside. Hence, any kind of policy-based assistance can only seek to support and to influence, at the margins, a radical reshaping of their economic systems.

It is obvious that the large-scale reorganization of productive structures currently under way has serious consequences for employment. The effects of rising unemployment in societies that have had little or no open experience of it emphasizes the critical importance of social safety nets. This becomes a crucial issue in program design since any provision for social transfers must be made at a time of acute budgetary stringency and when strong financial discipline is being applied to government as well as enterprise sectors. The provision of some form of income maintenance for individuals most severely affected must therefore be constructed so as to minimize the drain on the public exchequer. This could be done, for example, by setting up, on a temporary basis, a rationing scheme covering a basket of goods needed for maintaining minimum standards of health and nutrition and targeting its availability to those whose needs are self-identifying, such as the elderly, the disabled, pregnant and nursing women, and infants. Provision could also be made for self-targeted employment through public works at subsistence wages in order to temporarily cushion the impact of restructuring. Without such expedients, the initial experience with a market-oriented system could well create a backlash that would negate the process itself. If the international community becomes convinced of the criticality of this issue, social safety nets would need to be incorporated as an essential, rather than simply as a desirable, ingredient of Fund-supported programs.

Another issue that arises in the Eastern European context is the role of incomes policy as a complement to the application of financial discipline when the transition from central planning is being undertaken in a condition of high inflation, whether open or repressed. Even with a "hard" budget constraint, the freeing of prices can unleash a price-wage spiral, unless specific protections are built into the program. The de-indexation of wage contracts is one such step where indexation mechanisms were part of the wage determination process.

At the level of publicly owned enterprises, however, there may be a need to create strong restraints against the granting of large nominal wage increases, once the sanction of a centrally determined wage fixation arrangement is abandoned. Where such enterprises are operating in an imperfectly competitive environment, because of incomplete trade liberalization or because they service the nontradable goods sector, the need for effective wage containment becomes a critical element in program design.

This leads to another issue—the application of financial discipline at the microeconomic level. In most centrally planned economies, a number of devices have tended to shelter firms from the financial impact of macroeconomic policies, and indeed from the financial consequences of their own mistakes or failures. Firms were used to receiving special treatment—as regards taxes, access to subsidies, availability of credit or imported inputs, and so on. This meant that firms could escape the full brunt of, say, a credit squeeze introduced by the central bank as part of a macroeconomic policy package. In addition, an extensive network of inter-enterprise credits often dampened further the impact of overall financial discipline. Therefore, microeconomic discipline may become a prerequisite for macroeconomic balance.

Another issue relates to the comprehensiveness of economic reform packages. This is mainly because none of the essential elements of a market-oriented economy operates efficiently unless all other main elements are in place. It is not much use, for instance, to allow freedom of pricing (which implies decentralized decision making) unless the decision maker has full responsibility for the financial and other consequences of his decision. The Fund has worked with centrally planned economies in the past on the assumption that some decentralization of economic decisions and some use of realistic prices to guide such decisions were better than none and could help improve economic efficiency in a variety of political and institutional settings. Recent experience in Eastern Europe suggests that broader reforms are essential if the adjustment is to be carried out.

Finally, it is clear that the types of governmental institutions and the skills to operate them that are needed in the transition are quite different from those that were appropriate for operating a planned economy. As an example, the functions of a central bank that are critical to operating a complex monetary policy in a market economy differ markedly from the credit-allocation function of a central bank in a command economy. Only as money becomes a relevant variable can the financial programming approach of the Polak model be directly applied. In the meantime, the Fund must proceed in a rather experimental way.

10

The Monetary Character of the IMF

W.F. Duisenberg and A. Szász

Since May 1981, a number of communiqués of the Group of Ten have called for the preservation of the "monetary role" or the "monetary character" of the Fund, without however providing a clear indication what this "monetary character" involved. The 1985 Report of the Deputies of the Group of Ten on *The Functioning of the International Monetary System* is emphatic on the subject ("The Deputies emphasize the importance of preserving the monetary character of the institution..." (para. 85)), but it again... fails to be specific as to what is meant by this injunction. Why, 35 years after the establishment of the IMF, did its industrial members* feel it necessary to admonish the institution to live up to its middle initial? A middle initial, incidentally, which the institution acquired at a late stage, and for no very obvious reason, having spent most of its embryonic years as the United Nations (later: International) *Stabilization* Fund.**

---

*And only they: the expression never appeared in a communiqué of the Interim Committee. That Committee did stress "the monetary character of the SDR" (and conveyed the intended meaning of its statement by continuing) "which should not be a means of transferring resources" (paragraph 7 of its communiqué of April 10, 1986).

**The change from "stabilization" to "monetary" was made by the American drafters, in the tenth draft of the Joint Statement, in January 1944 in response to a British suggestion. J. Keith Horsefield, *The International Monetary Fund, 1945-1965* (Washington: International Monetary Fund, 1968), Vol. I, p. 54.

The authors thank D.H. Boot and C. Voormeulen for their help in preparing this paper.

Thus begins an unpublished paper by J.J. Polak.[1] He points out (paragraph 4) that "No general definition of 'monetary' would explain what is meant by the expression here discussed." Where an attempt to explain it is made, he finds it far from helpful. The absence of a published definition does not mean, however, that Polak did not deduct what the expression is intended to convey. "The call for preserving the monetary character of the Fund," he writes (in paragraph 6), "is . . . a code expression for constraint on the Fund's lending." But it is a code of which he clearly doubts the usefulness. In attempts made to substantiate the concept, reference is made to the need to preserve the Fund's liquidity position and to maintain the revolving character of its resources and Fund conditionality in order to contribute to the international adjustment process. In Polak's view, concern about the Fund's liquidity position seems exaggerated. As to the revolving character of the Fund's resources, he considers this (in paragraph 8) "important whether it undermines the liquidity position of the Fund or not. Concern for the system and the working of the adjustment mechanism should make the Fund insist on revolving use *by individual members*, even when its aggregate liquidity ratios are not at risk. Whether new drawings should be allowed—e.g., in the context of the debt crisis—needs to be considered on the merits of each case, not by some general concern about the monetary character of the institution." And he adds (paragraph 9): "If there is any lesson in all this with respect to the formulation of policy choices, it would be that it does not pay to present specific concerns by the use of allusive labels. That may initially provide some vague justification, but fails to focus attention on the precise issues that the institution must deal with."

In the end, Polak decided not to publish his paper, leaving it to us to decide whether we had anything meaningful to say, either about the monetary character of the Fund or about its use as an allusive label. It is not our intention to try to define the concept. Polak's notes are sufficiently discouraging in this respect. We do feel, however, that in spite of all its shortcomings the concept did serve a purpose. Hereafter, it will be examined whether this remains true in the present situation. First, however, some observations as to when and why the expression became fashionable.

---

[1] "Some Notes on 'The Monetary Character of the IMF'," August 18, 1989.

I. The Monetary Character in the Early 1980s

Origin

As mentioned by Polak, the reference to the Fund's monetary character emerges in the communiqué issued by the Group of Ten in May 1981. The summoning to preserve the Fund's character—though the word "monetary" is not used—is already implied in their communiqué published in September 1980: "At the same time, they stressed that the *basic* [italics added] character of Fund lending should be preserved and that changes in the Fund lending policies that are called for in the present circumstances should be kept under review." And even earlier, in mid-1978, a reference to the monetary role is made by the Dutch Executive Director Ruding, Polak's predecessor: "We should not forget that the Fund, in accordance with its Articles of Agreement, acts and should act as a monetary institution for bridging temporary balance-of-payments deficits by providing short- or medium-term credit. It is not a development aid institution for the financing of long-term development projects or programmes."[2]

That the monetary character of the Fund was not an issue at the international discussions on monetary matters for so long can be attributed to the fact that such a character was deemed self-evident for the Fund. Loans were provided to different countries at different times. Prolonged use was no acute problem. Nobody worried about the Fund's liquidity. Only when it became clear that these characteristics ceased to be evident, did the code expression become fashionable. Two developments can be distinguished that were important in explaining the role which the expression "monetary character of the IMF" was meant to play. One is that by this time industrial countries had ceased to draw on the Fund. The other is that the liquidity position of the Fund deteriorated markedly.

As to the first point, the Fund's debtors consisted exclusively of poor and middle-income developing countries. In itself this is not necessarily a worrisome situation. However, it led many to draw the conclusion that the IMF should no longer attach the same conditions to its lending as when industrial countries were still among its debtors. Developing countries, it was argued, had specific needs. The Fund should take them into account in fixing the amounts it lent, the duration, and the policy conditions attached. Political

---

[2]H.O. Ruding, "The IMF and International Credit," *The Banker* (London), June 1978, pp. 27–31, at p. 31.

pressure on Fund conditionality increased markedly in the wake of the second oil shock. Criticism was by no means limited to developing countries but was widespread in industrial countries as well. The report of the Brandt Commission published in 1980 is but one example of that pressure.[3] Monetary authorities in industrial countries faced the task of explaining, to an often uncomprehending public and parliament, the constraints to which Fund lending was subjected.

The constraints are a consequence of the aims of Fund credit, as laid down in Article I of its Articles of Agreement: "To give confidence to members by making the general resources of the Fund temporarily available to them under adequate safeguards, thus providing them with opportunity to correct maladjustments in their balance of payments without resorting to measures destructive of national or international prosperity." The Fund thus can help "to shorten the duration and lessen the degree of disequilibrium in the international balances of payments of members." Temporary balance of payments assistance implies that Fund conditionality has to focus on adjustment.

To many critics of the IMF this appeared to mean that the Fund gave priority to the restoration of balance of payments equilibrium over the maintenance of public expenditure to feed people and teach children. The explanation that the Fund's conditionality was a consequence of the Fund's purposes was not always accepted as convincing. Here was an institution with large reserves at its disposal: part of the resources of central banks of industrial countries. It did not need to compete for the scarce budgetary resources that industrial countries facing increasing financial pressures felt able to devote to developing countries. If its purposes, defined at a different time with different needs, stood in the way, then why not agree to change them? Ministers of finance and central bank governors of industrial countries had somehow to explain that one could not turn the IMF into an institution granting development aid while retaining its monetary resources. This was the message they wanted to convey when referring to the monetary character of the IMF.

The Fund's Liquidity Position

The reason why a situation where the balance sheet of the Fund consists of monetary resources on the one hand, and claims in the

---

[3] Independent Commission on International Development Issues, *North-South: A Programme for Survival* (Cambridge, Massachusetts: MIT Press, 1980).

form of development loans on the other, is neither possible nor desirable is illustrated by the Fund's liquidity position. In the early 1980s Fund lending increased steeply, from SDR 2.4 billion in 1980 to SDR 11.3 billion in 1984. The result was that between 1980 and 1984 the IMF's uncommitted own resources did not increase, notwithstanding a substantial quota increase, while its liquid liabilities tripled. As a consequence, the relation between these two, that is, the liquidity ratio, strongly deteriorated.

In the same period, the international debt problem became manifest. In 1982 Mexico led the way for a number of major developing countries in a massive rescheduling of debts to private banks. Most of these countries turned to the Fund at a stage when policy conditions had to be harsh and were therefore resented. The possibility could not be excluded that the international debt problem involving private banks would be followed by a debt problem involving the IMF.

If that would happen, the willingness of central banks in industrial countries to have part of their reserves at the disposal of the IMF would clearly lessen. That in turn would have consequences for the Fund, and, obviously, for the resources available to the debtor countries. For Polak the unease of some of the Fund's creditors, combined with the U.S. reluctance to contribute to the periodic quota increases, was a reason to revive an older idea in 1983, viz., to merge the General and Special Accounts in the IMF and put the Fund on an SDR basis. It would then lend by creating SDRs, thus providing creditors with an asset they might prefer to claims on the IMF. The idea was ingenious, as could be expected from Polak. But it could not allay the concern of central banks in several industrial countries. Those worried about the deteriorating liquidity position of the IMF and the implications for the liquidity of their claims on the Fund were even more concerned about what might happen if the constraint on Fund lending would thus seem to have been removed.

Discussions in the Group of Ten and the Monetary Committee

These concerns were not equally shared by all Group of Ten countries, certainly not initially. When the Dutch Group of Ten Deputies argued at the meeting held in April 1982 that prospective Fund lending should not be solely determined by demand, but that the availability of resources and the cause of the imbalances should also be taken into account, they were listened to in shocked disbelief by several of their colleagues. Yet, in August of that year the Monetary Committee of the European Community held a discussion on the implications of "Preserving the IMF as a Monetary Institution" on the basis of a note which the Dutch members had presented at the Committee's request. In February 1984, a modified version was presented to the Group of Ten Deputies.[4]

The Dutch Deputies found allies, among others, in the U.S. representatives who endorsed the criterion that the availability of Fund resources should be taken into account when deciding on prospective Fund lending. The U.S. authorities, in a paper also written as a preliminary study for the Group of Ten report on the "International Monetary System," believed that the key to the Fund's success and efficacy was its unique monetary character. They stressed the importance of a strong conditionality attached to Fund programs and advocated a forceful reduction in the Fund's access limits. The Fund itself was not particularly worried about its liquidity. It challenged creditor countries to make more frequent use of their reserve tranches, in order to raise the perceived liquidity of the claims.[5] Furthermore, it argued it was too simple to measure liquidity by a ratio between readily usable assets and liquid liabilities. However true this might be, the answer was not felt to be convincing because it failed to address the essential point: the lower the amount of usable currencies available to the Fund, the smaller the source from which payments can be made to countries that draw on their reserve positions.

Ultimately, a large part of the concerns brought forward by the Dutch Deputies was shared by the other Group of Ten members. It was reflected in the Group of Ten Deputies' report cited by Polak: "The Deputies... stress the need to safeguard its [the Fund's] monetary character and the revolving nature of its financing, as well as the importance of keeping it as a quota-based financial institution and its lending normally in line with quota resources. They also stress the need to continue to phase down the policy of enlarged access and to terminate it as soon as the situation of external payments permits, and to deal with the problem of prolonged use and arrears."[6]

---

[4] Note by the Dutch Group of Ten Deputies, "The Future Role of the International Monetary Fund and Its Monetary Character," February 20, 1984. The substance of this note has been published in a Dutch doctoral dissertation by A. Szász, *Monetaire Diplomatie* [Monetary Diplomacy] (Leiden: H.E. Stenfert Kroese BV, 1988).

[5] In 1986 the Netherlands made a symbolic reserve tranche drawing for repayments of a European Monetary System intervention debt.

[6] Deputies of the Group of Ten, *The Functioning of the International Monetary System* (June 1985), paragraph 112.

II. The Monetary Character in the Present Situation

The Fund's Liquidity Position

So where do we stand now, ten years after the code expression had emerged in the Group of Ten communiqués? Is it still worthwhile to be concerned about the Fund's middle initial? According to the Executive Board of the Fund it certainly is, as can be deducted from the 1990 *Annual Report*: "There was agreement by the Executive Board that...its basic monetary character...must be preserved by ensuring that the Fund would continue to provide balance of payments assistance on a temporary basis, that the Fund resources revolve, and that the Fund would continue to hold a level of usable assets sufficient to protect the liquidity and immediate usability of members' claims on the Fund, thereby maintaining members' confidence in and support of the institution."[7]

On the face of it, one could argue that the concern should have waned because one of the key indicators of the Fund's monetary character, its liquidity position, has improved markedly in the early 1980s. The ratio between the Fund's highly liquid assets and its liquid liabilities is now over 100 percent, whereas in 1982 it was less than 40 percent, while the Executive Board of the Fund seems to have reached consensus that about 70 percent is adequate. Yet, it is not the actual ratio that is a cause for concern. A shortage of liquidity is, in the words of Polak, "a potential rather than an actual risk."[8] This does not mean that it can be neglected. On the contrary, future developments have to be scrutinized closely and reviewed regularly in order to prevent the painful situation where the Fund would not grant assistance to an eligible country, because of a shortage of resources. In order to assess these potential risks, two considerations are important: the potential supply and demand of Fund credit and the nature of the Fund exposure.

Potential Supply and Demand

First of all, some general observations on the credit facilities of the Fund. As is well known, the Fund in 1981 established its enlarged access policy on Fund resources. Under this policy, access limits were raised from 100 or 165 percent[9] of a member's quota to a

---

[7]International Monetary Fund, *Annual Report, 1990* (Washington), pp. 47–48.
[8]"Some Notes on 'The Monetary Character of the IMF'" (cited in footnote 1), paragraph 8.
[9]Respectively, the limit for stand-by and extended arrangements.

cumulative total of 600 percent. It was clear from the outset that this could only be a temporary measure. Obviously in the long run the Fund would not be able to finance that much credit out of its own resources. The Fund staff has calculated a long-term sustainable ratio of around 250 percent. This is based on experience in the last decade where the ratio between the quotas of debtor countries and countries with weak external positions—whose currencies cannot be used for IMF drawings—and those of creditor countries is somewhere in the region of 30 percent versus 70 percent. It should be kept in mind, that this was the case in a situation where the IMF's debtors consisted only of developing countries. At present this is still a realistic assumption, but it neglects the wish that some industrial countries could in the future become Fund debtors as well. If a broadening of the group of Fund debtors were to occur, a considerable impact might emerge on the percentages just mentioned. The conclusion is obvious: access limits have to be brought down markedly. At least to 250 percent, preferably to an even lower number. Did this happen?

It did not. As in politics, one should not overestimate the significance of the expression "temporary." It can be regarded as an understatement for "wrong, but unavoidable under the circumstances." In September 1983, the communiqué of the Interim Committee explicitly acknowledged that "the policy of enlarged access . . . is of a temporary character."[10] In line with this observation the limits were lowered[11] to (cumulative) 408–500 percent from January 1, 1984. Two years later, the Interim Committee decided that for the moment only "modest adjustments" to the access limits were appropriate, while in the autumn of 1986 the Committee felt it could be even more generous. The temporary character was only given lip service, and the Committee refrained from reducing the limits any further. As from 1988, even this lip service has come to be considered superfluous. Moreover, the IMF recently decided to suspend the lower maximum limits under the policy of enlarged access in response to the crisis in the Middle East,[12] which in point of fact implies an increase of potential access. Of course, it was

---

[10] International Monetary Fund, *Annual Report, 1984* (Washington), p. 143.

[11] Though not nominal access, because quotas were increased simultaneously, on average by 50 percent.

[12] International Monetary Fund, Press Release No. 90/57, November 15, 1990, reprinted in *IMF Survey*, International Monetary Fund (Washington), Vol. 19 (November 26, 1990), pp. 365–66.

decided that it should be a temporary measure only, that is, until the end of 1991.

Whether this potential access will indeed be brought down substantially by the time the proposed increase in quotas has become effective, which is planned for the end of 1991, is uncertain. It is certain, however, that in the recent past *actual* access within these limits has risen. This development coincided with the implementation of the Brady initiative. One of the objectives of this initiative was that "the IMF and the [World] Bank could provide funding, as part of their policy-based lending programs, for debt or debt service reduction purposes."[13] This funding, known as "set aside accounts" and "augmentation for interest support" raised actual average access under stand-by and extended arrangements from around 40 percent of quotas to some 70 percent excluding and 110 percent including interest support. At the same time, the demand for Fund resources that can be expected in the near future is possibly considerable indeed. Balance of payments deficits on current account of the developing countries have again increased. Recent new commitments of Fund resources, SDR 11 billion in the financial year 1989/90, which is more than three times the amount recorded the year before, point in the same direction.

Furthermore, a new group of countries is knocking on the door. The former centrally planned economies of Central and Eastern Europe are increasingly demanding Fund resources. Their formidable task to reorganize the complete structure of their economies requires considerable financial assistance. The larger part of this probably needs to consist of funds with a structural character. Nevertheless, balance of payments assistance is necessary, too. What effects the Middle East crisis will have on the financial position of the Fund, we can only guess. For the moment, an oil element has been introduced in the compensatory and contingency financing facility, which enables countries that suffer from the oil price increase to draw 82 percent of quota at short notice with relatively weak conditionality attached to it.

Nature of the Fund Exposure

So, potential access is ample. Demand may be soaring. Moreover, prolonged use, which was already apparent in the early 1980s, has

---

[13] Remarks by the U.S. Secretary of the Treasury, Nicholas F. Brady, to a conference sponsored by the Bretton Woods Committee and the Brookings Institution, Washington, March 1989, *Third World Debt: The Next Phase*, ed. by Edward R. Fried and Philip H. Trezise (Washington: Brookings Institution, 1989), p. 73.

gained a new dimension: "super-prolonged use"—that is, overdue financial obligations to the Fund. In 1984 the Dutch Deputies stated that "more than half the outstanding Fund credit consists of claims on countries which have been more or less permanent IMF debtors for a period of ten years."[14] This implied that refinancing was in fact taking place. Nowadays, nearly *all* the debtors of the Fund are in such a position. In numerous countries, the exposure remains stubbornly high. Obviously, this constellation is at variance with the revolving nature of short-term balance of payments assistance.

This is even more true for the arrears to the Fund which—at the time this paper was written—were again on the increase, amounting to more than SDR 3.3 billion. Nobody will deny that overdue financial obligations are contrary to the Fund's monetary character, whatever the definition used. Moreover, as long as Fund resources are tied down in several member countries, they are not available to others. Whereas they should be, in a cooperative institution.

The Fund has sought to deal with this pressing problem in three different ways. First of all, to back up interest income forgone and to strengthen the Fund reserves, a burden sharing mechanism was introduced. It implies that creditors accept a lower rate of return on their remunerated reserve tranche position in the Fund, while the rate of charge on Fund drawings is raised. The consequence is that countries that actually service their debts, pay double. For instance, because of the arrears to the Fund of a certain African country, 82 countries, including 5 in Africa with per capita incomes equal to or below that of the country in question, have paid approximately SDR 13 million more in charges to the Fund than otherwise would have been necessary. A striking illustration of how arrears violate the cooperative nature of the Fund.

The burden sharing mechanism has its limitations. There is a limit as to how far the rate of charge can reasonably be raised without causing a "revolt" by the complying debtor countries that no longer wish to pay for their dissenting brothers. There is also a limit on the extent the rate of remuneration can be lowered: one cannot expect to allay the fears of creditor central banks about the effect the arrears have on the liquidity of their claims by eliminating the interest return on these claims.

As an alternative to the burden sharing mechanism, Polak set out a sophisticated plan on the back of an envelope. The idea was to temporarily reorganize part of the ninth quota increase in such a

---

[14]Referred to in footnote 4.

way that the Fund could save an annual SDR 300 million interest payments, roughly equal to the amount necessary at present to compensate for interest income forgone. An interesting suggestion that underlines the inexhaustible creativity Polak continues to demonstrate. However, it is also an illustration of how difficult it is to maintain orderly financial accounts in the Fund and to safeguard its reserves.

As a second measure, the Fund showed its collaborative grain. It introduced the possibility for the ineligible low-income countries with long-standing arrears to earn "rights" to drawings on the Fund as soon as a three-year shadow program had been successfully completed. Thus two birds are killed with one stone. That is, such was the aim. On the one hand, the country involved is provided with a—perhaps last—opportunity to improve its policies, supported by financial means from the international community. On the other hand, the Fund avoids having to depreciate its claims on these member states.

To prevent moral hazard, a third measure was initiated, and it was a rigorous one: an amendment of the Articles of Agreement, only the third in 45 years. It took the form of the possibility to suspend membership rights (i.e., mainly voting and representation rights) of a country that was judged to be insufficiently cooperative with the Fund in finding a solution to its long-standing arrears. The three decisions taken together constitute a solid, well-balanced approach, in principle. In practice, its efficacy is not beyond doubt because the underlying problem is not tackled. The failure to pursue adequate adjustment policies was—and is—at the heart of the problem. Whether the opportunity of receiving rights or the prospect of enhanced deterrent measures will at last turn out to be the appropriate incentive to improve on these policies remains to be seen.

III. Concluding Remarks

The monetary character of the Fund: defining it is difficult. It might be an allusive label. Yet it does serve a purpose. It conveys a simple message to the public at large: the Fund funds itself with the liquid reserves of its creditors, which they will only be prepared to continue to do, as long as proper constraints on the volume and character of Fund lending are adhered to. In this article, it has been argued that these constraints have been and possibly will be put to the test. As long as industrial countries are not prepared to draw on Fund credits, the consequences are twofold.

First, creditor countries will increasingly consider the Fund to be a development institution. This is emphasized by the potential worsening of the Fund's liquidity position. In these circumstances, creditor countries will see their reserve position in the Fund not as liquid investments, but more and more as a means of development assistance. Indications already exist that industrial countries consider the liquidity of their claims on the Fund as less liquid than foreign exchange reserves, as can be derived from remarks of the President of the Swiss National Bank.[15] Prospective members may be ready to accept this perceived inevitable cost of membership. However, the existing membership might become more hesitant to support any increase of its contribution to the Fund. This is illustrated by the fact that the preparedness to agree to the ninth quota increase was made dependent on a strengthening of the arrears strategy.

Second, it becomes more difficult to insist on strict conditionality on Fund drawings if it is obvious that the industrial countries themselves will never subject to it. The conditionality applied has indeed not succeeded in ensuring that countries are strict short-term users of Fund credit. On the contrary, adjustment programs have been insufficiently implemented, and Fund programs have tended to succeed one another quickly. The temporary policy of enlarged access, with its lengthened repayment periods and above-normal access, seems to be evolving into a more or less permanent feature. Extended arrangements have become more popular. An overwhelmingly large majority of debtor members has been indebted to the Fund for more than ten years continuously. Arrears keep rising; to cite again the *Annual Report*: "The reduction and elimination of overdue financial obligations to the Fund are essential for ensuring the cooperative nature of the institution and preserving its monetary character."[16]

---

[15] "By exchanging assets held in dollars for a creditor position with the IMF the National Bank would be giving up liquid assets for assets that were virtually illiquid; furthermore, the foreign exchange reserves held with the IMF are of relatively lower quality than those held in the currency of an internationally solvent state. The Fund's assets are effectively made up of loans to developing countries. Such debts clearly do not have the same degree of creditworthiness as those of the United States, for example. As the IMF has lent only to developing countries for nearly ten years now, holding debt at the Fund is equivalent to indirectly holding the debt of the most heavily indebted countries." Excerpt from a speech given by the President of the Swiss National Bank, Dr. Markus Lusser, at a conference organized by the Programme for Strategic Studies and International Security in Geneva on November 14, 1990.

[16] International Monetary Fund, *Annual Report, 1990* (Washington), p. 56.

The implication is not, however, that the Fund should curb its role of financier to the international community. Although IMF credits cannot and should not replace development loans, they ought to remain an important catalyst for other forms of financial assistance. Most important, the Fund should lay emphasis on what is its speciality: to provide proper and well-balanced advice on adjustment policies. Adequate conditionality is necessary not only to preserve the revolving character of its credits but also for the success of the government policies in the debtor countries. Yet Fund advice is best if political influences are kept at an ample distance. In this respect the Fund is like a central bank. If a central bank is not independent of political authorities, monetary policy may opt for the soft option: a premature lowering of interest rates and monetary financing of budget deficits. If IMF credits are granted on mere political grounds, without a solid analysis of the repayment capacity of the debtor country involved and of the preparedness of national government to pursue adequate adjustment policies, the risk is obvious: too much financing, too little adjustment, and, consequently, repayment problems. To use the allusive label, the monetary character of the institution is endangered.

Of course, the Fund is in reality subject to political influence. After all, member states choose their representatives on the Executive Board, the day-to-day decision-making forum of the Fund. As a result, Executive Directors have two hats. On the one hand, they are supposed to—and should—voice the views of the members of their constituency, that is, governments. On the other hand, as Board members of an international monetary institution, they hold an independent position; for they need to look after the Fund—and cherish its monetary character—like a good *paterfamilias* should. A proper balance between these two functions requires an Executive Director to be a person of formidable quality and stature. From 1981 to 1986, with the eminent and creative Polak, the Netherlands couldn't have fared better.

Current Issues in the Open Economy

PART FOUR

Current Issues in the
Open Economy

11

Prudential Supervision and Monetary Policy

H. Robert Heller

Central banking and the supervision and regulation of financial institutions and markets are key governmental functions in any modern economy. In general, the government reserves for itself the right to issue money—a privilege that is often enshrined in the constitution itself. But in a modern mixed economy, monetary functions tend to be shared by the central bank and commercial banks, be they public or private institutions.

Typically, the country's central bank is given the exclusive authority to determine the quantity of currency in circulation. It also exercises authority over other types of money, such as demand deposits, that represent liabilities of other financial institutions. These financial institutions play important roles as depository institutions, sources of credit, and as financial intermediaries. In addition to being creditors and debtors to the rest of the economy, the financial institutions also perform important payment services.

It is therefore appropriate to describe the financial system as the nerve center of a modern nation, without which it could not prosper.

Given this central role of the financial system, it is not surprising that governments take a keen interest in the health of financial institutions and markets as well as the payments system.

The key question to be addressed in this paper is whether the central banking function and the supervisory and regulatory functions should be combined in one institution, such as the central bank or the monetary authority, or whether supervisory and regulatory functions should be delegated to a separate supervisory agency.

Posing the question as a simple choice between the need for one or two institutions to exercise the central banking and supervisory and regulatory authority is probably an oversimplification of a complex set of problems and issues. The modern economy needs a broad range of financial institutions and markets, and the question as to which institutions should exercise, regulate, and supervise these functions is also highly complex. It is therefore no surprise that in the modern economy several regulators exercise these disparate functions. The search for a simple, all-encompassing framework will be difficult at best and lead to endless frustration at worst.

I. Policy Functions

Among the various financial functions that need to be exercised in a modern economy is first of all the monetary policy function, which encompasses the issuance of currency and the control of the monetary aggregates. Because liquid liabilities of depository institutions serve as money, the control over the aggregate amount of such monetary liabilities is a key element of monetary policy. Given the institutional structure of modern banking systems, this implies the need for control over reserve requirements and the total amount of reserves in existence. Without pursuing the point at this juncture any further, it is clear that whatever institution has authority over the required reserve ratio to be maintained by depository institutions will be involved in the monetary policymaking process as well as the bank regulatory process.

Second, there is the lender-of-last-resort function. In a two-tier banking system, some institution has to fulfill the role of being the banker's bank by standing ready to supply high-powered money to the depository institutions. This function is tied intimately to the central bank's role as the issuer of a nation's currency. In nations without their own currency, the lender-of-last-resort function may be exercised by the central bank of the currency-issuing country or a large private bank of unquestioned standing.

Traditionally, the central bank performs this lender-of-last-resort function through the discount window. By setting the discount rate, a monetary policy function, the central bank sets the terms at which the individual banks have access to the central bank's resources. Especially if the discount rate is set below the market rate at which reserves are traded in the free market, a need arises to administer the discount privilege. In turn this may necessitate a need for information to verify that this below-market discount rate privilege is not abused. If the discount rate is set above the market rate, such a need will not normally arise as banks have an incentive not to use the discount window, except as a true last resort. Under such circumstances, the fact that a bank actually utilizes the discount window may be an important indicator that has information value for the supervisory agency.

Of course, if the discount window privilege is used not only for liquidity purposes but also to hide the insolvency or impending insolvency of an institution, this would represent a source of concern. This danger is minimized if the central bank lends only against sound collateral because under these circumstances the act of liquefying an illiquid asset cannot help to hide insolvency. As long as the central bank lends only on the basis of sound collateral, the need for a direct supervisory role to prevent the abuse of the discount window is thereby minimized.

Third, there is the role of the central bank as the government's bank. As such, it serves as depository for liquid funds owned by the finance ministry or the treasury and manages and disburses these funds at the behest of the government. While these functions could also be exercised by private banks, governments need an institution of unquestioned integrity and reputation as their bank.

Fourth, there is the payments system function, which encompasses the clearing and settlement of checks and electronic payments. Typically, central banks play an important role in the payments system, with transfers on the books of the central bank constituting final and irrevocable payment.

Clearly, some or all of these functions can also be performed by private sector financial institutions. However, special precautions have to be taken to safeguard the system against the possible failure of a financial institution and the potential need to recast, or unwind a settlement.

But whereas a nation's central bank can well serve as the backbone of the national payments system, the issues involved are not at all clear when it comes to the international payments system. Nations are by nature reluctant to let official agencies of other countries perform this function and hence there is an important role for the private sector or an international agency.

So far we have discussed the functions of a central bank as it is more narrowly construed. We will now turn to the regulatory functions that may be exercised by the central bank or a supervisory and regulatory agency.

II. Bank Supervisory and Regulatory Functions

Rule-making authority is probably the broadest regulatory function that can be delegated to a bank supervisory agency. The legislature is the ultimate regular rule-making authority in the country—safe for a constitutional convention or the constitutional amendment process.

Due to the complexity of modern financial institutions and the ever-present need to adapt the regulatory environment to small institutional changes and market innovations, legislatures often find it convenient to delegate limited rule-making authority to regulatory bodies. This rule-making authority is generally confined to well-defined narrow problem areas, but on occasion disputes regarding the legislative intent of the limits to an agency's rule-making authority may emerge.

Rule making tends to follow a framework and set of procedures that is not unlike the legislative process itself. Typically, draft proposals are put out for public debate and comment and are implemented only after long and searching scrutiny.

In contrast, cases brought before the regulatory agency by various parties are handled in a manner that more closely resembles judicial procedures. Cases are brought either by regulated entities that wish to engage in additional activities or be relieved of restrictions imposed by previous regulatory decisions, or by other parties that wish to enjoin the regulated entities from engaging in certain activities or force them to offer additional services. By their very nature, cases are more closely related to the supervisory process and frequently arise out of the supervisory process itself.

Both rule making and case decisions can have profound influence on a country's banking structure. Over time, the cumulative effect of changes that are in and of themselves only marginal can be substantial and the regulatory agency can thereby exercise quasi-legislative functions.

Key areas of regulatory activities are in defining the charter provision for banks and the granting of charters under these provisions; the ongoing administration of banking institutions, including capital adequacy, liquidity, and related balance sheet requirements; the authorization to engage in specified activities; and the approval of expansions, mergers, and acquisitions. Finally, the ultimate supervisory responsibility rests in the authority to withdraw the charter and force the dissolution of the banking organization.

In addition to these regulatory and supervisory functions, financial institutions may also have to adhere to the rules and regulations established by other regulatory bodies. In particular, this may include the insurance funds for deposits in financial institutions. The interest of the insurance fund in regulatory issues will be heightened if the financial institutions to be insured have the option of seeking a charter from any one of several different supervisory and regulatory agencies. Under these circumstances, the insurance fund must make certain that the institutions are properly supervised and are adhering to certain minimum risk standards. This problem is less likely to arise in those countries where one single regulatory agency imposes a uniform set of standards upon all insured financial institutions. In that case, the insurance fund becomes a mere risk pooling device rather than an agency that is concerned with the establishment of uniform standards.

Moreover, there exists in many countries a whole panoply of governmental agencies, such as the tax authorities, the securities and exchange commission (or its equivalent), as well as labor and employee health and safety commissions that also have a role in regulating financial institutions.

III. Competing Interests

It is not surprising that in complex modern economies with sophisticated financial systems and a high degree of innovation, there exist competing regulatory interests and maybe even a degree of tension and competition among various regulatory bodies. This competition is particularly evident in large countries with a federal structure and in countries that have a complex and differentiated financial system.

An extreme example in this regard is the United States, where competing regional and sectoral influences are further exacerbated by a governmental structure that emphasizes checks and balances at the federal level and the preservation of states' rights at the regional level. This has resulted in a complex web of regulatory agencies that has resisted numerous attempts at reform designed to produce a more unified and coherent structure. It would be interesting to speculate to what extent a unified Europe might eventually resemble the complex U.S. regulatory structure a few decades from now.

IV. Basic Tenets

At this juncture it may be useful to establish some basic tenets that may guide us in arriving at an answer to the question whether supervisory and regulatory authority should be exercised by the central bank or lodged in a separate institution, and—if so—where the dividing line should be drawn.

One, the institutional structure of the regulatory, supervisory, and monetary authority should promote a safe and sound, stable financial system. It should also promote the development of dynamic markets.

Two, the role of the government supervisory and regulating agency should not be to micro manage the various financial institutions, but to prevent systemic failures and the risk of contagion.

Three, the freedom of action of the monetary, regulatory, and supervisory agencies should not be unduly impaired by conflicting goals and purposes.

The goal of a sound and stable financial system is the central focus of all governmental regulatory and supervisory activity as well as of monetary policy. It should include the activities of the government itself, such as the conduct of the government's budgetary policy.

A stable financial environment calls for a coherent and noncontradictory regulatory policy. Differences in regulatory and supervisory approaches will lead to competitive advantages and disadvantages among financial institutions and thereby engender financial instability.

The potential for regulatory laxity is another aspect of regulatory diversity. It is easy for industry groups to plead that they should be accorded easier regulatory treatment when there are various regulators that can be played off against each other. While the potential for competition in laxity among federal and state banking and regulatory agencies cannot be ruled out, the opposite—namely competition in stringency—is also a real possibility when the government or even the public at large is looking for scapegoats in difficult times.

But competition on a regional basis—such as between various state banking regulators—is perhaps even more difficult to control. On the one hand, there is the potential to attract entire branches of the financial service industry to one location by having a relatively permissive regulatory environment. This temptation on behalf of a state regulatory agency is particularly prcnounced when the existence of a federal safety net provides protection to depositors lured by high interest rates made possible by a very lax state regulatory environment. On the other hand, the existence of competition among states and state regulators helps to avoid the creation of an overpowerful federal bureaucracy.

In small countries, where there is no scope for the maintenance of several regional regulatory agencies, similar considerations may be brought into play by cross-border competition.

In sum, while a fragmented regulatory system may offer certain limited advantages by permitting experimentation and diversity in financial regulation, it is difficult to argue that regulatory diversity will promote stability, safety, and soundness of the financial system. For example, there is little evidence in U.S. financial history that suggests that the existence of a multitude of regulatory agencies has served to enhance the safety and soundness of the U.S. financial system.

The potential conflict between macroeconomic and microeconomic policy objectives is closely related to the question whether the central bank or a separate bank supervisory agency should be involved in the day-to-day supervision of financial institutions.

There are several reasons why one might want to argue that the central bank should be involved in the day-to-day supervision and regulation of financial institutions. First of all, the central bank will be able to garner valuable insights into the overall state of the economy by being involved in the day-to-day supervision and regulation of financial institutions. Second, being able to influence bank policy through regulatory pressure might give additional force and impetus to monetary policy measures. However, in exercising this additional power, the central bank might easily step across the line from impartial macro management of the economy to credit allocation and micro management of individual institutions.

One may even argue that there is a danger that impartial access to the discount window may not be given by a central bank that has regulatory powers in case of a regulatory conflict between the central bank and a bank that it supervises. In other words, one can see certain advantages in the existence of the central bank as an independent and neutral lender of last resort, rather than an institution that can leverage its own policy authority from one policy area to another policy area.

Central banks with supervisory and regulatory responsibilities have traditionally avoided such a conflict of interest by operating separate supervisory and monetary policy departments and have argued that the two functions are being conducted independently from each other. But if such "Chinese walls" exist within the central bank, then the argument that the supervisory and monetary policy functions should be exercised by one institution so as to take advantage of potential synergies does not hold water.

One can also easily envision situations in which the monetary policy function and the regulatory function might result in a conflict of interest. This potential for a conflict of interest is particularly strong in times when the central bank is forced to pursue such a tight monetary policy that the very survival of many financial institutions is threatened. In such a situation it may be difficult to separate the mandate for a sound monetary policy, which might have to drive interest rates so high that the very existence of many financial institutions is at stake, from the mandate to maintain safe and sound financial institutions. In such a conflict situation regulatory and supervisory actions may be delayed or not implemented so as not to exacerbate the impact of the monetary policy actions on the banking industry.

The alternative situation, namely that monetary policy is conducted with an excessive regard for supervisory concerns about the health of one or more financial institutions, is potentially even more dangerous as it might lead to the perpetuation of inappropriate monetary policies that might, in the long run, actually worsen the problems confronting the nation. Of course, a central bank without supervisory responsibilities might also feel that it is limited in its freedom of action in a situation where the banking system is in a precarious situation. However, under these circumstances, the possibility of a direct conflict of interest is not present and politicians and other observers cannot accuse the central bank of conflict of interest. Thus, it will be easier for the central bank to preserve its most cherished possession: its independence in the realm of monetary policy.

V. Preserving the Central Bank's Independence

This brings us to the essential point: preserving the independence of the central bank in monetary policy matters. In most countries, the central bank acts pursuant to authority granted to it by the congress or parliament. And whatever legislative powers the legislature grants, it can also take away again.

Bank supervision and regulation are functions much more closely related to the exercise of general governmental authority, that is, the executive branch. They are not functions that will ever be totally independent of the government, but other governmental agencies—such as the justice department—will be directly and substantially involved as well.

To put the matter differently, monetary policy is a macroeconomic activity that touches individual economic agents only indirectly, while regulatory and supervisory policies involve direct control by governmental agencies.

If the central bank assumes daily regulatory authority, it will get involved in the day-to-day exercise of governmental authority that may in extreme circumstances involve the central bank in partisan politics—thereby unavoidably endangering its independence.

This does not imply that the central bank cannot do an outstanding job in regulating and supervising financial institutions. As a matter of fact, I believe that the Federal Reserve has done an excellent job in that regard and has managed to stay clear of controversy and partisan politics. This has not been true for some other supervisory agencies in the United States. Just imagine the potential damage to the reputation of the central bank that might have resulted if the Federal Reserve had also been the supervisory agency for the thrift industry. At best, its prestige would have been blemished and at worst, its independence in monetary affairs might well have been challenged.

VI. The Track Record

It may be interesting to compare the track record of central banks that have supervisory responsibilities with the track record of central banks without supervisory responsibilities in achieving the central goal of monetary policy: a low inflation rate. Table 1 shows the inflation rate, as measured by the average annual increase in consumer prices during the period 1980–87, for central banks without supervisory responsibilities, for central banks that share the supervisory role, and for central banks that have main supervisory responsibilities.

Judging from the evidence provided by the limited sample of countries for which the evidence was readily obtainable, one may conclude that central banks without supervisory responsibilities were more successful in attaining a low inflation rate than central banks

Table 1. The Supervisory Responsibility of Central Banks and Inflation Performance[1]

Central banks without supervisory authority		
Canada	5.0	
Germany	2.9	
Japan	1.4	4.9 percent (3.3 percent without
Switzerland	3.9	Latin American countries)
Venezuela	11.4	
Central banks share supervisory authority		
France	7.7	
Italy	11.5	
Netherlands	2.3	6.5 percent
United States	4.3	
Central banks with supervisory authority		
Argentina	298.7	
Australia	7.8	
Brazil	116.3	
Ireland	10.2	66.2 percent (9.6 percent without
South Africa	13.8	Latin American countries)
Spain	10.7	
United Kingdom	5.7	

Sources: World Bank, *World Development Report, 1989* (New York: Oxford University Press, 1989); and Price Waterhouse.
[1] Inflation rates are average annual rates for 1980–87.

with shared or full responsibility in the supervisory area. The average inflation rate for 1980–87 for countries with central banks without supervisory responsibilities was 4.9 percent (or 3.3 percent if Venezuela, the only Latin American country in the group, is omitted). For the group of central banks that have shared supervisory responsibilities, inflation averaged 6.5 percent, while it reached an annual rate of 66.2 percent for countries with central banks that have full supervisory responsibilities (9.6 percent if the two Latin American countries in the sample, Argentina and Brazil, are excluded). This evidence would support the notion that central banks that concentrate all their energy on monetary policy tend to be more successful in achieving the goal of price stability than central banks that have major supervisory responsibilities.

Of course, it is possible that this apparent association between a good performance in attaining price stability and the absence of supervisory responsibilities may also be caused by the presence of other influences. One possibility that comes immediately to mind is the degree of independence of the central bank from the government. It may well be that independent central banks are better in attaining the goal of price stability and that these independent banks also do not tend to have supervisory responsibilities. But in a way, this argument, if found to be true, would support the basic hypothesis: namely that bank supervisory responsibility is a governmental function that is unlikely to be given to a truly independent central bank. In other words, the supervisory role for a central bank does tend to be associated with significant strings in terms of greater dependence on the government. Of course, exceptions to this general observation, like the highly independent Netherlands Bank, which also exercises supervisory authority, exist as well.

While a broader study that includes many more countries and a longer time period is clearly called for, the limited evidence presented here supports the notion that independent central banks without supervisory and regulatory responsibilities tend to do better in achieving the primary goal of monetary policy—a low inflation rate.

While supervisory and regulatory functions may impede the monetary policy function, the reverse is true as well. This is particularly so if the central bank in its role as regulator is empowered with rule-making authority. It is easy to conceive of situations in which the rule-making authority of the central bank overlaps or comes into potential conflict with the legislative function itself. In those situations it is not unheard of that legislators will directly approach the central bank and make their views felt.

Once this direct contact is established, two dangers emerge: one, legislators may also attempt to influence monetary policy actions and two, the central bank may defer regulatory actions in order to preserve its monetary independence. Under these circumstances, the regulated entities will not be served as well as they would be served by a regulatory agency for which such considerations do not apply, thereby permitting greater regulatory freedom.

Thus, one might conclude that, on balance, a central bank might be able to exercise its monetary policy responsibilities better if it is independent of primary supervisory and regulatory responsibilities. This has also been suggested by most of the task forces that have made recommendations regarding a possible restructuring of the U.S. monetary, supervisory, and regulatory authorities.

VII. The Role of the Central Bank in Supervision

Having stated that for various reasons the central bank should not be the primary regulatory agency, there is still an important role for the central bank in the regulatory process that will enhance and supplement its monetary policy function.

One can see this role of the central bank in setting rules that establish appropriate liquidity levels for the financial institutions and in monitoring adherence thereto. This includes the setting of reserve requirements to be held against monetary liabilities of the financial institutions. This role would supplement the central bank's role as the lender of last resort and a monetary policymaker by extending the central bank's authority over that part of the bank's activities that has a monetary impact.

Such a split in supervisory functions between liquidity concerns on the one hand and general supervisory and solvency concerns on the other hand exists already in some countries as well as in the international banking area. Here the Basle Concordat provides for supervision of liquidity matters by the host country, while the home country, or the country of the bank's domicile, has general supervisory authority, including solvency matters.

This proposal would extend the international division of labor to the domestic arena, with the central bank in charge of liquidity concerns and the other supervisory agency in charge of solvency and general supervision and regulation. For internationally active banks, this proposal would imply no significant changes, except that the home country supervision and regulation would normally be undertaken by a bank regulatory agency, while the supervision of foreign branches and agencies would be the responsibility of the foreign central bank.

VIII. Conclusion

We may conclude that, while central banks generally have a good track record as bank supervisors and regulators, there may also be times when the possible conflict of interest between regulatory and supervisory functions on the one side and monetary policy functions on the other side might result in a higher inflation rate than might be achieved by a truly independent central bank without supervisory responsibilities. Nonetheless, recognizing that the management of the nation's liquidity is a prime monetary policy function, it makes sense to give the nation's central bank limited supervisory functions in the liquidity area. This supervisory and regulatory role pertaining to reserve requirements and liquidity ratios can and should be exercised by the central bank.

This framework is similar to that agreed to in the Basle Concordat for international bank supervision, where the supervision of the liquidity position of foreign branches and agencies is delegated to the host country, while general supervision and regulation is performed by the regulatory and supervisory agency in the bank's home country.

By giving the major supervisory and regulatory responsibilities to a banking agency, while focusing the responsibilities of an independent central bank on monetary policy and supervision of liquidity, a possible conflict between supervisory and regulatory concerns and monetary policy objectives can be avoided. Under such an institutional arrangement, both national goals, the maintenance of a safe and sound financial system and an inflation-free environment may be more readily realized.

12

National and International Monetary Policy

J. de Beaufort Wijnholds

Monetary macroeconomics is quite segmented in a national and international component. General monetary theory deals with explanations of the nature and value of money and the functioning of a monetary economy at the level of a single country. International monetary economics is concerned with international liquidity, the functioning of the international adjustment process and, more broadly, the international monetary system. These two bodies of monetary theory seem to have developed largely separately from each other in recent decades. Similarly, discussions on monetary policy usually are conducted either on a national plane, dealing with policy questions of an individual country with little attention to international aspects, or are focused very much on international monetary problems—*systemic problems* in contemporary jargon—without much consideration for individual country positions.

A number of explanations can be given for the existence of this dichotomy. An obvious one is the far-reaching specialization that, as in other sciences, has become commonplace in economics. Among policy analysts and policymakers there also tends to be a considerable division of labor, with domestic monetary experts and international monetary specialists understanding each other but usually working and meeting largely independently of each other. Another factor appears to be the ideological split between (orthodox) monetarists, who focus almost exclusively on domestic monetary policy and believe that governments should not be externally constrained, and internationalists, who concentrate on the international monetary system and the discipline it can impart on governments.[1]

Looking to the future, however, one development can be singled out that may well lead to a greater integration of national and international monetary economics and a closer collaboration among the practitioners, namely the process of European monetary integration. Monetary integration among countries on a regional scale[2] combines elements of both main segments of monetary economics and requires knowledge of both national monetary structures and of international monetary relationships.

While the interrelationship between national and international monetary problems and policies has not received much attention over the past decades, there are some important exceptions. Twenty years ago Jacques Polak contributed an essay entitled "Money—National and International" to a *Festschrift*,[3] in which he examined the analogies between these two categories of money. His analysis led him to stress the differences rather than the similarities between these two, leading to his main conclusion that international monetary (or reserve) policy should not be geared toward demand management but focus on the long-run demand for reserves. In more recent publications various authors, particularly McKinnon[4] and the IMF staff[5] have demonstrated an interest in and a keen understanding of the relationship between domestic monetary policy and international exchange rate regimes. The relationship between domestic monetary policy and international liquidity remains, however, an underdeveloped area.[6]

In this paper an attempt is made to answer a number of questions pertaining to the relationship between domestic money supplies and domestic monetary policy on the one side, and international liquidity and international monetary policy on the other. The issues are

---

[1] Cf., for instance, Heller (1989).

[2] Proposals for monetary integration on a worldwide scale, such as a global common currency, deal with a different time horizon, as is acknowledged by some of their proponents; cf., for instance, Cooper (1991).

[3] Polak (1970).

[4] McKinnon (1984).

[5] Cf., for instance, Frenkel and Goldstein (1988).

[6] Some elements of this relationship have been addressed in Frenkel (1983). Frenkel suggests, inter alia, that the relative stability of the demand for international reserves, irrespective of the official exchange rate regime, implies that countries' domestic monetary policies have been influenced and constrained by their attempts to attain desired reserve holdings.

dealt with in a policy-oriented manner rather than from a theoretical point of view. In other words, an attempt is made to find generally formulated, practical answers to certain questions even thcugh the solutions may not be clear-cut on theoretical or empirical grounds. This approach of course reflects a policymaker's outlook, where operational—but sometimes flawed—answers are sought rather than elegant theoretical statements. In the real world which confronts government officials, central bankers, and IMF directors and staff—a world Jacques Polak knows intimately—this is often the only way to proceed without falling into the trap of procrastination.

The main theme of this contribution is the meaning and signifi- cance of the simultaneous occurrence during the past fifteen years or so of a central role for monetary policy in most large industrialized countries and a progressively declining interest in the conduct of international monetary policy, in the sense of control over interna- tional liquidity. In other words, while money still matters in the sphere of the domestic economy, most economists and policymakers do not seem to think it really matters in its international appearance. The paper first broadly traces the role of domestic monetary policy, showing that the monetarist revival has largely survived despite a period of waning influence during part of the 1980s. It then looks at the international liquidity question, concluding that the issue of control of international reserves has generally ceased to arouse economists and policymakers alike. In attempting to explain this development, the paper goes on to address the question of the relationship between domestic monetary policy on the one hand, and international reserves and international financial markets on the other. It then addresses the issue as to whether control over interna- tional liquidity is still a goal worth pursuing, concluding that to some extent this is still the case. Subsequently, the question whether international liquidity can actually be controlled is examined. The main conclusion is that traditional approaches are not feasible, but that prudential measures can have a significant impact on interna- tional bank lending and thereby on international liquidity and the international adjustment process. Finally, it is suggested that the question concerning the relationship between domestic monetary policy and international financial markets can be (imperfectly) ad- dressed by including in national monetary aggregates so-called ex- ternal monetary deposits, or by diminishing or eliminating non-in- terest-bearing reserve requirements to which banks are subject with respect to their domestic activities. European monetary integration is bound to solve these problems within the European Community

(EC), where the future European central bank will base its policy on a European monetary aggregate, and monetary policy instruments will be fully uniform or, in the case of decentralized execution of policy, highly harmonized.

I. National Monetary Policy

The low point in terms of faith in the effectiveness of monetary policy in the postwar era can be put at around 1960. Under the triumphant rule of Keynesian economics, the role of money and monetary policy was quite limited in most countries during the 1950s and the 1960s.[7] The quintessence of authoritative skepticism with respect to the role of monetary policy can be found in the report of the Radcliffe Committee, which concluded that "Monetary measures are aimed at the level of demand, but by their nature they are incapable by themselves of having an effect sufficiently prompt and far-reaching for their purpose, unless applied with a vigour that itself creates a major emergency."[8]

In the meantime, Friedman's monetarist counterrevolution was building up momentum, first in academic circles and in the 1970s also in central banks and governments. Monetary targeting by central banks commenced with the Deutsche Bundesbank's announcement in late 1974 of a target for the growth of central bank money in the following year. Soon the central banks of the United States (with targets for M1, M2, and M3), Canada, the United Kingdom, France, and Italy (more in the nature of projections) followed suit. Japan started publishing "estimates" for the growth of its broad money supply in 1978.[9]

---

[7] In countries such as Germany and the Netherlands a relatively strong monetary tradition nevertheless prevailed during that period.

[8] Committee on the Working of the Monetary System (Radcliffe Committee) (1959), par. 980.

[9] Among the smaller countries with very open economies, explicit monetary targets were adopted only by Switzerland (base money). Among the countries mentioned, Canada no longer announces monetary targets. In recent years, Spain adopted a target for a broad monetary aggregate. The Netherlands and Denmark intend to work with targets for domestic money creation (as distinguished from the overall money supply), in the framework of the monitoring of monetary policies of EC member countries under the first phase of the road to European monetary union.

The experience with monetary targeting has of course been mixed. During the early 1980s a number of central banks had increasing difficulties with the use of such targets. Money demand relationships shifted significantly, particularly in the English-speaking industrial countries, leading in a number of cases to an adjustment of money definitions and of the targeted aggregate. Generally this entailed choosing a broad monetary aggregate as the central focus of policy and moving away from M1 or base money. Various explanations have been given for the breakdown in the traditional relationships among monetary aggregates and for the instability of the demand for money. Large shifts took place between various types of monetary assets held by the public under the influence of widespread deregulation and liberalization of financial markets. The introduction of new types of assets (innovation), which was closely related to these developments, was another important factor. Underlying much of this upheaval were the dramatic changes in inflation and interest rates which took place during this period.[10] An interesting explanation for the breakdown of the traditional money demand functions is the notion that a change in central banks' behavior is involved. Tobin, for instance, argues that central banks, before monetary targeting, were generally accommodative in their monetary policy. The monetarists based their advocacy of monetary rules on evidence from the accommodative period in which increases in the (narrow) money supply and in income were strongly correlated. After central banks adjusted their behavior, the old relationships no longer obtained.[11]

Apart from redefining monetary aggregates and adjusting targets, a number of central banks reacted to the loosening of the relationship between money demand and income by de-emphasizing the importance of monetary aggregates and by affording a larger role to other indicators. In some countries the exchange rate came to feature much more prominently in monetary policy decisions during the 1980s. Also, such variables as changes in nominal national income or commodity price movements were considered by some monetary authorities to provide significant information on general monetary conditions. However, beginning in the late 1980s, in an

---

[10] Cf. Burger (1988). Optimism on the basic stability of the demand for money is reflected in Lucas (1988), who finds evidence of such stability in the United States over an extended period of time (1900–85).

[11] Cf. Tobin (1990), pp. 6–7.

environment of increasing inflationary pressures, sentiment shifted back at least some of the way toward a more central role for monetary aggregates. The predominant judgment now appears to be that "the difficulties in interpreting developments in the monetary aggregates due to financial innovation are normally not insurmountable."[12] In fact, for the United States "deregulation may have enhanced the usefulness of the monetary aggregates as long-run policy guides,"[13] as the focus has shifted to broader measures of money such as have been used for a long time in Germany and Japan. It can therefore be concluded that suitably adjusted. monetary targets have continued to play an important role in the United States, Germany, and France, whereas Japan has continued publishing its "estimates" for M2 plus certificates of deposit. The United Kingdom and, perhaps, Canada are in a different position. The only official monetary target (M0, or base money) left in the United Kingdom has little operational value, with the authorities emphasizing that vast changes in the financial system still render judgments on monetary aggregates hazardous. But the British case appears to be an exception among the largest countries in the early 1990s.

Whereas it is sometimes argued that further problems could be expected with monetary targeting,[14] for instance because of continuing structural changes affecting money demand, it appears that a stronger case can be made for expecting greater stability in the demand for money functions—at least for most of the large countries—in coming years. This case is based on the argument that liberalization and deregulation have largely, if in some cases for the time being not wholly, run their course in most of these countries, and that innovations in the financial system may also have reached their zenith. In fact, the difficulties experienced in the savings and loan industry and with the financing of leveraged buy-outs through junk bonds leading to an increasingly perceived fragility of the financial system in the United States may well spontaneously or institutionally act as a brake on further innovation.[15] Finally, it can

---

[12] Bank for International Settlements (1989), p. 143.

[13] Ibid.

[14] Some economists appear to have shifted back to the Radcliffe Committee views, stating that the money supply cannot be controlled by the central bank, and arguing the money creation is an endogenous process. Cf., for instance, Dow and Saville (1988). This view seems to be unduly colored by the British experience.

[15] In the EC a somewhat different development could be envisaged as in some countries considerable innovation may still occur in the scope of the establishment of the single internal market.

be argued that the credibility of domestic monetary policy has been enhanced or restored in countries such as the United States and Germany through attaining their quantitative monetary targets in recent years after a number of years of overshooting. It may well be that under conditions of stronger economic growth and mild inflationary pressures, with a slowing down of innovation, monetary aggregates have tended to revert to the traditional relationships with income and interest rates.[16] In conclusion, the use of domestic monetary policy aimed at controlling the growth of the money supply, based on the notion that money and prices are related in some fashion, on balance seems to have lost little of its importance over the past fifteen years or so.

II. International Monetary Policy

In contrast to developments with respect to national quantitative monetary policy, which has largely maintained or recouped its important role in individual countries, interest in international quantitative monetary policy has clearly waned in the past fifteen years. Control over international reserves is no longer an issue widely discussed in the literature or featuring on the agenda of international policymaking. This section starts with an analysis of how we arrived at this situation. Subsequently it examines whether this is a satisfactory state of affairs.

Under the Bretton Woods par value system, control over international reserves was generally considered an important matter, even if attempts at such control were not very successful. The inception of the SDR in 1968 was very much based on the notion that international reserves mattered and that managing such reserves was a desirable goal. It cannot be denied, however, that different countries held different views on what constituted adequate control over international reserves. European countries, for instance, at the time of the Committee of Twenty meetings insisted on asset settlement as a means of control, whereas the United States rejected any such

---

[16] Boughton (1990) mentions a—partly successful—renewed effort among economists to find stable long-run demand functions for money, while the Bank for International Settlements (1990, p. 169) observes that "New kinds of empirical research conducted by the Federal Reserve, the Bank of Japan and the Deutsche Bundesbank have established stable long-term relationships between the money stock and the price level."

proposals. After the collapse of the Bretton Woods system, divergences in views on international liquidity tended to become more pronounced at first. There were those who felt that the advent of a floating exchange rate regime greatly eased the problem of international liquidity, even if floating would be largely of the managed kind, as it turned out to be.[17] Others, especially Heller,[18] highlighted the large increase in world reserves in the early 1970s as a source of monetary expansion and inflation in the industrialized countries. In this view, which enjoyed a certain support, the stock of international reserves was considered to constitute an international monetary base. A logical consequence of this approach was to attempt to control international reserves. A proposal that fitted very much in this philosophy was that of the then Managing Director of the IMF, H. Johannes Witteveen, who advocated an agreement whereby countries would hold a certain minimum proportion of their reserves in the form of SDRs. By adjusting the volume of SDR allocations and/or the reserve ratios, global reserves could be managed.[19] The Heller-type approach, or international quantity theory as some dubbed it, was vigorously opposed, however.[20] Nor did Witteveen's proposal gather much support.

One way to trace how thinking on international reserves and whether there was a need to control them developed since the mid-1970s is to look at the views expressed at various conferences on international monetary issues organized or co-organized by the IMF. At a conference in honor of the late Marcus Fleming in 1976, the predominant view (although there were some important dissenters) was that the switch to floating rates had fundamentally changed the international liquidity situation and had more or less rendered the control of reserves a nonproblem. In his conference paper, Haberler (1977, p. 125) was outspoken in his views, emphasizing that "any correlation between changes in global reserves and in the world price level is apt to be spurious even if domestically the quantity theory works well." His conclusion was, therefore, that

---

[17] There has never been, and is unlikely to be (unless there is a world currency), an extended period of nonintervention in the foreign exchange markets. I pointed this out in an early examination of the need for reserves under flexible exchange rates; cf. De Beaufort Wijnholds (1974).

[18] Cf. Heller (1976), and also Khan (1979), who approached the problem empirically.

[19] Witteveen (1975).

[20] Cf. Sweeney and Willett (1977) and Williamson (1982).

"control of international reserves is no longer an important business for the IMF" (p. 130).

In 1983, at another IMF conference, support for the approach of reserves as international base money and for attempts to control international reserves appeared to be scant, also among European participants. In his conference paper De Grauwe (1983, p. 404) concluded that under the prevailing international monetary arrangements, "there is no clear causal link between international reserve stocks and money stocks," nor can it be said that the former causes the latter. He backed this up by empirical tests which showed that while the "international-monetary-base" hypothesis could not be rejected, the evidence in support of it was rather weak. In a comment, Thygesen (1983) dissented and advocated a return of international reserve control to the international agenda, without, however, specifying what form such control should take. The control of international reserves, which of course had been on the international agenda in the form of the unsuccessful discussions on a SDR-substitution account in 1979–80, did not reappear on that agenda.

By the time of an IMF co-sponsored conference in 1985, the view of the Fund staff had evolved further away from notions concerning reserve control. Dooley (1986, p. 97) stated in his conference contribution that "although the demand for reserves may appear to be little changed, the role of reserves in the current system is fundamentally different because the systemic constraints on the supply of reserves has changed." He pointed out that creditworthy countries could always obtain the reserves that they desired to hold, by borrowing from private financial markets at a cost equal to the spread between the marginal costs of obtaining such credit and the rate of return earned on the investment of their reserves (often in those same private financial markets). The implication of this situation is that for individual countries the demand for reserves is normally accommodated "with little or no change in overall economic conditions" (p. 109). Only countries without access to international financial markets are therefore constrained in their policies by the stock of their reserves, the supply of reserves not being elastic for them, according to Dooley.

In accordance with views such as espoused by Dooley, and before him Haberler, interest in the question of control of international reserves has all but vanished in recent years. Is this withering away of what used to be an important issue fully justified? The answer is not clear-cut. The central argument for neglecting international reserves under the present system is that the role of reserves has undergone a fundamental change. This is not so much because of the switch to floating exchange rates among the large industrial countries since the early 1970s. It has become clear that floating has been of the managed variety (with ups and downs), with different U.S. administrations discovering after a number of years that intervention might not be such a bad idea after all, and that the demand for reserves probably has not changed much in comparison to the days of the Bretton Woods system. That factor can therefore be eliminated from the analysis. The main change is to be found on the supply side, that is, the enormous growth of international financial markets and many countries' easy access to these markets for the financing of balance of payments deficits and for building up their international reserves.[21]

During the 1970s and the early 1980s international financial markets grew almost explosively. The phenomenon of the expansion of the Eurocurrency markets, to which not only industrialized countries but also Asian, Latin American, Eastern European, and some African countries had access, had a considerable impact on individual countries' reserve ease and adjustment behavior. Partly as a result of the—initially legitimate—need for recycling after the oil crises, many countries became habitual borrowers in the Eurocurrency markets. In a large number of cases this resulted in excessive borrowing, which was only sufficiently recognized by debtors and creditors alike when debt-servicing difficulties came to the fore. With the benefit of hindsight, it can be argued that international organizations were also late in recognizing the dangers of overborrowing at the time. The results of these developments are well known and need not be discussed here, except to mention that most developing countries came to be cut off from private financial markets after 1982. Thus developing countries generally returned to a situation in which the level of their reserves again became very much of a constraint to them in the conduct of their economic policies. Industrial countries, excluding Eastern Europe, continued to have easy access to financial markets and therefore were hardly, if at all, constrained in their policies by their reserve position. And since these countries dominate in the world economy in terms of output, international reserves, and so forth, it is their situation that

---

[21] On the explanation also for the loss of interest in the adequacy of international reserves, see Chrystal (1990), who follows a somewhat different argumentation.

determines the overall attitude toward international reserves and that led to a situation as described by Dooley.

In recent years we have, however, been able to observe that the lack of an external constraint on countries having access to international financial markets is not as permanent as has sometimes been made out. In a number of cases, industrial countries appear to have been taking adjustment measures at least partly as a precaution against an erosion of their creditworthiness. These are generally smaller industrial countries, the large countries being either in a comfortable external position, or able to run up external debt in their own currency, for example, the United States. The smaller industrial countries in particular seem to recognize that they could reach a point, which cannot be precisely quantified and may differ with countries' individual characteristics, where solvency considerations could come into play and affect their market access. This would force them to either adjust their policies on their own or turn to the IMF or the European Community for financial assistance, which would almost certainly lead to the adoption of adjustment policies.

Let us return now to the question whether the present lack of interest in control of international reserves is justified. One answer is that the size of international reserves is quite modest compared to the (estimated) world money supply, namely roughly 5 percent at the end of 1989 (see Table 1). This implies that a change in international reserves of 5 percent would have a direct impact of only $\frac{1}{4}$ of 1 percent on the world money supply. Secondary effects would add to this of course, but the overall effect would probably remain

Table 1. International Reserves, Trade, and Money Supply

	1975–80	1980–85	1986	1987	1988	1989
Annual percentage increase						
International reserves	13	1	15	39	1	6
International trade	18	−1	10	17	14	8

	1975	1980	1985	1986	1987	1988	1989
International reserves as percentage of							
International trade	27.8	23.9	26.6	27.8	32.7	28.8	28.2
World money supply	6.0	6.0	5.0	5.1	5.6	5.3	5.5

Note: International reserves have been measured in U.S. dollars and include gold valued at SDR 35 an ounce. International trade has been measured from the import side.

Sources: International Monetary Fund, *International Financial Statistics*; and author's calculations.

modest. While the impact of changes in international reserves on changes in the world money supply, and thereby on world inflation, should not be ignored, it is doubtful that they could exert a major influence under present conditions. Probably a considerably stronger influence could be exerted on the world economy by relatively high reserve levels and/or easy access to unconditional international credit by means of undermining the international adjustment process and thereby contributing to world inflation and payments imbalances. This view has probably been an important consideration in the opposition of some large countries to (sizable) new allocations of SDRs,[22] although other motives appear to have played a role too.[23] Obviously, controlling only SDR allocations while leaving other sources of reserve creation unrestrained cannot be an effective way of controlling international reserves. Also, without control of international credit, the control of international reserves would not achieve very much in terms of improving the functioning of the international adjustment process. In other words, if there is to be effective control it would have to encompass total international *liquidity*, not only reserves.

A separate case for controlling international credit extended through private financial markets can be made on the basis of the argument that such credit adds to the world money supply.[24] This is an issue that has not yet been satisfactorily resolved. Although it is widely recognized that endogenous money creation can take place in the Eurocurrency markets, it is not clear to what extent this is actually the case. However, most observers now tend to view money creation through the Eurocurrency markets as a limited affair on account of the small size of the multiplier, given the large leakages involved.[25] A pragmatic way of looking at this question is to relate the amount of nonbank deposits held in the Eurocurrency markets to the world money supply. A rough estimate would put this figure at around 7 percent (see Table 2). These deposits are generally not included in national monetary aggregates.[26] In some countries the external deposits held by nonbank residents constitute

---

[22] Cf., for instance, the recent analysis of the Deutsche Bundesbank (1990), especially pp. 40–41.
[23] On this matter cf. Polak (1988).
[24] Cf. Kessler (1980).
[25] Cf., for instance, Mayer (1979) and Johnston (1983).
[26] In the United States, very short-term external deposits held by nonbank residents are included in the money supply.

Table 2. External Deposits and World Money Supply

	1975–84	1985	1986	1987	1988	1989
	(Annual percentage increase)					
External deposits						
Dollar amounts	23	13	21	19	8	21
At constant exchange rates[1]	26	17	−1	5	0	26
Money supply						
Group of Ten (M2)	10	9	9	8	9	9
World (M2/M3)	16	19	16	14	12[2]	11[2]

	1975	1980	1985	1986	1987	1988	1989
External deposits as percentage of world money supply[3]	2.0	3.8	6.5	6.9	6.6	6.5	7.8

Note: External deposits are deposits held by nonbanks with international banks and are assumed to be (close) substitutes for (time) deposits with domestic banks. Local foreign currency deposits of nonbanks (constituting about 15 percent of the total) have been included as these are not counted as part of the domestic money supply in most countries.

Sources: Bank for International Settlements; International Monetary Fund, *International Financial Statistics*; and author's calculations (world money stock).

[1] Adjusted by means of a nominal effective exchange rate index.

[2] M1.

[3] World money supply as a stock figure based on a rough estimate. Externally held deposits are not included.

a considerably larger percentage of the money supply, however. Also, these deposits can from time to time show relatively high rates of expansion (for instance, recently in Germany) and should therefore not be ignored by the monetary authorities. The notion that control of the domestic money supply should be sufficient and that one need not be concerned about external monetary deposits appears to be too sanguine a view. One problem in this area is that some of the authorities have been coping with ambiguous feelings: on the one side feeling concern over a new source of money creation, on the other side worrying about their country's role as an international financial center, with the latter concern usually gaining the upper hand.

The foregoing suggests that the present neglect of control of international liquidity is not fully justified. International reserves and international credit matter, because any unbridled expansion of such liquidity tends to undermine the international adjustment process. It can also add to world inflation by means of increasing the world money supply, either through increases in international reserves or by means of money creation through the Eurocurrency markets. These monetary effects are usually believed to be of limited significance, however.

III. Can International Liquidity Be Controlled?

Having concluded that there still appears to be a case for attempting some control over international liquidity, we have to face the important operational question as to whether such control is feasible. It may be useful to recall what attempts have been made in the past to control international reserves and unconditional international credit, to see if any of them would be worth reviving, and to examine whether any other approaches could be useful.

As regards international reserves, attempts at control have never really materialized, partly as a result of important differences of opinion among countries on this issue. In the early 1970s, reserve control was one of the subjects discussed by the Committee of Twenty.[27] The United States favored a reserve indicator system, whereas the European countries wished to see the creation of reserves by way of U.S. balance of payments deficits checked through asset settlement. None of these schemes was adopted in the wake of the breakdown of the Bretton Woods system. Fears of a dollar glut persisted during the 1970s and were instrumental in the drawing up of a scheme for a substitution account by the IMF staff under Jacques Polak. The aim was to absorb the overhang of official dollar holdings by exchanging them for SDRs held in a special account. Disagreement on a technical problem, that is, the financing of losses that might result from the operation of the substitution account, prevented the scheme from coming into being.[28] Since then no new proposals for controlling international reserves have been made. The feasibility of reintroducing a proposal for asset settlement on the international monetary agenda is practically zero. The role of gold has been very substantially diminished, whereas the amount of SDRs outstanding is too small to act as a means of settlement for excessive dollar holdings. Moreover, the system has spontaneously

---

[27] Cf., Committee on Reform of the International Monetary System (Committee of Twenty) (1974).

[28] In the background, a recovery of the dollar exchange rate and the occurrence of the second oil shock undoubtedly contributed to a loss of interest in the substitution account.

developed more toward a multireserve currency system, with the share of dollars in total foreign exchange reserves declining steadily, from 73 percent in 1979 to 60 percent at the end of 1989. As to a substitution account, the notion remains a feasible one, and it is conceivable that it could be revived in the future if a serious loss of confidence in the dollar were to lead to large-scale support interventions by central banks in industrial countries. As has already been pointed out, however, control over international reserves alone would probably not be very effective from the point of view of preventing the international adjustment process from being undermined, since easy access to international financial markets would provide creditworthy, nonadjusting countries with sufficient leeway to continue as before.

There have been a few instances of attempts by the monetary authorities to influence the rapidly expanding international financial markets. In the early 1970s, when the Eurocurrency markets were just emerging from infancy, the central banks of the Group of Ten countries considered ways of constraining their growth. In 1971 they agreed to a standstill of the investment of their reserves in the Eurocurrency markets, as such investments tended to increase the liquidity of Eurobanks without a corresponding reduction of liquidity elsewhere. This understanding not to feed the Eurocurrency markets through central banks themselves was not very strictly adhered to, however, although it was (silently) reconfirmed in 1979. Also discussed among the Group of Ten central banks was the introduction of compulsory non-interest-bearing cash reserves against deposits held with Eurobanks. In this way, the competitive advantage of the strongly expanding Eurocurrency markets vis-à-vis domestic financial markets could be more or less eliminated. The last effort in this area dates from 1979 when cash reserve requirements against Eurodeposits on a consolidated basis were considered, at the instigation of the U.S. Federal Reserve System. The motive was primarily domestic, however, and the proposal enjoyed little support. What did ensue was an agreement by the Group of Ten central banks in 1980 on a closer surveillance of the macroeconomic aspects of the Eurocurrency markets and a strengthening of prudential control regarding international banking operations. Although the central banks concerned have continued to monitor developments in these markets, the macroeconomic exercise has been limited to an exchange of information.

In the prudential area, however, much more has been done in the past ten years. A number of important agreements have been reached, such as the delineation of responsibility for supervising solvency and liquidity by the supervisory authorities of the Group of Ten (the so-called Concordat) and, of particular importance, the agreement on capital adequacy standards. Under the latter agreement, reached in July 1988, the Group of Ten central banks decided that a minimum ratio of capital[29] to assets of 8 percent was to be adhered to by international banks supervised by them by the end of 1992, with an interim ratio of 7 1/4 percent to be reached by the end of 1990. The assets are weighted according to their perceived riskiness, with claims on the nonbank private sector and on governments outside the so-called preferential area (i.e., outside member countries of the Organization for Economic Cooperation and Development (OECD) and Saudi Arabia) weighing 100 percent and claims on central governments within the preferential area carrying a weight of 0 percent. In a number of countries, banks' risk-weighted capital ratios were at the outset considerably lower than the 8 percent minimum that has to be attained, so that a considerable effort is required by a sizable number of international banks to meet this standard. Clearly the weighting system "favors" the extension of loans to governments of OECD countries (some of whom do not actually enjoy top credit ratings in the markets), while "penalizing" loans to nonbanks in the private sector, both in the industrial and developing countries.

Given the present size of the Eurocurrency markets and the enormously increased financial integration in the world, agreements concerning the investment of (Group of Ten) central bank reserves cannot be expected to have a discernable influence on the growth of international financial markets. Furthermore, the strong movement toward deregulation and liberalization all but rules out measures of an overall monetary nature, such as the introduction of reserve requirements against Eurodeposits, aimed at controlling the expansion of such markets. It can therefore be concluded that the measures that were taken or contemplated in the past to exercise some control over the expansion of international financial markets do not constitute a meaningful option at present.

An alternative, of course, is to rely on market discipline. It is, however, questionable whether that would bring about a satisfac-

---

[29]Divided into core capital, including mainly equity and open reserves, and secondary capital, including items such as hidden reserves, general provisions, and subordinated loans.

tory outcome. International banks engaged in overlending to developing countries in the not too distant past, and although they can be assumed to learn from their mistakes, overall lending could well continue to expand more strongly than would be compatible with a smooth functioning of the international adjustment process. The fact that in recent years net international bank lending to industrial countries has grown considerably faster than domestic lending by banks in industrial countries has been a cause for some concern.[30] It also casts doubt on the view that the conduct of reasonably prudent domestic monetary policies by the (large) industrial countries would in itself be sufficient to keep the growth of the *total* of domestic and international bank lending within prudent limits, without having to raise interest rates to unduly high levels. Banks appear to economize very strongly on their reserve base as concerns their international lending activities.[31] Domestically such tendencies sometimes also exist, but these can be counteracted in various ways by the monetary authorities.

It is likely that the strengthening and international convergence of supervisory rules has a constraining influence on the expansion of international bank activity. Banks from countries that have previously enjoyed relatively light solvency rules, for instance, could well have to slow down their international lending if they are not able to increase their capital base at a commensurate pace.[32] This would be a welcome development from the point of view of improving the international adjustment process. Such a process could be strengthened by fostering an attitude among banks in which they show greater reluctance to continue lending to countries or entities that are rapidly building up external debt and are following inadequate adjustment policies. They should become more aware of the possibility that industrial countries can eventually also experience debt-servicing difficulties and that there is no assurance that they will be

---

[30] For an analysis of these developments, see the chapter on "International financial markets" in the *Annual Reports* of the Bank for International Settlements. It should be noted that bank lending to developing countries that are not members of the Organization of Petroleum Exporting Countries has actually contracted in recent years, reflecting debt conversion, asset sales, and write-offs.

[31] Heller (1979, p. 44) has pointed out that international banks do not hold liquidity reserves, but instead rely on the interbank market for funding and liquidity. See also Wallich (1979).

[32] There are reports that this has been the case recently for U.S. and Japanese banks.

bailed out by other countries or international organizations. The monetary authorities, national and international, could strengthen this awareness by expressing themselves clearly on the subject. The IMF, for instance, could be more forceful in pointing out to both the countries concerned and the international financial community that continued reliance on bank lending, without recourse to conditional credit, in order to escape necessary adjustment is undesirable and short-sighted. Banks should put pressure on nonadjusting countries to bring in official lenders, especially the IMF and the EC (as long as its lending is conditional), at an earlier stage.

In conclusion, the question whether control of international liquidity is feasible has to be answered largely in the negative. As concerns international reserves, introduction of a substitution account would be a possibility, but would not make much of an impact on total international liquidity. Control of international financial markets, and thereby of international bank lending, through traditional monetary measures does not appear feasible under current circumstances. Moreover, such measures would readily be seen as at odds with the widespread liberalization of international capital transactions that came about in the past decade or so. There is mounting evidence, however, that the ongoing strengthening of bank supervision, particularly the phasing in of international standards for minimum capital-assets ratios, is having a substantial impact on international banks' lending activities. While the rationale for such ratios is of a prudential nature, they could well produce significant macroeconomic or monetary effects. A more selective attitude by banks toward international lending, not only to developing countries but also to industrial countries, could help to strengthen the international adjustment process and to constrain money creation from external sources in individual countries. While this could be considered a welcome development, the fact remains that solvency ratios are set for prudential reasons, and that such ratios might not always be fully compatible with macroeconomic priorities.[33] At the same time, since bank supervision and monetary policy are in many industrial countries conducted by the same institution, that is, the central bank, a certain degree of compatibility could be expected.

---

[33] It would, however, seem worth considering bringing about a differentiation in the weighting for claims on governments in the preferential area (presently zero), for instance by distinguishing between claims that are denominated in the borrowing government's own currency (weight to remain zero) and claims denominated in foreign currencies, to which a positive weight would be attached.

Still, in times of less favorable cyclical conditions fears of a too rapid slowdown of bank lending as a consequence of the "bite" of solvency ratios are to be expected. The monetary authorities ought to be able to allay such fears by explaining their policies and the overriding need for maintaining a sound banking system, as well as by standing ready to provide liquidity support to the banks when they are faced with adverse developments beyond their control. The conditions of such support should, however, not be spelled out in advance in order to avoid as much as possible moral hazard problems.

A question that finally still has to be dealt with is that of the relationship between domestic monetary policy and international financial markets. As was stated in the previous section, the fact that international bank lending adds to the world money supply, albeit to a still relatively modest degree, could constitute a separate argument for constraining such lending or in some way taking into account its effects in the formulation of domestic monetary policies. It is of course conceivable that the external or cross-border component of the world money supply will no longer grow significantly faster than the domestic component, as the effects of liberalization of capital flows run out. This would, however, still not be a sufficient reason for ignoring cross-border bank activity of a monetary nature, since the fact remains that such activity constitutes a channel of money creation. Moreover, as long as cross-border bank activity is significantly less costly for lenders or borrowers or both, particularly because of the absence of non-interest-bearing reserve requirements, it is to be expected that the growth of external deposits will remain at least as strong as that of domestic money supplies.

The only acceptable instrument that can have a significant constraining influence on international bank lending and the monetary deposits it creates is—once again—the use of solvency ratios. Here, too, of course their indirect and uncertain overall effect on lending makes them a rather blunt tool for monetary policy purposes. There are other ways, however, in which the authorities can respond to the rapid growth of external monetary deposits and the loss of monetary control that it can entail for individual central banks. One way is to include such deposits in the monetary aggregates that serve as the intermediate target of monetary policy. Another way is to reduce or remove the competitive advantages of cross-border lending and depositing, not by making such transactions less profitable—as was intended in earlier proposals discussed in the previous section—but by making domestic banking activities more competitive. This can be done particularly by diminishing or even eliminating domestic non-interest-bearing reserve requirements.

As to the first possibility, it enables central banks to make explicit and take into account the growth of external monetary deposits in formulating their policies.[34] Since a central bank cannot directly control its residents' externally held deposits, as these fall outside its jurisdiction, the inclusion of such deposits in the monetary target variable implies that the central bank will have to act more vigorously on the other sources of growth of the overall aggregate at times when the aggregate tends to exceed the target. Although this does not appear to be a first-best solution, and in some cases is also subject to the problem of timely availability of data for external deposits, it nevertheless is a pragmatic approach that has attracted increasing attention. As was mentioned in footnote 26, the United States has followed this route to some extent, whereas in Germany the monetary authorities are now closely monitoring an alternative aggregate designated "extended M3," which includes deutsche mark deposits held abroad by German nonbanks. Other European countries are also increasingly looking at external monetary deposits held by their residents. It is to be expected that such deposits will be included in a European money supply concept, which concept will have to be developed in the course of the second stage of the European monetary union (EMU). In particular, such a concept should include short-term deposits held by nonbank residents of EC countries with banks in other EC countries. In a full-fledged monetary union (the third stage of the EMU), such deposits could no longer be termed "external," but would be an integral part of the European monetary aggregate or aggregates on the growth of which the European central bank would base its monetary policy decisions. In addition, deposits of a monetary nature held outside the EC could also be included in the aggregate, especially if they are denominated in EC currencies or European currency units.

---

[34]The monetary nature of external deposits is, however, not always clear-cut. In the case of the Netherlands, for which such deposits (denominated in all currencies) are very substantial (over 30 percent of domestic M2), it is estimated that about half of the total amount is held by so-called special financial institutions. These institutions are foreign holding companies that operate in the Netherlands largely for tax purposes and their deposits are not considered to have monetary characteristics. Of the remainder of the external deposits of the Netherlands, a sizable part is believed to be held by households practicing tax evasion; this part is probably more akin to long-term savings than to money.

The second approach mentioned—lowering or eliminating domestic non-interest-bearing reserve requirements—is also one that is being prudently pursued or studied in some countries. The United States started in this direction a number of years ago, whereas recently France has somewhat lowered the compulsory reserves held against certain deposits by its banks, partly as a response to a shift of French residents' funds to monetary deposits with banks in financial centers in which reserve requirements are absent. To the extent that central banks rely on non-interest-bearing reserve requirements to render their monetary policies sufficiently effective, this approach clearly has only limited possibilities. The fact is that compulsory reserves aimed at strengthening monetary control are applied in most European countries, as well as in the United States and Japan, although the importance attached to this instrument varies considerably among countries. It seems unlikely that in the near future central banks in all major industrial countries would agree to eliminate (a switch to interest-bearing compulsory reserves would have the same effect) or substantially lower reserve requirements. What is likely to emerge, however, is a greater harmonization in the application of this instrument in the European context. Monetary integration will bring to bear increasing pressure on central banks in EC countries to use monetary instruments that are compatible with developments in other countries, and that will not put the banking systems in their respective countries at a clear competitive disadvantage vis-à-vis banks in other EC countries. Once the European central bank is endowed with full powers, that is, in or near the third stage of the EMU, the continuation of such differences would be hard to imagine, even if the execution of monetary policy were to be highly decentralized (i.e., the national central banks playing a major role in implementing monetary policy). The problem of competitive advantage through differences in policies and regulations is therefore bound to disappear within the EC. As was suggested earlier, this problem is much less likely to vanish between industrial countries in general. This adds to the argument for a larger degree of coordination of monetary policies among the large industrial countries.

REFERENCES

Bank for International Settlements, *59th Annual Report* (Basle, 1989).

———, *60th Annual Report* (Basle, 1990).

Boughton, James M., "Long-Run Money Demand in Large Industrial Countries," IMF Working Paper No. 90/53 (Washington: International Monetary Fund, 1990).

Burger, Albert E., "The Puzzling Growth of the Monetary Aggregates in the 1980s," *Review*, Federal Reserve Bank of St. Louis (St. Louis), Vol. 70 (September/October 1988), pp. 46–60.

Chrystal, K. Alec, "International Reserves and International Liquidity: A Solution in Search of a Problem," in *The International Financial Regime*, ed. by Graham Bird (London: Surrey University Press, 1990).

Committee on Reform of the International Monetary System (Committee of Twenty), *International Monetary Reform* (Washington: International Monetary Fund, 1974).

Committee on the Working of the Monetary System (Radcliffe Committee), *Report* (London: H.M. Stationery Office, 1959).

Cooper, Richard N., "What Future for the International Monetary System?" Chapter 6 in this volume. Also published in *The Evolution of the International Monetary System: How Can Efficiency and Stability Be Attained?* ed. by Yoshio Suzuki, Junichi Miyako, and Mitsuaki Okabe (Tokyo: University of Tokyo Press, 1990).

De Beaufort Wijnholds, J.A.H., "The Need for Reserves Under Full and Limited Flexibility of Exchange Rates," *De Economist* (Leiden), Vol. 122, No. 3 (1974), pp. 225–43.

———, "Surveillance and Supervision of the International Banking System," *Quarterly Statistics*, De Nederlandsche Bank (Amsterdam), No. 2 (September 1980), pp. 85–98.

De Grauwe, Paul, "What Are the Scope and Limits of Fruitful International Monetary Cooperation in the 1980s?" in *International Money and Credit: The Policy Roles*, ed. by George M. von Furstenberg (Washington: International Monetary Fund, 1983).

Deutsche Bundesbank, "Die längerfristige Entwicklung der Weltwährungsreserven" (The longer-term trends in global monetary reserves), *Monatsberichte* (Frankfurt), Vol. 42 (January 1990), pp. 34–55.

Dooley, Michael P., "The Role of Reserves in the International Monetary System," in *Problems of International Money, 1972–85*, ed. by Michael Posner (Washington: International Monetary Fund and Overseas Development Institute, 1986).

Dow, J.C.R., and I.D. Saville, *A Critique of Monetary Policy: Theory and British Experience* (Oxford: Clarendon Press, 1988).

Frenkel, Jacob A., "International Liquidity and Monetary Control," in *International Money and Credit: The Policy Roles*, ed. by George M. von Furstenberg (Washington: International Monetary Fund, 1983).

———, and Morris Goldstein, "The International Monetary System: Developments and Prospects," NBER Working Paper No. 2648 (Cambridge, Massachusetts: National Bureau of Economic Research, July 1988).

Haberler, Gottfried, "How Important Is Control Over International Reserves?" in *The New International Monetary System*, ed. by Robert A. Mundell and Jacques J. Polak (New York: Columbia University Press, 1977).

Heller, H. Robert, "International Reserves and World-Wide Inflation," *Staff Papers*, International Monetary Fund (Washington), Vol. 23 (March 1976), pp. 61–87.

———, "Why the Market Is Demand-Determined" *Euromoney* (London), February 1979, pp. 41–47.

———, "Money and the International Monetary System," *Review*, Federal Reserve Bank of St. Louis (St. Louis), Vol. 71 (March/April 1989), pp. 65–71.

Johnston, R.B., *The Economics of the Euromarket: History, Theory, and Policy* (New York: St. Martin's Press, 1983).

Kessler, Geldolph A., "The Need to Control International Bank Lending," *Quarterly Review*, Banca Nazionale del Lavoro (Rome), Vol. 132 (March 1980), pp. 57–81.

Khan, Mohsin S., "Inflation and International Reserves: A Time-Series Analysis," *Staff Papers*, International Monetary Fund (Washington), Vol. 26 (December 1979), pp. 699–724.

Lucas, Robert E., Jr., "Money Demand in the United States: A Quantitative Review," in *Money, Cycles, and Exchange Rates: Essays in Honor of Allan H. Meltzer*, ed. by Karl Brunner and Bennett T. McCallum, *Carnegie-Rochester Conference Series on Public Policy* (Amsterdam), Vol. 29 (Autumn 1988), pp. 137–68.

Mayer, Helmut W., *Credit and Liquidity Creation in the International Banking Sector*, BIS Economic Papers No. 1 (Basle: Bank for International Settlements, 1979).

McKinnon, Ronald I., *An International Standard for Monetary Stabilization* (Washington: Institute for International Economics, 1984).

Polak, Jacques J., "Money—National and International," in *Essays in Honour of Thorkil Kristensen* (Paris: Organization for Economic Cooperation and Development, 1970), reprinted in *International Reserves: Needs and Availability* (Washington: International Monetary Fund, 1970).

———, "The Impasse Concerning the Role of the SDR," in *The Quest for National and Global Economic Stability*, ed. by Wietze Eizenga, E. Frans Limburg, and Jacques J. Polak (Dordrecht: Kluwer, 1988).

Sweeney, Richard J., and Thomas D. Willett, "Eurodollars, Petrodollars, and World Liquidity and Inflation," *Journal of Monetary Economics*, Supplementary Series (Amsterdam), Vol. 5 (1977), pp. 277–310.

Thygesen, Niels, "Comment" on paper by Paul De Grauwe, in *International Money and Credit: The Policy Roles*, ed. by George M. von Furstenberg (Washington: International Monetary Fund, 1983).

Tobin, James, "On the Theory of Macroeconomic Policy," *De Economist* (Leiden), Vol. 138, No. 1 (1990), pp. 1–14.

Wallich, Henry C., "Why the Euromarket Needs Restraint," *Columbia Journal of World Business* (New York), Vol. 14, No. 3 (Autumn 1979).

Williamson, John, "The Growth of Official Reserves and the Issue of World Monetary Control," in *The International Monetary System: A Time of Turbulence*, ed. by Jacob S. Dreyer, Gottfried Haberler, and Thomas D. Willett (Washington: American Enterprise Institute for Public Policy Research, 1982).

Witteveen, H. Johannes, "The Control of International Liquidity," address delivered in Frankfurt, October 28, 1975; reproduced in *IMF Survey*, International Monetary Fund (Washington), Vol. 4 (October 28, 1975), pp. 313–16.

13

Exchange Rate Arrangements, Seigniorage, and the Provision of Public Goods

Peter B. Kenen

I. Introduction

The Delors Committee Report on European monetary union[1] revived an old debate about fiscal policies in a monetary union. Believing that "divergent national budgetary policies would undermine monetary stability" and noting "that the centrally managed Community budget is likely to remain a very small part of total public sector spending and that much of this budget will not be available for cyclical adjustments," the Report concluded correctly that "the task of setting a Community-wide fiscal policy stance will have to be performed through the coordination of national budgetary policies" (Delors (1989), pp. 24–25). This conclusion, however, was followed by another that may be inconsistent with it and is controversial on its own (Delors (1989), p. 24):

I have benefited greatly from discussions with Alessandra Casella, from suggestions by Avinash Dixit, and from comments by participants in seminars at the Bank of Canada and Princeton University, but they bear no responsibility for the contents of the paper. Work on the paper was supported by the International Finance Section at Princeton University.
[1]Committee for the Study of Economic and Monetary Union, *Report on Economic and Monetary Union in the European Community* (Luxembourg, 1989); the Committee was chaired by Jacques Delors, President of the Commission of the European Communities. The report is cited hereafter as Delors (1989).

In the budgetary field, binding rules are required that would: firstly, impose effective upper limits on budget deficits of individual member countries of the Community, although in setting these limits the situation of each member country might have to be taken into consideration; secondly, exclude access to direct central bank credit and other forms of monetary financing while, however, permitting open market operations in government securities; thirdly, limit recourse to external borrowing in non-Community currencies.

These recommendations raise many questions, which can be grouped beneath three headings: stabilization, credibility, and seigniorage.

Stabilization

Having relinquished the use of monetary policy, does a member of a monetary union need to lean more heavily on fiscal policy to stabilize its own economy? The answer must be "yes" in principle, unless you believe that fiscal policy is completely ineffective or that the members of a monetary union should not expect to experience country-specific shocks to output and employment. In the United States, however, the world's largest monetary union, few state governments appear to follow contracyclical policies, and many are bound by balanced-budget rules, which have procyclical effects. Yet students of U.S. experience have also pointed out that the contracyclical behavior of the federal budget substitutes partially for local autonomy, and they have warned that a monetary union will not work well in Europe unless the budget of the European Community (EC) is made more flexible or supplemented by large-scale transfers to countries or regions that suffer adverse real shocks.[2]

Credibility

The debate about the Delors Committee Report has gradually revealed the main concern that caused its authors to recommend strict limits on national budget deficits. They were determined to protect the independence and credibility of the new European central bank, and its credibility will be impaired if it is expected to rescue member governments whenever they borrow their way into a debt crisis. It can be argued, however, that strict limits on new borrowing may not be necessary or sufficient for this purpose. They may not be necessary if capital markets can discipline national

---

[2]These issues and the relevant literature are reviewed in Eichengreen (1990).

governments by charging them more when they borrow more.[3] They may not be sufficient if national governments have large debts initially, because a debt overhang can lead to a debt crisis even when the debtor is not borrowing more.

Seigniorage

Some European governments have counted heavily on money creation to finance their budget deficits,[4] and they cannot expect to do that in a monetary union. This has led economists such as van der Ploeg (1990) to warn that a monetary union could produce a shortage of public goods. But Casella (1990) has come to the opposite conclusion. She has shown that a monetary union can help to prevent the excessive production of public goods that occurs when fiscal policies are not coordinated, and her analysis is the starting point for this paper.

Building on earlier work with Feinstein (Casella and Feinstein (1989)), Casella uses a two-country model to show how monetary arrangements can affect the supply of public goods. Each country has a private sector that produces and exports many varieties of a differentiated consumer good and a government that produces a single public good. An increase in output of the public good raises household welfare directly but reduces it indirectly by shrinking the number of varieties of the consumer good, and this indirect loss is shared by the two countries' households, which buy both countries' goods. Therefore, decentralized decision making leads each country to produce too much of the public good, and fiscal policies have to be coordinated to achieve the first-best allocation of resources. In Casella's model, however, the first-best allocation can be achieved by monetary coordination, because governments rely entirely on newly printed money to pay for the production of the public goods.

A monetary union is one form of monetary coordination, but it poses special problems in Casella's model, because country size and the strength of the demand for the public good affect the optimal distribution of new money. The particular characteristics of her model lead Casella to conclude that the smaller member of a two-country union will usually require and obtain more than proportional power in managing the union. Otherwise, it cannot count on

---

[3] A variant of this argument appears in Corden (1983).
[4] See, for example, Drazen (1989).

obtaining enough of the newly created money and will not join the union.[5]

Combining Inflation and Taxation

Casella assumes that governments are indifferent between two ways to pay their bills, issuing new money and collecting lump-sum taxes, and some of her results depend directly on this strong assumption. I will show what happens when it is relaxed—when governments are not indifferent between using the inflation tax and using lump-sum taxes and they differ in their policy preferences. The introduction of these preferences complicates the model greatly, forcing me to simplify it in some other ways. Accordingly, I have suppressed most of the cross-country differences featured in Casella's model and will not be able to say very much about the issue on which she concentrates—the effects of differences in country size on the appropriate constitution for a monetary union. But I will be able to analyze several other issues—the influence of various exchange rate arrangements on resource allocation, inflation rates, and tax rates, and the degree to which monetary coordination can substitute for fiscal coordination.

The first part of the paper outlines the basic model. It is an abbreviated version of Casella's presentation but makes some minor modifications and adds the national governments' policy preference functions.[6]

The second part solves the model for the national currency case, in which each country's households hold that country's currency (there is no currency substitution). It deals extensively with two policy regimes: a floating exchange rate with policy autonomy and a floating rate with comprehensive coordination. It asks what happens

---

[5]It should be noted that Casella's model and the adaptation here violate the injunction of the Delors Report that governments should not have direct access to central bank credit. A weak version of that injunction is introduced below, however, when the central bank of a monetary union is forbidden to discriminate in distributing new money.

[6]Casella's own model draws on the Dixit-Stiglitz (1977) representation of monopolistic competition and the trade-theoretic adaptation in Krugman (1981). Her basic conclusions, however, and those in this paper do not depend strongly on the use of that model; they can be obtained from old-fashioned trade models, where an increase in one country's spending on its public good will affect the welfare of the other country's households by affecting the terms of trade rather than the number of varieties of the consumer good.

in each instance when the two countries differ in size and in their policy preferences (DSP), when they are identical in size (IS) but differ in their preferences, and when they are identical in size and in their policy preferences (ISP).

The third part of the paper extends the analysis of the national currency case by looking at three more regimes: a floating exchange rate with partial policy coordination (monetary but not fiscal), a pegged rate with comprehensive coordination, and a pegged rate with partial coordination.[7]

The fourth part of the paper solves the same model for the common currency case, in which each country's households hold both countries' currencies (there is perfect currency substitution) or hold a single currency issued jointly by those countries. It examines three policy regimes: policy autonomy, comprehensive coordination, and partial coordination. The last two regimes are equivalent to monetary unions with and without fiscal coordination, and they will be analyzed under two arrangements—one in which the union's central bank can discriminate freely when issuing new money to its members, and one in which it is constrained to treat them identically. To limit the length of the paper and emphasize the influence of policy preferences, analysis of these common currency regimes is confined to the IS and ISP cases.

I will show that a floating exchange rate with comprehensive coordination is the first-best regime; it can accommodate differences in policy preferences but can still achieve the optimal allocation of real resources between each country's private and public sectors. A floating rate with partial coordination is a second-best regime; it cannot fully accommodate different policy preferences and thus leads to a less efficient resource allocation. Pegged exchange rates likewise interfere with the accommodation of policy preferences, distorting resource allocation, even when national policies are fully coordinated.

A common currency has interesting properties. When govern-

---

[7] It would be possible, of course, to have a pegged exchange rate without any policy coordination, but this regime cannot be modeled without adding another asymmetry; one central bank must lead and the other must follow. The analysis would be interesting, because the European Monetary System (EMS) has been described this way, which makes it the most appropriate benchmark for measuring the welfare effects of a European monetary union. But it is a difficult case to model, as we will see when we come to a similar case, where both countries issue a common currency but do not coordinate their monetary policies.

ments issue it independently, without any coordination, there is no equilibrium in Casella's model, yet that is not true here. But governments produce more public goods than in any other case, because they try to tax their partner's households by issuing larger amounts of money. A monetary union solves this problem, but it cannot accommodate differences in policy preferences. Hence, it tends to replicate the inefficiencies associated with pegged-rate regimes.

II. The Model

The model comprises two countries ($j = 1$, 2) having σ_j identical households and n_j identical firms. Each household supplies labor, earns wage income, pays lump-sum taxes, buys goods from the private sector, and partakes of the public good produced by its government. There is a one-period lag, however, between the time at which it receives its wage income and the time at which it pays taxes and buys goods from the private sector, and it holds a cash balance in the interim, since money is the only store of value.[8] Each firm produces its own variety of the differentiated consumer good under decreasing-cost conditions. Each household consumes all n varieties ($n = n_1 + n_2$).

The utility of the typical household in the jth country is represented by

$$u_j = (1 - g)\ln\left[\left(\sum_{i=1}^{n} c_{ij}^\theta\right)^{\frac{1}{\theta}}\right] + g \ln\left(z_j\sigma_j^{1-\mu}\right),$$

$$0 < g < 1, \quad 0 < \theta < 1, \tag{1}$$

where c_{ij} is the household's consumption of the ith variety of the consumer good and $\sigma_j z_j$ is total output of the jth country's public good.[9] The parameter μ is used to distinguish between two types of public good. When $\mu = 0$, the utility provided by the public good is independent of the number of households partaking of it. That is

---

[8]There are no other lags in the model, and I omit time subscripts whenever possible.

[9]Note that u_j is not affected by the output of the other country's public good. If that were true, an increase in one country's spending on its public good could be beneficial to the other country's households rather than being harmful, as it is in this paper.

Casella's specification. When $\mu = 1$, by contrast, households crowd each other out, and the utility provided by the public good varies inversely with the number of households. This distinction proves to be crucial for the effect of country size on household welfare.[10] Note that the parameters g, θ, and μ do not have country subscripts. Take this to mean that they do not vary from country to country. The elasticity of substitution between any two varieties of the consumer good is given by $1/(1 - \theta)$.

Labor is the only input in the model, and the quantity required by the ith firm to produce its own variety of the consumer good is

$$L_{ij} = \alpha + \beta X_{ij}, \tag{2}$$

where X_{ij} is total output of the ith variety, so that

$$X_{ij} = \sum_{j=1}^{2} \sigma_j c_{ij}. \tag{3}$$

Because the n_j varieties have the same labor requirements and figure identically in the utility function, they must have the same price, p_j, and profits must be zero with free entry:

$$p_j X_{ij} = w_j L_{ij}, \tag{4}$$

where w_j is the wage rate. Using equation (2) to replace L_{ij} and differentiating with respect to X_{ij}, we equate marginal cost to marginal revenue and can thus obtain

$$p_j = \left(\frac{\beta}{\theta}\right) w_j. \tag{5}$$

Hence, the output of each variety is

$$X_{ij} = X = \frac{\alpha\phi}{\beta}, \qquad \phi = \frac{\theta}{1 - \theta}. \tag{6}$$

Each firm chooses the same level of output, given by the tangency between its average-cost curve and demand curve. By implication, each country's private sector adjusts to policy changes and shocks by changing the number of varieties, not the output of each variety.

---

[10] A public broadcasting system exemplifies the first type of public good; a system of schools or hospitals exemplifies the second. But many public goods fall between these polar cases.

Changes in the number of varieties are achieved by the entry or exit of firms.

The two countries' goods prices are linked by the exchange rate, expressed in units of the first country's currency:

$$p_1 = ep_2. \tag{7}$$

Clearly, the exchange rate cannot be constant unless the two countries have the same inflation rates.

Under the assumptions imbedded in the utility function, the same fraction of each household's disposable income is spent on each variety of the consumer good. Accordingly,

$$c_{ij} = c_j = \left(\frac{1}{n}\right)\left(\frac{w_{jt-1} - w_{jt}\tau_j}{p_{jt}}\right) = \left(\frac{1}{n}\right)\left(\frac{\theta}{\beta}\right)\left[\left(\frac{1}{1 + \pi_j}\right) - \tau_j\right], \tag{8}$$

where π_j is the jth country's inflation rate and $w_{jt}\tau_j$ is the nominal lump-sum tax paid in period t, so that τ_j is the real lump-sum tax.[11]

The public good is produced under constant-cost conditions, and a suitable choice of units allows us to define the quantity of labor needed by

$$L_{jz} = \sigma_j z_j. \tag{9}$$

Production of the public good must be financed by taxation or money creation, which means that the jth government's budget constraint can be written as

$$z_j = \tau_j + m_j, \quad m_j = \left(\frac{1}{\sigma_j}\right)\left(\frac{M_{jt} - M_{jt-1}}{w_{jt}}\right), \tag{10}$$

where M_{jt} is the nominal money stock at the end of period t, so that m_j is the real increase in the money stock per household.

As labor is fully employed,

$$\sigma_j = n_j(\alpha + \beta X) + \sigma_j z_j = n_j\left(\frac{\alpha}{1 - \theta}\right) + \sigma_j z_j, \tag{11}$$

---

[11] Because the supply of labor is inelastic in this model, τ_j is equivalent in form and effect to a proportional tax on the current nominal wage, w_{jt}.

so that

$$n = \sigma\left(\frac{1-\theta}{\alpha}\right)\Gamma, \quad \sigma = \sigma_1 + \sigma_2, \quad \Gamma = \sum_{j=1}^{2} s_j(1 - z_j), \quad \text{and} \quad s_j = \frac{\sigma_j}{\sigma}. \tag{12}$$

Therefore, equation (1) can be rewritten as

$$u_j = A + (1-g)\phi\ln\Gamma + (1-g)\ln\left[\left(\frac{1}{1+\pi_j}\right) - \tau_j\right]$$

$$+ g\left[\ln z_j + (1-\mu)\ln s_j\right], \tag{13}$$

where

$$A = (1-g)\left[\phi\ln\left(\frac{1-\theta}{\alpha}\right) + \ln\left(\frac{\theta}{\beta}\right)\right] + \left[(1-g)\phi + g(1-\mu)\right]\ln\sigma.$$

Note that the term Γ contains the two z_j, which says that each country's decision concerning its z_j affects the utility of the other country's households. This is the basic externality in the model and the rationale for policy coordination.

This concludes the presentation of Casella's model and brings us to the governments' policy preferences.

Each government is deemed to maximize a welfare function containing the utility of the typical household and its own policy preference function:

$$W_j = u_j - \lambda Q_j, \tag{14}$$

The jth government's policy preference function is

$$Q_j = \frac{1}{2}\left[v_j\left(\frac{\tau_j}{z_j}\right)^2 + (1-v_j)\left(\frac{m_j}{z_j}\right)^2\right], \quad 0 < v_j < 1. \tag{15}$$

The cost of using a policy instrument, τ_j or m_j, rises quadratically as the government relies more heavily on it to finance production of the public good.

It might be more appropriate to write the policy preference function in terms of the inflation rate, π_j, rather than the cause of the inflation rate, m_j. We will soon see, however, that the two formulations are formally equivalent in the national currency case but that the use of π_j would complicate the common currency case, where the common inflation rate depends on both of the m_j. In other words, the use of π_j would introduce an additional externality. It might likewise be argued that the policy preference functions do not really belong in the model, as the costs of money creation and taxation are already reflected in the households' utility functions. But perfect internal consistency is not the ultimate virtue in a model too simple to be realistic.

As they are used repeatedly hereafter, it is worth writing out the partial derivatives of the policy preference functions:

$$\frac{\partial Q_j}{\partial \tau_j} = \left(\frac{1}{m_j}\right)^3 m_j q_j, \quad \frac{\partial Q_j}{\partial m_j} = -\left(\frac{1}{z_j}\right)^3 \tau_j q_j,$$

$$q_j = v_j \tau_j - \left(1 - v_j\right) m_j = v_j z_j - m_j.$$

This completes the model.

III. The National Currency Case

When households hold only their own country's currency, the demand for the currency must equal total wage payments, because households have to carry them forward from the period in which they earn them to the period in which they spend them. Therefore, money market equilibrium obtains when

$$M_{jt} = \sigma_j w_{jt},$$ (16)

so that

$$m_j = \frac{\pi_j}{1 + \pi_j}.$$ (17)

Equation (17) says that countries can have identical inflation rates if and only if $m_1 = m_2$. It also supports the assertion made earlier that it does not much matter whether the policy preference function is written in terms of m_j or π_j in the national currency case.

Using equation (17) to solve for π_j and replacing it in equation (13),

$$u_j = A + \left(1 - g\right)\left[\phi \ln \Gamma + \ln\left(1 - z_j\right)\right] + g\left[\ln z_j + \left(1 - \mu\right)\ln s_j\right].$$ (18)

Note that τ_j and m_j do not appear separately in equation (18). Hence, a government that wants merely to maximize u_j has simply to choose the appropriate z_j. That is what governments do in Casella's model. Putting the same point formally,

$$\frac{\partial u_j}{\partial \tau_j} = \frac{\partial u_j}{\partial m_j} = \frac{\partial u_j}{\partial z_j} = -(1-g)\left[\phi s_j\left(\frac{1}{\Gamma}\right) + \left(\frac{1}{1-z_j}\right)\right] + g\left(\frac{1}{z_j}\right).$$

Note further that

$$\frac{\partial u_1}{\partial z_2} = -(1-g)\phi s_2\left(\frac{1}{\Gamma}\right), \quad \frac{\partial u_2}{\partial z_1} = -(1-g)\phi s_1\left(\frac{1}{\Gamma}\right).$$

A Floating Exchange Rate with Policy Autonomy

With a floating exchange rate between the two countries' currencies and no international coordination of monetary or fiscal policies, the jth country's fiscal and monetary authorities will maximize W_j with respect to τ_j and m_j, and they will obtain these first-order conditions:[12]

$$\frac{\partial W_j}{\partial \tau_j} = \frac{\partial u_j}{\partial z_j} - \lambda\left(\frac{1}{z_j}\right)^3 m_j q_j = 0, \quad \frac{\partial W_j}{\partial m_j} = \frac{\partial u_j}{\partial z_j} + \lambda\left(\frac{1}{z_j}\right)^3 \tau_j q_j = 0. \quad (19)$$

Subtracting one from the other,

$$\lambda\left(\frac{1}{z_j}\right)^2 q_j = 0. \tag{20}$$

This condition cannot be satisfied, however, unless, $q_j = 0$, which gives us the optimal values of m_j and τ_j:

$$m_j = v_j z_j, \quad \tau_j = (1-v_j)z_j. \tag{21}$$

The marginal (and average) yield from each revenue-raising instrument is equated to the marginal cost of using it.

---

[12] The second-order conditions for this and other exercises are shown in Annex I.

When $q_j = 0$, moreover, equations (19) say that

$$(1-g)\left[\phi k_j\left(\frac{1}{\Gamma}\right) + \left(\frac{1}{1-z_j}\right)\right] - g\left(\frac{1}{z_j}\right) = 0, \tag{22}$$

where $k_j = s_j$.

As τ_j and m_j do not appear individually in equation (22), a government's policy preferences do not impinge on its decisions about z_j, the output of the public good, and it can partition its policy problem. It can use equation (22) to choose the appropriate z_j, then use equations (21) to choose the τ_j and m_j that minimize the cost of providing the public good.[13] For this same reason, moreover, a floating rate regime without coordination can accommodate different policy preferences. The governments' decisions about the z_j are interdependent, because both of the z_j appear in Γ, but their decisions about the τ_j and m_j can be taken independently. The latter are reconciled by the floating exchange rate, which offsets the gap between the inflation rates that arises when governments create different amounts of money per household.

Note finally that equation (22) puts strict limits on the z_j. It is, of course, impossible for them to be negative or larger than unity, but equation (22) narrows the limits. Feasible z_j must be positive and smaller than unity.

Before we carry the analysis further, let us look at the governments' problem with comprehensive policy coordination.

A Floating Exchange Rate with Comprehensive Coordination

With a floating exchange rate and comprehensive policy coordination, the two countries' monetary and fiscal authorities can be deemed to maximize a weighted sum of their welfare functions, with the weights based on the countries' populations:

$$W_T = s_1 W_1 + s_2 W_2. \tag{23}$$

---

[13] The policy problem in this particular case does not differ greatly from the one in Casella's paper, where the government chooses the optimal z_j and finances its spending by issuing money, levying a lump-sum tax, or using the two together. Whenever, $q_j = 0$, in fact, the results in this paper regarding the z_j match those in Casella's paper. (To replicate her results, we have merely to drop the policy preference function from the optimization problem by setting $\lambda = 0$.)

The first-order conditions for the jth country's instruments are

$$\frac{\partial W_T}{\partial \tau_j} = s_1\left(\frac{\partial u_1}{\partial z_j}\right) + s_2\left(\frac{\partial u_2}{\partial z_j}\right) - \lambda s_j\left(\frac{1}{z_j}\right)^3 m_j q_j = 0, \qquad (24a)$$

$$\frac{\partial W_T}{\partial m_j} = s_1\left(\frac{\partial u_1}{\partial z_j}\right) + s_2\left(\frac{\partial u_2}{\partial z_j}\right) + \lambda s_j\left(\frac{1}{z_j}\right)^3 \tau_j q_j = 0. \qquad (24b)$$

Subtracting one from the other, we obtain equation (20) once again and, therefore, equations (21) and (22), but with $k = 1$ instead of $k = s_j$.

Although the two governments engage in comprehensive coordination, each of them is still free to choose the τ_j and m_j that satisfy its preferences; the floating exchange rate continues to offset the gap between the π_j that arises when the governments have different preferences. Looking at this outcome from another standpoint, the governments seem to be coordinating their decisions about the τ_j and m_j but are really coordinating their decisions about the z_j. And that is what they should do in this model, where the externality involves the z_j.

Because the two regimes examined above yield very similar equations for the z_j (they differ only in the values of the k_j), the rest of the analysis can deal with them jointly.

Optimal Supplies of the Public Goods

To show how policy coordination affects household welfare, we must show how it affects the z_j. We begin by rewriting equation (22):

$$k_j(1-g)\phi(1-z_j)z_j - \Gamma(g-z_j) = 0. \qquad (25)$$

There are two such equations, of course, one for each country, and they must be solved simultaneously, because Γ appears in both. In the IS case, however, where the $s_j = \frac{1}{2}$, the two equations are the same and have only one feasible solution, $z_1 = z_2 = z$.[14] As $\Gamma = 1 - z$ in this case, the equations are easy to solve:

$$z = \frac{g}{H}, \qquad H = 1 + k(1-g)\phi, \qquad (26)$$

---

[14] See Annex II.

where $k = \frac{1}{2}$ with policy autonomy and $k = 1$ with comprehensive coordination. It will be useful, moreover, to define and evaluate total output of the public good, $z_T = z_1 + z_2$, to facilitate comparisons with other regimes. With policy autonomy,

$$z_T = \frac{2g}{1 + \frac{1}{2}(1 - g)\phi}, \tag{27a}$$

and with comprehensive coordination,

$$z_T' = \frac{2g}{1 + (1 - g)\phi}. \tag{27b}$$

Comprehensive coordination reduces total output of the public good $(z_T' < z_T)$.

Policy Coordination and Welfare

Policy coordination raises household welfare too, and this is easy to prove in the IS case. Using equation (26) to replace z_j in equation (13) and differentiating with respect to k,

$$\frac{\partial u_j}{\partial k} = \frac{g(1 - g)\phi^2(1 - k)}{(1 + k\phi)H}.$$

An increase in k raises utility when $k < 1$, and utility is maximized when $k = 1$. It would thus appear that a floating exchange rate combined with comprehensive coordination yields the first-best allocation of resources between the public and private sectors. The floating exchange rate accommodates the difference between the governments' policy preferences, and comprehensive coordination optimizes the number of varieties of the consumer good by reducing total output of the public good and releasing resources to the private sector.

Some Comparative Statics

Before examining other regimes, let us see how the optimal z_j are affected by the weight of the public good in the utility function and relative country size, how welfare is affected by relative size, and how it is affected by the size of the whole two-country world.

The first two questions can be answered by differentiating equations (25) with respect to the z_j, s_j, and g (remembering that $k_j = s_j$ with policy autonomy and $k_j = 1$ with comprehensive coordination), then evaluating the results for the IS case (in which $z_j = z$ initially):

$$\begin{bmatrix} (1-g)D + \frac{1}{2}(g-z) & \frac{1}{2}(g-z) \\ \frac{1}{2}(g-z) & (1-g)D + \frac{1}{2}(g-z) \end{bmatrix} \begin{bmatrix} dz_1 \\ dz_2 \end{bmatrix}$$

$$= (1-z) \begin{bmatrix} (1+kz\phi)dg - (1-g)z\phi dk_1 \\ (1+kz\phi)dg - (1-g)z\phi dk_2 \end{bmatrix},$$

where $D = 1 + k(1-z)\phi$, while $dk_j = ds_j$ with policy autonomy but $dk_j = 0$ with comprehensive coordination. With policy autonomy, then,

$$dz_1 = \left(\frac{1 + \frac{1}{2}z\phi}{H} \right) dg - (1-z) \left(\frac{z\phi}{D} \right) ds_1,$$

$$dz_2 = \left(\frac{1 + \frac{1}{2}z\phi}{H} \right) dg + (1-z) \left(\frac{z\phi}{D} \right) ds_1,$$

but with comprehensive coordination,

$$dz_j = \left(\frac{1 + z\phi}{H} \right) dg.$$

As one would expect, an increase in the weight of the public good raises output of the public good, with and without coordination. The effects of a change in the s_j, however, are felt only in the absence of coordination. An increase in the relative size of one country reduces its optimal z_j and has the opposite effect in the other country. This result is due to the basic externality that was built into the model and to the difference between the technologies used by the private and public sectors. If countries begin to differ in size, do not coordinate their policies, and did not adjust their z_j in response to the difference in size, both countries' households would experience a welfare-reducing reduction in the number of varieties of the consumer good. But governments will respond to the difference in size and will do so differently. The (newly) larger country has more influence on the number of varieties of the consumer good, so it will try to compensate its citizens by cutting output per household of the public good, releasing resources to the private sector, and raising the number of varieties of the consumer good. The (newly) smaller country has less influence on the number of varieties, so it will try to compensate its citizens by raising output per household of the public good, even though this will reduce the number of varieties of the consumer good.

The responses of the z_j to a change in the s_j do not depend on the nature of the public good (represented by the parameter μ). The nature of that good, however, is crucial for the ultimate effect on household welfare. Continuing to work with the IS case, consider the effect of increasing the size of the first country on the welfare of that country's households. From equation (13),[15]

$$\frac{du_1}{ds_1} = \frac{1}{z}\left(\frac{g-z}{1-z}\right)\frac{dz_1}{ds_1} + 2g(1-\mu).$$

We have therefore to deal with two pairs of possibilities:

(1) When the utility provided by the public good varies inversely with the number of households ($\mu = 1$), the last term of the expression drops out entirely. With comprehensive coordination, moreover, $(dz_1/ds_1) = 0$, so an increase in the relative size of a country does not affect its households' welfare. With policy autonomy, however, $(dz_1/ds_1) < 0$, so an increase in relative size reduces the households' welfare.

(2) When the utility provided by the public good is independent of the number of households ($\mu = 0$), an increase in the relative size of a country raises its households' welfare, with and without coordination. With comprehensive coordination, the first term of the expression goes to zero, as before, but the second term is positive. With policy autonomy, the first term is negative, the second term is positive, but the difference between them is positive.[16]

Finally, consider an increase in the size of the whole two-country world, measured by σ, the number of households, without changing the relative sizes of the countries. Using equation (13) again,

$$\frac{du_j}{d\sigma} = \frac{dA_j}{d\sigma} = \frac{1}{\sigma}\left[(1-g)\phi + g(1-\mu)\right],$$

---

[15] This formulation reflects the fact that $d\Gamma/ds_1 = 0$ in the IS case.
[16] Replacing (dz_1/ds_1) and simplifying, $(du_1/ds_1) = (1/D)[2g + (1-g)\phi z]$.

which is always positive, even when $\mu = 0$, because of the increase in the number of varieties provided by the increase in the number of households.

IV. Three More Policy Regimes

The two regimes examined in the previous section are similar in one vital way. They both rely on a floating exchange rate to offset the difference between national inflation rates arising from different policy preferences; inflation rates will differ when the m_j differ, and this will happen, even in the IS case, whenever the v_j differ. But the two regimes have different implications for resource allocation. As governments can use inflation and taxation to finance production of the public good, comprehensive coordination, covering monetary and tax policies, suffices to coordinate the governments' decisions about production of the public good. It prevents the excessive fall in the number of varieties of the consumer good that occurs when governments choose their z_j individually.

Nevertheless, a floating exchange rate cannot fully offset a difference in policy preferences when governments coordinate their monetary policies but do not coordinate their tax policies. Furthermore, comprehensive coordination cannot fully optimize the number of varieties of the consumer good when the exchange rate does not float. These are some of the results obtained in this section, which examines three more policy regimes: a floating exchange rate with partial coordination, a pegged rate with comprehensive coordination, and a pegged rate with partial coordination. (It is impossible to have a pegged rate without any coordination, because the exchange rate cannot be pegged in this particular model unless the two economies have the same inflation rates.)

For brevity and tractability, I confine the analysis to the IS case, where $s_j = \frac{1}{2}$. At times, in fact, I will have to go on to the ISP case, where the v_j are equal, too. This case was not considered before because the results for a floating exchange rate are not very interesting. As the m_j are equal in the ISP case, a floating rate cannot change. Put differently, pegging is redundant. That will be true here too, of course, but the ISP case will be the only one in which we can obtain solutions for the optimal z_j. (When comparing the z_j with those obtained before, however, we must keep in mind the special nature of the cases under study. The exchange rate cannot change. The importance of this point will be seen most clearly at the end of the section, when we look at the results for a pegged exchange rate with partial coordination; they will be the same as those for the corresponding floating rate case.)

A Floating Exchange Rate with Partial Coordination

With a floating exchange rate and monetary but not fiscal coordination, the monetary authorities will maximize W_T and the fiscal authorities will maximize the W_j. These are the first-order conditions for the jth country's instruments:

$$\frac{\partial W_j}{\partial \tau_j} = \frac{\partial u_j}{\partial z_j} - \lambda\left(\frac{1}{z_j}\right)^3 m_j q_j = 0, \tag{28a}$$

$$\frac{\partial W_T}{\partial m_j} = \frac{1}{2}\left[\frac{\partial u_1}{\partial z_j} + \frac{\partial u_2}{\partial z_j} + \lambda\left(\frac{1}{z_j}\right)^3 \tau_j q_j\right] = 0. \tag{28b}$$

Subtracting one from the other,

$$q_j = \tfrac{1}{2}(1-g)\phi\left(\frac{1}{\lambda\Gamma}\right)z_j^2. \tag{29}$$

Therefore, the optimal τ_j and m_j are

$$m_j = \left[v_j - \tfrac{1}{2}(1-g)\phi\left(\frac{1}{\lambda\Gamma}\right)z_j\right]z_j,$$

$$\tau_j = \left[(1-v_j) + \tfrac{1}{2}(1-g)\phi\left(\frac{1}{\lambda\Gamma}\right)z_j\right]z_j. \tag{30}$$

When the governments coordinate their monetary policies but not their fiscal policies, they cannot partition their policy problem; the ratio of τ_j to m_j is not independent of z_j, as it was before, but rises with z_j, and there is less reliance on m_j relative to τ_j for each and every z_j. It is, indeed, impossible to rule out solutions in which the m_j are negative.[17]

What happens to the z_j under this regime? Substituting the solutions for the τ_j and m_j into equation (28a),

$$\tfrac{1}{2}(1-g)\phi(2z_j - \tau_j)(1-z_j) - \Gamma(g-z_j) = 0,$$

---

[17] For more on this point, see Annex I, which examines the second-order conditions that correspond to equations (28a) and (28b).

or

$$\tfrac{1}{2}(1-g)\phi\left[(1+v_j) - \tfrac{1}{2}(1-g)\phi\left(\frac{1}{\lambda\Gamma}\right)z_j\right]z_j(1-z_j) - \Gamma(g-z_j) = 0.$$

(31)

There are, again, two such equations, one for each country, but they are cubic, even in the IS case. Therefore, we impose two simplifications. (1) We move on to the ISP case, where $v_j = v$, so that the two equations are identical. (2) We assume that the z_j are equal when the equations are the same.[18] Even after we impose these restrictions, the common equation is not easy to solve, but it can be used to define

$$z_T'' = \frac{2g + (1-g)\phi\tau}{1 + (1-g)\phi},$$

(32)

because the τ_j are the same when the v_j and z_j are the same. Using equations (27a) and (27b), it is then possible to show that

$$z_T'' - z_T' = \frac{(1-g)\phi\tau}{1 + (1-g)\phi} > 0,$$

$$z_T'' - z_T = -\frac{(1-g)\phi m}{1 + \tfrac{1}{2}(1-g)\phi} < 0 \quad \text{iff} \quad m > 0.$$

The cut in total output of the public good is smaller with partial coordination than with comprehensive coordination. When $m < 0$, indeed, the sum of the z_j is larger than it was with policy autonomy.[19] In brief, partial coordination cannot take us all the way to the first-best outcome and may indeed take us in the opposite direction.

A Pegged Exchange Rate with Comprehensive Coordination

To peg the exchange rate in this model, the two countries' central banks must equalize their m_j, but there are two ways to do that. One central bank can lead and the other can follow, as in many

---

[18] In the previous section, we relied on a *proof* that the z_j were equal before moving to the IS case. Here, we rely on a weaker proposition—the demonstration in Annex II that the assumption in the text does not produce a contradiction. (It does produce a contradiction under the first common currency regime studied in the next section.)

[19] Remember, however, that these results hold only for the ISP case, because equation (32) holds only for that case.

models of the EMS and of the earlier Bretton Woods system. Alternatively, they can coordinate their policies, by maximizing W_T with respect to a common value for the two m_j. I do not examine the first possibility, although it may be the best benchmark for appraising the welfare effects of European monetary union, being the closest approximation to the previous regime. I focus entirely on the second possibility, but distinguish, as before, between comprehensive and partial coordination.

With comprehensive coordination, the two countries' monetary and fiscal authorities can be deemed to maximize W_T by choosing optimal values for the τ_j and for the (common) m_j, denoted hereafter by $\tilde{m}$, and these are the first-order conditions:[20]

$$\frac{\partial W_T}{\partial \tau_j} = s_1\left(\frac{\partial u_1}{\partial z_j}\right) + s_2\left(\frac{\partial u_2}{\partial z_j}\right) - s_j\lambda\left(\frac{1}{z_j}\right)^3 \tilde{m}q_j = 0, \tag{33a}$$

$$\frac{\partial W_T}{\partial \tilde{m}} = s_1\left(\frac{\partial u_1}{\partial z_1} + \frac{\partial u_1}{\partial z_2}\right) + s_2\left(\frac{\partial u_2}{\partial z_1} + \frac{\partial u_2}{\partial z_2}\right)$$

$$+ s_1\lambda\left(\frac{1}{z_1}\right)^3 \tau_1 q_1 + s_2\lambda\left(\frac{1}{z_2}\right)^3 \tau_2 q_2 = 0. \tag{33b}$$

Subtracting equations (33a) from equation (33b),

$$s_1\left(\frac{1}{z_1}\right)^2 q_1 + s_2\left(\frac{1}{z_2}\right)^2 q_2 = 0. \tag{34}$$

Therefore,

$$\tilde{m} = \frac{s_1 v_1\left(\dfrac{1}{z_1}\right) + s_2 v_2\left(\dfrac{1}{z_2}\right)}{s_1\left(\dfrac{1}{z_1}\right)^2 + s_2\left(\dfrac{1}{z_2}\right)^2}. \tag{35}$$

In this instance, moreover, $\tau_j = z_j - \tilde{m}$. Accordingly, the τ_j will differ whenever the z_j differ, and that will happen whenever the v_j differ, even in the IS case, where the s_j are equal. Rewriting equations

---

[20] Although the analysis that follows deals only with the IS case, these first-order conditions are written for the general (DSP) case, so that they can be compared with their floating rate counterparts, equations (19) and (24).

(33a) for that case,

$$(1-g)\left[\phi\left(\frac{1}{\Gamma}\right)+\left(\frac{1}{1-z_j}\right)\right]-g\left(\frac{1}{z_j}\right)+\lambda\left(\frac{1}{z_j}\right)^3\tilde{m}\left(v_j z_j-\tilde{m}\right)=0,$$

which does not produce identical solutions for the two z_j unless we go to the ISP case, where the v_j are equal. In that case, however, exchange rate pegging is redundant, because comprehensive coordination will stabilize a floating rate.[21]

It is hard to solve for the z_j in the IS case, but we can say something about the solutions. It is clear, for example, that $\tilde{m}$ will be positive but that one of the τ_j can be negative:

$$\tau_1=\psi+\frac{z_1-z_2}{z_2^2\left[\left(\frac{1}{z_1}\right)^2+\left(\frac{1}{z_2}\right)^2\right]},\qquad \tau_2=\psi-\frac{z_1-z_2}{z_1^2\left[\left(\frac{1}{z_1}\right)^2+\left(\frac{1}{z_2}\right)^2\right]},$$

where

$$\psi=\frac{(1-v_1)\left(\frac{1}{z_1}\right)+(1-v_2)\left(\frac{1}{z_2}\right)}{\left(\frac{1}{z_1}\right)^2+\left(\frac{1}{z_2}\right)^2}>0.$$

But both τ_j cannot be negative because the sum of them cannot be negative:

$$\tau_1+\tau_2=2\psi+\frac{(z_1+z_2)(z_1-z_2)^2}{z_1^2+z_2^2}.$$

Furthermore, the sum of the two equations (33a) is

$$(1-g)\left[\phi\left(\frac{1}{\Gamma}\right)(z_1+z_2)+\left(\frac{z_1}{1-z_1}\right)+\left(\frac{z_2}{1-z_2}\right)\right]$$

$$-2g+\lambda\tilde{m}\left[\left(\frac{1}{z_1}\right)^2 q_1+\left(\frac{1}{z_2}\right)^2 q_2\right]=0.$$

---

[21] To confirm this assertion, assume provisionally that the z_j are equal when the v_j are equal and rewrite the previous equation for common values of the v_j and z_j. It becomes identical to the IS version of the corresponding equation for comprehensive coordination under a floating rate (in which case, of course, the z_j are equal because the solution is unique).

But the last term on the left side is zero, from equation (34), so that we can write

$$(1-g)\phi\left(\frac{1}{\Gamma}\right)\tilde{z}_T' - 2g = -(1-g)\left[\frac{z_1(1-z_2) + z_2(1-z_1)}{(1-z_1)(1-z_2)}\right],$$

where $\tilde{z}_T' = z_1 + z_2$. And using equation (27b), we obtain

$$\tilde{z}_T' - z_T' = -\frac{1}{2}\left[\frac{1-g}{1+(1-g)\phi}\right]\left[\frac{(z_1-z_2)^2}{(1-z_1)(1-z_2)}\right] < 0.$$

When governments engage in comprehensive policy coordination, total output of the public good is smaller with a pegged exchange rate than with a floating rate. The combination of comprehensive coordination and exchange rate pegging tends to *overcompensate* for the externality produced by policy autonomy and a floating rate. This result comes up again in the corresponding common currency case and thus echoes the result obtained by van der Ploeg (1990) that monetary union can cause a shortage of public goods. (He obtains his result from a different model, however, and ascribes it to monetary unification rather than exchange rate pegging.)

A Pegged Exchange Rate with Partial Coordination

When the governments peg the exchange rate by choosing $\tilde{m}$ jointly but do not coordinate their fiscal policies, the first-order conditions are given by equation (28a), for the maximization of the W_j with respect to the τ_j, and by equation (33b), for the maximization of W_T with respect to $\tilde{m}$. Subtracting the former from the latter,

$$2s_1s_2(1-g)\phi\left(\frac{1}{\Gamma}\right) - \lambda\left[s_1\left(\frac{1}{z_1}\right)^2 q_1 + s_2\left(\frac{1}{z_2}\right)^2 q_2\right] = 0, \tag{36}$$

so that

$$\tilde{m} = \frac{s_1 v_1\left(\frac{1}{z_1}\right) + s_2 v_2\left(\frac{1}{z_2}\right) - 2s_1s_2(1-g)\phi\left(\frac{1}{\lambda\Gamma}\right)}{s_1\left(\frac{1}{z_1}\right)^2 + s_2\left(\frac{1}{z_2}\right)^2}. \tag{37}$$

This equation replicates the basic result obtained for a partially coordinated float. There is comparatively less reliance on money creation than with comprehensive coordination, and we cannot rule out solutions in which $\tilde{m} < 0$. In the IS case, moreover,

$$\tilde{m} = \frac{v_1\left(\dfrac{1}{z_1}\right) + v_2\left(\dfrac{1}{z_2}\right) - (1-g)\phi\left(\dfrac{1}{\lambda\Gamma}\right)}{\left(\dfrac{1}{z_1}\right)^2 + \left(\dfrac{1}{z_2}\right)^2}.$$

This is the same result obtained for a floating rate with partial coordination and for a pegged rate with comprehensive coordination. The z_j are equal when the v_j are equal. When the v_j are equal, however, pegging is redundant, and the expression for $\tilde{m}$ becomes the same as the one for the (common) m_j obtained with a floating exchange rate and partial coordination. We need not carry the analysis further.

V. The Common Currency Case

When the two currencies are perfect substitutes or there is just one common currency, prices and wages cannot differ across countries, and the demand for money by the two countries' households must equal the sum of the money stocks supplied by the two central banks, whether they issue them separately or jointly. Therefore, equations (16) and (17) must be replaced by

$$M_{1t} + M_{2t} = \sigma w_t, \tag{38}$$

$$s_1 m_1 + s_2 m_2 = \frac{\pi}{1+\pi}. \tag{39}$$

The m_j should now to be interpreted as (1) the real increase per jth country household in the stock of the jth currency or in the stock of the common currency issued by the jth country's central bank, or (2) the real increase per jth country household in the stock of the common currency issued to the jth government by the central bank of a monetary union. They are formally equivalent.

Using equation (39) to solve for the common inflation rate, π, replacing π in equation (13), and setting $s_j = \frac{1}{2}$ to move to the IS case (which will be used through this section), we obtain the common currency version of the utility function:

$$u_j = A' + (1-g)(\phi \ln \Gamma + \ln G_j) + g \ln z_j, \tag{40}$$

where

$$A' = A + g(1 - \mu)\ln\tfrac{1}{2}, \quad \text{and} \quad G_j = 1 - \tfrac{1}{2}(m_1 + m_2) - \tau_j,$$

so that $G_1 = \Gamma + \tfrac{1}{2}(\tau_2 - \tau_1)$ and $G_2 = \Gamma + \tfrac{1}{2}(\tau_1 - \tau_2)$. Thus, the shift to a common currency introduces a second externality. The utility of the typical household depends on both z_j, which appear in Γ, and on both m_j, which appear in the G_j.[22] Therefore, the partial derivatives of the u_j with respect to the τ_j and m_j are no longer equal to their partial derivatives with respect to the z_j. Instead,

$$\frac{\partial u_j}{\partial \tau_j} = -\tfrac{1}{2}(1-g)\left[\phi\left(\frac{1}{\Gamma}\right) + 2\left(\frac{1}{G_j}\right)\right] + g\left(\frac{1}{z_j}\right),$$

$$\frac{\partial u_j}{\partial m_j} = -\tfrac{1}{2}(1-g)\left[\phi\left(\frac{1}{\Gamma}\right) + \left(\frac{1}{G_j}\right)\right] + g\left(\frac{1}{z_j}\right),$$

$$\frac{\partial u_1}{\partial \tau_2} = \frac{\partial u_2}{\partial \tau_1} = -\tfrac{1}{2}(1-g)\phi\left(\frac{1}{\Gamma}\right),$$

$$\frac{\partial u_1}{\partial m_2} = -\tfrac{1}{2}(1-g)\left[\phi\left(\frac{1}{\Gamma}\right) + \left(\frac{1}{G_1}\right)\right],$$

$$\frac{\partial u_2}{\partial m_1} = -\tfrac{1}{2}(1-g)\left[\phi\left(\frac{1}{\Gamma}\right) + \left(\frac{1}{G_2}\right)\right].$$

We will consider three policy regimes—national autonomy, comprehensive coordination, and partial coordination, and will interpret

---

[22] We noted earlier, moreover, that there would be a third externality if the Q_j were defined in terms of the inflation rate, because it depends on both m_j, and this can be demonstrated easily using equations (15) and (39). When the policy preference function is written in terms of the common inflation rate, π, rather than the increase in the money stock, m_j, it becomes:

$$Q_j = (\tfrac{1}{2})\left(\frac{1}{z_j}\right)^2 \left(v_j\tau_j^2 + (1-v_j)[\tfrac{1}{2}(m_1+m_2)]^2\right),$$

and each country's Q_j depends on both countries' m_j. But this interdependence vanishes in a monetary union if the central bank cannot discriminate freely when distributing new money. If the m_j are equal, we return to the result obtained in the national currency case, where it did not matter whether the policy preference function was written in terms of the π_j or the m_j.

the last two as monetary unions with and without fiscal coordination.

A Common Currency with Policy Autonomy

When the two countries can issue a common currency independently, each government has an incentive to subsidize its households—to replace lump-sum taxes ($\tau_j > 0$) with lump-sum subsidies ($\tau_j < 0$) and to finance the subsidies, as well as production of the public good, by issuing additional money. There is no limit to this process in Casella's model and, therefore, no well-defined Nash equilibrium.[23] But the policy preference functions limit the process in this model by making it increasingly expensive for governments to reduce the τ_j and raise the m_j.

The relevant first-order conditions resemble those pertaining to policy autonomy under a floating exchange rate between the two national currencies, but they cannot be written as they were before, because the partial derivatives of the u_j with respect to the τ_j and m_j do not equal their partial derivatives with respect to the z_j. They are

$$\frac{\partial W_j}{\partial \tau_j} = \frac{\partial u_j}{\partial \tau_j} - \lambda \left(\frac{1}{z_j}\right)^3 m_j q_j = 0, \quad \frac{\partial W_j}{\partial m_j} = \frac{\partial u_j}{\partial m_j} + \lambda \left(\frac{1}{z_j}\right)^3 \tau_j q_j = 0. \quad (41)$$

Therefore,

$$q_j = -\tfrac{1}{2}(1-g)\left(\frac{1}{\lambda G_j}\right) z_j^2. \quad (42)$$

When we use this expression to replace the q_j in equations (41), however, we obtain four quadratic equations in the τ_j and m_j (or, equivalently, the z_j and m_j). The problem is intractable even in the ISP case, because the strategy used before produces a contradiction here. Let the $v_j = v$ and assume provisionally that the z_j and m_j are equal in the ISP case.[24] Under these assumptions, equation (42) yields

$$\tfrac{1}{2}(1-g)z^2 + \lambda(1-z)(vz - m) = 0,$$

---

[23] To see that this is so, set $\lambda = 0$ in equations (41) below. There is no solution that can satisfy both of them.

[24] Under these conditions, the τ_j must be equal, and $G_j = \Gamma = 1 - z$.

and these are the optimal setting of the instruments:

$$m = vz + \tfrac{1}{2}(1-g)\left(\tfrac{1}{\lambda}\right)\left(\frac{z^2}{1-z}\right),$$

$$\tau = (1-v)z - \tfrac{1}{2}(1-g)\left(\frac{1}{\lambda}\right)\left(\frac{z^2}{1-z}\right). \tag{43}$$

There is comparatively more reliance on money creation than in the corresponding national currency case, and the lump-sum tax can give way to a lump-sum subsidy ($\tau < 0$). But when we use equation (43) to replace m in equations (41), we obtain

$$\left[(1-g)\phi z - 2(g-z) - (1-g)vz\right](1-z) - \tfrac{1}{2}(1-g)^2\left(\frac{1}{\lambda}\right)z^2 = 0, \tag{44}$$

and there can be *two* feasible solutions for z, which means that the z_j may not be equal.[25]

Consider a special symmetrical case, however, in which $g = \tfrac{1}{4}(1-g)^2(1/\lambda)$ and $\lambda[(1+\phi) + (1-v)] = (1-g)$.[26] The only solution for the output of the public good is $z = \tfrac{1}{2}$, so that

$$m = \tfrac{1}{2}\left[v + 2\left(\frac{g}{1-g}\right)\right], \quad \tau = \tfrac{1}{2}\left[(1-v) - 2\left(\frac{g}{1-g}\right)\right],$$

$$\text{and} \quad q = -\left(\frac{g}{1-g}\right).$$

In this same special case, moreover, $\tau < 0$ satisfies the second-order conditions corresponding to equations (41).[27] In other words, we obtain a well-behaved version of Casella's result. The lump-sum tax gives way to a lump-sum subsidy.

Finally, we can show that total output of the public good may be larger with a common currency and policy autonomy than in the corresponding national currency case. If the z_j *are* equal when the v_j are equal, even when there are two such solutions, equations (27a)

---

[25] See Annex II.

[26] The rationale for choosing this case is provided in Annex II.

[27] See Annex I for details.

and (44) can be used to obtain

$$\hat{z}_T - z_T = \left[\frac{2}{1 + \frac{1}{2}(1-g)\phi}\right]\left[(1-g)v(1-\hat{z})\hat{z} + \frac{1}{2}(1-g)^2\left(\frac{1}{\lambda}\right)\hat{z}^2\right] > 0,$$

where the $\hat{z}$ are the common currency values and $\hat{z}_T$ is the sum of those values.

Note that this last result pertains to the ISP case, where the exchange rate between the two national currencies did not change when the governments pursued independent policies. Hence, the result does not reflect any difference in exchange rate behavior between the common currency and national currency cases. It reflects instead the change in the governments' behavior produced by the externality introduced by a common currency. As part of each country's inflation tax is borne by the other country's households, both governments have an incentive to produce very large quantities of the public good.

A Common Currency with Comprehensive Coordination

When the two countries issue a common currency jointly or create a single central bank to issue it for them, they may be deemed to maximize W_T with respect to the m_j. When they coordinate their fiscal policies too, they may be deemed to maximize W_T with respect to the τ_j. The relevant first-order conditions resemble those obtained for comprehensive coordination under a floating exchange rate between the two national currencies, but they have to be rewritten:

$$\frac{\partial W_T}{\partial \tau_j} = \frac{1}{2}\left[\frac{\partial u_1}{\partial \tau_j} + \frac{\partial u_2}{\partial \tau_j} - \lambda\left(\frac{1}{z_j}\right)^3 m_j q_j\right] = 0, \tag{45a}$$

$$\frac{\partial W_T}{\partial m_j} = \frac{1}{2}\left[\frac{\partial u_1}{\partial m_j} + \frac{\partial u_2}{\partial m_j} + \lambda\left(\frac{1}{z_j}\right)^3 \tau_j q_j\right] = 0. \tag{45b}$$

Therefore,

$$\left(\frac{1}{z_1}\right)^2 q_1 = -\left(\frac{1}{z_2}\right)^2 q_2 = \frac{1}{2}(1-g)(\tau_2 - \tau_1)\left(\frac{1}{\lambda}\right)\left(\frac{1}{G_1 G_2}\right), \tag{46}$$

which says that the q_j cannot be equal unless they are zero, and they cannot be zero unless the τ_j are equal.

In Casella's model, comprehensive coordination has powerful effects when the s_j are equal. It offsets the externality arising from the use of a common currency, and it also offsets the tendency for governments to produce too much of the public good. In fact, the z_j given by this common currency regime are the same as the z_j given by the first-best national currency regime—the one with comprehensive coordination and a floating exchange rate.[28] Accordingly, Casella concludes that a currency union cannot be Pareto-superior to a floating rate regime but is not inferior to it in the IS case. (Her own paper, however, is chiefly concerned with the differences between a currency union and a floating rate regime when the s_j are not equal.)

In the model used here, by contrast, the common currency values of z_j differ from country to country and are thus different from their floating rate values (which are equal across countries). That is because the q_j cannot be equal in this model unless the τ_j are equal, and that will not normally happen unless the v_j are equal. When policy preferences differ, then, a currency union cannot precisely neutralize the tendency for governments to provide too much of the public good, even with comprehensive coordination.

There are two ways to illustrate this basic point without solving for the z_j explicitly. First, we can show that total output of the public good is smaller with comprehensive coordination and a common currency than with comprehensive coordination and a floating exchange rate. Using equations (27a), (45b), and (46),

$$\hat{z}'_T - z'_T = -\tfrac{1}{2}\left[\frac{1-g}{1+(1-g)\phi}\right]\left(\frac{1}{G_1 G_2}\right)(\tau_1 - \tau_2)^2,$$

where $\hat{z}'_T$ is the sum of the z_j with comprehensive coordination and a common currency. This difference is negative whenever the τ_j differ.

Second, we can use equation (46) to write

$$m_1\left(\frac{1}{z_1}\right)^2 + m_2\left(\frac{1}{z_2}\right)^2 = v_1\left(\frac{1}{z_1}\right) + v_2\left(\frac{1}{z_2}\right), \tag{47}$$

and this equation will allow us to show that comprehensive coordination in a currency union can yield results identical to those provided by a pegged exchange rate, not those provided by a floating rate, as in Casella's model.

---

[28] Once again, we can replicate Casella's result by setting $\lambda = 0$ in equation (45a) or (45b). The resulting equations are the same across countries and have only one feasible solution. Hence, $z_1 = z_2 = z$, and z is given by equation (26) with $k_j = 1$.

Suppose that the central bank of the monetary union cannot discriminate when issuing new money. It must issue identical amounts per household to both countries' governments.[29] Then equation (47) yields

$$m_j = m = \frac{v_1\left(\dfrac{1}{z_1}\right) + v_2\left(\dfrac{1}{z_2}\right)}{\left(\dfrac{1}{z_1}\right)^2 + \left(\dfrac{1}{z_2}\right)^2}.$$

This is identical to the result obtained with comprehensive coordination and a pegged exchange rate; it can be derived from equation (35) by setting $s_j = \frac{1}{2}$ to generate the IS case. It is possible to show, in fact, that a monetary union with $m_j = m$ combined with fiscal coordination is identical to a pegged rate regime with comprehensive coordination. The coordination or unification of monetary policies offsets the externality created by the use of a common currency. But precisely because it emulates a pegged rate regime, a monetary union tends to overcompensate for the externality affecting production of the public good. The effects of that externality always emerge when the v_j differ (except, of course, in the floating rate cases examined early in this paper).

A Common Currency with Partial Coordination

When the central bank of a monetary union cannot discriminate when issuing new money, but must issue the same amounts per household to both governments, and the governments do not coordinate their fiscal policies, the relevant first-order conditions are given by equations (28a) and (33b), as in the corresponding pegged rate case. Accordingly, the outcomes for a monetary union without discrimination or fiscal coordination are the same as the outcomes for a pegged rate regime with partial coordination. There is comparatively less reliance on money creation than with comprehensive coordination, and the amount of money creation, $\tilde{m}$, can be negative. In the IS case, moreover, the solution for $\tilde{m}$ is the same as the one obtained for a floating exchange rate and partial coordination.

---

[29] As was indicated earlier, this is a "weak form" of the recommendation in the Delors Report (1989) that the central bank of a European monetary union should not lend directly to national governments.

VI. Summary and Concluding Note

The main results of this analysis can be summarized succinctly by reviewing the principal effects of floating exchange rates, a monetary union, and fiscal coordination on total output of the public good and by comparing the results with those in Casella's paper.

Because it can insulate each economy from its partner's inflation rate, a floating exchange rate is the only regime that can prevent differences in policy preferences from affecting the allocation of resources between the public and private sectors. Accordingly, it sets the stage for policy coordination to optimize that allocation. By implication, the results in this paper strengthen the case for floating exchange rates implicit in Casella's paper.

When the members of a monetary union do not differ in size, the governments have the same policy preferences, and the governments coordinate their fiscal policies, the union does not distort resource allocation. Total output of the public good is the same as it would be with a floating exchange rate between the members' currencies and comprehensive coordination. When the governments have different preferences, however, a monetary union resembles a pegged rate regime, and total output of the public good is smaller than it would be with a floating rate. In other words, the monetary union *overcompensates* for the externality distorting resource allocation. Therefore, the results in this paper qualify those in Casella's paper.

When governments coordinate their monetary policies but do not coordinate their fiscal policies, there is comparatively less reliance on money creation than with comprehensive coordination or national autonomy. This result holds for floating and pegged rates and for a common currency. But total output of the public good tends to be larger than with comprehensive coordination and can sometimes be larger than with national autonomy. In brief, partial coordination does not always lead part way from the allocation under national autonomy to the first-best allocation under comprehensive coordination. These results have no counterpart in Casella's paper, because her model does not allow her to examine partial coordination.

A general cost-benefit analysis of the case for monetary union, in Europe or anywhere else, should take account of the issues studied in this paper. But others may be more important. How does exchange rate uncertainty affect capital formation? How high are the transactions costs imposed by using and holding many national currencies? How large are the costs of adjusting to country-specific shocks when nominal exchange rates are fixed or fused by a monetary union, when labor mobility is low, and when there are no endogenous fiscal transfers from one country to another? This list of questions is incomplete. The Commission of the European Communities (1990) has raised many more. The list is long enough, however, to warn that the model used in this paper deals with one corner of a complicated puzzle.

ANNEX I

The Second-Order Conditions

National Currency Regimes

In the national currency case, the second derivatives of the utility function are

$$\frac{\partial^2 u_j}{\partial \tau_j \partial \tau_j} = \frac{\partial^2 u_j}{\partial m_j \partial m_j} = \frac{\partial^2 u_j}{\partial z_j \partial z_j} = -(1-g)\phi\left[s_j\left(\frac{1}{\Gamma}\right)\right]^2$$

$$-(1-g)\left(\frac{1}{1-z_j}\right)^2 - g\left(\frac{1}{z_j}\right)^2 < 0,$$

$$\frac{\partial^2 u_1}{\partial z_2 \partial z_2} = -(1-g)\phi\left[s_2\left(\frac{1}{\Gamma}\right)\right]^2 < 0, \quad \frac{\partial^2 u_2}{\partial z_1 \partial z_1} = -(1-g)\phi\left[s_1\left(\frac{1}{\Gamma}\right)\right]^2 < 0.$$

The second derivatives of the policy preference functions are

$$\frac{\partial^2 Q_j}{\partial \tau_j \partial \tau_j} = \left(\frac{1}{z_j}\right)^4 m_j(m_j - 2q_j), \quad \frac{\partial^2 Q_j}{\partial m_j \partial m_j} = \left(\frac{1}{z_j}\right)^4 \tau_j(\tau_j + 2q_j),$$

$$\frac{\partial^2 Q_j}{\partial \tau_j \partial m_j} = \left(\frac{1}{z_j}\right)^4 [(\tau_j - m_j)q_j - \tau_j m_j],$$

which can be positive or negative (because q_j can be positive or negative).

A Floating Exchange Rate with Policy Autonomy

The jth government maximizes W_j, the first-order conditions are given by equations (19) in the text, and the corresponding second-order conditions are

$$\frac{\partial^2 W_j}{\partial \tau_j \partial \tau_j} < 0, \quad \begin{vmatrix} \dfrac{\partial^2 W_j}{\partial \tau_j \partial \tau_j} & \dfrac{\partial^2 W_j}{\partial \tau_j \partial m_j} \\[3mm] \dfrac{\partial^2 W_j}{\partial \tau_j \partial m_j} & \dfrac{\partial^2 W_j}{\partial m_j \partial m_j} \end{vmatrix} > 0.$$

But $q_j = 0$ when the first-order conditions are met, so that

$$\frac{\partial^2 W_j}{\partial \tau_j \partial \tau_j} = \frac{\partial^2 u_j}{\partial z_j \partial z_j} - \lambda v_j^2 \left(\frac{1}{z_j} \right)^2 ,$$

$$\frac{\partial^2 W_j}{\partial m_j \partial m_j} = \frac{\partial^2 u_j}{\partial z_j \partial z_j} - \lambda (1 - v_j)^2 \left(\frac{1}{z_j} \right)^2 ,$$

and

$$\frac{\partial^2 W_j}{\partial \tau_j \partial m_j} = \frac{\partial^2 u_j}{\partial z_j \partial z_j} + \lambda v_j (1 - v_j) \left(\frac{1}{z_j} \right)^2 ,$$

which satisfy the second-order conditions.

A Floating Exchange Rate with Comprehensive Coordination

The two governments maximize W_T, the first-order conditions are given by equations (24a) and (24b), and the second-order conditions are

$$\frac{\partial^2 W_T}{\partial \tau_1 \partial \tau_1} < 0, \quad \begin{vmatrix} \dfrac{\partial^2 W_T}{\partial \tau_1 \partial \tau_1} & \dfrac{\partial^2 W_T}{\partial \tau_1 \partial m_1} \\[3mm] \dfrac{\partial^2 W_T}{\partial \tau_1 \partial m_1} & \dfrac{\partial^2 W_T}{\partial m_1 \partial m_1} \end{vmatrix} > 0,$$

$$\begin{vmatrix} \dfrac{\partial^2 W_T}{\partial \tau_1 \partial \tau_1} & \dfrac{\partial^2 W_T}{\partial \tau_1 \partial m_1} & \dfrac{\partial^2 W_T}{\partial \tau_1 \partial \tau_2} \\[3mm] \dfrac{\partial^2 W_T}{\partial \tau_1 \partial m_1} & \dfrac{\partial^2 W_T}{\partial m_1 \partial m_1} & \dfrac{\partial^2 W_T}{\partial m_1 \partial \tau_2} \\[3mm] \dfrac{\partial^2 W_T}{\partial \tau_1 \partial \tau_2} & \dfrac{\partial^2 W_T}{\partial m_1 \partial \tau_2} & \dfrac{\partial^2 W_T}{\partial \tau_2 \partial \tau_2} \end{vmatrix} < 0,$$

and so on. Once again, however, $q_j = 0$, when the first-order conditions are met, so that

$$\frac{\partial^2 W_T}{\partial \tau_j \partial \tau_j} = s_j \left[\frac{\partial^2 u_T}{\partial z_j \partial z_j} - \lambda v_j^2 \left(\frac{1}{z_j} \right)^2 \right],$$

$$\frac{\partial^2 W_T}{\partial m_j \partial m_j} = s_j \left[\frac{\partial^2 u_T}{\partial z_j \partial z_j} - \lambda (1 - v_j)^2 \left(\frac{1}{z_j} \right)^2 \right],$$

$$\frac{\partial^2 W_T}{\partial \tau_j \partial m_j} = s_j \left[\frac{\partial^2 u_T}{\partial z_j \partial z_j} + \lambda v_j (1 - v_j) \left(\frac{1}{z_j} \right)^2 \right],$$

where

$$\frac{\partial^2 u_T}{\partial z_j \partial z_j} = - \left[(1 - g) \phi s_j \left(\frac{1}{\Gamma} \right)^2 + (1 - g) \left(\frac{1}{1 - z_j} \right)^2 + g \left(\frac{1}{z_j} \right)^2 \right] < 0,$$

while

$$\frac{\partial^2 W_T}{\partial \tau_1 \partial \tau_2} = \frac{\partial^2 W_T}{\partial \tau_1 \partial m_2} = \frac{\partial^2 W_T}{\partial m_1 \partial \tau_2} = \frac{\partial^2 W_T}{\partial m_1 \partial m_2} = -s_1 s_2 (1 - g) \phi \left(\frac{1}{\Gamma} \right)^2 < 0,$$

and it can then be shown, albeit laboriously, that the second-order conditions are satisfied.

A Floating Exchange Rate with Partial Coordination

The fiscal authorities maximize the W_j while the monetary authorities maximize W_T, the first-order conditions are given by equations (28a) and (28b), and the second-order conditions are

$$\frac{\partial^2 W_j}{\partial \tau_j \partial \tau_j} < 0, \quad \frac{\partial^2 W_T}{\partial m_1 \partial m_1} < 0, \quad \begin{vmatrix} \dfrac{\partial^2 W_T}{\partial m_1 \partial m_1} & \dfrac{\partial^2 W_T}{\partial m_1 \partial m_2} \\[2ex] \dfrac{\partial^2 W_T}{\partial m_1 \partial m_2} & \dfrac{\partial^2 W_T}{\partial m_2 \partial m_2} \end{vmatrix} > 0,$$

which must be evaluated at

$$q_j = v_j z_j - m_j = \tfrac{1}{2}(1 - g) \phi \left(\frac{1}{\lambda \Gamma} \right) z_j^2 > 0,$$

so that

$$\frac{\partial^2 W_j}{\partial \tau_j \partial \tau_j} = \frac{\partial^2 u_j}{\partial z_j \partial z_j} - \lambda \left(\frac{1}{z_j}\right)^4 m_j\left(m_j - 2q_j\right),$$

$$\frac{\partial^2 W_T}{\partial m_j \partial m_j} = \frac{\partial^2 u_T}{\partial z_j \partial z_j} - \lambda \left(\frac{1}{z_j}\right)^4 \tau_j\left(\tau_j + 2q_j\right),$$

and the cross-partial derivative has the same value as before. Clearly, the first second-order condition is satisfied when $m_j <$ or when $m_j > 2q_j$ (which confirms the statement in the text that we cannot exclude outcomes in which $m_j < 0$), and it is easy to show that other conditions are satisfied.

The pegged rate regimes are not examined here, because they resemble their floating rate counterparts in the ISP case, the only case in which they are tractable.

Common Currency Regimes

In the common currency case, the second derivatives of the household utility function are

$$\frac{\partial^2 u_j}{\partial \tau_j \partial \tau_j} = -\left[\tfrac{1}{4}(1-g)\phi\left(\frac{1}{\Gamma}\right)^2 + (1-g)\left(\frac{1}{G_j}\right)^2 + g\left(\frac{1}{z_j}\right)^2\right],$$

$$\frac{\partial^2 u_j}{\partial m_j \partial m_j} = -\left[\tfrac{1}{4}(1-g)\phi\left(\frac{1}{\Gamma}\right)^2 + \tfrac{1}{4}(1-g)\left(\frac{1}{G_j}\right)^2 + g\left(\frac{1}{z_j}\right)^2\right],$$

$$\frac{\partial^2 u_j}{\partial \tau_j \partial m_j} = -\left[\tfrac{1}{4}(1-g)\phi\left(\frac{1}{\Gamma}\right)^2 + \tfrac{1}{2}(1-g)\left(\frac{1}{G_j}\right)^2 + g\left(\frac{1}{z_j}\right)^2\right].$$

The other cross-partial derivatives are not needed here.

A Common Currency with Policy Autonomy

The jth government maximizes W_j, the first-order conditions are given by equations (41) in the text, and the corresponding second-order conditions are the same as those shown above for the corresponding floating rate case. Evaluating the relevant expressions for the special case where $g = \frac{1}{4}(1-g)^2(1/\lambda)$ and $z = \frac{1}{2}$,

$$\frac{\partial^2 W_j}{\partial \tau_j \partial \tau_j} = -\left[(1-g)(1+\phi) + 4g\right]$$

$$-4(1-g) - 4\left[\frac{(1-g)^2}{g}\right]m\left[m + 2\left(\frac{g}{1-g}\right)\right],$$

$$\frac{\partial^2 W_j}{\partial m_j \partial m_j} = -\left[(1-g)(1+\phi) + 4g\right] - 4\left[\frac{(1-g)^2}{g}\right]\tau\left[\tau - 2\left(\frac{g}{1-g}\right)\right],$$

$$\frac{\partial^2 W_j}{\partial \tau_j \partial m_j} = -\left[(1-g)(1+\phi) + 4g\right] - 2(1-g)$$

$$-4\left[\frac{(1-g)^2}{g}\right]\left[m\tau + \left(\frac{g}{1-g}\right)(\tau - m)\right].$$

The first condition is always met (because $m > 0$), and the second condition can be written as

$$4\left[\frac{(1-g)^2}{g}\right]\left(\left[(m-\tau) + 4\left(\frac{g}{1-g}\right)\right]\left[(1-g)(1+\phi) + 4g - 4(1-g)\tau\right]\right) > 0,$$

so that $\tau < 0$ is sufficient to meet it.

The other common currency regimes are not examined here, because they resemble their pegged rate counterparts in the IS case and their floating rate counterparts in the ISP case.

ANNEX II

Mapping Solutions for Optimal Output of the Public Good

A Floating Exchange Rate with Policy Autonomy or Comprehensive Coordination

Rewriting equation (25) of the text, using the version for the first country:

$$\left[s_1 + k_1(1-g)\phi\right](1-z_1)z_1 + \left[gs_1 + s_2(1-z_2)\right]z_1 - g\left[s_1 + s_2(1-z_2)\right] = y_1.$$

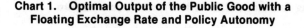

**Chart 1.   Optimal Output of the Public Good with a
Floating Exchange Rate and Policy Autonomy**

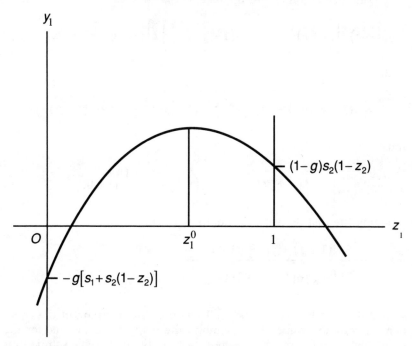

For feasible values of z_2, then, $y_1 < 0$ when $z_1 = 0$, and $y_1 > 0$ when $z_1 = 1$. Furthermore,

$$\frac{\partial y_1}{\partial x_1} = \left[s_1 + k_1(1-g)\phi\right](1 - 2z_1) + \left[gs_1 + s_2(1-z_2)\right],$$

and

$$\frac{\partial^2 y_1}{\partial z_1 \partial z_1} = -2\left[s_1 + k_1(1-g)\phi\right] < 0.$$

Therefore, y_1 reaches a maximum when

$$z_1^0 = \frac{1}{2}\left[1 + \frac{gs_1 + s_2(1-z_2)}{s_1 + k_1(1-g)\phi}\right],$$

so that $\frac{1}{2} < z_1^0 < 1$. These results are reproduced in Chart 1. When $0 < z_2 < 1$, there is only one feasible solution for z_1. But this proposition holds both ways, which means that there is only one such solution for the two z_j.

A Floating Exchange Rate with Partial Coordination

Rewriting equation (31) of the text,

$$\tfrac{1}{2}(1-g)\phi\left[(1+v)(1-z)-\tfrac{1}{2}(1-g)\phi\left(\frac{1}{\lambda}\right)z\right]z-(g-z)(1-z)=y,$$

so that

$$\frac{\partial y}{\partial z}=\tfrac{1}{2}(1-g)\phi\left[(1+v)(1-2z)-(1-g)\phi\left(\frac{1}{\lambda}\right)z\right]+[(1+g)-2z],$$

and

$$\frac{\partial^2 y}{\partial z\partial z}=-\left[2+(1-g)\phi(1+v)+\tfrac{1}{2}(1-g)^2\phi^2\left(\frac{1}{\lambda}\right)\right]<0.$$

Setting the first derivative equal to zero and solving,

$$z^0=\frac{(1+g)+\tfrac{1}{2}(1-g)\phi(1+v)}{2+(1-g)\phi(1+v)+\tfrac{1}{2}(1-g)^2\phi^2\left(\frac{1}{\lambda}\right)},$$

so that $0<z^0<1$ (because $g<1$). Therefore, the mapping of the equation for common value of z resembles the mapping of the one for the individual z_j in the previous section, with only one feasible solution for z.

A Common Currency with Policy Autonomy

Rewriting equation (44) of the text,

$$[(1-g)\phi z-2(g-z)-(1-g)vz](1-z)-\tfrac{1}{2}(1-g)^2\left(\frac{1}{\lambda}\right)z^2=y,$$

so that $y=-2g$ when $z=0$, and $y=-\tfrac{1}{2}(1-g)^2(1/\lambda)$ when $z=1$. Furthermore,

$$\frac{\partial y}{\partial z}=[1+(1-g)\phi+(1-v)+vg](1-2z)+2\left[g-\tfrac{1}{2}(1-g)^2\left(\frac{1}{\lambda}\right)z\right],$$

and

$$\frac{\partial^2 y}{\partial z\partial z}=-2\left[1+(1-g)\phi+(1-v)+vg+\tfrac{1}{2}(1-g)^2\left(\frac{1}{\lambda}\right)\right]<0.$$

**Chart 2.   Optimal Output of the Public Good with a
Common Currency and Policy Autonomy**

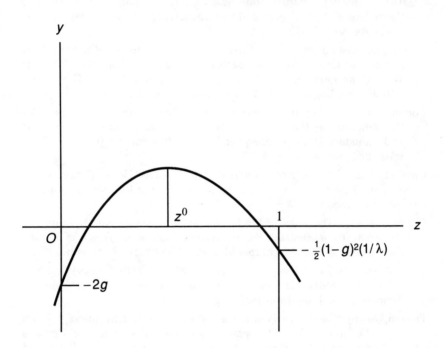

Therefore, y reaches a maximum when

$$z^0 = \left(\tfrac{1}{2}\right)\left(\frac{\left[1+(1-g)\phi+(1-v)+vg\right]+2g}{\left[1+(1-g)\phi+(1-v)+vg\right]+\tfrac{1}{2}(1-g)^2\left(\dfrac{1}{\lambda}\right)}\right) < 1.$$

These results are reproduced in Chart 2. There are two feasible solutions for z if $y > 0$ when $z = z^0$, one such solution if $y = 0$, and no solution if $y < 0$. When $g = \tfrac{1}{4}(1-g)^2(1/\lambda)$, however, $z^0 = \tfrac{1}{2}$, and the corresponding value of y is

$$y^0 = \tfrac{1}{4}(1-g)\left[(1+\phi)+(1-v)-(1-g)\left(\dfrac{1}{\lambda}\right)\right],$$

so that $y^0 = 0$ when $\lambda[(1+\phi)+(1-v)] = (1-g)$. The only solution for the output of the public good is $z = z^0 = \tfrac{1}{2}$, which is the special symmetrical case examined in the text.

REFERENCES

Casella, Alessandra, "Participation in a Currency Union," NBER Working Paper No. 3220 (Cambridge, Massachusetts: National Bureau of Economic Research, 1990).

——, and Jonathan Feinstein, "Management of a Common Currency," in *A European Central Bank? Perspectives on Monetary Unification After Ten Years of the EMS,* ed. by Marcello de Cecco and Alberto Giovannini (Cambridge, England: Cambridge University Press, 1989).

Commission of the European Communities, "One Market, One Money: An Evaluation of the Potential Benefits and Costs of Forming an Economic and Monetary Union," *European Economy* (Luxembourg), No. 44 (October 1990).

Committee for the Study of Economic and Monetary Union (Delors Committee), *Report on Economic and Monetary Union in the European Community* (Luxembourg, 1989).

Corden, W.M., "The Logic of the International Monetary Non-System," in *Reflections on a Troubled World Economy: Essays in Honor of Herbert Giersch,* ed. by Fritz Machlup and others (New York: St. Martins, 1983).

Dixit, Avinash K., and Joseph E. Stiglitz, "Monopolistic Competition and Optimum Product Diversity" *American Economic Review* (Nashville, Tennessee), Vol. 67 (June 1977), pp. 297–308.

Drazen, Allan, "Monetary Policy, Capital Controls and Seigniorage in an Open Economy," in *A European Central Bank? Perspectives on Monetary Unification After Ten Years of the EMS,* ed. by Marcello de Cecco and Alberto Giovannini (Cambridge, England: Cambridge University Press, 1989).

Eichengreen, Barry, "One Money for Europe? Lessons from the U.S. Currency Union," *Economic Policy* (Cambridge, England), No. 10 (April 1990), pp. 117–87.

Krugman, Paul R., "Intraindustry Specialization and the Gains from Trade," *Journal of Political Economy* (Chicago), Vol. 89 (October 1981), pp. 959–73.

Ploeg, F. van der, "Does Economic and Monetary Union Lead to a Too Small Public Sector in Europe?," paper presented to the Conference on Fiscal Aspects of European Economic Integration (New Haven, March 1990).

14

How to Warrant a Sufficient Level of Energy Supply to Future Generations

Jan Tinbergen

I. The Problem and Its Core

One of the hobbies that my long-time friend Jacques Polak, whom the Dutch call Koos, and I enjoy the most is building models. He has built some real beauties as we all know.[1] I hope he likes the one I dedicate to him on the occasion of his seventy-fifth birthday.

The problem dealt with in this essay is whether, and if so how, nonrenewable natural resources may be distributed between current and future generations. Since future generations are the children, grandchildren, and so on, of today's generation, it is natural to think that sharing the known reserves of natural resources poses a problem of equal sharing. In order to understand the most essential features of this problem, we simplify it to what we shall call its core. We assume that world population is stable and that the goal is to keep the standard of living of future generations equal to ours. The core question to be answered then is whether the *infinity* of future generations can be offered our standard of life (a quantity of goods and services) with the *finite* quantity of natural resources. The goods and services mentioned, although meant for consumption as well as for investment, will be called consumer goods.

---

[1]Take, for instance, J. J. Polak, *An International Economic System* (Chicago: University of Chicago Press, 1953; London: Allen & Unwin, 1954).

The answer to the core question is in the affirmative provided there is technological development. This means improvements in the production technology so that the quantity of resources needed to produce a unit of consumer goods diminishes over time. We choose the simplest assumption—albeit one not far from reality—that the quantity of resources needed decreases at a constant rate per annum, $p < 1$. If the quantity needed in year $t = 1$ is q, then the quantity needed in year 2 is qp, and in year t, qp^{t-1}. For all future years, a quantity Q is needed and

$$Q = q \sum_{t=1}^{\infty} p^{t-1} = q/(1-p).$$ (1)

If the known reserves of natural resources are

$$R = Q = q/(1-p),$$ (2)

it follows that the standard of life that can be warranted, q^*, as measured by the amount of natural resources used to produce a unit of consumer goods each period, is

$$q^* = R(1-p).$$ (3)

II. Permissible Consumption and "Optimum Moment"

The quantity q^* depends on the technology, characterized by p, and the resource reserves R. If actual consumption c rises at an observed rate of growth, we can calculate the time x it takes to make c equal to q^*. If $c < q^*$, x will be positive and the point where $c = q^*$ will be reached in the future. There are good reasons to call that point an *optimum moment*. It is the point of the highest value of c that warrants future generations our standard of life. These characteristics suggest a scenario starting with "underconsumption," reaching the optimum moment, and then entering a phase of overconsumption. The optimal policy is to attain the optimal point and to stay there. The optimal point is not constant: it changes with— mostly rising—reserves R and possible changes in technology p.

III. Some Interesting Computations

In this essay, two components (coal and natural gas) of the natural resource energy will be studied with the aid of data published by British Petroleum in its *Statistical Review of World Energy* and by the

World Bank. The same set of computations was made for coal and natural gas. First, efficiency changes per annum in producing consumer goods were estimated by dividing the annual rate of increase of consumer goods production (proxied by the annual rate of increase of gross national product (GNP)) by the annual rate of growth in the consumption of the energy type considered. This yields $1/p$. From it, $q^* = R(1 - p)$ is obtained. The time x needed to make $c = q^*$ is calculated with the aid of the annual growth of consumption $\dot{c}$. The relation used is

$$c(1 + \dot{c})^x = q^*,\tag{4}$$

which is solved for $x = \mathrm{Ln}(q^*/c)/\mathrm{Ln}(1 + \dot{c})$. (5)

For each type of energy, six alternative computations were made. Two alternative figures are used for the rate of growth in GNP, using data for the periods 1965–80 and 1980–87 obtained from the World Bank's *World Development Report, 1989*.[2] In addition, three alternative values for the rate of growth of energy consumption were used: the (geometrical) average of the period 1979–89 and those for the subperiods 1979–84 and 1984–89. These figures, as well as the reserves R at the end of 1989, are published in British Petroleum's *Statistical Review of World Energy*. In Sections IV and V, coal and natural gas will be considered.

Given the simplicity of the model and since all figures used may have random components, some of the results obtained seem very unlikely, particularly in cases where technological development appears to be absent. Of the two types of energy, coal seemed the least susceptible to this problem and provides therefore the clearest example of the scenario mentioned at the end of Section I. Natural gas was more susceptible to the impact of random forces. For these reasons, the discussion starts with the results for coal, followed by those for natural gas. The data used are shown in Annex I.

IV. Coal

Consumption in 1989, permissible consumption, and time needed to attain permissible consumption are shown in Table 1.

---

[2] World Bank, *World Development Report, 1989* (New York: Oxford University Press, 1989).

Table 1. Coal: Consumption in 1989, Permissible Consumption,
and the Time Needed to Attain It
(In years)

	Alternative Computations					
	I	II	III	IV	V	VI
Permissible						
consumption	11,251	4,683	16,810	4,972	25,610	13,275
Time needed	79	36	82	27	151	110
Memo item:						
Actual 1989						
consumption, 2,231						

The main feature of these results is that in each alternative compu-
tation, the permissible consumption is larger than consumption in
1989, and accordingly a positive time period is needed to attain the
"optimum moment." In terms of development policy, this means
that a policy of expansion of world production of consumer goods
may go on for at least 27 years, that is, during the next few decades,
without the threat of a coal shortage.

V. Natural Gas

For natural gas, the results are shown in Table 2. Here we find a
different situation. In two out of the six alternative scenarios, a
situation without technological development is found (i.e., $p \geq 1$),
where the possibility of warranting to future generations our stan-

Table 2. Natural Gas: Consumption in 1989, Permissible Consumption,
and the Time Needed to Attain It
(In years)

	Alternative Computations					
	I	II	III	IV	V	VI
Permissible						
consumption	1,079	· · ·	1,925	762	225	· · ·
Time needed	−26	· · ·	+6	−38	−53	· · ·
Memo item:						
Actual 1989						
consumption, 1,707						

dard of life does not exist. Of the four remaining alternatives, permissible consumption is lower than actual consumption in three cases and, accordingly, the optimal moment has been passed. In one case, short time is available before actual consumption reaches permissible consumption; otherwise, a shortage of natural gas may well develop, or the interests of future generations will be damaged.

VI. Conclusion

Summarizing our findings, the calculations from this simple model suggest that a further expansion of world production of consumer goods is not assured without damaging the interests of future generations. Coal would be available in sufficient quantities, but here the environmental consequences—too high an expulsion of carbon dioxide—may constitute a limit. This remains a topic of future research.

ANNEX I

Basic Data Used

Table 3. Consumption and Reserves

	Consumption (10^6 tons oil equivalent)			Reserves, End of 1989	
	1979	1984	1989	(10^6 tons oil equivalent)	(Other units)
Coal	1,819.5	1,973.6	2,231.3	722,267	1,083,403 million tons
Natural gas	1,271.0	1,412.2	1,707.4	101,700	113.0 10^{12} m^3

15

Current Issues in Transition Economics

John Williamson

Jacques Polak has been involved in most (or all?) of the debates on questions of international economic policy that have erupted over the past half century, so it seems fitting that a conference convened to honor his accomplishments should direct its attention to the issue of the moment. This is, without question, what has been termed "transition economics": the task of converting the former centrally plannned economies into market economies.

This debate was initiated little over a year ago, following the liberation of Eastern Europe and the belated recognition it brought in its train that the Soviet leadership was sincere (if not necessarily serious) in its professed intention of converting the Soviet Union into a market economy. It took little time or controversy to delineate the series of reforms that would be needed to accomplish this transformation. It is taking a lot more effort to flesh out the substance of the needed reforms. But by far the most lively debate has centered on the question of the relationship among the various reforms; in particular, on their *sequencing*.

I write as one of the many economists who have never claimed any expertise on either Eastern Europe or the economics of socialism, but who have nonetheless had the good fortune to become engaged in the debate. My involvement has largely been with external questions like convertibility and exchange rate policy, but in

I am grateful to Stanley Fischer and Reuven Brenner for comments on a previous draft.

this paper I venture beyond my comparative advantage to cover broader issues of sequencing on which I have until now been a passive spectator. Given this lack of expertise, the conclusions suggested should be treated as tentative.

I. The Scope of Reform

A typical list of the various reforms that are needed to transform a planned economy to a market economy would be something like the following:

1. Establish property rights (legalize private property, enact contract and bankruptcy laws).
2. De-etatize: abolish state orders and the planning mechanism, and make enterprises autonomous units.
3. Decontrol prices, which should be market-determined.
4. Harden budget constraints (abolish subsidies, eliminate automatic access to bank credit to cover losses, and prevent easy resort to inter-enterprise credit).
5. Establish commodity convertibility (i.e., give enterprises the right to spend their money balances).
6. Legalize firing of workers.
7. Break up monopolistic state enterprises.
8. Introduce antitrust legislation.
9. Regulate natural monopolies.
10. Privatize.
11. Establish a competitive commercial banking system (which may involve recapitalizing the banks).
12. Create a social safety net.
13. Charge the central bank with the duty of controlling inflation.
14. Eliminate any monetary overhang (through monetary reform, asset sales, and/or inflation).
15. Establish market-clearing interest rates.
16. Reform the tax system.
17. Secure fiscal discipline.
18. Permit inward foreign direct investment.
19. Establish convertibility for current account transactions at a single, competitive exchange rate.
20. Liberalize trade, by first tariffying quantitative restrictions and subsequently reducing tariffs.

Once these 20 reforms have been implemented, the market economy will be in place. The first 11 of the reforms create the institutions of a market economy; the twelfth aims to provide conditions under which workers could reasonably be expected to accept the elimination of their traditional forms of security; the next 5 aim to establish the macroeconomic conditions under which a market economy has a chance to function effectively; and the last 3 provide for integrating the country into the world economy.

II. Gradualism versus a Big Bang

The list of necessary reforms is far longer than that which has been involved in the discussions of sequencing to be found in the previous literature. Reforms (15) through (20) are standard, but no reforming developing economy has needed to create anything like the full range of the institutions of a market economy. Even where the topics overlap, as with privatization, the scale is vastly different; privatization in Latin America referred to at most a few hundred state enterprises producing perhaps 20 percent of gross national product (GNP), whereas in the socialist economies it involves several thousand enterprises producing 90 percent or more of GNP.

Even though the problem of reform was so much less all-embracing in, say, the Southern Cone of South America in the late 1970s, it is generally agreed that it was badly mishandled. One of the criticisms that is now widely accepted is that too much was done too quickly: in particular, the capital account of the balance of payments was liberalized prematurely, before what are now regarded as necessary preconditions (a liberalized domestic financial system, a well-established nontraditional export sector) had been put in place.[1] Some draw a general moral from this experience about the dangers of trying to rush reform. And it is not difficult to think of other countries that tried to implement reforms before preconditions were in place, with the result that the reforms were aborted: the British declaration of sterling convertibility in 1947 is a classic case in point.

The idea of a carefully sequenced program of gradual reforms that "would minimize economic disturbance" (International Monetary Fund and others (1990, p. 2)) is attractive. The problem is, as the

---

[1]See, for example, Corbo and de Melo (1985), Edwards (1984), and McKinnon (1991).

authors of the joint report go on to acknowledge, that "we know of no such path." The closest to common ground is that macroeconomic stabilization needs to come at the start of the reform program[2] (assuming that stabilization is needed, which is true in most but not all cases, the notable exception being Czechoslovakia, at least prior to its decision to destabilize itself by overdevaluing). But views differ sharply on, for example, whether price liberalization should be undertaken simultaneously with stabilization;[3] on the priority to be accorded to liberalization of the commercial banking system;[4] and on the urgency of opening the economy.[5]

But it is not just our inability so far to have derived any robust, widely agreed generalizations about optimal sequencing that motivates support for a "big bang." Both the literature and many conference discussions are full of assertions that x cannot occur until y has been done, most of which appear highly convincing. Everything, it seems, needs doing first. As Lipton and Sachs (1990, p. 99) argue:

> The transition process is a seamless web. Structural reforms cannot work without a working price system; a working price system cannot be put in place without ending excess demand and creating a convertible currency; and a credit squeeze and tight macroeconomic policy cannot be sustained unless prices are realistic, so that there is a rational basis for deciding which firms should be allowed to close. At the same time, for real structural adjustment to take place under the pressures of tight demand, the macroeconomic shock must be accompanied by other measures, including selling off state assets, freeing up the private sector, establishing procedures for bankruptcy, preparing a social safety net, and undertaking tax reform. Clearly, the reform process must be comprehensive.

---

[2] As it happens, I questioned the universal validity of even that conclusion, on the basis of experience in Mexico and Turkey, in commenting on a paper of Vittorio Corbo and Stanley Fischer (Williamson forthcoming).

[3] The Shatalin Program (1990), Genberg (1990), and Kemme (1991) argue for simultaneity; Fischer and Gelb (1990) and McKinnon (1991) argue for making macroeconomic stabilization the priority.

[4] The Shatalin Program (1990) and Brainard (1991) both treat this as a priority, while Fischer and Gelb (1990) and McKinnon (1991) argue that early liberalization carries a threat of exorbitant real interest rates such as to impair the creditworthiness of many borrowers, thus raising the Stiglitz-Weiss (1981) threat of adverse selection.

[5] Richard Portes (1991) reports that Mario Nuti's "fairly conventional sequencing" places this reform near the end of the sequence (followed only by liberalization of the capital account), while he, like the report of the International Monetary Fund and others (1990), urges that it be given a much higher priority.

Experience with gradual reform programs has in general been disappointing. This is most conspicuously true in the Soviet Union, where five years of *perestroika* seem to have transformed a stagnant economy into one that is on the verge of collapse. But gradual reforms also led to problems rather than progress in Poland prior to the big bang at the beginning of 1990. Hungary and Yugoslavia fared somewhat better, but neither of them has as yet emerged as a functioning market economy, and it is not obvious that either is yet notably better off than they would have been had they persevered with traditional central planning—though admittedly as determined a reformer as Kornai (1990) advocates maintenance of the gradualist strategy. Even if they do ultimately complete the transition without a more comprehensive package than any yet implemented, one can reasonably wonder whether more rapid access to the benefits of reform might not have been worth the costs of more disruption during the adjustment process.

The one country that seems to have reaped real and substantial benefits through partial reforms is China. Perhaps it is no coincidence that China still has a massive agrarian component to its economy and that its earliest and most far-reaching reforms concerned agriculture, which is presumably more self-reliant than other sectors. Perhaps it would nonetheless have made good sense for other countries to emulate the Chinese example and liberalize agriculture even before a more comprehensive reform package could be prepared. Be that as it may, one has to admit that China provides an exception.

One explanation for the disappointing performance of gradual (and therefore partial) reform, China aside, seems to be the general theory of the second best. Ever since the theory was developed by Lipsey and Lancaster (1956), there has been an undercurrent of disagreement as to whether second-best theory dealt with pathological cases of no practical relevance, whether it destroyed the scientific basis for all reform proposals (given that in practice it is inconceivable that all but one of the conditions for Pareto optimality will be satisfied simultaneously), or whether it contained important implications for economic policy from which reformers can benefit rather than be paralyzed. The analysis of the failures of partial reform efforts points to the third conclusion. Let me give a couple of examples.

One of my favorite anecdotes (due to the oral presentation of Jeffrey Sachs at the Brookings Panel on Economic Activity in April 1990) is of how Poland had become an exporter of semitropical flowers prior to the big bang. This is an activity for which Poland's climate denies it a comparative advantage; central planners, for all their failings, would be most unlikely to choose to export such flowers. However, once the central planning mechanism is relaxed to the point where an autonomous, profit-maximizing enterprise can decide how best to react to a set of prices that include energy priced at about 6 percent of the world market level, activities with such conspicuous negative value-added become entirely possible.

A much more familiar anecdote is of how hens and pigs were (are) fed subsidized bread. Once again, this is a negative value-added activity that would surely never be ordered by a planner, but that becomes attractive to decentralized entrepreneurs facing heavily distorted prices. Partial reform that decentralizes decision making without reforming prices can and does lead to welfare losses, just as second-best theory explains can happen. I know of no study that attempts to quantify the costs of these second-best losses, but the impression one gets from exposure to the anecdotes is that they must be cumulatively massive.

The danger perceived in the appeal to second-best theory has always been that it makes the best the enemy of the good. If we take seriously the conclusion that only comprehensive reform can guarantee improvement, we may postpone action indefinitely. Václav Klaus (1991) responded that comprehensive reform need not imply waiting until one can do everything at once, but can be accomplished by taking several steps in the proper sequence, but that of course takes us back to the problem that there is still no consensus on what the proper sequence might be. In the next section I advance the hypothesis that there is sufficient validity in the big bang thesis to justify making a biggish bang the central element in an analysis of the optimal sequence.

III. The Minimum Critical Size of Bang

Let us explore the hypothesis that a lot of things have to be done simultaneously in order to overcome the problem of sabotage by the second best. At the same time, limitations of administrative feasibility argue for restricting the number of things that are done simultaneously to the minimum range that is essential in order to overcome the second-best problem. Thus each of the 20 reforms that were listed in Section I will be examined to see whether it is an essential component of the big bang, or whether it can be undertaken before or after what I shall term "M-Day" ("M" for the day on which a market economy starts to function).

Specifically, each of the reforms will be placed in one of the following categories:

1. A precondition for M-Day, that is, something that has to be in place by M-Day (it may be introduced either before or on M-Day).[6]
2. A part of the minimum critical bang; that is, something that must be introduced on M-Day.
3. Post-M-Day reforms; that is, those that can be postponed until a market economy is functioning.
4. Reforms with flexible timing; that is, those that can be introduced before, on, or after M-Day.

Property Rights

A move to a market economy is not possible until the legal institutions of a market economy are in place. Legislation permitting the private ownership of property and establishing contract and bankruptcy laws must be passed before M-Day. Thus we have here a precondition.

De-Etatization

The essence of a market economy is that agents should make economic decisions for themselves, reaping the rewards and suffering the penalties that those decisions may bring, rather than following the edicts of others. Clearly, therefore, enterprises must be autonomous on and after M-Day, and state orders and the planning mechanism must be eliminated. But second-best analysis points clearly to the dangers (illustrated by the anecdotes quoted in Section II) of allowing enterprises autonomy in the absence of the other essential features of a market economy, notably a set of prices that reflect scarcity. Thus de-etatization falls in category (2), an essential element of the M-Day reforms. (In practice de-etatization has not usually been a clearcut once-over change; it has sometimes started before M-Day, leading to the second-best problems noted above, and sometimes been incomplete after M-Day, limiting the gains expected from moving to a market economy.)

---

[6] Semantic purity might suggest that these would more appropriately be called conditions rather than preconditions, but the literature seems to use the latter term.

Price Decontrol

As argued above, enterprise autonomy works in a socially benign way only in the presence of market-determined, scarcity-reflective prices. Price decontrol is thus a central element of the M-Day reform package.

Hard Budget Constraints

Enterprises have no incentive to act responsibly until they face hard budget constraints. But it is impractical to confront them with hard budget constraints and therefore with the possibility of bankruptcy until they are autonomous. Thus the hardening of budget constraints is another essential feature of M-Day.

Commodity Convertibility

Autonomous enterprises must be able to spend their reserves of purchasing power as they see fit. Enterprises without hard budget constraints, in contrast, need to be restrained from spending money balances that happen to have accrued in their name from arbitrary pricing practices, and even more to be restrained from spending money balances that they do not have but that would be supplied automatically if they were to spend more. Thus commodity convertibility should be a part of M-Day.

Firing

Autonomous enterprises must be able to fire workers whose marginal productivity fails to match their cost. There would seem no harm in legalizing firing before M-Day, *once the safety net is in place*; some enterprises might thus be enabled to make an early start on necessary restructuring. Thus the legalization of firing falls in category (1), but has its own precondition regarding establishment of the social safety net.

Breakup of Monopolistic State Enterprises

It is surely desirable that when enterprises start to function autonomously they should already be in a form that is expected to endure indefinitely, and not expect to be reorganized even before they have a chance to adapt to life in a market economy. This suggests that ideally the breakup of monopolistic state enterprises should be accomplished no later than M-Day. On the other hand, industrial restructuring is such a lengthy process that to make this a precondition for M-Day would threaten to delay reform unduly. Thus this reform is most appropriately placed in the flexible category (4).

Antitrust Legislation

The other leg of domestic antimonopoly policy is the introduction of antitrust legislation. This is, perhaps, a reform that is slightly less urgent than the others; M-Day is hardly likely to collapse if some enterprises get away with operating cartels for a few months. It seems appropriate to place it in the flexible category (4).

Regulation of Natural Monopolies

Rather similar comments apply to this subject, except that it hardly makes sense to tackle the issue prior to the general price liberalization that creates the need for regulation. An exception might be made to the general policy of price decontrol on M-Day in order to provide a temporary regime until satisfactory arrangements for regulation can be implanted. Thus this reform can be placed in category (3).

Privatization

Privatization sometimes seems to be equated to establishment of a market economy. This is surely mistaken: enterprises can function autonomously, pursuing socially benign goals at least for a time, without the transfer of ownership claims into private hands. This is demonstrated by British experience with privatization, where the most impressive productivity gains have typically come not *after* privatization but while a public enterprise was in the process of *being prepared* for privatization (Walters (1991)). I presume that this is because both managers and workers knew that they could expect a cut in the proceeds of privatization, which gave them an incentive to raise efficiency before the sale occurred. Some Eastern European countries, notably Poland, are planning to give employees the right to buy a portion of the shares at a concessional price, which gives them a similar incentive. Others, notably Hungary, are making a point of avoiding any such concessions, which seems to me a sad mistake.

Given that privatization is a complex process that needs time to be done properly and that there is no technical need to include it in the package of measures to be launched on M-Day, it falls in category (3). This is not to suggest that the process of privatization should be unnecessarily prolonged. The good incentive effects of expecting to be privatized cannot be expected to carry much weight if the expectation is that privatization may be delayed for several decades, which is all too possible if the case-by-case approach used in the United Kingdom and other market economies is emulated in countries where virtually the whole of industry has been socialized in the past. There is thus much to be said for proposals for giving away a large proportion of the shares to the citizenry, either through a voucher scheme as contemplated in Czechoslovakia or through giving the shares to mutual and pension funds, and then in turn distributing claims on those intermediaries to the public at large, as is under discussion in Poland.[7] Moreover, there may well be a good case for initiating "small privatization"—the sale of retail stores, restaurants, farms, housing, and so on—much sooner, partly in order to help absorb any monetary overhang.

Commercial Banks

Views differ sharply on the priority to be accorded to establishing a system of competing commercial banks. The essential feature of the banking system in this context is its loans to industry and commerce on the asset side of the balance sheet, not the economist's traditional principal concern, namely the money stock that constitutes the liability side of the balance sheet. The point is that banks typically have a network of branches that gives them a capacity to lend to myriad small borrowers, at least once they have learned the art of assessing creditworthiness. In some countries, like Germany, banks are indeed the principal source of loan capital even to large companies, and may also hold equity claims and play an active role in supervising management. Many observers would like to see the

---

[7] However, it is not obvious that every single enterprise is best treated in this way. It appears that some of the labor-management cooperatives have been functioning reasonably satisfactorily in Poland. On the old principle that one should not fix that which is not broken, one might wonder whether it would not be sensible to allow an enterprise to choose to remain a cooperative, subject to the condition that it pay a higher rate of value-added tax so as to compensate the state for use of its inherited capital stock. (The proceeds of asset sales would still need to accrue to the state so as to avoid evasion of this obligation, and the problem of policing asset sales at knockdown prices to insiders would remain.)

banking system quickly start to play a similar role in the economies of Eastern European countries.

Controversy concerns not so much the desirability of this development as its feasibility. Bank officers in socialist countries had no training or experience in assessing creditworthiness. The question is whether this deficiency can be made good rapidly by crash training programs, or whether it can only be expected to evolve gradually over time as bank managers grow into new responsibilities. Pessimists like McKinnon (1991) argue that initially banks will not have much credit to lend because the government will appropriate most of the savings, and that even as this changes they will initially be well advised to restrict their lending to safe and self-liquidating assets ("real bills"). On this view enterprises had better reckon on being essentially self-financing through retained earnings for a prolonged period. Clearly, this implies that a competitive banking system able to transfer savings to enterprises with promising investment projects is not going to evolve until well after M-Day, so I tentatively assign this reform to category (3).

Social Safety Net

Economic security under socialism was provided primarily by the guaranteed availability of a job. That security will vanish once enterprises are allowed, and indeed expected, to fire those who contribute less to the value of output than to the cost of production. It will need to be replaced by the sort of unemployment insurance provided in a typical market economy, at the latest by M-Day. Hence this reform falls in category (1).

Central Bank

Virtually all Eastern European countries have already formally reorganized their banking systems so as to split off the commercial banking part of the system from a central bank. However, the substantive economic step is not so much this administrative reorganization as the redefinition of the responsibilities of the central bank. Until a market economy is born and prices start to reflect scarcity, the central bank still has to play the role it was assigned under central planning, of ensuring that enterprises are not prevented from fulfilling their planned assignments by a shortage of cash. Once M-Day comes, however, budget constraints must be hardened, and accordingly the central bank must change its responsibilities fundamentally, taking up its new responsibility of seeking price stability. While the administrative reorganization will need to precede M-Day, the critical change in how the central bank behaves is a part of the minimum reform package, category (2).

Monetary Overhang

Price decontrol in the presence of a monetary overhang will lead to inflation: indeed, that provides one of the mechanisms by which a monetary overhang can be absorbed. As in other contexts, however, I would argue that inflation is a suboptimal technique. It enables those with accumulated money balances to outcompete those who have to rely on regular income until such time as the overhang has been absorbed, which is undesirable if the legitimacy of the balances is in doubt. But it extinguishes a large part of the real value of the money balances themselves, which is unjust if the balances were on the whole legitimately acquired, and also jeopardizes the prospects of successful small privatization since the potential entrepreneurs tend to be those who have already built up some money balances. In either event the outcome is ethically objectionable, as well as being inefficient.

A more appropriate strategy is surely to decide explicitly whether to expropriate the holders, taking account both of the legitimacy by which the balances were acquired and the role that the holdings can play in jump-starting the private sector. If expropriation is chosen, there should be a monetary reform. If not, the monetary assets should be swapped for real assets owned by the state. A mixed approach, in which holdings of balances in excess of some norm were swapped for (say) an additional allocation of the mutual funds being created to privatize large enterprises, would also be feasible. Allowing the holders of balances to compete with income earners, thus forcing the latter into initiating a wage-price spiral that is likely to be hugely expensive to eradicate subsequently, is a very short-sighted way of dealing with a monetary overhang.

If the above argument is accepted, elimination of the household component of the overhang should be accomplished before or at the time of the move to the market economy. It falls in category (1).

In contrast, the enterprise component of the overhang might more appropriately be dealt with by a monetary reform at the time of liberalization. Every enterprise would receive an initial endowment of liquidity, while past assets and liabilities, including inter-enterprise credits, would be consolidated and doubtless written down in value, perhaps to zero. A monetary reform is best done on M-Day.

Interest Rates

The ultimate objective of reform is a market-clearing interest rate. However, experience in Latin America has demonstrated the dangers of freeing interest rates where confidence is lacking and uncertainty is excessive. Interest rates rise to incorporate a large risk premium, the Stiglitz-Weiss problem of adverse selection enters, and debts start to escalate out of control.

To pre-empt this vicious circle, monetary policy should in the first instance establish a positive but nonprohibitive real interest rate. This will suffice to give enterprises a rate of return on financial assets that deprives the hoarding of inventories of its past attractions, and to give savers a return that limits the motivation to place their funds abroad. A "realistic" interest rate, as one may term a rate with those properties, should certainly be in place on M-Day. That first stage of reform belongs in category (1).

The liberalization of interest rates to respond to market forces and take over the primary responsibility for rationing credit comes at a later stage, when reconstruction is clearly in train, confidence has in consequence revived, and a competitive commercial banking system is emerging. This second stage of reform falls in category (3).

Tax Reform

A large part of the government's revenue in a centrally planned economy arose from the surpluses of enterprises whose output prices were set arbitrarily above their costs. These surpluses were deposited with the state bank and were in effect treated as revenue by the central government, without any need to promulgate a formal tax system. To provide motivation to enterprises, they have increasingly been allowed to retain some part of their surpluses in special funds. The government's fiscal position has in consequence eroded.

Fiscal discipline will never be restored without tax reform that substitutes alternative and explicit taxes for the implicit taxes of the past, which are incompatible with a market economy. The needed taxes are the same as those found in the typical market economy: a value-added tax with broad coverage but moderate rates, excise taxes at much higher rates on sin goods and luxuries (and, in the future, probably on goods with a harmful environmental impact as well), a comprehensive personal income tax that exempts the poor and avoids penal marginal rates, and perhaps—though this is a complex tax to administer, and in any event McKinnon (1991) argues it should wait till the need for self-financing of investment is over—a corporate profits tax. Since tax reform is a precondition for the re-establishment of fiscal discipline, it is appropriately placed in category (1).

Fiscal Discipline

It was noted in Section II that the closest to a consensus that has yet emerged in the literature on the sequencing of economic reform is that stabilization—meaning above all fiscal discipline—should come at the start of a reform program. Although I confessed in footnote 2 that I had questioned the conclusion that no progress could ever be made on liberalization without stabilization being achieved first, I would not recommend a country to decontrol prices until it had got, or was taking measures to get, demand under control. At times it may be expedient for a country to combine fiscal stabilization with liberalization because of an unwillingness of the populace to accept price increases except in the context of a program sufficiently comprehensive to bring some prospect of benefits as well as costs, and indeed there is often a natural link inasmuch as price decontrol may be needed to eliminate subsidies that are a drain on the budget. But the restoration of fiscal discipline is not an essential element in the minimum critical bang: at times it may be perfectly feasible to stabilize before liberalizing, or there will be no need to stabilize if macroeconomic discipline has been maintained. Thus this reform belongs in category (1).

Foreign Direct Investment

Laws permitting foreign investment on the same basis as domestic investment are unlikely to have a great impact until after M-Day, since the prospect of operating in an economy where access to supplies is regulated by the planners is unappealing to most businessmen, but there seems no obvious reason to delay the necessary legislation until after M-Day. On the other hand, foreign direct investment has always been, and is likely always to be, a marginal addition to investment rather than something that is essential to getting reform off the ground. Hence this reform falls in the flexible timing category (4).

Current Account Convertibility

Convertibility for current account transactions (the concept of convertibility embodied in the IMF's Article VIII) is an essential element in the transition to a market economy, as Polak (1991) argues in a paper prepared for a conference that I organized. The reason is that current account convertibility and an absence of trade restrictions are necessary if a country's goods markets are to be integrated into the world economy, so as to give it the demonstrated advantages of outward orientation and the stimulus of competition from the rest of the world.

Both Poland and Czechoslovakia have already demonstrated that they attach a far higher priority to the establishment of convertibility than was given by the countries of Western Europe during their period of postwar reconstruction. There are good reasons for this. The countries of Western Europe had suffered great physical destruction and were in consequence experiencing acute shortages, but one thing they all had was a functioning market economy that provided a set of prices that more or less reflected scarcity and that subjected domestic producers to competitive pressures. The countries of Eastern Europe, in contrast, lack both a rational structure of relative prices and domestic competition (due to the planners' search for economies of scale, which typically led them to concentrate production in a single plant in each country, or even a single plant for the whole Council for Mutual Economic Assistance area). The only quick way of remedying these deficiencies is to import them, which requires reasonably free trade and current account convertibility.

It would not be sensible to establish convertibility prior to M-Day. Current account convertibility means decentralizing the decision as to whether imports should be allowed. To pass that decision to enterprises before commodity convertibility was established and budget constraints had been hardened would simply result in all the demands that planners did not approve getting funneled into the foreign sector and adding to the demand for imports, with predictable results for the balance of payments.

However, there is also a strong argument for not delaying convertibility until after M-Day. Price decontrol is a central feature of the move to a market economy. Yet market-determined prices can be expected to work satisfactorily only if enterprises are subject to the sanction of losing customers and thus jeopardizing their continued viability if they set prices too high. The introduction of competitive pressures is essential if that sanction is to be a real one. The only place from which they can realistically be expected to come in the short run is from abroad, however vigorously monopolistic enterprises are broken up. Hence I conclude that establishment of convertibility falls in category (2), something that should be an integral part of M-Day.

Convertibility will be jeopardized by a payments deficit unless aggregate demand is under control and the exchange rate is competitive. Previous sections have dealt with the control of aggregate demand, via absorption of the monetary overhang, fiscal discipline, and positive real interest rates. A competitive exchange rate is something that could be achieved prior to M-Day, and is certainly necessary by then. It thus falls in category (1).[8]

Unification of the exchange rate, in the sense of eliminating multiple exchange coefficients, is also necessary by the time of M-Day, inasmuch as the latter is intended to import a rational price system. However, a dual rate is an alternative way of providing transitional protection of the general character urged by McKinnon, and so unification of the exchange rate is perhaps best placed in the flexible timing category (4).

Trade Liberalization

As noted above, integration of a country's goods markets into the world economy requires not just that the currency be convertible but also that trade be relatively free. It seems to be widely agreed that trade liberalization should be broken down into two stages. In the first, quantitative restrictions would be replaced by tariffs. In the second, the tariffs would be reduced gradually to the sort of low rates that are now typical on trade among industrial countries.

The first stage should logically be implemented at the same time as convertibility is established, as an integral part of the move to a market economy. Without the first stage, foreign prices could not be

---

[8]I have throughout discussed convertibility on current account only. Capital account convertibility (abolition of exchange controls) is generally agreed to be a much lower priority: this is the only robust conclusion of the literature on the optimal sequencing of financial reforms in developing countries. To allow capital account convertibility in Eastern Europe in the next few years, with the great uncertainties and difficulties those countries are confronting, would be to invite capital flight at a time when they need capital at home to reconstruct their economies. No one should imagine that exchange controls will be able to prevent entirely the export of capital by households, but there is all the difference in the world between a parallel market that allows the retail export of capital at a premium and an official market that allows the wholesale export of institutional savings with no penalty. The time for relaxing capital controls is when reconstruction is complete, in perhaps ten or twenty years if all goes well in the interim.

imported to provide a relative price structure and the discipline of foreign competition would be absent. Of course, the existence of tariffs will mean that the price structure that is imported will not be the world price structure, but that structure as modified by the tariff schedule. But if the transitional tariffs are chosen rationally, so as to allow domestic producers that previously benefited from (in particular) cheap energy and materials a breathing space in which they can adapt their productive processes to the new (world) relative input prices, and to permit enterprises with positive but low value-added at the new prices to continue producing something until newly profitable export activities can expand and absorb their labor, it is this modified price structure that will transmit the appropriate incentives to enterprises.

Views differ quite sharply, however, on the modalities of transitional tariff protection: on desirable initial tariff levels, on the speed with which tariffs should be reduced, and on whether the timetable for tariff reduction should be immutable. McKinnon (1991) argues for very substantial transitional tariff protection coupled with an immediate move to world market prices for inputs. The official report on liberalization of the Soviet economy (International Monetary Fund and others (1990)) suggested maximum tariff rates of 30 percent with a minimal degree of dispersion, supplemented by a temporary 50 percent border tax on energy exports. At the other extreme, Jeffrey Sachs (1991) has argued that nothing short of immediate free trade will confront Eastern European producers with the right price incentives.

Similarly, one finds proposals for a fixed three-year period for phasing out transitional tariffs, whereas others would prefer to see a five-year target with some flexibility to modify the rate of tariff reduction according to macroeconomic circumstances (motivated by the experience of postwar reconstruction in Western Europe, where trade liberalization was suspended or even reversed when payments problems arose). Unless one subscribes to the view that nothing except immediate free trade will do, however, there is no difficulty in placing tariff reduction in the reform sequence: it clearly belongs in category (3), something that must be done after M-Day.

IV. Summary and Comparisons

It is time to summarize the argument developed above. What I have sought to provide is a way of drawing together the principal lines of thought regarding the key issue of sequencing the transition to a market economy. It seems to me that most, though not all, participants in the debate have been moving toward the conclusion that a market economy may never emerge from a gradual decentralization of economic authority, because piecemeal changes raise second-best problems that worsen economic welfare and in that way undermine support for reform. This points to a need for a decisive break with the old regime, a day when a number of complementary changes are introduced simultaneously.

This day has been labeled M-Day, the day when a market economy comes into being. It was January 1, 1990 in Poland, the country that invented the idea of making a sudden break with the past. It was July 1, 1990 in the former German Democratic Republic, and January 1, 1991 in Czechoslovakia. Hungary, in contrast, has not had an M-Day; it continues to pursue a gradualist strategy.

Why call this event "M-Day" rather than a "big bang"? The reason is that the number of things that have to be done simultaneously—the minimum critical size of bang—is much more modest than the number of things that were in fact done at the same time in Poland. Consider Table 1, which summarizes the position of each of the 20 reforms whose sequencing was discussed in the previous section. (Note that 3 of the reforms are split in two, and 1 into three, so that the table actually has 25 entries.) Eight reforms are listed as essential features of M-Day: de-etatization, price decontrol, the hardening of budget constraints, assumption by the central bank of responsibility for controlling inflation, a monetary reform and debt consolidation for enterprises, current account convertibility, and the tariffication of quantitative restrictions on trade. A further 8 reforms are listed as conditions that should have been satisfied by M-Day. In the Polish case, most of those, including notably the stabilization measures, were introduced simultaneously with the move to a market economy. In Czechoslovakia, by contrast, the reforms introduced on M-Day were pretty much the minimum critical list. And in east Germany, virtually all reforms other than privatization were introduced simultaneously, in a number of cases by simply adopting the institutions of the Federal Republic of Germany.

But the purpose of this paper is less that of suggesting definitive answers to the substantive issues of sequencing than to suggest a way of thinking about the problem. One starts off by asking whether it is indeed true that second-best considerations suggest a case for making a number of simultaneous complementary moves to put in place a market economy. One then asks what is the minimum

Table 1. Classification of 20 Reforms

Preconditions

(1)	Property rights
(6)	Legalization of firing
(12)	Social safety net
(P14)	Elimination of monetary overhang of households
(P15)	Positive real interest rates
(16)	Tax reform
(17)	Fiscal discipline
(P19)	Competitive exchange rate

Minimum critical bang

(2)	De-etatization
(3)	Price decontrol
(4)	Hard budget constraints
(5)	Commodity convertibility
(13)	Central bank responsibility for inflation
(P14)	Elimination of monetary overhang of enterprises (and consolidation of debts)
(P19)	Current account convertibility
(P20)	Tariffication of quantitative trade restrictions

Post M-Day

(8)	Antitrust policy
(10)	Privatization (some, especially small privatizations, could come earlier)
(11)*	Competitive commercial banking system
(P15)	Market-clearing interest rates
(P20)	Tariff reduction

Flexible timing

(7)	Breakup of monopolistic state enterprises
(9)	Regulation of natural monopolies
(18)	Liberalization of foreign direct investment
(P19)	Unification of exchange rate

Note: P signifies a part of the relevant reform; and * signifies doubts as to appropriate classification.
Source: See Section III.

critical size of the package of moves needed to lay the ghost of sabotage by the second-best. The next step is to classify reforms into either an element of the critical package, a condition for the package, or something that can be postponed till after M-Day. Perhaps this approach will help recognition that, while there are merits in making a decisive break with the past, there is also a danger that a reform program could be threatened by making unrealistic demands of the administrative machinery. I would hope that this is the sort of sensible, undramatic cause of which Jacques Polak will approve.

REFERENCES

Brainard, Lawrence J., "Reform in Eastern Europe: Creating a Capital Market" (Amex Bank Prize Essay, 1990), in *Finance and the International Economy: 4*, ed. by Richard O'Brien and Sarah Hewin (Oxford: Oxford University Press, 1991).

Corbo, Vittorio, and Jaime de Melo, eds., *Liberalization with Stabilization in the Southern Cone of Latin America*, a special issue of *World Development* (Oxford), Vol. 13 (August 1985).

Edwards, Sebastian, *The Order of Liberalization of the External Sector*, Princeton Essays in International Finance No. 156 (Princeton, New Jersey: Princeton University Press, 1984).

Fischer, Stanley, and Alan Gelb, *Issues in Socialist Economy Reform*, World Bank Working Paper No. 565 (Washington: World Bank, 1990).

Genberg, Hans, "On the Sequencing of Reforms in Eastern Europe" (unpublished, 1990).

International Monetary Fund, World Bank, Organization for Economic Cooperation and Development, and European Bank for Reconstruction and Development, *The Economy of the U.S.S.R.* (Washington, 1990).

Kemme, David M., *Economic Transition in Eastern Europe and the Soviet Union: Issues and Strategies* (New York: Institute for East-West Security Studies, 1991).

Klaus, Václav, "A Perspective on Economic Transition in Czechoslovakia and Eastern Europe," *Proceedings of the World Bank Annual Conference on Development Economics, 1990* (Washington: World Bank, 1991).

Kornai, Janos, *The Road to a Free Economy, Shifting from a Socialist System: The Example of Hungary* (New York: Norton, 1990).

Lipsey, R.G., and Kelvin Lancaster, "The General Theory of Second Best," *Review of Economic Studies* (Oxford), Vol. 24, No. 1 (1956), pp. 11–32.

Lipton, David, and Jeffrey Sachs, "Creating a Market Economy in Eastern Europe: The Case of Poland," *Brookings Papers on Economic Activity: 1* (1990), Brookings Institution (Washington), pp. 75–147.

McKinnon, Ronald I., *The Order of Economic Liberalization: Financial Control in the Transition to a Market Economy* (Baltimore: Johns Hopkins University Press, 1991).

Polak, Jacques J., "Convertibility: An Indispensable Element in the Transition Process in Eastern Europe," in *Currency Convertibility in Eastern Europe*, ed. by John Williamson (Washington: Institute for International Economics, 1991).

Portes, Richard, *The Transition to Convertibility for Eastern Europe and the U.S.S.R.*, Discussion Paper No. 500 (London: Centre for Economic Policy Research, January 1991).

S.S. Shatalin, *Transition to the Market*, translated by the Cultural Initiative Foundation, Moscow (Moscow: Arkhanagel'skoe, 1990).

Sachs, Jeffrey, "Sachs on Poland," *The Economist* (London), January 19, 1991, p. 61.

Stiglitz, Joseph E., and Andrew Weiss, "Credit Rationing in Markets with Imperfect Information," *American Economic Review* (Nashville, Tennessee), Vol. 71 (June 1981), pp. 393–410.

Walters, Alan, "Misapprehensions on Privatization," *International Economic Insights*, Institute for International Economics (Washington), Vol. 2 (January/February 1991), pp. 28–30.

Williamson, John, "On the Rationale of Adjustment Lending," forthcoming in a World Bank volume on structural adjustment lending.

PART FIVE

External Adjustment and Policy Assignment

16

The Design of Macroeconomic Policy in the World Economy
Proposals for Reform

Victor Argy

I. Introduction and Background

Dissatisfaction with the macroeconomic performance of the world economy, particularly from the early 1970s, has been the catalyst for a great variety of proposals in recent years for the redesign of macroeconomic policy in the world economy. This paper reviews some of these proposals, focusing particularly on their application to the Group of Three countries (the United States, Japan, and Germany).[1]

Summary Performance of the Global Economy

Table 1 summarizes the global performance of the world economy for the period 1967–89 based on six measures: inflation, unemployment, external balances, real interest rates, the real wage gap, and exchange rate volatility. The table is self-explanatory, revealing a

---

This paper draws on the DE ROOS lecture delivered by the author at the Free University in Amsterdam on September 21, 1990.
[1]Polak had a continuing and enduring interest in international policy reform. Polak's papers that are closest to the themes developed in this paper are (from his bibliography; see Chapter 1, Annex I in this volume) 1950a, 1951a, 1953, 1956, 1962b, 1963, 1965, 1967b, 1970a, 1971a, 1976b, 1979a, 1981a, 1983a, 1984b, and 1990b.

Table 1. Macroeconomic Performance in Industrial Countries, 1967–89

	Percent Change in Consumer Prices[1]	Unemployment Rates in OECD Countries[2]	Averages of Current Account as Percent of GNP/GDP (Unsigned)[2]		Real Interest Rates[3]			Real Wage Gap (OECD Europe)[4]	Exchange Rate Volatility[5]			
			Group of Three Countries	Group of Seven Countries	United States	Japan	Germany		Pound sterling	Deutsche mark	French franc	Japanese yen
1967	2.9	3.0	0.9	0.9	2.3	2.9	5.4	96.2	4.81	0.00	0.00	0.00
1968	3.9	3.0	1.1	1.2	1.5	1.7	4.9	95.8	0.00	0.00	0.00	0.00
1969	4.7	2.9	1.0	1.2	1.3	1.8	4.9	96.5	0.00	2.45	3.61	0.00
1970	5.6	3.1	0.7	0.8	1.5	−0.5	4.9	98.9	0.00	0.00	0.00	0.00
1971	5.2	3.5	1.0	1.0	1.9	1.0	2.8	100.1	0.63	1.01	0.72	1.58
1972	4.6	3.6	1.0	0.8	2.9	1.8	2.4	100.3	1.89	0.63	1.64	0.97
1973	7.6	3.3	0.7	0.8	0.6	−4.3	2.3	100.7	2.03	4.95	3.93	2.98
1974	13.1	3.6	1.3	2.1	−3.4	−13.9	3.4	102.8	1.97	3.20	3.49	2.76
1975	11.1	5.2	0.7	1.1	−1.1	−2.6	2.6	105.9	1.81	2.62	2.82	1.13
1976	8.3	5.3	0.6	1.0	1.8	−0.7	3.5	104.9	2.59	1.02	1.27	0.90
1977	8.5	5.2	1.0	0.9	0.9	−0.9	2.5	104.4	0.99	1.55	0.78	1.68
1978	7.2	5.1	1.3	1.4	0.8	1.9	3.1	103.0	2.31	2.53	2.22	3.62
1979	9.2	5.2	0.5	0.8	−1.9	4.0	3.3	103.0	2.53	1.45	1.39	2.32
1980	11.9	5.9	0.9	1.0	−2.0	1.5	3.1	104.1	2.11	2.79	2.66	3.58
1981	10.1	6.7	0.4	1.2	3.6	3.8	4.1	104.3	3.13	3.83	3.46	2.47
1982	7.5	8.0	0.5	1.1	6.8	5.4	3.7	102.8	1.58	2.78	3.60	3.92

1983	5.1	8.6	1.3	1.1	7.9	5.5	4.6	101.1	2.01	1.89	1.77	2.01
1984	4.8	8.1	2.3	1.0	8.2	4.5	5.4	98.8	2.40	3.08	2.95	1.95
1985	4.2	8.0	3.1	1.3	7.0	4.3	4.7	98.2	4.14	3.60	3.52	3.25
1986	2.4	7.9	4.1	1.7	5.8	4.3	6.1	97.1	1.67	1.86	2.13	3.30
1987	2.9	7.4	3.7	2.1	4.6	4.2	5.5	97.1	2.56	2.80	2.33	3.19
1988	3.4	6.9	3.1	2.2	4.8	3.6	4.8	96.3	3.06	2.60	2.50	2.51
1989	4.5	6.4	2.8	2.5	3.7	2.8	4.3	96.1	2.53	3.19	3.07	2.16

[1] International Monetary Fund, International Financial Statistics—industrial countries.
[2] Organization for Economic Cooperation and Development, Economic Outlook, various issues.
[3] Long rate less rate of inflation, International Monetary Fund, International Financial Statistics.
[4] OECD calculations 1970–73 = 100. Compensation per employee in real terms divided by labor productivity.
[5] Standard deviation of monthly proportionate changes over the year (International Monetary Fund, International Financial Statistics).

record that has been anything but satisfactory (Argy (1988)). Has there been progress in recent years?

On the one hand, by the end of the 1980s inflation had finally been brought down to levels comparable to the mid-1960s (although more recently it has been creeping upward again). By most measures, too, the real wage gap had by the mid-to-late 1980s largely disappeared in most countries. On the other hand, despite the steady improvement in the employment position in the second half of the 1980s, unemployment rates were by 1989 still at levels on average more than twice the 1960s rate.[2] Real interest rates were also still at historically high levels, although down somewhat from the peaks around the mid-1980s. Moreover, our measure of global external imbalance (misalignment) reveals a substantial deterioration since the early 1980s.

Finally, exchange rate volatility is included as a measure of performance to represent the view frequently expressed that this volatility has been excessive, and that such volatility has harmful effects on the economy.[3] There is no obvious trend in volatility discernible, at least since the float; the important point to note, however, is that there has not been a noticeable diminution in volatility.

Reform Proposals

Protagonists of such proposals contend that a rerun of history with different policy packages would have improved on macroeco-

---

[2] Averages are a little misleading here. The United States and Japan are only marginally worse off; the big deterioration is in Europe. The continued high unemployment, notably in Europe, raises questions about the appropriateness of the real wage gap as an explanation of unemployment. The point to note here is that although profit shares (as measured by the real wage gap) have returned to levels in the late 1960s (see Table 1), the profit rate (i.e., the return to capital) has either not recovered to the same degree or has actually deteriorated. For an explanation of these divergent trends, see Organization for Economic Cooperation and Development (1987).

[3] Volatility is obviously excessive relative to a fixed rate regime; it may also be excessive relative to some anticipation originally formed about how flexible rates would perform. However, exchange rate volatility is not "excessive" relative to other "auction" prices (e.g., equities, interest rates) which have in fact been demonstrably more volatile (Frenkel and Goldstein (1988)). As for potential effects on trade, theory is ambiguous about the direction of the effect; econometric evidence is also mixed on the trade effects; moreover, if there are adverse effects on trade why is this bad? Finally, the more relevant question is whatever the costs, these must be traded off against presumed benefits from exchange rate flexibility.

nomic performance and will improve performance in the future. All such reform proposals of course have to be evaluated in terms of the key macroeconomic objectives of policy. What are these?

For the medium term governments seek:

— A low rate of inflation (the "optimal" rate is still a matter of debate).
— Rapid convergence following a disturbance toward a rate of unemployment that reflects frictional-structural (predominantly voluntary) unemployment.
— A satisfactory external balance (although this particular target is being increasingly questioned).
— A right mix between consumption and investment.

Over the short term we also want to minimize fluctuations in prices, employment-output, real interest rates, and nominal-real exchange rates (all around a trend).

The reform packages that we will review are directed at improving the overall performance on these fronts. Obviously, any regime that promotes one of these without adversely affecting another must be counted as an improvement.

II. Reform Proposals

Modest Reforms Directed Primarily at Moderating Exchange Rate Volatility

These reforms address the concern already noted that exchange rate volatility has been excessive. There are two general types of proposals: First, policies to limit capital flows at the short end of the market, aimed primarily (although not always exclusively) at stabilizing exchange rates. Second, more formal coordinated exchange rate management aimed at moderating the fluctuation in key exchange rates.

Restricting Capital Movements

Several prominent economists (notably Tobin (1978) and Dornbusch (1982)) have expressed concern at the ease with which capital currently flows across frontiers and the magnitude of the amounts involved and have proposed that restrictions be placed on capital flows. The principal advantage these proponents see in limiting capital flows is that it will moderate exchange rate volatility.

The proposals have taken a variety of forms: the reintroduction of capital controls, a small tax on foreign transactions, a real interest rate equalization tax. Tobin's proposal to impose a small tax on foreign transactions (including trade transactions) has easily received the most attention.

Suppose a tax of the order (t) on foreign transactions is imposed (on each trip). Then, simplifying the mathematics a little, we have (without capital controls as such)

$$rd = Ee - E/E + rf - 2t/k,$$

where rd and rf are, respectively, the annualized interest rate at home and abroad; $Ee - E/E$ is the expected percent devaluation of the currency; t is the tax rate on the value of the transaction; and k is the time period of the transaction ($k = \frac{1}{12} = 1$ month; $k = 2 = 2$ years, etc.). Of course, if $t = 0$, we have the open interest parity condition. Suppose $Ee - E/E = 0$ and $t = 0.02$, then if $k = \frac{1}{12}$, $rf - rd = 0.48$; and if $k = 2$, $rf - rd = 0.02$. A monthly roundtrip requires that the foreign interest rate exceed the home interest rate by nearly 50 percent; a two-year round trip requires a difference of only 2 percentage points.

This serves to emphasize the important fact that a tax of this form will strongly discourage very short-term capital movements while penalizing only slightly long-term flows. If, in fact, it were true that the former are "destabilizing" while the latter are "productive," the strategy serves to discourage short-term destabilizing capital while "letting off" more productive capital. At the same time, trade will only be marginally affected.

Frankel (1988a) distinguishes two groups of speculators: spot traders who hold destabilizing exchange rate expectations and investor-fundamentalists who hold regressive stabilizing exchange rate expectations. If the former (latter) dominate in the short term, Tobin's tax is likely to stabilize (destabilize) exchange rates. Frankel himself provides some evidence of the possible dominance of the former. Most commentators agree that, in general, the effect on exchange rate volatility is ambiguous.

Argy (1989) attacks the question differently. He asks how, in a macroeconomic model, exchange rate volatility is affected by integration in the face of disturbances of domestic or foreign origin. In general, he concludes that reduced integration would moderate exchange rate movement; but what is important here is that we also need to address how reduced integration would affect output, interest rate, and price volatility; moreover, we might also want to know how it affects policy effectiveness.

The following seem to be the more interesting of the results of the effects of integration.

(1) For almost every disturbance (including a real expenditure disturbance at home, if capital mobility is already relatively high) the movement in the real exchange rate is amplified.
(2) Interest rate volatility is amplified for external shocks but mitigated for shocks originating at home.
(3) Output volatility is almost certainly enhanced by integration for most shocks.
(4) Home price volatility is enhanced by external shocks but it is unclear what home shocks do.

Argy (1991) also analyses the role of speculation in the presence of trade lags and J-curves in the face of a current account disturbance. Restricting speculation in this context is likely to destabilize the exchange rate.

An almost universal reaction to the proposal is that unless it were very widely implemented internationally, the tax could be evaded by shifting the transaction to a tax free zone. Frankel (1988a, p. 185) puts it as follows: "If the United States were to impose a tax on foreign exchange transactions, the business would simply go to London and Tokyo. If the G-10 countries were to impose the tax simultaneously, then the business would go to Singapore." Not everyone, however, accepts this argument (Cooper (1991)).

Another common criticism of the proposal is that it would have adverse efficiency-allocation effects. Frenkel and Goldstein (1988, p. 208), for example, cite a number of potential benefits from free markets: "lower spreads between lending and deposit rates, increased returns to savers, a lower cost of capital to firms, and better hedging instruments against a variety of risks."

A final comment made is that since the stock market is more volatile than the foreign exchange market and to avoid one potential "distortion," a similar tax should also be imposed on stock market transactions (see, e.g., Summers (1987)). A parallel argument could be made about money market transactions at home.

Coordinated Exchange Rate Management—Reforms

A distinction needs to be made between *unilateral* intervention by a single country (e.g., Germany and Japan) to stabilize its currency and *coordinated* intervention (which also involves the United States as an active intervenor in agreement with other Group of Three and

Group of Seven countries). We are concerned here only with the second and in particular whether it has something to offer in addition to the first and the form exchange rate management should take.

The Reagan administration, during its first four years of office, took the strong view that exchange rates should not be interfered with and should be left alone to be determined by market forces. However, by late 1984 and early 1985, with large and continued current account imbalances, protectionist stirrings in Congress, and the continuing very strong U.S. dollar, the U.S. administration did an about-turn and decided there was now a case for a more activist approach.

Recent Experience with Coordinated Intervention. Since 1985, acting on this change of heart by the United States, there have been periodic bursts of coordinated intervention as well as intermittent official announcements signaling the appropriateness or otherwise of market exchange rates. Four particular phases can be readily identified.

The first phase came after the long upward movement in the U.S. dollar starting in mid-1980. In September 1985, the Group of Five Plaza meeting agreed that "some further orderly appreciation of the main non-dollar currencies against the dollar is desirable" and that the Group of Five governments would "stand ready to cooperate more closely to encourage this when to do so would be helpful." (Obstfeld (1988), Funabashi (1988).) It was agreed to sell up to $18 billion to bring the dollar down by some 10–12 percent over a short period of six weeks. (This would have corresponded very roughly to short-term targets of ¥ 215 and DM 2.55 per US$1 at a time when the actual rates were ¥ 240 and DM 2.85 per US$1.)

These short-term objectives were realized but the dollar continued to fall. In the course of 1986 the fall in the dollar had begun to acquire a momentum of its own.

The second phase came in early 1987. The Group of Six ministers and governors, meeting in Louvre in February 1987, now issued a strong statement that currencies were now "within ranges broadly consistent with underlying economic fundamentals" (given the policy commitments undertaken).

It is widely reported that the Group of Six ministers agreed to stabilize the deutsche mark and the yen within ±5 percent ranges of DM 1.825 (DM 1.734–1.916) and ¥ 153.5 (¥ 145.8–161.2). As exchange rates approached those limits intervention would be "expected to intensify." At the 5 percentage limit there would be mandatory "consultation on policy adjustment." None of this was, however, publicly announced (Obstfeld (1988, p. 9)).

The Louvre resolutions were soon put to the test. In the months that followed sentiment continued strongly against the dollar, particularly vis-à-vis the yen. There was now massive coordinated intervention (including a U.S. contribution of the order of $4 billion of foreign currency sales), a large interest rate realignment favoring U.S. investment, and strong official supportive statements, including a Japanese announcement of an easier fiscal stance.

Despite these efforts the dollar continued to fall (Table 2) and indeed by late 1987 had substantially breached the Louvre Accord, particularly so with respect to the yen rate. According to Funabashi

Table 2. Deutsche Mark-U.S. Dollar and Japanese Yen-U.S. Dollar Rates, 1985 – 90

(In averages of month)

	1985	1986	1987	1988	1989	1990
Germany						
January	3.17	2.44	1.86	1.65	1.83	1.69
February	3.29	2.33	1.83	1.70	1.85	1.68
March	3.31	2.26	1.83	1.63	1.87	1.70
April	3.08	2.27	1.81	1.67	1.87	1.69
May	3.11	2.23	1.79	1.69	1.95	1.66
June	3.06	2.24	1.82	1.76	1.98	1.68
July	2.92	2.15	1.85	1.84	1.89	1.64
August	2.79	2.06	1.86	1.89	1.93	1.57
September	2.84	2.04	1.81	1.87	1.95	1.57
October	2.64	2.00	1.80	1.82	1.87	1.52
November	2.59	2.03	1.68	1.75	1.83	⋯
December	2.51	1.99	1.63	1.76	1.74	⋯
Japan						
January	254.2	200.1	154.5	127.6	127.2	145.1
February	260.2	184.6	153.5	129.2	127.8	145.5
March	258.6	178.9	151.5	127.3	130.4	153.1
April	251.7	175.6	143.0	124.9	132.1	158.5
May	251.5	166.8	140.5	124.8	138.4	153.5
June	249.0	168.0	144.5	127.1	143.8	153.8
July	241.8	158.6	150.2	133.1	140.7	149.3
August	237.2	154.0	147.6	133.6	141.1	147.4
September	237.0	154.7	143.0	134.4	145.1	139.0
October	214.7	156.0	143.5	129.0	141.9	129.7
November	203.7	162.6	135.3	123.2	143.5	⋯
December	202.8	162.3	128.6	123.6	143.7	⋯

Source: International Monetary Fund, *International Financial Statistics*.

(1988) the yen-dollar rate was then rebased, the new 5 percent range being now ¥ 139.04–153.3.

The third phase came with the strong upward thrust of the U.S. dollar, beginning at the end of 1988 and lasting to mid-1990. At each meeting of the Group of Seven during this period some statement was made about the need to coordinate on exchange rates, to keep these in line with "fundamentals." Typical of such statements was one in September 1989 asserting that the rise in the dollar to then had been "inconsistent with longer-run economic fundamentals" and that further appreciation or an excessive decline "would adversely affect prospects for the world economy." At several points substantial coordinated sales of U.S. dollars occurred.

The fourth phase is too recent to comment on. In recent months the U.S. dollar has fallen substantially. With the sharp rise in the yen there were also reports that the U.S. and Japanese officials had agreed to now (October 1990) target the rate at ¥ 122–123.

A Tentative Evaluation of the Recent Experience. One way of evaluating the experience is in terms of the presumed immediate objective that the authorities had set for themselves. This was to nudge the exchange rate closer to the target exchange rate than would have been the case otherwise. Put in those terms the question is very difficult to answer. We might break down the question into three parts. First, did they succeed in *moving* the currencies by coordinated intervention? Second, did they move them closer to *their* targets? Third, were their targets *right* to begin with?

What does theory say about the effects of intervention on the currency? Intervention that is sterilized in a world of near-perfect asset substitution, in itself is likely to have only a marginal impact on the currency. However, the act of coordinated intervention (albeit sterilized) may also have an announcement (signaling) effect that could be substantially more significant. Finally, coordinated monetary intervention (i.e., unsterilized) will certainly have an impact on the exchange rate. A view also widely held is that the signaling effect will be more durable and substantial if supported by changes in monetary policy (although one can think of situations, e.g., in the face of J-curves and long trade lags where a signaling effect could be significant without monetary backing). (See on all this Edison (1990).)

So did the authorities have an effect on the currencies? It seems that most of the intervention was in fact sterilized; indeed, it is not easy to find significant instances of monetary intervention, nor indeed of changes in relative monetary policies directed primarily at the exchange rate. This leaves us only with a potentially significant signaling effect. There is plenty of anecdotal evidence that intervention did exercise a signaling effect at least for brief periods (see Bank for International Settlements, *Annual Reports*, Federal Reserve Bank of New York, *Quarterly Reviews*, Dominguez (1990), and Obstfeld (1988)); there is as well some evidence that coordinated intervention had a more significant signaling effect than unilateral intervention (Dominguez (1990)) and that public intervention is much more significant than secret intervention (Dominguez and Frankel (1989)). But, on the other hand, the Bank for International Settlements in its 1990 *Annual Report* has also argued that more recently "the impact of intervention was beginning to wear off and that...more and more of it was required to achieve the same result" (p. 194).

A further point worth making in this context is that on occasion conflicting signals have been given by officials (e.g., in the course of 1986 when the dollar was falling sharply).

Did the signaling effect work in the right direction? At most the Plaza Agreement helped to nudge the U.S. dollar down. In due course, however, the fall acquired a life of its own, possibly overshooting the mark from the authorities' perspective. At Louvre they tried to stabilize the currencies with some (modest) success in the first six months; after that the dollar resumed its fall. The target yen-dollar rate was apparently eventually revised, faced with the continuing appreciation of the yen (an apparent concession to the "wisdom" of the market forces?). When the U.S. dollar finally rose it acquired a new momentum against which coordinated intervention seemed powerless.

This record is hardly a good one. Indeed, there were signs that by mid-1990 the Group of Three had themselves become a little disenchanted with coordinated intervention. It seems that in this fourth phase, with the U.S. dollar again collapsing, there is now little official support for a rescue operation (France appears to be the exception here).

Finally, it is well known that there are huge differences in points of view about the fundamental-equilibrium rate and how it should be calculated, so one could question the reference points used by the authorities. (See Williamson (1990), Frenkel and Goldstein (1986) for methods of calculating equilibrium rates.) Some economists are totally skeptical about arriving at an equilibrium rate (Krugman (1988)); others lean on some version of purchasing power parity; others again prefer a rate that achieves a target current account. To illustrate these difficulties, purchasing power parity calculations suggest an equilibrium yen rate of about ¥ 160 and a deutsche mark rate of DM 2.27. A rate based on a current account target would be more like ¥ 100–110 and DM 1.41 (closer to more recent rates) (Williamson (1990)). In any event, it seems the authorities did change their perceptions of the fundamental rate but primarily in response to market forces.

Reform Proposals. The official view (perhaps now abandoned), implicitly represented above, is that coordinated intervention may be helpful at times in signaling a direction to the exchange rate. There are two other (completely opposing) views about coordinated intervention and exchange rate management.

The first view argues that intervention, as practiced to date, does not go far enough and should be extended and formalized. This view is represented by Bergsten (1990) and Williamson (1989). The reforms they propose are: zones should be wider (10 percent around a central rate) than those adopted (e.g., in Louvre); the central rate should be defined in real, not nominal, terms calculated more scientifically and should be announced; also, there should be a much firmer commitment on all sides to defend the zones by interest rate policies.

Completely on the other side is the second view which argues not only that intervention should not be undertaken but that it may actually be (and indeed has been) positively harmful. This view is represented most forcibly by Feldstein (1989). Feldstein's argument is that monetary policy should be used to attack inflation, not to stabilize exchange rates. As an illustration Feldstein argues that had monetary policy been used in say 1984/85 to stop the upward thrust of the dollar, the budget deficit would effectively have been financed by money creation, which would have been inflationary. He also argues that in the spring of 1987 when the U.S. dollar was very weak and the United States actually raised interest rates to counter this fall, the rise precipitated the stock market collapse, which in turn provoked a reversal of interest rates. Had this reversal not occurred, the sharp rise in rates might have pushed the U.S. economy into recession.

The key Feldstein argument is that there may be benefits from stabilizing real exchange rates around fundamental rates but there may also be costs. This takes us into much broader issues, well beyond the scope of this paper. (On the question of optimal intervention, see Argy (1990).)

Variants of National Monetarism

What is common to national monetarists is the conviction that once stable and proper macroeconomic policies in the leading economies are in place, the world economy would perform satisfactorily. Their emphasis is on the application of simple rules with an eye on achieving medium-run objectives. At the same time, and importantly, once the leading economies agree to adopt monetarist-type policies there are no further demands made on policy coordination.

Under this heading we discuss three proposals: Friedman's monetarist package, extensions to Friedman's monetary rule, and Sargent-Wallace's medium-run monetary-fiscal coordination at home.

Friedman's Monetarist Package

Friedman has relatively simple prescriptions. First, keep money growth on a fairly steady path so as to achieve an inflation rate of about zero. Second, let the exchange rate float without any management or capital controls. Third, balance the budget on an ex ante basis, that is, projected annual receipts should be equal to projected expenditures. Fourth, keep domestic markets (including labor markets) free and reduce the size and the role of government (Friedman (1948, 1959, and 1983)).

The contention is that with rates of inflation low and stable and budgets on average in balance, exchange rates should also be much more stable. Current account imbalances will also reflect only private sector decisions to save and invest and provided these decisions are optimally made the current account will then also be optimal.

Extensions to Friedman's Monetary Rule

A variation on the Friedman monetary rule is to allow monetary policy to respond directly to inflation. An early proposal along these lines was one by Wicksell in 1898 (Wicksell (1936)). In its modern form, the rule requires the monetary authorities to select a particular price index and use money stock or interest rate policy to stabilize that price index. Barro (1986) has proposed a rule of this kind. Such a rule has become very fashionable recently, being widely debated. In New Zealand and Canada, a rule along these lines has actually been adopted.

Meltzer's variation (Meltzer (1988)) on the Friedman theme is to allow base money growth to adjust in line with recent variations in base velocity, as follows:

$$bt = \bar{y}t_{-1} - \bar{v}t_{-1}, \tag{1}$$

where b is the current growth rate of base money, $\bar{y}$ is the moving average of the growth rate of domestic output, and $\bar{v}$ is the moving average of the growth rate in base money velocity.

McCallum (1987 and 1988) extends Meltzer's rule further. The specific rule he proposes, for quarterly adjustment, is

$$bt = 0.00739 - \tfrac{1}{16}\left(vt_{-1} - vt_{-17}\right) + \lambda2\left(x^*t_{-1} - xt_{-1}\right) \tag{2}$$

(all in logs),

where 0.00739 is a 3 percent annual growth rate, the second term represents an adjustment (à la Meltzer) for the growth rate in base money velocity averaged over the previous four years, and the third term represents further adjustment for the gap between actual GNP (x) and its target path (x^*)($\lambda2 > 0$).

Sargent-Wallace's Monetary-Fiscal Analysis

These writers are concerned with the question of maintaining the long-run consistency of monetary and fiscal policy (Sargent and Wallace (1981), Minford and Peel (1983), and Brunner (1986)). If the monetary authorities call the tune (as they should) by setting the growth of base money at its optimal level, then the deficit should be set at a level that will allow the growth of debt to equal the growth of money. Debt cannot grow for long at a rate faster than money.

Notation
   B = stock of home bonds
   Mo = money stock
   D = primary deficit (excluding interest payments)
   r = interest rate
   DEF = public sector deficit
   Y = nominal income
   g = growth rate of nominal income.

In equilibrium, bonds must grow at the same rate as money, which is predetermined at g.[4] In this context, g represents the money growth rate that, over the medium run, will generate a

---

[4]We focus only on the case where the real interest rate exceeds the real growth rate but it is only in this case that problems of consistency arise. If the real growth rate exceeds the real interest rate then it is known that the primary fiscal deficit (excluding interest payments) can be set independently of monetary policy.

satisfactory rate of inflation.

$$\frac{\Delta B}{B_{-1}} = \frac{\Delta Mo}{Mo_{-1}} = g.$$ (1)

In equation (1), dividing both sides by Y_{-1} and adding $\Delta Mo/Y_{-1}$ to both sides and noting that $DEF = \Delta B + \Delta Mo$ we also have

$$\frac{DEF}{Y_{-1}} = \frac{B_{-1} + Mo_{-1}}{Y_{-1}} \cdot g.$$ (2)

Effectively this tells us that given the independent monetary stance, represented by g, and the money-bond ratio, there is only one sustainable public sector deficit, as a percent of GNP, that is compatible with this monetary stance.

We know too that

$$\frac{D}{Y_{-1}} + \frac{rB_{-1}}{Y_{-1}} = \frac{\Delta B + \Delta Mo}{Y_{-1}} = \frac{DEF}{Y_{-1}},$$ (3)

where D is the primary deficit (excluding interest).

Substituting equation (2) into equation (3) gives

$$\frac{D}{Y_{-1}} = -(r-g)\frac{B_{-1}}{Y_{-1}} + \frac{Mo_{-1}}{Y_{-1}} \cdot g.$$ (4)

Drawing on equations (2) and (4) Table 3 illustrates some of these results. For example, if $g = 0.02$ and $(Mo_{-1} + B_{-1})/Y_{-1} = 0.5$, the sustainable budget deficit as a percent of GNP is about 1 percent. If the growth rate were multiplied fourfold and the money-bond ratio

Table 3. Sustainable Public Sector Deficits for Different Values of Parameters

(DEF/Y_{-1}) (D/Y_{-1})	g	Mo_{-1}/Y_{-1}	B_{-1}/Y_{-1}	r
0.01 (0.0025)	0.02	0.25	0.25	0.03
0.02 (0.005)	0.02	0.5	0.5	0.03
0.08 (0.03)	0.08	0.5	0.5	0.10

doubled, the sustainable deficit is 8 percent. In the first case the primary deficit is less than 0.3 percent and in the second it is 3 percent (given $r > n$).

Comments on National Monetarism

(1) On the one hand, without the discipline imposed by a simple money growth rule the authorities might be tempted to abuse the system and overinflate (Barro and Gordon (1983) and Fischer (1988)). On the other hand, there are clearly situations when discretion can be welfare improving. Two good illustrations from the last 15 years come readily to mind. First, after the two oil price shocks a case could be made that some monetary accommodation was appropriate. Second, and more important, during the 1980s, financial deregulation and innovations in many industrial countries distorted the relationship between money aggregates and income; in these instances a more flexible monetary policy is appropriate (see Argy and others (1990)).

Frankel (1989, p. 10) notes for example for the United States that between the second quarter of 1982 and the second quarter of 1986 M1 growth averaged some 10.3 percent, while nominal GNP grew by some 8 percent a year. Had the authorities in those years persisted with a substantially more modest growth of M1 (e.g., 3 percent) nominal GNP would have grown by less than 1 percent a year, almost certainly extending over several more years the 1981–82 recession.

(2) In the light of recent shifts in velocity produced by distortions to, and uncertainties associated with, the money aggregates, the Meltzer-McCallum rules must be judged an improvement over Friedman's rule. They achieve some discretion where it really counts without courting serious risks of inflation.

(3) The author has recently investigated in some detail the policy proposal to target nominal income (Argy (1991)). He finds that theory is fairly supportive of such a proposal, particularly in the face of demand disturbances (but not necessarily so in the face of productivity or supply disturbances). He does, however, argue that theoretical analysis has tended to be biased in favor of such a proposal. Moreover, econometric evaluations of the proposal are not all supportive.

(4) Friedman's fiscal rule appears extreme. It is likely to generate instability in the short run (a projected downturn has to be confronted by, e.g., a rise in the tax rate); finally, it is not clear in the

light of the issues raised by Sargent-Wallace how consistent such a policy is in the long run with a money growth rule.

(5) The Sargent-Wallace monetary-fiscal framework centers attention on the very important longer run links between monetary and fiscal policies but it needs to be put in a broader open economy framework.

More Radical Reforms to Exchange Rate Regime

We turn now to proposals to radically reform the exchange rate regime. The proposal is not simply to tamper a little with the flexible rate regime since 1973, as with proposals to manage exchange rates, but rather to break dramatically with the past and to establish radical new rules. There are essentially two types of proposals here: one is to return eventually to a permanently fixed exchange rate regime. The other is to retreat to a new version of the old Bretton Woods system.

Proposals to Permanently Fix Exchange Rates

In recent years the three leading exponents of a return to a permanently fixed exchange rate regime, at least for the big three, are Mundell (1983), McKinnon (1984 and 1988), and Cooper (1984 and 1991). To be fair, the authors recognize that there may need to be a fairly long transitional period during which the "world" economy would gradually converge toward this ultimate objective.

Mundell (1983) proposes a return to a managed gold standard. Although it is now over fifty years since the collapse of the second gold standard, the idea of restoring the gold standard in some form has never completely died. The most recent support for its reinstatement came from the supply-side economists in the United States, who, for a while at least, had the support of the Reagan administration. The proposals, however, although they received wide publicity, never had much support and were the object of widespread criticism (see Cooper (1982)).

McKinnon's (most recent) proposals are fairly straightforward: permanently fixed exchange rates, symmetrical unsterilized intervention in the key participating countries, and coordinated monetary policy directed at stabilizing the world price of traded goods.[5]

---

[5]McKinnon is somewhat less explicit on the design of fiscal policy. Over the medium term he would assign fiscal policy to the current account.

Cooper would go even further than McKinnon. He would like ultimately to see a common currency established for the industrialized democracies.

A permanently fixed exchange rate regime would require resolution of the following key issues. First, what will be the initial set of equilibrium exchange rates that will be established? Second, who will have responsibility for setting the "world" rate of inflation? A related question is, will the system be symmetrical in so far as adjustment is concerned? Third, will there be restrictions on the reserve currencies available under the system? Fourth, and related to the last point, how will the system provide for the secular growth in world reserves?

On the first question, McKinnon would fix exchange rates on the basis of purchasing power parity based on a comparable basket of traded goods. Some calculations along these lines have been made by McKinnon.

On the second question, both McKinnon and Cooper take the view that it would be a joint decision. Under fixed rates, the rate of inflation, other things being equal, would be determined by the "world" money supply, which in turn is the sum of the domestic assets of the "combined" central banks. Central banks would have responsibility for adjusting their domestic assets to achieve the inflation objectives.

Cooper (1991; see this volume, p. 144) is explicit about the institutional arrangements.

> The institutional aspects of a common currency are not so difficult to imagine: they could be constructed by adaptation of the U.S. Federal Reserve System, which is an amalgam of 12 separate Reserve Banks, each of which issues its own currency. One could imagine an open-market committee for all or any subset of the industrial democracies that would decide the basic thrust of monetary policy for the group as a whole. On it could sit representatives of all member countries, with votes proportional to gross national product. At one extreme the representatives could be ministers of finance; at the other they could be outstanding citizens chosen by their governments for long terms solely for the purpose of managing the monetary system. An obvious interim (and possibly permanent) step would be to appoint the senior governors of existing central banks.

Under both schemes adjustment would be "symmetrical," in the sense that regional money supply would be regulated by its overall balance of payments. However, it is also possible to envisage a scheme that is asymmetrical in the sense that a single large key economy would determine the rate of inflation, sterilizing its own balance of payments flows, while the other countries did not in fact sterilize. This approaches the Bretton Woods case, under which the United States played a similar role; it is also not unlike the role of Germany today in the European Monetary System (EMS). The adjustment mechanism is quite different under a symmetrical and an asymmetrical system (Argy, McKibbin, and Siegloff (1989) and Argy (1991)).

The last two issues were, of course, debated in great detail in the 1960s. It is possible to have a single reserve asset, for example, the U.S. dollar or the SDR, or allow freedom of choice in the reserve asset. How the system provides for the secular growth in reserves depends on how the last issue is resolved. More precise control is possible only if the SDR were the only reserve asset; however, what is gained in terms of monitoring the growth of reserves is lost in terms of restricting the choice.

A New Bretton Woods?

Kenen (1988) has proposed a return to a Bretton-Woods-type system, but with substantially wider bands than existed at the time of the demise of Bretton Woods. In effect he would like to see the Group of Three adopt a variation of the exchange rate arrangements in the EMS.

Krugman (1988) has recently argued that, increasingly, changes in exchange rates do not produce real external adjustment. Exchange rate volatility itself, together with the substantial sunk costs involved in entering a foreign market, have combined to "delink" trade from exchange rate changes. In essence he is saying, "We should avoid a system in which massive exchange-rate changes occur all the time for no very good reason, so that exchange-rate changes will be effective when we need them" (p. 100). Hence, his change of heart, "I am now an advocate of an *eventual* return to a system of more or less fixed rates subject to discretionary adjustment" (p. 99).

This provokes three comments. First, Krugman is factually wrong about the delinking of exchange rates from the real economy because of weakening passthrough (Frenkel and Goldstein (1988)). Second, even if it were true, there are still valuation effects that improve the external balance, whatever the currency in which the external balance is denominated. Third, again even if true it is only one potential consideration in evaluating an exchange rate regime, for example, the stability of the macroeconomy may be at least as important (see Section III and also Taylor (1989)).

Global Activist Assignment Rules

We consider under this heading proposals concerned with assigning specific roles to monetary and fiscal policies in the medium term in the achievement of macroeconomic targets of policy, the emphasis being on readily implementable assignment rules. We summarize Williamson-Miller's (WM) blueprint and the Boughton-Genberg-Swoboda (BGS) proposal.

The Williamson-Miller (WM) Blueprint

Williamson and Miller (1987) have proposed a blueprint for the conduct of global macroeconomic policy. There are three prongs to their proposals. First, exchange rate target zones would be defined for the leading currencies. The center of a target zone would be calculated with an eye on securing long-run current account objectives. A margin of 10 percent would be allowed on each side of the center. Each central bank would defend the upper and lower points by adjusting its interest rate.

Second, national fiscal policies would also be adjusted so as to achieve national target rates of growth of domestic demand. However, if fiscal deficits are already too high or the ratio of public debt to gross domestic product excessive, the rule that fiscal policy should be expansionary when nominal demand growth has stalled would be suspended.

Third, the average level of the world interest rate should be adjusted so as to achieve the target growth of nominal demand for the participating countries.

The Boughton-Genberg-Swoboda (BGS) Framework

We focus here on the spirit of the BGS framework, extended to the large country case (Boughton (1989) and Genberg and Swoboda (1987 and 1989)). Assume a two-country world with flexible rates. Each of the two countries is assumed to target internal and external (current account) balance and the real interest rate (to achieve a desired mix of consumption and investment); at the same time, we have four policy instruments, monetary and fiscal policies in each of the two countries. Since the current account target is common to the two countries we have, in essence, as many instruments as targets.

Monetary policy has unambiguous effects on income (internal balance) in both the short and the medium run. The only difference is in the partition between "real" and price effects (the latter dominating over the medium run, the former over the shorter run). Monetary policy also has unambiguous effects in the shorter run on real interest rates and real exchange rates, but is likely to have no effects on either over the medium run. Monetary policy has weak but ambiguous effects on the current account in the short run and is likely to have no effect over the medium run.

Fiscal policy has ambiguous effects on income in the short to medium run (e.g., a rise in taxes potentially increasing wage claims) but an unambiguous effect on the real interest rate and on the current account.

Given these comparative effects on the targets, they propose that over the medium run the two monetary instruments be assigned to each country's internal balance (nominal income), that one fiscal instrument be assigned to the common external balance, and the other be assigned to the real interest rate target. Thus, whereas no coordination is strictly needed on the monetary front (except an initial agreement to abide by these rules), coordination is obviously necessary on the fiscal front.

Swoboda (1990) provides a simple illustration of how fiscal policy in the two countries might in the medium run be assigned to the current account and real interest rate targets, assuming each monetary policy has taken care of its nominal income targets (and the world economy is at full employment).

Chart 1 reproduces Swoboda's graphical presentation. The CA schedule represents the combinations of government expenditures in A and B that maintain the common external balance. Clearly if G(A) increases, G(B) must also increase to maintain the same current account. The rw schedule represents the combinations of fiscal policy that maintain an "acceptable" common real world interest rate. If G(A) were to rise, pushing up rw, GB must now fall to keep the real interest rate at its desired level.

If A represents the United States today and B say Japan and Germany, then clearly we would have to place the world economy in quadrant 2 where A has a current account deficit (B a surplus) and rw is "too high." If the world economy were at Q, where the CA deficit is relatively small but the real interest rate is very high, both A and B must adopt tight fiscal policies (A's being the tighter) to reach O. If the economy were at P, where the deficit is the overriding problem (but less so the real interest rate), A must

Chart 1.   Fiscal Policy Coordination

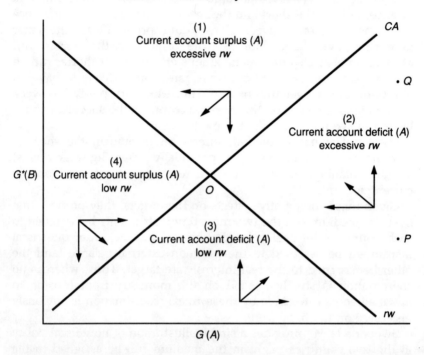

tighten and B must ease its fiscal policy. (A tightening by more than B eases.) Alternatively, A could be assigned the task of securing the real interest target and B the task of correcting current account imbalances. Arrows point in the direction in which each country would proceed.

WM and BGS Compared

There are three principal differences between the WM and the BGS frameworks. First, WM want to target the real exchange rate, BGS do not (although BGS are not committed as such to a flexible rate regime). Second, and most important, the assignment is reversed in BGS. In WM, monetary policy is assigned to the real exchange rate (but ultimately to achieve current account objectives); fiscal policy is assigned to internal (nominal demand) balance, but global monetary policy is assigned to global internal balance (raising questions about too many instruments doing the same job). BGS, as already indicated, basically reverse this assignment, assigning money to the internal balance and fiscal policy to the current account. The extra fiscal instrument goes to the real interest rate. Third, the WM blueprint probably makes greater demands on coordination than the BGS framework.

Comments on the Assignment Rules

(1) Insofar as medium-run analysis is concerned, the BGS framework appears more plausible. (In the short term and for reversible disturbances, however, the WM framework becomes more viable, see Section III.)

(2) Genberg and Swoboda correctly argue that their framework can also be applied to a fixed rate regime. In this case, the combined domestic assets of the central banks could target the common "world" inflation (à la McKinnon), while fiscal policies can be treated as in the flexible rate regime.

(3) The idea of assigning fiscal policy to the current account raises the possibility that this has the effect of shifting the problem onto fiscal policy: domestic bond accumulation may simply replace foreign bond accumulation.

(4) The idea that the current account ought to be a target of policy is being increasingly questioned (Pitchford (1990) and Corden (1991)). For example, suppose a current account deficit reflects a private sector imbalance between savings and investment. If decisions on saving and investment are made "optimally," the case for targeting the current account is weakened. However, we do know that these decisions to save and invest are made on the basis of economic variables that are themselves far from optimal (e.g., real interest rates, taxes, relative unit labor costs in a common currency). So the outcome is not optimal. This is not to say, of course, that we can readily identify such distortions, so in the end this may not bring us any closer to a resolution of the problem.

(5) A variation on this general theme is to target national wealth, the change in which comprises investment and the current account (as proposed by the New Keynesians in the United Kingdom (Weale and others (1989)). Wealth enters more directly into households' utility function. The implications of targeting "wealth" in lieu of the current account are quite different; for example, a surge in private investment matched by a current account deficit does not change wealth and hence does not need correcting.

This still prompts a lot of questions. Suppose there is a drop in private sector savings ending up in a current account deficit and a decumulation of wealth. Why should this receive attention?

(6) If the current account is dropped as a target, what is there left for fiscal policy to do? If we retain the real interest rate as a target (as

a means of partitioning consumption and investment—itself potentially questionable), we free up one fiscal instrument (perhaps to combine with monetary policy to achieve exchange rate targets or perhaps employment?).

Labor Market Reforms

We noted in Section I that unemployment was still a problem. The monetary-fiscal assignments reviewed above do not in themselves address the question of unemployment. In particular, there is an urgent need to counter the tendency for unemployment to persist once a new level is reached.[6]

We need, therefore, policies that directly attack the question of unemployment. Monetary-fiscal policies need to be supplemented with labor market reforms, which would aim at achieving greater real wage flexibility in the presence of unemployment. Such reforms would improve macroeconomic performance, facilitating a more rapid convergence toward full employment once the economy strays from it (i.e., avoiding unemployment persistence).

At the more technical level, wages policy would now appear as additional instruments in the design of policy. Consider again a two-country world and a BGS-type framework. We have two countries, two targets of inflation, one real interest rate and one external target, and two "full employment" targets. In principle, these could all be achieved by assigning the two fiscal policies to real interest rate and external targets and the two monetary policies to inflation targets (as we have already seen), but now the two wages policies are assigned to the two full employment targets (see Annex I). This general framework, with emphasis on labor market reforms (but not necessarily the monetary fiscal assignments), is precisely the one highlighted by the New Keynesian economists (see Meade (1982) and Weale and others (1989)).

Unfortunately, while there would be almost universal agreement among economists that greater medium-run real wage flexibility would ameliorate macroeconomic performance, there would be considerable disagreement on how to do this; indeed, many would be skeptical as to the likelihood of success on this front.

---

[6]The phenomenon of unemployment persistence has inspired a rash of new theories, collectively known as hysteresis. See Blanchard and Summers (1986), Bean (1989), Layard and Bean (1988), and Lindbeck and Snower (1986, 1988, and 1989).

How then does one proceed? Perhaps a good place to start is to look first at differences in unemployment performance, to relate these differences in performance to differences in real wage flexibility, and then to try and identify differences in labor market institutions that might account for these differences in real wage flexibility. The final step is to see if one can transplant some of the more successful labor market institutions to improve performance. As an extension, one can also explore new ideas and policies that have not been extensively put into practice. Clearly, this is a very tall, if not an impossible, order.

Consider first unemployment performance. On the surface at least the strong performers have been Austria, the Nordic countries, and Switzerland. The United States has also been a strong performer, but particularly so since 1983. In general, the poor performers are mostly from continental Europe and the United Kingdom, Ireland, Australia, and New Zealand. Some of these last, however, notably Germany, the United Kingdom, and Australia have recorded considerable success recently in reducing their unemployment.[7]

Consider now performance in terms of real wage flexibility. There are numerous studies, but fortunately there is a reasonable convergence in results. (For a recent summary of these studies, see Andersen (1989).) These show that Japan and Switzerland are easily the best performers here; Austria, Norway, and Sweden also perform well. The United States is more controversial. Notwithstanding the lack of hard core empirical support, the consensus view now appears to be that the United States has performed well in this regard, particularly so in more recent years (Organization for Economic Cooperation and Development (OECD) (1989)). At the other end of the scale, we have relatively poor performers such as France, Germany, the United Kingdom, Finland, Canada, Belgium, Italy, Denmark, and the Netherlands. (For an econometric study of the macroeconomic implications of increased real wage flexibility, see Barbone and Poret (1989).)

---

[7]Unemployment rates in themselves, however, can be deceptive as indicators of performance. First, they do need adjusting to take account of absorption into public employment and retraining schemes (strikingly so in the case of Sweden), immigrant labor (as in Austria and Switzerland), and definitional concepts (Japan's unemployment rate needs to be adjusted upward). Second, unemployment could be improved, at least for a while, at the expense of higher potential inflation (perhaps the case of Sweden) or a deterioration in external balance.

Unemployment performance is a function not only of real wage flexibility but also, importantly, of the magnitude of shocks to labor markets. Two countries with the same degree of real wage flexibility will perform differently if they are exposed to different degrees of, say, adverse supply shocks. Despite this obvious proviso there appears to be a good relationship between real wage flexibility and unemployment performance (see Grubb and others (1983) and Organization for Economic Cooperation and Development (1989)).

Next, it is not difficult to identify important differences among countries in terms of labor market institutions. The key areas of differences are (1) wage bargaining arrangements; (2) welfare state characteristics and the regulatory framework; and (3) direct government involvement in wage negotiations and in manpower (retraining) schemes. Actual differences in labor market institutions aside, there are as well innovative ideas on this front that have received a good deal of attention, for example, profit sharing schemes and a tax-based incomes policy.

What sorts of measures might serve to improve the degree of real wage flexibility, focusing on these fronts?

Is it possible, in other words, to improve the workings of labor markets by reforms to the wage bargaining arrangements, by dismantling part of the welfare state and the regulatory framework, and by greater direct involvement by the government in wage setting and retraining schemes?

Wage Bargaining Arrangements

The more important elements here are the industrial relations environment, the length of the wage contract, the degree of synchronization of wage negotiations, the degree of indexation (and the rapidity with which wages adjust to the cost of living), the level of bargaining, and the degree of unionization and of trade union power.

All of these considerations have received some attention in the literature. We, however, choose to focus primarily on the last two, which have attracted particular attention in recent years. We also very briefly discuss profit sharing schemes, seen by some as a panacea for labor market problems.

The Level of Bargaining and Degree of Corporatism. Bargaining can be centralized or it can take place at the industry (intermediate) level or at the enterprise (decentralized) level. The term corporatism embraces more than the level of bargaining. An economy is said to be more corporatist the more centralized the bargaining, the greater the degree of government involvement in wage negotiations, and the greater the "consensus" between labor and firms with shared perspectives on the goals of economic activity (Calmfors and Driffill (1988)). Many economists have tried to construct rankings in terms of corporatism and to show that more corporatist economies perform better (Bruno and Sachs (1985), Organization for Economic Cooperation and Development (1988), and Newell and Symons (1987)).

In a careful paper, Calmfors and Driffill (1988, p. 17) rank industrial countries in terms of centralization (defined as "the extent of inter-union and inter-employer cooperation in wage bargaining with the other side") and successfully relate this measure to macroeconomic performance (defined as the rate of unemployment plus the current account in percent of GNP) and to indicators of real wage flexibility.

Centralized economies include the Scandinavian countries plus Austria; intermediate economies include Germany, the Netherlands, Belgium, Australia, and New Zealand; and decentralized economies include France, the United Kingdom, Italy, Switzerland, the United States, Canada, and Japan. They find evidence of a hump-shaped relationship: the best performers are to be found among the centralized and the decentralized economies, while the worst performers are among the intermediate economies. Importantly, they provide a theoretical rationale for such a relationship.

There is a certain vagueness surrounding this literature, making it difficult to come to terms with its central propositions (see Jackman (1989)).

Performance is by no means uniform among a particular group (e.g., Denmark and Finland are as centralized as Norway and Sweden but their unemployment has been relatively high): among the decentralized are France, the United Kingdom, and Italy, whose performance as a group is inferior to Germany's, which is intermediate. Clearly, centralization can only be one element, if at all, in the total explanation. Finally, the internal dynamics and stability of regimes may be important (see Newell and Symons (1987)). For example, as Calmfors and Forslund (1989, p. 1) note on Sweden, "the traditional Swedish model of centralized wage setting, with private-sector employers and blue-collar workers playing the dominating role, has recently begun to crumble, partly because of the emergence of new strong collectives of wage earners, and partly because of a tendency to shift the emphasis in negotiations from the central to lower levels.''

Minford (1988) also notes that there are positive as well as negative aspects of corporatism, more broadly defined. Centralized bargaining is associated with strong unionization; this in turn tends to be associated with political leverage, which in turn encourages "welfare state" characteristics that may be unfavorable to employment.

From our perspective it is not evident what its central message is. Assuming they could, should intermediate economies move up or down?

The Degree of Unionization and of Trade Union Power. Unionization in itself is less important than the way in which power is used. High unionization combined with low (high) coordination may be a poor (good) mix (Layard (1990)).

It is not difficult to find theoretical support for the view that the exercise or the exploitation of trade union power can reduce economy-wide employment (Blanchflower and others (1989)). Lindbeck and Snower (1989) also show how trade union power can increase unemployment in an insider-outsider framework. There is as well some empirical support for this (Minford (1988) and Blanchflower and others (1989)).

One obvious way, therefore, to attack unemployment is to try to reduce trade union power. This is the route Thatcher took in the United Kingdom, where unions have had a reputation for militancy and aggressiveness. From 1979 she passed legislation to reduce trade union power. It is not, however, evident that she met with much success in terms of its impact on macroeconomic performance (Brown and Wadhwani (1990) and McConnell and Takla (1990)). In the United States, too, trade union power may have lessened in recent years (Kahn and Weiner (1990)).

Profit Sharing Schemes. Broadly, there are two types of profit sharing schemes: one relates basic pay directly to profits (revenue or value added); in the other, employees acquire an equity (through share ownership) in their firm. There are plenty of illustrations of the two variants to be found in industrial countries (Estrin and others (1987)). The most celebrated and most widely discussed application of the first is the case of Japan where a bonus payment is made twice a year as a supplement to the base wage (it represents about a quarter of the base wage and in principle is supposed to be dependent on the profitability of the enterprise, although there is some debate about how responsive it is to profit fluctuation). On a lesser scale, in the United States too in recent years schemes of this kind have become increasingly popular (Bell (1989)).

The recent debate over the merits of profit sharing has predominantly focused on the first type to which we also briefly limit ourselves.

There are three claims made for profit sharing. The first is that it will improve morale, the industrial relations environment, and productivity. This is outside our own interest. The second is that it represents a form of wage flexibility, with actual earnings depending on the state of the economy. This is probably the strongest case that can be made for profit sharing (Argy (1991)). The third is that, if it were widely introduced, under certain circumstances it would have the effect of pushing the economy permanently toward full employment; indeed, there would be a constant excess demand for labor. This is the principal argument made by Weitzman (1984 and 1985).

Not every one, however, has been convinced by the theoretical arguments, particularly the last one. Moreover, empirical work, both on Japan and on countries where some firms have experimented with profit sharing schemes is not very supportive of the claims made (Estrin and others (1987), Blanchflower and Oswald (1986), and Wadhwani and Wall (1990)).

Welfare State Characteristics and the Regulatory Framework

The two most eminent proponents of the view that the welfare state and the regulatory framework have, in combination, tended to stifle and inhibit economic adjustment, with adverse effects on employment are Giersch (1987) and Lindbeck (1988). (For a careful analysis of the impact of the size of government on unemployment and growth see Tullio (1987).)

Of the big three, Germany has the most advanced welfare state. Japan and the United States are well down in the OECD rankings in this respect. Government outlays as a percent of GNP is 48 percent in Germany, 36 percent in the United States, and 33 percent in Japan. At the same time, the direct regulatory environment is much more "oppressive" in Germany than in either the United States or Japan.

The level of unemployment benefits and their duration, minimum wage legislation, high taxes (on income and on employment), employment protection laws, and regulations imposed to foster social justice all have some potential implications for labor market flexibility. These have received wide attention in the literature. (For an application to Germany, see Soltwedel (1988), Dombois (1989), and Beuchtemann (1989); see also Emerson (1988) for a general review of industrial countries.)

We focus below briefly on the role of unemployment benefits only.

Despite the ambiguous econometric evidence, one would expect high unemployment benefits, other things being equal, to increase unemployment by reducing the relative return from work. Increased benefits increase search time, hence the duration of unemployment. They also increase the bargaining strength of workers (see Jackman and others (1990)). Such benefits, other things being equal, are likely to reduce the degree of real wage flexibility. Reform here need not take the form of reducing unemployment benefits, which for reasons of equity may be undesirable, but rather of tightening eligibility conditions for benefits.

Minford (1988) highlights the differences in unemployment benefits and eligibility conditions in accounting for differences in unemployment performance between continental Europe, the United States, and Switzerland-Sweden. The last two offer generous unemployment benefits and monitoring is strict and the duration of the benefit is limited in time (after which, in Sweden the unemployed are automatically absorbed in community work). (See also Burda (1988).) Layard (1990) highlights the importance of the duration of unemployment benefits.

Direct Government Involvement in Wage Negotiations and in Manpower (Retraining) Schemes

Government involvement in wage setting can take several forms: a "guidelines" type policy, a "mandatory" wage policy, a wage-tax trade-off, an employment subsidy, or a tax-based market-oriented wage policy. The general verdict on traditional incomes policies is that they have had at best modest but temporary success. To quote Jackman and Layard (1987, p. 8), "While traditional incomes policies have had temporary successes (especially in the later 1970s), they have not generally been able to last long. This is because they set an absolute limit on the level of wage growth for individual grades of employee. This eliminates free collective bargaining (making it unacceptable to the unions) and severely reduces the scope for employers to raise wages, to recruit, retain and motivate workers (except by fiddles like regrading)." This particular verdict may be too harsh

(Layard (1990) acknowledges the recent success of a guidelines type policy in Australia).

Wage-tax trade-offs have also been tried, notably in a number of Nordic countries but it seems with little, if any, success (Calmfors and Nymoen (1990)).

Employment subsidies to employers were fashionable in the 1970s, with many countries implementing variations on this theme (Argy (1981) and Jackman and others (1990)), but there has been considerable disenchantment in recent years with such schemes.

A case for a tax-based wage policy has been made over many years now by Layard and his colleagues at the London School of Economics. To quote Jackman and Layard (1987, p. 8), ''The obvious solution is to have a fixed norm for the growth of average earnings in each firm (without regard to grade structure), and to tax heavily any excess earnings growth—while not making it unlawful. This would exert a strong downwards pressure on excess wage growth, while leaving much of the needed flexibility intact.''

Retraining schemes may also be helpful. One theory of hysteresis (unemployment persistence) is that unemployment erodes human capital (skills), rendering the unemployed less employable. One would thus expect, in principle, the long-term unemployed to exert less pressure on downward wage push than the short-term unemployed. (For some evidence of this see Blanchard and Summers (1986) and Cotis (1988).)

To counter this source of unemployment persistence there are two routes to take. One is to allow greater wage flexibility (the loss of skill would be reflected in lower wages). A better route is to implement retraining schemes. As Layard and Bean (1988, p. 36) note, ''it is striking that long-term unemployment is very much smaller in countries such as the U.S., Sweden, Norway, Finland and Austria in which benefits are not available beyond 6–12 months, except for those on special work or training schemes. Targetted training and job programmes for the unemployed, as in Sweden, also have a crucial role.''

Conclusions

A very interesting (but controversial) paper by Layard (1990) allows us to summarize some of our own explorations and provides a good basis for thinking about some of these issues. Layard tries to explain, by econometric analysis, cross-section differences in unemployment rates (1983–88) in 20 OECD countries in terms of two broad sets of factors: wage bargaining arrangements and unemployment policies. He has three key variables to represent the first: unionization (coverage and density), trade union coordination, and employer coordination. He has four key variables to represent the second: the replacement ratio (the level of the unemployment benefit), the duration of the unemployment benefit, the level of active labor market spending, and the change in the inflation rate between 1982 and 1988 (a measure of demand pull). Layard argues on a priori grounds that high unionization (in itself) ought to increase unemployment but high coordination ought to reduce unemployment (à la Calmfors-Driffill); at the same time, a high replacement ratio or a long duration of unemployment benefit ought to increase unemployment, while active labor market spending should reduce unemployment; finally, a fall (rise) in the inflation rate should increase (reduce) unemployment. All these expectations are perfectly realized; the signs are all right, the seven variables combined explaining over 90 percent of the cross-section variation in unemployment. Roughly half is explained in terms of wage bargaining arrangements and the other half in terms of unemployment policies.

Jackman and others (1990) reach rather similar conclusions, using an unemployment-vacancy (Beveridge curve) framework. Unemployment is explained by the vacancy rate, and additionally by the benefit duration, replacement ratio, corporatism, labor market policies, and lagged unemployment.

What then can we finally conclude? One cannot be dogmatic that reforms of the kind proposed would necessarily improve the macroeconomy. Moreover, there will clearly at times be a potential trading of equity against efficiency. Finally, and most important, it is not at all clear that characteristics that appear to improve labor market performance in one economy can be transplanted elsewhere with similar effectiveness (see Alogoskoufis and Manning (1988) and Emerson and Dramais (1988)).

Monetary-Fiscal Policy Coordination

It is convenient to begin by making a distinction between three levels of coordination. At the lowest rung we have periodic intergovernmental exchanges of information, consultations, and declarations of policy intent. At a second-order level we have what Wallich has called "a significant modification of national policies in recognition of international economic interdependence" (Wallich (1984, p. 85)). At a third-order level we have full-fledged coordination in the sense of the cooperative maximization of some joint welfare function.

Few would quarrel with coordination of the first order. On the other hand, very few if any would seriously contemplate moving in the direction of coordination of the third order (Frankel (1988b)). We can, therefore, safely limit our remarks to second-order coordination that has some support among economists.

Second-Order Coordination

It is known that, particularly since 1985, the major industrial countries have "coordinated" on macroeconomic policy to a greater degree than previously. Greater coordination has occurred on several fronts: the setting of exchange rate policies and targets (reviewed earlier), some commitment on the setting of monetary and fiscal policies, and the use of indicators to determine target compatibility and the appropriateness of policy in relation to set targets.

There was one well-advertised instance of monetary coordination: in March–April 1986, the central banks of several major countries lowered their discount rates in synchronization, the aim being to encourage growth without altering exchange rate relationships.

There has been some coordination on fiscal policies as well. At the Plaza meeting, the United States indicated that it was firmly committed to reducing the budget deficit. Other participant countries also produced some, but very vague, statements about their policy intention.

It was not till the Louvre meeting, however, that somewhat firmer commitments were made on the fiscal front. Germany and Japan undertook to ease their fiscal policy stance, while the United States pledged to cut its federal deficit to 2.3 percent of GNP in 1988. Similar commitments were repeated at the April 1988 meeting of the Group of Seven.

The indicators approach to coordination was first given public exposure at the Tokyo summit of May 1986. At that meeting, a new Group of Seven finance ministers was formed to work more closely and to meet more frequently between summit meetings. One of the tasks assigned to this new Group of Seven was to "review their individual economic objectives and forecasts, using a wide range of indicators, with a particular view to examining their mutual compatibility." The particular indicators chosen were GNP growth rates, inflation rates, interest rates, unemployment rates, fiscal deficit ratios, current account and trade balance, money growth targets, reserves, and exchange rates. This multilateral surveillance was to be undertaken in close collaboration with the International Monetary Fund.

Frenkel and Goldstein (1988, p. 210) justify the use of indicators as a means of assisting the process of coordination as follows: "These indicators are employed to help gauge the international implications of domestic policy changes; to spot likely inconsistencies among policy objectives—both within and across countries; to monitor whether short-term developments are 'on-track' in terms of longer-term objectives; and as early-warning signals of emerging global inflationary or deflationary trends."

At the Venice summit in June 1987, the list of indicators was reduced to six: growth, inflation, trade balances, government budgets, monetary conditions, and exchange rates. At the Toronto summit in June 1988, the Group of Seven added a commodity price indicator to the list.

Did coordination, as summarized immediately above, and earlier, actually make a difference to the course of the leading economies, à la Wallich?

If exchange rate management had small but uncertain impacts on exchange markets, as we concluded, "agreements" on fiscal policies probably had even lesser impact. A very reasonable case can be made for the view that none of the big three did much that they would not have done anyway (Shinkai (1990)).

Finally, insofar as the indicators approach is concerned, there is little evidence that it has altered policies in a way that would not have happened otherwise.

All of this suggests that there has been very little serious second-order coordination.

III. An Evaluation of Some Reform Proposals

In Section II we reviewed and summarized a number of proposals to reform the design of macroeconomic policy in the leading economies. This section tries to evaluate some of these proposals.

There are two ways to proceed here: one theoretical, the other empirical. One can undertake an analytical evaluation of the policy proposals or one can undertake empirical simulations with econometric models of the proposals.

Theoretical Analysis

We can evaluate some of the proposals in terms of medium-run and short-run objectives. These were defined in Section I.

Medium-Run Evaluation

Which policy packages are most likely to achieve the medium-run objectives?

Virtually all the proposals in one guise or another address the problem of inflation. McKinnon has a target rate of inflation that is to be achieved by coordinated monetary policies; Friedman has target rates of inflation for each country to be achieved by an appropriate growth in the national money stock; Williamson-Miller (WM) have a target growth of domestic demand (that explicitly accommodates a target inflation), with fiscal policy as the primary instrument; Boughton-Genberg-Swoboda (BGS) have target rates of nominal income/inflation that, as in Friedman, are addressed by appropriate national rates of money growth; McCallum, who targets the growth of nominal income, has base money growth as the appropriate instrument.

A key difference is between a fixed rate regime (à la McKinnon), where the target rate of inflation is common and a flexible rate regime, where countries would be free, in principle, to set their own rate of inflation (as in Friedman). If optimal rates of inflation are different across countries and if the problem of discipline can be overcome (e.g., by giving more independence to the central bank and requiring it to have responsibility for inflation), this is an advantage for flexible rates.

None of the proposals seriously addresses the problem of unemployment. The New Keynesians have given the most thought to this. Friedman believes he would take care of the problem by "deregulating" labor markets. There is still a need to integrate labor market analysis into a macroeconomic framework.

BGS and WM (the latter through a real exchange rate target) explicitly address the question of external balance. In Friedman, as already noted, medium-run external balances will reflect private sector savings/investment decisions, which are implicitly assumed to be optimal. The New Keynesians, as noted, have a broader (wealth) target, the change in which comprises not just the external balance but also the rate of capital formation.

BGS are the most explicit, in a large country framework, in defining goals and instruments. Their framework accommodates one additional target: the real interest rate (directed at the consumption/investment mix).

In the final analysis, then, insofar as the medium-run intention is concerned, there is probably little to choose between the different proposals. But, as we have seen, there is still an important question of which proposal has got the assignment of instruments to targets right; there is also the important question of what macroeconomic variables ought to be targeted.

"Short-Run" Analysis

There is now an extensive literature that analyses the insulating properties of fixed and flexible rate regimes (Argy (1990)). In a recent analysis, Argy (1991) shows that the large country choice between a fixed or a flexible rate regime will depend on (1) the type of disturbance (expenditure, monetary, or productivity); (2) the country origin of the disturbance; (3) the loss function (i.e., which targets appear important to the authorities and the weights attaching to each); (4) the structural coefficients of the model; and (5) institutional considerations, for example, if wage contracts are indexed or otherwise. This is about as far as one can take "short-run" analysis; at this theoretical level substantive differences do emerge between fixed and flexible rate regimes.

Econometric Analysis[8]

What does econometric work tell us?

Fixed versus Flexible Rates

Taylor (1989), using his own multicountry model, evaluates alternative simple monetary strategies. Briefly, his basic comparison is between, on the one hand, a flexible rate regime where central banks use interest rate policy to stabilize the price level and, on the other hand, a fixed rate regime where central banks adjust the "world" interest rate, again to stabilize the price level. He finds that flexible rates work better "according to almost all measures of internal economic stability" (p. 130).

Frenkel-Goldstein-Masson (1989) (FGM) carry out simulations of alternative policy strategies, using the IMF's MULTIMOD. From our perspective, two simulations are of particular interest. They report root mean square deviations for a number of key variables for two simple rules: a money target with flexible rates; and an asymmetrical fixed rate regime (where the United States is assumed to sterilize). In one simulation they use historical shocks (1974–85) while holding

---

[8]For more details on some of the work reviewed see Argy (1991).

fiscal policy neutral. In a second simulation they generate shocks from a much longer historical base (40 years against 12 years).

They report results for the United States, Japan, and Germany. Interestingly, for the two simulations there is essentially very little difference between the regimes, at least insofar as price output outcomes are concerned.

McKibbin and Sachs (1989) (MS), using the McKibbin-Sachs Global Model (MSG), evaluate three simple rules: a fixed money growth rule with flexible rates, a symmetrical fixed exchange rate regime, and a fixed rate regime, where the Group of Three monetary authorities target the world price level (as in McKinnon). They report results for individual disturbances. Through these simulations fiscal policy is held neutral. The three disturbances are an expenditure shock, an oil price shock, and a money demand shock (the first and last originating in one of the Group of Three countries).

Their solutions are presented in Table 4, which is self-explanatory. Insofar as fixed-flexible regimes are concerned, the results conform to theoretical expectations. For the country of origin, a fixed rate is on balance better for a money disturbance; a flexible rate is better for an expenditure disturbance. The outcomes are similar for an oil price shock. McKinnon's rule, not surprisingly, performs best on inflation.

Assignment Rules

Consider now empirical work on assignment rules. The basic comparisons here are between the WM blueprint, the BGS reverse assignment, and the "historical" performance. There are three econometric studies that bear most on this: FGM (1989); Currie and Wren-Lewis (1989) (CW); and MS (1989).

FGM's exercises are extensions of those noted above for historical and generated shocks. They compare the blueprint with the reverse assignment. The results are very similar for historical and generated shocks. In general, on the key variables (output, inflation, and the real effective exchange rate) the blueprint outperforms the reverse assignment.

CW undertake econometric simulations for the Group of Three, using the National Institute Global Econometric Model (GEM) over the years 1975–86. The simulations are designed to evaluate the relative performance of the blueprint, the reverse assignment and history. Their conclusions are easily summarized: "Both schemes improved welfare compared to history over this period, but the

Table 4. Standard Deviations of Variables in Response to Three Shocks

	Flexible Rate	Symmetrical Fixed Rate	McKinnon Rule
U.S. real demand shock			
United States			
Output	149.53	164.22	56.79
Inflation	72.13	89.76	19.87
Japan			
Output	25.17	11.07	25.30
Inflation	47.45	8.63	13.56
Real exchange rate	216.11	104.78	82.38
Germany			
Output	89.79	64.44	22.03
Inflation	47.11	11.04	25.13
Real exchange rate	157.35	59.25	59.88
U.S. money demand shock			
United States			
Output	21.72	14.57	0.34
Inflation	18.11	9.67	0.12
Japan			
Output	1.79	4.65	0.15
Inflation	7.33	0.84	0.08
Real exchange rate	66.35	6.27	0.49
Germany			
Output	9.30	6.18	0.13
Inflation	4.08	4.66	0.15
Real exchange rate	59.65	9.97	0.36
Oil price shock			
United States			
Output	3.00	3.07	8.43
Inflation	4.59	4.56	0.68
Japan			
Output	0.49	0.47	2.46
Inflation	3.66	0.31	0.44
Real exchange rate	4.48	4.83	4.81
Germany			
Output	3.82	3.94	2.12
Inflation	3.27	0.56	1.47
Real exchange rate	4.30	4.95	3.34

Source: McKibbin and Sachs (1989).

gains associated with [the blueprint] were generally larger and more substantial'' and ''our model suggested that fiscal policy had a comparative advantage over monetary policy in directly controlling demand at a national level'' (p. 268).

Thus, although the model is different, the methodology used is different, and the design of policies different, this study in essence agrees with FGM that the blueprint outperforms the reverse assignment.

In the same study referred to earlier, MS evaluate a large number of policy proposals, including assignment rules. It turns out that the best results are obtained when fiscal policy is primarily linked to the real exchange rate and monetary policy is primarily linked to nominal income, especially so for U.S. money demand and real demand shocks. So this study, if anything, appears to be critical of the WM blueprint, and appears to endorse the reverse assignment.

Conclusion

There is something quite frustrating about not being able to resolve key policy issues either in analytical or empirical terms. Sadly, this is the case. It seems that the more work is undertaken the less we appear to advance.

ANNEX I

The Medium-Run Model Underlying the Thesis in the Section on "Labor Market Reforms"

1. $ya = \alpha_1(e + pdb - pda) - \alpha_2\,ra + \alpha_3\,gra + \alpha_7\,yb$
2. $yb = -\alpha_1(e + pdb - pda) - \alpha_2\,rb + \alpha_2\,grb + \alpha_7\,ya$
3. $moa = ya + pda - \alpha_5\,ra$
4. $mob = yb + pdb - \alpha_5\,rb$
5. $ra = rb = rw$
6. $ya = \alpha_6(wa - pda) + \alpha_6/k_1u_3a$
7. $yb = \alpha_6(wb - pdb) + \alpha_6/k_1u_3b$
8. $wa = pa + \pi_{12a}(ya - ya^*)$
9. $wb = pb + \pi_{12b}(yb - yb^*)$
10. $pa = \alpha_{15}\,pda + (1 - \alpha_{15})(e - pdb)$
11. $pb = \alpha_{15}\,pdb - (1 - \alpha_{15})(e - pda)$
12. $(CA/X_o)a = \alpha_{20}(e - pda + pdb) - (ya - yb)\alpha_{20} > \alpha_1$
13. $ya^* = u_3a$
14. $yb^* = u_3b$

Notation (a, b, represents the two countries)

y = output
mo = money stock
$r = rw$ = common interest rate
pd = home prices
w = wage rate

e = exchange rate

p = consumer price index

g^* = fiscal policy

y^* = full employment output

CA/X_o = current account balance as a proportion of initial exports.

The two-country model is fairly standard. Equations (1) and (2) represent the real demand for goods. Equations (3), (4), and (5) represent the monetary sector. Equations (6) and (7) represent the supply side of the economy. u_3 is a productivity disturbance. The wage rate in each country is determined by the consumer price index and by the gap between actual output and full employment output. π_{12} is the degree of real wage flexibility, as in the text. Policies would be aimed at increasing π_{12}. When $\pi_{12} \rightarrow \infty$, output will return to its full employment level. Assuming the elasticity of supply of labor is zero, full employment output is determined by productivity (as in 13–14).

The six instruments of policy are π_{12a}, π_{12b}, moa, mob, gra, and grb. The targets are rw, pa, pb, CA/X_o, ya^*, and yb^*.

REFERENCES

Alogoskoufis, George, and Alan Manning, "Wage Setting and Unemployment Persistence in Europe, Japan, and the U.S.A.," *European Economic Review* (Amsterdam), Vol. 32 (March 1988), pp. 698–706.

Andersen, Palle S., *Inflation and Output: A Review of the Wage-Price Mechanism*, BIS Economic Papers No. 24 (Basle: Bank for International Settlements, January 1989).

Argy, Victor, *The Post-War International Money Crisis: An Analysis* (London: Allen & Unwin, 1981).

———, "The World Economy in the 70s and 80s—Lessons from Experience —Prospects and Current Policy Proposals," *Australian Professional Publications* (Sydney, 1988).

———, *International Financial Deregulation—Some Macroeconomic Implications*, Pacific Economic Papers No. 168 (Canberra: Australian-Japan Research Centre, February 1989).

———, "Choice of Exchange Rate Regime for a Smaller Economy: A Survey of Some Key Issues," in *Choosing an Exchange Rate Regime: The Challenge for Smaller Industrial Countries*, ed. by Paul De Grauwe and Victor Argy (Washington: International Monetary Fund, 1990).

———, "Nominal Income Targeting: A Critical Evaluation," IMF Working

Paper No. 91/92 (Washington: International Monetary Fund, October 1991).

——, Warwick McKibbin, and Eric Siegloff, *Exchange-Rate Regimes for a Small Economy in a Multi-Country World*, Princeton Studies in International Finance No. 67 (Princeton, New Jersey: Princeton University Press, December 1989).

Argy, Victor, Anthony Brennan, and Glenn Stevens, "Monetary Targeting: The International Experience," *Economic Record* (Burwood, Victoria, Australia), Vol. 66 (September 1990), pp. 37–62.

Bank for International Settlements, *Annual Reports*, 1985–90 (Basle).

Barbone, Luca, and Pierre Poret, "Structural Conditions and Macroeconomic Responses to Shocks: A Sensitivity Analysis for Four European Countries," *OECD Economic Studies* (Paris), No. 12 (Spring 1989), pp. 131–58.

Barro, Robert J., "Recent Developments in the Theory of Rules versus Discretion," *Economic Journal* (Oxford), Supplement to Vol. 96 (1986), pp. 23–37.

——, and David B. Gordon, "Rules, Discretion and Reputation in a Model of Monetary Policy," *Journal of Monetary Economics* (Amsterdam), Vol. 12 (July 1983), pp. 101–21.

Bean, Charles, "Capital Shortages and Persistent Unemployment," *Economic Policy* (Cambridge, England), No. 4 (April 1989), pp. 11–53.

Bell, Linda A., "Union Concessions in the 1980s," *Quarterly Review*, Federal Reserve Bank of New York (New York), Vol. 14 (Summer 1989), pp. 44–58.

Bergsten, C. Fred, "The World Economy After the Cold War," *Foreign Affairs* (New York), Vol. 69, No. 3 (Summer 1990), pp. 96–112.

Beuchtemann, Christoph F., "More Jobs Through Less Employment Protection? Evidence from West Germany," *Labour* (Rome), Vol. 3, No. 3 (Winter 1989), pp. 23–56.

Blanchard, Olivier J., and Lawrence H. Summers, "Hysteresis and the European Unemployment Problem," in *NBER Macroeconomics Annual 1986*, ed. by Stanley Fischer (Cambridge, Massachusetts: MIT Press, 1986).

Blanchflower, D.G., and A.J. Oswald, "Profit-Sharing—Can It Work?" Discussion Paper No. 255 (London: Centre for Labour Economics, London School of Economics, October 1986).

——, and N. Millward, "Unionization and Employment Behavior," Discussion Paper No. 339 (London: Centre for Labour Economics, London School of Economics, March 1989).

Boughton, James M., "Policy Assignment Strategies with Somewhat Flexible Exchange Rates," in *Blueprints for Exchange Rate Management*, ed. by

Marcus Miller, Barry Eichengreen, and Richard Portes (London: Academic Press, 1989).

Brown, William, and Sushil Wadhwani, "Economic Effects of Industrial Relations Legislation Since 1979," Discussion Paper No. 376 (London: Centre for Labour Economics, London School of Economics, March 1990).

Brunner, Karl, "Fiscal Policy in Macro Theory: A Survey and Evaluation," in *The Monetary versus Fiscal Policy Debate: Lessons from Two Decades*, ed. by R.W. Hafer (Totowa, New Jersey: Rowman & Allanheld, 1986).

Bruno, Michael, and Jeffrey D. Sachs, *Economics of Worldwide Stagflation* (Cambridge, Massachusetts: Harvard University Press, 1985).

Burda, Michael, "'Wait Unemployment' in Europe," *Economic Policy* (Cambridge, England), No. 7 (October 1988), pp. 391–425.

Calmfors, Lars, and John Driffill, "Bargaining Structure, Corporatism and Macroeconomic Performance," *Economic Policy* (Cambridge, England), No. 6 (April 1988), pp. 13–47.

Calmfors, Lars, and Anders Forslund, "Wage Setting in Sweden," Seminar Paper No. 430 (Stockholm: Institute for International Economic Studies, University of Stockholm, January 1989).

Calmfors, Lars, and Ragnar Nymoen, "Real Wage Adjustment and Employment Policies in the Nordic Countries," *Economic Policy* (Cambridge, England), No. 11 (October 1990), pp. 397–448.

Cooper, Richard N., "The Gold Standard: Historical Facts and Future Prospects," *Brookings Papers on Economic Activity: 1* (1982), Brookings Institution (Washington), pp. 1–45, reprinted in *The International Monetary System: Essays in World Economics* (Cambridge, Massachusetts: MIT Press, 1987).

———, "A Monetary System for the Future," *Foreign Affairs* (New York), Vol. 63, No. 1 (1984), pp. 166–84, reprinted in *The International Monetary System: Essays in World Economics* (Cambridge, Massachusetts: MIT Press, 1987).

———, "What Future for the International Monetary System?" Chapter 6 in this volume and in *The Evolution of the International Monetary System: How Can Efficiency and Stability Be Attained?* ed. by Yoshio Suzuki, Junichi Miyake, and Mitsuaki Okabe (Tokyo: University of Tokyo Press, 1990).

Corden, W. Max, "Does the Current Account Matter? The Old View and the New," Chapter 18 in this volume.

Cotis, Jean-Philippe, "Fund Staff Study Finds Evidence of 'Hysteresis' in Europe," *IMF Survey*, International Monetary Fund (Washington), Vol. 17 (August 15, 1988), p. 257.

Currie, David, and Simon Wren-Lewis, "Evaluating Blueprints for the Conduct of International Macro Policy," *American Economic Review*,

Papers and Proceedings (Nashville, Tennessee), Vol. 79 (May 1989), pp. 264–69.

Dombois, Rainer, "Flexibility by Law? The West German Employment Promotion Act and Temporary Employment," *Cambridge Journal of Economics* (Cambridge, England), Vol. 13 (June 1989), pp. 359–71.

Dominguez, Kathryn Mary, "Market Responses to Coordinated Central Bank Invervention," *Carnegie-Rochester Conference Series on Public Policy* (Amsterdam), Vol. 32 (Spring 1990), pp. 121–63.

——, and J. Frankel, "Some New Tests of Foreign Exchange Intervention: The Portfolio and Expectation Effects" (unpublished; Cambridge, Massachusetts: Harvard University, 1989).

Dornbusch, Rudiger, "Equilibrium and Disequilibrium Exchange Rates," *Zeitschrift für Wirtschafts- und Sozialwissenschaften* (Berlin), Vol. 102, No. 6 (1982), pp. 573–97.

Edison, Hali J., *Foreign Currency Operations: An Annotated Bibliography*, International Finance Discussion Papers No. 380 (Washington: Board of Governors of the Federal Reserve System, International Finance Division, May 1990).

Emerson, Michael, "Regulation or Deregulation of the Labour Market," *European Economic Review* (Amsterdam), Vol. 32 (April 1988), pp. 775–817.

——, with André Dramais, *What Model for Europe?* (Cambridge, Massachusetts: MIT Press, 1988).

Estrin, Saul, Paul Grout, and Sushil Wadhwani, "Profit-Sharing and Employee Share Ownership," *Economic Policy* (Cambridge, England), No. 4 (April 1987), pp. 14–62.

Federal Reserve Bank of New York, *Quarterly Reviews*, 1985–90 (New York).

Feldstein, Martin, "The Case Against Trying to Stabilize the Dollar," *American Economic Review, Papers and Proceedings* (Nashville, Tennessee), Vol. 79 (May 1989), pp. 36–40.

Fischer, Stanley, "Rules versus Discretion in Monetary Policy," NBER Working Paper No. 2518 (Cambridge, Massachusetts: National Bureau of Economic Research, February 1988).

Frankel, Jeffrey A. (1988a), "International Capital Mobility and Exchange Rate Volatility," in *International Payments Imbalances in the 1980s*, Conference Series No. 32, ed. by Norman S. Fieleke (Boston: Federal Reserve Bank of Boston, October 1988).

—— (1988b), *Obstacles to International Macroeconomic Policy Coordination*, Princeton Studies in International Finance No. 64 (Princeton, New Jersey: Princeton University Press, December 1988).

——, "International Nominal Income Targeting: A Proposal for Overcoming Obstacles to Policy Coordination" (unpublished, April 1989).

Frenkel, Jacob A., and Morris Goldstein, "A Guide to Target Zones," *Staff Papers*, International Monetary Fund (Washington), Vol. 33 (December 1986), pp. 633–73.

——, "Exchange Rate Volatility and Misalignment: Evaluating Some Proposals for Reform," in *Financial Market Volatility* (Kansas City: Federal Reserve Bank of Kansas City, 1988).

——, and Paul R. Masson, "Simulating the Effects of Some Simple Coordinated versus Uncoordinated Policy Rules," in *Macroeconomic Policies in an Interdependent World*, ed. by Ralph C. Bryant and others (Washington: Brookings Institution, Centre for Economic Policy Research, and International Monetary Fund, 1989).

Friedman, Milton, "A Monetary and Fiscal Framework for Economic Stability," *American Economic Review* (Nashville, Tennessee), Vol. 38 (June 1948), pp. 245–64, reprinted in *Essays in Positive Economics* (Chicago: University of Chicago Press, 1953).

——, *A Program for Monetary Stability* (The Millar Lectures, No. 3) (New York: Fordham University Press, 1959).

——, "Less Red Ink," *The Atlantic* (New York), February 1983.

Funabashi, Yoichi, *Managing the Dollar: From the Plaza to the Louvre* (Washington: Institute for International Economics, 1988).

Genberg, Hans, and Alexander K. Swoboda, "The Current Account and the Policy Mix Under Flexible Exchange Rates," IMF Working Paper No. 87/70 (Washington: International Monetary Fund, 1987).

——, "Policy and Current Account Determination Under Floating Exchange Rates," *Staff Papers*, International Monetary Fund (Washington), Vol. 36 (March 1989), pp. 1–30.

Giersch, Herbert, "Eurosclerosis—What Is the Cure?" *European Affairs* (Amsterdam), No. 4 (Winter 1987), pp. 33–43.

Grubb, Dennis, Richard Jackman, and Richard Layard, "Wage Rigidity and Unemployment in OECD Countries," *European Economic Review* (Amsterdam), Vol. 21 (March/April 1983), pp. 11–39.

Jackman, Richard, "Wage Formation in the Nordic Countries Viewed from an International Perspective," Discussion Paper No. 335 (London: Centre for Labour Economics, London School of Economics, January 1989).

——, and Richard Layard, "Innovative Supply-Side Policies to Reduce Unemployment," Discussion Paper No. 281 (London: Centre for Labour Economics, London School of Economics, May 1987).

Jackman, Richard, Christopher Pissarides, and Savvas Savouri, "Labour Market Policies and Unemployment in the OECD," *Economic Policy* (Cambridge, England), No. 11 (October 1990), pp. 449–90.

Kahn, George A., and Stuart E. Weiner, "Has the Cost of Disinflation

Declined?" *Economic Review*, Federal Reserve Bank of Kansas City (Kansas City), Vol. 75 (May–June 1990), pp. 5–24.

Kenen, Peter B., *Managing Exchange Rates* (London: Routledge, 1988).

Klau, Friedrich, and Axel Mittelstadt, "Labour Market and Flexibility," *OECD Economic Studies* (Paris), No. 6 (Spring 1986), pp. 8–45.

Krugman, Paul R., *Exchange-Rate Instability* (Cambridge, Massachusetts: MIT Press, 1988).

Layard, Richard, "Wage Bargaining and Incomes Policy: Possible Lessons for Eastern Europe," Discussion Paper No. 2 (London: Center for Economic Performance, London School of Economics, May 1990).

——, and C. Bean, "Why Does Unemployment Persist?" Discussion Paper No. 321 (London: Centre for Labour Economics, London School of Economics, August 1988).

Lindbeck, Assar, "Consequences of the Advanced Welfare State," *World Economy* (Oxford), Vol. 11 (March 1988), pp. 19–37.

——, and Dennis J. Snower, "Wage Setting, Unemployment, and Insider-Outsider Relations," *American Economic Review, Papers and Proceedings* (Nashville, Tennessee), Vol. 76 (May 1986), pp. 235–39.

——, "Long-Term Unemployment and Macroeconomic Policy," *American Economic Review, Papers and Proceedings* (Nashville, Tennessee), Vol. 78 (May 1988), pp. 38–43.

——, "Demand- and Supply-Side Policies and Unemployment: Policy Implications of the Insider-Outsider Approach," Seminar Paper No. 439 (Stockholm: Institute for International Economic Studies, University of Stockholm, April 1989).

McCallum, Bennett T., "The Case for Rules in the Conduct of Monetary Policy: A Concrete Example," *Economic Review*, Federal Reserve Bank of Richmond (Richmond), Vol. 73 (September/October 1987), pp. 10–18.

——, "Robustness Properties of a Rule for Monetary Policy," *Carnegie-Rochester Conference Series on Public Policy* (Amsterdam), Vol. 29 (1988), pp. 173–204.

McConnell, S., and L. Takla, "Mrs. Thatcher's Trade Union Legislation: Has It Reduced Strikes?" Discussion Paper No. 374 (London: Centre for Labour Economics, London School of Economics, January 1990).

McKibbin, Warwick J., and Jeffrey D. Sachs, "Implications of Policy Rules for the World Economy," in *Macroeconomic Policies in an Interdependent World*, ed. by Ralph C. Bryant and others (Washington: Brookings Institution, Centre for Economic Policy Research, and International Monetary Fund, 1989).

McKinnon, Ronald I., *An International Standard for Monetary Stabilization* (Washington: Institute for International Economics, 1984).

——, "Monetary and Exchange Rate Policies for International Financial Stability: A Proposal," *Journal of Economic Perspectives* (Nashville, Tennessee), Vol. 2, No. 1 (Winter 1988), pp. 83–103.

Meade, J.E., *Wage-Fixing, Vol. 1: Stagflation* (London: Allen & Unwin, 1982).

Meltzer, Allan H., "On Monetary Stability and Monetary Reform," in *Toward a World of Economic Stability: Optimal Monetary Framework and Policy*, ed. by Yoshio Suzuki and Mitsuaki Okabe (Tokyo: University of Tokyo Press, 1988).

Minford, Patrick, "Wages and Unemployment Half a Century On," Discussion Paper Series No. 262 (London: Centre for Economic Policy Research, August 1988).

——, and David Peel, *Rational Expectations and the New Macroeconomics* (Oxford: Martin Robertson, 1983).

Mundell, Robert A., "International Monetary Options," *Cato Journal* (Washington), Vol. 3 (Spring 1983), pp. 189–210.

Newell, A., and J.S.V. Symons, "Corporatism, Laissez-Faire, and the Rise in Unemployment," *European Economic Review* (Amsterdam), Vol. 31 (April 1987), pp. 567–614.

Obstfeld, Maurice, "The Effectiveness of Foreign-Exchange Intervention: Recent Experience," NBER Working Paper No. 2796 (Cambridge, Massachusetts: National Bureau of Economic Research, December 1988).

Organization for Economic Cooperation and Development, *Economic Outlook*, No. 42 (Paris, December 1987).

——, *Economic Outlook*, No. 43 (Paris, June 1988).

——, *Economies in Transition: Structural Adjustment in OECD Countries*, Chapter 2 (Paris, 1989).

Pitchford, John, "The Role of the Current Account: A Study of Select Industrial Countries" (unpublished; Washington: International Monetary Fund, December 1990).

Sargent, T.J., and N. Wallace, "Some Unpleasant Monetarist Arithmetic," *Quarterly Review*, Federal Reserve Bank of Minneapolis (Minneapolis), Fall 1981, pp. 1–17.

Shinkai, Yoichi, "Evaluation of the Bretton-Woods Regime and the Floating Exchange Rate System," in *The Evolution of the International Monetary System: How Can Efficiency and Stability Be Attained?* ed. by Yoshio Suzuki, Junichi Miyake, and Mitsuaki Okabe (Tokyo: University of Tokyo Press, 1990).

Soltwedel, Rudiger, "Employment Problems in West Germany: The Role of Institutions, Labor Law, and Government Intervention," in *Stabilization Policies and Labor Markets, Carnegie-Rochester Conference Series on Public Policy* (Amsterdam), Vol. 28 (Spring 1988), pp. 153–220.

Summers, Lawrence H., "A Few Good Taxes," *New Republic* (Washington), November 30, 1987, pp. 14-15.

Swoboda, Alexander K., "Financial Integration and International Monetary Arrangements," in *The Evolution of the International Monetary System: How Can Efficiency and Stability Be Attained?* ed. by Yoshio Suzuki, Junichi Miyake, and Mitsuaki Okabe (Tokyo: University of Tokyo Press, 1990).

Taylor, John B., "Policy Analysis with a Multicountry Model," in *Macroeconomic Policies in an Interdependent World*, ed. by Ralph C. Bryant and others (Washington: Brookings Institution, Centre for Economic Policy Research, and International Monetary Fund, 1989).

Tobin, James, *A Proposal for International Monetary Reform*, Cowles Foundation for Research in Economics, Discussion Paper No. 506 (New Haven, Connecticut: Yale University, October 1978).

Tullio, Giuseppe, "Long Run Implications of the Increase in Taxation and Public Debt for Employment and Economic Growth in Europe," *European Economic Review* (Amsterdam), Vol. 31 (April 1987), pp. 741-74.

Wadhwani, Sushil, and Martin Wall, "The Effects of Profit-Sharing on Employment, Wages, Stock Returns and Productivity: Evidence from U.K. Micro-Data," *Economic Journal* (Oxford), Vol. 100 (March 1990), pp. 1-17.

Wallich, Henry C., "Institutional Cooperation in the World Economy," in *The World Economic System: Performance and Prospects*, ed. by Jacob A. Frenkel and Michael L. Mussa (Dover, Massachusetts: Auburn House, 1984).

Weale, Martin, and others, *Macroeconomic Policy: Inflation, Wealth and the Exchange Rate* (Winchester, Massachusetts: Unwin Hyman, 1989).

Weitzman, Martin L., *The Share Economy: Conquering Stagflation* (Cambridge, Massachusetts: Harvard University Press, 1984).

———, "The Simple Macroeconomics of Profit Sharing," *American Economic Review* (Nashville, Tennessee), Vol. 75 (December 1985), pp. 937-53.

Wicksell, Knut, *Interest and Prices* (London: Macmillan, 1936).

Williamson, John, "The Case for Roughly Stabilizing the Real Value of the Dollar," *American Economic Review, Papers and Proceedings* (Nashville, Tennessee), Vol. 79 (May 1989), pp. 41-45.

———, "Equilibrium Exchange Rates: An Update" (unpublished, October 1990).

———, and Marcus Miller, *Targets and Indicators: A Blueprint for the International Coordination of Economic Policy* (Washington: Institute for International Economics, 1987).

17

The Current Account and the Policy Mix Under Flexible Exchange Rates

Hans Genberg and Alexander K. Swoboda

The policy mix and assignment problems that figured so prominently in the economic literature of the 1960s fell somewhat out of fashion with the adoption of floating exchange rates by major industrial countries in the early 1970s. The Meadian conflict between external and internal balance and the Mundellian assignment of monetary policy to the balance of payments and of fiscal policy to internal balance did not seem of great practical relevance to a world in which the exchange rate, nominal and/or real, would adapt automatically to ensure equilibrium in the official settlements balance of payments. Although concern with the structure of the balance of payments was occasionally mentioned in the policy-mix literature, that was not a principal focus of the analysis. At a theoretical level, the assignment issue fell out of fashion as questions of effectiveness of monetary policy (the rational expectations-policy ineffectiveness debate) and fiscal policy (the Ricardian equivalence proposition) dominated the research agenda. Furthermore, to the extent that monetary and fiscal policies were considered together, it was suggested that the most appropriate way to analyze their interaction was to use an optimizing approach in which one single policymaker determines the appropriate stance of both policies simultaneously.[1]

---

[1] See Niehans (1968).

420

This paper returns to the tradition of the policy-mix and assignment literature but does so in the context of flexible exchange rates. There are a number of reasons why such an approach to contemporary international macroeconomic policy is appropriate. In the first place, flexibility of exchange rates has not removed external balance from the agenda of policy discussions. As concern began to mount about the increasingly large current account imbalances of the 1980s, the current account became an important subject of national and international policy discussions. Second, while some early optimism concerning the efficacy of sterilized interventions in the foreign exchange market seemed to suggest that the monetary authorities could manage both internal and external balance in the economy by a suitable combination of monetary control and intervention policy, it has become increasingly recognized that the room for independent monetary and exchange rate policies is extremely limited in the context of major industrial countries and regions.[2] Other policy instruments have consequently been brought back into focus, notably fiscal policy and commercial policy.

Once it is recognized that several policy instruments controlled by autonomous agencies must be used in order to attain the economy's macroeconomic goals, the question of coordination between these agencies reappears. It cannot be taken for granted that monetary policy, fiscal policy, and commercial policy will be determined in a coherent fashion as if they were set by a single optimizing policymaker. The central bank which sets monetary policy, the treasury or parliament which controls fiscal policy, and the foreign trade ministry which is responsible for trade policy are each subject to different political influences and constraints. Without some assignment of responsibility to each agency, it is quite conceivable that the desired macroeconomic targets will never be attained.[3]

Furthermore and perhaps more fundamentally, the assignment approach to policymaking can be justified on the basis of limited information both about the structure of the economy and the exact

---

[2] See Obstfeld (1990) for a recent evaluation.

[3] Policy discussions in the United States in the mid-1980s seem to be a case in point. There was considerable pressure on both monetary and commercial policy to deal with the mounting current account deficit. While these pressures do not seem to have derailed monetary management significantly, it can perhaps be argued that threats to use commercial policy to influence the balance of trade as a result of failure to consider alternative policy assignments led to a deterioration of the climate in multilateral trade negotiations.

nature of the disturbances that perturb it.[4] That is, the problem of assigning (adjusting) instruments to (discrepancies between actual and desired values of) target variables would arise with limited information even if all instruments were controlled and all targets set by one and the same policymaker.

A paper that attempts to deal with concrete policy problems is almost always inspired by specific historical events. The present one is no exception. The main arguments presented below were developed when the authors were visiting the International Monetary Fund in the spring of 1987.[5] At the time the persistently large deficit in the U.S. current account balance, in spite of the depreciation of the dollar from its peak in March 1985, was a major policy issue. Other concerns of the time were high real interest rates, low growth, and the threat of recession in a large number of countries.

At the time several schools of thought as to the appropriate policy response could be identified reflecting not only the difficulty of the problem but also a lack of agreed-upon framework of analysis. At one extreme there were those who argued that policymakers should not pay any attention to the current account on the grounds that it reflects optimal borrowing and lending plans of the private sector. Moreover, changes in fiscal policy would in any event have no significant influence on the current account because compensating changes in private sector saving would occur.[6]

Other analysts discounted the relevance of the Ricardian argument and stressed that correction of fiscal imbalances would have beneficial effects on current accounts. However, while some put the responsibility of adjustment primarily on the United States, others argued instead that fiscal policies should be expanded in Germany and Japan. This would have the same effect as a U.S. contraction as far as the current account was concerned, but it would not lead to a contraction in overall world demand at a time when recession was a genuine possibility.

For many economists the real foreign exchange value of the dollar was the main variable to focus on. What was needed was a further

---

[4] See Swoboda (1972).

[5] Genberg and Swoboda (1987 and 1989) were written during that visit. The paper published in 1989 contains many of the more analytical arguments. The present paper draws freely on the 1987 working paper of the same title which contained much of the policy analysis.

[6] Arguments and empirical evidence along these lines were presented in Evans (1986).

depreciation. Trade adjustment would follow in due course once J-curve effects had disappeared. How a real depreciation was to come about was less clear. "Talking down" the dollar was an approach that seemed to be favored by the U.S. Treasury, while using expansionary monetary policy was advocated by others who also thought a fall in interest rates was desirable on its own.

Finally, one should mention the frequently expressed view that attributed the current account deficit of the United States to restrictive trade practices elsewhere. The implied solution was to press for the opening of foreign markets (notably Japan), and, failing this, to impose trade restrictions at home.

Although the arguments in this paper were first conceived against the background of these events and opinions, we believe that they are more generally applicable and that they can be used as a guide for policy discussion today as well. One reason for this is that current account imbalances remain a significant feature of the world economy. It would not be surprising if they again become the source of tensions between surplus and deficit regions. The apparent demise of the Uruguay Round of trade negotiations may give a push to protectionist sentiments in many countries. As we witnessed in the mid-1980s, lingering trade imbalances could be used as "proof" of unfair trade practices and lead to calls for retaliation unless other, more appropriate, policy measures are taken. Similarly, threats of recession in deficit countries could make beggar-my-neighbor exchange rate policies seem attractive. In addition, the investment needed to rebuild the economies of Eastern Europe and the Soviet Union will certainly put a strain on available resources in the rest of the world which in turn will put upward pressure on real rates of interest. Unless an appropriate mix of policy responses in industrialized countries is forthcoming, the required capital movements may not come about, with harmful consequences for growth and development in Eastern Europe. The goal of this paper is to examine the principles on which such a policy mix should be based both at the national and at the world level.

The analysis starts in Section I by a brief discussion of the motivations for taking the current account as a target of policy. That section also contains a description of the main features of the principal alternatives to the assignment rules proposed in this paper, as well as a few remarks on the targets-instruments approach to policymaking and on the macroeconomic model that underlies much of the subsequent discussion. Section II deals with the small open economy case. It shows that, under floating exchange rates, fiscal policy has a comparative advantage in dealing with the current account and monetary policy with internal balance under fairly general conditions. It also shows that an assignment of policy instruments to targets based on the principle of effective market classification will be stable.

Section III turns to a multicountry model to discuss the causes of policy failures and their resolution. Its first part deals with the problem of securing enough instruments (here two monetary and two fiscal policies) to attain the targets of policy (here the two output or price levels, the world rate of interest, and current account balance). A second part discusses the assignment problem: how to assign specific instruments to specific targets in such a way as to converge on targets rather than diverge from them in a world of limited information. Part of the answer is seen to depend on the relative size of countries. Individual relatively small countries should aim their fiscal policy at their own current accounts; countries that are very large relative to the rest of the world should aim their fiscal policy at the world rate of interest.

Section IV reviews the conclusions of recent attempts to compare alternative assignment rules within the context of simulation models of the world economy, and Section V contains a summary of the main themes of the analysis.

It should be obvious by now that the themes of this paper are close to Jacques Polak's concerns and writings. On policy coordination, though we share some of his skepticism, we search, like him, for some simple rules. And our approach to the trade balance and the current account owes much to the absorption approach that he so perceptively helped pioneer.

I. The Current Account as a Policy Target, Alternative Assignment Rules, and Other Preliminaries

That the current account *should* be a target of macroeconomic policy is far from obvious; that it actually *is* seems a fact of life.

In a world of small countries, with full and symmetric information, competitive markets, flexible prices, and no externalities, there is no reason why the current account (or for that matter any "real" macroeconomic variable) should be a target of policy. Current account surpluses or deficits would simply reflect differences in productivity and/or time preference among countries and be a consequence of the efficient reallocation of capital from regions with an excess of saving over investment to regions with an excess of investment over saving. Respect of intertemporal budget constraints would ensure solvency and an appropriate time path of current accounts along "stages of the balance of payments" lines.

From a theoretical point of view, there are a few legitimate reasons why governments may want to influence their current accounts in a world of less than perfect competition. A large country with an influence on the rate of interest at which it borrows and lends may want, from a national though not a cosmopolitan perspective, to impose an "optimum tax" on capital movements. Some market failures may likewise suggest intervention in international lending and borrowing—but can usually be shown to be second best. In some instances, the government may have different time preference than the public and may wish therefore to interfere with capital movements, again usually a second best way to deal with the issue. On the whole, there appear to be few general analytical reasons for which the current account should be a target of policy.[7]

In practice, there are three main reasons why current accounts have become a target of policy. The first is that net exports are a component of aggregate demand and some governments see policy-engineered manipulation of the trade balance as a major tool of control of effective demand for their country's output. The second reason is concern with a country's net indebtedness position. This concern may be legitimate when the current account does not reflect "basic" differences between productivity and time preference at home and abroad. But it should be noted that in both of these first two cases the current account becomes a target because of inappropriate government policies, or an inappropriate policy mix, in other areas of economic life. The current account becomes a target of policy, as it were, because of the unwanted side effects of existing government policies.

A third reason for concern with current account imbalances is the protectionist sentiment to which they give rise, particularly in deficit

---

[7] For a fuller discussion of the current account as a target of policy and an indication of the argument's applicability to contemporary imbalances, see Corden (1991).

countries. The U.S. example comes immediately to mind. With higher net exports, employment and the manufacturing sector would fare far better, it is argued. The argument is of course incorrect and, again, related to failure of policy (or simply poorer-than-desired economic performance) in other areas. It is domestic plus foreign demand that governs total employment; it is relative competitiveness that governs the share of manufacturing versus other production in total output; and it is the current account that then reflects discrepancies between national saving and investment, public and private.

Be that as it may, it appears that the current account has become a target of policy. This paper analyzes the consequences under floating exchange rates in a simple macroeconomic framework that is consistent with a fairly wide class of standard static macroeconomic models of the open economy. The model is more fully developed in Genberg and Swoboda (1989) and little needs to be said here about its underlying structure other than that it is in the Mundell-Fleming tradition. It should be noted, however, that, as used below, it abstracts both from the dynamics that arise from the process of asset accumulation that follows from current account imbalances and from expectational dynamics. It also abstracts from asymmetrical wealth effects. Furthermore, for simplicity, fiscal policy is represented by government spending, tax revenue being assumed fixed. The analysis thus neglects the implications of tax versus spending changes and those of variations in the structure of government spending (as, for instance, between home and foreign goods).[8]

The central argument in this paper is that in a small economy with a flexible exchange rate aggregate fiscal policy should be assigned to the maintenance of external balance and monetary policy should be concerned with internal balance. In a world setting, a redundancy problem is obviously present in view of the summing-up constraint on current account balances. It is argued that this problem be solved either by a constraint on worldwide government spending or by assigning the maintenance of a target level of the world real interest rate to the fiscal instrument of the largest country in the system.

Other proposals have considered essentially the same targets of policy but have concluded that policy assignments should be differ-

---

[8]Some of these implications are discussed in Genberg and Swoboda (1989). Note also that the neglect of current account dynamics is not too damaging if the target value of the current account target is one of balance.

ent. Early exchange rate target zone proposals, for instance, were built on the idea that the exchange rate is the main causal variable behind trade balance adjustments. Since monetary policy exerts a strong influence on the exchange rate in a floating rate environment, it was concluded that monetary policy should be given the task of maintaining external balance.[9] Later versions of the target zone idea, especially the so-called "blueprint for international policy coordination,"[10] maintained the assignment of monetary policy to external balance and added the requirement that fiscal policy should be used to sustain an appropriate growth rate of domestic nominal aggregate demand. In addition, the average world real interest rate was to be adjusted so as to prevent the aggregate world level of nominal income from deviating substantially from the sum of the national target levels. Coordinated monetary policies would presumably be responsible for steering the average real interest rate.

Boughton (1989) suggests a pattern of assignments of monetary and fiscal policies that is closely related to that proposed here and in Genberg and Swoboda (1987). One feature of our analysis that is not treated explicitly by Boughton concerns the implications of the size of the country for the international aspect of the assignment rule.

Finally, a discussion of proposals for international policy coordination would be remiss unless it contained some reference to the recommendations made by McKinnon, even if these focus only on the international coordination of monetary policies and do not treat the assignment problem within each country.[11] McKinnon proposes an international monetary system essentially based on fixed exchange rates where $n-1$ countries target nominal exchange rates and the nth country steers the world rate of monetary expansion in such a way as to stabilize an index of world prices of traded goods. This proposal is thus quite different in spirit from the others in that it explicitly advocates substantial stability, if not complete fixity, of nominal exchange rates, whereas our, Boughton's, and Williamson's strategies are all set in a floating rate environment.

In the next two sections we present what we believe to be a solid theoretical case in favor of our assignment rules. A selective critical survey of some simulation studies that attempt to assess the stabilizing properties of alternative rules in the context of comprehensive empirical multicountry econometric models is given in Section IV.

---

[9] See Williamson (1983) and, for a critique, Genberg (1984).
[10] Williamson and Miller (1987).
[11] McKinnon (1988).

II. The Small Economy Case

Policy mix prescriptions to achieve internal and external balance in an open economy have two parts. The first, "static" component, is to ensure that there be as many independent instruments of policy as there are targets so that the targets can indeed all be achieved. The second, "dynamic" component, is Mundell's assignment rule that requires instruments to be assigned to targets, when there is limited information, in such a way as to ensure that the path of the economy converges to the targets and that the value of the instruments converge to their "optimal" setting. Mundell's famed solution to the conflict between internal and external balance under fixed exchange rates was first to show that capital mobility made it possible to use monetary and fiscal policy as independent instruments in the pursuit of the two objectives of internal balance and external balance, the latter defined as equilibrium in the official settlements balance of payments. Mundell then showed that assigning monetary policy to the balance of payments and fiscal policy to internal balance led to convergence to the targets while the reverse assignment was destabilizing to the economy.

It will be convenient to begin our discussion of the policy mix and assignment problems under floating exchange rates with the case of a small open economy unable to influence economic variables (prices, incomes, interest rates) abroad. This case, which abstracts from foreign repercussions and feedbacks, is also that most thoroughly investigated in the literature dealing with a fixed exchange rate regime. To allow comparison with that literature, it will also be convenient to carry the analysis below in terms of the simplest, fixed domestic price, version of the Mundell model under floating exchange rates. It should be noted, however, that the analysis holds qualitatively also for most more sophisticated static models of the open economy provided there is high enough a degree of capital mobility. A more general approach using a "semi-reduced form" version of standard macroeconomic models is used in Section III for the two-country case. It can easily be checked that most results below will also hold for that more general form.[12] As the standard Mundell-Fleming version is most familiar and very transparent, it is used in the small open economy case for expository purposes.

---

[12] See Genberg and Swoboda (1989).

The economy is in equilibrium when the demand for goods and services is equal to the supply, the demand for money is equal to the fixed supply, and the ex ante current account is equal to the net ex ante capital outflow.[13]

Suppose the authorities have a specific current account (or external) target, $\tilde{T}$, and a specific output (or internal) target, $\tilde{Y}$. What combination of instruments will allow these targets to be achieved? The answer is illustrated in Chart 1. The two instruments are the money stock and government spending (remember that the exchange rate is an endogenous variable and not a policy instrument). The internal balance line ($Y = \tilde{Y}$) slopes downward because an increase in government spending creates an excess demand for goods and services, the elimination of which requires a fall in the money supply that raises the interest rate and appreciates the currency—and hence decreases net export demand. When capital is perfectly mobile the internal balance line becomes horizontal. This reflects the well-known result that, with perfect capital mobility and for a small Mundell-Fleming country, a change in government spending crowds out an equal amount of net exports through the appreciation of the domestic currency it causes (and hence aggregate demand remains the same). Since the domestic interest rate stays at the level of the given world rate of interest, there is only one level of the money stock that is compatible with internal balance. The external balance schedule slopes upward because an increase in the money stock depreciates the currency and hence improves the

---

[13] The model can be written as:

$$S(Y) - T(Y, e) - I(i) - G = 0 \tag{1}$$
$$L(Y, i) - M/P = 0 \tag{2}$$
$$T(Y, e) + K(i, i^*) = 0 \tag{3}$$

where T is the trade balance and, neglecting interest income, also the current account; the remainder of the notation is conventional. Note that money balances are deflated by the price of domestic output which is assumed to be fixed (and can henceforth be set equal to 1), that is, output is assumed to be infinitely elastic with respect to the price of domestic goods. The main implication of deflating money balances by a general price index into which the exchange rate is weighted is that an increase in government spending now results in some expansion of domestic output and in less-than-full crowding out of net exports even in the case of perfect capital mobility. Note also that saving and the trade balance depend on output and not on expenditure and that saving and hence expenditure do not depend on the terms of trade. Note, finally, that in this simplest version of the Mundell-Fleming model capital flows depend on the level of the home and foreign interest rates and that the model neglects asset accumulation and its consequences.

Chart 1.   Policies for Internal and External Balance

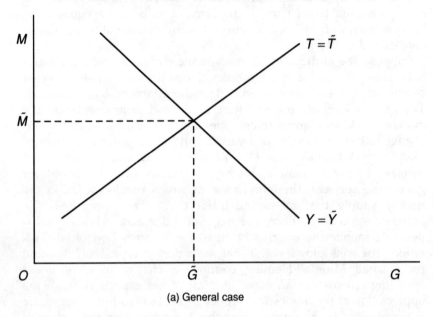

(a) General case

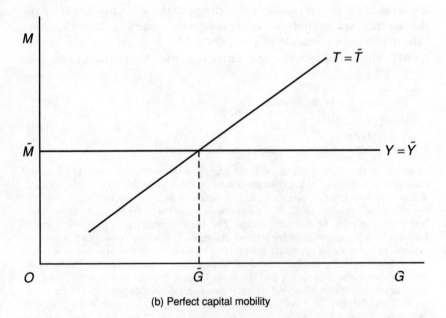

(b) Perfect capital mobility

balance of trade (the Marshall-Lerner condition is assumed to hold); an increase in government spending is required to deteriorate the balance of trade either by bringing about an increase in output and hence imports, or by appreciating the currency, or both.

With perfect information and no constraints on instrument values, all that is required to achieve internal and external balance simultaneously is to set M at $\tilde{M}$ and G at $\tilde{G}$ and let the economy converge to equilibrium.

With imperfect information, the assignment problem becomes relevant. Two assignments suggest themselves. The first would let fiscal policy deal with the current account (raise government spending whenever there is a surplus in the current account relative to target) and monetary policy deal with internal balance (increase the money stock to fight unemployment). The second ("reversed") assignment would have government spending increase whenever there is unemployment and the money stock decrease whenever there is an excess trade surplus in order to appreciate the domestic currency and hence decrease net exports.[14] The fact that the current account is equal to the sum of the excess of private saving over investment and of the government budget surplus would suggest that fiscal policy has a comparative advantage in dealing with the current account and that the first assignment is preferable to the second. That comparative advantage becomes evident as the degree of capital mobility increases since, with perfect capital mobility, a change in government spending has a one for one effect on the trade balance and no effect on output. Hence, the first pairing of instruments to targets will be called the "natural assignment," and the second the "reversed assignment" below.

The two assignments are illustrated for the case of perfect capital mobility in Chart 2. The diagram suggests, and mathematical analysis confirms, that, though both assignments eventually converge, the natural pairing leads directly to policy equilibrium whereas the reversed assignment is likely to result in a cyclical approach to equilibrium (with corresponding cycles in output, interest, and exchange rates). This likelihood decreases as capital becomes less and less mobile. This analysis confirms the comparative advantage of using fiscal policy to deal with the current account balance. It

---

[14] It can be shown that trying to get rid of a surplus by increasing the money stock to increase output and induced imports while aiming fiscal policy at internal balance would put the economy on an explosive path.

Chart 2.   Alternative Assignment Rules

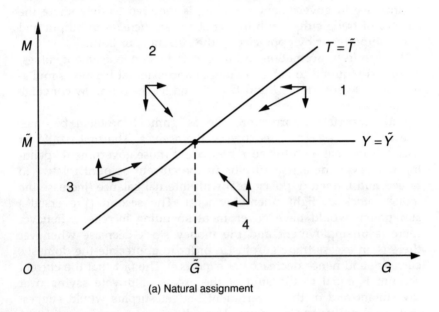

(a) Natural assignment

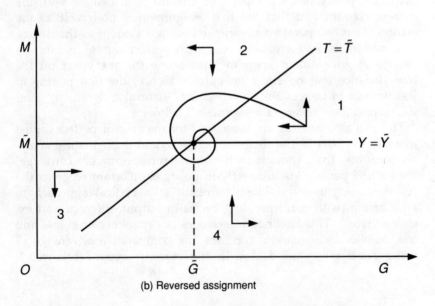

(b) Reversed assignment

1: Inflation/deficit   3: Unemployment/surplus
2: Inflation/surplus   4: Unemployment/deficit

suggests, moreover, that trying to use other means, in particular trying to influence the current account indirectly by using the exchange rate as an intermediate target of monetary policy with the current account as the ultimate objective, is likely to provoke cycles that may ultimately prove destabilizing to the economy as a whole whenever it is subject to shocks and once expectations effects are taken into account.

It is important to notice that the result of the previous paragraph is not sensitive to the particular assumptions that we have imposed on the model used here. We have shown elsewhere (Genberg and Swoboda (1989)) that the comparative advantage of fiscal policy as a current account instrument obtains also if the exchange rate influences the money market equilibrium directly via a consumer price index that deflates nominal money balances. Furthermore, incorporating into the model an aggregate supply structure based on a labor market in which there is some degree of wage indexation does not alter this result. Fiscal policy should still be assigned to the external balance target whether nominal wages are completely rigid or completely indexed to the domestic consumer price index. Finally, the result does not depend critically on the static expectations assumption. Introducing forward-looking exchange rate expectations does not alter the assignment rule if export- and import-demand functions are sufficiently price elastic.

To ensure that the world economy moves towards its desired state is, of course, the motivation for analyzing the assignment problem. Lest the importance of designing proper assignment systems be underestimated, it may be worth noting that many of the policy problems of the 1960s and, to some extent, the breakdown of the Bretton Woods system, can be attributed not only to a shortage of instruments but also to an inappropriate assignment (under fixed exchange rates) of monetary policy to the pursuit of internal balance. Improper assignment leads to increasing discrepancies between actual and target values of economic variables and, eventually, to abrupt reversals in policies or the breakdown of the system.

One may, however, ask why an assignment that leads to a direct rather than cyclical approach to policy equilibrium should be preferred if both assignments ultimately converge. One reason is simply that a cyclical approach may involve reversals in resource allocation that are likely to be costly and could be avoided if the approach were direct. Another reason is that an assignment that makes for a direct approach is likely to be more robust than one that implies a cyclical approach to equilibrium; at the limit the cyclical approach can veer to the borderline case where the system oscillates endlessly around equilibrium without ever reaching it. Finally, there are "practical" reasons why a direct approach would appear preferable. First, a cyclical approach of target variables to their long-run values implies a cyclical approach of instruments to their long-run values that may well be politically and administratively difficult to justify. Second, a cyclical approach implies that, at least over some ranges, some disequilibria will grow temporarily larger. This may well be taken as a sign of policy failure and lead to policy reversals that would prove destabilizing and damaging to the economy.[15]

III. The Policy Mix in a Multicountry Setting

So far it has been assumed that the country undertaking policies to achieve its various goals was small. This part of the paper turns to a two-country model of the policy mix to analyze some problems both of national policy and of coordination when countries are large enough for foreign repercussions to be important.

Our concern will be mainly with "policy failure" and how to prevent it. That is, why would targets fail to be achieved and what can and should be done to correct the situation. Policy mix models typically focus on two sources of policy failure: a shortage of instruments relative to targets due either to an overabundance of targets or to constraints on allowable values of instruments; and an improper assignment of instruments to targets in the presence of limited information, leading to movements away from rather than toward targets.[16]

---

[15]The discussion has proceeded on the assumption that G and M could actually be set at their optimal values. In practice, however, there are often limits on the values that policy instruments can take, especially in the short run. For instance, the political process may prevent government spending from being lowered sufficiently. The consequences of such limitations are discussed in Genberg and Swoboda (1987). That paper also considers alternatives to fiscal policy, such as capital controls and "talking currencies up or down," as instruments for attaining current account targets. It finds them seriously wanting.

[16]There are other possible sources of failure, for example, multiple solutions, linearly related targets, breakdown of systematic relationship between targets and instruments (policy ineffectiveness), model disagreement, disagreement as to the actual state of various economies, and inconsistent (conflicting) target values for "shared" variables, such as the current account, across countries, and so forth. These are not analyzed below even though some of them are mentioned in passing.

To make some headway and to keep the exposition relatively simple, we will make use here, unlike in Section II, of "semi-reduced form" relationships between targets and instruments that can be more formally deduced from a variety of versions of standard two-country macroeconomic models (of which the two-country version of the Mundell-Fleming model is one, but only one, example).[17] These relationships, or derivatives of target variables with respect to instruments, are "medium run" in the sense that interest rates, the exchange rate, and either income or prices are allowed to adjust. We neglect, however, as we did in Section II, the effects of adjustments in asset stocks and the dynamics they imply, as well as the dynamics that arise from explicitly taking into account expectations formation mechanisms.[18] The argument considers two polar cases: rigidity of the domestic currency price of national outputs and full price flexibility. It also assumes perfect capital mobility (in the sense that domestic interest rates are equalized across countries in the static equilibria that are analyzed).

The relationships we assume are summarized in Table 1 both for the rigid prices/unemployment and for the flexible prices/full employment cases. The results are familiar ones. Consider, first, the main entries in the unemployment case. A domestic monetary expansion lowers interest rates worldwide (r_w), causes a depreciation of the home currency (an increase in e), an improvement in the trade balance (T), an increase in output at home (Y), and a fall in output abroad (Y^*). Had prices been flexible and output at full employment, the increase in the home money supply would have been neutral and would merely have increased home currency prices (P) and the exchange rate by an equal amount, leaving foreign variables, the interest rate, and the real exchange rate (eP^*/P) unaffected. For the unemployment case, the signs in parenthesis refer to the Mundell model when the home country becomes very

---

[17] See, in particular, Mundell (1968), Chapter 18 and Appendix. See also Frenkel and Razin (1987) for a recent exposition of the Mundell-Fleming model together with some indications of its shortcomings, and Mussa (1979) for an analysis of transmission mechanisms under alternative exchange rate regimes. It is of interest to note that Mussa (p. 180) mentions in passing that the differences in transmission mechanisms that operate under fixed and flexible exchange rates suggest that policy assignment under floating rates should be the opposite of that recommended for fixed rates. He does not elaborate further on this remark, however.

[18] For a fuller analysis that incorporates some of these factors and concentrates on the current account, see Genberg and Swoboda (1989).

Table 1. Effects of Instruments on Target Variables

	Instruments			
	M	M^*	G	G^*
Targets				
	Rigid prices			
Y	+	−	+ (0)	+
Y^*	− (0)	+	+ (0)	+
T	+	−	− (−1)	+ (0)
r_w	− (0)	−	+ (0)	+
e	+	−	? (−)	? (+)
	Flexible prices			
P	+	0	+	+
P^*	0	+	+	+
TB	0	0	−	+
r_w	0	0	+	+
eP^*/P	0	0	−	+

Note: The values in parentheses refer to the special cases where $(Y/Y^*) \to 0$ and the Mundell-Fleming structure is assumed. They are given for these cases where they tend to the limiting values of 0 or 1, or where they differ from the general case.

small relative to the rest of the world (the starred country), the case discussed in Section II above. In that case a domestic monetary expansion fails to have any effect abroad.

Turning to fiscal policy, an increase in government spending at home (an increase in G) raises interest rates, attracts capital from abroad (thus financing the trade deficit it causes), and results in an increase in output both at home and abroad. The effect on the nominal exchange rate (and hence on the real exchange rate with fixed home currency prices) is ambiguous, although there is a presumption that the home currency will appreciate unless behavior parameters differ widely across the two countries. For a very small country, an increase in government spending merely crowds out exports, deteriorating the balance of trade by an equal amount, via the appreciation in the home currency, leaving all other variables unchanged. In contrast, for a very large country (the world in the limit), it is investment that gets crowded out, though usually not by an equal amount, by a rise in government spending, and the balance of trade is left unchanged. In the full employment case, it is price levels rather than incomes that rise in both countries whenever there is a fiscal expansion anywhere. This follows from the fact that, with perfect capital mobility, interest rates rise everywhere. What gets affected differentially depending on the origin of the fiscal policy is the trade balance, which deteriorates for the country where the increase in government spending originates, and the real exchange rate which appreciates for that same country.

One feature of these by and large familiar results is worth special emphasis. Under floating exchange rates with capital mobility it is fiscal policy that generalizes to the world economy. This result offers a striking contrast with a fixed exchange rate regime where it is monetary policy that generalizes to the world: domestic monetary policy affects output, price levels, and interest rates to the extent that it affects the world money stock and in proportion to its share in the latter; fiscal policy is, as it were, "country-specific." Under floating rates the reverse is true: with a high degree of capital market integration national fiscal policy has a worldwide impact since it affects interest rates everywhere; monetary policy, on the other hand, tends to be "country-specific." This insight is pursued further, and turns out to be important, in the discussion of the policy mix that proceeds in two steps. We begin with an examination of the comparative statics of the policy mix: how can instruments be combined to reach various targets in our two-country context? And what can cause policy failure in that context? We then turn to a discussion of the dynamics of the assignment of instruments to targets when information on the structure of the world economy is limited. We pay particular attention to the role of the relative size of countries in that context.

The Policy Mix: Statics

For a single country, the two targets of internal and external balance could be reached by an appropriate combination of monetary and fiscal policy, provided no constraint was put on the range of the instruments. The two-country counterpart suggests a surfeit of instruments. We have four instruments, monetary and fiscal policy in each of the two countries, to reach three independent targets: internal balance at home and abroad, and current account equilibrium. That there are only three independent targets of policy derives of course from the fact that the home country's current account surplus is the rest of the world's current account deficit. The $n-1$ problem, of fixed exchange rate fame, resurfaces: one of the four instruments can be used to pursue some additional policy goal. Failure to reach all policy targets in a static, perfect information context can arise from three reasons: (1) constraints on the value of instruments; (2) the introduction of additional targets; and (3) failure to agree on what constitutes current account equilibrium. We discuss the perfect information, static, two-country case briefly in the present section.

Beginning with the rigid prices/unemployment case, suppose, first, that the two countries are only concerned with internal balance. The two internal balance targets can be reached indifferently through the use of monetary policy in both countries, of fiscal policy in both, or of fiscal in one and monetary policy in the other, as Chart 3 illustrates. Ignore the dashed, trade, or current account, equilibrium schedules for the moment. The slopes of the home and foreign internal balance schedules, II and I^*I^*, can be determined from the derivatives in Table 1.[19]

The internal balance schedules are drawn for given values of the remaining (unused for internal balance) instruments. As the chart makes clear, it is always possible to find a combination of values of the two used instruments that allows for fulfillment of the two countries' output targets. This combination, given the values of the redundant instruments, is unique except in the case of perfect capital mobility where government expenditure at home and abroad are used to obtain target outputs, the case illustrated in panel (b).

That case deserves further discussion. With perfect capital mobility, it is the sum of government spending at home and abroad (given taxes) that, given the money stocks in the two countries, determines both the world interest rate and world output, the sum of outputs in the two countries. In other words, as shown in Genberg and Swoboda (1989), perfect capital mobility and fixed prices make it possible to add the two countries' IS and LM curves into a world IS and LM curve that determines the world's output

---

[19]The relative values of the slopes of the schedules can be derived from specific model formulations as well as more general (stability) considerations. For instance, in panel (a), II will be steeper than I^*I^* if the effect of a change in M on home output Y, (dY/dM), is greater than its effect on foreign output (dY^*/dM), a reasonable condition on, or outcome of, most standard models.

and interest rate. There exists a unique *sum* of government expenditures for which, given the two money supplies, world output will be distributed among the two countries in such a way as to ensure that full employment obtains simultaneously in both countries. From such a point, suppose home government spending decreases and foreign spending increases by the same amount: the world interest rate is unaffected and hence, given the money supplies in the two countries, national outputs are unaffected.[20] Since the interest rate and output levels are unaffected, the current account of the home country must have improved by an amount exactly equal to the decrease in home government spending. The home currency depreciates to effect the change in the trade balance (the crowding in of exports).[21]

Adding a current account target to the internal balance goals of the two countries is easily accommodated within Chart 3 as long as the two countries agree on what that target is. Assume for simplicity that a zero current account balance is the sought-after target. This target is represented by the dashed *CA* lines in the chart. There will always exist a combination of the two remaining instruments that ensures that the three target lines intersect at the same point. The "only" problem is that the two remaining instruments cannot be used independently; the redundancy of the fourth instrument must be respected lest the system be overdetermined.

The fourth instrument could also be used to pursue an additional goal. There is one additional goal that naturally suggests itself in the present context: the world interest rate. Suppose, for instance, that a low interest rate becomes a target in order to foster investment and growth in the long run; suppose also that countries agree on what that low interest rate should be. The four targets—two internal balances, current account equilibrium, and a given world rate of

---

[20] In terms of panel (a), the internal balance schedules depend on home and foreign government spending. The decrease in G shifts II to the right by an amount Z, the increase in G^* shifts it back to the left by the same amount, leaving II in its original position. Similarly the net effect of the two changes is to leave I^*I^* in its original position. The dashed curve, however, shifts to the left showing that at M_0, M_0^*, the home country now has a current account surplus.

[21] This discussion abstracts from possible Laursen-Metzler effects of the change in the terms of trade on saving, from influences of the exchange rate on the domestic price level and hence on real balances, from exchange rate induced wealth effects, and from the direct influence of the exchange rate on aggregate supply. Incorporating these factors into the analysis would make the II and I^*I^* schedules in Chart 1 panel (b) distinct. Unique values of G and G^* could then be determined in this case as well.

Chart 3. The Pursuit of Internal Balance

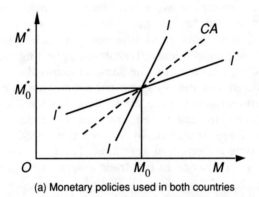

(a) Monetary policies used in both countries

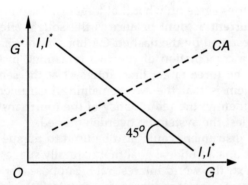

(b) Fiscal policies used in both countries

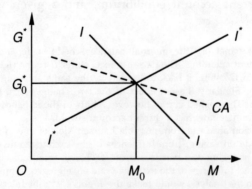

(c) Monetary policies at home, fiscal policies abroad

interest—can in principle be attained with the four instruments—the two monetary and the two fiscal policies. This is illustrated in Chart 4 in the G, G* plane for the case of perfect capital mobility.

Before proceeding to the illustration, it will be convenient to examine the determinants of the slope of the CA line. It stands to reason that the CA line should be upward sloping. An increase in home government expenditure deteriorates the balance of trade and must be compensated by an increase in government expenditure abroad if current account balance is to be maintained. More precisely, the slope of the CA line is $-(dT/dG)/(dT/dG^*)$. Since the size of the derivative of the trade balance with respect to G is inversely related to the size of the country, the slope of the CA line will go from ∞ (vertical) when the home country is infinitesimally small to 0 (horizontal) when the foreign, starred, country is infinitesimally small. More precisely, the slope of the CA line is given by

$$\frac{dG^*}{dG}\bigg|_{CA} = \frac{Y^*}{Y} \cdot \Omega,$$

**Chart 4.   Fiscal Policies for Current Account and
Real Interest Rate Targets**

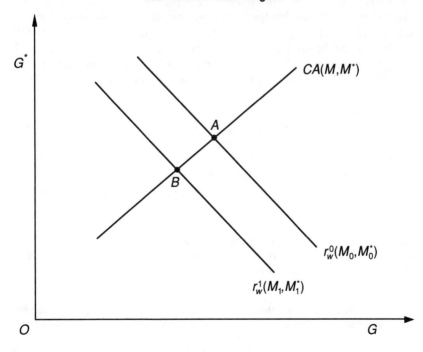

where Ω is a constant that depends on the behavior parameters in the two economies. If these behavior parameters are identical across countries, that is, if countries differ only in size, Ω will be equal to one.[22]

Turn now to Chart 4. Suppose that all four targets are initially met at point A, but that the authorities in both countries wish to see the world interest rate lowered. The II, I^*I^* line has been rebaptized r_w to indicate that along that line, given the two money supplies, the rate of interest is constant. What should be done to lower the rate of interest from r_w^0 to r_w^1? One obvious suggestion would be to lower the sum of G and G^*. To maintain current account balance the sum should be lowered so as to maintain the proportion Ω (Y^*/Y): the two countries should decrease government spending by the same percentage of their respective gross national products. The reduction in government spending, however, would create an excess supply of output unless matched by an increase in money supplies. For the world as a whole, the leftward shift in the IS curve has to be accompanied by a rightward shift of the LM curve to keep world output constant at a lower interest rate. How the rise in money supply is to be apportioned among countries will depend on the value of various behavior parameters in the two countries. If the countries differ only with respect to size, the two money supplies should be increased by the same percentage; in that case, the CA curve will remain unaffected and the new equilibrium will be at B.

The precise combination of instrument values that will achieve all targets simultaneously would be extremely difficult to estimate in practice. This suggests that one may want to consider a decentralized system of response to ensure a converging approach to policy equilibrium. Some aspects of this question will be examined in the next section. In the meantime, we note that the discussion so far suggests that the sum of governmental spending in the two countries plays a crucial role in determining the world rate of interest and that their difference determines the current account balance. This, in turn, suggests the pairing of instruments and targets given in Table 2.

To determine whether such a pairing is dynamically stable or not, and whether other pairings are unstable, requires a full mathematical analysis that is beyond the scope of this paper, although some elements of an answer are presented in the next section.

---

[22] It can be checked that these conclusions hold both for the rigid and for the flexible prices standard models.

Table 2. Pairing of Instruments and Targets

Target	Instruments
r_w	$G + G^*$
CA	$G - G^*$
Y	M
Y^*	M^*

Consideration of the full employment, flexible price case, however, suggests that it is the correct pairing. For, in that case, money is neutral and the Y, Y^* targets can be replaced by P and P^* targets. Neutrality of money ensures that the r_w and CA lines in Chart 4 are independent of the money supplies, M and M^* (in Table 1, $(dT/dM) = (dr/dM) = (dT/dM^*) = 0$). In other words, in a run long enough for money to be neutral, there is no substitute for fiscal measures to achieve current account equilibrium at an appropriate level of real interest rates.

The Assignment Problem: Dynamics

Even if there are as many instruments as there are targets, reaching the latter is no mean task unless information is perfect. If it is, all that is needed is to set the instruments at their optimum static value and wait for the economic system to reach all targets; better still, if one also knows the full dynamics of the system, one should move the instruments to their final value at a speed that maximizes some social welfare function that takes adjustment costs into account. Unfortunately, knowledge of the behavior parameters underlying the derivatives of Table 1 is far from perfect;[23] knowledge of the system's dynamics is even more imperfect and the economy is continually subjected to unpredictable shocks. Supposing that available information is confined to the signs of the derivatives mentioned above and to the state of the economy at a moment in time (whether there is a surplus or a deficit in the current account, whether there is unemployment or inflation, etc.), can one design a system of policy adjustment, or response, which is robust in the sense that it will lead to eventual convergence toward the targets of policy or at least not systematically away from them? This is the

---

[23] See, for instance, Frankel (1988).

motivation for Mundell's assignment proposition that enjoins that instruments be assigned to targets according to their comparative advantage in reaching those targets. The principle was illustrated in Section II for the case of the small open economy.

Analysis of various assignments when the number of targets is larger than two becomes rather complex. A few points about assignment in the two-country case can nevertheless be made. First, consider the pursuit of internal balance in the two countries, neglecting current account balance considerations. It turns out that the following pairing of instruments to targets are all stable: both countries use monetary policy, both countries use fiscal policy, one country uses monetary policy and the other fiscal policy. This can be shown formally but the analysis is too cumbersome to be repeated here. Adding a current account target and assigning one of the remaining instruments to it does not add an obvious element of instability for some assignments and not for others. If countries are similar in terms of behavior parameters (they differ mainly in size), various assignments all appear to be stable.

There is, however, one important sense in which fiscal policy should be assigned to the current account in that case. In the long run monetary policy loses its influence on the current account and, by necessity, fiscal policy has to be assigned to it. Although price rigidities may render monetary policy effective for current account adjustment in the short run, this should not be used to propose a strategy in which monetary policy is assigned to external balance even if such a strategy could be shown to lead to a convergence of the economy to the desired values of the target variables.[24] The reason is that such an assignment would have to be reversed in the medium to long run in order to be consistent with the effects of monetary policy at that horizon. It is not at all clear how such a switch in policy responsibilities could be effected, and the resulting uncertainties would almost certainly be used as an excuse for inaction in the transition.

Formal analysis of the assignment problem when all four instruments are used to attain all four targets is quite complex and has not been carried out yet. We suspect, however, that any assignment

---

[24] In a true dynamic model in which expectations about the future play an important role it is also possible that policy rules which imply that a nominal policy instrument should try to steer a real variable may be unstable. This could come about even if monetary policy is not neutral in the model in question over the short run. For a further illustration of this point, see Section IV.

other than the one suggested in Table 2 will prove unstable; this assignment is, after all, the floating rate counterpart to the fixed exchange rate rule that requires monetary policy to be devoted to the overall balance of payments (and fiscal policy to internal balance) if policy convergence is to be attained. Again, this proposition must be true in the long run when the ability of monetary policy to affect real variables such as the real rate of interest, the real exchange rate, or output levels weakens.

In fact, we can say something more precise about the assignment problem when money essentially controls national price levels. There remains the problem of achieving the target levels of the real interest rate and of the current account. Consider once more the G, G^* plane and the CA and r_w lines as in Chart 4. Suppose that our country and the rest of the world agree on the appropriate real rate of interest and state of the current account. Given perfect information this agreement would be sufficient to determine government spending in the two regions. In the absence of perfect information, however, is there any way of reaching point A without knowing its exact location? Suppose that we let the home country adopt the following rule: increase government spending whenever you experience a current account surplus (and vice versa in case of a deficit); and the foreign country lower its government spending whenever the interest rate is above r_w^0 and raise spending whenever r_w is too low. The outcome is illustrated by the arrows of motion in panel (a) of Chart 5. As the path from B to A indicates, this division of tasks leads to convergence to the policy targets.[25] Note that letting, instead, the home country target the rate of interest and the rest of the world target the current account would also lead to convergence, as illustrated in panel (b). It would seem that it does not matter who looks after what target as long as a clear division of tasks is adopted.

In fact, it turns out that who should target what variable depends on the relative size of countries. If one country is quite small and the other quite large, the first should use fiscal policy to adjust the current account and the large country should target the world rate of interest if the approach to equilibrium is to be direct rather than cyclical. Why a direct approach is preferable was discussed at some length in Section II. This proposition is illustrated in Chart 6. Recall that the slope of the CA line is an inverse function of the home country's size. As the home country becomes infinitesimally small

---

[25] Genberg and Swoboda (1987) contains a formal proof.

Chart 5. Assignment Rules for Fiscal Policies in a Two-Country World

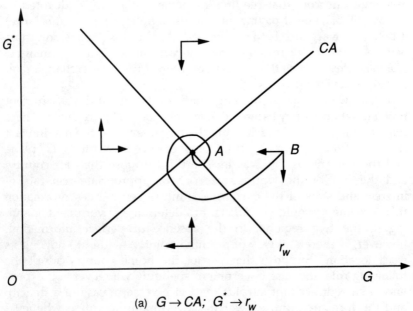

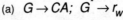

(a) $G \rightarrow CA; \; G^* \rightarrow r_w$

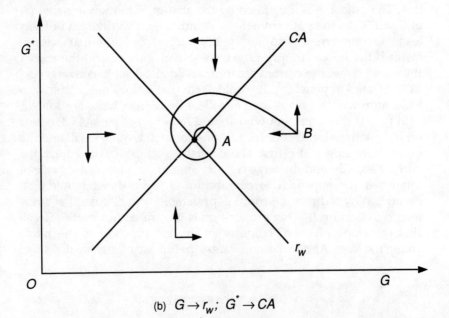

(b) $G \rightarrow r_w; \; G^* \rightarrow CA$

Chart 6.   Assignment Rules When Countries Are of Different Size

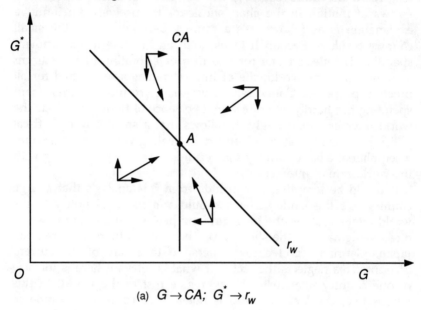

(a) $G \rightarrow CA;\ G^* \rightarrow r_w$

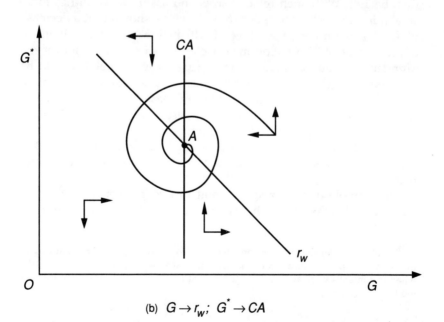

(b) $G \rightarrow r_w;\ G^* \rightarrow CA$

relative to the other country, the *CA* line becomes vertical. The arrows of motion in the chart speak for themselves. An intuitive explanation is as follows. As a country becomes small, the small country result of Section II takes hold: an increase in government spending is reflected one for one in a deterioration of the current account while the world rate of interest remains unaffected for all practical purposes. Conversely, a very large country's government spending has hardly any effect on its balance of trade but affects the world interest rate strongly. It follows that a small country's fiscal policy has a comparative advantage in dealing with current account disequilibria, a large country's government spending in dealing with the world rate of interest.

It would be tempting to conclude from this analysis that a large country like the United States should aim its fiscal policy at the world interest rate in the long run (and perhaps at sustaining world effective demand in the short run) leaving it to others, for example, Japan, Germany, and a few others, to take care of the current account. This neglects the fact that what is relevant here is the size of one country relative to the aggregate rest of the world. In this perspective, the United States is not a large country: the ratio of U.S. output to rest of the (relevant) world output would perhaps be of the order of 1:3 (the ratio of U.S. output to world output would then be 1:4). With such relative sizes and assuming countries to be similar in their behavior parameters, it can be shown that a decrease in U.S. Government spending of $10 billion would result in an improvement of $7.5 billion in that country's current account if the Mundell two-country model under perfect capital mobility is to be believed. The relative size criterion thus does not support the notion that it is up to the rest of the world to increase its spending to solve the U.S. current account problem, unless it is argued that world interest rates are too low. There is, of course, also the complication that the rest of the world is not a single country, which makes assigning the responsibility for the world interest rate a difficult matter.[26]

The example does, however, point to two problems. In the first place, coordination through assignment rules becomes much more

---

[26] Swoboda (1990) suggests that an alternative to the relative size criterion may be to assign the task of current account adjustment to the fiscal policy of deficit countries when real interest rates are too high and to that of surplus countries when they are too low.

difficult when the world is composed of several medium-sized countries: there is no clear criterion for assigning responsibility for the world interest rate to any one of them even though it would seem natural for each to aim its fiscal policy at its current account. Second, agreement on the target value of shared variables (the world interest rate or the current account) may become much more difficult to reach.

IV. Evidence on Assignment Rules from Simulation Models

The position taken in this paper (and by Boughton (1989)) that monetary policy should, under floating exchange rates, be used to achieve internal balance and that fiscal policy should be assigned to external balance is not shared by everyone. In Section I we noted that the well-known extended target zone proposal essentially advocates the reversed assignment. Since it is not possible to show conclusively that one assignment is stable and all alternatives are not even in simple symmetric models, it appears that some form of empirical evidence is needed to decide which set of rules is superior. Once more complicated models are considered, especially those incorporating endogenous dynamic adjustment and expectations, the need to go beyond analytical evaluations of alternative policy rules becomes even more acute, since in the more comprehensive models the assignment problem soon becomes analytically intractable.

In response to the difficulties in obtaining analytically clear-cut results, a number of studies have recently been undertaken using multicountry simulation models with the aim of evaluating the performance of alternative policy rules. Those that attempt to deal specifically with the type of assignment rules considered in this paper include Currie and Wren-Lewis (1989), Frenkel, Goldstein, and Masson (1989 and 1990), and McKibbin and Sachs (1989). The typical procedure followed in these studies is first to specify a baseline path of the model which often is intended to replicate a given historical period. Fluctuations around this baseline path are generated by subjecting the model to stochastic shocks. These shocks are temporary in nature so that the economy has a natural tendency to return to the baseline. Next, alternative policy rules are incorporated into the model and the stochastic simulation is calculated in each case. The policy rules are always specified in such a way that the target values that they try to reach correspond to the *known* baseline path of the target variable. Finally, the policy rules are compared according to some statistic measuring the variability of the economy around the baseline (target) path.

The results that have emerged from these studies are not conclusive. Currie and Wren-Lewis suggest that the assignment implicit in the extended target zone proposal yields a superior performance than the alternative proposed here. The results obtained by Frenkel, Goldstein, and Masson are somewhat less categorical in that they identify circumstances in which one or the other rule dominates. McKibbin and Sachs report long-run stability problems with their implementation of the extended target zone proposal, but they do not report results pertaining to our alternative policy assignments.

While the results from these simulation studies are interesting, they do not yet answer the questions addressed in this paper. The reason is the procedure used in setting up the simulations.[27] As already noted, this procedure implies that the researcher is investigating the economy's fluctuations around the baseline path which represents the steady-state path as well as the target path of the economy. But the procedure is not capable of shedding any light on what would happen if that steady-state path were changed as a result of a permanent shock to the system or if the target path were defined independently from the baseline. In other words, the simulation studies carried out so far are incapable of answering how alternative policy rules would perform when the exact nature of the new steady-state path is not known and when the desired values of the target variables are defined without reference to the simulation model itself. But these are precisely the problems posed in the assignment literature and which the analysis presented in this paper has attempted to address. This implies that, to be able to propose policy assignments that can be implemented by a policymaker who has only limited information about the nature of the economy and the shocks to which it is subjected, and who has to specify what his targets for policy are, we still must rely on theoretical arguments for guidance. In this respect we believe that the assignment rules proposed in this paper are preferable.

---

[27]McCallum (1990) criticizes the standard simulation approach followed in most studies from a methodological standpoint.

V. Capital Mobility, Fiscal Policy, and Coordination: A Summary

One consequence of capital mobility is that it makes for a great deal of macroeconomic interdependence under floating exchange rates, an interdependence that under fixed exchange rates would exist even in its absence. The nature of the interdependence, however, differs as between the two exchange rate regimes. Under fixed exchange rates, it is the world money stock that is the "world instrument," affecting interest rates (and hence outputs) in the short run and the world price level (but not interest rates) in the long run. Under fixed exchange rates, the price level is a common variable. Under floating exchange rates, it is the sum of individual countries' fiscal policies ("world fiscal policy") that is the "world instrument" affecting the world level of interest rates in the short and long runs; under floating exchange rates, monetary policy is country-specific, at least in the long run.

It is the nature of this interdependence that, together with long-run neutrality of money, gives "world fiscal policy" its comparative advantage in dealing with the world rate of interest, the common variable under floating. The comparative advantage of the sum of national government expenditures (and taxes) in dealing with r_w and that of the differences in government expenditure and tax levels in dealing with the current account constitutes a second main theme of this paper. Ultimately, the main general instrument (and one of the only relatively efficient ones) for dealing with current account imbalances is fiscal policy.

A third theme concerns the implications for policy coordination. Successful policy coordination in practice has three key ingredients: ensuring that there are enough instruments; assigning them to targets in stabilizing fashion; and securing international agreement on the target value of shared (common) variables.

This paper has concentrated attention on four target variables in a two-country setting: the two output levels (price levels in the long run), the current account, and the world level of interest rates. It has identified four instruments to deal with these targets: the two monetary and the two fiscal policies. Constraints on the admissible values of monetary policies are likely to be less severe than those on fiscal instruments. This suggests that restoring flexibility in fiscal policies, at least in the long run, is a first requirement to avoid that a shortage of instruments leads to policy conflict and failure to achieve real interest rate and current account balance targets.

With an equal number of targets and instruments, policy equilibrium exists but may not be reached unless the assignment of targets to instruments is appropriate. We have given a number of reasons why the assignment suggested in Table 2 should be appropriate. One part of the assignment turns out to be crucial from a long-run perspective: the assignment of the sum of governments' expenditures to the world rate of interest, that of their difference to the current account. If that assignment is to be achieved in a decentralized fashion—in the sense that each country sets its level of government spending independently of the other's—we have also suggested that, in a two-country context, the small country's fiscal policy be aimed at the current account, the large country's at the world rate of interest.

Finally, equality of the number of target variables and instruments, together with proper assignment, will not succeed in eliminating conflict if various countries insist at one and the same time on different values for a shared variable. Goal agreement is indispensable. Such agreement in practice can be achieved in some bargain that concerns both target and instrument values (that moves instruments in the direction suggested by the proper assignment of instruments to targets).

An efficient bargain is one that is consistent with the long-run logic of interdependence under the ruling exchange rate regime, respects the direction of proper assignments, and incorporates goal agreement on shared variables. Efficiency is a requirement for credibility of the bargain; and without credibility the bargain would, in any event, be defeated by markets and be ineffective.

REFERENCES

Boughton, James M., "Policy Assignment Strategies with Somewhat Flexible Exchange Rates," in *Blueprints for Exchange-Rate Management*, ed. by Marcus Miller, Barry Eichengreen, and Richard Portes (London: Academic Press, 1989).

Corden, W. Max, "Does the Current Account Matter? The Old View and the New," Chapter 18 in this volume.

Currie, David, and Simon Wren-Lewis, "An Appraisal of Alternative Blueprints for International Policy Coordination," *European Economic Review* (Amsterdam), Vol. 33 (December 1989), pp. 1769–85.

Evans, Paul, "Is the Dollar High Because of Large Budget Deficits?" *Journal of Monetary Economics* (Amsterdam), Vol. 18 (1986), pp. 227–49.

Frankel, Jeffrey A., "Ambiguous Policy Multipliers in Theory and Empirical Models," in *Empirical Macroeconomics for Interdependent Economies*, ed. by Ralph C. Bryant and others (Washington: Brookings Institution, 1988).

Frenkel, Jacob A., and Assaf Razin, "The Mundell-Fleming Model a Quarter Century Later: A Unified Exposition," *Staff Papers*, International Monetary Fund (Washington), Vol. 34 (December 1987), pp. 567–620.

Frenkel, Jacob A., Morris Goldstein, and Paul R. Masson, "Simulating the Effects of Some Simple Coordinated Versus Uncoordinated Policy Rules," in *Macroeconomic Policies in an Interdependent World*, ed. by Ralph C. Bryant and others (Washington: Brookings Institution, Centre for Economic Policy Research, and International Monetary Fund, 1989).

——, "The Rationale for, and Effects of, International Economic Policy Coordination," in *International Policy Coordination and Exchange Rate Fluctuations*, ed. by William H. Branson, Jacob A. Frenkel, and Morris Goldstein (Chicago: University of Chicago Press, 1990).

Genberg, Hans, "On Choosing the Right Rules for Exchange-Rate Management," *World Economy* (Oxford), Vol. 7 (December 1984), pp. 391–406.

——, and Alexander K. Swoboda, "The Current Account and the Policy Mix Under Flexible Exchange Rates," IMF Working Paper No. 87/70 (Washington: International Monetary Fund, 1987).

——, "Policy and Current Account Determination Under Floating Exchange Rates," *Staff Papers*, International Monetary Fund (Washington), Vol. 36 (March 1989), pp. 1–30.

McCallum, Bennett, "Specification of Policy Rules and Performance Measures in Multicountry Simulation Studies" (unpublished; Washington: International Monetary Fund, August 1990).

McKibbin, Warwick J., and Jeffrey D. Sachs, "Implications of Policy Rules for the World Economy," in *Macroeconomic Policies in an Interdependent World*, ed. by Ralph C. Bryant and others (Washington: Brookings Institution, Centre for Economic Policy Research, and International Monetary Fund, 1989).

McKinnon, Ronald I., "Monetary and Exchange Rate Policies for International Financial Stability: A Proposal," *Journal of Economic Perspectives* (Nashville, Tennessee), Vol. 2 (Winter 1988), pp. 83–103.

Mundell, Robert, *International Economics* (New York: Macmillan, 1968).

Mussa, Michael, "Macroeconomic Interdependence and the Exchange Rate Regime," in *International Economic Policy: Theory and Evidence*, ed. by Rudiger Dornbusch and Jacob A. Frenkel (Baltimore: Johns Hopkins University Press, 1979).

Niehans, Jürg, "Monetary and Fiscal Policies in Open Economies Under Fixed Exchange Rates: An Optimizing Approach," *Journal of Political*

Economy (Chicago), Vol. 76, No. 4, Part II (July/August 1968), pp. 893–920.

Obstfeld, Maurice, "The Effectiveness of Foreign-Exchange Intervention: Recent Experience, 1985–1988," in *International Policy Coordination and Exchange Rate Fluctuations*, ed. by William H. Branson, Jacob A. Frenkel, and Morris Goldstein (Chicago: University of Chicago Press, 1990).

Swoboda, Alexander K., "On Limited Information and the Assignment Problem," in *Stabilization Policies in Interdependent Economies*, ed. by Emil Claasen and Pascal Salin (Amsterdam: North-Holland, 1972).

——, "Financial Integration and International Monetary Arrangements," in *The Evolution of the International Monetary System: How Can Efficiency and Stability Be Attained?* ed. by Yoshio Suzuki, Junichi Miyake, and Mitsuaki Okabe (Tokyo: University of Tokyo Press, 1990).

Williamson, John, *The Exchange Rate System* (Washington: Institute for International Economics, 1983).

——, and Marcus Miller, *Targets and Indicators: A Blueprint for the International Coordination of Economic Policy* (Washington: Institute for International Economics, 1987).

18

Does the Current Account Matter?

The Old View and the New

W. Max Corden

In this paper I shall contrast the "old view" and the "new view" of the current account. I subscribe to the new view, but I shall devote much of this paper to exploring possible qualifications to it. Given that the two "views" are by now well known, the contribution of this paper is the pursuit of these qualifications. The old view is that the current account certainly does matter and that, in general, so-called current account imbalances are undesirable and require some policy action, especially if they are unlikely to be "sustainable." The new view is that the current account does not matter from a policy point of view at all, even though various elements that determine it are certainly relevant for policy.

The old view will be described in Section I, the new view in Section II, and possible qualifications to the new view in Section III. Section IV looks at the implications of the Barro-Ricardo debt neutrality theorem for the issue under discussion here. Section V sums up. I shall limit the scope of the paper in one particular way: it will deal only with countries that have current account deficits. While the new view is applicable also to surplus countries, as is also the discussion of qualifications, there are some special features applying to the surplus cases that will not be dealt with here.

Jacques Polak did not directly write on this subject.[1] But during

---

[1] Proposals for coordinating current account targets were especially common after the first oil shock, but also since. Jacques has been unsympathetic to such views, which suggests that he would tend to agree with what is called the new view here. It is also worth noting that he does not believe that countries have current account objectives anyway. See Polak (1989, pp. 378–79).

his long and fruitful reign, an important paper came out of the Research Department of the IMF—namely, Salop and Spitäller (1980)—which was, in fact, one of the earliest statements of the new view.[2] I recall Jacques citing this paper to me with approval several years later. So the new view is hardly new now, no more than the New Economics was new when Keynesian economics finally reached Washington in 1961. But it is new in the sense that only lately has it crept into the International Monetary Fund's *World Economic Outlook*, its *Staff Studies for the World Economic Outlook*, and the *Economic Outlook* of the Organization for Economic Cooperation and Development (OECD), as well becoming widely accepted in the academic world as "obvious."[3] Yet, the old view still lives, at least implicitly, with continuing concerns about "imbalances" or expressions of delight that these imbalances have been declining and may decline further.

Before launching into details, let me make two general points. First, this issue can be compared with the free trade-protection debate. The usual way in which economists approach the free trade-protection issue is to begin with the principle of comparative advantage, a principle not widely understood outside our profession, and endlessly expounded and defended by economists worldwide. This principle is, in my view, comparable with the new view. It is where one must begin, even though qualifications have to be considered. But, as we well know, given specified conditions, sound arguments for protection or intervention of some kind can be made. They do not negate the principle of comparative advantage but qualify its practical conclusions in particular cases. The issue is whether the conditions for particular arguments for protection exist, and specifically whether various arguments would actually outweigh the basic principle significantly so as to destroy the presumption in favor of free trade. The qualifications to the new view that I will explore are comparable to the explorations of arguments for protection. They may qualify the new view without destroying it.

The second point concerns the attitude one should take to the perception of "problems." The world is full of problems, and it is

---

[2] I stated it in Corden (1977) and elaborated it further in the third (1985) edition of that book, also exploring some qualifications. The present paper is really a development of the arguments in that book. See also Congdon (1982) where the main point was taken up, developed further, and popularized in the United Kingdom.

[3] See International Monetary Fund (1990), Artis and Bayoumi (1990), and Organization for Economic Cooperation and Development (1989).

certainly a role of economists to study them, to draw attention to problems that may not be widely perceived, and to urge policy changes that will avoid problems in the future. But it is surely important not only that problems be well defined but also that we do not divert our attention to imaginary problems. For example, I would argue that when German capital was moving into Spain on a large scale in recent years, that was hardly a problem in itself. Rather, it was a natural movement of funds from a high savings economy to an economy with emerging investment opportunities. Of course, conceivably it could lead to problems, as any movement of factors or goods could, but to suggest that current account imbalances within Western Europe were a problem per se is to manufacture artificial worries in a world that has enough real problems to worry about.

I. The Old View

Consider the following simple case. A country is committed to a fixed exchange rate regime. For whatever reason, there is little or no private international capital mobility. If it does exist potentially, the private sector has little or no borrowing capacity abroad. Finally, the government or central bank cannot borrow abroad, other than short term for emergency purposes. Apart from such short-term emergency borrowing, notably through the IMF, a current account deficit must thus be financed by use of the country's own foreign exchange reserves. This broadly describes the situation that did exist for all countries other than the United States in the early years of the Bretton Woods system.

In this situation, a country can run a current account deficit for a limited period. But no positive deficit is sustainable indefinitely. It must come to an end. If it keeps going, well before the foreign exchange reserves run out, there is likely to be a foreign exchange crisis generated by expectations of devaluation. Perhaps there is a steady and predictable inflow of direct investment, as there was into Western Europe in the 1960s. This makes a prolonged current account deficit possible, but no greater than the capital inflow. Hence, the sustainable deficit may not actually be zero.

The practical conclusion is that the current account must be carefully watched so as to avoid a sudden crisis. An increase in a current account deficit, or a shift from surplus or balance into deficit, is a matter of concern, even when the deficit is seen to be temporary and hence self-correcting. On the other hand, its causes—for example, whether an increase in it is caused by a rise in private investment, a fall in private savings, or an increase in the budget deficit—are irrelevant. Any current account deficit that is expected to be lasting for a longer period in the absence of a policy change, and that exceeds predictable direct investment inflows, is "worrisome" or "a matter for concern," to use some popular official phrases.

This is the simplest way of making sense of the old view. The trouble is that times have changed. There *is* private capital mobility, and in addition governments that wish to maintain their exchange rate can and do borrow on the international capital market directly to finance deficits. For all developed countries, as well as some developing ones, that is surely a correct description of their situation since the early 1970s and, to some extent, even earlier. Yet the old view has survived, at least until very recently.

It is obvious that a current account figure is a flow figure and what matters, even for the old view, is the movement to a stock situation —that is, the running down of foreign exchange reserves in the example I have given to a level that would lead to crisis. Thus, it would be a cheap criticism of the old view to say that it makes no sense to have flow targets. The only target can be a stock, such as a target foreign exchange level, combined with a view about the optimal time profile of current account flows to attain the stock. Thus, I do not distinguish the old view from the new on this ground. It seems reasonable to presume that the believers in the old view know the difference between stocks and flows. When they show concern about a current account situation or prospective path of the current account, they are concerned that it is not falling fast enough to attain the desired stock level (or ratio of the stock to, say, imports or gross national product).

The old view has been implicit in a mass of writing in this field coming from the Fund, the OECD, the Bank for International Settlements, many governments, and independent commentators, including some authors from the Institute for International Economics. The problem for me here is that any clear theoretical foundation has not been provided. The view has, indeed, only been implicit. It is reflected in extended discussions of current account imbalances and their prospects and brief remarks suggesting that reductions are welcome and represent "progress" toward an objective.

It is important not to be unfair here. It is possible that concern about current account imbalances has been based not on the logic that has just been advanced—that is, on a model where an international capital market is not available to a country—but rather on a judgment, often implicit, that one or more of the qualifications to the new view discussed in Section III below are empirically so important that they outweigh the simple logic of the new view itself. This would suggest that the new view is not new even in the minds of those who have apparently put forward the "old view."[4]

The empirical evidence that the old view has influenced actual government policies is perhaps more important than what is written down. It appears that governments have deliberately sought to avoid or moderate current account imbalances, though this has been less so in the 1980s than earlier. This conclusion emerges from the search by Bayoumi (1990) and Artis and Bayoumi (1990) for explanations of the correlations between national savings and national investment, originally noted by Feldstein and Horioka (1980) and attributed by the latter to low capital mobility.[5]

II. The New View

In its most general form, the new view may be put as follows. The current account is the net result of savings and investment, private and public. An increase in a current account deficit can be caused by an increase in investment or a fall in savings, or any combination of these, again distinguishing private and public investment and savings. Indeed, there are many kinds of investment, and many different agents who may save, so it is not just a matter of four variables. If, just for exposition, we simplify by aggregation and suppose that there are just two agents, the private sector and the public sector, and just two decisions for each, the investment decision and the

---

[4]I am indebted for this line of thought to some comments made by John Williamson at the conference.

[5]In Polak (1989, p. 378) Jacques questions whether governments have views or objectives on the current account at all. In a footnote he remarks perceptibly that, "If countries did attach great importance to their current account balances as guides to policy, they would be sure of having good statistics for them. The fact that in recent years the world's current account statistics summed up to a combined deficit of about $100 billion instead of the theoretical zero is proof in itself that the current account is not uppermost in governments' minds as they plan their policies." This is an interesting thought, but is difficult to relate to the Artis and Bayoumi (1990) conclusion cited here.

savings decision, one can conceive of an optimal outcome when all four decisions are optimal.

There are problems about this approach because the four decisions are not necessarily independent, and I shall come back to this point in Section IV. But, to proceed, the optimal outcome will carry with it a particular current account level at any point in time. Yet, this cannot really be described as the "optimal current account" at which policy should aim, because it could result from various combinations of savings and investment, public and private, and not just from the optimal combination. The current account that would result from the optimal levels of saving and investment could also be a by-product, for example, of a situation where the budget deficit was too high and private investment too low. Looking at the current account figure on its own tells us nothing. One must look at the separate decisions.

An increase in a current account deficit might have been caused primarily by an increase in the budget deficit, as in the case of the United States since 1982. Alternatively, it might have been caused by an increase in private investment combined with a decrease in private savings, as in the case of the United Kingdom and Australia recently. These are very different situations and require very different policy changes, if indeed they require policy changes at all. For example, if investment increased because the perceived productivity of investment had increased, and there is reason to believe that it is equal to or greater than the rate of interest on borrowed funds abroad, no policy change at all would be required. There are numerous factors determining optimal savings and investment, and also divergences between actual levels of these and the optimal levels, and it is these that are relevant for policy consideration.

A simple parallel from trade theory can be drawn here. I shall abstract from terms of trade effects for the moment, and assume that we are concerned with a small country facing given terms of trade and a given world interest rate. The trade volumes and trade patterns resulting from free trade are then optimal for a country if there are no "domestic distortions," that is, if underlying production and consumption decisions are not distorted by taxes, subsidies or controls, lack of information, and so on. If there are distortions, the first-best policy is to remove them. Looking at what happens to the volume of trade tells us absolutely nothing about the distortions, and it is impossible to determine what the optimal trade volumes and trade patterns are, other than by seeing what happens, or speculating what might happen, if the distortions were removed. In a decentralized system, it is necessary to get the traffic signs and signals right—which includes providing appropriate taxes and subsidies or other incentives to deal with externalities—and then the optimal traffic flow will result.

There are now many theoretical papers that either imply or clearly state the new view and that provide intertemporal analyses of external balance. They usually assume that private (or national) savings and investment are determined independently and optimally, so that a time path for the optimal current amount emerges endogenously.[6] This recent literature represents a considerable advance on earlier models that, rather misleadingly, identified current account imbalances with net national wealth decumulation or accumulation, hence assuming away domestic investment.

I put the new view in its strongest form in Corden (1977, pp. 50–51). One should assume that private savings and investment decisions are optimal unless there are particular reasons to believe to the contrary. There is no reason to presume that governments or outside observers know better how much private agents should invest and save than these agents themselves. These private decisions should not be a matter for public policy concern, other than to ensure that there are no government-imposed distortions. ''Various divergencies between social and private costs and benefits should be corrected, so that private decisions are made on the basis of price signals that indicate social and not just private costs and returns. But there is no need for concern with particular quantitative outcomes, and certainly not for any public-policy quantitative targets.'' On the other hand, public sector behavior—that is, the budget balance—is a matter for public policy concern and the focus should be on this. This does not mean that budget balances should be zero (however calculated), but only that a public policy issue of the appropriate fiscal policy does arise.[7]

It follows that an increase in a current account deficit that results from a shift in private sector behavior—a rise in investment or a fall

---

[6] See, especially, Bruce and Purvis (1985, pp. 844–54), Frenkel and Razin (1987), Obstfeld (1987), Stockman (1988), and Pitchford (1989). These papers contain further references. Incidentally, earlier indications of the new view can be found in McKinnon (1978) and Cooper (1981), and most recently it has been advanced by Makin (1989) who put his references to ''imbalances'' always in quotation marks.

[7] See the extensive discussions in the United States of this fiscal policy issue, for example, in the symposium on the budget deficit in the *Journal of Economic Perspectives* (Yellen and others (1989)).

in savings—should not be a matter of concern at all. In the United States, there is widespread confusion as to whether the problem (if any) is the budget deficit or the current account deficit, since they have tended to move together since 1982. Sometimes it has hardly seemed necessary to make the distinction. But, by contrast, recent developments in the United Kingdom and Australia have highlighted the issue raised in this paper. In both countries the central budgets have moved into rough balance or even surplus, while current account deficits have increased owing to private consumption and investment booms. Thus, these countries do not have twin deficits, and one can clearly distinguish the current account issue, which is the focus of this paper, from the fiscal policy issue which is, in principle, quite distinct.

The official position in Australia has been that the current account deficit is certainly a problem, and this view has support in the financial community and from others. But John Pitchford—in Pitchford (1990) and elsewhere—has strongly put forth the argument suggested here that there is indeed no problem, and in Australia the new view is known as the "Pitchford line." When the United Kingdom went into current account deficit in 1988, the "Lawson doctrine" propounded the same view, though it was much disputed. As noted above, it was put forth earlier in Congdon (1982).

There was a similar situation in Chile from 1979 to 1981.[8] The budget had been brought into balance, but there was massive private sector borrowing abroad, generating a large current account deficit. This is possibly the only example of this kind of situation since 1973 in a developing country. The official position was that, for the reasons given here, the current account deficit was not a problem. The unfortunate outcome in that case was that, when the debt crisis came, the government was compelled by foreign creditors to take over the private sector debts. It is a kind of situation to which I shall return below when discussing qualifications.

III. Qualifications and Complications

Let us now assume that a country's current account deteriorates, perhaps quite suddenly and sharply, owing to a private spending boom, that is, a rise in private investment or a fall in savings. The

---

[8] See Corbo (1985) and Mellor (1990).

interest rate will tend to rise, which draws in capital from abroad, and the real exchange will appreciate as a result of some combination of rise in domestic prices and nominal appreciation. If the authorities wish to avoid temporary inflation—leading possibly to the generation of inflationary expectations and hence longer-term problems, these developments will be associated with some monetary contraction, which may avoid the rise in domestic prices and which will appreciate the nominal exchange rate further. In any case, there will be a real appreciation, with familiar redistributive effects affecting tradable goods producers adversely, and probably raising real wages, at least in the nontradable sectors. We assume that there is no change in fiscal policy, though the budget balance could, of course, be affected by these developments. Naturally foreign debt will build up as a result. The question now is, again, whether the current account deficit and buildup of foreign debt are matters for public policy concern. One can think of several channels through which, conceivably, they might be.

Unsound Private Borrowing and the Signaling Role of the Current Account

Perhaps the spending boom is unsoundly based. This could be because the government or central bank is understood to have provided implicit or explicit guarantees for domestic borrowers (a moral hazard problem) or because, for whatever reason, the country is just experiencing the usual unsound boom destined to end in a bust. Even without guarantees involving the possibility of rescue operations, private losses are bound to be spread to the public sector, if only through reduced tax collections.

Basically I am assuming now either that there is a divergence between private and social interest (a domestic distortion) or that myopic private agents subject to a boom mentality do not really know what is best for themselves, and in doing themselves and their shareholders and creditors harm, they are also harming the society as a whole. One recognizes the Chilean case—where the government ended up taking over private debts—and also negative views of private sector decision making that are frequently expressed, for example, in Australia recently. Anyone familiar with the recent activities of various Australian entrepreneurs is likely to have some sympathy for such views.

There may then be a case for policies that either moderate the boom through monetary contraction, or that offset its effects through fiscal contraction. The move into sharp current account deficit can then be regarded as a warning signal of a problem. The deficit matters in the sense that it needs to be watched.

This argument does not mean that a current account deficit must always be moderated or avoided, but only that a spending boom that caused it possibly should be.[9] It is still necessary to look in detail at the sources of the deficit, as taught by the new view. Not all booms are "unsound," or even partially so, and justify second-guessing by the authorities. Furthermore, there would also be a problem if the boom manifested itself not in a current account deficit, but in higher interest rates, leading to crowding-out of "sound" investment. The new view is not really dented by this consideration.

Contamination Effect

The more private agents or governments borrow, the larger the share of their equities or the debt instruments they issue in international portfolios. The larger this share, the greater the risk factor will be, and thus the interest rates borrowers have to pay, or the lower the prices of their equities.[10] This is obviously not an argument for keeping current account deficits to zero, since there cannot be any presumption that the existing stock of the nation's financial assets held abroad happens to be optimal to start with. Furthermore, the risk factor surely depends also on the state and prospects of the economy, which depend, among other things, on the way in which

---

[9] If there is no moral hazard problem, the suggestion that an "unsound" boom may justify public policy action to restrain it implies a belief that the official authorities may have more knowledge or judgment than the private agents creating the boom. Our modern Cartesians, working from standard first principles currently accepted by many economists, would query this: why should governments know better, when would we know that they know better, and can they be relied upon to act appropriately even when they do know better? I do not subscribe to the Cartesian position as religiously as some, but it was certainly implied in my own statement of the new view, in Corden (1977).

[10] This does not refer to the effects of exchange rate expectations on the domestic interest rate nor to the effects of exchange rate risk resulting from exchange rate uncertainty. It can be assumed here that all debt is denominated in foreign currency, so that the relevant interest rate is the foreign one. In the case of debt, the concern is thus with default risk. If borrowing is in the domestic currency (as in the case of the United States), one must separate the exchange rate and default risk elements, the focus here being on the latter. (But the risk of unexpected inflation would, in that case, be a form of default risk.)

the borrowed funds have been used. The expected time paths of the debt-GDP and debt-export ratios may shed some light on the risk factor, though that is the most that can be said about these favored and much cited statistics.

All this is not really relevant for the central issue of whether the current account—as distinct from the buildup of *public* debt held at home or abroad—should be a matter of public policy concern. The real issue is whether changes in the risk factor resulting from increased borrowing are wholly internalized for the various agents, private and public, or whether there is some externality or "contamination" effect. If they were wholly internalized—so that increased borrowing by one agent would not raise the risk factor facing another agent—there would be no public policy issue resulting from current account deficits. This is the key point. There has to be an externality. If there is not, then there is no need to make elaborate calculations, for example, of the likely growth in the share of U.S.-issued assets in the world's financial portfolios, or of changes in the U.S. debt-GDP ratio. Individual agents will incorporate expected adverse effects of increased borrowing in their own borrowing—and hence savings and investment—decisions. In the absence of externalities, the new view stands completely.

Yet there is surely a possibility that borrowers *do* contaminate each other, so that there is an externality. Markets are concerned with country risk and do look at a country's total debt ratios. It is not unreasonable to presume that the more some private agents of a country borrow, the higher have to be the interest rates that are paid both by the government of the country and by other private agents. Perhaps this is not always so, and if markets are sensible, they will also look at the details—how much went into consumption, how much into investment, and so on. Yet, such a concern of markets with country risk is not wholly irrational and can be explained by considerations already discussed.

Governments may have to rescue private agents in trouble, and so may encounter more financial difficulties themselves as a result of excessive private borrowing (hence increasing the need for rescheduling their own debts, for example), and, conversely, private agents may have to rescue governments in trouble through paying higher taxes to finance mounting sovereign debt-service obligations. Furthermore, if some private agents get into trouble, governments may have to raise taxes or reduce government services to finance their rescue, and this would then create financial problems for other private agents.

We have thus a genuine qualification to the new view resulting from the existence of country risk: from this aspect, at least, the current account as a whole, and not just the sources of its changes, is relevant, and increases in the deficit are "worrisome." Decentralized decision making could lead to excessive borrowing from a national point of view. But this qualification will only become relevant once debt ratios and current account deficits exceed certain levels, and particularly when increased borrowing is for consumption rather than for investment.

There is an additional factor in the case of a very large borrower in world terms—that is, the United States. The more such an economy borrows, for whatever purpose, the more it raises world interest rates for a given risk factor and not just interest rates facing the United States. If it is a net debtor, this has an adverse effect on the economy as a whole (like any deterioration in the terms of trade), an adverse effect which will not be internalized. This kind of effect provides a standard argument from a strictly national point of view for taxing capital inflow.[11] Of course, it provides no basis for targeting the current account, but only for an optimal tax (with the tax rate changing over time) that would have the net effect of reducing the stream of current account deficits to some extent. More relevant in present conditions are the international effects of the rise in interest rates brought about by growing U.S. net indebtedness. Debtors lose and creditors gain as a result; it could be argued that the loss to developing country debtors is an undesirable international redistribution effect that U.S. policies should take into account.

The Present and Future Real Exchange Rate

Much of the concern with current account deficits and their sustainability appears to be connected with exchange rate considerations and with changes in the absolute and relative positions of the tradable and nontradable sectors of the economy, as well as real wages. In other words, it is not concerned with optimal borrowing or lending considerations at all, but with relative price and distributional effects of changes in current accounts.

If a current account goes into deficit in the way described earlier, the problem can be of two kinds. First, the actual distributional effects of the change may be thought undesirable, and will certainly

---

[11] See Kemp (1962) and Corden (1974, Chapter 12).

be perceived as such by losers. Thus, the move into deficit is likely to be associated with a real appreciation (whether through domestic prices rising as a result of the boom, or nominal appreciation resulting from capital inflow, or both), and this will adversely affect the tradable goods producers. Second, the current account deficit may be predicted to be temporary, being based perhaps on an inevitably temporary investment boom, or it may be "unsustainable" because of a growing debt-GDP ratio or growing ratio of the country's debt instruments in international portfolios, leading to an increasing risk factor and an inevitable adjustment to a lower deficit. The temporary nature of the deficit, and hence of the real appreciation and national output patterns that go with it, are often thought undesirable because, presumably, they are sources of instability.

These two concerns—the immediate distributional effect and the dislike of a temporary shock—are somewhat contradictory. If distributional effects are temporary, they are, presumably, less sectorally damaging than if they were permanent. And if they are known to be temporary, they should not lead to costly reallocations of resources that will later be regretted as the real exchange rate depreciates again when the boom and the capital inflow come to an end.

Indeed, there seems to be some confusion about the desirability or otherwise of an "unsustainable" deficit. Is a development necessarily undesirable because it is not likely to, or indeed cannot, go on forever? Must a private consumption or investment boom, and the associated current account deficit, necessarily be stopped because eventually it will stop in any case? An investment boom may be perfectly "sound"—the expected marginal productivity of capital exceeding the foreign rate of interest—yet it will inevitably be temporary. It can be interpreted as a sound stock adjustment—a switch in the nation's asset portfolio out of financial assets into real assets because the expected profitability of real assets has improved. Similarly, an apparent consumption boom is often really a boom in the acquisition by households of consumer durables and here, again, it can be regarded as an adjustment of asset portfolios. The policy literature shows an extraordinary concern with "sustainability." But we might bear in mind that the rate of growth of a teenager is also not sustainable. Does that make it nonoptimal?

Nevertheless, it can be conceded that stability of the real exchange rate, and hence of the size and profitability of the tradable relative to the nontradable sectors, could be desirable, other things being equal; it could be one of a number of arguments in a plausible social welfare function. Indeed, only by introducing real exchange stability

as a separate concern, independent of optimal borrowing and lending, can one rationalize a great deal of policy advocacy in this field.[12]

This suggests that some public policy action designed to modify or
offset, at least in part, the current account and real exchange rate
effects of a private sector boom could be justified. Intervention in
the foreign exchange market designed to prevent appreciation would
be inflationary and hence fail to avoid real appreciation, unless there
were a simultaneous fiscal contraction. With high capital mobility,
monetary contraction would have little effect in reducing private
spending. Hence there would have to be offsetting action in the
form of fiscal contraction. This, of course, may lead to a nonoptimal
budget balance—government spending becoming too low or taxes
too high—an adverse effect that would have to be traded off against
the objective of real exchange rate stability. But such stabilization
policy aimed at the real exchange rate is subject to all the modern
critiques of short-term demand management and stabilization
policies.

At this point, one might also reflect on the "hard landing"
scenario put forth frequently in the mid-1980s, and apparently
providing an argument in favor of reducing the U.S. current account
deficit because of its probable exchange rate effects.[13] The argument
was that a depreciation of the dollar, implicitly not just nominal but
also real, was inevitable, and at some stage this would lead to a
sudden shock-depreciation that would have further adverse repercussions, apparently both inflation and recession.

It has never been clear to me why a depreciation that was so
widely expected, and did seem to follow logically from many forecasts, should have to happen suddenly and in a crisis atmosphere.
As we know now, it has not done so. One can concede that a
depreciation could have adverse effects (more inflation for given
overall employment), and that reduction of the current account
deficit would be associated with a real depreciation. But why would
it be desirable to bring this about earlier rather than later? Possibly
the argument was really that the budget deficit was excessive, and
that it needed to be—and would eventually have to be—reduced.

---

[12] Various reasons for seeking to manage exchange rates are discussed in Kenen
(1988). One concern of advocates of exchange rate targets or intervention of some
kind has been with the effects of exchange rate "bubbles" resulting from speculation,
these being quite distinct from fluctuations or "misalignments" that are caused by
changes in investment, savings propensities, or fiscal policies. This is one element in
the analysis in Williamson (1985).

[13] See Marris (1985), which was for a time a very influential study.

The current account and exchange rate effects would be adverse by-products of the inevitable adjustment. If this was the position, it would fit in with the new view, since the policy issue was really concerned with the budget deficit.

Current Account Deficits Generate Protectionism

The following line of thought is well known. In the United States the current account deficit is said to give rise to protectionist pressures, this presumably being a response to the adverse effects of the deficit, or of the real appreciation, on import-competing producers. Thus the argument is not that the distributional effects themselves are bad but that the pressures that result from the distributional effects have an adverse effect on the national economy.

It is worth noting that, given a floating or flexible exchange rate system, there is no presumption that increased protection would actually improve the current account—that is, increase savings or reduce investment (Corden (1990)). Furthermore, protection would just yield gains to the protected import-competing producers at the expense of the nonprotected (or less protected) ones; thus it would reshuffle, not reduce overall, the losses suffered in the tradable sector as a whole as a result of the real appreciation.

It can hardly be disputed that better ways to resist such pressures should be sought if there are no other reasons for wishing to reduce the deficit. But, if it is true that a deficit or increased deficit does generally generate such pressures and these become effective in producing more protection, there is possibly some argument here for moderating a current account deficit, even though this would be a second-best approach. But is it true? One has no difficulty thinking of some surplus countries that are by no means free traders, nor countries (such as the United Kingdom and Australia) where a shift into deficit has not led to increased protection. But the relationship between current account balances and protection is an empirical question suitable for a Ph.D. thesis.

Thinking about surplus countries, one might go on to assume that the effect could be symmetrical, deficits leading to increases and surpluses to decreases in protection. One would then expect that the effect of the Japanese and German surpluses—which have been, more or less, the mirror images of the U.S. deficit—would have been to reduce protection in those countries. This appears to have been true for Japan, but not Germany. If there were actually symmetry, the basic argument would really be destroyed. World current account imbalances would not necessarily bring about increases in world protection as a whole, since higher protection by the deficit countries (or by countries that have shifted into higher deficit) would be offset by reduced protection by the surplus countries. A reduction in the U.S. deficit associated with real depreciation of the dollar might be expected to lead to increased protection (or greater reluctance to liberalize) by other countries. Thus, the argument actually assumes an asymmetrical reaction.

Two More Qualifications?

In my determined search for qualifications to the new view, I shall try to give precise content to two other popular arguments.

(1) The first argument applies to the United States, which borrows in domestic currency. It is said that the larger the stock of dollars held abroad as a result of U.S. current account deficits, the greater is exchange rate volatility—a dependence of the exchange rate on the fickle views of foreigners. This argument should be distinguished from the one discussed above, which concerned real exchange rate instability in the medium run.

There appears to be a flaw in the argument, insofar as it focuses on current account deficits as the source of the problem. Given international capital mobility, the larger the holdings of liquid dollar-denominated assets by foreigners *or by U.S. residents*, the more likely are big swings in the exchange rate owing to asset market effects—that is, owing to short-term changes in expectations. Possible capital flight presents just as much of a problem in a country like Brazil where the local-currency-denominated assets (whether or not described as "money") are held wholly by domestic residents. When the pool of liquid assets in a particular currency builds up, there can indeed be a problem, but this also comes about when local savers rather than foreigners hold large amounts of domestic money or short-term government debt.

The problem is, again, the budget deficit and not the current account. In the case of the United States, one can surely assume that the vast holdings of liquid dollar assets by U.S. residents are more than enough to ensure that the foreign exchange market will respond rapidly and possibly with large movements to changes in "news."

(2) Next I come to the argument that continued current account deficits lead to increased and undesirable foreign ownership and control of the domestic economy. This view is at present popular in the United States, especially with regard to Japanese investment. There is a vast literature on this supposed foreign ownership prob-

lem, much of it stimulated by the postwar flow of U.S. investment abroad.[14] Let us grant for the purpose of the discussion that there is a public good (or "public bad") factor here: at the margin, at least, domestic control of capital is better than foreign control, and this consideration does not enter the private decision-making calculus. The first-best policy is then to tax income from direct investment by foreigners above the rates of tax appropriate for other reasons.[15] Taxing income from all foreign investments, including income from portfolio capital and debt instruments (where no foreign control is involved), would be second-best or worse.

The outcome of a tax, whether on income from all foreign capital inflow or only on income from direct investment alone, would be to raise the domestic interest rate and the return on equities, and this would possibly increase domestic savings and certainly reduce domestic investment, the latter, at the margin, being foreign financed. Thus the outcome would indeed be a reduction in the current account deficit below the level it would have reached otherwise. But the first-best approach is surely to impose an (estimated) optimal tax on direct investment—if one really believed that reducing foreign control is a public good—and then allow the market to determine the savings, investment, and hence current account outcomes. The alternative old view approach of aiming directly at a current account target would nonoptimally discourage also foreign capital inflow that does not involve control, so that the attempt to deal with one distortion would yield a new, by-product, distortion. In addition, and most importantly, a current account target would disregard numerous factors that would normally influence and change savings and investment and that a free market modified by given rates of taxation would automatically take into account.

IV. The New View and the Barro-Ricardo Theorem

In view of the immense attention that the Barro-Ricardo debt neutrality theorem has received in the fiscal policy literature, it can

---

[14] The largest body of literature has come from Canada. I hope that the recent U.S. preoccupation with this problem will not involve a complete rediscovery of old ideas in new language.

[15] There are some complications here; these are discussed in Corden (1974, pp. 335–47), which reviews various factors determining the optimal taxes on foreign investment, taking into account also taxes on domestic capital.

hardly be ignored here.[16] The basic idea is that government deficits or surpluses affect future expected taxes, and these expectations would, in turn, affect private sector savings. For given government spending, a reduction in current taxes would raise the budget deficit, and this would be offset, at least to some extent, by a rise in private savings designed to provide for increases in taxes in the future. In the extreme case there would be a full offset: a shift from tax finance to debt finance would not change total national savings.

The evidence seems to suggest that there is sometimes a tendency in that direction but certainly not a full offset. This tendency can be found in the recent British and Australian episodes referred to earlier, though the shift of the Australian current account into large deficit appears to be explained primarily by an investment boom, and I am not convinced that the Barro-Ricardo story is the right explanation for the consumption booms in the two countries. These booms are more likely to have been caused by financial liberalization that made borrowing easier. The United States since 1982 has been a laboratory experiment for the proposition, and it is obvious that private savings in the United States have not responded in the way suggested.[17]

The implication for our present discussion is that government and private savings or dissavings are possibly related, and certainly should be related, if individual private agents are to behave optimally from their own point of view, or from the point of view of themselves and their heirs and successors combined. This leads to an issue concerned with optimal savings. For any given level and pattern of private and government investment, given expected productivity improvements and expected terms of trade, there is, in principle, an optimal path of national savings (public and private combined). If there were an increase in the expected productivity of investment or an expected future improvement in the terms of trade, optimal national savings would fall, since some of the expected future gains should be passed back to the present, allowing present consumption to rise. In other circumstances, national savings might need to increase. If these and similar circumstances did not change (and there were no change in social time preference), national savings should stay constant.

---

[16] Barro (1989) is a convenient statement of this point of view. For criticisms, see Gramlich (1989).

[17] See Gramlich (1989).

The next step is to disregard distinctions among citizens, and to assume that the average taxpayer at any point in time is also the average saver. If the private sector were to behave optimally from a national point of view (future generations being included in "the nation"), it should then offset any changes in public sector savings. If the Barro-Ricardo theorem applied in its extreme form, the private sector would indeed do so. A shift from tax finance of government spending to debt finance would not alter national savings and hence the current account. Of course, the current account balance could still change because of changes in public and private investment levels and, in addition, optimal national savings may change for various reasons, and this would change the current account through appropriate changes in private sector savings.

It follows that *if* one made the assumption that private agents were able to "see through" the implications of switches between taxing and debt finance, and, in addition, behaved optimally from a national (including future generations) point of view, private savings decisions would ensure the optimality of national savings, and any change in the current account resulting apparently from changes in savings should not be a matter of concern. One might also like to assume that private investment is always optimal, given available information, in which case only changes in the current account resulting from changes in government investment would be matters of concern. The moral is then that one should look directly at government investment, since most sources of changes in the current account would result from optimal decisions.

It has already been observed that, even ignoring the Barro-Ricardo theorem, it is hardly reasonable to assume that private savings and investment decisions are always made on the basis of undistorted signals, nor that private agents always behave optimally even from their own point of view. But now we have an additional complication or problem. The evidence seems to be pretty clear that private agents do not fully (or at all) "see through" the future tax implications of government debt finance or, even if they see through it, do not respond in their savings behavior in the extreme way that the simplest version of the Barro-Ricardo theorem suggests. There is then an additional source of nonoptimality. In fact, public debt finance gives rise to an additional "domestic distortion," leading to a divergence between private sector savings behavior and the optimal savings from a national intergenerational point of view. Public debt finance is likely to lead to national savings that are too low, and the greater the debt-financed deficit, the greater the discrepancies between actual national savings and optimal savings (unless there are other distortions pushing in the opposite direction).

All these complications do not alter the main message of the new view. It is pointless only to look at changes in the current account. The distinction between changes originating in the private sector and the public sector, and between changes in investment and changes in savings, must still be made.

Yet, having said that, I shall continue my relentless search for qualifications to the new view. The Barro-Ricardo idea may give one a lead to understanding the common intuitive reaction that a budget deficit financed by domestic savings is likely to be less of a problem for the future than a budget deficit financed through a current account deficit.

Let us compare two countries—call them the United States and Italy—both of which have bond-financed budget deficits of similar size (relative to GDP), with the deficits having similar implications for future taxpayers.[18] Let us also assume that private investment in both countries is optimal in the sense that the expected marginal social return is equal to the expected world interest rate over the relevant periods. But the United States has low private savings, just sufficient, say, to finance private investment, so that the U.S. current account deficit matches the inflow of foreign funds to finance the budget deficit. On the other hand, Italy has high private savings sufficient to finance both private investment and the budget deficit. Thus, Italy does not have a current account deficit. Actually, for the argument it is necessary only that Italian savings are higher (relative to GDP) than in the United States, but the case I describe is a very clear-cut one.

What this example does say is that the higher current account deficit of the United States reflects its lower private savings ratio. The current account deficit of the United States is then a problem if the U.S. savings ratio is too low. In practice, the current account deficit could also reflect a higher investment ratio resulting from greater investment opportunities, but we assume that this is not so in this case.

Now the question is whether Italy is saving too much or the United States too little. The intuitive view is that it is the United States and not Italy that has a problem in this case. The implicit

---

[18] This is not the actual situation. Italy's deficit is much higher and partly it has been financed by an inflation tax.

theory could be the following. Italian taxpayers, present and future, are Barro-clever and can see through the veil of debt finance, and, furthermore, they show foresight and a concern for their heirs, and save more as a result. Thus, they ensure that there will be no problem for them in the future because of the budget deficit. By contrast, Americans have not pierced the debt veil or—more likely—do not show foresight or a concern for future generations—so that they do not save much, if at all, just because of the budget deficit. The farsighted Barro-Ricardo-thinking policy adviser or policymaker sees the U.S. problem, which manifests itself as a problem of foreign debt accumulation. The central point is that the low savings of the United States could conceivably be attributed to a failure of private savers to take into account the dissavings of the government. But it still remains true that just looking at the current account deficit is not enough, since this deficit also depends on investment.

V. Conclusion

In conclusion, one might ask whether the various qualifications and complications that have been discussed here seriously dent the new view of the current account. I do not think that they do.

First, one can concede that the current account (as distinct from the fiscal balance) is worth watching as a signal of problems in private saving and investment decisions: spending booms may be "unsound" or subject to distortions. But the new view is not even dented because one must still look at private investment and saving separately and directly, and search for distortions or signs of foolish decision making.

Second, if there are contamination effects owing to country risk, the *nation's* debt (possibly relative to GDP, or relative to exports) becomes relevant, and not just separate agents' debts. In this case, the actual and expected path of the current account deficit must indeed be watched. But this consideration only becomes significant once debt ratios are fairly high; one may guess that it is not significant for the United States or the United Kingdom but could be significant now for Australia.

Third, there is the concern with real exchange rate stability. Here, of course, it is the real exchange rate, and not actually the current account, that matters, but the two are closely related. The question really is whether there ought to be as much emphasis on real exchange rate stability as one finds in the literature. It certainly has to be set against other objectives, notably that saving and investment, private and public, be as close to optimality as possible. Is it really sensible to forgo an investment boom because it leads to instability of the real exchange rate?

Fourth, there is the argument common in the United States that the current account deficit generates protectionist pressures that become effective and impose familiar losses on the economy. This is essentially an empirical question where the evidence (on casual empiricism) seems to be somewhat ambiguous. But perhaps this argument could justify policies—essentially second-best policies—designed in some circumstances to reduce a deficit below where it would be otherwise. The weakest link in the argument is that it assumes a lack of symmetry.

Fifth, there is the concern with foreign ownership. Even if one grants this (and I hesitate to do so), the new view is not dented at all in this case since the relationship between the current account and the increase in foreign control is quite indirect; taxes directed specifically to this concern would be first-best.

Finally, national savings may be below the optimum when there is a debt-financed fiscal deficit because of the failure of private agents to compensate fully by increasing their own savings. The evidence suggests that they are unlikely to behave like perceptive Barro-optimizers. But this consideration does not dent the new view; in fact, it fully supports it because it means that the source of the problem is specifically the budget deficit. As stressed in the new view, the budget deficit is that determinant of the current account balance which one should watch most closely to see whether there is a policy problem.

REFERENCES

Artis, Michael, and Tamim Bayoumi, "Saving, Investment, Financial Integration, and the Balance of Payments," in *Staff Studies for the World Economic Outlook* (Washington: International Monetary Fund, 1990).

Barro, Robert J., "The Ricardian Approach to Budget Deficits," *Journal of Economic Perspectives* (Nashville, Tennessee), Vol. 3 (Spring 1989), pp. 37–54.

Bayoumi, Tamim, "Saving-Investment Correlations: Immobile Capital, Government Policy, or Endogenous Behavior?" *Staff Papers*, International Monetary Fund (Washington), Vol. 37 (June 1990), pp. 360–87.

Bruce, Neil, and Douglas D. Purvis, "The Specification and Influence of Goods and Factor Markets in Open-Economy Macroeconomic Models," in *Handbook of International Economics*, Vol. II, ed. by Ronald W. Jones and Peter B. Kenen (Amsterdam: North-Holland, 1985).

Congdon, Tim, "A New Approach to the Balance of Payments," *Lloyds Bank Review* (London), No. 146 (October 1982), pp. 1–14.

Cooper, Richard N., "Comments on Sachs," *Brookings Papers on Economic Activity: 1* (1981), Brookings Institution (Washington), pp. 269–73.

Corbo, Vittorio, "Reforms and Macroeconomic Adjustments in Chile During 1974–84," *World Development* (Oxford), Vol. 13 (August 1985), pp. 893–916.

Corden, W. Max, *Trade Policy and Economic Welfare* (Oxford: Clarendon Press, 1974).

———, *Inflation, Exchange Rates and the World Economy* (1st ed., Chicago: University of Chicago Press, and Oxford: Oxford University Press, 1977; 3rd ed., Oxford: Clarendon Press, 1985).

———, "Trade Policy and the Current Account," in *The Direction of Trade Policy*, ed. by Charles S. Pearson and James Riedel (Cambridge, Massachusetts: Basil Blackwell, 1990).

Feldstein, Martin, and Charles Horioka, "Domestic Saving and International Capital Flows," *Economic Journal* (London), Vol. 90 (June 1980), pp. 314–29.

Frenkel, Jacob A., and Assaf Razin, *Fiscal Policies and the World Economy* (Cambridge, Massachusetts: MIT Press, 1987).

Gramlich, Edward M., "Budget Deficits and National Saving: Are Politicians Exogenous?" *Journal of Economic Perspectives* (Nashville, Tennessee), Vol. 3 (Spring 1989), pp. 23–35.

International Monetary Fund, *World Economic Outlook, May 1990* (Washington, 1990).

Kemp, Murray C., "The Benefits and Costs of Private Investment from Abroad: Comment," *Economic Record* (Sydney), Vol. 38 (March 1962), pp. 108–10.

Kenen, Peter B., *Managing Exchange Rates* (London and New York: Routledge, 1988).

Makin, John, "International 'Imbalances': The Role of Exchange Rates," *The Amex Bank Review, Special Paper No. 17* (London: American Express Bank Ltd., November 1989).

Marris, Stephen, *Deficits and the Dollar: The World Economy at Risk* (Washington: Institute for International Economics, 1985).

McKinnon, Ronald I., "Exchange Rate Instability, Trade Imbalances, and Monetary Policies in Japan and the United States," in *Issues in International Economics*, ed. by Peter Oppenheimer (London: Oriel Press, 1978).

Mellor, Patricio, "Chile," in *Latin American Adjustment: How Much Has Happened?* ed. by John Williamson (Washington: Institute for International Economics, 1990).

Obstfeld, Maurice, "International Finance," in *The New Palgrave*, Vol. 2, ed. by John Eatwell and others (London: Macmillan, 1987).

Organization for Economic Cooperation and Development, *Economic Outlook* (Paris, December 1989).

Pitchford, J.D., "Optimum Borrowing and the Current Account When There Are Fluctuations in Income," *Journal of International Economics* (Amsterdam), Vol. 26 (May 1989), pp. 345–58.

———, *Australia's Foreign Debt: Myths and Realities* (Sydney: Allen & Unwin, 1990).

Polak, Jacques J., "Comment," in *Macroeconomic Policies in an Interdependent World*, ed. by Ralph C. Bryant and others (Washington: Brookings Institution, Centre for Economic Policy Research, and International Monetary Fund, 1989).

Salop, Joanne, and Erich Spitäller, "Why Does the Current Account Matter?" *Staff Papers*, International Monetary Fund (Washington), Vol. 27 (March 1980), pp. 101–34.

Stockman, Alan C., "On the Roles of International Financial Markets and Their Relevance for Economic Policy," *Journal of Money, Credit and Banking* (Columbus, Ohio), Vol. 20 (August 1988), pp. 531–49.

Williamson, John, *The Exchange Rate System*, Policy Analyses in International Economics, No. 5 (Washington: Institute for International Economics, 2nd ed., 1985).

Yellen, Janet L., and others, "Symposium on the Budget Deficit," *The Journal of Economic Perspectives* (Nashville, Tennessee), Vol. 3 (Spring 1989), pp. 17–93.

19

The Quantity Theory of Money in an Open Economy

Variations on the Hume-Polak Model

Robert Mundell

The problem of adapting the quantity theory of money to the balance of payments adjustment mechanism presented a dilemma for the economists of the eighteenth and nineteenth centuries that was never completely resolved. Whereas, in a closed economy, an increase in the money supply would raise prices, in an open economy, subject to the law of one price, the domestic price level cannot rise by more than the world price level. Even Hume, co-discoverer[1] of the self-regulating mechanism of the balance of payments, stumbled on the dilemma, failing to make clear that demand could alter the balance of payments without changes in relative prices.

The classical literature after Hume reached an unhappy compromise in the formulation of the "price-specie-flow mechanism," according to which balances of payments were supposed to be corrected by price level increases in the surplus countries and price level decreases in the deficit countries. In the Mill-Taussig-Viner theory, changes in relative prices did not violate the law of one price because they meant changes in the terms of trade. For over a century, the high authority of this school perpetuated an embarrass-

---

[1] With Antonio Serra, Isaac Gervaise, and Richard Cantillon. See Mundell (1989a) for a recent discussion of the development of the mechanism.

ment in the modern literature.[2] The confusion is based on the neglect of the wealth effects that provide equilibrating adjustment even at unchanged prices.

The Cunliffe Report of 1918 is the locus classicus of the error in twentieth century literature. Between this report and the late 1950s there was very little progress on the monetary aspects of adjustment theory. The wartime and postwar literature were dominated by Keynesian multiplier models that completely ignored monetary elements. Writing in 1957, Jacques Polak, pioneer of the formalization of the monetary approach to the balance of payments, commented on the distressing state of the literature in passages of which the following are excerpts (pp. 1–2):

> ...existing analytical studies rarely succeed in integrating monetary and credit factors in the explanation of income or of payments developments...an adequate theoretical basis...seems to be lacking.
>
> The failure to accommodate monetary factors in the analysis probably becomes most evident when questions are raised concerning the effects of specified monetary changes on income or on the balance of payments....
>
> The embarrassing inability to handle such questions contrasts strikingly with the ease with which nonmonetary problems are approached in income analysis....
>
> But the customary income analysis cannot handle monetary questions. Even where it is pushed to a considerable degree of refinement, it not infrequently omits monetary factors altogether....
>
> Perhaps the failure to develop empirical monetary analysis on the basis of [Keynes's] General Theory is less surprising than the fact that an empirical income analysis was developed from it.

What followed made history. To Polak goes the credit for developing for the first time an explicit quantitative model of the monetary adjustment process. Polak made strong assumptions to get quantitative results. He assumed a constant income velocity of money and selected an income period to make velocity equal to unity; income became the demand for money and expenditure the supply. Imports were assumed to be a function of income and exports were assumed to be exogenous. On the basis of these simple assumptions, Polak was able to construct the edifice that inaugurated an era of quantita-

---

[2] For reviews of the literature on the monetary approach see Frenkel and Johnson (1976, Chapter 1), Frenkel (1976), Samuelson (1980), and Humphrey and Keleher (1982).

tive monetary analysis of the balance of payments. A deficit has cumulative effects on the money supply that reduces the quantity of money until income and imports have changed by enough to restore equilibrium. Associates, colleagues, and Polak himself developed the ideas further in articles that have been incorporated in the IMF's 1977 publication on the subject, itself a suitable monument to Polak's powerful influence in this field.

When I came to the Fund in September 1961, Polak and Marcus Fleming set me to work on problems like the monetary-fiscal policy mix, capital mobility, flexible exchange rates, forward markets, commodity-reserve currency plans, and the monetary-structuralist controversy on inflation in Latin America. But I couldn't resist toying also with the Polak model which conjured up to me visions of the early classical analysis of Hume. My interest was less in its quantitative aspects than the theory which I tried to formalize more generally in what I then called the "Hume-Polak" model.[3] What came to be called the monetary approach to the balance of payments[4] was a combination of Hume's monetary equilibrium concept, banking theory, Polak's analysis of the role of money in balance of payments analysis, and an application of general equilibrium techniques to the monetary analysis of an open economy.

Three books[5] have now been published that include "monetary approach to the balance of payments" in their title; but the issues raised by the monetary approach have been by no means resolved. To this date there does not exist in the literature even a static model complete and accurate enough to analyze the hypothetical experiments Hume attempted. Lacking a complete static framework, it

---

[3] When I first presented the model at an IMF seminar in 1963, Marcus Fleming resented its non-Keynesian orientation; it was there he made his flippant remark that the only Keynesians left in the Fund were himself and the Managing Director (Per Jacobsson)! He later penned a memorandum to me entitled "Lament for Economics"; my paper thus never saw the light of day as an IMF paper. Shortly after I had left the Fund, Marcus had a chance to use his "lament" officially in commenting on my presentation at a World Bank conference in 1965, which was later published in Adler (1967); it became Chapter 8 in my *International Economics* (1968) and was reprinted in Frenkel and Johnson (1976, Chapter 3).

[4] I introduced the phrase "monetary approach to the balance of payments" in my article on "The Balance of Payments" written in 1965 for the *International Encyclopaedia of the Social Sciences* (1968).

[5] Frenkel and Johnson (1976); International Monetary Fund (1977); and Humphrey and Keleher (1982). See Hahn (1977) for a critical review article with the same title. See also Putnam and Wilford (1986) for a related title.

goes without saying that there has been inadequate analysis of the monetary dynamics of the adjustment process.

The first part of this paper will develop a model suitable for analysis of changes in the quantity of money in one country in the context of a world in which relative prices are fixed and the law of one price holds. It is shown that the effects of Hume's experiment—an increase in the quantity of money in one country—cannot be determined outside the context of a global model that allows for both changes in the world price level and in the redistribution of the world capital stock associated with changes in the balance of payments.

The second part of the paper explores monetary dynamics, identifying the stability conditions corresponding to alternative adjustment postulates. The dynamic complexities associated with the banking system help to discriminate between the stability conditions of the price-specie-flow mechanism and the alternative postulates of the monetary approach.

I. Monetary Statics

Hume[6] started with one hypothetical experiment in which "four-fifths of all the money in GREAT BRITAIN" was "annihilated in one night" (pp. 62–63) and another in which the money supply is multiplied fivefold. Two pillars of his analysis stand out: First, that there is an equilibrium quantity of money in a country and that it is proportionate to its resources, productive power, or output. Thus: "wherever I speak of the level of money, I mean always its proportional level to the commodities, labour, industry, and skill, which is in the several states" (p. 66). Second, prices at home and abroad cannot differ by more than the cost of transport: "All water, wherever it communicates, remains always at a level" (p. 63). An increase in the money stock might initially increase industry and lead to a higher equilibrium stock but if it does not do so, the equilibrium money supply will be restored: "the increase of money, if not too sudden, naturally increases people and industry, and by that means may retain itself; but if it do not produce such an increase, nothing will retain it except hoarding" (pp. 197–98).

---

[6] See Rotwein (1955).

In analyzing the effect of an increase in money, it is first necessary to confirm what Hume means by money. In the following passage, Hume makes it clear: "Suppose that there are 12 millions of paper, which circulate in the kingdom as money ... and suppose the real cash of the kingdom to be 18 millions: Here is a state which is found by experience to be able to hold a stock of 30 millions" (p. 68).

Paper circulates *as* money but only specie is real cash. When he supposes an increase in money, he means an increase in *specie*. Because he also analyzes the effect of an increase of credit or paper money, it is necessary to incorporate both specie and paper money in Hume's model.

Hume is not explicit about events in the rest of the world. If the money stock in the rest of the world is constant, the global money stock increases by the amount of the increased national money; but if the world money stock is constant, the increased money in one country must be associated with an equal decrease in the rest of the world. In the former case, the world price level must rise; in the latter case there is a world redistribution of wealth that cannot fail to have a permanent effect on equilibrium. Hume's sketch of the adjustment process ignored or obscured these issues.

A Gold Standard Model

To analyze Hume's model, it will be convenient to use the following symbols:

p = price of commodities
π = price of gold
e = price of home currency in terms of foreign currency
O = output
R = nongold resources
L = demand for money
M = supply of money
G = stock of gold
α = gold reserve ratio
k = money supply per unit of income
ϕ = ratio of output to resources.

With primes to denote the foreign country, Hume's model can be represented as follows:

$$L = kpO; \qquad L' = k'p'O'; \qquad\qquad (1, 1')$$

the demand for money is proportionate to money income.

$$\pi G = \alpha M; \qquad \pi' G' = \alpha' M'; \tag{2, 2'}$$

the value of gold reserves is proportionate to the money supply.

$$O = \phi R; \qquad O' = \phi' R'; \tag{3, 3'}$$

output is proportionate to resources.

$$e = \pi'/\pi; \tag{4}$$

the exchange rate is the ratio of the foreign currency price of gold to the home currency price of gold.

$$p = p'/e; \tag{5}$$

the law of one price and purchasing power parity.

$$W = \pi G + pR; \qquad W' = \pi' G' + p' R'; \tag{6, 6'}$$

money wealth is equal to the value of gold and resources.

$$M = \pi G + D; \qquad M' = \pi' G' + D'; \tag{7, 7'}$$

the money supply is composed of specie (gold) and domestic credit.

$$G + G' = G^*; \tag{8}$$

the sum of the gold stocks is equal to G^*, the world gold stock.

$$R + R' = R^*; \tag{9}$$

the sum of the resources of the two countries is equal to the world stock.

When the above equations are solved for the price levels in the two countries, we get

$$p = \pi G^*/(\alpha k \phi R + \alpha' k' \phi' R') \tag{10}$$

$$p' = \pi' G^*/(\alpha k \phi R + \alpha' k' \phi' R'). \tag{10'}$$

It will be convenient to define a term H for the denominator in these expressions so that

$$H = \alpha k \phi R + \alpha' k' \phi' R' = (\alpha k \phi - \alpha' k' \phi') R + \alpha' k' \phi' R^*.$$

From equations (10) and (10') it can be seen that price levels are proportionate to the *world* stock of gold and to the respective gold prices in the two countries. As long as the international distribution of resources is constant, the equilibrium price level is independent of the distribution of the world gold stock.

Further propositions[7] can be noted. (1) An increase in the price of gold π—devaluation—in one country raises the equilibrium price level in that country, but leaves unchanged the equilibrium price level in the rest of the world. (2) An increase in the world gold stock causes a proportionate increase in the price level of each country. (3) An increase in α, the gold reserve ratio in either country increases gold requirements and thus lowers the world price level. (4) An increase in k, the demand for money as a proportion of output, in either country lowers the world price level because it raises gold requirements. (5) An increase in resources (growth) in either country's resources lowers the price level in both countries.

In the special case where gold-resource ratios are the same in the two countries, the world price level will depend on the level of global resources and not on its distribution between countries. Gold-resource ratios are now equal to

$$\pi G / pR = \alpha k \phi \tag{11}$$

and

$$\pi' G' / p' R' = \alpha k \phi, \tag{11'}$$

the same in the two countries. The price levels in the two countries now reduce to

$$p = \pi G^* / \alpha k \phi R^* \tag{12}$$

and

$$p' = \pi' G^* / \alpha k \phi R^*, \tag{12'}$$

which shows that (apart from currency prices of gold) price levels depend on global endowments of gold and resources, not on their international distribution.

Let us now consider the equilibrium distribution of gold in the two countries. After substituting for p / π and p' / π' from equations (12) and (12') into

$$G = \alpha k \phi pR / \pi \tag{13}$$

and

$$G' = \alpha' k' \phi' p' R' / \pi' \tag{13'}$$

---

[7] In his interesting paper Collery (1971) develops a two-good two-country model of the gold standard. The model in this section is complementary to his in that his model allows for the possibility of changes in the terms of trade (mine does not), whereas my model allows for resource redistribution effects (his does not).

we can obtain the ratio of the gold stocks in the two countries:

$$G/G' = (\alpha k \phi / \alpha' k' \phi') \; R/R'. \tag{14}$$

The ratio of the gold stocks is proportionate to the ratio of resources. A country's share in world gold reserves can be increased by (1) an increase in its reserve ratio; (2) a decrease in foreign reserve ratios; (3) an increase in the demand for money per unit of output; (4) a decrease in the demand for money in the rest of the world; (5) an increase in productivity; (6) a decrease in productivity abroad; (7) an increase in resources; or (8) a decrease in resources abroad.

Monetary Experiments

Consider now the effect of an increase in the stock of gold in the home country, the gold holdings of the rest of the world remaining constant; the national gold stock, G, and the world gold stock, G^*, increase by equal amounts. The effects of this windfall increase in the quantity of money can be split into its global effect on prices and its redistribution effect on wealth.

The increase in the stock of money, while increasing the home country's wealth, upsets the balance between money and resources. The new equilibrium requires that the home country exchange excess gold on world markets for resources. This raises the world price level, eroding some of the windfall gains of the home country. At the new equilibrium both the stock of resources and the *real* value of gold will be higher in the home country and lower in the rest of the world.

Because the home country can dispose of its new-found riches only at higher prices, both the realized increase in wealth of the home country and the realized loss of wealth of the rest of the world is smaller than it would have been had the price level remained constant. The windfall of money to the home country acts like a tax on the rest of the world, part of the burden of which is reduced by the rise in the price of resources.

The redistribution of wealth complicates the determination of the price increase if the equilibrium money-resource proportions are different at home and abroad. By differentiation of equations (10) and (10′) we can solve for the change in the price levels:

$$dp/p = dp'/p' = dG^*/G^* - dH/H, \tag{15}$$

where $dH/H = (\alpha k \phi - \alpha' k' \phi')dR / [(\alpha k \phi - \alpha' k' \phi')R + \alpha' k' \phi' R^*]$.

The normal result, predicted by the quantity theory of money, is that the price level rises in the same proportion as the quantity of money. This result, however, will only hold if H is constant. H will be constant only if (1) the gold-resource ratios are equal at home and abroad; or (2) the monetary expansion does not change the distribution of resources between the two countries.

Because of the redistribution of resources to the home country, the proportionate increase in the world price level will be less or greater than the proportionate increase in the world gold supply depending on whether equilibrium gold-resource ratios are higher or lower in the home country than abroad. The proportionate change in the ratio of home to foreign gold holdings will be equal to the difference between the home and foreign changes in resources.

How will the increase in money affect the international distribution of the stock of gold? From equation (14) it can be seen that the effect of the monetary change on the international distribution of gold depends on the distribution of resources. The proportionate change in the ratio of the gold reserves (G/G') is equal to the proportionate change in resources (R/R').

The increase in gold supply of the home country is a gift that acts like a tax on the rest of the world, the proceeds of which accrue to the home country. Hume correctly recognized (after prompting by his friend Oswald) that the windfall of money balances would raise resources and thus lead to higher money requirements; but he neglected to take into account the increase in the world price level occasioned by the redistribution of gold stocks and the consequent increase in gold requirements to maintain the real value.

Diagrammatic Analysis

For the diagrammatic explication of Hume's problem, assume that the home country is trivially small relative to the rest of the world; this means that prices are constant. In Chart 1, put output on the abscissa and gold on the ordinate. The equilibrium level of output and the equilibrium quantity of gold can then be determined by the intersection, at Q, of two schedules, GA and GR.

GA, the gold availability schedule, is a kind of efficiency frontier, reflecting the fact that gold has an opportunity cost in the form of a sacrifice of the output that could be produced by exchanging the gold for resources. The GA schedule has a negative slope because a reduction in gold holdings invested in resources results in a larger income; the slope, which can be derived by differentiating (with

Chart 1.   Small Country Case

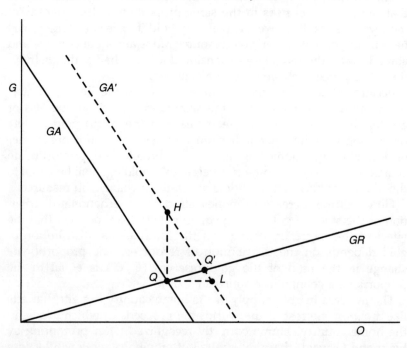

wealth constant) the wealth constraint equation,

$$W = \pi G + pR = \pi G + pO/\phi,$$

is, with a negative sign, the resource-output ratio, $1/\phi$ multiplied by the gold price of commodities, p/π.

GR is the gold-requirement schedule. Given constant prices of gold and commodities, it is the relation between income and gold at which the demand for gold equals supply. It has a positive slope because money requirements rise with national income; the slope, derived from the equation

$$\pi G = \alpha k pO,$$

is the product of α, the gold-reserve fraction and k, the money supply per unit of output, multiplied by the gold price of output, p/π.

Consider now Hume's experiment where the gold supply increases by the amount QH. This creates a disequilibrium in the form of an excess supply of monetary gold and an excess demand for resources. Gold is shipped abroad in exchange for resources, which increases productive power, income, and the demand for money. As the exchange continues, a falling supply of gold meets a rising demand for it until a new equilibrium at Q' is reached. At Q' the equilibrium levels of both gold and money income are higher than before the increase in the quantity of money.

The case depicted in Chart 1 is the extreme case where the home country is able to exchange its excess gold into resources without raising the price level. When the small country assumption is relaxed, the exchange of excess gold could only be effected at higher commodity prices and the real value of the increase in wealth would be less than its nominal value. To allow for price changes, it is necessary to specify the distribution of the information associated with the price change. Suppose first generalized knowledge in the world as a whole of the monetary experiment and also rational expectations. Assuming reserve ratios are the same everywhere, the increased supply of gold results in predictions of a proportionate increase in the world price level. This has two effects. It lowers the real value of the increased gold stock of the home country and it raises the demand for money. Because gold can now command fewer resources, the new gold availability line GA' (see Chart 2) is steeper; and because the demand for money rises, the gold requirements curve GR' shifts upward. The new equilibrium is at Q'' where both real income and gold are higher than at Q; but income is lower and gold is higher than at Q' (the result had prices not changed at all).

When information about the increased gold stock is restricted to the recipients, the result is of course better for the home country (and worse for the rest of the world). Some purchases of resources are made at prices close to the original prices so that the resource value is higher than when prices adjust instantaneously. The new equilibrium will be at a point on GR' like Q''', which involves a higher gold stock than at Q' or Q'', and a higher real income than at Q'' (but of course lower than at Q').

A Non-Hume Experiment

Consider now a quite different experiment from the one posed by Hume. Instead of a miraculous increase in money, suppose there is a miraculous increase in resources. In the special case where repercussion effects are ignored (small country assumption), the final result is exactly the same as in the case where the stock of gold is

Chart 2.   Global Price Effects

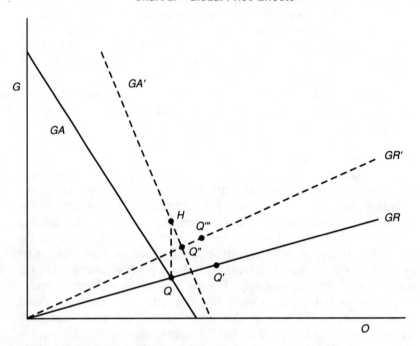

increased, given equal increases in wealth. As long as gold and resources can be exchanged on the international market at constant prices, the only thing that matters is the extent of the increase in wealth, not its composition. An increase in the stock of resources yields an increase in output that increases demand for transactions balances and gold imports in exchange for resources until portfolio balance is restored. In Chart 1, an increase in resources equivalent to QH of gold would yield an increased output equal to QL. At the point L, there is an excess demand for money and an excess supply of resources that results in an exchange of resources for gold until the equilibrium Q' is reached.

The situation is much different, however, when the country is not of insignificant size and when full account is taken of repercussions. The exchange of resources for goods results in a fall in the international price of resources, which lowers the demand schedule for money (in both countries), reducing the home country's money requirements, and worsens the terms of exchange for the home country. Assuming generalized knowledge of the increase in world resources, the price level would fall in the same proportion that output has increased. These effects are depicted in Chart 3, where the additional resources of QL lower the price level, flattening the slope of GA to GA', resulting in a new equilibrium at N, below and to the right of L. Note that the country gains more by an increase in wealth manifested in real resources than it does by an equivalent increase in wealth in the form of gold.

II. Monetary Dynamics

Up to now the analysis has not paid any attention to the time frame in which the disturbances to equilibrium are worked out. We have investigated the effect of a change in the initial conditions on the equilibrium, but we have not investigated the path to the new equilibrium or even ascertained whether the new equilibrium is reached. We have analyzed the comparative statics of the distur-

Chart 3.   Increase in Resources

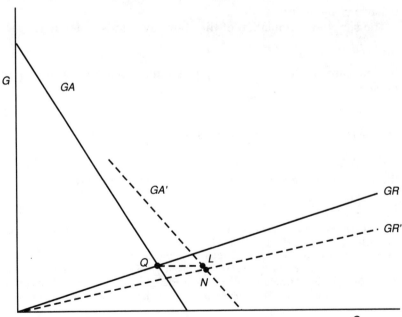

bance but not the dynamic adjustment to the new equilibrium.[8] That is the purpose of this part of the paper.

Because of its prominent place in the literature, it will be useful to analyze first the dynamics of the price-specie-flow mechanism theory. A good theory is likely to be robust in the face of alternative tests of its stability, whereas a bad theory is likely to be sensitive to present difficulties in connection with formulating dynamic tests. One feature of the Mill-Taussig-Viner theory of the adjustment mechanism is its potential instability.

The Quantity Theory Version

To simplify the dynamical analysis, assume that the country is small relative to the rest of the world and that there are no output effects. The basic propositions of the adjustment process according to the Viner interpretation of Hume include the following:

1. The money supply increases or decreases at a rate equal to the balance of payments.

2. The price level increases or decreases—income remaining constant—according to whether the money supply increases or decreases.

3. The change in the price level brings about a correction of the balance of payments.

The simplest formulation of the above system is as follows:

$$dM/dt = B, \tag{1}$$

the increase in the money supply is equal to the balance of payments;

$$B = g(p), \tag{2}$$

the balance of payments is a function of the price level;

$$p = h(M), \tag{3}$$

the price level is a rising function of the money supply.

---

[8] Hume himself was aware that monetary disturbances occur overnight but are not eliminated overnight. Hume noted that the self-regulating mechanism might take some years to work itself out: "Suppose twenty millions brought into Scotland; suppose that, by some fatality, we take no advantage of this to augment our industry or people, how much would remain in the quarter of a century? Not a shilling more than we have at present." See Hume's 1750 letter to James Oswald in Rotwein (1955, p. 198).

Chart 4.   The Price-Specie-Flow Mechanism

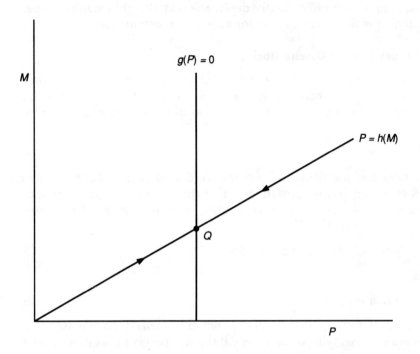

Chart 4 depicts money on the ordinate and the price level on the abscissa. The balance of payments is in equilibrium on the line $g(p) = 0$ and the price level is governed by the quantity of money. The point Q represents equilibrium.

It is by no means certain that the equilibrium position Q will be stable or unique. Given the positive slope of the $h(M)$ line, the equilibrium will not be dynamically stable unless $g'(p) < 0$, a condition equivalent to the familiar Marshall-Lerner criterion. In the stable case where $g' < 0$, the balance of payments will be positive or negative according to whether the price level is higher or lower than equilibrium p; the arrows on $h(M)$ will point toward Q ensuring that it will be reached. But if $g'(p)$ is positive, the arrows would point in the opposite direction. In this case, there may be more than one equilibrium line on either side of $g(p) = 0$; and if $g'(p) = 0$, there might be an infinite number of "equilibrium" lines.

The theory of rational behavior gives us no clue as to the sign of $g'(p)$. Situations of multiple equilibrium or indeed an infinity of equilibria might exist.[9] The problem, however, is that the above equations may not correctly depict the way the gold standard operated. It is necessary to look for alternative formulations.

Money Market Disequilibrium

Let us now relax the rigid form of the quantity theory of money defined in equation (3). Assume, along traditional lines, that the demand for money is a linear function of money income, $Y = pO$ so that

$$L = kpO, \tag{4}$$

where L is the demand for money and O is output. Let us assume that output (O) is constant and that the price level rises in proportion to the excess supply of money, so that, instead of the above system, we have

$$dp/dt = \beta(M - L) = \beta(M - kpO) \tag{5}$$

and

$$dM/dt = g(p). \tag{6}$$

These two differential equations, when linearized, have equilibrium solutions that will be stable only if the real parts of the latent roots of the characteristic equation,

$$\lambda^2 + \beta kO\lambda - \beta g' = 0,$$

are negative, which will be true if and only if $g' < 0$. Superficially, therefore, it appears that the introduction of some sluggishness in the adjustment of prices to the excess supply of money does not alter the stability conditions. A closer look, however, shows that the answer is more complicated. Unless

$$kO > 2\sqrt{-(g'/\beta)}, \tag{7}$$

the approach to equilibrium will be cyclical.

Except for money income instead of the price level on the abscissa, the static configuration in Chart 5 is analogous to that in

---

[9] Could the Hicks-Samuelson Correspondence principle be invoked to justify an assumption of stability? The answer is yes, *if* the actual gold standard exhibited characteristics of stability; *and* the equations above correctly portray the gold standard. Whether the latter is true is the subject under investigation.

Chart 5. Money Market Disequilibrium

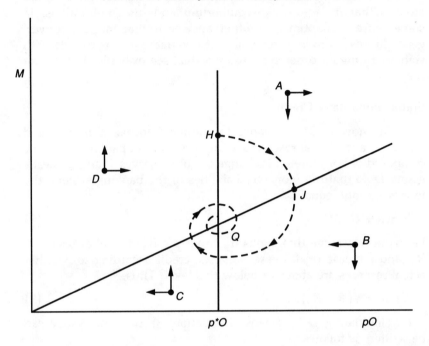

Chart 4. But the possibility of disequilibrium positions off the *LM* line introduces more complex dynamics. The arrows in the four quadrants indicate the direction of the variables when the system is not in equilibrium. Consider a Hume-type disequilibrium point like *H*, where there is an excess supply of money. The path to equilibrium will move into quadrant *A*, intersect the *LM* line at a point like *J* and enter quadrant *B*. Whether the path then moves directly toward *Q* or moves as indicated, depends on inequality (7), which expresses the relative strength of the forces operating on prices and money. From *J* the path is more likely to be direct rather than cyclical, for any given propensity to hold money, the more rapidly prices respond to an excess supply of money (the higher is β) and the lower is the elasticity factor g'. Notice the curious fact that, whereas the elasticity factor has to be high enough to promote stability ($g' < 0$), high values of it interfere with the directness of convergence; at *J*, a very high payments deficit tends to push the money supply below its equilibrium level, causing overshooting and a later correction that creates a (convergent) cycle.

Why should we care about cyclicity and overshooting? One answer is that it prolongs disequilibrium and disequilibrium is, in some sense, suboptimal. Another answer is that indirect convergence in lower order systems almost invariably means trouble with stability in higher order systems. We shall see examples in the next sections.

Endogenous Bank Credit

Let us now make allowance for nongold forms of money and introduce a fractional reserve banking system. Let banking assets be composed of both foreign exchange or gold reserves R and domestic assets D so that the monetary liabilities of the banking system, the money supply, equals

$$M = R + D. \tag{8}$$

Let us now assume that banks try to keep a fixed level of reserves, R_o, and increase or decrease domestic credit according to whether actual reserves are above or below this level. Thus,[10]

$$dD/dt = \gamma(R - R_o). \tag{9}$$

After eliminating D by means of equation (8), the new system can be written as follows:

$$dP/dt = \beta(M - kpO) \tag{10}$$
$$dR/dt = g(p) \tag{11}$$
$$dM/dt - dR/dt = \gamma(R - R_o). \tag{12}$$

Equilibrium will be stable only if the roots of

$$\lambda^3 + \beta kO\lambda^2 - \beta g'\lambda - \beta g'\gamma = 0 \tag{13}$$

have negative real parts. The absence of positive real roots requires that all the coefficients of λ in equation (13) be positive, which will be the case if and only if (given the other known signs) $g' < 0$; again, the elasticity condition is the determining factor. However, in this more complicated system, $g' > 0$ is not sufficient for stability. It is also necessary to rule out complex roots with positive real parts. The Routh conditions require that the product of the coefficients λ^2

---

[10]This assumes that all the gold is in the hands of the banking system. Allowance for private holdings of gold involves introducing an additional equation to determine portfolio balance between gold and bank money for the private sector.

and λ in equation (13) exceed the last term, that is,

$$kO > \gamma/\beta, \tag{14}$$

an additional condition for stability imposed by allowance for noninstantaneous adjustment in the banking system.

A high propensity to hold money is conducive to stability, as is a low γ and a high β. Notice the family resemblance between the stability inequality (14) and the criterion for cyclicity of the simpler system, inequality (7).

Banking Reserve Ratios

Let us now assume that banks, instead of trying to keep a fixed level of monetary reserves, strive to keep a fixed proportion of their actual, but fluctuating, monetary liabilities. Let desired reserves R^* be proportionate to the money supply so that

$$R^* = \alpha M. \tag{15}$$

As before, in addition we assume that banks expand or contract their domestic assets according to whether

$$dD/dt = \gamma(R - R^*). \tag{16}$$

The revised system of equations is now

$$dp/dt = \beta(M - kpO) \tag{17}$$

$$dR/dt = g(p) \tag{18}$$

$$dM/dt = dR/dt + \gamma(R - \alpha M), \tag{19}$$

which has a characteristic equation

$$\lambda^3 + (\beta kO + \alpha\gamma)\lambda^2 + (\beta kO\alpha\gamma - \beta g')\lambda - \gamma\beta g' = 0. \tag{20}$$

For the coefficients of λ in equation (20) to be positive, g' again must be negative. To rule out complex roots with positive real parts it is required that

$$(\beta kO + \alpha\gamma)(\beta kO\alpha\gamma - \beta g') + \gamma\beta g' > 0 \tag{21'}$$

or

$$\gamma kO[\beta kO + \alpha\gamma - \beta g'/kO] > (\alpha - 1)\gamma g'/\alpha. \tag{21}$$

This condition is satisfied if $\alpha = 1$ (or higher); high reserve ratios contribute to stability. Given that $\alpha < 1$ and $g' < 0$, all the terms in inequality (21) are positive. The closer to unity is α, the lower is the term on the right-hand side of inequality (21) and the greater the chance for stability. Given $g' > 0$, a *sufficient* (but not necessary) condition for stability is that

$$kO > (1 - \alpha)\gamma/\beta. \tag{22}$$

Note that the more rapidly prices adjust to excess supply in the money market relative to the speed of adjustment in the banking market, the more likely it is that the equilibrium will be stable. Note also that inequality (22) is a weaker condition than inequality (14), so that the adjustment mechanism of this model may be stable even when the system, based on fixed reserve targets, is unstable.

The Monetary Approach

The preceding analysis has been characterized by two assumptions that need to be modified. First, it applies to an open economy a theory of prices strictly applicable only to a closed economy; the postulate that the price level rises in response to an excess supply of money, as it would in an isolated economy, needs to be modified to allow for arbitrage whenever the domestic price level rises above its equilibrium level. This was precisely the criticism levied at Hume by his friend James Oswald prior to the publication of Hume's essay on the balance of trade; Hume promised to amend his draft to make clear that prices would not rise to as great an extent if part of the money was at once spent on imports.[11]

---

[11] Hume's final draft is tantalizingly ambiguous and has led to considerable controversy. See, for example, Viner (1937), Collery (1971), Staley (1976), Samuelson (1971 and 1980), and Humphrey and Keleher (1982). There are two basic issues: (1) Was Hume aware of the possibility that a fortuitous increase in the money supply could be eliminated without price changes? and (2) which type of price changes did Hume have in mind?

Consider the first issue. In an early version of his exposition of the adjustment process, Hume puts the entire burden of adjustment on a change in prices; see his letter to Montesquieu in Rotwein's 1955 edition of Hume. This letter supports Samuelson's 1980 interpretation that at that time, Hume was guilty of ignoring expenditure effects at unchanged prices. In the later correspondence with Oswald, Hume goes part way toward correcting his omission, and in his published essay (1752), he advances from error to tantalizing ambiguity! I am inclined to accept the generous interpretation of Hume suggested by Humphrey and Keleher (1982) in their excellent review of the entire literature on the monetary approach.

Hume thought the prices of some commodities would have to change. Because Hume accepted the law of one price, Viner interpreted Hume's price changes to mean changes in the terms of trade (or more generally relative prices of home-produced goods). Collery (1971, p. 28) rejects Viner's interpretation as "so silly that its wide acceptance must forever remain one of the puzzles in the history of economic thought." See Staley (1976) for a discussion of this issue.

The other adjustment that is required is in the balance of trade equation. The equation $B = g(p)$ implies that the balance of trade can only be changed by a change in the price level, although the sign of the derivative $g'(p)$—the elasticity condition—cannot be determined by the theory of rational behavior. In contrast to this elasticity approach, the monetary approach makes use of the absorption-approach relation between income, expenditure, and the balance of trade and relates the expenditure function to income and the excess supply of money.

Although the monetary approach does not depend on a rigid form of the law of one price it is, of course, consistent with it. To show how adjustment is modeled in the absence of price changes, assume that arbitrage is instantaneous so that the domestic price level cannot diverge from the price level, expressed in domestic currency, abroad. Thus,

$$p = p^*,\qquad(23)$$

where p^* is the international price.

The next assumption of the monetary approach involves a theory of total spending (domestic expenditure). Theoretically, domestic expenditure is the aggregate of individual spending decisions based on intertemporal utility maximization subject to the wealth constraint. A simplification of this theory equates expenditure to income raised or lowered by a factor related to the gap between actual and desired wealth. Early in the discussion of the monetary approach, a simplification of this relation was introduced by Prais (1961). In the Prais equation, expenditure is equal to income plus a factor proportionate to the excess supply of money. We shall use this equation to illustrate the monetary approach, modifying it, however, to allow for net outward transfers.[12] Thus,

$$E = pO - T + v(M - kpO) = (1 - vk)pO - T + vM,\qquad(24)$$

---

[12] The monetary approach does not stand or fall with this particular form of the expenditure function. Because equation (24) relates expenditure (including investment) rather than consumption to the independent variables, it allows for the possibility that the marginal propensity to consume is less than unity. An implicit assumption is that net transfers are completely financed or spent by decreases or increases in spending, that is, the marginal propensity to spend out of transfers is unity. It would of course be possible to allow for differential spending propensities out of produced income and transfers. Account could also be taken of liquidity

where T denotes outward transfers.[13] We have also the following equations:

$$pO = E + B, \tag{25}$$

the definition from the national income accounts;

$$dM/dt = B - T, \tag{26}$$

the balance of payments equation relating the balance of payments to the change in the money supply. For simplicity assume that $T = 0$.

Chart 6 plots money on the ordinate and both income, pO, and expenditure, E, on the abscissa. LM denotes the money equilibrium line and also the line at which expenditure is equal to income. Given money income, p^*O, the E-line represents desired expenditure for every level of the money supply. Consider now a Hume-type experiment. The money supply is increased to the level indicated by H.

---

requirements associated with transfers along the lines of the next footnote.

Unilateral transfers should be distinguished from capital movements such as loans. Whereas the former involves a redistribution of wealth and should therefore increase current consumption in the receiving country, the latter does not change wealth (except indirectly through rents) and should therefore have its impact mainly on investment. The difference between the two types of transfers—unilateral transfers and loans (or investments)—does not affect the level of expenditure so much as the division of expenditure between consumption and investment.

More generally, the expenditure equation, looked at as a theory of spending, should be related to the differential between actual and desired wealth rather than between actual and desired liquidity. For analysis of the short-run mechanism, however, the present formulation suffices.

[13] I have not made allowance for any adjustment in the demand for money equation to allow for the effect of transfers on the demand for money, the subject of the Robertson-Viner controversy in the *Quarterly Journal of Economics* in the late 1930s. Their arguments were couched in terms of the assumed constancy of income velocity versus expenditure or "final-purchases" velocity. In my terminology Robertson contended that the demand for money L depends on income Y, whereas Viner argued that it depends on expenditure, $E = Y - T$. My own view is a little closer to Viner's than to Robertson's, but both, in their concentration on the *distribution* of the demand for money between payer and payee, neglect the increase in the global demand for money due to the additional transactions caused by capital movements. Moreover, as I have noted in Mundell (1991), a complete analysis requires a division of the demand for money between households and firms. The issue becomes important in assessing the effects of transfer on the flow of gold or the balance of payments (under fixed exchange rates) or the exchange rates, given existing money supplies.

Because transfers are exogenous and held constant in the present analysis, failure to take transfers into account in the demand for money does not introduce any distortion of the conclusions.

Chart 6.   The Monetary Approach

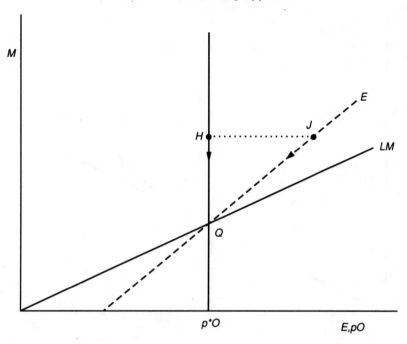

This increases expenditure in excess of income by *HJ*, creating a balance of payments deficit equal to *HJ*. The money supply therefore declines even though prices have remained constant. The path of income and money is determined by the arrow at *H*, and the path of expenditure and money is indicated by the arrow from *J*.

The adjustment paths assumed in Chart 6 imply that expenditure is allocated to consumption rather than investment, with no increase in resources. If, on the contrary, the new wealth is exchanged for resources, the money income line, p^*O would shift[14] to the right by $dO = \phi dR$, where ϕ is (as before) the average product of resources, *R*. In this case (see Chart 7), the new equilibrium is on *LM* to the northeast of *Q* at *Q'*. *HQ'*, the income-money path to *Q'*, has a slope[15] equal to the resource-output ratio, $1/\phi$. Because of the

---

[14] This abstracts from lags between the spending, the increase in resources, and the consequent increase in output.

[15] This assumes choice of units so that the gold price of commodities is equal to unity.

Chart 7. Increase in Resources

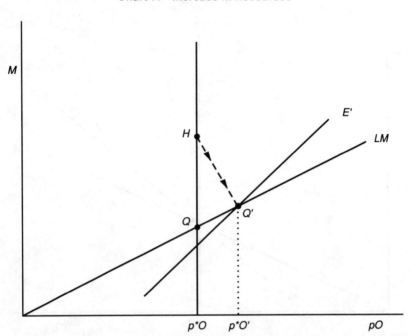

increase in income, the expenditure line shifts to the right until, at the final equilibrium, it intersects *LM* at the point Q'. The increase in income at the new equilibrium, as a proportion of the increase in wealth (equal to the initial increase in the stock of money) is equal to $\phi/(1+k\phi)$. The increase in the equilibrium money stock, as a proportion of the increase in wealth, is $k\phi/(1+k\phi)$.

The Monetary Approach and Price Adjustments

Adjustment in the preceding case, based on the law of one price, occurs entirely without price changes. But the monetary approach does not stand or fall according to whether this law holds. If arbitrage is not instantaneous, domestic prices can diverge for a time from the international level. I assume that arbitrage tends to increase or decrease the price level according to whether it is below or above its purchasing power parity equivalent. I shall also allow for the possibility that an excess supply of money can exert a direct effect on prices. In order to explore the stability of the system under more complicated dynamic assumptions, we reintroduce the banking system.[16] The equations are as follows:

$$dp/dt = \beta(M - kpO) + \Theta(p^* - p),\qquad(27)$$

where β and Θ indicate the weights attached to each disequilibrium.[17] We have also the following equations:

$$E = pO - T + v(M - kpO) = (1 - vk)pO - T + vM\qquad(28)$$

$$pO = E + B\qquad(29)$$

$$dR/dt = B - T\qquad(30)$$

$$R^* = \alpha M\qquad(31)$$

$$M = R + D\qquad(32)$$

$$dD/dt = \gamma(R - R^*)\qquad(33)$$

$$T = T^o.\qquad(34)$$

Domestic assets D can be eliminated using equations (32) and (33); desired reserves R^* can be eliminated using equation (31); the balance of trade B can be eliminated using equation (29); and expenditure E can be eliminated using equation (28). The system can thus be reduced to three equations:

$$dp/dt = \beta(M - kpO) + \Theta(p^* - p)\qquad(35)$$

$$dR/dt = v(kpO - M) - T^o\qquad(36)$$

$$dM/dt = dR/dt + \gamma(R - \alpha M).\qquad(37)$$

The solution of the system depends on the roots of the following

---

[16] No account is taken of the possibility of investment spending and an increase of resources in this section.

[17] An alternative formulation could relate the rate of price increase to the difference between (1) the sum of expenditure and the trade balance and (2) income, which under certain definitions would equal the rate of reduction in national inventories.

characteristic equation

$$\lambda^3 + (\alpha\gamma + \Theta + \beta kO + v)\lambda^2$$
$$+ \left[(\Theta + \beta kO)\alpha\gamma + v(\Theta + \gamma)\right]\lambda + v\gamma\Theta = 0. \tag{38}$$

All the coefficients of λ are positive, so there are no positive real roots in the system. It is readily shown that there are no complex roots with positive real parts[18] so the equilibrium is stable.

The elasticity criterion that figures so prominently in the stability conditions of models of the previous section—depicting the Mill-Taussig-Viner adjustment theory—has no role in the stability conditions of the monetary approach. In the Mill-Taussig-Viner theory, a deficit in a country's balance of payments reduces the money supply and the price level, switching spending onto domestic goods, correcting or worsening the balance of payments according to whether the (terms of trade) elasticities exceed unity or fall short of unity. If it turns out that the elasticities are exactly equal to unity, the balance of payments can never be corrected!

By contrast, the monetary approach does not rely on changes in relative prices of different goods. A spontaneous increase in the stock of money raises expenditure above income and leads to deficit and a loss of reserves that eventually brings the stock of money back to its equilibrium level.[19] In the interim, the excess supply of money can exert an effect on the price level, but arbitrage mitigates this disturbing factor.

In order to show how the two forces working on the price level contribute to stability, consider extreme cases. Suppose $\beta = 0$. This has the effect of reducing the values of the coefficients of λ^2 and λ in the stability equation (38), decreasing what turns out to be a stabilizing force, but not by enough to create instability. If prices are not directly influenced by any excess supply of money, the arbitrage equations are sufficient to ensure stability.

The other case, $\Theta = 0$, is not so fortunate. It results in a zero root so that the system will not converge to its equilibrium. Whereas the adjustment of prices to excess demand for money contributes to stability when it is accompanied by the arbitrage equation, it cannot operate by itself.

---

[18]The reader can satisfy himself that the Routh criterion, that the product of the coefficients of λ^2 and λ^3 minus the last term be positive, is necessarily satisfied because the only negative term cancels out.

[19]We are again assuming here no global redistribution of wealth of the kind analyzed in Section I of this paper and, of course, no change in the world price level.

Another interesting case is where arbitrage is instantaneous. In this case, relative price levels play no part in the adjustment process and the system is again necessarily stable.[20]

III. Conclusion

This paper addressed some neglected issues in the development of the Hume-Polak model. A two-country static framework was first developed to provide solutions for Hume's monetary experiments. A sudden increase in the supply of specie in one country would raise world prices in proportion to the world increase in specie and thus raise domestic prices but by only a fraction of the percentage by which the domestic money supply increased. Thornton was the first to develop the implications of monetary policy in one country on the rest of the world.[21]

It was then shown that the increased money would result in a redistribution of resources toward the country in which the money supply had increased, and that the monetary change in the home country makes it better off while making the rest of the world worse off. It was then shown that an increase in resources of a small country would have the same effect on that country's real income—supposing that world prices remain constant—as an equivalent increase in money. However, when allowance is made for changes in the global price level, an increase in resources results in a fall in the world price level and a redistribution of income that raises the real income of both countries, the home country gaining less than the full benefit of its increase in resources.

Section II of the paper explored the monetary dynamics of the price-specie-flow mechanism and the monetary approach to the balance of payments. It was shown that even in the simplest case a dynamic form of the Mill-Taussig-Viner theory of adjustment resulted in overshooting and cycles; and that in more complicated cases, involving endogenous bank credit, the cyclicity degenerated

---

[20] If arbitrage is instantaneous, the speed Θ is infinite. Divide the characteristic equation (38) by Θ and then set $\Theta = \infty$. The cubed term drops out and the characteristic equation reduces to $\lambda^2 + (az + c)\lambda + cz = 0$, which has only either negative real roots or complex roots with negative real parts.

[21] See Mundell (1989a and especially 1989b) for an exposition of the empirical importance of the Thornton effect in creating "exported inflation" in the past two centuries of the international monetary system.

into instability. By contrast the monetary approach, relating the balance of payments to the excess demand for money, resulted in stability conditions that were satisfied.

A final note. The theory of monetary dynamics of adjustment is still in its infancy. The sketch of alternative monetary dynamics outlined above shows some of the rich alternatives open for future analysis. Much work remains to be done both on the formal analysis of the dynamic equations and on testing the empirical validity of alternative dynamic hypotheses.

REFERENCES

Adler, John H., ed., *Capital Movements and Economic Development* (London: Macmillan; New York: St. Martin's Press, 1967).

Claassen, E., and P. Salin, eds., *Recent Issues in International Monetary Economics* (Amsterdam: North-Holland, 1976).

Collery, Arnold, *International Adjustment, Open Economies, and the Quantity Theory of Money*, Princeton Studies in International Finance No. 28 (Princeton, New Jersey: Princeton University Press, 1971).

Frenkel, Jacob A., "Adjustment Mechanisms and the Monetary Approach to the Balance of Payments: A Doctrinal Perspective," in *Recent Issues in International Monetary Economics*, ed. by E. Claassen and P. Salin (Amsterdam: North-Holland, 1976).

———, and Harry G. Johnson, *The Monetary Approach to the Balance of Payments* (London: Allen & Unwin, 1976).

Hahn, Frank H., "The Monetary Approach to the Balance of Payments," *Journal of International Economics* (Amsterdam), Vol. 7 (August 1977), pp. 231–49.

Humphrey, Thomas M., and Robert E. Keleher, *The Monetary Approach to the Balance of Payments, Exchange Rates and World Inflation* (New York: Praeger, 1982).

International Monetary Fund, *The Monetary Approach to the Balance of Payments* (Washington, 1977).

Mundell, Robert A., *International Economics* (New York: Macmillan, 1968).

——— (1989a), "Trade Balance Patterns as Global General Equilibrium: The Seventeenth Approach to the Balance of Payments," *Rivista di Politica Economica* (Rome), Vol. 79 (June 1989), pp. 9–60.

——— (1989b), "The Global Adjustment System," *Rivista di Politica Economica* (Rome), Vol. 79 (December 1989).

——, "The Great Exchange Rate Controversy: Trade Balances and the International Monetary System," in *International Adjustment and Financing: The Lessons of 1985–1991,* ed. by C. Fred Bergsten (Washington: Institute for International Economics, 1991).

Polak, J.J., "Monetary Analysis of Income Formation and Payments Problems," *Staff Papers,* International Monetary Fund (Washington), Vol. 6 (November 1957), pp. 1–50.

——, "International Coordination of Economic Policy," *Staff Papers,* International Monetary Fund (Washington), Vol. 9 (July 1962), pp. 149–79.

——, and William H. White, "The Effect of Income Expansion on the Quantity of Money," *Staff Papers,* International Monetary Fund (Washington), Vol. 4 (August 1955), pp. 398–433.

Polak, J.J., and Lorette Boissonneault, "Monetary Analysis of Income and Imports and Its Statistical Application," *Staff Papers,* International Monetary Fund (Washington), Vol. 7 (April 1960), pp. 349–415.

Prais, S.J., "Some Mathematical Notes on the Quantity Theory of Money in an Open Economy," *Staff Papers,* International Monetary Fund (Washington), Vol. 8 (May 1961), pp. 212–26.

Putnam, Bluford, H., and D. Sykes Wilford, eds., *The Monetary Approach to International Adjustment* (New York: Praeger, 1986).

Robertson, Dennis H., "Indemnity Payments and Gold Movements," *Quarterly Journal of Economics* (Cambridge, Massachusetts), Vol. 53 (February 1939), pp. 313–14.

——, "Rejoinder," *Quarterly Journal of Economics* (Cambridge, Massachusetts), Vol. 53 (February 1939), p. 317.

Rotwein, Eugene, ed., *David Hume: Writings On Economics* (Madison: University of Wisconsin Press, 1955).

Samuelson, Paul A., "An Exact Hume-Ricardo-Marshall Model of International Trade," *Journal of International Economics* (Amsterdam), Vol. 1 (February 1971), pp. 1–18.

——, "A Corrected Version of Hume's Equilibrating Mechanisms for International Trade," in *Flexible Exchange Rates and the Balance of Payments,* ed. by John S. Chipman and Charles P. Kindleberger (Amsterdam: North-Holland, 1980).

Staley, Charles E., "Hume and Viner on the International Adjustment Mechanism," *History of Political Economy* (Durham, North Carolina), Vol. 8 (Summer 1976), pp. 252–65.

Thornton, Henry, *An Enquiry into the Nature and Effects of the Paper Credit of Great Britain (1802),* ed. by F.A.v. Hayek (The Library of Economics Series; London: Allen & Unwin, 1939).

Viner, Jacob, *Canada's Balance of International Indebtedness, 1900–1913* (Cambridge, Massachusetts: Harvard University Press, 1924).

——, *Studies in the Theory of International Trade* (New York and London: Harper, 1937).

——, "A Reply," *Quarterly Journal of Economics* (Cambridge, Massachusetts), Vol. 53 (February 1939), pp. 314–17.

Wu, Chi-Yuen, *An Outline of International Price Theories* (London: Routledge, 1939).